Consumer Choice Behavior

A Cognitive Theory

Flemming Hansen

Drawing on research done both in the United States and Europe since 1966, the author has constructed a systematic framework for the study of consumer behavior both based in individual psychology theory and related to traditional macroeconomic and microeconomic theory. Studying the consumer's role within the marketing system, and how the system operates, he takes into consideration the relation of the market researcher, the marketer, the consumer, and society itself to the marketing system as an integrated part of the total economic system.

After an introductory chapter, Professor Hansen presents the psychological background for a model of consumer choice behavior. He then proposes a model of individual consumer choice behavior, discusses its implications, and then moves to the consumer decision process and its relation to collective decision-making, particularly within the family. He concludes by discussing possible problems in the future study of consumer behavior.

CONSUMER CHOICE BEHAVIOR

A Cognitive Theory

by Flemming Hansen

The Free Press, NEW YORK

Collier–Macmillan Limited, LONDON

The Free Press
A DIVISION OF THE MACMILLAN COMPANY
866 Third Avenue, New York, New York 10022

Collier-Macmillan Canada Ltd., Toronto, Ontario

Library of Congress Catalog Card Number: 72–143513

printing number
1   2   3   4   5   6   7   8   9   10

Contents

PART THREE

A Model of Individual Consumer Choice Behavior

PART FOUR
Research and Findings

PART FIVE
Consumer Decisions and Market Behavior

PART SIX
Integrated Models of Markets

Appendixes

Preface

Consumer Choice Behavior: A Cognitive Theory serves three purposes. It presents a general model of consumer behavior, it relates existing evidence to this model, and it presents findings from a number of experiments especially designed to test crucial aspects of the model.

This attempt to construct a systematic framework for the study of consumer behavior grew out of a project started in Copenhagen in 1966. The original purpose was to provide a review of existing literature, but very soon I realized that this would require a general model of consumer behavior; a model that did not exist at the time. I therefore worked out the framework for such a model while in Copenhagen and later in Durham, New Hampshire, in 1967.

As the work progressed it became clear to me that a thorough understanding of consumer behavior must be based in individual psychological theory and that it must build bridges from here to traditional macroeconomic and microeconomic theory, for two reasons. First, research has shown that a number of more or less aggregated approaches to consumer behavior do not work when they are applied to individual behavior. If they made it possible to answer all the questions we would like to ask at an aggregated level there would be no problem; but they do not. These attempts have still left businessmen and national economists faced with considerable risk and uncertainty in the area of consumer behavior; consequently models based in individual behavior may have important advantages over traditional approaches.

Second, within psychology a significant body of theory and findings exists concerning individual human behavior. To apply this knowledge, however, raises a problem: Psychologists are rarely concerned with the problems of aggregation inherent in the models with which they work, so that to relate the material to consumer behavior requires that the study of consumer behavior start at the individual level. To apply psychological models or variables to markets, completely neglecting the problems of aggregation, violates the assumptions of these models. Nevertheless this use of psychological theory has been most common among students of consumer behavior over the last two decades.

For these reasons, the present approach is strongly devoted both to consumer behavior at the individual level and to the problems that arise when the models are applied to aggregated markets. Eventually, these problems may be found to be those most characteristic of the study of consumer behavior compared with related areas.

An important consequence of the view just promoted is that much less is said about the application of the consumer behavior model in decision-making situations than is said of the structure and implications of the model. The first problem is not considered to be minor as it is sincerely believed that these applications are the most fundamental purpose of the study of consumer behavior; rather, the emphasis in the following chapters reflects an attempt to economize with resources. The areas dealt with are largely unexplored. Moreover, when first a reasonable framework for thinking about consumer behavior has been established, its application involves minor problems only, problems that have parallels in microeconomics, in operations research, and in systems analysis—all areas where a large and valuable literature is available.

The work presented here could not have been completed had it not been for practical and moral support from a number of individuals. In early phases in Denmark, particularly, Professor Arne Rasmussen encouraged and guided me; my colleague Otto Ottesen has in discussions provided valuable suggestions.

Since 1967 I have been associated with The Whittemore School of Business and Economics at the University of New Hampshire, and here also a number of individuals have been of valuable assistance to me. Particularly, I would like to express my gratitude to Dean Jan Clee, who not only made it possible for me to get the time for the project but also has given me practical and moral support along the way. I have received similar help from Assistant Deans Richard Mills and John Haskell.

I would also like to express my gratitude to the Computation Center, the Central University Research Fund at the University of New Hampshire, and the Whittemore School, all of which have contributed to making my experiments possible. Professor of Psychology Gordon Haaland, Assistant Professor of Sociology Thomas Burns, and Assistant Professor of Economics William Hosek have provided valuable comments.

Many people with whom I have discussed the project have in one way or another influenced my thinking. It is impossible to mention all, but I would like to express my gratitude to Associate Professor M. Venkatesan, University of Massachusetts, and Assistant Professor Stewart Bither, Pennsylvania State University. Similarly, I am extremely grateful to Associate Professor George Haines, Jr., at the University of Rochester, who has reviewed the entire manuscript and contributed extremely valuable comments. In late phases of the project Professor Erik Johnsen, the Copenhagen School of Business Administration and Economics, and Professor Olof Henell, Lund University, have been extremely helpful also.

The practical completion of the manuscript has involved many individuals but my two graduate assistants, Ray Locatelli and Robert Phelps, have provided particularly good help in proofreading and suggesting stylistic improvements. Similarly my secretaries, Mrs. M. Watkins and Mrs. E. Vachon, have worked with unsurpassed patience and skill on various versions of my not always easily read drafts. Finally, my class in consumer behavior in the fall of 1969 at the University of New Hampshire, which used the manuscript as a textbook, has provided valuable suggestions.

Most important of all, my wife Birgit has followed the work with patience, interest, and criticism. Without her support and positive attitude it would never have been completed.

FLEMMING HANSEN

About the Author

FLEMMING HANSEN is Vice-President of T. Bak Jensen, Management Consultants, Copenhagen. He was most recently an Associate Professor at the Whittemore School of Administration at the University of New Hampshire.

PART ONE

Introduction

Chapter 1

THE BACKGROUND FOR STUDIES OF CONSUMER BEHAVIOR

1. *Concern with Consumer Behavior*

1. Research on Consumer Behavior

The consumer in modern society has been studied within economics, business economics (particularly marketing), and home economics. Each of these areas has been concerned with different aspects of consumer behavior, and questions have been raised which reflect varying levels of aggregation. In studies of the total economy the marketing system has been dealt with at a highly aggregated level. In this context the single consumer is unimportant and the single products and services are interesting only to the extent that they constitute segments of a larger economy. Within business economics the concern is with the individual company and its products. Here the single consumer is important only in that he is the basic unit of which larger markets are composed. Finally, home economics is concerned with the consumer and his problems. Here the level of aggregation is low. Usually the single household and its use of products and services is studied.

Problems relevant to consumer behavior have also been dealt with in sociology, psychology, social psychology, and anthropology. In these areas the concern is with human behavior in general, and the goal is to understand behavior rather than to be able to suggest solutions to specific decision problems.[1] Finally, material relevant to studies of consumer behavior may be found in functionally oriented sciences such as statistics, mathematics, and computer science.

[1] Of course ultimately all research is problem oriented; only the distance from basic research to applied research is greater in such areas as sociology and psychology than in economics or business economics.

The main emphasis in the following chapters will be upon psychological and sociological models as a foundation for studies of consumer behavior. Occasionally other material will be touched upon, but an extensive coverage of other areas is not attempted.

2. Application of Findings

The researcher may be interested in the role of the consumer in the marketing system because he wants to know the system and to learn how it operates. However, interesting as such an understanding may be, alone it does not warrant extensive studies. Rather, an understanding of the consumer as a part of the marketing system is important because it makes improved decision-making possible for the marketers, the consumers, and the state and federal officials concerned with regulating the system.

The marketer is interested in the system because he wants to select strategies which allow him to achieve his profit, sales, and other goals; therefore he wants models which makes it possible to deduce normative decision rules with respect to price, product, and promotional strategies (Kotler 1967 and Palda 1969). Many such decision rules can be derived from existing models, but when they are analyzed closely they appear to rest upon assumptions about consumers which have little or no basis in available evidence.

The consumer wants to "get the most out of the system," and he is interested in models which make it possible to deduce normative consumer decision rules (Burk 1968 and Carman 1969). However, only slight progress has been made with such models, perhaps because the goals with respect to which normative consumer decision-making rules should be evaluated are extremely difficult to formulate.

Society is interested in the marketing system because it is an integrated part of the total economic system and because its malfunctioning may have severe consequences for society's total well-being. Traditionally, economists have provided guidelines for decisions in this area (Hansen 1955, Parsons and Smelser, 1956). Often, however, unpredicted effects have been observed, and frequently they can be traced back to invalid assumptions about consumers' reactions.

3. The Influence of the Marketing System upon Society

In recent years, a number of authors have pointed at problems associated with the functioning of the marketing system (Packard 1957, Galbraith 1958, and Toynbee 1962). Often this discussion rests upon misconceptions about the marketing system but, nevertheless, important problems are pointed at. It is not our purpose to review this literature here; but, because of the extreme importance of some of the problems, a few points should be made.

There can be little doubt that governmental agencies and others concerned with the functioning of our society will become increasingly concerned with the functioning of the marketing system. They will display a concern which will not be limited to the system's influence on the total economy, but which will also cover the role which the marketing system plays in shaping the total society and its values.

However, any attempt to regulate the marketing system's influence upon society's values and norms will have to rest upon some kind of consensus about the goals the system is supposed to serve. Traditionally, it has been seen as a primary goal of the marketing system that the economy function properly, and the system has been disturbed only when it was necessary to insure that this goal was met. The attempt to regulate the marketers' influence upon consumers' values and product choices, however, cannot be valued with respect to this goal. Possible strategies must be appraised in relation to goals concerning preferable values and choices. Assuming that such goals can be established and disregarding the dangers inherent in establishing them,[2] the marketing system can be influenced in three ways. Influence can be aimed at the marketers, at the consumers, or at the rules which govern the interaction between marketers and consumers.

The first approach has been suggested by many critiques of the marketing system. However, how successful it will be is questionable. In a free economic society, business enterprises work toward such goals as profit maximization, survival, market-share, and the like. Given the marketing system and the rules under which it operates, and given the consumers and the way in which they respond, business enterprises will select strategies which are likely to insure that these goals are met (Hansen 1955). They may do so more or less intelligently, but as long as their goals remain the same, it is not likely that major change in their behavior can be brought about. Consequently, through influence upon business enterprises the marketing system can be changed only if new goals can be imposed upon the marketers. Such goals can result from major changes in the ownership or in the organizational structure of companies. For example, an increased number of consumer corporations, employee-owned corporations, or nationalized companies, may bring about such changes. The creation of a business sector dominated by such companies, however, may have such drastic effects upon society that it becomes questionable whether such change really is wanted by a majority of the population.

A second approach is to control the marketing system by laws regulating the interaction between marketers and customers. Several types of such laws are already in existence, as for example regulation of competition, public control in particular industries (utilities, transportation, and the like), and of certain products (drugs, liquor, cigarettes, and so on). However, such

[2] For example, to pursue a policy that encourages consumers to purchase some products rather than others implies a limitation on the consumer's "free choice," an effect which may violate values held by some in the society.

legislation often has a limited effect or is burdened with significant secondary effects. The first drawback can be exemplified by a law regulating the information which must be provided on product labels or by one specifying how interest rates must be given in connection with credit purchases. Such attempts of control will hardly have major negative secondary effects, but it can be questioned how much they will change the marketing system.

The complete prohibition of television advertising can serve as an example of the second kind of regulation. This action would definitely influence the marketing system. However, it would also have major effects on particular industries (prohibiting television commercials would completely change the structure of the television industry), and it would make marketing more expensive. The latter effect requires a few comments.

The major function of the marketing system is to overcome the distance between marketers and consumers, a distance which is increasing as the society is growing in complexity. If some of the more efficient ways in which the company can communicate with its market are eliminated, the company will have to choose more expensive and less efficient communication channels, and this change will result in more expensive products for one or both of two reasons. Either the same distance has to be overcome by more expensive means, or changes in the production sector towards smaller companies will result. The latter method reduces the distance between company and consumer, but at the same time it will result in higher production costs. Moreover, there is no guarantee that the new promotional activities will be preferable to those which were restricted in the first place. Severe limitation of the use of one kind of communication will result in an increased use of other forms, for example, personal communication such as canvassing and door-to-door selling. Similarly it will encourage manufacturers to increase their influence upon retailers, or it will make it easier for retailers to gain control over manufacturers.

These side effects are fairly obvious when major regulations of marketing activities are considered. However, minor changes will have similar effects, only to a lesser extent, and in general attempts to curtail the marketing system will have costs in terms of decreased efficiency of the system. This is not to say that regulations are unwanted, but that any legislation should be evaluated in terms of the impact it will have upon the marketing system and the costs associated with operating it. However, such an evaluation requires a detailed understanding of how consumers will react under the new conditions.

Finally, the marketing system may be influenced through the consumers. Basically marketers adapt to the consumers, regardless of how they behave. Consequently, if a change is wanted which results in more "rational" consumption, consumers should change so that "more ethical" marketing strategies become profitable. However, it is as difficult to generate such a change as it is for the marketers to force a product through the marketing system which does not fit into the values and purchase patterns of consumers. This does not mean that such changes cannot be brought about, but it does imply that they will require far-reaching strategies, such as basic changes in school and university education, major investments in consumer education, and the like. Nevertheless, it is possible that in the long run these strategies are preferable, since they will have less significant secondary effects upon the economy and other aspects of the society. However, the proper design of such policies requires detailed understanding of consumer decision-making.

2. *The Formal Structure of Models in Economics and Psychology*

As background for the following chapters, the present section discusses formal models through a comparison between the models used in economics and psychology. The most advanced models are found in these two areas, while models in marketing and sociology have few or no formal characteristics of their own. A comparison of models in the two areas also points at difficulties encountered when findings are introduced from different areas.

A model can be described by an equation which includes the variables and parameters of interest, as follows:

$$f_i(x_1, x_2, \ldots, x_n; a_1, a_2, \ldots, a_k) = 0 \qquad (1.\text{I})$$
$$\text{for } i = 1, 2, \ldots, m$$

where n is the total number of variables, k the number of parameters, and m the number of dependent variables. If n is greater than m, there are $n - m$ independent (exogenous) variables, that is, variables which have to be determined outside the model. When the system consists of m independent relationships $(m = n)$, the model is closed and all endogenous variables can be determined. When there are fewer equations the system is underdetermined and may have many solutions. When there are more than m equations, the system is overdetermined.

Frequently the researcher is not particularly interested in the formulation in (1.I). Rather he deals with the reduced system which can be written as:

$$x_i = g_i(x_{m+1}, x_{m+2}, \ldots, x_n; a_1, a_2, \ldots, a_k) \qquad (1.\text{II})$$
$$\text{for } i = 1, 2, \ldots, m.$$

In this system there are still k parameters, m endogenous variables, and $n - m$ exogenous variables, but the system is arranged so that endogenous variables are determined directly from the parameters and the exogenous variables. If this system has $(m) \times (n - m)$ parameters different from zero, it is completely interdependent and can only be solved simultaneously. If, however, one or more of the parameters are zero, it is possible to make a causal arrangement of the relationships that will reveal how changes in exogenous variables are transmitted to the endogenous variables.

1. Intervening Variables

It is common to represent economic models as in (1.I) or (1.II); and psychological models, although they are normally not thought of in this way, can be studied within a similar framework. The psychologist, however, is rarely interested in the reduced system. Rather, he is concerned with a formulation which lies somewhere between (1.I) and (1.II). This formulation can be illustrated with an example. (In the following linear system, the a's are parameters and the x's are variables.)

$$0 = a_1x_1 + a_2x_2 + a_3x_3 + a_4x_4 \qquad \text{(1.IIIa)}$$
$$0 = a_5x_1 + a_6x_2 + a_7x_3 + a_8x_4 \qquad \text{(1.IIIb)}$$

Now imagine that x_2 and x_3 are exogenous variables and that a_1 is equal to -1, and a_4 and a_6 are equal to zero, and a_8 is equal to -1. With these assumptions the reduced system will look as follows (after solving (1.IIIb) for the endogenous variable x_4) and simplifying by substituting $a_2x_2 + a_3x_3$ for x_1):

$$x_4 = a_2a_5x_2 + (a_3a_5 + a_7)x_3 \qquad \text{(1.IV)}$$

The psychologist, however, is often interested in the following partially reduced system.

$$x_1 = a_2x_2 + a_3x_3 \qquad \text{(1.V)}$$
$$x_4 = a_5x_1 + a_7x_3$$

The difference between (1.IV) and (1.V) is that in (1.IV), x_1 has been eliminated from the system, whereas in (1.V), x_1 plays a crucial role as a tie between the first and second equations. Such *intervening variables*, which can formally be reduced out of the system, appear frequently in psychological models. Often, they reflect processes within the individual which cannot be observed directly; their functioning, however, can be inferred from studies of relationship among dependent and independent variables.

In economic models, the role of such variables is taken over by the *parameters*. When (1.IV) and (1.V) are compared, it can be seen that instead of x_1 in (1.IV) two complex parameters, $(a_2 + a_5)$ and $(a_3a_5 + a_7)$, appear. In economics, models are commonly formulated so that parameters perform the functions of the intervening variables in psychological models. Price elasticity is a typical example. In an economic model, this elasticity defines how the exogenous variable *price* determines the endogenous variable *quantity*. A psychological model describing the same relationship could look as follows: Price (exogenous variable) determines an attitude towards the product (intervening variable), and the quantity of the product which will be demanded (endogenous variable) is determined by the attitude towards the product.

Another similarity between parameters in economic models and intervening variables in psychological models appears in connection with identification problems (or quantification of the parameters). An economist is interested in parameters in the original model and tries to estimate them from observations of parameters in the reduced system. Correspondingly, the psychologist will try to learn about the intervening variables from his observation of the dependent and independent variables.

An economist could argue that the psychologist might as well get rid of the intervening variables as formally they cannot add to the understanding of the system. However, the intervening variable is redundant only if the model is completely autonomous, that is, if the phenomenon with which the model deals is independent of all factors not considered in the model. Furthermore, intervening variables can be eliminated only if all of the functional relationships are known. When it is realized that few models are really autonomous and many relationships cannot be established, it is seen to be advantageous to maintain the intervening variable.

While the psychologist's interest in intervening variables is explained by his concern with such aspects of human behavior as can rarely be observed, the absence of intervening variables in economic models is related to the normative character of these models. An economic model tries to describe a piece of reality with the purpose of determining how changes in exogenous variables will influence the endogenous variables. Frequently, the exogenous variables are decision variables such as tax rates, money supply, and prices, whereas the endogenous variables are those the economist is interested in manipulating, that is, goal variables such as national income, interest rates, and price levels. The intervening variables are interesting to the economist only to the extent that they make it possible to explain relationships between the decision and the goal variables. In the psychological model, the exogenous variables are often stimuli which act upon the individual and the endogenous variables are responses. The psychologist, however, is not much interested either in the exogenous or in the endogenous variables. Rather, he is concerned with the processes which connect the two sets of variables.

2. Dynamics in Economic and Psychological Models

The question of dynamics is dealt with differently in economic models and psychological models. The concept can be illustrated with a psychological model, McClelland's personality model as presented in Madsen (1960). This model is illustrated in Figure 1.1.

Like most psychological models, McClelland's consists of stimuli variables, hypothetical variables, and response variables. Madsen (1960) describes McClelland's stimuli variables as follows (p. 48): "Signal value reflects the similarity with previous situations in which a particular habit has been reinforced." "Meaning represents the content which the individual's culture ascribes to the particular stimulation," whereas stimulus "Incitement measures the situation's positive or negative character."

The remaining variables in Figure 1.1 should be self-explanatory.

If it is assumed that the variables are additive, and if they are symbolized as in Figure 1.1, the model can be rewritten as follows:

$$H_3 = a_1S_1 + a_2S_2 + a_3H_4 \qquad (1.\text{VIa})$$
$$H_2 = a_4S_3 + a_5H_6 \qquad (1.\text{VIb})$$
$$H_1 = a_3S_2 + a_7H_5 \qquad (1.\text{VIc})$$
$$R = a_8H_1 + a_9H_2 + a_{10}H_3 \qquad (1.\text{VId})$$

In this model there are 10 parameters $(a_1\text{-}a_{10})$, four endogenous variables $(R, H_1, H_2,$ and $H_3)$, and six exogenous variables $(S_1, S_2, S_3, H_4, H_5$ and $H_6)$.

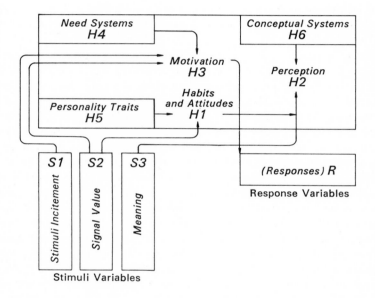

FIGURE 1.1.   McClelland's personality theory. After K. B. Madsen's "Moderne psykologiske teorier" (p. 49).

Among the endogenous variables are three intervening variables, $(H_1, H_2,$ and $H_3)$.

The H-variables $(H_1\text{-}H_6)$ constitute six hypothetical variables. The first three H-variables are also frequently discussed as *functional* variables, whereas the latter three H-variables are *disposition* variables. Disposition variables are important in psychological models because they make it possible to deal with dynamic aspects of behavior within the framework of a static model. Frequently in psychological models truly dynamic formulations are avoided by the use of such variables. Disposition variables depend on impressions received at some earlier time, but how they relate to these impressions is often left unspecified. Hypothetical disposition variables make it possible not only to relate a static model to processes that have occurred at some earlier time but also to tie the model in with future events.

The hypothetical disposition variables also play another role in the psychological model. By adding such variables to the model, one can always establish a sufficient number of relationships that, formally, all endogenous variables can be determined. By introducing a sufficient number of disposition variables, one can close the model. However, when the variables cannot be measured, the autonomy of the model is somewhat artificial. Nevertheless, such variables are frequently used because the psychologist assumes that they correspond to underlying psychological processes that he will be able to measure at some future time.

3. Choice of Dependent and Independent Variables

In a completely determined system (like 1.I) the distinction among parameters, exogenous variables, and endogenous variables is arbitrary. In a system with n functional relationships and m endogenous variables, $(n - m)$ exogenous variables can freely be chosen and the remaining k variables can be treated as constants (parameters).

In economic models the choice of variables is rarely a problem. The economist's normative approach makes it possible to distinguish between goals and means. The endogenous variables will then be the goals, whereas the means are found among the exogenous variables. When goals and means are determined, a sufficient number of other exogenous variables (preferably variables which can be estimated) and endogenous variables (preferably variables which cannot be determined outside the system) are chosen whereby the model becomes determined.

Among psychologists a normative view is rare, and it is not always obvious which variables are endogenous and which are exogenous. This problem has not always been realized, and psychologists have been faced with some difficulties as a result.

Many psychological models like Figure 1.1 consist of stimuli variables, hypothetical variables, and response variables. In such models interaction can occur among variables within each of the three categories, and frequently the interaction among different H-variables is important. But the relationship among the three categories of variables is ordered so that the S-variables determine the H-variables, which in turn determine the R-variables. This ordering automatically makes the R-variables endogenous and the S-variables exogenous, whereas the H-variables can be exogenous as well as endogenous. This way of looking at things results from the psychologist's unexpressed assumption that behavior is to be explained. Recent findings, however, have revealed the dangers that follow from such an approach. Within dissonance theory, for example, it has been observed (Festinger 1957) that the traditionally endogenous variable *behavior* may explain part of the traditional intervening variable *attitude*. Similarly, studies of information selectivity have suggested that H-variables may be important determinants of the S-variables (the stimuli) to which the individual will be exposed.

These interactions among S-, H-, and R-variables make the choice of exogenous and endogenous variables less obvious, and they may cause particular difficulties in studies of consumer behavior. This is the case when, for example, purchase behavior is studied as a function of attitudes, because the consumer's attitudes may be adjusted in accordance with the purchases he has made. Of course, if sufficiently small time intervals are used it will be possible to isolate the two effects in separate time periods. However, the problem of the length of the time periods to be studied has rarely been dealt with in connection with psychological models.

4. Problems in Aggregation

It is the nature of economic and psychological models to operate at different levels of aggregation. Nevertheless, it is possible to illustrate how the two types of models are connected and how they relate to other behavioral models.

Within economics, models range from macroeconomic models dealing with the total society to microeconomic models dealing with minor segments of the society, such as single company, a geographical area, or the market for a particular product.

Psychological models represent only a single level in the hierarchy of behavioral models. It is possible to arrange these models according to their level of aggregation:

1. Genetic models (dealing with molecules and molecular structures).
2. Physiological and neurological models (dealing with cell bodies, particularly nerve cells).
3. Psychological models (dealing with the individual).
4. Social-psychological models (dealing with the individual and his environment).
5. Sociological models (dealing with larger segments of the society).
6. Anthropological models (dealing with complete societies).

In this classification microeconomic models belong to a level between social-psychological and sociological models, whereas macroeconomic models normally operate between sociological and anthropological models. Consumer behavior can be studied at several of these levels. In the following pages it is a vital assumption that the study of aggregated consumer behavior should be based upon models of individual behavior. This, however, makes the aggregation problems extremely important, as it is not always possible to go directly from one to another level of aggregation. As an example, consider Figure 1.2.

In Figure 1.2a the same model is applied to four different individuals and

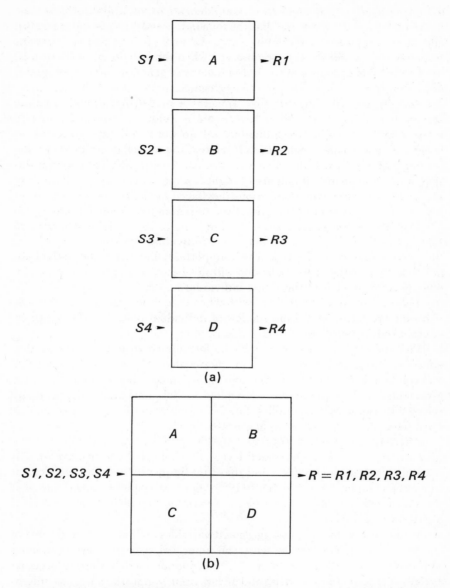

FIGURE 1.2.   Application of the same model to (a) four single individuals and (b) the same four individuals in a group.

the responses R_1, R_2, R_3, and R_4 to the independent variables S_1, S_2, S_3, and S_4 are predicted. Now assume that the four individuals are placed in a group and faced with the same stimuli, S_1, S_2, S_3, and S_4. It is possible that the responses then differ from those observed when the individuals were studied separately. The grouping of the individuals may generate interaction that is not automatically considered in the aggregated model (Figure 1.2b).

An example will illustrate this: Imagine a model that describes how a certain communication will influence an individual's behavior. Such a model may predict what the individual will answer in a situation where he is faced with a particular stimulus. If it is a realistic model, it can predict what several individuals will do when they are faced with different communications. Now if these individuals are brought together in a group and if they are exposed to the same communications they faced alone, responses may occur that are totally different from any of the responses that occurred previously.

This interaction effect results because none of the individual models in Figure 1.2a is autonomous. As long as the individuals are studied separately, the open character of the model is unimportant. But when the individuals are brought together their behavior will not be predicted by a model built directly upon models of the single individual's behavior.

These problems must be dealt with when models of aggregated consumer behavior are formulated from models of individual behavior. They can be approached in two ways.

The less aggregated models may be formulated so that the interaction effect can be controlled when they are aggregated. This will make it possible to explain the R-variables in the aggregated model based upon the same S-variables as those in the less aggregated model. This approach, normally referred to as *reductionism*, implies that the variables in the aggregated models must have counterparts at less aggregated levels.

Alternatively, new aggregated variables can be formulated that have no counterparts at less aggregated levels. Psychological constructive models are built upon such variables, and they also frequently occur in sociological models. Examples are Lazarsfelt's (1955) global variables or a variable such as "group cohesiveness"—a sociological variable to which no psychological variables correspond.

Within economics highly aggregated variables are common, and some of the problems in connection with consumer behavior in microeconomics may have to do with aggregation. Macroeconomic models were formulated before microeconomic models, and it has been tempting to suggest microeconomic models that apply variables more or less borrowed from macroeconomic models. This, however, may be dangerous since macroeconomic models use variables that do not necessarily have any meaning at less aggregated levels.

3. *Consumer Behavior in Models of Markets*

1. The Single Consumer

The aim of the present book is to explore the possibility of improved models of markets. To show that a better understanding of consumer behavior is imperative for this task, the present section will outline some integrated models of markets.

Comparisons between present knowledge and the requirements of formal models suggest that the most immediate task is to identify and define the variables that must enter into such models. In an attempt to do so, attention is directed to the single consumer. A consumer can be seen as a unit that receives some input (stimuli) from the environment and produces a certain output (responses). Such a view underlies Figure 1.3 and suggests three important classes of variables: stimuli, responses, and variables intervening between stimuli and responses.

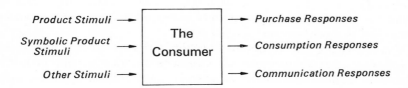

FIGURE 1.3. *The consumer as a system intervening between stimuli and responses.*

2. Consumer Responses[3]

In the individual's role as a consumer, three categories of responses are particularly important:

1. The purchases the consumer makes and his activities before making them (purchasing behavior).
2. The use the consumer makes of the product (consumption behavior).
3. The communication that the consumer provides to other consumers (communication behavior).

The purchasing behavior is of the most immediate significance for the marketer. It includes the purchase itself, as well as the preceding acts such as choice of supplier. When the purchase is made, consumption behavior starts. Through the purchase the consumer becomes the owner of a product or he

---

[3] Part of the following has appeared in Hansen (1966a).

obtains a right to use a service, and in connection with the purchase some kind of payment is involved. These two things do not necessarily take place simultaneously; however, when the consumer gains possession of the goods, he makes a commitment to pay for it. Consequently purchase responses can be defined as those preceding and including the change in possession and commitment to payment.

Consumption behavior is important because subsequent purchases are influenced by previous consumption. However, it is not always obvious what is meant by *consumption*. Within economics it is defined as occurring when a product is purchased. (Only the consumption of one's own house is an exception; here the purchase is considered an investment.) This view has influenced students of marketing to such an extent that almost all studies of consumer behavior deal with purchases only. This is unfortunate. A number of products are not destroyed in a single use but remain available for use over a considerable period of time. Moreover, consumers frequently purchase in quantities so large that the subsequent consumption goes on for some time. Finally, the services the consumer buys may include some future rights (as for example, insurance). In all of these instances consumption may occur in other periods than the one in which the purchase is made, and in such cases it is misleading to make consumption identical with purchase. In the following, consumption is seen as the set of those responses through which goods are used and destroyed.

Communication responses occur when the consumer acts as a source of information for other consumers or when the consumer provides informational feedback to retailers and producers. The consumer can convey information both through oral communication and through demonstration of products. To the first category belong instances when the consumer talks about brands, products, or other consumption-related topics. To the second category belong those instances when other consumers observe him using the product. Both kinds of communication occur primarily within the social groups to which the consumer belongs. They are particularly important when the consuming unit consists of several individuals and when the product is not both purchased and consumed by the same individual.

3. The Consumers' Stimuli

It is common to consider the factors that influence the consumer as identical with those that can be manipulated by the marketer. However, the single consumer receives many more impressions of importance for a product than those coming from the producer. All the stimuli received can be classified according to either their source or the nature of the information they provide. A classification based upon the first approach will be discussed in subsequent chapters. The nature of the information suggests distinctions among:

1. Stimuli of which the product itself is a part.[4]
2. Stimuli in which the product is symbolically represented.
3. Other stimuli of importance for the consumer's behavior.

The consumer is exposed to the product itself when he consumes it. Thereby, consumption responses become important as feedback, which influences subsequent consumption behavior. The consumer also meets the product when he observes other consumers using it. In these cases other consumers, more or less voluntarily, act as information sources. Finally, the consumer can inspect the product in stores and other places where it is exhibited.

Symbolically, the product can appear in personal and mass communication. Mass communication can be received from a large number of sources (TV, newspapers, radio, and the like), as can personal communication. Important personal information sources are the members of the individual's primary groups and salesmen or other representatives of the marketer.

Finally, the consumer receives information not directly related to products that nevertheless influences his behavior with regard to particular products. Information of this kind may concern income, the distribution of products, legal regulations, and competing product alternatives.

It should be noted that the stimuli that influence the consumer may be present when the choice is made or they may have acted upon the consumer sometime earlier. In the latter case the exposure defines a special situation with its own, often internal, responses. Only if such responses occur will the exposure influence subsequent behavior. This time lag between exposure and behavior makes intervening variables extremely important.

4. Intervening Variables

As just suggested, the consumer's behavioral responses cannot normally be related directly to the stimuli he receives. Problems follow from the time lag between stimuli and responses, and each single response is related to a large number of stimuli. Consequently the interaction between stimuli and responses will have to be studied through intervening variables. Such variables are attitudes, values, beliefs, motives, and so on. As several of the following chapters deal with them, a detailed discussion is not given here.

The introduction of intervening variables raises questions about their definition and their relationship with external (stimuli and response) variables. Preferably, it should be possible to make inferences about intervening variables based upon observations other than those to be explained by the variables. Such inferences can be based upon the consumer's response to rating scales and other measurement devices.

[4] Here *product* can have many different meanings. It can be a brand, a group of products, or a store.

5. Aggregating Individual Consumer Behavior

Markets are made up of individual consumers, and a study of marketing systems must begin with them. Commonly, however, as concern is with markets composed of many consumers or decision-making units, it is necessary to go from the single consumer to aggregated market variables.

When consuming and purchasing units are composed of more than one individual, the family or the household frequently is of interest. Here, the input is still stimuli working upon individuals, and output is individual responses. However, some input may be received by one member of the decision-making unit and the response to it be controlled by another member. In such instances, it is important to explain how interaction within the family links the independent to the dependent variables.

When individual consumers (or consuming units) are aggregated to form total markets, purchases and consumption responses must be dealt with as distributions of purchase or consumption frequencies, purchase or consumption sizes, and the like. But this is normally not the complete solution. As these responses have a feedback effect individually, they must also be considered a feedback mechanism in the aggregated market. Moreover, the individuals' communication responses act as stimuli for other individuals and must be considered as feedback to the market. Again, the concern must be with the frequency and the nature of such responses: Who communicates with whom? How frequently? What kind of information is transmitted?

Other stimuli variables must be examined from the viewpoint of the consumers. The advertising the marketer is buying must be converted to actual exposures of the consumers to it, and the price strategies he chooses must be dealt with in terms of the retail prices perceived by the consumer.

Frequently, intervening variables are measured by rating scales. It is not always possible to aggregate such measurements. The procedures that can be applied depend upon the kind of scale used. If the scale is nominal or ordinal, the aggregation of measurements is severely limited compared with operations that can be applied when the data correspond to an interval or ratio scale (Stevens 1959).

Moreover, intervening variables raise problems because the single consumer is frequently described in terms of a number of different variables. For example, he may have four or five different attitudes relevant to a particular product. Even though these single attitude measures can be aggregated, important information can thereby be lost. If, for example, a certain purchase can be predicted when a consumer scores over a certain level on all the attitude dimensions, it may still be difficult to make predictions from the aggregated score because many summarized attitude measurements will not reveal how many consumers scored higher than the required level on all the dimensions.

A third problem exists because many intervening variables are not stable, that is, they fluctuate over time. For example, if a need like *thirst* is measured, the measurement will depend on how much time has passed since the individual last had something to drink. When variables of this kind are summarized, measurements may be difficult to interpret.

Figure 1.4. illustrates the type of model that emerges from the preceding discussion of individual consumer behavior. The model rests upon a number of simplifying assumptions, but it shows some of the more important aspects of the total system. Particularly, it is a static model. The framework, however, as will be discussed in subsequent chapters, lends itself easily to dynamic formulations.

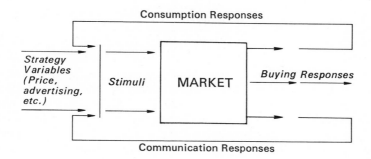

FIGURE 1.4.   *A simplified model of a market.*

6. Models of Aggregated Consumer Behavior

The marketer is related to the market in two ways. He receives payments for goods and services that he sells, so that his profit is determined by the consumers' buying responses. Second, through his product and communication strategies he can influence the stimuli to which the consumers are exposed. If it is assumed that there is only one seller who sells only one product, then a system like that in Figure 1.4 is completely determined. Under these conditions there are no other goods or services, and the consumers receive only stimuli that are controlled by the marketer, follow from their own consumption, or are generated by other consumers. The marketer, through his selection of product and communication strategies, controls all external influences upon the system; and if all relationships are specified, it is possible to quantify how sales will vary with changes in product and communication strategies. Under these assumptions a formal model can be formulated. If cost relationships are added to the system, it is possible to identify the product and communication strategies that will maximize the marketer's profit.

The functional relationships that must be known are:

1. Relationship among the marketer's strategies and stimuli that are acting upon the consumers of whom the market is composed.

2. Relationships among stimuli and intervening variables (including those between feedback and intervening variables).

3. Relationships between intervening variables and responses.

4. Relationships between strategies and costs, and between purchase responses and sales revenue.

Relationships of the first two categories have been studied within communication theory, and studies of consumer behavior have dealt with the third type of relationship.

The simplified market illustrated in Figure 1.4 deviates in two important ways from the more complex real markets. First, there is no "distance" between the company and the market. That is, there are no distribution channels and no media. Second, there are no competitors and no external environment to provide the consumers with competing stimuli.

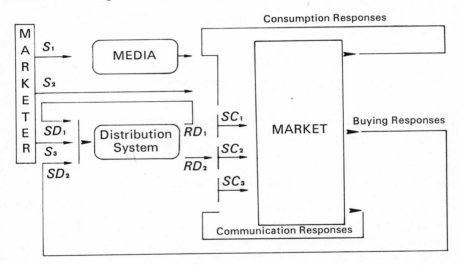

FIGURE 1.5. *A simplified model of a market, extended version. S_1, S_2, S_3: Marketer's strategy variables. SC_1, SC_2, SC_3: Stimuli acting upon consumers. RD_1: Responses from distribution system acting as feedback. RD_2: Responses from distribution systems acting as stimuli upon consumers. SD_1, SD_2: Stimuli acting upon the distribution system.*

When a market is considered in which the marketer has to work through media and distribution channels, a system like that suggested in Figure 1.5 emerges. The introduction of media and distribution channels means that the marketer's control over the stimuli that act upon the consumer decreases. This is a minor problem in connection with media, as the marketer has considerable influence upon the messages he is sending and the media through which they come. But even here his control is not perfect, as he has only little influence upon the environment in which the messages appear; the quality of the presentation is also often beyond his control.

The distribution system in its own right is composed of organizations just as the market is composed of consumers, and it must be studied in terms of its input (stimuli) as well as its output (responses). Here the important responses are those which determine the stimuli the consumers will face. Moreover, the distribution system has its own feedback mechanism and consumer responses add feedback to it. Before formal models of more complex marketing systems can be formulated, a detailed understanding of this system is required.

In summary, in addition to the relationships already mentioned, the introduction of media and a distribution system make it necessary to deal with:

5. Relationships between, on the one hand, the company's product and communication strategies and, on the other hand, the stimuli that act upon the distribution system.

6. Relationships among the stimuli acting upon the distribution system (including feedback effects) and the system's intervening variables.

7. Relationships among the distribution system's intervening variables and its responses.

8. The modifying effects of media upon the company's messages.

These additions increase the complexity of the model, but the total system is still completely determined. If the relationships can be specified, optimal decision rules can be derived. However, the marketing system becomes even further complicated when competitors are considered. Their introduction into the model makes it necessary to introduce relationships between the competitors and the distribution system, between the competitors and the consumers, and between the marketer and his competitors. Moreover, analysis of the stimuli that act upon the distribution system and the consumers becomes more complicated as stimuli are now provided from two or more sources.

Whether such an enlarged system can be completely determined is questionable. It would require that the relationship between the marketer and his competitors must be known to such an extent that the competitors' behavior can be either predicted or controlled. The ultimate goal for a theory of competition must be to make such predictions possible. This should be accomplished through studies of the relationships between the marketer's strategies and the competitors' choices of strategies, a task that will involve extensive work with game-theoretical models. Particularly, these relationships may be predictable for a group of only a few major companies. Under such conditions close ties exist between the price, advertising, and quality strategies of the single marketers (Rasmussen 1955).

Still further complexity is added when it is considered that the consumers as well as the competitors and the distribution system are influenced by society in general. Such influences may be in the form of legal regulations or may occur as information that influences the consumers' evaluation of products. They often come to the consumer in the form of stimuli that are not closely related to the product.

Thus, two final sets of relationships must be added:

9. Competitive relationships.
10. Relationships between society and the marketing system.

All these relationships (1-10) define areas that must be studied before more formal models of the marketing system can be established; communication theory, the theory of competition, and studies of consumer behavior deal with some of them.

4. *Outline of Following Chapters*

The preceding pages have described how individual consumer behavior forms a foundation for models of markets. In the following chapters consumer behavior will be studied as choice behavior. The discussion will be grounded in psychological studies of choice and conflict. Although consumer behavior constitutes a large part of the individual's behavior, large parts of psychological theory are less important for the present approach. Therefore the discussion of psychological models of conflict and choice can be limited to the extent that the particular characteristics of consumer choice behavior can be identified.

In a given choice situation the individual may have more or less freedom of choice, the choice may be more or less important, and it may be more or less easily reversed. The nature of the choice process will depend upon these aspects of the situation: Compared with other conflict situations, consumer choices give the individual considerable freedom of choice, that is, they have a high degree of volition. Also, consumer choices are commonly irreversible, that is, once the choice is made it is difficult to change it. Finally, consumer choices are less consequential than choices concerning professional occupation, health problems, and child rearing. On the other hand they are more consequential than a choice between the left and right hands for removing one's glasses. Even though consumer choices cover a wide range of situations, it is still possible to avoid complex conflicts such as those studied in connection with abnormal or psychic behavior or very inconsequential routinized choices such as those in animal learning experiments.

Human behavior is motivated. Many psychological theories deal with motives that vary from basic (such as hunger and thirst) to very inconsequential ones (such as the positive evaluation associated with certain foods). As will be discussed, consumer choice behavior is primarily governed by less basic motives: the affective values associated with alternatives. Basic motives are normally satisfied equally well by most of the alternatives the consumer considers. Basic motives are very strong, and if they were not satisfied they would dominate the individual's behavior. Therefore, in the marketplace, no single competitor is allowed to monopolize a single basic motive. Rather, a considerable number of alternatives are always available that will satisfy basic motives equally well and that differ only in the extent to which they harmonize with less consequential affective values. The major concern of consumer research must be with such affective values, and basic motivation will have to be considered only to the extent that it influences them.

Although these limitations of consumer behavior as a subset of human behavior provide limits to our discussion, still many subjects will have to be considered. In Part Two the psychological background for a model of consumer choice behavior is presented. These chapters rely heavily upon contemporary psychological theory, but the various psychological approaches are not dealt with as in most psychology textbooks and books on consumer behavior that treat theories of learning, theories of perception, theories of motivation, and the like as independent areas. Rather, relevant findings are introduced with an integrated model in mind.

In Part Four, a model of individual consumer choice behavior is proposed and its implications are discussed. Chapters 11 to 13 present original experimental evidence from the author's own research on consumer choice behavior.

Part Five deals with aggregated consumer behavior. It concentrates on the complete consumer decision process, and relates it to collective decision-making, particularly within the family. This approach makes it possible to discuss aggregated consumer behavior in Six. In the concluding chapter, future problems in the study of consumer behavior and normative applications of the model are discussed.

This book draws upon psychology and sociology as well as studies of consumer behavior. It was necessary to be highly selective because of the large number of findings extant in the first two areas. Emphasis has been placed upon recent findings, and findings most directly relevant to models of consumer behavior. Moreover the degree of consensus within the particular area from which findings are reported has been considered. Where disagreements exist, the more important views have been given, and consequently more findings discussed in such areas. Findings are included regardless of whether they support or disagree with the view proposed here.

Studies of consumer behavior are included according to a slightly different criterion: Here a wider selection has been made, and studies not included have been rejected because of either their quality or a lack of information with which to rate them. These criteria have been applied as uniformly as possible, although the evaluation of each single study is not included, for reasons of space.

PART TWO

Psychological Foundations for a Theory of Consumer Choice Behavior

Chapter 2

CONSUMER RESPONSES

Consumer markets can be described as systems that transform environmental stimuli into consumption, communication, and purchase responses. The nature of these responses will now be explored through an analysis of the dependent variables that have been used in studies of consumer behavior. This approach highlights the problems facing students of consumer behavior, but it does not guarantee that all potential variables are included, as new and superior variables may be introduced in the future. Nevertheless, to identify the variables used in the past and to examine the ways they are related directs the attention to some of the problems with which a model of consumer behavior will have to deal.

In the following pages a few selected examples illustrate the variety of measures applied and show how these variables reflect responses chosen in particular situations. Attention is directed to the nature of the consumer's responses in the last part of the chapter, where responses are analyzed from a psychological point of view.

1. *Dependent Variables*

1. Measuring Consumer Behavior

Practically all aspects of consumer behavior can be, and have been, measured both directly and indirectly. Direct measures rely upon information obtained from the consumers themselves. Such information can be gathered with the use of observational procedures, or it can be based upon the consumer's verbal responses. An example of the first method is in-store observations of purchases; the latter method is exemplified by the consumers' own verbal accounts of their previous purchases. Indirect measures reflect variations in consumer behavior without studying it directly. Examples of such variables are data from the company's own sales records, information obtained from store panels, or consumption data based upon production and similar statistics. When indirect methods are used, they are always a substitute for measurements that could have been obtained directly. That is, for each indirect measure it is possible to think of a corresponding direct measure that would give the same information. For that reason the present concern is with direct measures alone. However, this does not mean that indirect measures are not important, for they may have considerable advantages such as being less expensive and more easily available. An explanation of direct variables will automatically provide an explanation of the indirect measures as well.

2. Observational Measures

Generally, observational measurements are the most reliable, but they are also the most expensive and often difficult to obtain. It is a fundamental problem that the observer almost always influences the observed behavior. Furthermore, in observational studies, a record must be kept, perhaps in the form of a movie or a written report. However, in both instances inaccuracies will occur. A film can report only part of the total situational setting, and thereby important aspects are lost. If a written report is used, inaccuracies will occur in the observer's report. It is not possible to get all details down in a report, and the observer may (unknowingly) disturb the observations by relying upon his own experiences to interpret the observed behavior. Nevertheless, observational studies (although presently scarce) are possible. First and foremost, motion and time studies seem promising. These techniques have successfully been used over the last half century in studies of organizational behavior (see for example, Niebel 1967). Future application of such methods as stopwatch time studies, work sampling, and filming may provide extensive information about consumer behavior. Modified attempts of this nature have been made by Schwartz (1964), Steiner (1966a), Wells and LoSciuto (1966), Alexis et al. (1968), and Granbois (1968).

3. Studies Relying upon Personal Reports

It is possible to ask individuals to tell about their own behavior by asking them what they did on various occasions in the past or requiring them to keep a log of their own behavior. The first approach is the easiest and least expensive, but also the least reliable. Errors with which the market researcher is familiar may occur when respondents are asked about what they did in the past. Respondents do not remember, or they will not report correctly. They may want to be kind to the interviewer, or they may purposely try to give an inaccurate picture of themselves. In all instances doubtful results are forthcoming from this approach. Nevertheless, studies based on simple interviewing have been used successfully in a number of instances.

Log-keeping can be used in two different ways. The researcher may ask the respondent to complete a log for some previous time period, or the respondent may be required to keep the log himself as the action proceeds, when usually he receives the log with the instruction that he is to keep it for a certain period, and then return it. Both methods have advantages and disadvantages. The first approach may easily result in the same errors as simple interviewing. On the other hand, the keeping of a current log may influence the action, as does the presence of the observer in direct observation. Whichever approach one chooses, the response rate is a major problem. With this kind of study a response of 15% to 25% is not uncommon (Foote 1966). With a response rate this low, the use of probability sampling is meaningless, and judgment samples may be the only possible solution.

2. *Behavioral and Internal Responses*

Consumer behavior variables reflect aspects of responses that occur in particular situations, but they cover only part of these responses. As psychological theory concerns the individual's choice of responses, it is important to point out similarities and differences between the measurements upon which consumer behavior variables rest and the responses with which the psychologist deals. Only then can the study of consumer behavior be tied in with psychological theory.

To the psychologist, a response is a reaction to a specific situation. It can be an observable act (such as picking up a brand), but it can also be a completely internal reaction (such as a decision about some future behavior). The first is a *behavioral response*, while the latter can be labeled an *internal response*. In specific situations an individual may respond with either of the two or with a combination of both. In one situation a consumer may respond by picking a brand, in another by *thinking* that he will buy a certain brand sometime later, and in still another situation he may pick a substitute brand and at the same time decide that he will buy his regular brand as soon as it becomes available. Commonly, however, the student of consumer behavior limits his interest to either the behavioral or the internal response. Thus, consumer variables often reflect only part of the responses that the consumer considers and chooses. When, for example, a consumer is exposed to a TV commercial, his response may be extremely complex, consisting of internal components (for example, a change in beliefs) and a behavioral component (for example, a switch to another channel). However, the market researcher who studies the effects of the commercial may attempt to register the internal component only. Similarly, when a purchase is made, it may be accompanied by various internal responses, but the researcher be concerned only with the purchase itself.

When it is realized that the researcher wants only to explain the change in beliefs or the purchase and not the total behavior of the individual, this concern with only part of the complete response may be excusable. It is unfortunate, however, when it is believed that the consumer's behavior can be understood only as reactions to a particular situation. But because of the market researcher's limited focus, he records in his data only the particular response that he has decided beforehand to measure. He does not often realize that it may be just as significant to study what substitute responses the consumer considers and how frequently they are chosen. It may be as important to know how frequently a consumer postpones a certain purchase as it is to know when he makes it. Moreover, the consumer's choices cannot be explained so long as all the alternatives considered are not taken into account.

3. *Responses Underlying Dependent Variables*

1. Behavioral Responses

Although students of consumer behavior have rarely dealt with the entire set of response alternatives in a particular situation, they have been concerned with both behavioral and internal responses. As these variables are usually studied in different contexts, we will treat them relatively independently. Behavioral responses include purchases, several activities preceding purchases, consumption, and communication responses.

PURCHASE VARIABLES

Purchases can be studied by observation and by means of the consumers' own reports. Logically, it is possible to learn only about purchases that have been made. Nevertheless, the researcher may be interested in knowing something about future purchasing behavior. In such cases, measures of purchase intentions and simulated choices have been substituted for measurements of past purchases.

In many ways, purchase responses are the most important part of consumer behavior, and other aspects of consumer behavior are often dealt with only to help explain purchase responses. Much of the concern with consumers' reactions to mass communication is motivated by a wish to better understand their purchase responses.

Basically, the purchase response is simple: the chosen response must be registered in terms of what and how much was purchased, where the purchase was made, when it was made, which price was paid, and the like. It was previously suggested that a purchase is made whenever a consumer commits himself to pay for the product, but it may be operationally difficult to specify the time of the purchase. For example, in a supermarket, is the purchase made when the article is picked up from the shelf or when it is paid for at the cashier? Moreover, it may be difficult to obtain accurate measurements even when the purchase itself is conceptually well-defined.

Information about purchases can be used to distinguish between buyers and nonbuyers. However, several more complex statistics are often computed, being derived from combinations of two or more aspects of the underlying responses, such as the following measures.

Brand Loyalty: When a sequence of purchase reponses is studied, several different patterns may be found in the data. On the one hand, the sequence may consist of a number of purchases of the same brand. The consumer for whom such a pattern is observed is said to be loyal to that brand. On the other hand, the sequence can consist of as many different brands as there are purchases, in which case no loyalty exists. Of course, many other combinations can be found. For example, in a market with many different brands, a consumer can make the following sequence of purchases of the brands A and B:

$$A\text{-}A\text{-}B\text{-}A\text{-}B\text{-}A\text{-}B\text{-}A\text{-}A\text{-}A\text{-}A\text{-}B$$

This consumer can be said to be partially loyal to A, or to be first-brand loyal to A and second-brand loyal to B. In general, depending upon the length and number of the different runs, various degrees of loyalty can be defined. Definitions applied in studies of consumer behavior are discussed by Brown (1953), Cunningham (1956), Kuehn (1962), and Massy et al. (1968).

Store and Other Loyalty: When the concern is with the genetic product choices (for example, orange juice or tomato juice), with the place of the purchase, or with product family choices (for example, Campbell or Heinz soups), product, store, or product-family loyalty can be defined. For example, the relationship between store and brand loyalty is discussed by Cunningham (1961) and by Wickström (1965).

Private-Brand Proneness: As a consumer can concentrate his purchases on few or many individual brands, he can make few or many purchases of private brands. Private-brand proneness is defined as the frequency of private-brand purchases (Frank and Boyd 1965, and Myers 1967). Similarly, the consumer can more or less frequently make use of deals, special offers, and coupons; this activity defines the extent to which he is *deal-prone* (Frank and Massy 1965).

Other aspects of purchases of frequently bought products can be used to classify consumers. A few examples will suffice: The frequency and size of purchases form the basis for a distinction between *heavy* and *light users* and the proportion of purchases devoted to small packages identifies *package-size proneness* (Frank 1967b).

With major purchases and with new products, the concern is usually with the *timing of the single purchase* rather than the pattern of purchases. For new products, innovators (those purchasing early) are distinguished from followers (those purchasing later). With repeat purchases the single purchase can be studied relative to the last similar purchase, relative to a fixed time where intentions were measured, or relative to the beginning of a new advertising campaign.

Of course, many other combined measures can be and have been applied. Like the others, these variables are derived from simple registration of purchase responses. The variables used by Massy et al. (1968) can serve as an example. These authors studied consecutive purchases of coffee, tea, and beer, using 31 different measures of purchasing behavior. Five are simple statistics, based upon aggregation, for example, the number of units of the product purchased and the number of shopping trips on which the product is purchased. Seven are statistics based on ratios of different kinds, such as the proportion of the units of the product devoted to the favorite brand and the proportion of the units of the product bought in the favorite store. The remaining 19 statistics are based upon the order of purchases, for example number of brand runs, number of brand runs greater than one purchase long, average length of brand runs measured in trips, and average lengths of brand runs measured in units of product. The authors conducted a factor analysis of these measures and identified seven basic factors that in the subsequent analyses were used as dependent variables. Examples of the factors are a loyalty factor reflecting the overall tendency for loyalty, with stores and brands combined; a brand loyalty factor reflecting a tendency for brand loyalty; a store loyalty factor; and a factor reflecting the amount of activity exhibited by families with respect to the product.

CONSUMPTION VARIABLES

Considerably less research has been concerned with consumption behavior than with purchase behavior. One reason is the tendency to define consumption as identical with purchases. Only in recent years has it been realized that future purchases can be explained only if the consumer's previous experiences with the same and similar products are studied.

Often, consumption is difficult to observe because it takes place privately and at times when observations are difficult to make. Consumption, unlike purchase and prepurchase behavior, is part of almost all human activity.

In an attempt to reveal patterns in consumption behavior, total time spending has been studied (Foote 1966). Because such studies also provide information about the environment in which consumer behavior takes place, they will be discussed in the following chapter where situational influences on consumer behavior are dealt with. Other studies have relied upon factor analysis of purchase, use, and interest data (Wilson 1966 and Pessemier and Tigert 1966).

Extensive studies of individual products have been conducted only in connection with the consumer's use of mass media as information source, and concern such aspects as the extensiveness and frequency of use, the time spent on different media, and the like. Similar measures could be applied in studies of the use of other products as well, but so far research of this kind has been conducted only by companies, and findings have not been published. (A single exception is the study presented by Cerha in 1967.)

In spite of the scarcity of data and methodology, it is obvious that studies of consumption behavior must rest upon measurements of responses chosen by consumers in specific situations and that these measurements must underlie all aggregated variables.

COMMUNICATION VARIABLES

Here and in the following a distinction is made between instances in which consumers receive information (exposure variables) and instances where they provide information to others (communication responses). This distinction may seem a little subtle in that whenever a communication response occurs, somebody is also exposed to the information. It is maintained for several reasons. First, the nature of the response is completely different in the two cases. Second, in aggregated market systems (Chapter 18) communication responses play a unique role. Finally, some exposures occur in all choice situations, whereas communication responses are found in only a few.

Like purchase and consumption responses, communication responses represent observable action, and like consumption behavior these responses have given rise to only limited research. Most frequently they have been studied from consumers' own reports (Katz and Lazarsfeld 1955; Arndt 1968b; and Silk 1966), either when information has been requested from the consumer or when the source is the initiator of the conversation. In both cases the response is tied to a specific situation, and any attempt to understand the nature of such responses must begin in studies of the situations in which they occur.

In this area observational methods have rarely been used, but studies of family interaction processes (Chapter 17) and of customer-salesman interactions (Chapter 9) suggest that such responses could be studied observationally in semi-experimental settings.

2. Internal Responses

The market researcher is interested in internal responses either when no behavioral response occurs, or when the behavioral response is unrelated to the problem the researcher is studying. Such responses are often found prior to purchases, and they can appear as changes in beliefs, values, or intentions following exposure to marketing communication or as cognitive changes when the consumer is thinking about brands, products, and the like. The first type will be labeled *exposure responses*, the latter *deliberation responses*. The introduction of such internal responses makes it possible to relate subsequent purchases, consumption, and communication to exposure and thinking occurring prior to the particular situation in which the behavioral response is chosen.

EXPOSURE VARIABLES

The purchase can be observed, but the response to exposure is rarely observable. Therefore the measurements used to study exposure reflect that exposure has taken place, or they try to identify some internal response generated by the exposure. These measures can be direct (for example, obtained through interviews) or indirect (for example, circulation data), but only direct measures are considered here.

Direct measures can be observational (for example, in store studies of exposure to display material) or be based upon reports from the consumers (for example, recall of advertising material). Observational records of exposure vary considerably in detail. Somewhat crude measures, such as the number of individuals observing a billboard, give information only about where or when the exposure occurred. Somewhat more detailed measures also tell who was exposed; and the most detailed records, such as measurements of eye movements, give information about the length of the exposure, what material was attended to, and so on.

When interviewing is used, exposure is registered by means of recall or recognition techniques, which can provide more or less detailed information. Like purchase data they are subject to errors following from inaccuracies in the consumer's memory, and they are subject to biases that can occur when the accuracy of the respondent's replies cannot be controlled. A discussion of these methods is available in Robinson et al. (1968).

As the concern rarely is with the exposure itself, but rather with the impact it subsequently may have upon purchases, a number of measures have been applied in an attempt to trace these effects. These may be observational or based upon direct questioning. The first are exemplified by measurement of pupil size, foot pressing, dynamic skin responses, and the like (Advertising Research Foundation 1957 and Lucas and Britt 1963); the second by measures of changes in knowledge, intentions, or attitudes (see, for example, Cerha 1967).

Although less obvious than purchase responses, these measures reflect reactions in response to particular stimulation. Because of the diversity of exposure situations, the basic measures taken are many and varied. As an example, Halbert (1966), in "a study about how new families learn about the market," uses 28 different dependent variables, some reflecting the nature and the frequency of exposure, others dealing with different kinds of effects.

Combined and aggregated variables exhibit considerable variations also. A case in point is the wide variety of readership measures that can be applied. Here, even slight variations in the underlying records result in considerable differences in the aggregated measures. For example, Schyberger (1965) discusses how recall measures related to particular issues (the *issue* method) differ from those obtained when the respondent's reading pattern in a certain time interval is explored (the *time* method). Finally, exposure measures may be made as a foundation for complex aggregated variables such as Starch's (1964) Netap variable or the variables used in multiple coverage studies (Broadbent 1964 and Agostini 1961).

OTHER PREPURCHASE VARIABLES

It would not be necessary to deal with other prepurchase variables if autonomous relationships could be established between exposure and purchase. However, the complexity of consumer behavior rarely makes it possible to quantify such relationships. Therefore attention must be devoted to the consumer's behavior between exposures and purchase. This implies a concern with mostly internal cognitive processes, which, like exposure effects, are difficult to trace. These processes occur in specific situations, and often the nature of the situation determines the cognitive activity. For example, a consumer may begin to consider whether or not he can afford a new car in a situation where the old one is performing poorly, or a housewife may consider buying more bread when she realizes that there is no more bread in the refrigerator. These cognitive processes, which occur prior to purchases and often tie exposure to purchase, will be labeled *deliberation responses*. Subsequently it will be discussed how these internal responses occur as reactions to more or less important conflicts.

Because of the internal character of these responses, they are difficult to quantify, and thus in most instances their effects must be inferred from indirect measures. Probably the most elaborate measure is the deliberation index developed by Katona and Mueller (1954) which is composed of five independent measures reflecting circumspectness (length of planning period, amount of family discussions, and other alternatives considered), information seeking[1], choosing with regard to price, choosing with respect to brand, and the number of features considered.

Rogers (1962) discussed the different steps of the prepurchase process in connection with the adoption of new products and practices. In his description of the single stages he writes: "At the awareness stage the individual . . . *seeks additional information*" (p. 82). "At the evaluation stage . . . *a sort of mental trial occurs . . . and information and advice from peers is likely to be sought*" (pp. 83–84). "At the trial stage the individual *uses the innovation on a small scale*" (p. 84) and finally, "Adoption implies continued use" (p. 86) (all italics added).

Similar attempts to identify variables to be used in studies of prepurchase

---

[1] In the present approach the term *deliberation* is used to refer to prepurchase activities *other* than information acquisition.

behavior are discussed by Lavidge & Steiner (1961). They suggest that advertising can be studied as a force that moves consumers from a cognitive over an affective to a conative (behavioral) phase, and they point at variables such as awareness, interest, knowledge, conviction and intentions that reflect the different steps in the process.

Still other variables have been used in studies of purchase intentions (Juster 1964) and in studies of problem solving and decision making (Brim et al. 1962). Interesting attempts are also Lewin's (1958) and Bilkey's (1953) use of prepurchase tension ratings, the studies of perceived risk (Cox 1967a), and of dissonance (Engel and Light 1968). All these approaches will be explored further in later chapters.

This review suggests that the kinds of dependent variables used in studies of consumer behavior can be traced back to responses occurring in specific situations. They are aggregated measures of the individual's behavior. Therefore, to improve our understanding of these variables, it is necessary to deal with the type of responses chosen and the specific situations in which the choices are made.

4. *The Nature of Responses*

1. Behavioral Responses

The study of consumer behavior requires that the behavior to be described be meaningfully defined. Here an attempt is made to do this.

To the observer, the behavior of an individual may look like a continuous stream of action. Clearly this does not agree with the view that human behavior can be studied as responses to specific situations. However, a closer inspection will reveal that the stream of behavior is composed of a number of distinguishable elements. Mandler (1964) has studied such elements of behavior, which he labels "organized responses." Though Mandler is not too clear on this point, he does mention sequences as complex as "driving home" and "eating a meal." In clarification he writes: " . . . any organized response has the same inevitability of completion that we readily accept in short organized responses such as swallowing, lever-pressing, kicking or speaking a word. And they are acquired in much the same way. There is nothing qualitatively different about learning how to write and learning how to strike a single typewriter key" (pp. 165–66). The individual's stream of behavior can be seen as composed of such organized responses, the nature of which will be discussed subsequently.

Mandler maintains that a tendency towards completion is present in the individual as soon as a sequence has been started. This concept is especially important to the student of consumer behavior who must be concerned with interruptions of behavioral responses. Since the fact that a sequence has been started implies a tendency towards completion, any interruption will create some kind of conflict. Further, when faced with interruptions the individual will attempt to apply one of the following strategies:

1. Persist to completion.
2. Find substitute responses.
3. Exhibit emotional disturbances.

Mandler presents considerable evidence in favor of his formulation. He finds that the more firmly established a sequence is, the more conflict (arousal) will follow an interruption and the more attempts will be made towards completion of the sequence. The better organized a sequence is, the more easily subjects recover from an interruption, and the less relevant to the sequence the disruption is, the slower the recovery will be.

When the same behavioral response is performed on a number of different occasions it will be found to have a large number of single acts in common, but variations can also be observed. The way in which the response is structured may vary, and so may the way in which the single acts are carried out. Some of these variations represent adjustments to minor changes in the environment for which the individual has some tolerance and to which he— within limits—is able to adjust the performance. These adjustments in the performance relate to the degree of perfection to which the responses are learned, a matter that will be discussed in more detail in connection with learning processes (Chapter 7).

2. Choice Processes and Conflict

It is also important to look at the behavior that occurs between two adjoining responses. When a response terminates, a new one will be picked; and similarly, when it is interrupted, new action is chosen. In such situations the individual is faced with several internal alternatives as well as behavioral alternatives. These instances will be labeled *conflict situations*, and the behavior in these situations is discussed as *choice processes*. Although several subsequent chapters deal further with choice behavior, it is necessary to say a few words about choice-processes here in order to clarify the response concept.

Choice processes vary greatly in duration. In extreme cases one behavioral response may seem to follow directly after another; however, on other occasions the individual may be observed between two behavioral responses. In such instances it will commonly be found that he interacts actively with his environment. The amount of conflict that can be inferred may vary widely among different situations. In some instances the situation seems immediately to supply the cues necessary for the next behavioral response. This will especially be the case with choice processes occurring as a result of interruptions. In such instances the interrupting agent will often initiate the subsequent behavior also. To illustrate: If the telephone rings while one or another sequence is being performed, the action will stop and a new sequence, "answering the telephone," will be generated. Here the telephone both caused the interruption and directed the subsequent behavior.

3. The Stream of Action

Altogether, the behavior of the single individual may be seen as a string of behavioral responses with choice processes in between. This concept makes it possible to describe the total behavior of the single consumer along a time axis, as is done in Figure 2.1, where it can be seen that responses and choice processes follow each other. Some of the choices occur between different responses, and others represent interruptions.

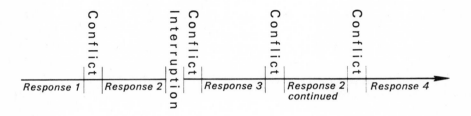

FIGURE 2.1.   *A sequence of behavioral responses and conflicts.*

A view like the one illustrated in Figure 2.1 makes it possible to improve our understanding of purchase, consumption, and communication behavior in connection with particular products. If the choice processes are isolated which are relevant to the product, then those occurring prior to the purchase constitute the purchasing behavior and those following the purchase, the consumption behavior. Among both, instances can be found when communication responses are chosen. Moreover, if it is known what factors will influence the choices and how these factors will interact, then the outcome of the choices can be predicted; and if it can be predicted also what choice processes will occur, the consumer's total stream of behavior can be explained.

4. Cognitive Aspects of Behavior

Until now, behavior has been discussed in terms of sequences of behavioral responses; however, "something within the mind" accompanies the behavior, and when choices are made intellectual processes are important. The fact that the environment may interrupt the behavior implies cognitive processes also. Altogether, behavioral responses and choice processes consist not only of action but also of cognitive processes. Three different kinds of cognitive processes will be discussed:

1. Cognitive processes governing the behavioral responses.
2. Cognitive processes occurring in choice processes.
3. Cognitive processes accounting for interruptions.

Cognitive aspects of behavioral responses may be seen as programs directing the action (Hilgard and Bower 1966). In a sense, they are ordered arrangements of cognitive elements corresponding to the components of the chain of action. The behavior and the accompanying cognitive processes are two aspects of the same reality. The cognitive aspects governing the action are quite independent of the environment. Normally, when behavioral responses are performed, the environment does not directly influence the cognitive processes. On the contrary, when such interaction occurs, inter-ruptions result. The functioning of such control hierarchies is dealt with in Chapter 7.

Cognitive aspects of choice processes can be studied as conflict solving (Simon 1967a), and these internal processes are the main concern in sub-sequent chapters. In contrast to the programs governing behavioral responses, they are greatly influenced by and in close interaction with the environment. Information is picked up, and eventually the environment is manipulated in order to facilitate such information search.

A particularly important class of cognitive processes associated with choice processes are those internal responses which can help terminate the aroused conflict. In a given conflict situation the selected response may be a chain of thoughts, which in some cases may result in a commitment con-cerning future behavior. Such responses have much in common with behavioral responses. They may be seen as learned sequences, and they may be more or less firmly established. But they differ from behavioral responses in two aspects. They cannot easily be observed, and they have no immediate impact on the environment.

It is much more complicated to deal with internal responses than it is to study behavioral responses. Behavior can be observed directly, whereas cognitive processes can only be inferred. Nevertheless, when cognitive processes can help to explain and predict behavior, they become valuable tools in the hand of the model-builder; therefore, it is important to decide whether the study of behavior should limit itself to observable behavior or deal also with cognitive variables. This issue is probably the single most-discussed issue in psychology (see, for example, Skinner 1953). It has been argued that only behavioral aspects of action should be dealt with as it is impossible to know what goes on within the individual. But it has also been maintained that cognitive and other internal processes are fundamental to the study of behavior.

This study adheres to the view that properly defined behavioral responses make it possible to avoid dealing with the cognitive processes governing these responses. If it is known that certain acts will be performed in the course of an organized sequence, the study of the behavioral response can be limited to this chain of action. In contrast, choice processes can not be explained from observation of the action itself. In choice processes, several internal alternatives as well as behavioral response alternatives are available; and, in order to explain which will be chosen, it is necessary to consider the cognitive processes involved in the choice. Thus the following chapters concern the cognitive functions in conflict situations.

5. *Consumer Behavior Variables: An Overview*

Just as it is possible to illustrate how traditional consumer behavior variables can be traced back to responses chosen in particular situations, it is possible to start with the psychological responses and then show how consumer behavior variables emerge. Eventually this approach will result in a more complete coverage of consumer behavior variables than a discussion limited to the variables that have actually been studied.

Responses have been classified as behavioral and internal, and the former divided into (1) purchase responses, (2) consumption responses, and (3) communication responses. Each response, internal as well as behavioral, may be at one or more levels in a hierarchy ranging from individual brands to the total economy of the individual or of the society. Cerha (1967) suggests a distinction among (1) brand level, (2) assortment level, (3) manufacturer (or store) level, and (4) product level. This classification rests upon analysis of the nature of the response (for example, whether it concerns brand or product class choices).

Consumer behavior variables reflect aspects of choices made by single individuals in specific situations, but they can also be aggregated to represent behavior at the household level, at a level corresponding to segments of markets, or at a level corresponding to total markets. Taken together the three classifications can be illustrated as a cube, as in Figure 2.2. The figure summarizes the kinds of dependent variables with which students of consumer behavior can be concerned. However, most of the following discussion will be at the individual choice level because relatively little has been done in this area, because findings from psychological studies may thus be linked to consumer behavior, and because variables at higher levels of aggregation can be traced back to responses in specific situations. Chapters 17 to 19 will consider the problem of aggregating the individual choice variables.

The present chapter has discussed the ultimate dependent variables in studies of consumer behavior and compared them with responses as dealt with by psychologists. An individual's continuous stream of action has been described as a string of behavioral responses that vary in the extent to which they are well established and alternate with brief moments of conflict.

When faced with conflicts, humans engage in choice processes that terminate when the conflict is eliminated and new behavior decided upon.

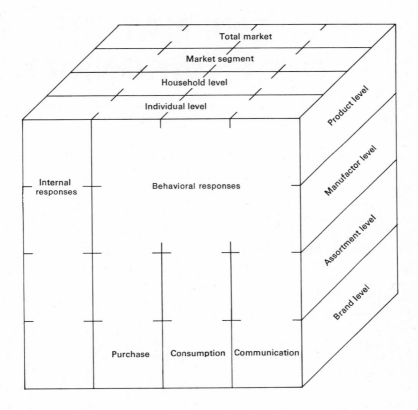

FIGURE 2.2.   *Types of consumer behavior variables.*

In solving the conflict, choices are made among internal as well as behavioral responses. The variables used in studies of consumer behavior can be traced back to such responses, but the student of consumer behavior has rarely been concerned with all the response alternatives available to the consumer.

Choice processes must be studied in relation to the specific environment in which they occur, as the nature of the alternatives considered and the choice process itself depend upon the problem facing the consumer and the environment.

Chapter 3

THE NATURE OF
THE ENVIRONMENT

1. *Situational Influence on Behavior*

1. Personality and Situational Variables

Are stable traits residing within the individual the major source of variation in behavior, or is such variation mainly ascribable to differences in the situations people encounter? Within psychology this issue is an old one, but it has recently gained renewed attention. For example, Hunt (1965) accuses personality theorists of sticking to the fallacious belief that "the source of most of the variation in behavior resides within the person" (p. 80), and he claims that personality traits have generally been able to explain only from 4% to 25% of the total variation in behavior.

Among attitude theorists this question has gained renewed attention, and difficulties in explaining behavior by measuring attitudes have been ascribed to the neglect of situational factors, most explicitly by Rokeach (1967), but Bauer (1968), Fishbein (1967), and Ehrlich (1969) have maintained similar positions.

Neither personality nor situational factors can be neglected. Even if it were found that situational variations explain all variations in behavior, the question must still be asked how the individual transforms the situational input to behavioral output, which makes it necessary to look at the individual's internal processes.

2. Studies of Situational Influence in Psychology and Sociology

The question of situational influence upon behavior has been raised most directly by Endler et al. (1962), and by Hunt (1965). These authors have studied variations in anxiety responses in 11 specific situations where the frequencies of 14 different modes of response were measured. The responses were preselected according to their association with anxiety, and the procedure was repeated with different groups of subjects. The findings consistently showed that more variation is explained by situational factors than by individual differences, and that interaction between the two sources of variation accounts for more variation than either of the two sources taken separately. Moreover, Endler et al. (1968) report similar findings from a study of hostility responses.

A related study reported by Brim and Hoff (1957) examined individual and situational differences in the desire for certainty and found it highly dependent upon situational factors. Brim et al. (1962) report related findings from a study of choices among child-rearing practices. They presented groups of parents and individual parents with four different conflict situations and studied their choices in terms of problem identification, information search, identification of strategies, evaluation of strategies, selection of strategies, and action. Behavior at various steps was reflected in variables such as desirability of alternatives, expectations concerning different outcomes, importance placed on immediate versus delayed results, number of outcomes considered, complexity of the selected strategy, and the like. A total of ten dependent variables were applied. When intersubject and intersituational differences were compared, it was found that situational factors dominate the individual differences and that considerable interaction occurs between individuals and situations.

Further evidence of situational influence is found in a number of studies that deal with children's behavior in different school and other settings. Rausch et al. (1959), Soskin and John (1963), Goffman (1963) and Gump et al. (1963) all report relevant findings.

A very extreme formulation with interesting evidence has been presented by Bem (1965 and 1967). Bem deals with attitude measurements, maintaining that responses to attitude questions are self-descriptive statements based on situational clues (among which is observation of one's own behavior). Bem (1967) writes:

... many of the self-descriptive statements that appear to be exclusively under the discriminative control of private stimuli may, in fact, still be partially controlled by the same accompanying public events used by the training community to infer the individual's inner states. (p. 185)

Consequently, he argues, other individuals should be able to predict the responses made by subjects in attitude experiments, provided that they are supplied with the necessary situational clues. This method of interpersonal replication has been used in a number of "classic" dissonance studies. In Bem (1965) a successful replication is reported of a study by Brehm and Cohen (1962), and in Bem (1967) two other replications of classical dissonance studies are reported. Although these interpersonal replications have been met with severe criticism (Mills 1967 and Freedman 1969), the results do lend support to the hypothesis that situational aspects are extremely important in determining responses.

Supporting evidence may be found within various other research traditions also. A number of older studies have shown the existence of situational distortions of reasoning—the so-called atmosphere effect—(Woodworth and Sells 1935 and Sells 1936); and among more recent studies several on decision making and utility theory bear on the issue. (For a review see Edwards 1954a and 1961, and Becker and McClintock 1967. Some of these findings are also discussed in Chapter 9.) Preferences are often found to be inconsistent, and in many instances this is ascribed to differences between the choice situations (Davis 1958 and Dolbear and Lave 1967).

Similarly, a number of studies showing the inability of attitude measurements to predict behavior have been cited as evidence for situational influence. Probably the most widely known examples are reported by LaPiere (1934), Holman (1956), and DeFleur and Westie (1958). In addition, various methodological studies support the proposition that situational aspects are important determinants of behavior. Clues as to the experimenter's hypothesis that subjects pick up during an experiment may completely distort their responses. A general discussion of this phenomenon is given by Orne (1962), and a classical example of its consequences is presented by Rosenberg (1965a).

The evidence strongly supports the proposition that situational factors, separately and in interaction with personal variables, influence behavior; consequently, it is important to ask whether this influence also applies to consumer behavior. As consumer behavior constitutes a considerable part of the individual's total behavior, there are no a priori grounds to believe that it should not; nevertheless, it is possible to throw some more light on the issue.

3. Situational Influence on Consumer Behavior

Research on consumer behavior has mainly been interested in personal variables, as in motivation research (Ferber and Wales 1958), attitude studies (Crespi 1965), image studies (Mindak 1961), and recent attempts with personality measures. (See, for example, Brody and Cunningham 1968.) However, a number of authors have pointed at the neglected situational variables.

Lavidge (1966) maintains that for many products consumption is closely related to specific situations, and he cites evidence from media and other studies. Longman (1968) makes the same point but relates it to attitude measurements and consumer planning studies.

Among Swedish researchers the problem has gained special attention, and Sandell (1967, 1968a, and 1968b) has reported findings from several studies. In an early experiment (Sandell 1967), two choice alternatives (unfamiliar cigarette brands) were conditioned to either "stress" or "sleepiness," represented by typed versions of the similar Swedish words. The conditioning was obtained by showing the cigarette brands by means of a tachistoscope immediately following exposure to either one of the two words. In the experimental presentation each subject always had the same brand paired with the same word. Exposures were very brief (just above the absolute threshold), and they were repeated 24 times for each pair of associates. In order to conceal the purpose of the experiment, the experimenters told the subjects that they were testing a tachistoscope-exposure method. None of the subjects indicated that they had understood that a learning task was involved. After the exposures subjects were artificially brought into either stressed or boring situations, and at the end of this manipulation they were offered a choice between the two cigarette brands. The brand choices clearly confirm that situational aspects influenced the choice. In the stressed choice situation the brand associated with "stress" was chosen 16 out of 18 times, and in the "sleepy" condition the brand associated with "sleepiness" was chosen 19 out of 24 times.

In a later and modified replication of this experiment similar results were obtained. Here each of the same unknown cigarette brands was associated with one of two well-known brands of beer. Beer brands were chosen as "situational aspects" partly in order to obtain advance measures of attitudes toward the brands and partly because the product (being complementary to cigarettes in consumption) could act as a situational clue. Besides confirming the results of the first experiment, this study showed that preferences for either one of the "situational aspects" could not account for the paired choice. In five out of 14 cases the cigarette brand associated with the most-preferred beer brand was chosen (not significant), whereas in 11 out of 14 cases (significant with $p < .05$) the cigarette brand which had been paired with the beer brand offered in the choice situation was chosen.

Finally, in a later study (Sandell 1968a) a somewhat different approach was used. Ten different beverages (alcoholic and nonalcoholic) were preference-rated. Respondents next were asked to rate the beverages in connection with a specific situation, such as "for breakfast," "with lunch," or "at a party." An analysis of variance of these data showed that the largest part of the total variance was explained by the situational factor. That is, the tendency for different subjects to choose the same beverages in the same situations was greater than the tendency for subjects to remain loyal to the same beverages. Furthermore, factor analysis of preference ratings (obtained without situational association) revealed a number of factors which could be identified as "situational." For example, the first factor was loaded heavily on brandy and beer (which in Sweden is commonly associated with *smörgosbord*), another was heavily loaded on liquor and wine (typical Swedish female party drinks).

Other evidence of situational influence upon consumer behavior can be found in a number of studies which have come upon the phenomenon more or less accidentally. For example, studies of impulse purchases have provided some evidence (reviewed in Chapter 15) that factors such as location in the store and the use of display material influence the in-store behavior. Similarly, studies of personal and mass communication have found that even minor variations in the information available in exposure situations may have tremendous impact on the consumer's response (see Chapters 10 and 15). Methodological studies have also revealed situational influence on consumer behavior. In a test of his "tension-rating procedure" Bilkey (1957) found considerable inconsistency ascribable to variations in the test situations, and similar results have been reported by Kamen and Eindhoven (1963), Bengtson and Brenner (1964), and Stout (1969). Finally, Day (1970) shows how controlling for disturbing situational influences improves the predictive power of simple attitude measures.

The findings reviewed here do not allow detailed specification of the conditions under which situational influence occur, but they do warrant the conclusion that the consumer's immediate environment is an important factor in explaining his behavior.

2. *The Situation*

1. Observation of Behavior Settings

In a sense, all the situations which surround the individual are unique. Close study will reveal differences between any two situations. However, various situations in which choices are made may be grouped into categories which have significant aspects in common.

Over a little more than a decade a very interesting line of research has been carried out in social psychology following earlier work by Lewin (1935). Important contributions have been published in Barker and Wright (1955), Barker et al. (1961), Dickman (1963), and Wicker (1968). In these studies of the relationship between behavior and its environment, behavior has been studied in terms of behavior episodes and the environment seen as behavior settings.

Behavior episodes, much like organized responses, are characterized as integrated units of action of a limited time range and directed towards completion. These episodes should be studied in relation to the situation in which they take place. Barker (1963) maintains that the behavior setting can be dealt with meaningfully. He writes: "Behavioral settings can be identified and described reliably without an explicit theory and by means of a variety of techniques" (p. 21), and he goes on to discuss how a situation may be described in terms of the entities and actions of which it is composed; that is, the physical objects and people present and the processes going on. For example, the environment in which TV viewing occurs may be described in terms of the TV set, chairs, and other pieces of furniture and elements present, in terms of the people watching, and in terms of the show going on.

If these elements are studied, it will be found that they represent a pattern which may be almost predictable. In the TV example, the TV set is placed with the screen facing the viewers, and all heads are directed towards it. Moreover, the situation has an easily definable boundary. In the TV viewing situation, for example, the environment is limited to the room in which the action occurs.

How the situation should be described depends on what is being studied. Sometimes the situation should be dealt with as a whole, but in other instances the people present or the way in which the elements are structured can be the keys to understanding the relationship between the situation and the behavior. Situations, however, must be studied with caution. Two situations which at first glance look very much alike can later turn out to be significantly different. For example, two shopping trips to the same store may seem to be carried out in identical environments, but a closer inspection will often reveal that the shopping environment has not remained unchanged. At the time of the second trip a new brand may have been introduced or special offers given, and this change may influence the outcome of the trip. Two situations may also look very different, but to the actor function identically. For example, an organized response like "washing hands" may be performed perfectly the same in quite different environments.

Altogether, how the actor perceives the situation is as important as the actual elements found in the physical environment. For that reason a digression will be made, and a few basic principles of perception will be discussed.

2. Perceiving the Environment

The total environment may be described as a number of potential stimuli, some of which are perceived as differing from the background (Restle 1961). Just what is perceived and the rules governing this process have been the subject of considerable study within perception psychology. It is beyond the scope of the present presentation to review this area in any great detail. The reader may turn to such sources as Allport (1955), Dember (1960), or Vernon (1962), or to the briefer marketing-oriented presentations like Crane (1965) or Douglas et al. (1967). In Chapter 6 more will be said about the perception of choice alternatives. Here the discussion is limited to a few aspects basic to understanding the role of the environment.

Perception depends upon the sense organs receiving stimuli from the environment and upon internal processes structuring this sensational input. Essentially, sensation is a differentiation process. That is, all sensational processes imply differentiation between a stimulus and its background. For this the eye, the ear, the nose, the skin, or the mouth may be used; dimensions such as smell, light, sound, taste, temperature, and touch are perceived.

For all sense dimensions a lower limit of stimulation (the *absolute threshold*) exists. Sound must be of a certain intensity before it is perceived; a certain minimum of light is required before it can be detected. These thresholds are not always easy to determine as they vary with personal and environmental factors. There are also limits to the individual's ability to detect differences between stimuli. Differences are perceived only when they are of a certain magnitude, that is, when they exceed the *differential threshold*. Nor is this threshold constant. Besides individually and environmentally determined differences, it depends on the absolute magnitude of the stimulus. For example, a consumer judging an orange may be able to distinguish between one weighing 4 ounces and another weighing $4\frac{1}{2}$ ounces, but the same consumer cannot detect whether a box of detergent containing 2 pounds differs from one containing 2 pounds and a half ounce (Weber's Law).

The absolute and the differential thresholds are important when environmental settings are discussed. For an element in the environment to be perceived, it must exceed the absolute threshold; and for any change in the situation to be perceived, it must exceed the differential threshold.

The perception of the environment is not influenced only by the capabilities of the sense-organs. Only a limited number of the potential stimuli are actually observed. That is, part of the total environment is selectively differentiated from the background. This process of selection has been studied in great detail but a brief account of the basic factors is given by Berelson and Steiner (1964): "Which stimuli get selected depends upon three major factors: the nature of the stimuli involved; previous experience or learning as it affects the observer's expectations (what he is prepared or "set" to see) and the motives in play at the time" (p. 100).

Besides selective processes, organizing processes are important also. The observed stimulus becomes structured. For example, in a supermarket a housewife does not see 10 apples, but a bag of apples. Similarly, a box of detergent is not perceived as a printed piece of carton with certain colors, a name, and some pictures. It is seen as a unit, to such an extent that the observer, just after perceiving it, may be unable to tell which color it had or what the illustration was. Organization of stimuli depends on learning, and is influenced by important factors like similarity, proximity, continuity, shape, and contrast with the background.

Organizing tendencies may even destroy reality. In a stimulus object perceived as a whole, a number of disturbing elements may be neglected and missing elements may be added. For example, a consumer may recognize a cigarette brand at a distance where he cannot read the name or see any details of the package. A few aspects such as the shape and the color of the package are sufficient for identification. The same consumer also may be faced with a new cigarette brand which has a package not too different from the one he regularly buys. Even though the name is different and clearly visible on the package, he may pick the new brand, thinking he is buying his regular brand.

The selection and organization of stimuli is important for a discussion of situational settings. It explains which aspects of the situation will be of significance, and how they may be structured.

How a total situation is perceived depends on the aspects in the environment to which the individual attends. A situation is identical with a previous one when the individual perceives the same aspects on both occasions, and similarly the extent to which two situations are perceived as different depends on how many different aspects are perceived in the two situations. Extending this idea, Restle (1961) looks at the perceived aspects of situations and compares the number of similar aspects in different situations. According to this analysis he can characterize a number of different relationships. First, he defines identical situations as those with exactly the same perceived aspects. Second, situations with no perceived aspects in common are completely different situations. Moreover, since most situations fall between these two extremes he suggests that the degree of difference can be thought of as the number of common aspects relative to the total number of perceived aspects. Finally, Restle discusses a situation that consists of all the aspects in another situation, plus some more; he calls the first situation *more complex* than the second. These concepts make it possible to compare different situations meaningfully, and they should be kept in mind when similarity and complexity of situations are discussed. Extending this notation to situations where consumers are faced with product information makes it possible to analyze the stimuli acting upon the individual in terms of potential and perceived aspects of the situation. For example, a consumer in a store will often be faced with a number of brands (each representing a potential aspect of the situation), and other aspects may be surrounding these brands such as displays, price signs, and competing products. To understand the consumer's behavior in the particular situation it is necessary to study what aspects he perceives and to examine how this situation, defined in terms of those particular aspects, compares with situations he has experienced previously. Similarly, a consumer faced with an advertisement in the press is confronted with three classes of situational aspects: the advertisement, the editorial environment of the advertisement, and the environment in general, each of which can be specified further. For example, the advertisement may be broken down into an illustration, a logo, two or three bodies of print and the like. To understand the consumer's response to the advertisement it is necessary to know the nature of the attention he pays to the different potential aspects.

3. General Aspects of Situations

A few variables relate to situational settings in general. Berlyne (1960 and 1967) suggests that a situation may be characterized in terms of its *novelty, change, surprisingness, complexity,* and *incongruity.* These variables reflect the individual's perception of the situation, and they depend on factors in the surrounding environment.

The extent to which a situation is *novel* to an individual depends on learning. Because repetition and recency are important factors in learning, novel aspects are those to which the individual has not recently been exposed and those to which he has never or only infrequently been exposed. Berlyne (1960) suggests that in the beginning all stimuli have the same ability to "create interest," but as a result of habituation, some of them lose part of this ability. He also suggests that a novel situation is more complex and conflict-inducing than a familiar one and that its arousing potential results from that reason. Thus, the extent to which a situation is novel depends on (1) how often situations with similar aspects have been experienced, (2) how recently they have been experienced, and (3) how many aspects they have in common with the present situation.

Moving or in other ways changing observed objects has been found to have consequences very much like those associated with novelty (Berlyne 1960). The amount of *change* can be thought of as the difference between the emerging and the original situations. The importance of change depends on whether or not it is noticed, which in turn depends on the magnitude of the change and on whether the change is expected. Strictly speaking, the environment is never completely static, but the change must exceed the differential threshold before it is observed; and generally, the more change, the more likely it is to be observed.

When a change is expected, it will have little or no effect, whereas unexpected changes will be very consequential. The effect of unexpected change is considered in the variable *surprise*, which also reflects the extent to which a new situation is unexpected. *Surprise* depends on the contiguity of situational aspects in the past. The more frequently an aspect has occurred together with a certain other aspect, the more the second aspect will be expected when the first is perceived; consequently, the more surprising the absence of the second aspect will be. On the other hand, the less frequently they have been encountered together, the more surprising it will be to meet them together. Similarly, the more frequently a specific change has been observed in a certain environment, the less likely it is to be specifically noticed. Osgood (1957) suggests an explanation for this phenomenon: "The greater the frequency with which stimuli events A and B are associated in the input to an organism, the greater will be the tendency for the central correlates of one, *a*, to activate the central correlates of the other, *b*." Essentially, it is the organizing tendencies involved in perception that account for the expectation (or lack of same) that in turn explains the surprise with which a certain stimulus or a total situation is met.

Complexity, like novelty, depends on learning. What is perceived as complex is what the individual finds unfamiliar. However, it is possible to point out some factors especially associated with complexity. First, an increase in the number of perceived aspects increases the complexity. As was pointed out earlier, a situation consisting of all the aspects inherent in another situation plus some more is more complex than the other. As an example, a department store with a narrow selection of dresses is a less complex dress-shopping environment than a large specialty store with a very wide selection. Second, the more different aspects are in the environment, the more complex it is. For example, a situation in which a sportsman is faced with a number of lures is more complex than one in which he is faced with a similar number of weights, as the lures will be judged along many more dimensions than the weights.

Finally, *incongruity* relates to expectations established through learning. Congruent stimuli are those believed to "belong together," and incongruent stimuli are those which violate some previously held belief (see Chapter 6).

These variables are closely interrelated, and it may be that, rather than being five separate factors, they reflect the same underlying dimension. In a sense they all have to do with the amount of information in the situation, particularly the amount of information that is new to the individual, and it makes sense to talk about them as one single variable. Such a view is proposed by Walker (1964), who talks about environmental complexity as the one crucial variable, discussing it as dependent upon novelty, congruity, and so on. Similarly, Hebb (1966) talks about the total amount of environmental stimulation.

4. Specific Aspects of Situations

Environmental complexity is an overall dimension along which the total situation can be described. In many instances, however, concern is not with the total situation, but with single aspects (stimuli) occurring in the situation. Often a single or, at the most, a few aspects of the situation are the highly significant ones; if so, it greatly simplifies the analysis to concentrate on them.

Single stimuli can of course also be studied in terms of their novelty, surprisingness, change, and complexity, but other dimensions may be more important. They may vary in size, strength, volume, and magnitude. Strong versus dim light, loud versus mellow sound, color versus black and white print, large versus small objects are some examples. Stimuli may also vary in their motivational relevance for the individual. Food for a hungry person and water for a thirsty one have special stimulus properties. Finally, stimuli may have affective value. For example, some kinds of food may be more liked than others, and some persons may be preferred to others.

Much psychological experimentation uses systematic variation of one or a few aspects of the subject's immediate environment. Behavior is compared in two or more settings which differ only along a single dimension; for example, different motivating agents, obstacles, or disturbing elements may have been introduced. In social psychological experiments much the same procedure is applied, but the experimental variations are frequently more complex. Informational messages or more or less complicated tasks are used. Basically, however, much of this research can be interpreted as comparisons among behavior in environments where all but a few elements are identical.

In the consumer's environment, the stimuli that are particularly important relate to the products and brands used by the consumer. They may occur in the form of personal or mass communication, and they may vary widely in content.

3. *The Consumer's Environment*

It has been maintained that the consumer should be studied in the situations in which he makes choices, but is it possible to specify such situations? Specific situations can be described, and some of the dimensions used in such descriptions have been discussed. However, if the consumer's environment is too varied and no systematic patterns exist, the task may be so complex as to be impracticable.

Unfortunately, no studies have attempted to classify the different environments in which consumer choices are made. As consumer behavior constitutes a large part of human behavior, such classification would be easy if studies of the environments in which people in general spend their days were available. However, such studies have not been reported. Total time-spending studies come closest to what is sought. Concerned with the different activities in which humans engage, these studies tell about the variability of human behavior and indirectly reveal the stability of the environments in which this behavior occurs. Such studies have been carried out since the early thirties by Lundberg et al. (1934), Sorokin and Berger (1939), Robinson and Converse (1966), Foote (1966), and Andreasen (1967).

In these studies human behavior is found to consist of a relatively limited number of different activities, an observation which suggests that the individual's environment is quite predictable. Commonly, it has been possible to work with classifications consisting of from 100 to 200 different episodes.

1. Consumer Choice Situations

For the study of consumer behavior the specific situations where conflict is aroused and where choices are made are particularly important. Eventually these situations are reflected in the total environment of the consumer, as changes of environment (a new home, a new town, a new job) will result in changed situations. Nevertheless, for the sake of clarity, a distinction between specific *situations* and the overall *environment* will be maintained in the following pages.

In a choice situation, three things happen (see Chapter 4):

1. The individual receives information from the environment.
2. Cognitive processes occur.
3. A response is selected.

In some cases information acquisition is the most important aspect of consumer behavior. In other cases the main aspect is cognitive change, and in still others response selection is the most important part. For example, where the focus is on purchase behavior, the researcher is interested in the final responses. However, in earlier phases of the decision process he is more interested in changes in cognitive elements and the information to which the consumers are exposed. This suggests a distinction between *exposure situations*, *deliberation situations*, and *response choice situations*. It should be emphasized, however, that this distinction is not made among situations where only exposure, deliberation, or response selection occurs. In all choice processes all three elements exist. The distinction rests upon the researcher's judgment as to what is his major concern.

Response choice situations can be of different kinds. In some, a final purchase is made; in others some observable action occurs that the researcher wants to explain. The action can be to go to a store, to approach an insurance agent, to use a product, or to communicate about products. Generally, as consumer responses can be classified as consumption, communication, and purchase responses, response choice situations will be *purchase, communication,* or *consumption* situations.

As *purchase situations* result in some observable behavior, they are usually relatively easy to identify. If the ultimate dependent variable is the total demand for a product or brand, the situations that must be defined are those where a final purchase of the product or brand is made. For a few marketers, this may involve a single situation, namely, where the product is available only in one particular environment, as for example in vending machines. More often, however, a number of different situations will have to be specified. A beer manufacturer, for example, will have to deal at least with instore purchases and restaurant purchases. Frequently each of these purchase situations can advantageously be broken down further.

It may be necessary to deal with a varying number of *consumption situations* also. Some products have several uses or move through a process of preparation. When all the different aspects of consumption are important, several consumption situations must be considered. However, as some products have only a single use, which always occurs in the same way, it may sometimes be possible to deal with a single consumption situation.

In *situations* where a *communication* response is selected the responses will always be in the form of information provided to somebody else. The diversity and importance of this information determines with what detail such situations should be specified.

Exposure situations can be defined relatively easily. Although the response does not have to be observable, these situations involve interaction with information sources. Consequently exposure situations can be defined in terms of this interaction. The researcher who studies exposure situations in their own right will have to define the situations in which he is interested. The researcher who is concerned with exposure situations only as they influence subsequent purchases must define them so that all that relate to the particular purchase he wants to explain are included. For the particular product or brand, this may involve few or many situations, depending upon the nature of the marketing communication and the diversity of personal communication.

It is possible to identify a number of different types of exposure situations. One distinction rests upon the type of information to which the consumer is exposed, such as television exposure situations and magazine exposure situations. Another distinction is based upon the type of response which follows the exposure. Often the immediate response is purely internal, as follows most exposure to television advertising. In other instances, however, a behavioral response may be elicited, as when a consumer makes an "impulse purchase" after exposure to a product display. In the latter case the exposure situation is also a purchase situation, and in that case it is often easier to study the relationship between exposure and subsequent purchases. Unfortunately such situations are the exception rather than the rule.

Another important distinction can be based upon the way the exposure is generated. In some instances the consumer himself seeks out information sources, either in the immediate environment or by performing some action that exposes him to the information. These exposure situations are labeled information *acquisition situations*, and they are opposed to situations where information is more or less forced upon the consumer. The latter, labeled *forced learning situations*, occur when the exposure results because information is provided in environments where the consumer had not intended to seek out that particular kind of information. For example, television exposure often belongs to that category.

Finally, exposure may result as a secondary effect of some other activity, most commonly when the consumer uses the product and thereby becomes exposed to it. These instances have been labeled *experience formation situations*. (Behavior in different exposure situations is explored further in Chapter 9.)

Exposure and response choice situations are relatively easily identified, as they involve some observable action. This is not always so with deliberation situations. Only extensive studies of purchase sequences can identify the deliberation situations important to a particular product. Deliberation situations can be more or less closely tied in with a particular environment. The closer the ties, the more easily the situation can be defined. However, when the deliberation occurs relatively independent of environmental factors an indirect approach can be used. It is possible that the cognitive changes which occur between exposure situations or between exposure and purchase situations are systematic in such a way that they can be predicted from knowledge of the exposure and purchase situations.

Exposure, deliberation, and response choice situations can be defined in terms of the particular settings in which they occur, in terms of the problem they concern, or both. It would be nice to be able to list all the settings in which consumers make choices, but clearly this cannot be done. Situations must therefore be specified relative to the particular product or brand studied. However, a number of important situational settings may be mentioned, such as the home, the supermarket, the car, the job, the street, the club, and the department store. The examples suggest that the important parts of consumer behavior occur in rather few settings.

The problems of consumers in particular situations may be classified along a number of dimensions. Distinguishing among situations that concern different products results in one such classification. Others are equally important. In particular, it is possible to distinguish between prepurchase and postpurchase (consumption) behavior. The first occurs in all situations preceding a particular purchase, regardless of whether the situation is an exposure, deliberation, or response choice situation. Consumption takes place after the purchase.

It is always possible to classify single situations meaningfully, but when aggregated consumer behavior is studied, several problems have to be considered. Here the researcher will be interested in how many different choice situations occur, how many consumers enter into the different types, and how they respond to these situations. The researcher's approach to the definition of situations has important implications for the overall structure of his model. The more in detail he specifies the situations, the more homogeneous will be the situations he will be concerned with; but he will also have to study more different situations. Homogeneity makes it easier to predict outcomes in each single situation, but it also requires much more detailed information about the pattern of choices that characterizes different consumers. If only a few broad situations are specified great variability will be found in each of them, and the problems of explaining consumer behavior are not much different from those facing the market researcher when he has not specified environmental conditions at all. An improved understanding can be gained only if consumer behavior is segmented in terms of the different situations in which it occurs.

2. Specific Aspects of Consumer Choice Situations

Each situation can be characterized in terms of its complexity. For that the total situation will have to be considered, but within most situations single aspects particularly relevant to the individual's role as a consumer can also be found. First and foremost are the stimuli which represent information relevant to products and brands, and these stimuli can be classified by their content or their source. In Chapter 1, a distinction was made among stimuli representing the product or brand being studied, stimuli that represent it symbolically, and other stimuli. This classification points at important differences among kinds of information. The symbolic representation of the product differs from those instances when the product or brand is present itself. First, with symbolic communication a source will always be involved, and as will be discussed subsequently, the nature of the source may greatly influence the way the consumer responds to the information. Second, the symbolic representation may differ significantly from the product or brand; it may neglect some aspects and overemphasize others, and it may even attempt to convey "untrue" information. Third, symbolic communication is almost entirely limited to visual and auditory information.

The marketer can influence the stimuli the consumer faces through his product strategies, that is, through the way he defines the offer he is bringing to the market in terms of price, quality, service, credit conditions, and the like. In addition he can exert influence through his communication activities, such as advertising, personal selling, information on packages, and so on (Ottesen 1969). But he cannot completely control the stimuli the consumer faces, because the marketer's efforts compete with the efforts of others in the marketing system and because the consumer may reject or attend to whatever pleases him. Therefore there is not a simple direct relationship between the marketer's strategies and the information the consumer receives. It is important to study the marketer's decision variables as they relate to the stimuli the consumer perceives. Stimuli can be grouped as (1) those the marketer can influence to a high degree (for example, advertising), (2) those he can influence somewhat (for example, retailer's sales effort), and (3) those he cannot control (for example, information from governmental agencies or consumer unions).

When the stimuli acting upon the consumer are classified in accordance with their source, a slightly different grouping emerges. Cerha (1967) has suggested a classification distinguishing among primary communication (experiences derived directly from the product), secondary communication (mass communication), tertiary communication (information acquired in stores, at exhibitions, and in similar places), and personal communication. These distinctions can be illustrated as in Figure 3.1. Just as Figure 2.2 specifies the responses the consumer can choose in a particular choice situation, Figure 3.1 presents the dependent variables influencing these choices. Subsequent chapters will be concerned with the choice mechanisms of interaction between the two classes of variables.

4. *Changes in the Consumer's Environment*

It has been maintained that relevant aspects in consumer choice situations may be quantified, and these aspects have been shown to be important determinants of behavior. However, this does not necessarily imply that studies of consumer behavior should begin with the situations in which

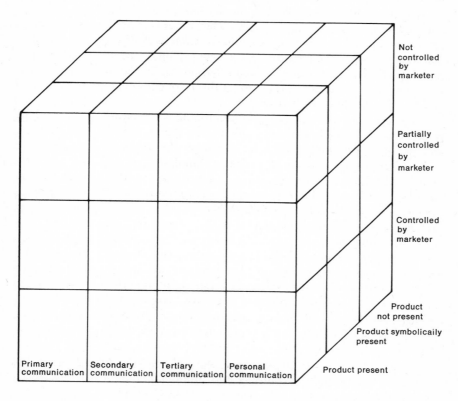

FIGURE 3.1. *Independent variables in consumer choice situations.*

choices are made. If consumers day after day and year after year bring themselves into the same situations, then the situational aspects are not a major cause of variations in consumer behavior.

The consumer's choice situations will change to the extent that his total environment changes. The consumer's environment may vary because of changes introduced by the outside world, especially the marketers, or it may vary because the consumer himself introduces changes. That the present-day consumer lives in a dynamic world needs no documentation. His environment constantly changes. Some of these changes are ongoing processes with an impact on the consumer that is hardly traceable, but others come suddenly and have an immediate effect on behavior, such as changes in gun laws, new highways, new schools in the consumer's area. Similarly the social groups to which the consumer belongs may change or may introduce changes into the world of the consumer, as in the case of a friend who gets a new car or a new family across the street. All this may directly or indirectly cause situational changes which in turn will influence the individual's behavior.

Furthermore, changes occur in the market: prices change; new advertising campaigns are introduced; new sales techniques are used; deals, coupons, premiums and new credit-terms are offered. Even more directly, the changing marketplace meets the consumer with new products, services, and forms of distribution. The acceptance of such offerings has in recent years been the subject of research (Seipel 1971), and a theory of consumer adoption of new products is emerging (Robertson 1968).

New products also influence consumption, as is clearly illustrated by products such as the automobile, the TV, or the second home. These, and all other major durable products, have changed the consumption of a number of substituting and competing products. Similarly, new services and new nondurables have impact. Changes in air transportation facilities, credit services, and food products' degree of preparation have all directly and indirectly changed the consumer's way of life.

This constantly changing market place presents the consumer with new situations influencing his behavior. However, even without these changes consumers would constantly be faced with new situations, as the consumer himself changes his environment. First of all, the individual consumer grows older. A number of major events mark especially important changes in the consumer's total situation. Some of these are "moving away from parent's home," "marriage," and "having children." These observable changes in the consumer's life have led to the formulation of the *family life cycle* concept. The consumer is seen as moving through a number of stages, each of which results in major changes in his environment. Several different definitions of life cycles have been proposed (Lansing and Morgan 1955 and Madsen 1964). Lansing and Morgan deal with these categories of people:

1. Young (under 45 years of age) single.
2. Young married, no children.
3. Young married with children, youngest child under 6.
4. Young married with children, youngest child over 6.
5. Older (head of household 45 or over) with children.
6. Older married, no children under 18.
7. Older single.
8. Other.

Other important changes occur in connection with a new job, change in income, change in work time, retirement, or moving to a new area all of which result in new situations to which the consumer must adapt.

Finally, new situations occur simply because the consumer acts as a consumer. That is, he uses products. Nondurable products are used up, new stock is needed, or durable products break down or need repair.

Altogether, the consumer lives in a constantly changing environment, and again and again he will find himself in a situation which is significantly different from previous ones. Each major change in the environment translates into new aspects in one or another specific situation. The consumer is constantly presented with new situations. The consumer himself changes, and so does the world in which he lives. Consequently, the interaction between changing situations and behavior is important. Without changes in the environment consumer behavior would become highly habitual, but new elements in the environment repeatedly interfere with this.

Chapter 4

CHOICE PROCESSES AND AROUSAL

Consumer behavior has been described as a composite of habitual responses, each labeled a *behavioral response*; within each pair of responses a choice process occurs. When the same responses have followed each other on a number of occasions, the choice process deteriorates and eventually disappears completely. A new and larger behavioral response is then established.

If environmental changes did not occur, enduring behavioral responses could be established; or, to put it differently, behavior would be extremely habitual. But the environment does change, and this change necessitates adjustments in behavior. The more change in the environment a consumer experiences, the more adjustment is needed and, consequently, the less firmly established and the shorter the behavioral responses will be. With any given environment an ideal amount of adjustment exists, and to this a certain amount of interaction corresponds. To the extent that this amount of interaction is realized, it minimizes the amount of effort needed to cope with the surrounding world.

Stated a little differently, the problems are: How many and how conflicting choice processes will occur? How are they triggered, and how do individuals respond when they occur? To answer these questions it is necessary to take a closer look at the elements of choice process: It must be asked: How and why do choice processes vary? The answer lies in the different amounts of psychological energy released for making the choice. This in turn brings the attention to a specific motivational center, the *reticular arousal system*, which has been related to the overall activity of the individual. It is possible to point at variables that reflect variations in arousal and studies of these variables have isolated some of the factors causing variations in choice process behavior.

1. *The Choice Process*

1. Elements in the Choice Process

A choice process occurs when more than one response alternative is aroused. Choice processes vary widely in duration; many are barely observable, and the stream of action pauses only for a fraction of a second before the next response is selected. However, in other instances, the choice process is distinct and observable.

Strictly speaking, the choice itself has little or no duration in time. Just before and just after the choice different activities can be observed that are closely associated with what is chosen, but the choice itself only marks a brief interval in time when a reponse is selected. The response selection is a psychological process of extremely brief duration. Behavior just before and just after the choice can be seen as a number of different activities existing in their own right but distinguishable from most other responses. Commonly they are very short. Those occurring before the response selection are related to what is being chosen in such a way that it would be impossible to predict the outcome if they were not considered. Similarly, those occurring immediately after the response selection serve functions in connection with the choice. Moreover, internal responses dominate; and the observable behavior, such as exploration and expressions of doubt, is closely related to the internal cognitive processes. For these reasons choice processes will be considered to cover the whole range of associated activities.

Many studies have described responses in connection with decisions and choices. It is not always made clear whether the described choice process occurs in a brief interval of time or whether it may be spaced out in time with many other activities occurring inbetween. However, researchers specifically dealing with choices as continuous processes in time (Brim et al. 1962, Lanzetta 1963, Festinger 1964a, and Gerard 1967a) mention steps such as problem identification, information search, production of possible strategies, evaluation, selection of strategy, and actual performance. These and similar labels are descriptive terms attached to the activities observed in connection with the choice process. They do not explain what is going on, but they give an impression of the diversity of activities to be found.

A somewhat more restrictive, but also more informative description is provided by Lanzetta (1963) and Gerard (1967). They consider the choice process as composed of information gathering, information processing, response selection, and post-choice adjustments. This conceptualization is the background for the present discussion, in which two kinds of activities will be considered in connection with choices. Some relate to the environment and the individual's orientation to it; others are completely internal and may be described as shorter or longer chains of thoughts. The first category is referred to as *exploration* (Berlyne 1960), and the second is commonly described in such terms as "thinking," "problem solving," and "memorizing." For these latter activities the term *deliberation* will be used.

2. Exploration

Exploratory behavior consists of responses made in an attempt to change the individual's perception of the environment. Exploration activities are closely associated with attention, and they are used to bring stimulus into the focus of sense organs. Berlyne (1960) writes: "They do so by intensifying or clarifying stimulation from objects that are already represented in the stimulus field, and thus reducing uncertainty about the properties of those objects, or else by bringing receptors into contact with new stimulus objects" (p. 79).

Commonly, exploratory behavior is observable, but it is also accompanied by important internal processes. Internal as well as external aspects serve a number of functions. By allowing the individual to concentrate on some aspects and neglect others, they increase the effectiveness with which significant aspects are perceived. In other instances, by increasing the sensitivity of the sense organs in general, they prepare the individual for whatever may occur, and they facilitate perception of the same stimulus objects by more than one sense organ.

In the individual's exploration of his environment several progressive steps can be identified: *orienting behavior, locomotor exploration*, and *investigatory exploration*.

Orienting behavior involves a change in the sense organs or in the posture of the observer. The eyes may be directed towards a stimulus object, the individual may "concentrate" on hearing, smelling, or tasting better, or a total increase in the alertness of the individual can result. Berlyne (1960) writes: "Orienting behavior forms part of a whole constellation of physiological processes, permeating the entire organism, that can be elicited by the onset, termination, intensification, weakening or modification in any other way of any kind of stimulation" (p. 81).

Orienting behavior is subject to learning. It is elicited by specific situational conditions, but if the same conditions recur often, it may be extinguished. On the other hand the individual can learn that certain stimuli signal important changes, and consequently these stimuli may gain signal value and be extremely effective in eliciting exploration.

Locomotor exploration occurs when the individual moves in order to gain access to stimuli. It is immediately observable. The shopper who moves closer to a stand in a supermarket in order to see better performs locomotor exploration, and so does the consumer who walks around a car on a used-car lot and examines it. Locomotor exploration brings stimuli into the stimuli field which were previously not available or only partly available.

Investigatory exploration goes one step further. Here the individual not only moves, gut he also directly changes the stimuli field. That is, items are picked up for inspection, or other items are moved away, so that previously invisible or partly visible objects will become available.

So far exploration has been described as increasing the amount of interaction with the environment and raising the efficiency of perception. However, instances occur in which the informational intake is modified in the opposite direction. These instances have been labeled "adaptive" or "defensive" reactions, but they will be referred to here as *negative exploration*. They result in changed perception of the environment, but they differ from positive exploration in that they tend to decrease or distort the information which is picked up from the environment. That is, they reduce stimulation. Such responses are as important as positive exploratory responses and may be seen as their counterpart.

Adaptive responses protect single organs from overstimulation. For example, an increase in light will cause a reduction in the pupil size; generally extreme stimulation will decrease the sensitivity of the related sense organs.

Defensive reactions are more general. They include a whole range of withdrawing, avoiding, and distorting responses, of which only some relate directly to the perception of the environment. In the discussion of negative exploration, only those which involve intake of information from the environment are considered. Examples are "overlooking unpleasant aspects of the environment," "avoiding seeing alternative brands in the store," and so on.

In the choice process, exploration is used to obtain information relevant to the choice. However, such information may be obtained in another way. The consumer may decide to perform a behavioral response that will make information available. Examples would be a shopper who decides to postpone a decision concerning a dress in order to go to another store or a consumer who chooses to obtain a catalogue before making a final choice of a TV brand.

Like exploration, behavioral responses involving extended search supply the consumer with relevant information, but they differ from exploratory behavior in several other ways. They are longer and more complex responses, they may bring the individual into new situations, and they are not necessarily performed immediately before or after the conflict to which the information is relevant. The last two differences are important. They imply that the information sought is not present (or expected to be present) in the immediate environment, and that the outcome of a choice can be to search for more information. The term *information search* is here reserved for those instances that involve a separate behavioral response, and the term *exploration* is used only in connection with information acquisition in the course of the choice process.

3. Deliberation

Deliberation occurs immediately preceding or immediately following the choice, and it can substitute for or complement exploration. The recovery of information from memory is especially important (Norman, 1968 and Shriffrin and Atkinson, 1969), but deliberation may also involve handling of information made available by exploration. Exactly where perception ends and where deliberation takes over can be difficult to decide, but no doubt the exploratory behavior gives rise to thought processes far removed from the actual perception of the environment.

Other deliberation responses are strings of thoughts connected with the choice. Silently reciting such sentences as "I think I made a good buy" performs important functions in the choice process. They may reinforce whatever cognitive structure is present, or they may modify it. Such chains of thoughts may also be concerned with unavailable alternatives and other irrelevant matters. For example, Festinger (1964a) writes: "A goodly portion of the time that a person spends making a decision may actually be spent not in collecting and evaluating information, but in trying to discover new alternatives or in thinking about better alternatives that are not actually available to him" (p. 130). By means of such processes the salient cognitive structure is constantly being modified, and it is important to learn what will terminate these activities.

Deliberation, like exploration, may be positive as well as negative. Negative deliberation is the counterpart of defensive exploratory behavior. It can take the form of denial of or withdrawal from the problem. On the other hand, positive deliberation corresponds to positive exploration. In broad terms these activities may be described as *problem solving* but it should be remembered that many responses may occur that are only vaguely related to the forthcoming choice.

The choice process consists of the response selection together with exploration and deliberation. The present section has dealt with the latter two activities. Treatment of the response selection itself will have to wait until a more thorough discussion of choice processes has been completed.

2. *The Environment, Arousal,*
and Choice Process Behavior

1. Variations in Choice Processes

Choice processes vary widely. The same consumer may on separate occasions approach the same choice very differently, and other consumers may attack the same problem in different ways. These common observations have been confirmed in several studies. Wells and LoSciuto (1966), Alexis, et al. (1968) and King (1969) observed systematic patterns in consumers' shopping behavior, as did Kollat and Willett (1967) in their study of impulse purchases. But the latter authors also report important individual differences. Convincing also are the findings presented by Brim et al. (1962). In their study of decision processes considerable variations were found in subjects' ways of handling problems.

Consumers spend different amounts of energy on various choices, and these differences must be explained in terms of varying amounts of motivation at the time of the choice. Recent developments within physiological psychology have pointed at a "motivational center" that seems to explain these differences. This center is related to Hull's (1952) general drive concept and has commonly been referred to as the *reticular arousal system* (RAS). One of its main functions is to direct the amount of *activation* or *arousal*.

In the following, it will be proposed that the initiation and the extensiveness of the choice process is determined by the RAS. That is, the amount of exploration and deliberation as well as the way the response is selected depend on the amount of arousal at the time of the choice. However, before this suggestion can be reviewed in light of available evidence, it is necessary to explain what arousal implies and to discuss the factors which determine arousal.

2. The Reticular Arousal System

A detailed understanding of the processes of the brain is not necessary in order to explain the interaction between, on the one hand, internal and external stimulation and, on the other, arousal and choice process behavior. However, a brief review of some of the main processes involved helps clarify the issue and also lends support to the postulated relationships.

It is not our purpose to give a detailed analysis of brain functioning, nor shall we review the underlying evidence. Only a few basic processes will be described, and for specific evidence the reader will have to turn to the sources which will be mentioned.

Two main centers in the brain are needed for an explanation of the role of arousal in connection with choice processes.[1] They are the reticular arousal system and the cerebral cortex, both illustrated in Figure 4.1.

The cerebral cortex is located in the upper parts of the brain, and like the rest of the nervous system it consists of nerve cells, each with a large number of nerve fibers. These fibers, varying in length, connect the different cell bodies in a highly complex network. Different perceptions and cognitive processes correspond to activation of specific combinations of nerve cells. Once source of such activation is the RAS.

The reticular arousal (or activating) system is located in the brain stem and consists of a network of nerve fibers and nerve cells, but in contrast to the cortex, it is not divided into distinct areas. It receives activation from various sources, and in turn it activates the body and the cortex in various ways.

---

[1] The following description deals with only some main features of arousal and activation systems. Recent discussions (Glickman and Schiff 1967 and Routtenberg 1968) point in the direction of two or more simultaneously working and interacting arousal systems.

Thus it serves as a general activating center; among other functions, it governs sleep and waking activity.

The functioning of the arousal system is reflected in the electrical activity

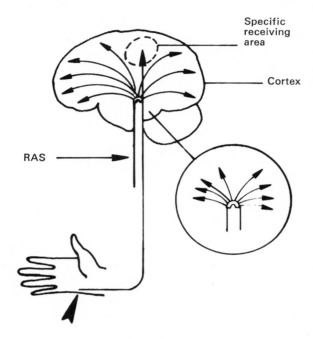

FIGURE 4.1.   The Functioning of the arousal system.

"Schematic drawing showing how a touch stimulus to the hand is relayed to a specific receiving area in the cerebral cortex. The sensory channel also sends collateral branches into the reticular activating system (RAS), which in turn projects alerting stimulation to many areas of the cerebral cortex. The inset shows the cortical projections arising from the forward end (thalamic section) of the reticular formation."
(From Theories of Learning, third edition, by Ernest R. Hilgard and Gordon H. Bower, copyright © 1966. Reprinted by permission of Appleton-Century-Crofts, Educational Division, Meridith Corporation. Special permission for reproduction of the illustration granted by Behavioral Research Laboratories.)

in the brain, which may be measured by electroencephalograph (EEG). It has been found that normal relaxed but awake adults produce certain medium-frequency, moderately large reticular oscillations (α waves). In sleep or when highly active they generate different waves: Sleep produces waves with lower frequency, whereas deviations such as fear, excitement, and the like cause high-frequency, low-amplitude waves.

The RAS performs several functions. It sends a constant stream of activation or "energy" to all parts of the brain. That is, it constantly bombards nerve cells in the cortex, the intensity of the bombardment being measurable in terms of the electrical activity in the brain. Special parts of the upper brain stem stimulate specific areas and retard others and thus influence what will be attended to. Finally, the RAS is connected with the body to which it also supplies energy.[2]

The activity of the RAS depends on what is being perceived. Any observation from the environment is directed to the cortex by means of a specific projection system, but the environment also influences RAS through collateral fibers from the nerve channels connecting the sense organs with the cortex. Bower (Hilgard and Bower, 1966) explains this as follows: " . . . new sensory information stimulates the RAS, which relays the presence of some kind of stimulation to various sensory receiving areas of the cortex. This diffuse stimulation alerts the cortex essentially telling it that some kind of news is arriving. The alerted cortex is then better able to deal with or process the specific information arriving over the specific sensory input channel to the cortex" (p. 440).

The RAS also receives stimulation from two internal sources. The composition of the blood reflects changes in the basic physiological state of the organism, and ongoing processes in the cerebral cortex provide feedback to the RAS. Both of these sources may cause changes in arousal.

Altogether, the RAS is influenced by external stimulation, by processes going on in the cortex, by nerve connections from the body, and by the bloodstream. In turn it activates the brain and the various motor functions of the body. In sleep, in normal relaxed behavior, and in states of extreme excitement, the organism's overall level of activity is determined by the RAS.

3. *Factors Determining Arousal*

1. Correlates of Arousal

A rise in arousal will be accompanied by a number of symptoms, some of which are:

1. Changes in sense organs, such as pupil dilation, that lower absolute thresholds of perception.
2. Changes in skeletal muscles that direct sense organs, such as opening the eye widely and turning the head.
3. Changes in general skeletal musculature, such as interrupting ongoing action, a rise in general muscular tonus, diffuse bodily movements, and increase in muscular electrical activity (that may be observed by electromyograph).
4. Changes in the central nervous system, reflected in electroencephalograph waves (EEG waves).

[2] The role of the RAS in connection with bodily activity and the performance of a number of vital reflexes is quite complicated. The present discussion is mainly concerned with the RAS's influence on cognitive activities.

　　5. Vegetative changes, such as expansion and contraction of blood vessels (measurable by plethysmograph) and changes in the electrical conductance of the palm (measurable and usually referred to as galvanic skin responses).

　　6. Finally, reaction time and measures of perceived uncertainty and conflict revealing aspects of the underlying arousal.

The most important indicators are the EEG waves, galvanic skin responses (GSR), blood pressure, pulse rate, pupil reactions, and measures of conflict and uncertainty. By means of these indicators it has been possible to infer a good deal about the factors determining arousal.

Many of these measurements have been applied in studies of consumer behavior (Edfelt 1960, Krugman 1964, 1966 and 1971, Hess 1968, and Birdwell et al. 1969). Most studies have dealt with responses to advertising material. For example, attempts have been made to relate galvanic skin responses to attention (Lucas and Britt, 1963) and measurement of pupil size to choice and preference ratings (Krugman 1964). Occasionally some, but certainly not perfect correlations have been reported. A major problem is the difficulty of interpreting the measurements. In a statement concerning galvanic skin responses which reflects the general feeling, Lucas and Britt (1963) write: "Certainly interpretations of the meaning of galvanic patterns have not become definitive. Extreme fluctuations of the record may indicate excitement, attraction, repulsion, perplexity—or what?" (p. 157). It seems very likely that future attempts with these and similar techniques may gain significantly if the attempted interpretations are based on arousal theory. In particular, a badly needed theory of attentional processes may be developed along these lines.

The Reticular Arousal System receives stimulation from a number of different sources; and it acts as if it estimated from this stimulation how much activation subsequently will be needed. In the following, the factors increasing the activity of the RAS will be labeled the *arousal potential* (Berlyne 1960). They fall into three broad categories (Simon 1967a):

　　1. Environmental stimulation via collateral fibers from primary sensory channels.

　　2. The organism's internal states through changes in the blood passing through the RAS.

　　3. Cognitive processes in the cerebral cortex by means of nerve fibres from cortex to the RAS.

2. Environmental Stimulation

Various aspects of the environment will generate different amounts of arousal. Figure 4.1 illustrated how a sensory input influences the system, but it is not clear from the illustration whether a specific sensation will result in a smaller or larger amount of arousal. Novelty, change, surprise, and incongruity will have more effect than extreme simplicity and lack of novelty and change (Berlyne 1960, Hebb 1966, and Rosenzweig 1966). The aspects of the environment that can increase arousal can be labeled the *environmental arousal potential.* When this potential is moderate, it will generate a proportionate amount of arousal or activation, but an extremely complex environment will cause a steep drop in arousal. A kind of defensive "closing the eyes" can occur, or other avoiding responses can be applied. Similarly, when the environmental arousal potential is extremely low, it may result in a rise in arousal. This phenomenon has been ascribed to boredom or to a perceptual conflict occurring because the stimulation is close to the absolute threshold (Berlyne 1960).

3. Physiological Conditions

The RAS would be of little value as a coordinator of human activity if no means were supplied by which bodily changes could be taken into account. Such a function is performed by the bloodstream and by nerve connections from various internal organs. Changes in bodily conditions are reported to the RAS by nerve signals or changes in the chemical composition of the blood. Hunger, thirst, sex, sleepiness, and aggression influence the RAS in this way.

Increased arousal caused by internal processes will often build up gradually and diminish abruptly when the need is satisfied which caused the stimulation. The blood will normally carry the elements which cause the increased arousal until the specific need is satisfied or in other ways extinguished; therefore bloodstream variations will often result in more lasting changes in the arousal level.

4. Cognitive Activity

Cognitive processes correspond to activities in the cerebral cortex, and they are related to the RAS in two different ways. Cognitive activities both depend on stimuli outgoing from the system and feed stimuli back to it; through feedback they can either activate the RAS to increase arousal or they can inhibit increases in arousal. For the present approach cognitive processes are important because: (1) Like environmental stimuli and physiological processes, they can cause increased arousal. (2) They govern the perception of the environment. (3) They constitute a major part of the activity in choice processes.

Simon (1967a) describes how cognitive processes can cause interruptions. Besides "loud stimuli" and physiological needs, he suggests that cognitive processes can be interrupted by "cognitive associations—loud stimuli evoked not by sensory events, but by associations in memory, for example anxiety arousal" (p. 37). These interruptions occur when cognitive processes governing the behavioral response accidentally lead to associations that call for special attention. It is difficult to decide how frequently conflicts are aroused in this manner, but it is unquestionable that they occur.

Perception is governed by cognitions, and in this connection expectations and habituation are important. *Expectations* can be understood as associations between stimuli presently working on the sense organs and other stimuli previously experienced with the present stimuli. Moreover, cognitive processes may create expectations more or less directly related to the situation. Expectations supply clues to what will come next, and in doing so they govern anticipatory adjustments in arousal. Depending on the specific character of the expectations, the changed arousal may result in a general rise in alertness or take the form of specific preparations, the latter being the case when expectations supply clues as to just what is likely to come next. If, for example, the expected development is relevant to the visual sense organs, the state of readiness may be concentrated in them.

Habituation may be seen in connection with expectations and perceived complexity. The immediate effect of a new stimulus object is a rise in arousal caused by the collateral fibers outgoing from the nerve channels that connect the specific sense organ with the RAS. However, when a stimulus object remains in the field of vision this activation ceases, and RAS receives instead inhibitory signals from the cerebral cortex. This influence is believed to be related to processes by which the individual becomes habituated to the stimulus object.

If the stimulus object is not new, the habitually determined inhibitory tendencies may start at the very beginning of the sensation. This explains why new aspects of the environment tend to cause more arousal than well-known ones. Similarly, if expectations have been caused by elements perceived before the stimulus appears, the inhibitory tendencies may be at work even before the stimulus is perceived. The effect of change and especially of surprise may be ascribed to the absence of such anticipatory inhibition. Finally, the more complex the stimulus object is, the longer it will be before habituation occurs, and consequently the more arousal will result.

Whatever the cause of the conflict, cognitive processes will become important, and sooner or later they will be concerned with possible response alternatives. When the first effects of the external stimulation, the physiological disturbance, or the cognitive association have ceased, the major source of input to the RAS becomes the cognitive processes that have been started. The amount of such stimulation depends on uncertainty, involvement, and conflict.

Uncertainty may be induced by elements in the situational setting, but it can also be characteristic of cognitive processes occurring in the cerebral cortex. That is, *perceived uncertainty* may be of two different kinds; first, the individual may be uncertain as to "what is out there," meaning that he is not quite sure what the perceived stimulus object really is. Second, uncertainty may relate to the possible responses; the individual is uncertain about "what to do." As it turns out, the two kinds of uncertainty are closely related. The response alternatives may be immediately or symbolically present in the environment, or the perceived aspects of the environment may be closely associated with possible response alternatives. In theories of learning dealing with stimulus selection, the two factors are identical. When it is determined which stimulus the individual will attend to, then the response is automatically determined (Bush and Mosteller 1955, Bush and Estes 1959, and Restle 1961).

A measure of uncertainty has been proposed within information theory (Shannon and Weaver 1949). Berlyne (1960) has suggested an application of this measure to perceived uncertainty, and with a slight modification, this fits our purpose nicely. In any situation where an individual is faced with a number of possible response alternatives, uncertainty is present. Assume that a *response strength* is associated with each of the alternatives, that is, each of the alternatives is seen as being more or less attractive.[3] Now let there be n different alternatives, and let A_i be the attractiveness of alternative number i. It is then possible to define the relative attractiveness of alternative i as follows:

$$B_i = \frac{A_i}{\sum_{i=1}^{n} A_i} \tag{4.I}$$

Using this measure of relative attractiveness and the information-theory measure of uncertainty, we may define the response uncertainty as follows:

$$U = \sum_{i=1}^{n} B_i \log_2 B_i \tag{4.II}$$

This measure has a number of advantages. First, when n is equal to one, B_i will be one also, and then the measure of uncertainty equals to zero. Second, with a fixed number of alternatives which are all equally attractive, the measure takes on a maximum value; and furthermore, the more alike the alternatives are in attractiveness, the larger the measure of uncertainty will be. Finally, when the number of alternatives increases, the measure of uncertainty will also increase.

In spite of these properties the measure of perceived uncertainty presents one problem. Intuitively it would be expected, whatever the number of alternatives, that if the two most attractive responses are equally attractive then a considerable amount of response uncertainty will be present. This, however, is reflected in the expression only where just two alternatives are considered. In a case with more alternatives, when the two best ones are equally attractive, the effect of the additional alternatives may be to make the total uncertainty measure quite low.

As cognitive uncertainty increases, the cerebral cortex increases its stimulation of the RAS, and consequently arousal increases. But uncertainty itself is not sufficient to elicit any significant amount of arousal. The "importance of" or the "involvement with" the problem must be considered

---

[3] The concept of attractiveness will be dealt with in detail in Chapter 6, and response strength is discussed further later in this chapter.

also. If the matter is trivial, extreme uncertainty may be neglected, whereas if the problem is highly involving, only a little uncertainty is needed for considerable conflict to result.

Together the importance of the problem and the cognitive uncertainty define the amount of *cognitive conflict* (Sieber and Lanzetta 1964). A multiplicative relationship has been suggested (Berlyne 1960). That is, uncertainty and importance are together the necessary and sufficient conditions for conflict to occur, and the absence of either one of them will eliminate the conflict. The nature of the interaction between uncertainty and involvement, however, is not fully understood. For example, it is perfectly possible that the kind of uncertainty that results when involvement is low is entirely different from that which occurs in highly involving situations. In the first case the uncertainty may be seen as a kind of indifference, whereas in more involving situations the uncertainty is more similar to the uncertainty concept in information theory (Shannon and Weaver 1949). Lanzetta and Driscoll (1968) report findings that suggest that under some circumstances the relationship between involvement and uncertainty may be additive.

5. Substitution Among Different Arousal Potentials

The total activation of the RAS is the sum of the situational, the physiological, and the cognitive stimulation. The level of arousal, i.e., the stimulation of the cerebral cortex provided by the RAS, is a function of all these sources, and in this sense the different sources of arousal (or arousal potentials) may substitute for each other. However, a question is whether a change in one arousal potential can be counteracted by manipulation of another source of arousal.

On the one hand, as will be discussed, there are limits to the amount of adjustment attainable through manipulation of physiological arousal potential, and there probably are such limits—although less narrow—to altering the other potentials for arousal. On the other hand, it is fairly obvious that some substitution among different arousal potentials occurs. For example, an extremely complex environment may be dealt with by selective attention, but cognitive distortions may also be applied. It is not possible to specify how far such substitution may go, but it presumably occurs.

4. *Response Strength, Involvement, and Uncertainty*

Response strength, involvement, and uncertainty have characteristics common with the variables in several major psychological traditions. To explain the nature of these variables and to review the possibilities for quantifying them, existing research into them is discussed briefly.

1. Types of Response Strength Variables

RESPONSE STRENGTH AND ATTITUDES

Commonly the *"response strength"* reflects the net amount of motivation directing the individual towards an alternative. Generally it is expected that the alternative that arouses the largest response strength is the one that will be chosen (Hull 1952, Tolman 1955, and Berlyne 1960), but some authors have perceived the variable probabilistically (Luce 1959a, Restle 1961). Here the response strength is translated into a probability reflecting the likelihood that a specific alternative will be chosen. In a marketing context, experiments with aggregated variables of this nature have been reported (Weiss 1968 and Kuehn et al. 1966), with somewhat successful results for four unidentified private brands.

In line with this use of the term is the attitude concept as it has been used by many authors. As far back as Allport (1935), it has repeatedly been stated that an attitude towards an object is a predisposition to act towards that object, and in this sense the attitude has much in common with the response strength or the attractiveness of the alternative. Attitude measures as predictors of behavior will be discussed in Chapter 9.

THE NET VALENCE CONCEPT

Lewin (1935) suggests a concept of positive and negative forces determining a net valence that explains whether or not an alternative will be chosen. In accordance with his theory it is possible to measure the net valence in terms of a net desire and a net resistance in connection with the alternative. Bilkey (1951 and 1953) has used this approach in studies of purchasing decisions. In Figure 4.2 his model is illustrated.

It can be seen that the net valence is thought of as composed of separately measurable forces, and the difference between these forces reflects the response strength. Attempts to measure these variables have been rather unsuccessful (Bilkey 1957).

MILLER'S APPROACH-AVOIDANCE MODEL

As in Lewin's concepts of positive and negative valences, Miller (1944) (see also Holzman 1958) in his models of conflict assumes that the choice alternative has positive as well as negative aspects. The positive aspects will give rise to approaching behavioral tendencies, whereas the negative aspects will generate avoiding tendencies. The actual behavior will be determined by the difference between the approaching and the avoiding tendencies. Miller, however, adds further assumptions: he suggests that both the approaching and the avoiding tendencies increase in strength as the choice alternative comes closer to one's reach and that the avoiding tendencies increase faster than the approaching tendencies. This implies that a point can be reached

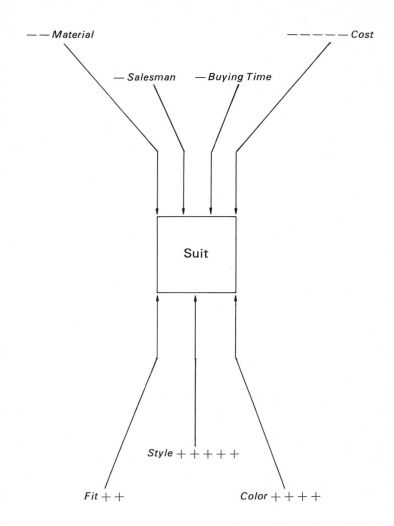

FIGURE 4.2.   *"Hypothetical psychic tension relationship for a person buying a suit. Each arrow represents a force direction or vector regarding the suit (hence the term vector hypothesis), and the strength of these vectors is represented by the valences (plus and minus signs) shown on them. Assumptions are that he likes the suit's color, style and fit, and that he dislikes the salesman, the material, buying time involved, and the cost. This relationship aggregates to 11 +'s and 9 —'s or to a net difference of 2 +'s; hence the suit would tend to be purchased." (Reprinted from W. J. Bilkey: "A Psychological Approach to Consumer Behavior Analysis," Journal of Marketing Vol. 18, no. 1, July 1953, published by The American Marketing Association.)*

where the two tendencies are equally strong. Such a point of maximum conflict is shown in Figure 4.3.

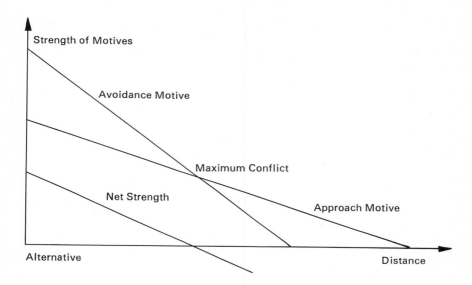

FIGURE 4.3. *Response strength as a function of approach and avoidance motives.*

Miller is primarily interested in predicting when a lasting conflict will result. In order to do this he must assume that both the approaching and the avoiding tendencies remain constant over some period of time and that no substitute alternatives are available. This situation, however, is very unlikely in consumer behavior. The net approach tendency determined by the two opposing tendencies reflects essentially the same thing as the response strength.

UTILITY CONCEPTS

In traditional utility theory (Kauder 1965) each alternative has a fixed utility associated with it. In recent formulations, choice depends not only upon this utility, but also upon the subjective probability associated with it. In these models the concept of subjective expected utility (S.E.U.) is important (Edwards 1962). Used to reflect the overall evaluation of the alternatives, it is defined as the subjective probability of the outcome multiplied by its expected utility. The subjective expected utility can be seen as a kind of response strength. Attempts to measure this variable are discussed in Chapter 9.

ACHIEVEMENT MOTIVATION

Out of McClelland et al.'s (1953) theory of achievement motivation has grown a concept of response strength (Atkinson and Feather 1966). In its original formulation, the achievement motive is seen as a disposition governing the extent to which the individual will strive to obtain success in economic, competitive, and other social contexts (Brown 1965). The achievement motive is composed of a positive motive towards achievement of success (M_s) and a negative motive towards avoidance of failure (M_f). Each motive can be dealt with separately, and they reflect important personality traits. Atkinson's (1964) formulation deals with how motivated an individual will be towards a certain response alternative. In connection with each alternative, a probability of success (P_s) and a probability of failure (P_f) are introduced together with an incentive value of success (I_s) and an incentive value of failure (I_f). Atkinson suggests that the net response strength can be computed as follows:

$$R = M_s \times P_s \times I_s - M_f \times P_f \times I_f$$

This formulation explicitly points out how the response strength is a function of individual predispositions $(M_s$ and $M_f)$ of attributes of the alternatives $(I_s$ and $I_f)$ and of the individual's perception of the situation $(P_s$ and $P_f)$.

2. Problem Importance and Involvement

Although involvement has been an important variable in many psychological studies (for example, Brehm and Cohen 1962, Lanzetta 1963, Eagly 1967), a distinction is rarely made between problem importance and subjective involvement. The latter can be thought of as reflecting the extent to which the individual is engaged in the particular situation, whereas importance reflects aspects of the problem with which the individual is faced, such as the amount of money at stake or the severity of the consequences of the choice. Often, importance has been manipulated experimentally, and it has seemed to influence involvement. For example, Sieber and Lanzetta (1964) varied involvement by telling subjects that they were taking a test that would affect their grades, whereas the remaining subjects believed that they were simply evaluating an experimental device.

A few attempts to relate involvement to an individual's cognitive structure have been reported. In studies of perceived risk (Cox 1967a) subjects have been asked to rate the subjectively perceived importance of the consequences of different choices (see Chapter 5); and Rokeach (1960) suggests that the importance of a problem depends upon the centrality of the issue in relation to the total belief-value structure of the individual (see Chapter 7). Finally, Sherif et al. (1965) have suggested a procedure by which involvement can be measured (see Chapter 7).[4]

[4] It has been argued that this approach measures the subjective importance of the overall problem rather than involvement (Krugman 1967).

Only a single attempt to measure involvement in the particular situation has been reported. Krugman (1967) attempted to quantify involvement with particular advertisements through the amount of interaction with the advertisement. That is, the measurement is based upon observation of the subject's behavior in the exposure situation. However, in the present context this procedure is not ideal, as it measures the involvement by means of characteristics of the behavior involvement is supposed to determine.

3. Perceived Uncertainty

Uncertainty depends on the response strengths, but like involvement, it can be manipulated experimentally and be measured by having individuals rate their perceived uncertainty. Both approaches have been applied (Lanzetta 1963, Atkinson and Feather 1966, and Cox 1967a). In contrast to involvement and response strength experiments, useful measurements have been obtained, and Driscoll et al. (1966) find good correlation between different measures of perceived uncertainty.

Chapter 5

THE OPTIMAL AROUSAL LEVEL

1. *The Rationale Behind an Optimal Arousal Level*

The relationship between arousal potentials and the total amount of activation available for cognitive processes is not straightforward. A number of built-in feedback mechanisms make the relationships considerably complex (Routtenberg 1968). Important aspects of this complex relationship can be dealt with through the introduction of an optimal arousal level.

Humans must adapt to a constantly changing environment. If the individual is always extremely alert, he may manage such adjustments with ease and be likely to choose the right action quickly enough. But, if the organism is constantly kept at a high level of activation, the bodily equipment wears out very soon. Most people have experienced how prolonged periods of concentration result in fatigue and other signs of bodily degeneration. Consequently, an intermediate level of readiness or an intermediate level of arousal is preferable, because it corresponds to an optimal amount of arousal the size of which depends on environmental requirements and the state of the organism. Berlyne (1960) writes: "This level may represent something like the prevailing level of arousal required of the organism in its particular circumstances, susceptible to modification if the circumstances alter." (p. 184)

The optimal level does not correspond to a single value, but rather it represents a certain range of tolerable amounts of arousal. It might be more appropriate to talk about an optimal range, as some variations in the arousal potential can normally be observed that do not produce the effects normally associated with deviations from the optimal level. However, it is not known whether this phenomenon is an artifact of the insensitivity of the measurement

78

devices or whether it reflects a significant aspect of the functioning of the RAS. The following discussion will be in terms of an optimal level, but the idea that this corresponds to a certain range should not be neglected.

2. *Maintenance of an Optimal Level of Arousal*

Because the amount of activation outgoing from the RAS varies with the amount of stimulation the system receives, the maintenance of an optimal level of arousal requires that the arousal potential must be modified or that the optimal amount of arousal be adjusted in advance to correspond to the amount of stimulation that subsequently will be present. Advance adjustment can occur when the required amount of arousal can be predicted and when it is not extremely large. This condition is met when the individual is so familiar with the situation that no aspects of it present extreme amounts of arousal potential and his expectations and habituation can direct the amount of arousal that subsequently will be needed. But these requirements are not always present. Changes in physiological and cognitive arousal potential can rarely be predicted, and the environment may produce unexpected stimulation; consequently, the arousal may exceed or fall short of the optimal level. In such instances balance must be achieved in other ways, which imply modifications of the input to the system or an application of specific cognitive processes aimed at restoring the balance. Such adjustments may be aimed at reducing or increasing the arousal potential. When the optimal arousal level is exceeded by environmental stimulation, the individual may attempt to eliminate environmental complexity; if the optimal arousal level exceeds the stimulation working on the system, then excitement, complexity, and the like may be sought out.

1. Manipulation of Situational Arousal Potential

When moderate deviations occur, responses that can restore the balance between arousal and external stimulation will be sought; but when the environmental complexity is very great or very low, other strategies may be applied. Extreme amounts of stimulation may result in a drop in arousal; and, similarly, very low amounts may generate increased arousal. With moderate deviation one of the following strategies can be applied:

1. When the environmental stimulation falls below the optimal level, exploration may aim at revealing more complexity or new elements in the environment. Both will tend to increase arousal.

2. When the environment is more complex than can be tolerated, exploration may be used to reduce arousal. Here continued occupation with the same objects may make them more familiar and less complex.

3. Finally, the individual can maintain the optimal level by deliberately picking responses which ensure that external stimulation does not become too complex or too trivial.

2. Manipulation of Physiological Arousal Potential

Assume for a moment that the physiological arousal potential can be studied with no regard to other sources of arousal. If this potential is just sufficient to maintain an appropriate level of activation, there are no problems, but if it is either very large or very small, he question becomes whether the organism can modify the physiological ir pact on the RAS to such an extent that an intermediate arousal level is stored. Evidence shows that such processes may occur (Brehm et al. 1964), but the very nature of the physiological arousal potential suggests that there will be a limit to the extent of the modification. Very naturally, responses will be made that eliminate the physiological disturbance that caused the increased stimulation. For example, it is possible that certain amounts of hunger can be suppressed; but as hunger increases, other arousal-reducing devices must be applied. In the case of hunger, responses involving food intake will be chosen.

3. Manipulation of Cognitive Arousal Potential

Assume for a moment that sources of arousal other than cognitive arousal potential can be neglected. The question then becomes what will happen when the cognitive arousal potential exceeds or falls short of what is required for the maintenance of an intermediate level of arousal. As with the situational arousal potential, a high amount of cognitive arousal potential will be expected to generate cognitive processes aimed at reducing this potential. Such processes may produce selectivity in recall, search for meaning or for cognitive balance, suppression, and distortion of conflicting cognitions. On the other hand, too little cognitive arousal potential may lead to increased cognitive activity aimed at increasing cognitive conflict by searching for stimulating thoughts, daydreaming, and the like.

A deviation from the optimal level of arousal caused by one kind of arousal potential will often trigger strategies aimed at adjustments in the same potential. However, discrepancies will not always be met in this way. Within certain limits different arousal potentials can substitute for each other; and, for example, a rise in the situational arousal potential may be counteracted by strategies aimed at decreasing the cognitive arousal potential.

3. *Determinants of an Optimal Level of Arousal*

Behavioral responses and choice processes relate to the optimal amount of arousal. While a behavioral response is being performed, the arousal potential corresponds to the arousal level. This is not to say that the level of arousal remains constant, but as long as the individual is continuously able to establish relevant expectations as to what will be next, the arousal level can be adjusted in advance. However, sudden environmental changes or the termination of fixed responses may increase the level of arousal and a choice process be generated. When that happens, arousal has to be brought back to the optimal level before the behavioral response can be completed or before new action can be started.

The optimal arousal level brings to mind the previously described changes between conflict and behavioral responses. Both reflect the organism's attempt to adjust to external factors, and they may be closely related. In circumstances where behavioral responses are long and choice processes are few and associated with only little conflict, the arousal level may be lower than in circumstances where conflict is frequent and important.

In brief, an intermediate arousal level will be sought which depends on internal states and environmental circumstances. In the short run, internal and external stimulation may generate deviations; and in turn, responses will be sought out which tend to restore the intermediate level of arousal. Deviations from the intermediate level imply conflict, and generate a choice process which will terminate when a choice is made of a behavioral response which can restore balance.

Only little systematic evidence is available concerning the determinants of the optimal level of arousal, but there is some indication of a link between the prevailing short-time fluctuations in the arousal and the subsequent optimal level. This relationship is discussed by Berlyne (1960):

We can picture the tonus level of arousal as creeping upward or downward if a level above or below an earlier tonus level is sustained for some time. How much arousal potential of a particular kind an individual will tolerate depends not only on the level of arousal tonus, but also on how promptly and easily he has been able to assuage the arousal induced by similar conditions in the past. (p. 212)

Thus, when short-time fluctuations are explained, much is also said about changes in the optimal level.

The optimal level reflects that level which the individual has learned will be appropriate under the given circumstances. Thus, it depends on accumulated previous experiences. When an individual has learned that a relatively high amount of arousal is optimal for him under some specific circumstances, he is willing to accept considerable complexity and conflict. On the other hand, when the individual has a low optimal level of arousal, only little complexity and conflict is tolerable. Berlyne (1960) suggests that the optimal level of arousal depends on a diversity of factors:

We can expect personality factors, cultural factors, learning and psychological states all to play their parts in determining the level at which arousal tonus is maintained. Consequently, the rate of arousal potential that is optimal can be presumed to vary widely from individual to individual and from occasion to occasion. (p. 211)

4. *Research Interpreted in Terms of an Optimal Level of Arousal*

1. The Search For Optimal Arousal

In a particular situation, it is predictable that the individual will seek out exciting stimulation when the environment provides too little stimulation and will avoid stimulation when the environment is too complex. The validity of this proposition can be tested by presenting individuals with extremely low or extremely high arousal potentials. An illustration of such a study is provided by Sokolov (1958). In studying reactions to electrical stimulation of the skin, he found that an increase in stimulation at first creates orientation (or positive exploration) responses but that later, when a certain intensity of stimulation has been reached, negative exploration takes over.

Other illustrative evidence is provided by Dember and Earl (1957) and by Berlyne (1958). Berlyne presented children and adults with pictures varying in complexity, and he found a marked preference for more complex patterns. However, in a later study (Berlyne 1960) considerably more complex material was used, and this time no definite preference was observed. Presumably, in the second experiment the complexity of the alternative illustrations corresponded approximately to the optimal arousal level.

In line with these findings are studies of stimulus deprivation. The optimal arousal level concept implies that individuals will seek out stimulation when the arousal potential is very low. Considerable evidence confirms this proposition. Extreme stimuli deprivation is experienced as very unpleasant, and it may result in uncontrollable hallucinations and a search for more arousing stimulation (Jones et al. 1960, and Kubzansky and Leiderman 1961). For example, Heron (1961) reports: "Twenty-five of the twenty-nine subjects reported some form of hallucinatory activity. Typically, the hallucinations progressed from simple to complex. . . . They had little control over the content of their hallucinations, nor were they able to start or stop them" (pp. 17–18).

2. Effects of Repeated Exposure

When a subject is presented with a new and highly complex stimulus pattern, the expected immediate reaction will be withdrawal (provided the initial arousal potential exceeds the optimal level). However, as exposure is repeated, the stimulus object loses some of its novelty and complexity; and after a number of exposures, correspondence between arousal and arousal potential is achieved. As the sequence of exposures is continued, habituation will occur, and eventually, the stimulus object will produce less than the optimal level of arousal. Consequently, repeated exposure should produce withdrawal, interest, and boredom in the order mentioned, and Grass and Wallace (1969) present evidence in favor of a model that predicts that repeated exposure to TV commercials will first generate increased attention and interest, later followed by a decrease in the same variables.

3. Adaption and Aspiration Level Theories

A different line of research has presented evidence that may be interpreted in terms of a quest for an optimal amount of arousal. The adaption-level theory of McClelland et al. (1953) suggests that the amount of reward associated with an upcoming event depends on how its appearance relates to what was expected. If the stimulus falls extremely below or above expectations, it will be judged to be unpleasant, whereas stimuli deviating somewhat less will be judged as more pleasant than stimuli corresponding to expectations. The formulation has gained widespread interest, and several confirmative results have been reported (McClelland et al. 1953, Haber 1958, and Conners 1964).

Interpreted in terms of arousal level, the theory says that stimulus patterns with no deviations from expectancies, i.e., with no surprise or novelty, are less rewarding than those with moderate novelty, surprise, or complexity, and that extreme overstimulation will also be negatively evaluated. The theory suggests a butterfly-shaped relationship between stimulation and response (Figure 5.1). However, often it has been impossible to identify the lower part of the relationship (Locke 1967 and Verenis et al. 1968). In such cases the model comes close to competing formulations, namely the theory of aspiration levels (Lewin et al. 1944) and adaption levels (Helson 1964 and 1966).

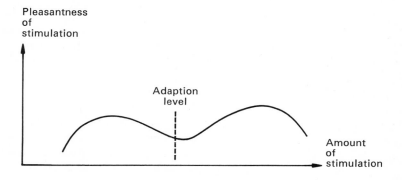

FIGURE 5.1. *The relationship between amount of stimulation and pleasantness of stimulation.*

The aspiration level theory deals with situations in which the individual performs a task where the outcome is partly controlled by himself. In such cases expectations take the form of goals or "aspirations" towards which the individual strives. The goals are set so that the individual has a fair chance of reaching them (Harvey and Sherif, 1951) and will strive hard to achieve them. Moreover, subsequent aspirations are adjusted in accordance with previous experiences, so that future achievements are likely at least to come close to, and commonly to exceed, what is expected. Seen in this light, adaption-level theory may be related to arousal in the following way: In achievement situations, expectations will secure the amount of arousal needed to deal with the subsequent arousal potential; and, moreover, responses are selected that tend to produce this arousal potential.

It is beyond the scope of the present discussion to review the extensive research conducted in connection with aspiration-level theories, and only a single example will be provided. Festinger (1942) presented subjects with a task whose outcome, unknown to the subjects, was manipulated so that achievement of the aspired level was obtainable for some, but not all subjects. This made it possible to study how aspiration levels change. Among subjects who had experienced success, 51% raised their aspirations and 41% showed no change, whereas only 8% decreased their aspiration levels. Among subjects who failed to reach their aspiration level, adjustments were in the reverse direction. 64% reduced their level of aspiration, 29% did not change, and only 7% increased their aspirations.

An excellent summary of some of the basic findings from this research is given by Katona (1960):

    1. Aspirations are not static; they are not established once for all times.
    2. Aspirations tend to grow with achievement and decline with failure.
    3. Aspirations are influenced by the performance of other members of the group to which a person belongs and by that of reference groups.
    4. Aspirations are reality oriented; most commonly they are slightly higher or slightly lower than the level of accomplishment rather than greatly different from it. (p. 130)

The aspiration-level formulation has given rise to a number of hypotheses concerning consumer behavior (March and Simon 1958, Katona 1960, Nicosia 1966, and Hansen 1967a; see also Chapter 9). In brief, the theories hold that consumers have rather stable expectations as to what they will accept. As long as the products they buy and consume satisfy these aspiration (satisfaction) levels, consumption and purchases will be repeated without much conflict; but when significant negative deviations occur, the consumer will begin to search for new alternatives. On the other hand, when significant positive deviations are experienced, the satisfaction levels are raised. These hypotheses have not been followed by extensive experimental research. They rely heavily upon findings reported by psychologists; but, like the underlying theory, they relate to arousal and can be interpreted in terms of an optimal level of arousal.

Somewhat contrary to the aspiration-level theory, Helson (1964 and 1966) has proposed an adaption-level theory whose emphasis is placed on expectations generated by the overall situation rather than upon aspirations. The model suggests that stimuli will be judged relative to an adaption level that depends upon previous and present focal and background stimuli. The theory is interesting because it suggests the existence of optimal or neutral levels in human judgment of environmental events. As Helson (1964) writes: "Adaption levels appear as neutral or indifferent zones in bipolar responses" (p. 26). The model has been applied primarily to perceptual phenomena, but a few studies with attitude material have been reported. At present, its applicability outside a perceptual context is questionable (Insko 1967).

4. Conflict Solving

Conflict solving, decision making, problem solving, and choice behavior are some of the headings under which human response selection has been studied. Many different approaches have been used and many theoretical suggestions put forward (see, for example, Cartwright and Festinger 1943, Miller 1944, Edwards 1954a, Simon 1958, Janis 1959a, Gagne 1959, Festinger 1964a, Howard and Sheth 1967, and Engel et al. 1968). Many of these approaches will be dealt with subsequently, but only a single aspect will be discussed here.

Most studies of conflict and choice have one thing in common. They suggest that a conflict is an unpleasant state of affairs, which motivates the individual to attempt to reduce the unpleasant aspects of the situation. Janis (1959a) writes: "This state of tension which occurs whenever there is a decisional conflict which implicates important personal or group goals will motivate the person to work out some form of resolution whereby the subdominant consideration can be ignored, minimized or eliminated" (p. 21), and similarly, Festinger (1964a) states: "Indeed this pre-decision period can be and has been considered to be synonymous with a period of frustration" (p. 3). In fact, this observation has been made so often that many have been inclined to argue that such a response pattern will occur in all circumstances. That this is not the case has been shown in the previous sections, and it must be repeated that whether an individual will respond with arousal-increasing or arousal-reducing responses cannot be answered uniformly with "yes" or "no." The response will depend upon the optimal arousal potential.

Conflict has frequently been studied in terms of uncertainty and involvement (Chapter 4), and exploratory behavior has been the dependent variable. Exploration can be used to increase as well as to decrease conflict. The specific nature of the exploration will depend on the relationship between the arousal potential and the optimal level of arousal. If the arousal potential is high, exploration will be used to reduce the perceived conflict, by reducing uncertainty or involvement. Contrarily, if the arousal potential is low, exploration may be used in an attempt to increase the conflict; and here, uncertainty and involving stimulation may be sought out.

Another model, which sees exploration as depending upon uncertainty and importance, is proposed by Irwin and Smith (1956 and 1957) and Irwin et al. (1956). To test the model Irwin and Smith (1957) asked subjects to guess whether the numbers printed on a card deck had a mean above or below zero. The subject paid a price for each card he decided to see before making his guess. Furthermore, the subject received a prize if his guess was correct. This setup made it possible to vary uncertainty by using card decks with means more or less close to zero (.5 and 1.5 were used) and by using card decks with differences in variance (2.0 and 7.5 were used). The importance of the decision was varied by using prizes at two different levels (50 cents and one dollar). Within these experimental variations, increased uncertainty and importance made the subjects purchase more information. If it can be assumed, and it seems plausible, that the choice situation was so complex that conflict-reducing responses were sought, the findings confirm that exploration (information purchases) was used to decrease uncertainty. However, even more interesting is another finding the authors report. After each choice, the subjects were asked to rate how confident (certain) they felt about their guesses. None of these ratings varied significantly among the experimental conditions, an opinion which may be interpreted in terms of an optimal arousal level. Presumably, subjects continued their information buying until they had reached a certain level of certainty (corresponding to a certain level of arousal) and then made their choices. An interpretation supported by findings reported by Morlock (1967).

Other evidence is provided by Siegel and Goldstein (1959). Following a sequence of exposures to "light" or "no light" events, they asked college student subjects to predict whether an upcoming event would be "light" or "no light." As the sequences were not randomly arranged, it was possible to measure variations in the quality of the performance. It was predicted that involvement (labeled *conflict* by the authors) would influence the responses. To test this prediction three experimental conditions were applied. In the first condition, the subjects were not offered any payment; in the second condition, the importance of the conflict was increased by payment for correct predictions; and in the third condition, further increases in the perceived conflict were introduced by requiring the subjects to pay back their earnings when they were wrong. If it can be assumed that this experimental setup created a considerable amount of conflict, the arousal-level hypothesis predicts that the amount of deliberation will increase from condition one to condition three. Moreover, if it can be assumed that increased deliberation will result in improved performance, then the performance should improve from the first to the third condition. This was actually the result.

Further, Zajonc and Burnstein (1961) have studied the influence of uncertainty upon deliberation. In an experiment they found support or a relationship between uncertainty, cognitive changes, and message distortion. With a condition of increased uncertainty, subjects tended to interpret information in favor of the alternative that was initially least uncertain. Because such distortions will reduce the perceived uncertainty, the findings suggest that not only quantitative aspects of exploration but also cognitive manipulation of information may be applied in attempts to reduce arousal.

Other authors have approached similar problems in a slightly different way. Lanzetta (1963) reports an experiment in which he studied exploratory behavior in relation to the initial level of uncertainty and to the rate with which the uncertainty could be reduced. It was found that in three experimental conditions, exploration continued until uncertainty was reduced to approximately the same level, and then the choice was made. The nature of the findings is suggested in Figure 5.2, where it can be seen that the subjects did not search for information until complete knowledge was gained. Rather, they stopped their information acquisition when a certain level of uncertainty was reached, a level which did not depend on the initial amount of uncertainty or on the speed with which the uncertainty could be reduced.

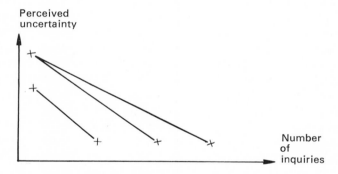

FIGURE 5.2. *Exploration and choice as a function of uncertainty in three experimental conditions (Lanzetta, 1963).*

Together, Sieber and Lanzetta (1964 and 1966) have reported findings that relate directly to Berlyne's arousal tonus hypothesis. In their first study, they dealt with the complexity of choice-process behavior in terms of amount of search, expressed doubt, amount of new information generated, time spent on processing information, and aspects of the solution given. These variables were related to uncertainty and importance, and both were found to influence all but one measure of the complexity of the decision process. Similarly, Driscoll and Lanzetta (1964 and 1965) and Lanzetta and Driscoll (1968) present findings which support a relationship between, on the one hand, arousal, complexity and conflict and, on the other hand, exploratory behavior. Lanzetta and Driscoll (1966) report a study that shows that individuals will acquire information about an uncertain outcome, even though the outcome is unavoidable and the information is useless. These findings suggest that exploratory behavior serves purposes other than supplying information for "rational" decision making.

Related findings have been reported by Green et al. (1964, 1966, and 1968) and Green (1966) on the consumer's use of information. For an evaluation of the findings, it is necessary to describe briefly the model which has governed this research.

Based on the normative utility model (Chapter 10), using a Bayesian approach (Miller and Star 1967), it is possible to set up conditions under which an optimal amount of information can be determined. When an individual is faced with a conflicting choice, he may decide to acquire more information or to make a choice based on the information available. How much more information it is advantageous to buy depends on the cost of the information, the initial amount of information, the quality of the information, and the potential gains and losses associated with the decision. Using an experimental game procedure much like the one used by Irwin and Smith (1956 and 1957), it is possible to manipulate the variables of importance for the optimal amount of information. In a number of experiments reported by Green (1966), he found that individuals do have a preferred amount of information they will tend to acquire. Almost all subjects bought some information, and none bought all the information available. Furthermore, the individual's preferred amount of information was not closely related to the optimal amount of information that would be prescribed by a normative decision model.

Of special interest is the following finding. The Bayesian model predicts that useless information will be avoided. Considerations based on arousal predict that excessive amounts of arousal generated by a conflicting situation will be reduced and that if this can be achieved only by purchasing information, then that strategy will be preferred, even though the normative guiding value of the information is zero. The findings strongly confirm this prediction. When the experimental conditions were manipulated so that information was useless, subjects still bought information. In fact, they bought even more information in this case than when information was valuable, a result that suggests that the lack of reduction in uncertainty made the subjects extend their exploration.

5. Perceived Risk

The concept of risk has a prominent tradition in economics and business theory, and recently it has gained attention from students of consumer behavior (Bauer 1960, Cox 1967a, Popielarz 1967, and Hughes et al. 1969). Traditionally, risk has been seen as a function of the uncertainty of the outcome and of the significance of the problem in question; in recent approaches it is perceived in a similar way. Bauer (1960) and Cox (1967a) define risk as a function of uncertainty as perceived by the consumer and of the consequences that the consumer associates with the decision. Unlike traditional approaches, their definition includes not only monetary consequences, but also the use of the product and the social consequences inherent in using it.

Probably the best-known research dealing with perceived risk has been conducted at Harvard. Most of the findings have been reported in Cox (1967a). Perceived risk has rarely been measured in specific choice situations, but rather researchers have attempted to quantify the amount of risk that consumers associate with products and brands in general. The main purpose has been to show how consumer behavior can be explained as responses aimed at reducing or avoiding risk. (Until recently the possibility that consumers may attempt to increase perceived risk has not been explored.) Risk can be reduced either through information search or through purchase strategies. The latter occurs when a consumer becomes loyal to a brand or when he avoids buying new products.

Cunningham (1966) found different amounts of perceived risk associated with headache remedies, fabric softeners, and dry spaghetti, and he also reports that some consumers perceive more risk than do others. Moreover, he found that people who perceived high risk were most likely to have discussed the product recently and to have observed advertising. Similarly, individuals with high perceived risk tended to be more brand loyal than individuals perceiving less risk (Cunningham 1967a).

In line with this, Arndt (1967b), in a study of the introduction of a new coffee brand, reports that consumers with high perceived risk are most likely to be brand loyal and least likely to switch to a new brand. However, Arndt did not find that consumers with high perceived risk were more likely to engage in word-of-mouth advertising, a finding he suggests is due to the fact that the higher degree of brand loyalty among these consumers overrules the necessity for reducing perceived risk by means of communication.

In another study reported by Cox and Rich (1964) it was found that shopping by telephone related to perceived risk. The more risk consumers perceive in connection with a certain product, the less likely they are to buy it by telephone. If it can be assumed that telephone shopping is more risky than regular shopping, the fact suggests another strategy consumers may apply in attempts to reduce or avoid risk. From the same study, findings indicate that perceived risk is associated with familiarity with the alternatives. It was found that products with low purchase frequency are more likely to be perceived as risky than are products with high purchase frequency.

All the Harvard studies have dealt with situations in which consumers are trying to reduce risk. However, under certain circumstances it may be unwise to avoid risk. Or to put it a little differently, the reduction of risk by avoiding risky alternatives is achieved at a different kind of "cost." Just as it is unwise to purchase a new product if it will be unsatisfactory, it may be unwise *not* to buy a new product if it will be better than the one presently used. That is, there is a possible risk of not obtaining the advantages inherent in a new product that really is superior. This formulation conforms to arousal theory as the quest for an intermediate level of arousal will secure a strategy that balances the two counteracting "risks." Popielarz (1967) has tested hypotheses derived from this formulation, based on research carried out by Pettigrew (1956). He suggests that people with broad cognitive categories tend to be more willing to deal with the type of risk associated with new products. He confirmed this hypothesis by conducting a study in which perceived category width was found to be correlated with willingness to try new products.

6. Cognitive Consistency, Dissonance, and Balance

Relationships between cognitive elements have been studied in terms of dissonance (Festinger 1957 and Brehm and Cohen 1962), cognitive balance (Heider 1958 and Abelson and Rosenberg 1958), cognitive congruity (Osgood and Tannenbaum 1955), and belief congruence (Rokeach and Rothman 1965). These and other formulations predict that inconsistency between salient values, attitudes, or beliefs will generate tendencies aimed at reducing this inconsistency. Over the last 15 years hypotheses derived from these formulations have been among the most tested within social psychology. Generally it has been found that incongruity-reducing responses are applied, but also that they are certainly not so universal as originally believed (Rosenberg 1965b). Although this whole area is discussed in the following chapter, a few comments are made here.

The conditions that will cause inconsistency-reducing responses have most explicitly been studied within dissonance theory (Brehm and Cohen 1962). Some of the more important variables that have been found to trigger such responses are commitment (involvement), number of alternatives involved (complexity), and the extent to which alternatives are alike (uncertainty). These conditions characterize a high amount of arousal potential, which supports the suggestion that dissonance reduction, achievement of cognitive balance, and the like are arousal-reducing responses. In this respect dissonance, balance, and congruity approaches may be seen as opposed to Brehm's (1966) reactance formulation (Chapter 7). The former focus on arousal-reducing responses, the latter on arousal-increasing responses. The acceptance-rejection formulation of Sherif et al. (1965) and Feather's (1967a) congruity model can be seen as first steps towards a unification of these opposing formulations. In these models, attitude change will occur or be counteracted, depending on the extent to which the attitude material is "new" or incongruent relative to the individual's initial position (Chapter 7).

Related to those models are also a number of studies of selectivity in exposure to communication (Chapter 9). Here it has repeatedly been found that the occurrence of selectivity is highly dependent upon the entire situation, and that conditions exist that favor a choice of inconsistent information as well as conditions favouring congruent information.

Altogether, the studies of repeated exposure, of aspiration and adaption levels, of conflict solving, of risk and information handling, and of the acceptance of attitude statements suggest that individuals, in their interactions with their environment, have some kind of an optimal level for perceived conflict, novelty, uncertainty, and so on. In this connection, it is enlightening to cite Hunt (1965):

Whatever the essential character of this informational organism-environment interaction and its relationship to arousal turns out to be, there appears to be an optimal amount of it for each organism at any given time. I suspect that this optimum is to a considerable degree a function of experience, and that it may obey Helson's (1959) notion of the adaption level. (p. 137)

Chapter 6

CONCEPTS AND COGNITIVE STRUCTURES

A conflict may generate more or less arousal, from which more or less complex cognitive processes will result. Cognitive processes imply manipulation of *salient* cognitive elements that have been established through learning. (The term *salient* is here used to distinguish activated cognitive elements from nonactivated elements.) What has been learned must be stored in memory, and this storage can be accomplished in several ways. Among these, one is of special importance: the registration and storage of learned *concepts*, which are the informational units with which cognitive processes work.

In order to explain what response will be chosen in a given choice situation, it is necessary to predict which cognitive elements will become salient. Several factors influence this. Among the more important are (1) the amount of arousal, (2) the specific motivation of the individual at the time of the choice, (3) environmental factors, and (4) associations among different cognitive elements.

In the present approach, motivation is one of the factors that determine what the salient elements will be; and the salient cognitive elements in turn perform motivational functions.

The fact that a concept is salient in a choice-process does not imply that the individual is also aware of it. A number of factors may cause salient concepts to remain more or less unconscious.

The single choice should be studied in terms of the salient cognitive elements that appear in the choice process. However, chains of related choices can frequently be observed. An important factor in explaining such sequences is the notation of motivational sets, i.e., the way in which individuals can be "set" on something.

92

1. *Memory*

As background for the discussion of information-storing systems, a few comments on physiological aspects of memory are in order. Memory provides a link between impressions received at one time and responses selected at some later time. Consider the following example. A consumer sees a certain advertisement, and sometime later he purchases the product promoted in the advertisement. If it can be established that the product would not have been purchased had the advertisement not been seen, then the observation of the advertisement must have caused something to change within the individual that then was stored and subsequently influenced his behavior. This "something which is stored" provides links between events occurring at different times, and it is referred to as *memory*.

A brief discourse into some of the phenomena underlying memory will make the following discussion easier. Memory traces are located in the neurons that compose the total nervous system (Wooldridge 1963, Hebb 1966, Hilgard and Bower 1966, Rosenzweig and Leiman 1968, and Pfaff 1969). A neuron consists of a number of input channels (fibrils or dendrites) at the receiving end, a cell body, and a single output fibril (the axon). Both the dendrites and the axon are conductors, and respectively they receive and transmit electric stimulation from and to other neurons. The cell body may also receive stimulation directly from axons coming from other nerve cells. Through these processes on the input side, each neuron is connected with a large number of other neurons, but normally it has only one axon. However, as this axon will often have a number of branches (collaterals), it may reach a considerable number of other neurons.

Dendrites and axons transmit electric current in very different ways. The dendrites (and the cell body) constantly register all incoming activation, but the axon will be activated and "fire" only if the summated input exceeds a certain level. Activation of a memory trace requires that the involved neurons fire; and, as most neuronal processes are duplicated in that many units perform parallel functions, variations in memory strength will result from variations in the number of activated parallel systems.

Theories concerning the exact nature of human information storage are rapidly changing, and a detailed discussion of the various hypotheses will not be provided here (see, for example, Bernback 1967). However, a single aspect important for the following discussion should be mentioned. Humans are often believed to be equipped with two or more different memory systems (Melton 1963, Wooldridge 1963, Hilgard and Bower 1966, Norman 1968, and Shriffrin and Atkinson 1969). Most authors talk about a short-term memory, a medium-term memory, and a long-term memory, all of which are closely interconnected. The appropriate functioning of the first two seems to be a necessary condition for establishing long-term memory, although some recent theories have thrown doubt on this relationship (for a review see Rosenzweig and Leiman 1968).

The characteristics of the three memory processes are most easily understood by considering how a visual impression ends up as a long-term memory. Observation of an environmental event will first result in registration in the sensory receptors, accounting for visual perception. This activation—corresponding to the short-term memory—does not last long. However, if the brain directs attention to what is perceived, the picture may be transferred to the medium-term memory, where the picture will be stored somewhat longer. However, if the picture is not transferred to a long-term memory, it will eventually disappear.

The process involved in establishing long-term memory from medium-term memories are not known. Most recent theories assume that the short- and medium-term memories are ascribable to temporary activation of specific memory traces. Long-term memory, on the other hand, is explained in terms of biochemical changes in the nerve cells (Hilgard and Bower 1966, and Schneider 1967). In the following the primary concern is with long-term memories, although some aspects of short-term memories and medium-term memories are important for understanding the salience of cognitive concepts.

It is possible to speculate a little about how stored information may provide a link between previous experiences and subsequent responses. Logically three possibilities exist.

1. Information may be stored as raw data (as a movie film of environmental events) and then processed at the time of the response (Miller 1968).

2. Information may be stored as action programs where each input to the system results in immediate corrections in existing programs or in establishment of new programs that can be performed at an appropriate time.

3. Finally a number of combinations between these two extremes are possible. For example, information may be coded and then stored so that, at the time of the response, the coded information can be regenerated from the memory and the final response selection can take place.

In studies of brain processes and memory, analogies are often made with digital computers (Wooldridge 1963 and Simon 1967a). Although such comparisons can be misleading, they can help explain the nature of the different storage systems. Consider for example a computer connected to a number of cash registers in a department store. Such a computer may handle information in several different ways. It may register all the single transactions as they occur and at some later time perform sorting and computations, or it may immediately compute the necessary totals so that it is able at any time to provide totals for all important figures. However, in the second case the original raw data will normally not be stored. Finally, it may carry out some sorting and processing when the data are received and then later complete the more complex calculations. The first procedure would correspond to a human memory system that continuously registers all events as they occur, the second to an immediate adjustment in a person's behavior program, and the last to an "inbetween" solution.

Actually men seem to make use of all three kinds of storage systems. A few examples will illustrate this.

1. Stored programs seem to explain most routinized behavior such as walking or breathing. These programs are established early in the life of the individual, they are normally not revised, and they are available for execution at any time (Hebb 1966).

2. Human beings are able to store sequences of events in such a way that they can be reproduced very much as they occurred. In a number of experiments electric stimulation of the cortex has resulted in detailed accounts by the subjects of previous episodes. For example, Penfield and Roberts (1959) report that a patient stimulated in a certain area of the cortex told them that she could hear an orchestra playing a number which she did not herself know how to sing or play and which she only vaguely could remember having heard before. The authors described this phenomenon as follows:

> When, by chance, the neurosurgeon's electrode activates past experience, that experience unfolds progressively, moment by moment. This is a little like the performance of a wire recorder or a strip of cinematographic film on which the individual was once aware . . . the things he selected for his attention in that interval of time. Absent from it are the sensations he ignored, the talk he did not heed. (p. 53)

3. Other experiments with applying electric stimulation to the brain have resulted in temporary forgetting of well-known words and concepts. Penfield and Roberts (1959) report that a subject presented with a picture of a foot while stimulated in a certain part of the brain was unable to recall the word *foot* but made use of various other means to describe the picture: "Oh, I know what it is, that is what you put in your shoes."

As a number of other experiments have given similar results (for a review see Wooldridge 1963), it seems warranted to conclude that human beings store behavior programs and sequences of events just as they have a storage system for language, concepts, images, and other nonverbal concepts. This latter system is appropriate for coding and simplifying the extremely complex environmental input the individual constantly receives.

Information can be stored in various locations. Often memory is associated with the cerebral cortex; images, concepts, and sequences of events are stored in it; but memory is not restricted to this area. A number of very elementary responses have their "programs" stored in the spinal cord or in other nerve channels. For example, the sensory input channel linking the eyes with the sensory reception areas can engage in some data processing and also store some information (Hebb 1966). Another important area is the cerebellum, which is found in a special part of the lower brain. It coordinates more complex behavior patterns such as walking and breathing. Consequently, fairly complex behavior programs must be stored in this part of the brain, and it is likely that parts of the programs controlling the performance of organized responses are found here. These responses were described as complex behavioral units to which elaborate and firmly established programs correspond. Such programs do not have to be in the form of a complete unit stored in one specific location in the brain. They may involve a number of subroutines controlled by some higher-order integrating mechanism. For example, the spinal cord may direct elementary routines involved in walking, whereas the coordination of all the different bodily movements required for this activity is provided by the cerebellum and the processes involved in directing the individual "where to go" originate in the cortex.

There is no doubt that choice behavior, as it is dealt with here, should be studied in connection with information located in the cortex (Wooldridge 1963, Hebb 1966). Many subroutines may be located elsewhere, but the selection of the higher-order program will involve cortical processes. For example, "to write one's name" may be represented in the cortex by a single informational signal; when transmitted to the cerebellum or to other control centers, this signal is transformed into a detailed behavior program that controls the necessary action. The important thing is that the selection of the responses of interest here involves some kind of cerebral activity.

With this in mind, it is possible to ask, what kind of information storage system do human beings rely upon when making choices? To what extent do they use a continuously registering memory system? And to what extent do they rely upon the memory system that primarily stores single units of information in the form of concepts and images? Answers to these questions have major implications for the kind of choice model which will emerge. Unfortunately, it is not presently possible to give a final answer. However, the following considerations have guided the present search for principles underlying consumers' response selection.

If all events are registered in great detail in memory, it is almost inevitable that such a memory system make use of a coding device to translate the diverse sensory input into more manageable informational units.[1] If not, it is doubtful whether the available brain capacity would be sufficient to store all the impressions an average person encounters during his life (Wooldridge 1963). If such a coding system is applied, it is reasonable to expect that it makes use of the coding units that have already been shown to exist, namely, images and concepts.

Second, it is perfectly possible that not every single episode is stored in the memory. Although it is well documented that people have more detailed memories than has previously been thought, it may still be that only selected episodes are remembered. Such episodes may not appear to be of any special significance at the time of the experimental recovery, but they may have been quite important when they were stored. Moreover, it is possible that memories which are not used will fade away. Studies of forgetting indicate that such a process occurs.

Third, even if only a limited number of episodes are stored, it is still

---

[1] Memory saving could result because more complex images would have to be stored in detail only once; on subsequent occasions they could be referred to by means of a simpler code.

likely that a coding system is employed in the process of memory formation. If this were not the case, the storage requirements would still be large; and the fact that perception of the episodes employs coding suggests that the storing of the same episodes does also.

Finally, even if a complete registration of events takes place or if a considerable part of all events is registered, it is unlikely that response selection could be explained in terms of a memory system of this kind. The process would be extremely complex if the total memory had to be alerted each time a choice was made. One or another selective mechanism must govern what will be involved in a given response selection; such a mechanism is handily available in the coding system, as perception of a choice situation implies that a number of elements from the coding system are alerted and used.

It is suggested that the cognitive elements that become salient provide a clue to understanding what is involved in the selection of responses. This possibility will be examined further, but first it is necessary to take a closer look at the coding system men use when they perceive and deal with their environment.

2. *The Information Coding System: Concepts*

In the course of their lives human beings receive an astronomical number of impressions. In even a single situation the number of aspects that could be perceived is extremely large. In order to cope with an unlimited number of colors, shapes, sounds, tastes, and the like and all the possible combinations of these inputs, human beings have to systemize their sensory inputs. They can do so by establishing categories or classes into which they sort the various elements, events, and other things which they perceive. Such categories or concepts may be thought of as informational units in the language of the brain (Newell et al. 1958). Each concept represents a number of elements, events, or other phenomena, all of which have something in common. Bruner et al. (1956) describe the use of categories as follows:

To categorize is to render discriminately different things equivalent, to group the objects and events and people around us into classes and to respond to them in terms of their class membership rather than their uniqueness. (p. 1)

Similarly, Geer and Jaspers (1966) suggest "that S (subject) has a concept if he has a disposition on the basis of which he can make nominal classificatory statements or responses ('This is X, that is not X')" (p. 149).

Concepts are established through learning. They are general in the sense that humans are able to refer a new phenomenon to a concept in spite of the fact that the phenomenon was never encountered during the process of learning.

The individual's total system of concepts may be compared to the spoken language, although the systems are not identical (Bruner 1964 and Paul and Paul 1968). The English language consists of more than 100,000 words. Each word represents a concept, and furthermore, a concept may correspond to a combination of two or more words. However, this definition does not enable us to estimate the total number of concepts an individual uses. First, only a few people are familiar with all the words in the language. Many people may know and use fewer than 10,000 words, and great variability in usage exists among individuals. Second, there are concepts to which no words correspond, that is, concepts that can be used to deal with input from the environment but that cannot be verbalized. One important class of such concepts are those learned very early, that is, before any formal language is formed. Others deal with perceptions of taste, music, and so on. Moreover, basic elements of the conceptual system may be combined to form larger units or images (Hebb 1968). The total number of informational units constituting the memory system is thus very large.

The coding system serves a number of different purposes. Reviewing a few of these gives a more detailed understanding of the nature of concepts (Bruner et al. 1956) and facilitates perceptional comparison processes. When an individual is faced with an element in the environment, he is able to compare what his perceptional system observes with the various concepts he has available, and thereby he arrives at a conclusion as to "what is out there."

As a second major function, concepts act as the "unit of operation" for thinking and cognitive processes. When people are solving problems, thinking, or performing other cognitive activities, they are operating in terms of concepts. They are relating them, comparing them; and from this activity they are drawing conclusions.

Third, concepts are used in interhuman communication. The language is a subset of the total coding system, and communication is possible only to the extent that there is some degree of agreement between the concepts different individuals use.

Fourth, the coding system is used in memory formation. The environment is perceived as if composed of a number of distinct elements such as houses, trees, and roads, which reduces the capacity requirement for memory space.

Finally, the categorical system works as a memory device in its own right. As concepts are being learned, it stores information from the learning experience in such a way that the information is handily available for future use.

3. *Attributes of Concepts*

A concept may be thought of as a record of information. It may represent as complex a phenomenon as the image of a person, or it may be as simple as the figure one.

As in any other information coding system, each concept in the cognitive system has an identification tag. Each concept is described along one or more dimensions, and anything that falls within certain intervals along these dimensions is judged to belong to a particular category.

Second, each concept is related to other concepts. For example, to some individuals the concept *sports car* may be related to the concept *traffic accident*. Such relationships are represented in terms of information stored in connection with the concept (Wicklegren 1969).

Third, many concepts are evaluated more or less positively or negatively, i.e., information about the concept's affective properties must be stored. Other types of information may be stored as well,[2] but in the present context, these three kinds are the most important.

Concepts are thought of as single informational units, but this does not imply that all the information relevant to a certain concept is stored in one single location in the brain. Recent findings indicate that all the different information that constitutes a single concept may be stored in a number of different places (Hebb 1966 and Rosenzweig and Leiman 1968). In the present discussion, however, concepts are considered as single informational units regardless of their actual location in the brain.

1. Defining Attributes[3]

Consider the following situation. An individual who has a concept of a car is faced with a phenomenon in the environment. How does he decide whether it is a car or not?

A car may be described along a number of dimensions. It has four wheels, a certain shape, size, and color, and examination reveals that it has features such as an engine, steering wheel, brakes, and so on. Several combinations of these and other attributes will define *a car* in a unique way, and it is likely that the individual relies in some instances on one combination of clues and in other instances on another set of attributes. However, not all attributes are equally useful. Some are more *critical* than others, in the sense that the probability that the phenomenon possessing them is a car is larger for some attributes than for others. In some instances, the presence of a single highly critical attribute may be enough to determine to which category a certain phenomenon belongs. More commonly, however, several attributes have to be present before a proper judgment can be made, and often such judgments are probabilistic in nature. That is, the judgment implies that "because these aspects are present," it is likely that the phenomenon belongs to "that specific category."

[2] For example, Feldman (1966b) suggests that the potency dimension of concepts, which is usually revealed when the Osgood et al. (1969) semantic differential technique is used, can be seen as a measure of the arousal potential of the concept. Day (1970) maintains that the involvement properties of a concept may be completely independent of the polarity of the evaluation of the concept.

[3] The following discussion of concepts relies heavily upon Bruner et al. (1956).

Normally, individuals will discover that some attributes discriminate better than others, and they will learn to make greater use of them. Such highly critical attributes facilitate quick and easy identification of the observed phenomenon, but it is also important that the critical attributes secure a maximum amount of accuracy in the judgment.

To the extent that the identification process can be simplified, the speed and the ease with which it can be completed will be increased. Besides relying upon the more critical attributes, the individual can reduce the effort needed for identification by learning to perceive not the single attributes, but the total object as a complete unit. How such *Gestalts* are formed and how they operate has been the subject of considerable study (see for example Humphrey 1963). A very clear example of how this ability to generalize is achieved is the way that an individual learns to read. The student first becomes familiar with single letters, later he perceives complete words; finally, some learn to read complete sentences at a time.

The development of "unit identification" facilitates perception and cognition, but it does not eliminate the function of single attributes. In cases where the individual is in doubt about a particular phenomenon, the unitary approach is insufficient, and the individual will return to the single attributes. In reading, for example, if there is doubt about a certain word, the student can look at the single letter and literally spell out the word.

2. Evaluating Attributes

Of all the many situations and individual encounters, some are rewarding, others are neutral, and still others are unpleasant or punishing. There is no general agreement as to exactly what is involved when a situation is rewarding. Within learning theory, several suggestions have been made; for example, conditions are considered rewarding if they increase the probability that whatever action occurred when they were present will be repeated when they reappear (Bush and Estes 1959 and Hilgard and Bower 1966). Brain physiologists, on the other hand, suggest that the rewarding properties of events can be explained in terms of stimulation of certain parts of the lower brain (Wooldridge 1963, Madsen 1965, and Rosenzweig and Leiman 1968). Whatever the underlying processes are, if a certain concept has been associated primarily with rewarding conditions, this fact will be reflected in the evaluation of the concept. In contrast, concepts mainly associated with unpleasant conditions will be negatively evaluated. If a concept is positively evaluated, it will favor approaching behavior tendencies, whereas avoiding tendencies will be enhanced if the concept is negatively evaluated.

Described in this way, the evaluative attributes of concepts resemble such variables as attitudes, values, and affect—all variables of major concern to attitude theory. Because this area has provided many findings important for the present discussion, a few comments are in order on relationship between attitudes and the evaluative attributes of concepts.

Katz (1960) suggests in his functional analysis of attitudes that one of the major functions of an attitude is the "instrumental, adjustive or utilitarian function." He describes it as follows:

The child develops favorable attitudes towards the objects in his world which are associated with the satisfactions of his needs and unfavorable attitudes towards objects which thwart him or punish him. Attitudes acquired in the service of the adjustment function are either the means for reaching the desired goal or avoiding the undesired one. . . . (p. 170)

It can be seen that this function resembles the evaluative aspects of a concept as they are described here.

An important line of research has been conducted by Hovland and his coworkers (Hovland et al. 1953, 1957, and 1959, and Rosenberg et al. 1960). These researchers maintain that an attitude is composed of three different elements, namely, an affective, a cognitive, and a conative component. These components are shown in Figure 6.1. It can be seen that the affective component has much in common with the evaluative attributes of concepts. If in Figure 6.1 "attitude" is replaced by "concept"[4] then the affective component emerges as an attribute directly related to the concept.

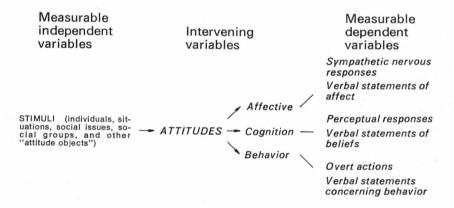

Measurable independent variables

STIMULI (individuals, situations, social issues, social groups, and other "attitude objects")

Intervening variables

ATTITUDES

Affective

Cognition

Behavior

Measurable dependent variables

Sympathetic nervous responses

Verbal statements of affect

Perceptual responses

Verbal statements of beliefs

Overt actions

Verbal statements concerning behavior

FIGURE 6.1. *Schematic conceptualization of attitudes. (Reproduced with permission from M. J. Rosenberg et al., Attitude Organization and Change, Yale University Press, 1960, p. 3.)*

Other researchers have studied the meaning of concepts. Using the *semantic differential*, Osgood et al. (1957), Osgood (1967), and Tannenbaum

[4] A substitution that is in line with other approaches. For example, Osgood et al. (1957) introduce a "mediating response" intervening between external stimulation and responses.

(1966) have shown that most concepts can be described along three dimensions: an evaluative dimension (represented by scales such as "good-bad," "kind-cruel," "honest-dishonest"), a potency dimension ("strong-weak," "hard-soft," "heavy-light"), and an activity dimension ("active-passive," "fast-slow," "hot-cold"). In the terminology of these authors the evaluative dimension reflects the attitude and is identical with the evaluative attributes of concepts as they are discussed here.

Still other researchers have concentrated on a two-dimensional attitude concept. Although the terminology varies somewhat, the approaches have much in common. Rosenberg (1956), Peak (1958), and Rosenberg and Abelson (1960) suggest a model in which an attitude toward an object is determined by the importance of the underlying values with which the object is associated (*value-importance*) and by the strength of these associations (*perceived instrumentalities*). Similarly, Zajonc (1954) deals with a *valence factor* that can be compared with the value importance factor and a *prominence factor* that corresponds to the perceived instrumentality in the work by Rosenberg (1956) and others. It has been suggested (see, for example, Insko and Shopler 1967 and Phillips 1967) that the value-importance factor (and hence the value factor) is identical with the affective component in the conceptualization presented in Figure 6.1, which in turn corresponds to the evaluative attributes of concepts as they are discussed here.

A closely related position, which also ties in with the work by Osgood et al. (1957), is taken by Fishbein (1963, 1965, and 1967b) and by Fishbein and Raven (1967). These authors explicitly reserve the term *attitude* for the evaluative aspects of concepts, and they suggest that relationships among concepts (the cognitive components) represent a completely separate variable for which they suggest the term *beliefs*.

In spite of the confused terminology, it appears that the evaluative attributes of a concept have much in common with attitudes. According to some authors, it is identical with attitude, whereas other authors consider the evaluative aspect to be only one of two or more components of which an attitude is composed. In order to avoid confusion, the use of the term *attitude* will henceforth be avoided, and instead *evaluative attributes of the concept* or simply *value attributes* will be referred to.

It should be emphasized that evaluative attributes are seen as unidimensional, that is, they reflect the concept's ability to elicit approaching or avoiding behavior tendencies, whatever the issue is and however these tendencies have been established. Some recent work seems to disagree. For example, Komorita and Bass (1967) conducted a factor-analytical study that found that the evaluative dimension of the semantic differential can be decomposed into three separate factors (a functional-utilitarian factor, an affective-emotional factor, and a moral-ethical factor). However, in the view of the present author, these multidimensional aspects reflect variations in the relational attributes of concepts, which do not require the introduction of multidimensional evaluative attributes.

3. Relational Attributes

Beside their affective or evaluative aspects, concepts have relational, cognitive, or instrumental aspects. Some authors consider these aspects to be part of the concept (attitude), but other authors suggest that they are completely different variables. For example, Phillips (1967) says: "*Perceived Relations* and *evaluations* can be usefully dealt with as two distinct constructs" (p. 486). As each concept is related to other concepts in a unique way, these relationships are here dealt with as attributes of the concept. Such attributes can be seen as learned expectations or beliefs, and they correspond to information that is stored in memory.

Relational attributes can be of many different kinds. For example, the concepts *aspirin* and *headache* may be related as follows: "aspirin *reduces* headache" or as "aspirin *is indifferent* to heachache." Such connections imply that one concept has an influence on, or is related to, the other concept. Many relations are based upon experience, but the situation may establish such relationships directly. For example, a consumer may read that "aspirin causes heart diseases." This piece of information establishes a relationship between two already familiar concepts (aspirin and heart diseases), and if it is stored, it can be activated at some later time.

Relationships among concepts have been analyzed from many different points of departure. Most fundamental is the distinction between positive, negative, neutral, and ambivalent relationships. It has been suggested by Heider (1946 and 1958), Osgood et al. (1957), Festinger (1957), and Abelson and Rosenberg (1958), and it appears in most later writings on the subject. Examples of positive relationships are: *likes, helps, serves, promotes*; of negative relationships: *dislikes, inhibits, prevents*; and of neutral relationships: *does not affect, is indifferent to, does not interest*. Finally, ambivalent relations are those to which a single sign cannot be assigned. An example would be the following: person *A* is seen as liking person *B*, whereas person *B* is perceived as disliking *A*; here, no single sign describes the overall relationship and, as suggested by Cartwright and Harary (1956), it is necessary to deal with each relationship separately. Although stable ambivalent relationships are most common in interpersonal relationships, they are of minor importance to the kind of choice alternatives dealt with here; consequently, in the following they will not be considered in any detail.

Other criteria have been suggested by Osgood et al. (1957) and by Fishbein (1967b). The latter distinguishes between *beliefs in* (the existence of), and *beliefs about* (the nature of) concepts. His *beliefs about* have much in common with relational attributes, and he suggests a classification that stated with his own examples, looks as follows:

1. Beliefs about the component parts of the object (Negroes have dark skin).
2. Beliefs about characteristic qualities or attributes of the object (Negroes are athletic).

3. Beliefs about the object's relation with other objects or concepts (Negroes are equal to white men).
4. Beliefs about whether the object will lead to or block the attainment of various goals or valued states (Negroes inhibit free expression of ideas).
5. Beliefs about what should be done with respect to the object (Negroes should be respected).
6. Beliefs about what the object should or should not be allowed to do (Negroes should not be allowed to hold government jobs) (Adapted from Fishbein 1967b, p. 259).

Fishbein also suggests that relational attributes (beliefs about) can be seen as learned informational units that can be described along a number of dimensions, and that themselves can be related through other relationships. However, in spite of this, it is normally not difficult in a specific context to determine what are concepts and what are relationships.

A more systematic classification has been suggested by Insko and Schopler (1967). They deal with four different kinds of connections, namely, (1) affective, (2) instrumental, (3) logical, and (4) spatial or temporal proximity. Each of these connections can be positive, negative, or neutral. This system is presented in Table 6.1 with some examples.

TABLE 6.1

Cognitive relations

Sign	Affective	Instrumental	Logical	Spatial or Proximal
Positive	likes loves admires is interested in	facilitates brings about helps causes	follows from is equivalent to is the same as is equal to	stands by is next to comes after is close to
Neutral	is indifferent to	has no effect on	is not the same as	is far away
Negative	hates dislikes disparages	hinders acts against harms	is inconsistent with contradicts is dissimilar to	

Reproduced with permission from Insko and Schopler, "Triadic Consistency," *Psychological Review*, Vol. 74, No. 5, 1967, p. 363, © American Psychological Association.

Insko and Schopler's (1967) classification gives only the basic dimensions along which relationships among concepts may vary. Relationships may involve several of the four basic relations at once. The authors suggest, for example, that "ownership may involve a combination of affect, spatial proximity and instrumentality" (p. 363). Furthermore, two concepts may be related in two or more ways, and these relationships may eventually oppose each other to make the overall relationship ambivalent. For example, two concepts can be positively related with regard to affect and at the same time oppose each other logically (McGuire 1960a, b).

4. *Salience of Concepts*

The categorical system consists of an extremely large number of concepts, but only a few will be activated in any single choice process. The distinction between an individual's *latent conceptual system* and his *salient cognitive structure* is therefore important. It is assumed that a concept must be salient before it can influence choice-process behavior and response selections, a position taken in most cognitive theories. For example, Osgood (1960) writes: "We have varying attitudes towards myriads of people, things and events, many of them potentially incongruent, imbalanced, or dissonant as one's theory would have it, but these cognitions are not continuously interacting—only when they are brought together in some way" (p. 351). Similar positions are taken by Newcomb (1956), Cartwright and Harary (1956), Festinger (1957), and Abelson and Rosenberg (1958).

It is important to explain just what concepts will be salient in a specific choice process. Concepts with their attributes are informational units stored in neurons in the cerebral cortex. Each neuron registers all the input it receives, but it fires only if the total input exceeds a certain level. This means that the information stored in a single neuron is activated only when the neuron receives so much activation that the critical level is exceeded; consequently, for a concept to become salient, the activation of the nerve cells storing the information corresponding to the concept must exceed a certain level. Moreover, as parallel memory systems exist and different attributes may be stored in different locations, it is possible for a concept to be more or less salient; and similarly, it is possible that only some of the concept's attributes are evoked.

Assume that several different sources can generate stimulation that acts upon the nerve cells storing a certain concept. It would then be possible for the concept to become salient, either because it receives small amounts of stimulation from two or more sources or because it receives large amounts of stimulation from one single source. The important thing is that it is the total amount of stimulation, independent of its source, that determines whether or not a concept will be salient. Consequently, to explain what concept will become salient, it is necessary to ask what potential sources of activation may eventually stimulate the memory traces where the concept is stored. The following pages will discuss four such sources of activation, (1) the reticular arousal system, (2) situational influences, (3) physiological states of the organism, and (4) relationships among concepts.

Another question is, how long will an aroused concept remain salient? First, salience will depend on the degree to which the concept is activated. The more neurons involved in storing the concept activated, the more likely it is that the concept will remain salient for some time. Secondly, the activation that originally made the concept salient may continue to work, keeping the concept salient. Third, once a concept has been made salient, it is possible for it to remain so even though the activation that originally aroused it decreases. For some time after a memory trace has been activated, it requires a smaller amount of stimulation in order to be reactivated. Hence, once a certain concept has been made salient, it is likely to remain so for some time.

1. Arousal

The reticular arousal system is continuously activating the cerebral cortex, but this activation is normally not enough to arouse specific concepts. However, variations in arousal imply variations in the overall activity of the cerebral cortex. As this stimulation increases, the amount required from other sources will be reduced. A general increase in arousal will thus cause more concepts to become salient, but what these concepts will be depends upon the activation received from other sources.[5]

For example, Berlyne (1967), after reviewing a number of recent studies, concludes that increases in arousal facilitate learning, remembering, and recall, all of which may indicate the more elaborate cognitive processes involved under conditions of increased arousal. Other relevant findings are reported by Schachter and Singer (1962). In a study of emotions, they increased arousal by injecting adrenalin and found that this stimulation influenced the nature of the cognitive processes. Related evidence is also reported by Peak (1960), who artificially manipulated arousal by having half her subjects participate in a 15-minute quiz-test before an experiment and found that arousal influenced instrumentality beliefs and attitudes. Finally, correlations have been reported between cognitive processes and variables usually believed to indicate arousal. For example, Bockhout (1966) found that attitude change was accompanied by changes in the heart rate.

2. Sensory Stimulation

Sensory stimulation works in two ways, as illustrated in Figure 4.1, presenting a major problem when sensory stimulation is studied as a factor which can arouse concepts. Hebb (1966) describes the two functions neatly: "Sensory stimulation has two quite different functions. The first can be called a cue function: a guiding or steering of informational affect. The second is the arousal function: it determines the level of excitement or excitability or wakefulness of the animal without determining what the animal's behavior will be" (p. 209). It is difficult to separate these two functions experimentally.

---

[5] There is some evidence that RAS may perform some directive functions as well. For example, it can activate visual receptors and inhibit others. However, this stimulation is general in the sense that it is the complete visual area in the cortex which is activated, not particular concepts (Wooldridge 1963).

For example, in the work by Peak (1960) just mentioned, it is possible that the effect should be ascribed to the cue function as well as to the arousal function.

In most instances, however, sensory stimulation influences the salience of concepts in a very straightforward way. The perception of sensory input implies that concepts are applied, and these concepts will become salient simply as a result of the perceptional process.

3. Physiological Stimulation

The physiological state of the organism influences cognitive structures. But again, this factor is not easy to isolate. It often interacts with other processes. First, physiological states may themselves be generated by environmental factors and cognitive processes. For example, observation of food can influence cognitions and thereby give rise to hunger. The aroused hunger may then feed back and activate relevant concepts. Second, the reticular arousal system is influenced by changes in the physiological state of the organism and in turn may increase arousal. Internally generated hunger will influence the cerebral cortex through the reticular arousal system as well as directly, and it is difficult to separate these two effects.

In spite of these difficulties, there can be no doubt that the physiological states of the organism are important directive determinants of cognitive processes. For example, it is a common observation that food deprivation will cause food-related concepts to become salient; the same is true of thirst and other physiological needs. Findings that show relationships between cognitive processes and underlying motivational states are reported by Brehm and Cohen (1962), by Brehm (1962), and by Brock and Grant (1963). In a dissonance context, they have shown how variations in thirst and hunger influence cognitions and cognitive processes.

4. Relationships Among Cognitive Elements

Cognitive elements are related to each other by means of beliefs, expectations, and the like. The more closely two concepts are associated, the more likely it is that the arousal of the one will result in the subsequent arousal of the other. If, for example, the concept "vacation" is salient, it is likely that concepts such as *travel*, and *hotel* will be activated. Bruner et al. (1956) talk about "the person's manner of grouping and relating information about his world" (p. 46) as a major factor explaining how people are able to add new information to whatever is present in the environment. Similarly, Peak (1958) suggests a special kind of relationship among concepts when she talks about "the probability that the arousal of a given element results in the arousal of another element" (p. 352). Whether such "probabilities" can be identified as separate variables independent of beliefs and expectations is a question which future research must answer.

The individual's total categorical system is not randomly organized, and the way the single concepts are related will influence what concepts will be aroused together. For example, concepts may be related as means-ends chains (Chapter 16). When certain "ends" are made salient, it is likely that "means" with which they have previously been associated will be aroused also. Similarly, concepts are systematically related in accordance with their level of generality (Hansen 1966b). For example, the concept *house* could be seen as composed of several lower-level concepts such as *stone houses, frame houses,* and *brick houses.* Each of these can in turn be divided into concepts at still lower levels. Similarly, a concept can itself be a member of a higher-order concept. *House,* for example, is one of several concepts belonging to the category *buildings.* When concepts are salient at one level of such a hierarchy, they may activate concepts at other levels of the same hierarchy.

In some instances, the lower-order concepts are identical with the defining attributes of the higher-order concept. For example, the concept corresponding to a specific brand of toothpaste can be defined in terms of such attributes as the toothpaste's color, taste, and consistency. These attributes, however, may themselves be seen as concepts: *brand X taste, brand X color,* and *brand X consistency.* Moreover, the same lower-order concept can belong to several higher-order hierarchies. Using the same example as before: *brand X's taste,* besides being an attribute of brand X, can be a lower-order concept in the category *taste of toothpaste.* Such ties between sub-segments of the total conceptual structure will influence what concepts become salient.

5. *The Salient Cognitive Structure*

1. Balanced and Unbalanced Structures

The salient cognitive structure consists of the aroused concepts and the relationships among them. The relationships can be positive, negative, or neutral; and the elements themselves can be positively, negatively, or neutrally evaluated. The overall nature of the cognitive structure depends upon the signs associated with the concepts and the relationships, the topic of many studies of cognitive structures in terms of their *balanced-state* (Heider 1946 and 1958), *congruity* (Osgood and Tannenbaum 1955), *structural balance* (Cartwright and Harary 1956 and Harary 1959), *cognitive consonance* (Festinger 1957), and *cognitive balance* (Abelson and Rosenberg 1958). These consistency theories are excellently reviewed by McGuire (1966b), Feldman (1966a), and Insko (1967); and formal statements of the underlying model are presented by Lambert (1966) and by Phillips (1967).

To illustrate what is meant when it is said that a cognitive structure is balanced, consider the following example: "I" (concept) "like" (relationship) "chocolate" (concept). "I" also "am opposed to" (relationship) "anything which is fattening" (concept). Finally, "chocolate" "is" (relationship) "fattening." This structure is represented in Figure 6.2(a), where positively evaluated concepts and positive relationships are assigned a plus sign, and negatively evaluated concepts and negative relations are assigned a minus sign. If the specific relationships and concepts are left out, the nature of the cognitive structure can be illustrated as in Figure 6.2(b).

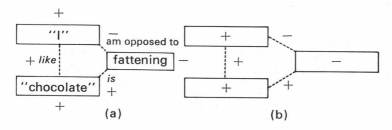

FIGURE 6.2.   *Graphic representation of simple cognitive structure.*

In Figure 6.2, each single substructure (consisting of two concepts with a relationship between them) is balanced or unbalanced, depending on the combination of signs. If two positively evaluated concepts or two negatively evaluated concepts are associated with a positive relationship, then this part of the total structure is balanced. If, however, either of them is related to a negative relationship, this substructure is unbalanced. Similarly, if a positively evaluated concept and a negatively evaluated concept are connected with a positive relationship, then this substructure is unbalanced, whereas the same substructure is balanced if the relationship is negative. In general, a substructure with one or with three negative signs will always be unbalanced, whereas a substructure with two or no negative signs is balanced. It can now be seen that the structure in Figure 6.2a is composed of two balanced ("I-chocolate," "I-fattening") and one unbalanced ("chocolate-fattening") substructure, and the total structure therefore is unbalanced.

When a larger number of concepts are salient, the analysis becomes more complicated, but the concept of balance applies equally well. For example, in a structure consisting of six concepts, it is possible to analyze the cognitive system by means of the matrix in Table 6.2, where the degree of balance in the total structure is reflected in the ratio of balanced to unbalanced substructures.

It is not always easy to determine whether a complex cognitive structure is balanced or not, and several shortcuts have been suggested. Abelson and Rosenberg (1958) use a procedure that essentially tests each single part relationship. Cartwright and Harary (1956) have proved the following

TABLE 6.2

Structure matrix topic : having an honor system at Yale. (Larger cognitive structure. p = positively associated, n = negatively associated, and o = not associated.)

	Ego (p)	Honest Student (p)	Report Cheater (n)	Feel Trust (p)	Cheat by Few (n)	Honor System (p)
Ego (the subject himself (p)	p	p	n	p	n	o
The honest student (p)	p	p	n	p	o	p
Report cheaters (n)	n	n	p	o	n	p
Feel trust (p)	p	p	o	p	o	p
Cheating by a few (n)	n	o	n	o	p	n
An honor system (p)	o	p	p	p	n	p

Reproduced with permission from R. P. Abelson and M. J. Rosenberg, "Symbolic Psycho-Logic : A Model of Attitudinal Cognition," *Behavioral Science*, Jan. 1958, p. 2.

theorem: "As S-graph (cognitive structure) is balanced if and only if its points can be separated into two mutually exclusive subsets such that each positive line joins two points of the same subset and each negative line joins points from different subsets" (p. 319). According to this theorem, a balanced structure is one that represents a completely "black and white" picture. In such a structure, some concepts are positively evaluated and others negatively evaluated. The important thing is that all relationships among positively evaluated concepts are positive (or neutral), all relationships among negatively evaluated concepts are positive (or neutral), and all relationships among positively and negatively evaluated concepts are negative (or neutral).

When a cognitive structure is unbalanced it is possible to talk about the *degree* of balance present in the structure. Degree of balance will vary with the number of unbalanced relationships, with the strength of the relationships, and with how positively or negatively the concepts are evaluated. If, on the one hand, the unbalanced substructures are composed of concepts that are only slightly positively or negatively evaluated, and if the relationships are not strong, the overall structure can still be relatively well balanced. If, on the other hand, a single unbalanced substructure is present that contains a very positively and a very negatively evaluated concept and if the relationship is strong, then the total structure can be highly unbalanced; consequently, variations in the evaluative attributes and in the strength of relationships are important for the degree of balance of the overall structure.

2. Cognitive Structures in Choice Processes

Certain of the individual's concepts are of special importance for the student of consumer behavior. He must study response selection in terms of the perceived choice alternatives and the positively or negatively evaluated concepts associated with them. This more narrow focus implies a drastic reduction in the number of concepts to be dealt with. While the total system of latent concepts is extremely large, concentration on relevant values eliminates many concepts. First, many concepts are neutrally or very weakly evaluated, which means that they are of minor importance. Second, a number of the individual's more significant values can be assumed to be unimportant in consumer choice processes because they are not normally related to the choice alternatives. Finally, only a limited number of values will be activated in any single choice process.

The salient cognitive structure before the response is selected should be studied in terms of alternatives, values, and relationships. The alternatives can be positively as well as negatively evaluated, but often the consumer's alternatives are themselves not very strongly evaluated. However, following the choice, the chosen alternative will become positively evaluated, and the rejected alternatives will become negatively evaluated. This change in the structure is in line with the very nature of the choice process. The selection of an alternative implies that the individual associates himself with one alternative and rejects others. In the evaluation of alternatives the consumer can be seen as "testing" the amount of balance which will follow if he commits himself to a certain alternative.

Both the pre- and the post-choice structures can be described as matrices composed of the perceived response alternatives together with the related salient values. Other concepts may be salient too, but if they are neutrally evaluated or if they are not connected with the response alternatives, they are of no significance for the choice. As the choice alternatives are normally unrelated, it is possible to decompose such matrices into as many smaller matrices as there are choice alternatives. For example, in a choice between two brands of a minor durable product, the only salient concepts may be *durability*, *expensiveness*, and *efficiency*. Here, the cognitive structure can be described in a five-by-five matrix as in Table 6.3a; but it can also be looked upon as two four-by-four matrices, one for each of the choice alternatives (Table 6.3b).

The extent to which the pre-choice structure is balanced depends upon the evaluation of concepts and alternatives. If it is assumed that the concepts of *durability* and *efficiency* are evaluated positively and the concept *expensiveness* negatively, and if it furthermore is assumed that the first alternative is perceived as the most durable and efficient and the least expensive, then the five-by-five matrix will look like Table 6.3a.

If the first alternative is chosen and becomes more positively evaluated than the second alternative, the emerging structure will be completely balanced. It can be difficult to see from the larger matrix which alternative will result in the most balanced structure, but when the structure is broken down as in Table 6.3b, it appears that both submatrices are completely balanced if the first alternative is chosen (and thereby becomes positively

TABLE 6.3

Matrices of salient cognitive structures in the choice process
(p = positive ; n = negative ; o = neutral)

		A1 (o)	A2 (o)	D (p)	E (p)	P (n)
Alternative 1	(o)	o	n	p	p	n
Alternative 2	(o)	o	o	n	n	p
Durability	(p)	p	n	o	o	o
Efficiency	(p)	p	n	o	o	o
Price Expensiveness	(n)	n	p	o	o	o

a   5×5 matrix of a structure composed of two alternatives and three values.

		A1 (o)	D (p)	E (p)	P (n)
Alternative 1	(o)	o	p	p	n
Durability	(p)	p	o	o	o
Efficiency	(p)	p	o	o	o
Price Expensiveness	(n)	n	o	o	o

		A2 (o)	D (p)	E (p)	P (p)
Alternative 2	(o)	p	n	n	p
Durability	(p)	n	o	o	o
Efficiency	(p)	n	o	o	o
Price Expensiveness	(n)	p	o	o	o

b   Two 4×4 matrices of a structure composed of 2 alternatives and 3 values.

evaluated) and the second alternative rejected (and thereby becomes negatively evaluated). This balance can also be shown in a graph as in Figure 6.3. Here, the total structure is broken down into two substructures; the first one contains all positively evaluated concepts and the second one all negatively evaluated concepts. Within these substructures, all relationships are positive, whereas all relationships between elements in each of the two substructures are negative. Consequently, in accordance with the Cartwright-Harary (1956) theorem, the structure is completely balanced. The structure also represents the "black and white" picture discussed earlier. The first alternative is "better" than the second one, along all salient value dimensions.

The example discussed is extremely simple. For several reasons, analysis of cognitive structures may be considerably more complicated. First, it is possible that two or more of the salient values are related in such a way as to make the total structure unbalanced. If, in the example, the individual perceives price as closely associated with durability, further changes in the cognitive structure are required before a completely balanced structure emerges.

Second, it is possible that none of the alternatives are positively associated with all positive values and negatively associated with all negative values. In the example, this would be the case if the second alternative were seen as considerably more durable than the first one. Then the first alternative

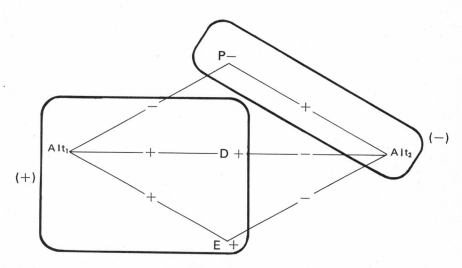

FIGURE 6.3. *S-graph of completely balanced conceptual choice structure.*

would be negatively associated with durability and the second one would be positively associated with durability. In that case, a division like that in Figure 6.3 cannot be made.

Third, it is possible that none of the alternatives are related with salient values in such a way that a balanced structure can result. In the example, this would be the case if neither of the two alternatives was perceived as being efficient.

Fourth, only cognitive structures containing two alternatives have been considered. Although more alternatives do not change the nature of the analysis, they make it more complex.

Finally, complications result because it is necessary to study how positively or how negatively the concepts are evaluated. In a choice process, the evaluation of relevant concepts can be referred to as the *value importance* of the concept. Similarly, the strength of the relationships between the alternatives and salient values should be considered. This strength can be referred to as the *perceived instrumentalities* of the alternatives (Abelson and Rosenberg 1958). Again referring to the previous example: The more positively evaluated a concept such as *durability* is, the more of an impact it will have upon the degree of balance in the overall structure. That is, the more important the value is and, similarly, the more strongly an alternative is related to the value, the more significant that part of the total cognitive structure is.

Altogether, the submatrices corresponding to each of the choice alternatives show the perceived instrumentalities of the alternative, the value importance of the salient concepts, and the relationships among the values themselves.

All types of consumer choices can be approached in this manner. For example, in connection with exploratory behavior, alternative information sources can be seen as substructures composed of values and instrumentality relations; and the impact of perceived information can be studied in terms of changes in the salient cognitive structure (Newcomb 1953) (see also Chapter 9).

3. Attractiveness, Balance, and Conflict

The amount of conflict in the cognitive structure can be discussed in terms of the attractiveness of the alternatives, where the attractiveness of an alternative depends upon the way it relates to the salient values. The more positively an alternative is associated with positive values and the more negatively it is associated with negative values, the more attractive it is. (Operational measures of attractiveness are discussed in Chapters 10 and 11.)

Attractiveness defined in this way corresponds to the response strengths discussed in Chapter 4; and as conflict increases with uncertainty, it follows that the more equal in attractiveness the alternatives are, the more cognitive conflict will be present. Moreover, as conflict also depends upon involvement, it means that the more important the salient values are, the more conflict a certain set of alternatives can generate.

The attractiveness of an alternative is also reflected in the submatrix corresponding to that alternative (Table 6.3b). The more balanced the submatrix will be if the alternative is chosen (and becomes positively evaluated), the more attractive that alternative is. Consequently, even with only a single salient alternative, conflict can still be present if the alternative is represented by an unbalanced cognitive structure.

When more alternatives are salient, the amount of conflict is reflected in the degree of balance in the total cognitive structure. A situation with minimal conflict is one in which one of the alternatives is extremely attractive and the remaining alternatives are not attractive at all. But as was shown in Figure 6.3, this situation corresponds to a salient cognitive structure that is highly balanced.

In conclusion, the less balanced a certain cognitive structure is, the more conflict it will arouse. Moreover, the degree of balance in cognitive structures in choice processes is reflected in the attractiveness of the alternatives. First, the less attractive the best alternative is, the less balanced the cognitive structure. Second, the more equal in attractiveness the alternatives are, the less balanced the structure.[6] Consequently, any change in the salient cognitive structure that generates a more attractive alternative or which differentiates the most attractive alternative from the competing ones will change the degree of balance in the structure resulting in a reduction in conflict. This implies that deviations between actual and optimal arousal can be reduced by such changes in the cognitive structure that bring about appropriate changes in the attractiveness of the alternatives.

6. *Motivation and Evaluative Attributes of Concepts*

1. Three Concepts of Motivation

Motives or needs are usually seen as internal forces directing behavior and inferred from observation of behavior. Berelson and Steiner (1964) suggest that: "A motive is an inner state that energizes, activates or moves and that directs or channels behavior towards goals." Madsen (1964), in his analyses of motivational theories, suggests that motivation should be seen as "all variables which arouse, sustain, and direct behavior." In the preceding pages, such variables have been discussed in three different contexts. First, the reticular arousal system influences the overall level of activity. Second, physiological processes in the organism can direct behavior and can influence which concepts become salient. Third, the evaluative attributes of concepts have motivational properties. When a concept becomes salient, it will direct behavior towards or away from objects and events to which the concept relates.

The functioning of the reticular arousal system has already been explored. In the present section, the other two concepts of motivation will be discussed. They are markedly different. Physiological motivational processes are concerned primarily with behavior which must be performed in order to keep the bodily equipment intact. Valued concepts are less directly related to basic needs, but they are important in connection with the individual's overall adjustment to his environment. The two motivational processes also differ in the extent to which they involve cognitive processes. When evaluative attributes perform motivational functions, cognitive activity is always implied. This is not necessarily the case with physiological motives.

Within traditional motivational theory, several distinctions run parallel with the one applied here. For example, Hull's (1952) "primary motivations" are centrally located drives reflecting inherited biological needs, and are contrasted to his "secondary motivation," which is seen as evaluative aspects of external stimuli established through association between stimuli and satisfaction of primary motives. In the same way, Lewin's (1935) "basic biological needs" and his opposed "determining tendencies" reflect a distinction between micro and macro motivational processes.

---

[6] Strictly speaking, this applies only when the alternatives are not ideal. It is perfectly possible to have a completely balanced cognitive structure composed of ideal alternatives equal in attractiveness.

2. Primary Motivation

Changes in physiological states of the organism will initiate signals to be sent over the nerve channels or changes in the chemical composition of the blood. Both kinds of impulses are registered in special centers in that part of the lower brain closely associated with the reticular arousal system—the hypothalamus. From these centers activation can be transmitted to the cerebral cortex. It is not known exactly how many primary motivational centers human beings have, but at least the following have been demonstrated: hunger, thirst, sex, maternal motivation, temperature motives, pain motives, evacuation motives, and breathing motives (Madsen 1966 and Hebb 1966). All these and possibly other primary motives are activated by biochemical changes in the body, and they may or may not influence cognitive processes.

Primary motives influence human behavior in two ways. Under normal circumstances, most of them act as a homeostatic mechanism to secure a sufficient amount of food, water, oxygen, and the like. They perform these functions without involving cognitive activity. For example, the very complicated muscular behavior involved in breathing works perfectly well without cognitive control. Only when disturbances occur will cognitive processes be involved. For example, an individual deprived of oxygen will direct all his cognitive and behavioral activity towards one single aim: to restore the free inflow of air.

Many primary motives (for example, temperature and breathing motives) are of little importance for choice processes. They will influence cognitive response selection only when they give rise to cognitive activity, but most commonly they will be satisfied long before they can cause such disturbances. Other motives such as hunger, thirst, and sex frequently influence cognitive activities. Instances of such cognitive activation have been described by Simon (1967a) as emotional interruptions of cognition, and it has been discussed how they can cause conflict and generate choice processes. This kind of motivational influence upon behavior is well documented (see, for example, Beier and Griffin 1963), and a single study can serve to show its influence on consumer behavior. Bjuvman and Schött (1966) had cigarette smokers stop smoking for 24 and 48 hours; and in a tachistoscope test they found that the longer the subjects had been deprived of cigarettes, the more easily they recognized cigarette brands. In these and similar experiments, stimulation generated by physiological processes may be acting upon the cortex so that a smaller amount of environmental stimulation is sufficient to arouse the relevant concepts.

Besides triggering cognitive processes, physiological motives are important in another way. Many authors have suggested that the evaluation of concepts learned in the very early stages of human development is largely influenced by the way they have been associated with satisfaction of primary motives. Some concepts learned early (for example, *mother*) can be motivationally loaded to such an extent that other concepts later associated with them will become positively or negatively evaluated depending on the evaluation of the original concept.

3. Secondary Motivation

Assume that human behavior is largely governed by the cognitive structures salient when the behavior is decided upon. Furthermore, assume that one attempts to uncover a limited number of underlying motivational variables from inferences based on observing actual behavior (including answers to questions). What one would then find would be motivational variables defined in terms of the concepts most commonly occurring in choice processes. Essentially, this is the result of many studies of human motivation. In his work on personality, Murray (1938) defines between 30 and 40 such needs and related variables. For example, his "need for exhibition" is described as follows: "To make an impression. To be seen and heard. To excite, amaze, fascinate, entertain, shock, intrigue, amuse or entice oneself" (p. 170). This need is seen as governing behavior such as "self-display," "to make the self conspicuous by wearing unusual or colorful clothing," "to seek the lime-light," "pose for effect," "enjoy it when all eyes are upon the self," "to wear little clothing or go naked," "to join a nudist colony" (p. 171). It can be seen that such motives really describe a number of concepts with various positive or negative evaluative attributes.

In the present approach such intervening variables are avoided, and instead the concepts and values acting in the different choice processes are dealt with directly. This is a more micro-oriented view of motivation, but hopefully also a more realistic one. A similar view inherent in much work on attitudes has been formulated explicitly by Janis (1959a) and by Feldman (1966b), who suggests that evaluative attributes of concepts correspond to approaching and avoiding tendencies and that behavior will be determined by interaction among salient values.

7. *Conscious and Unconscious Processes*

In the present discussion, unconscious processes play only a minor role. This formulation is defensible, provided that one can assume that it does not matter much whether the individual is aware of the response selection process. To examine the validity of this assumption and the special research methodologies applicable to unconscious processes, the nature of such processes will be discussed briefly here.

The *unconscious* most often refers to some internal, usually guiding, selecting, or directing process that can be inferred from behavior without the individual's being able to tell about the process. A related phenomenon is *extra-sensory perception* (ESP), a term used to describe the common observation that human beings are able to react to stimuli of which they are not, or least not fully, aware. A number of studies have shown the operation of unconscious cognitive elements in conflict and choice situations. Brock and Grant (1963) used hypnosis to show that a cognition made salient without the subject's awareness can influence behavior. Other studies have shown that subjects can make use of clues presented in the environment without knowing that they are doing so. For example, Maier (1931) reports that in a problem-solving task, subjects unconsciously made use of clues that they did not see as connected with the problem, and similar findings have been reported by Mendelsohn and Griswold (1966) and by Guthrie and Wiener (1966).

The distinction between conscious and unconscious cognitive processes is not absolute. That is, there may be several degrees between the two extremes of "complete awareness" and "absolutely no awareness." Adams (1957), after reviewing a number of studies dealing with different aspects of the unconscious control of behavior, concludes that at least four different conditions can exist: (1) Subjects may know the specific nature of the cue being introduced, (2) subjects may know the general nature of the cues, (3) subjects may believe that cues are being given but not know anything about the nature of the cues, and finally (4) subjects may not believe that any cue is being given. Cognitive elements may be unconscious for one or more of the following reasons:

1. Behavior can occur completely without cerebral or cognitive activity.
2. Cognitive processes can operate at a low level of arousal so that awareness does not occur.
3. Suppression of cognitive elements can occur.
4. Cognitive processes can involve concepts to which no verbal counterparts correspond.

1. Behavior Without Accompanying Cognitive Activity

Human beings are capable of performing many different activities without any cognitive control. They are able to breathe, walk, and carry out a number of reflexes which are completely controlled by the lower parts of the nervous system (Wooldridge 1963 and Hebb 1966). These activities will give rise to cognitive activity only "when something goes wrong." For example, if a person loses his balance while walking, his attention will then be directed to the ongoing activity, and the selection of the appropriate corrective action will involve cognitive processes. Normally, however, such behavior occurs without awareness. Unconscious processes of this kind are of little importance to consumer choice processes.

2. Unconsciousness Ascribable to Low Amounts of Arousal

Concepts may be activated to such an extent that they influence behavior, but not to a degree sufficient to make the individual aware of them. For example, Staats and Staats (1958), Staats et al. (1960), and Insko and Oakes (1966) report that although awareness does influence the amount of change, it is not a necessary condition for attitude change to occur. Similarly, Laird (1932) reports that housewives were significantly influenced in their choice of stockings by technical quality aspects of which they were not aware.

Unconscious processes like those discussed here are common in consumer behavior because many consumer choice processes generate only moderate amounts of arousal. Many "blind product tests" have revealed unconscious choice processes, but little of this material is published. However, a single study illustrates the phenomenon. Naylor (1962) gave subjects a choice among 7, 8, and 9 ounce packages of potato chips without informing the subjects that the choice alternatives differed only in weight. It was found that the actual weight of the packages influenced the choices even though the consumers had no conscious perception of the weight differential. Presumably, subjects were able to discriminate among the alternatives without being aware of the discrimination process.

In analysing choice behavior, it is important to ask whether concepts operating at a low level of arousal have the same impact on response selection as if they had been fully conscious. The findings by Staats and Staats (1958) suggest that there are differences depending upon the level of awareness; but on the other hand Festinger and Macoby (1964) found that distraction may influence the effectiveness of persuasive communication, a finding which Haaland and Venkatesan (1968) were not able to confirm. However, it is possible to conclude that even though a concept is not consciously held, it can still exert influence on choices. The specific nature of this effect, however, needs further examination.

3. Suppression of Cognitive Elements

A number of concepts and values may be consciously unacceptable to the individual. A discussion of reasons for this is given by Sarnoff (1961), Blum (1966), and Mendelsohn and Griswold (1967). An example is the young child who acquires a number of positively evaluated concepts only to learn later that the values are unaccepted by his parents or by society in general. In such instances, the values may still influence his behavior, but without ever reaching the level of consciousness.

In this area, most of the documentation comes from clinical experiences and hypnotic studies. Classic, of course, is the work by Freud (1938a and b). More recent work is reviewed by Spence (1967) and an experiment reported by Deering (1963) can serve as an example. In an attempt to reveal how the operation of inhibitory forces can influence cognitive processes, he found that affective stimulus words are not recalled as easily as neutral words.

It is difficult to tell how important such processes are in connection with consumer behavior. Most of the work by Dichter (1960 and 1964) and by others dealing with motivation research has been aimed at revealing such unconscious motivation, and there can be little doubt that unconscious processes of this nature occur in consumer behavior.

4. Concepts Without Corresponding Verbal Labels

If cognitive activity were to be described solely according to verbal reports, it would be tempting to conclude that cognitive processes rely upon the same language as human communication. To a certain extent, this may be the case, but the difficulty of verbalizing concepts related to areas such as taste, sound, and physical sensation often explains the absence of such concepts in reports on cognitive activity. In any event, there is some evidence that human beings react differently to different degrees of stimulation, such as taste variations, even though they are not able to verbalize or consciously perceive any difference. It is common knowledge among market researchers with experience in taste studies of cigarettes, beverages, and food products that consumers can show a significant preference for one alternative although they are not able to point out any consciously perceived difference in the taste of the tested products. What is available of this work clearly confirms the proposition. Gridgeman (1966) conducted an experiment in which the subjects compared strawberry and raspberry jams differing in sweetness. He found that even differences the respondents could not verbalize had significant influence upon their preferences. In another area, Quenon (1951) showed that housewives are able to discriminate among children's shorts along a number of dimensions they are usually not able or used to verbalizing.

Again, the question arises whether the fact that consumers are not consciously aware of the categories they are using affects response selection. Although no evidence is present, it is tempting to suggest that when unawareness is ascribable to lack of "ability to verbalize," it does not significantly reduce the concept's impact on the choice.

8. *Motivational Sets as Directing Forces*

The preceding pages may give the impression that elements of the conceptual system are either resting or salient, and that only in the latter case do they influence behavior. This does not account for the commonly observed phenomenon that individuals may be "set" on something. That is, human beings can, over extended periods of time, maintain a certain amount of "preparedness" for action. In connection with problem solving, this preparedness or *problem-einstellung* has been studied by German psychologists; and in American literature, it is often discussed as *determining tendencies* or *motivational sets* (Humphrey 1963). In consumer behavior, the phenomenon is common. The consumer may solve an aroused conflict by deciding to do something later (buy a product, acquire additional information), and in such instances he can be said to have made an internal commitment. Very often when the appropriate circumstances arrive the behavior will be executed, the crux of the matter being that the particular response would not have resulted had the commitment not been made. An explanation is needed of how the situation in which the behavior is elicited became able to generate that specific response.

The nature of internal commitments or motivational sets can be understood from the preceding discussion of motivation and unconscious processes. It has been pointed out that a concept will become salient if sufficient stimulation is provided. Such stimulation can come from different sources; it is perfectly possible that some cognitive elements constantly receive some stimulation, but not enough to make the concept important for choice processes. If this limited but constant inflow of stimulation is derived from internal sources, only little additional external stimulation is required to make such partly activated concepts salient. Hebb (1949) has suggested a mechanism which might explain such *states of readiness*.[7] He suggested that chains of nerve cells may form internal circuits that are continuously activated by self-stimulation. These internal circuits correspond to smaller or larger amounts of related information, and they may account for the effects of internal commitments. It is possible that a commitment results in starting such a circuit, and that the circuit will remain activated until behavior has been elicited or until it is destroyed in other ways. Whether these speculations will hold up will have to be shown by future research. In the meantime, they suggest a hypothetical construction that may help to conceptualize the working of internal commitments.

Explicit commitments are not the only course for motivational sets. More loosely made commitments may have similar, although less strong, effects, as may unsolved problems (Manis and Ruppe 1969). For example, Gerard and Fleisher (1967) and Claeys (1969) report that under certain conditions conflicting cognitions are more easily recalled than balanced ones. Finally, the effects of primary motivation may sometimes be explained in terms of motivational sets. For example, Nisbett and Kanouse (1969) show how food deprivation can significantly influence shopping behavior in supermarkets. Motivational sets and internal commitments relate to buying intentions as discussed by Juster (1964), and in Chapter 14 this relationship will be discussed further.

[7] Hebb's idea was originally meant to explain memory in general, but for this purpose it is now largely abandoned (Hilgard and Bower 1966).

Chapter 7

LEARNING OF RESPONSES AND CONCEPTS

The system examined in the preceding chapters is almost entirely a static one. A number of variables were introduced, but only little attention was paid to the processes through which these variables become established, and to how they gradually are modified, the topic of the present chapter.

1. *Learning of Behavioral Responses*[1]

Organized responses are important for the individual's interaction with his environment. By integrating basic elements of behavior into larger units, the individual saves energy for other purposes and can develop more complex skills. For example, if the same amount of conscious cognitive control were needed for walking as for target shooting, walking would be badly constrained. Organized responses also make performance easier. It is a common experience that too much cognitive control of behavior may decrease its efficiency. The experienced typist who suddenly starts thinking about where the letters are located will reduce her speed considerably and at the same time make more errors.

The very young child has a limited behavioral repertoire, but adults command a large number of behavioral responses. New responses are

[1] A thorough treatment of the formation of behavioral responses may easily involve large parts of the psychology of learning. For more detailed discussions the reader may turn to such sources as Keller (1954), Berelson and Steiner (1964), Hilgard and Bower (1966), and Deese (1967) or for more marketing oriented presentations, Howard (1963a), Engel et al. (1968), and Markin (1969).

constantly learned, less firmly established ones are improved, and others are modified or extinguished.

The learning of organized responses has been dealt with in many different contexts, as in a classic study of a student learning telegraphic code (Bryan and Harter 1899). This experiment is interesting because it illustrates how minor sequences are integrated into larger units. Bryan and Harter found that their subject's performance did not improve in accordance with any straightforward growth curve. If performance were measured in terms of the number of letters received per minute, the learning curve tended to level out at various points. One such example is shown in Figure 7.1, and similar results have been found in other studies. This curve has been interpreted as showing shifts from one level of learning to another.[2] At first the subject received one letter at a time, and after approximately 20 weeks he had achieved the maximum speed possible. No further improvement occurred until he started to receive whole words at a time. Then he could start building larger behavioral sequences and thereby improve the performance. Essentially this step is involved when a minor behavioral reponse has been fully learned and is used as a building block in the construction of more complex behavioral units.

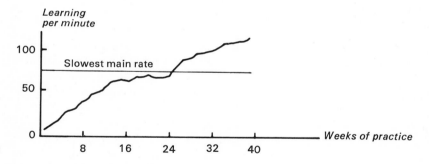

FIGURE 7.1. *Learning curve with plateau for learning of telegraphic code. (Bryan and Harter 1897, p. 49, with permission from © American Psychological Association.)*

1. Simple Responses and Complex Sequences

As Bryan and Harter's experiment indicates and as we discussed earlier, organized responses may be decomposed into very small units. It is important to ask what the basic units are and how they are formed. The answers to both questions require a brief review of basic learning processes.

[2] It has been argued that such plateaus are artificial and may be explained in terms of changes in motivation (Keller 1958).

One approach, Pavlov's (1927) and Watson's (1914) classical conditioning, can be illustrated with the following example. A child reacts naturally with withdrawal when he touches a hot bottle. But if a bell rings whenever the child meets the hot bottle, he may eventually react to the bell exactly as he originally did to the bottle. That is, the child has learned to react with withdrawal to the sound of the bell (Figure 7.2). Here the first unconditioned stimulus (UCS) represents the hot bottle. The response is withdrawal. As a result of learning, the response becomes conditioned to the second stimulus, the *conditioned stimulus* (CS) (the sound of the bell).

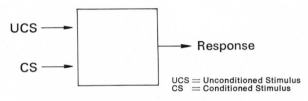

FIGURE 7.2.   *Classical conditioning.*

Simple conditioned responses form the basic units in organized responses. How such responses may be established is illustrated in Figure 7.3. Let the figure illustrate a consumer lighting and smoking a cigarette. In the upper part of the figure, S_1 represents the stimulus to which the consumer originally reacts (R_1) by reaching for a package of cigarettes. S_2 is the package of cigarettes now brought into the situation. This stimulus now elicits the response "reaching for matches," R_2, which in turn brings the matches (S_3) into the situation, which in turn elicits the next response (R_3), "lighting the cigarette." The chain continues until the cigarette is smoked and the stimulus S_n, "the cigarette butt," elicits the final response (R_n), "extinction of the cigarette." Such a chain is built of simple conditioned responses, and it is perfectly possible to imagine a consumer performing the chain for the first time, provided he has previously learned each of the single responses. However, as the sequence is being repeated the stimuli in the environment become less important. Each single response may now be generated directly by the completion of the previous one. The environment has to meet a number of requirements; but, if it does so, it becomes only a necessary condition for the performance of the sequence.

Unexpected changes in the environment may disturb the response, but how much variation is tolerable? To answer this, the attention must be directed to the generalization and discrimination processes.

Generalization is the process that enables the individual to respond

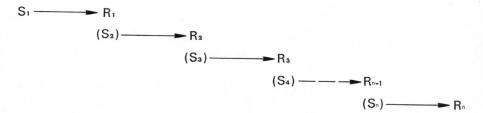

FIGURE 7.3. *Chaining of simple responses to an organized sequence.*

to a new stimulus as he has learned to respond to a similar but not identical stimulus in the past. Berelson and Steiner (1964) write:

Once a conditioned response has been established, it will be elicited not only by the conditioned stimulus actually used during training but also by a variety of similar stimuli ("stimulus generalization"); the magnitude of the response, however, decreases with the difference between the conditioned stimulus and the similar ones. (p. 138)

In most situations a certain amount of variation can be tolerated without the behavioral reponse being disrupted. Consider, for example, the response "to turn on the television set." This can be performed in many different settings, but there are limits to the acceptable amount of variation. These limits are associated with the process of discrimination. Unlike generalization, discrimination has to be learned. Again Berelson and Steiner (1964) explain the process:

Stimulus generalization occurs as an automatic part of the conditioning process, until the subject is specifically conditioned to discriminate between the conditioned stimulus and similar stimuli. Such "discrimination training" requires extinction of the response to the similar stimuli through a series of trials in which the stimuli involved are presented, but only the appropriate one is followed by the unconditioned stimulus. (p. 139)

Before a stimulus can cause an interruption, it must be discriminated. As an example, consider the behavioral response "buttering a piece of bread." This sequence may be performed with butter within quite a range of temperatures; but if the butter is too cold (and hard) or too warm (and melting), the sequence will be interrupted. Exactly when discrimination occurs varies widely from individual to individual; the same person may have very narrow tolerance limits in some areas, whereas in other areas he is able to make broad generalizations. His behavior depends on how the response has been learned and should be explained in terms of interaction between generalization and discrimination.

2. Instrumental Conditioning

It may be argued that in order to learn anything by means of classical conditioning, highly controlled learning situations must be set up. Consequently, some psychologists have suggested a different formulation (Thorndike 1898 and Hull 1952). This formulation, *instrumental conditioning* or trial-and-error learning, holds that in any situation a number of different responses are possible, and many of them will be tried in turn. However, the one which turns out to be the most rewarding will gradually become dominant, and when it is performed 100% of the time, learning is complete. As an example, a small child may have access to a drawer containing baby food. Whenever he is hungry, he goes to it and picks a jar. In the beginning, the selection of jars is completely random. Soon, however, the child will realize that some jars contain better-tasting food than others; and consequently, the child begins to make a non-random selection of the jars. Ultimately the child may choose only jars containing desserts. The process is illustrated in Figure 7.4. Here R_1, R_2, and so on represent different baby foods, among which R_d represents desserts. After a number of trials all responses but R_d will be extinguished.

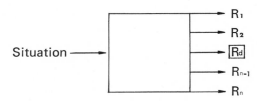

FIGURE 7.4.   *Instrumental conditioning.*

Like classical conditioning, instrumental conditioning deals with learning of single responses; but since such responses may be combined, it can also explain learning of more complex behavioral responses. Therefore the question becomes: classical or instrumental conditioning? If Figures 7.2 and 7.4 are compared, it will be seen that they have much in common. In classical conditioning, the contiguity between conditioned and unconditioned stimuli is stressed, whereas in instrumental conditioning, the reward is the crucial factor. However, classical conditioning cannot be established completely without rewards; and the trial and error situation also contains a number of stimuli, some of which work as unconditioned stimuli. Together the two basic forms of learning may be seen as special cases of more general simple motoric learning (Madsen 1966).

3. Cognitions Governing the Behavioral Response

Basically models of simple motoric learning connect observable stimuli in the environment with observable responses. However, as cognitive processes must be involved and connected to organized responses, they are of major importance. Such processes may be described as *cognitive cards* (Tolman 1932), *learning sets* (Harlow 1949), or *control hierarchies* (Hull 1952 and Newell et al. 1958). Consequently, in connection with behavioral responses it is possible to concentrate on the learning of the chain of actions or on the learning of the control hierarchy governing the execution of the behavior.

A control hierarchy may be described as follows: Imagine the sequence "to go and have a glass of water." At the very highest level the sequence may be governed by the program (adapted from Simon 1967a):

1. Go to the kitchen.
2. Pour a glass of water.
3. Drink it.

But, each of the three subroutines is in turn governed by a program. The first subroutine may look like this:

1. Take one step with left foot.
2. Take one step with right foot.
3. If kitchen is reached then proceed to 4, otherwise return to 1.
4. Stop.

Eventually, each step in the subroutine may be seen as composed of minor programs, so that the complete control hierarchy may look like Figure 7.5.

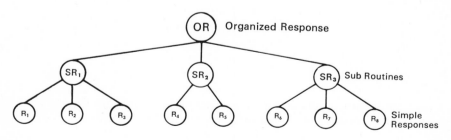

FIGURE 7.5.   *Control hierarchy.*

As human beings grow, they form still larger programs; and when a control hierarchy at one level is firmly established, it may be used to establish higher-level hierarchies. In this way learning proceeds, and firmly established behavioral responses will be governed by control hierarchies that are integrated into fixed units. Less completely learned sequences may be seen as sequences in which the controlling cognitive system is not yet integrated into one single operational unit.

4. Factors Facilitating Learning

The individual's responses constantly undergo changes. Responses already learned may be integrated into larger units or they may be extinguished, and those not yet completely learned may become more firmly established. Many factors influence the ease with which responses are learned or extinguished. Here it is possible to cover only a few of the more basic ones. For more detailed discussions the reader will have to turn to sources such as Berelson and Steiner (1964) and Hilgard and Bower (1966).

First and foremost, the frequency with which the response is performed influences how well it is learned, a result supported by all studies of learning. However, repetition may interact with other factors, three of which will be discussed: (1) reward, (2) previous learning, and (3) individual factors.

The more rewarding a response is, the more easily it is learned. The amount of reward depends on the individual's motivation when the response is performed, and it depends on how relevant the response is to this motivation. The reward may be imbedded in the behavior itself as, for example, is the case with "to watch television," or it may follow only indirectly from the completion of the response, as with "doing dishes," when, if not directly associated with the behavior, reward may follow with shorter or longer delay. Generally, rewards imbedded in the sequence or following immediately after are the most gratifying. Finally, rewards may be negative, that is, a response may be completed in order to avoid punishment.

Rewards may be complete or partial, that is, they may be associated with each and every performance of the sequence, or they may occur on some occasions but not on others. The more frequent the reward, the more easily the sequence is learned; but learning following a 100% reward schedule is more easily forgotten than learning following a schedule by which the rewards are spaced properly. This spacing of the reward may vary in many ways, which too will influence learning and retention. Behavioral sequences such as "smoking a cigarette," "driving a car," or "watching television" may be difficult to extinguish because of the considerable and partly unpredictable variations in reward.

Previous learning influences the ease with which new responses become established. This is self-evident, if one considers how the control hierarchy may be built from minor elements learned on previous occasions. These effects of previous learning are related to "transfer." The extent to which the consumer has previously established similar but not identical responses may retard or advance the learning of new ones. Whether the transfer will be positive or negative depends on the extent to which either generalization or discrimination is at work. A previously learned response may be so close to the one being learned that the individual has difficulty in discriminating and eventually, by means of generalization, mixes them up. In such instances the learning task consists not only of learning the response, but also of learning to discriminate it from the one previously learned. In other cases, however, generalization may favor learning. Essentially this process is involved when minor responses are integrated into new and larger ones.

Finally, individual differences may account for marked differences in learning. Individuals may vary in their ability to learn, i.e., in intelligence, and they may vary in motivation and personality. These differences will influence what responses will be learned and how fast and how firmly they are acquired.

5. The Environment, Learning, and Interruptions

The preceding discussion of learning makes it possible to connect situational factors with consumers' behavior and to show how they may account for interruptions. As discussed in Chapter 3, the situational factors are important as:

1. A background condition for the performance of well-established behavioral responses (or as a background that provides guiding clues for the performance of incompletely learned responses).
2. Factors that cause interruptions in behavioral responses.
3. Factors interacting with cognitions in choice processes.

Consider for a moment how a well-organized response has been learned. Take the response "to go to a refrigerator and get a glass of juice for breakfast." This sequence, provided certain circumstances are present, may be performed automatically. However, at some earlier time this response was two distinct responses, with a conflict intervening: "going to the refrigerator," *choosing*, and "picking up a glass of juice." As these responses have been performed a number of times, and as the same choice has been repeated, the conflict and the choice process become less noticeable. As the learning of the response progresses, less energy is needed for its performance. In terms of the cognitive processes involved, the controlling hierarchy becomes highly integrated and independent of external stimuli. Moreover, the choice of juice, which first had to be explained in terms of a particular conflict, now must be approached in terms of the conflict in which the response is chosen that incorporates the act of picking the juice. That is, the integration of the juice choice into the larger sequence forces the researcher to direct his attention to a new type of conflict situation.

The formation of behavioral responses requires that a number of conditions be met. In terms of the previous example: A refrigerator must be present, juice must be available, a glass must be available, and so on. All these conditions must be present in the situation, and they work as necessary conditions for the performance of the response. If one of them is missing, the response is interrupted and a conflict is aroused.

The same conditions must be met as long as the learning of the response is going on. If the situation changes too frequently, the larger response will never be organized; but the function that the external stimuli perform in the learning of a response differs from the role they play when that response has been learned. An actor memorizing a monologue will rely heavily upon his text as long as the sequence is not completely learned; but when the monologue has been learned, the clues coming from the text are no longer necessary. Situational factors are still important; they determine when the actor will start on his monologue, and they may interrupt him, but they do not govern each single element in the performance. In terms of the accompanying cognitive processes a fundamental difference exists. The completely learned response is governed by a highly integrated controlling hierarchy, which is largely independent of environmental stimulation. In contrast, the imperfectly learned response relies heavily on a number of situational stimuli controlling the single behavioral components in the larger response. When such a response is performed, a number of instances occur in which several response tendencies are present, and here the selection of the next response depends on the surrounding stimuli. Too-frequent changes in the environment may prevent perfect learning. Each repetition will improve the performance somewhat; but when an interruption occurs, it will retard it. The phenomenon is illustrated in Figure 7.6; the quality of the performance is measured along the vertical axis. Repetition improves the quality of the performance, and trials with an imperfect situational setting (i.e., T5, T12) set it back. If all trials were carried out in completely identical situations, learning would proceed as illustrated by the dotted curve.

As the figure shows, if interruptions occur with a certain regularity, learning will never be complete and the response will not be perfectly established. The quality of the performance will fluctuate at one level or another, according to the ratio of perfect to imperfect situations. The more frequently interruptions occur, the lower the average level of performance will be.

The individual's learning of a particular response does depend not only upon his experience with the situation. He may generalize from other more or less similar situations also. To show what the existence of such other situations implies, consider an intervening choice process in an imperfectly learned response. In the choice situation, several aspects are significant. In the previous example, a number of aspects may be associated with breakfast, such as coffee, toast, juice, and milk. However, the consumer will experience other situations where the same stimuli are present. For example, advertising

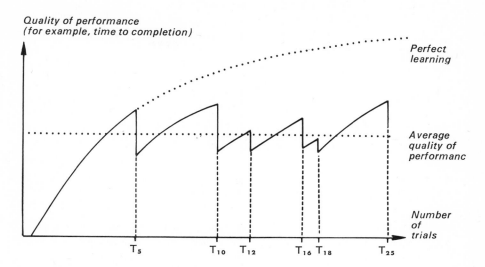

FIGURE 7.6. *Quality of performance varying with situational setting.*

about the advantages of milk for breakfast can establish a competing response tendency that is aroused the next time he enters into the particular situation. The competing tendency may never be followed; but as long as it exists, the organized response will not be firmly established. Only when the response has been completed a sufficiently larger number of times without the competing response tendency being reinforced will the organized response be completely learned. Consequently, it is possible to define a completely learned behavioral response as one which is performed without competing response tendencies, and conversely a choice situation occurs whenever competing response tendencies are aroused.

This generalization between situations has important implications for marketing strategies. It means that a particular choice situation must be understood not only in terms of its appearance in the past, but also in terms of more or less similar situations from which generalizations can be made. For a particular purchase situation, previous related exposure situations are also important. A good many conflicts have very little element of choice left, as is often the case with choice processes occurring in organized responses learned to a high, but not perfect, degree. Of the consumer's different behavioral responses, consumption responses are most likely to be integrated into larger units with little or no conflict. While communication and, particularly, purchase responses will normally arouse some conflict, many aspects of consumption may become completely habitual. When that occurs, the student of consumer behavior will have to be concerned with that choice process that decides the particular behavioral response of which consumption is a part. In other words, whereas purchases and exposure must be explained in terms of conflict-solving in particular situations, studies of consumption behavior may imply a concern with parts of the consumer's entire behavioral repertoire.

2. *Learning and Modification of Concepts*

While behavioral responses are being learned, changes occur in the cognitive elements that control the performance of the responses. But changes in cognitive elements may result also where there are no easily observable changes in the behavior. The remaining part of this chapter will be concerned with such changes.

As with behavioral responses, both forgetting and learning occur in connection with concepts. Whereas forgetting is a process that goes on continuously, learning takes place when concepts are salient.[3] A detailed analysis of how concepts are learned and modified, and especially how values change, will require a thorough review of a considerable number of studies of attitude formation and change. Such a discussion falls outside the limits of the present approach, and excellent presentations are available elsewhere: A review with special emphasis on mass communication is presented by Klapper (1960), and some of the basic problems are discussed by Cohen (1964). Moreover, the issue as it relates to marketing problems is discussed by Crane (1965), Nowak et al. (1966), and Myers (1968). Here the emphasis is on the relationship of this work to the present approach, which raises two questions. First, how are the three major attributes of concepts (defining, evaluative, and relational) being learned? Second, are the attributes and the concepts themselves related in such a way that a change in one attribute or in one concept automatically necessitates adjustment in others?

1. Learning of Defining Attributes

How do humans learn what attributes to rely upon in making judgments about persons, events, and phenomena in the environment? The problem has been studied in terms of *concept attainment*. A thorough discussion can be found in Bruner et al. (1956), and a review of recent findings and emerging problems is presented by Geer and Jaspars (1966).

In concept attainment, *generalization* and *differentiation* are important. To make the judgment that a certain phenomenon belongs to one or another category is a generalization, and by means of differentiation the individual learns to distinguish among phenomena he previously saw as identical.

[3] Shiffrin and Atkinson (1969) suggest a model of memory that implies that forgetting does not occur. What is being observed as forgetting is seen as a result of the fact that a still-growing amount of information stored in memory makes it increasingly difficult to recover old material.

Concepts are learned in the process of human development. A detailed discussion of how children develop their conceptual structure can be found in the work of Piaget (Inhelder and Piaget, 1964), and attempts to relate this work to other approaches have been made by Gyr et al. (1967) and Furth (1968).

Concepts are not formed and changed only in early stages of human development. Any choice process will result in some modification of the conceptual system; consequently, the total system constantly adapts to the changing requirements facing the individual.

How differentiated and detailed are the set of concepts belonging to an individual will depend on the extent to which he has had use for more or less detailed classifications. For example, the average consumer may have only a few very crude concepts concerning coffee, whereas the professional coffee blender may be operating with an extremely large number of specific concepts corresponding to different raw products, roasting procedures, and blends.

2. Learning of Evaluative Attributes

We have discussed how exposure to new and complex stimuli can at first create a high amount of arousal accompanied by withdrawal and dislike. With repeated exposure the stimulus will seem less complex and become more positively evaluated; finally, after a considerable number of exposures, it can become boring and be less positively evaluated. If a large number of exposures is required before the decrease in liking occurs, then in most practical cases repeated exposure to unfamiliar stimuli will result in increased liking. This is exactly what Zajonc's (1968) *mere exposure* hypothesis proposes. He maintains that positive evaluation may result from repeated exposure alone. He compares the evaluation of more or less frequently used words and finds a strong positive correlation between exposure and liking, with the more frequent words being the most positively evaluated. However, as Zajonc himself points out, from this study it is not obvious whether the most frequent words have become most positively evaluated *because* they are frequent or whether they are used more frequently because they are positively evaluated. Consequently he reviews studies where exposure has been experimentally manipulated, and he shows how the subjects' liking of nonsense words, figures resembling Chinese characters, and photographs increases with the number of exposures.

The mere exposure hypothesis is promising for studies of the advertising process, and Krugman's (1965, 1968) *low-involvement* advertising model assumes the operation of such a principle. Moreover, findings which suggest its applicability are reported in Krugman's (1962) study of learning of preferences, in simulated exposure experiments reported by Wells (1964), in Wells and Chinsky (1965), and in Grass and Wallace's (1969) study of satiation effects of advertising.

However, as Jacobovitz (1968) and Harrison (1968) point out, mere exposure can be a dominant factor only where new and uninvolving concepts are presented. When concepts are familiar they will become associated with known concepts, which may counteract the mere exposure effect, as when a new concept results from a combination of two or more already-known ones (Heise 1969). For example, the concept *a flying car* will be new to most people. It is built from two well-known concepts, namely *flying* and *car*. The evaluation of such a concept will depend upon the evaluation of the two original concepts. Osgood and Tannenbaum (1955) and Osgood et al. (1957) have studied how the evaluation of such new concepts relates to the evaluation of the concepts already known. They suggest that the new concept will be evaluated somewhere between the two original ones. That is, if *car* is very positively evaluated and if *flying* is only slightly positively evaluated, then *flying car* will be less positively evaluated than *car* but more positively than *flying*. Moreover, the authors suggest that the firmness with which a value is established is reflected in the polarity of its evaluation and that the more firmly it is established, the more it will influence the evaluation of the new concept. That is, in the present example, the *car* value is more firmly established than the *flying* value, in that it deviates more from a neutral evaluation. Consequently the theory predicts that the evaluation of *flying car* will be closer to the evaluation of *car* than that of *flying*. For this *congruity principle*, Osgood et al. (1957) suggest the following formula to determine the evaluation of the new concept:

$$E_{12} = \frac{|E_1|}{|E_1| + |E_2|} E_1 + \frac{|E_2|}{|E_1| + |E_2|} E_2 \qquad (7.1)$$

Here E_1 is the evaluation of the first concept, E_2 the evaluation of the second concept, and E_{12} the evaluation of the emerging concept. Evidence in favor of the formula has been presented by Osgood and Tannenbaum (1955), Osgood et al. (1957), Tannenbaum (1966), and Tannenbaum et al. (1966).

A somewhat similar position has been taken by Staats (1967) and by Rhine (1958). These authors also see the formation of values associated with concepts as a conditioning process much like the one implied in the Osgood model; and Staats and Staats (1957 and 1958), Rhine and Silun (1958), Staats et al. (1960), and Geer (1968) have presented supporting evidence.

In these formulations the emerging value results from an averaging of the values associated with the original concepts. The possibility that two or more concepts that are brought together may interact in such a way that a new concept emerges that is evaluated even more positively or negatively than any of the original ones has been explored by Rokeach and Rothman (1965). As a result, they have suggested a modification that they have formulated in their *principle of belief congruence*. This principle predicts that the new concept can be more positively or negatively evaluated than Osgood's congruity principle would predict if the new concept is seen as being more *important* or *relevant* than any of the original concepts. In an extensive test, the authors show that in a number of instances this modified principle predicts evaluation better than the straightforward congruity principle.

Other researchers have suggested that the resulting evaluation of the concept should be computed not as an average, but as the sum of the evaluations of all concepts with which the new one is connected. Evidence in favor of an additive method is presented by Rosenberg (1956), Triandis and Fishbein (1963), Fishbein and Hunter (1964), Anderson and Fishbein (1965), and Chalmers (1969) (see Chapter 10).

The problem becomes even more complicated when an already existing concept is connected with some other evaluated concept. As long as the concepts are only moderately involving, it is likely that the principles described above will apply. That is, the evaluations of the two concepts will move in the direction of each other, and the most involving concept will exhibit the least change. Consequently, if the existing value is considerably more involving than the one with which it is being associated, then the original concept will change only a little.

However, when more involving concepts are at stake, other processes may interfere with the straightforward conditioning effects. When an individual is strongly committed to a certain position, or when he is highly involved with the concept in question, the association of this involving concept with another concept evaluated very differently may trigger defensive reactions, which in turn will disturb or even reverse the assimilation process. That is, the effect depends upon whether the suggested relationship (belief) is accepted or not, a problem raised in the following section.

3. Learning of Relational Attributes

What happens when a certain concept is experienced in connection with another concept with which it has not previously been related ? And what happens when a belief about a concept is communicated which disagrees with beliefs already held? There are two possible answers. The new experience or the new belief may be accepted and thereby result in a modification of the salient cognitive structure, or it may be turned down and have no influence. What will happen depends upon involvement and upon the discrepancy between the initial and the communicated position.

Sherif and Hovland (1961) and Sherif et al. (1965) have suggested a model which deals with this issue. Briefly the model may be described as follows. On a given issue on which an individual takes a stand there will be some positions he is willing to accept, some which he will reject, and some towards which he is indifferent. These positions may be arranged to form a scale, on which the acceptable positions lie close to the stand the individual takes, those rejected are far away from the individual's own position, and the positions towards which the individual is indifferent lie between. Based on this observation, Sherif et al. (1965) define a *region of acceptance*, a *region of rejection,* and a *region of indifference.* These regions are illustrated in Figure 7.7.

The size of the regions will vary with the involvement in (or importance of) the issue.[4] For an individual who is only little involved, the region of

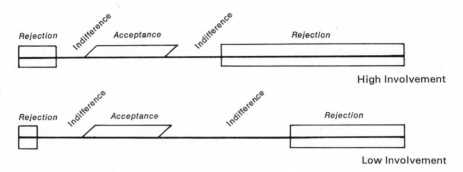

FIGURE 7.7. *Regions of acceptance, rejection, and indifference (in accordance with Sherif et. al. 1965).*

rejection will be smaller and the region of indifference will be wider (the lower graph of Figure 7.7). With more involved individuals, the opposite will be the case (the upper graph of Figure 7.7). Hovland et al. (1957), Sherif et al. (1958 and 1965), Carlman (1966), Atkins et al. (1967), and Peterson and Koulack (1969) present evidence in favor of the model. They show that the way a certain communication will be perceived depends upon its location in relation to the three regions. If the message is too close to the individual's own stand, it will be attended to, but it will not result in any significant amount of attitude change. On the other hand, defensive reactions will occur if it lies in the region of rejection. Only when the message deviates moderately from the individual's own stand, will attitude changes occur.

Predictions based on the model have striking similarities with predictions based on arousal-level theory. Restated in terms of arousal, the model says: If a message deviates considerably from an individual's present stand, i.e., if it is too novel, it will elicit arousal-reducing responses (defensive reactions such as avoidance and rejection). If, however, the message deviates only moderately from the individual's present stand, i.e., presents only a limited amount of novelty, it will generate moderate amounts of conflict and exploration, deliberation, and eventually acceptance may occur in the process of reducing conflict. Moreover, the difference in the size of the three regions implies that if the individual is highly involved, then the amount of additional arousal potential that can be dealt with is small; whereas if the individual is only slightly involved, then he is able to cope with considerably more additional arousal potential.

[4] Miller (1965) reports a study that failed to find this relationship. However, the experimental manipulation of involvement applied is highly complex, and it may be questioned whether the primary effect really was a modification of involvement. Moreover, some conformative evidence is reported by Ward (1966).

Findings which further highlight the relationship between arousal and affective stimulation are presented by Byrne and Clore (1967). These authors devised an index of arousal used in a series of experiments to study the relationship between arousal and the attraction of different stimuli. Their findings show that attraction increases as arousal increases, but with extreme amounts of arousal the relationship was reversed.

An interesting model proposed by Feather (1967a), based on Atkinson's (1964) achievement motivation model (Chapter 4), suggests that new information will be approached or avoided depending on the individual's *tendency to avoid inconsistency* and his *tendency to seek consistency*. If the message is expected to be highly inconsistent with the individual's present position, the avoidance tendency will dominate, but if the information is expected to be only slightly inconsistent, the approaching tendency will take over. That is, the strengths of the two tendencies vary with the amount of the discrepancy. Moreover, Feather suggests that the strengths of the avoiding and approaching tendencies are modified by a third variable he describes as the *usefulness* of the information. If information is expected to be highly useful or in other ways rewarding, then the approaching tendencies will increase, whereas information that is expected to be less useful or eventually unpleasant will strengthen the avoiding tendencies. Feather himself (1967a) reports some confirming evidence, but a more detailed evaluation awaits further evidence. However, his model has striking similarities to the one proposed by Sherif et al. (1965). Both models attempt to specify conditions under which information will be approached or avoided; they both point to *usefulness* or *involvement* as crucial variables, and they both emphasize the importance of the discrepancy between the information and the individual's own stand.

Both the Feather and Sherif-Hovland models are concerned with instances where pressure towards compliance is moderate. Brehm (1966), in his "Theory of Psychological Reactance," has discussed effects of stronger pressure towards compliance. Basically, his theory predicts that an individual whose response alternatives are eliminated will try to make the eliminated alternatives reappear; if this is not possible, other substituting responses may occur. The essence of the theory is contained in the following statement: "When a person feels he is free to engage in a given behavior if he wants to, the elimination of that freedom will arouse psychological reactions in him" (Hammock and Brehm 1966). Interpreted in terms of arousal, the model says that when a person has established a certain level of readiness (arousal) in preparation for a conflict, then an environmental change that reduces the conflict would be counteracted. This interpretation gains further support when it is noted that two of the basic factors shown to influence the occurrence of reactance are the importance of the situation and the number of alternatives eliminated (i.e., the reduction in complexity). The theory has been supported by findings reported by Brehm and Sensening (1966), Horowitz (1968), and Sensening and Brehm (1968). The latter studies in particular show that attitude change may be in a direction opposite to the advocated position if the pressure towards compliance is sufficiently great.

Another prediction based on this theory is that the eliminated choice alternative will be evaluated more highly after its elimination than before (Hammock and Brehm 1966), a prediction tested in a marketing context by Brehm (1966), who found that a strong attempt to influence shoppers' choice of bread can decrease the frequency with which the promoted bread is purchased. This finding reminds one of reactions found in studies of loyalty; for example, Tucker (1964) reports that adding pennies to choice alternatives induced brand switching, but not in favor of the promoted alternative. The phenomenon is worthy of further exploration in connection with consumer behavior. It would be premature to conclude that excessive amounts of promotion will have negative effects, but the evidence certainly warrants further study.

In this connection the work by Rokeach (1960, 1963, and 1968a) should be mentioned. He is mainly interested in what Fishbein (1967b) would label *beliefs in* and he deals with six different categories of such beliefs. The beliefs vary in centrality to the individual. The most primitive beliefs are the most central ones and are considered to be very firm and unchangeable, whereas the less central beliefs are more easily influenced. It seems that the centrality of beliefs in Rokeach's formulation comes close to the involvement variable of Sherif et al. (1965).

TABLE 7.1

Beliefs of varying centrality

Types of Beliefs	Definition	Examples
Type A Primitive Beliefs	A belief which is uncontroversial because everyone in a position to know believes it too.	I believe this is a typewriter. I believe the sun rises in the east. I believe my name is Milton Rokeach.
Type B+ Primitive	A belief which is uncontroversial because I continue to believe it regardless of what others may think.	I believe I am intelligent. I believe I am rational. I believe I am a kind person.
Type B—		I believe I am abnormal. I believe others cannot be trusted. I believe I am no good.
Type C Authority Beliefs	Beliefs about which authorities can and cannot be trusted.	The Church, the President, Einstein, scientists, parents, and the like.
Type D Peripheral	Beliefs which are derived from authority.	I believe divorce is immoral. I believe Jupiter has twelve moons.
Type E Inconsequential Beliefs	Beliefs which, if changed, leave other beliefs unaffected.	I believe a vacation at the beach is more enjoyable than one in the mountains. I believe Sophia Loren is prettier than Elizabeth Taylor.

(Reproduced with permission from Rokeach, 1968. Copyright July 1964, Trans-Action, New Brunswick, New Jersey.)

Depending upon the nature of the relationships among the elements in the belief structure, Rokeach distinguishes between open and closed-minded subjects. Closed-minded subjects have peripheral beliefs (Figure 7.8) which are highly dependent upon their authority beliefs, whereas open-minded subjects are more willing to face conflicts between their own beliefs and those of their authorities.

Recently it has been pointed out (Powell 1966, and Hunt and Miller 1968) that the *open and closed mindedness* dimension may be identical with Hovland and Sherif's *latitude of rejection-acceptance* dimension. It has been found that closed-minded subjects take more extreme stands, have a wider latitude of rejection, and less tolerance for inconsistency. This suggests a relationship between the belief structure of the individual and the amount of conflict an individual is willing to accept in a particular situation. The relationship deserves further study because it suggests that important aspects of a consumer's choice behavior can be predicted from knowledge of his belief structure.

4. Interaction Among Attributes of Concepts

Indirect effects may occur when a change in one attribute results in changes in other attributes of the same concept. Theoretically, such indirect effects may occur as: (1) changes in evaluative and relational attributes resulting from changes in defining attributes, (2) changes in defining and evaluative attributes resulting from changes in relational attributes, and (3) changes in defining and relational attributes resulting from changes in evaluative attributes.

A change in defining attributes will normally imply that a concept is manipulated so that two or more new concepts emerge or that a new concept is formed from existing ones. It has been discussed how the evaluation of the new concept will depend on the values associated with the original concepts. In the same way the relational attributes of the new concept will depend upon the relational attributes of the original ones.

As an example of a concept divided into two new individual concepts consider the concept *hot cereal* divided into *regular hot cereal* and *instant hot cereal*. What will be the evaluative and relational attributes of the new concepts? Of course their evaluation will depend on experiences and learning in situations involving the two newly established concepts, but this is not the complete answer. The value and beliefs associated with the old concept will influence the new ones, in various ways. It is possible that both concepts become evaluated and get almost the same relationships as the original one, but it is also possible that the positive attributes will be concentrated on one of the new concepts and the negative ones on the other (Cohen 1964).

The evaluative attribute of a concept will often change when the concept is related to new concepts, or when existing relationships are modified. This is a common observation. For example, Carlson (1956) and Rosenberg and Abelson (1960) in studies of cognitive consistency show that changes in perceived relationships generate changes in the evaluation of the concept. Similarly Rokeach (1960 and 1968a) and Stein (1966) found that interpersonal and, particularly, racial values are highly dependent upon the beliefs individuals hold about other persons. On the other hand, Kelman (1958) points out that, at least temporarily, beliefs may change without accompanying changes in evaluative attributes. He suggests that attitude change occurs as a three-step process composed of compliance, identification, and internalization and that only changes in values occur in the last phase.

Changes in relational attributes may also lead to the formation of new concepts. For example, when strongly positively evaluated concepts become related to negatively evaluated concepts, this opposition can be resolved by dividing the original concepts into two separate ones, one of which is related to positive value concepts and the other primarily to negative value concepts (Cohen 1964). For example, a pipe-smoker may be exposed to strongly negative information relating smoking and health, and as a result he establishes two new concepts, *pipe-smoking* and *other smoking*, of which the first concept carries all the positive associations of smoking and the second takes on all the negative ones.

It is difficult to tell whether changes in evaluative attributes can bring about modifications in defining and relational attributes. Only little evidence is available. One reason for this is that it is difficult to change value attributes experimentally without simultaneously influencing beliefs. However, Rosenberg (1960a and 1960b) made an attempt to overcome this difficulty. He changed evaluative attributes through hypnosis and found that the modified evaluations resulted in changes in the relational attributes of the concepts. His use of hypnosis, however, makes it difficult to generalize these findings.

In conclusion, a concept's different attributes are not independent of each other. Changes in one attribute can generate changes in others. Changes in expectations, beliefs, and other relational attributes will result in modifications of evaluations, and changes in defining attributes will lead to changes in relational and evaluative attributes. Finally, changes in value attributes may cause modifications in beliefs.

5. Interaction Among Concepts

When cognitive conflict is aroused, more or less complex cognitive structures will be salient. As a change in one concept can influence its relationship with another concept, and as this alteration in turn can influence the other concept, it can be expected that a change introduced in one part of a salient cognitive structure will spread to other concepts in the structure. Many experiments have suggested that such changes occur, but most of these have also introduced change into the cognitive structure directly, and it is difficult to isolate the effects which result merely from bringing a number of cognitions to act upon each other. However, McGuire (1960a and b) found that when cognitions were made salient together they would influence each other. He first asked his subjects to indicate to what extent they believed that a number of related statements were true, and then he had them rate how positively or negatively they evaluated these statements. When the same measurements were obtained a week later, it was found that subjects had adjusted their beliefs to make them more logically consistent. McGuire writes: "Merely stating his beliefs on related propositions results in the respondent's adjusting his beliefs toward greater mutual consistency" (p. 82). Similar findings have been reported in Dillehay and Insko (1966),[5] by Holt and Watts (1969); and in a marketing context Roman (1969) presents related evidence.

The kind of changes in concepts just discussed are important because they explain why concepts closely related in the conceptual system tend to be adjusted to each other. When a change is generated in a concept at one level in a categorical subsystem (Chapter 6), it is likely that sooner or later this change will be transplanted to concepts at other levels in the same subsystem because closely related concepts are likely to become salient together. For example, if a concept like *cigarettes* is changed, it is likely that this change, within a certain period of time, will influence evaluations and beliefs concerning lower-level concepts such as *filter cigarettes* and *non-filter cigarettes*. On the other hand, if a new cigarette brand being introduced is perceived as being less dangerous than the usual brands, it eventually may modify the overall evaluation of the higher level concept *cigarettes*.

The available evidence does not allow a specification of the conditions that will cause adjustments in salient cognitive structures. However, it is tempting to suggest that a situation where actual arousal exceeds the optimal level will be one where incongruity-reducing adjustments are most likely.

In this connection a problem relates to the kind of adjustments that are most likely when individuals strive for congruity. At least three possibilities exist. First, concepts themselves can be changed, that is, they may be decomposed so that more balanced substructures emerge. Second, the evaluative attributes of the concepts can be changed, and third, beliefs can be modified.

As pointed out earlier, a number of investigators hold that when two concepts are related, the one having the least affect associated with it will be the one that changes most (Osgood and Tannenbaum 1955). A related prediction is made by McGuire (1960a and b). He suggests that when two beliefs are incongruent, the most distorted one (that is, the one involving the largest amount of wishful thinking as opposed to logical reasoning) will be the one most likely to change.

Other authors have suggested that the concepts that are most isolated, that is, have the fewest ties with other cognitions, will be most likely to change (Cartwright and Harary 1956, Festinger 1957, and Zajonc 1960). Moreover,

---

[5] Although the authors raise some doubt about the specific model based on which McGuire (1960a) makes his predictions.

when a change can be made either in the evaluation of the concept or in its relationship with other concepts, the latter is the most likely to occur (Rosenberg 1956). Also, when balance can be restored either by making a positive sign negative or by making a negative sign positive, then the sign change from negative to positive will be preferred (Harary 1959 and Rodriques 1967).

Concepts change because of new experiences and as a result of communication. Furthermore, the mere fact that concepts act upon each other may lead to changes in their attributes. Altogether, the categorical system is a constantly changing language with which cognitive processes work. New elements are regularly added, others are dropped, and still others change meaning.

PART THREE

*A Model
of Individual
Consumer
Choice Behavior*

Chapter 8

THE CHOICE PROCESS

An explanation of consumer behavior requires answers to three questions:

1. How and when do consumers enter situations in which they make choices?
2. In these situations, what alternatives are considered and what factors influence the consumers' evaluation of these alternatives?
3. How do these factors interact to determine what alternatives will be chosen?

In this and the following chapters a model is proposed to answer these questions at an individual level, and a number of hypotheses derived from the model are tested.

1. *The Salient Cognitive Structure*

What concepts will be aroused by a stimulus depend upon a number of factors interacting in a complex manner, as is illustrated in Figure 8.1.

The figure shows the variables interacting between the situational setting (S) and the actor's behavior (R). Its dependent variables are the behavioral responses that are selected, and the ultimate independent variables are the aspects of the situation and the physiological states of the organism.

From the figure it can also be seen how environmental stimulation will influence the salient cognitive structure and the arousal center, which in turn will influence the cognitive activity. Similarly, the physiological states of the organism influence cognitive activities directly as well as indirectly. The reticular arousal system (RAS) works as a general energizing unit triggered by stimulation from the environment, from primary motives, and from cognitive processes. In addition, it influences cognitive processes, the more

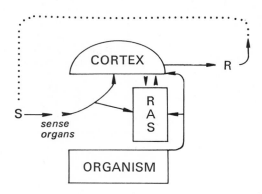

FIGURE 8.1.   *Cognitive processes and their relationship with RAS, the environment, and the organism.*

specific nature of which is directed by environmental factors, associations, and primary motivation. Such cognitive processes are of major importance for the selection of responses.

The salient cognitive structure will always contain one or more *action programs* or *alternatives*. If the mechanism illustrated in Figure 8.2 gives the signal *go*, then the most attractive action program will be executed. Subsequently, the action will change the environment, the physiological stage of the organism, and the salient cognitive structure. This change results in a renewed comparison between actual and optimal arousal, and if this test again shows that the two variables do not deviate significantly from each other, action is continued. In this way behavior will go on without interruption as long as a balance between actual and optimal arousal is maintained. However, if the arousal changes, so that it deviates from the optimal level, one of the following two cases may result.

If arousal falls short of the optimal level, action will be interrupted, and exploratory behavior and deliberation will take its place. Exploration will be aimed at more exciting or stimulating environments and alternatives, and it will result in changes in the salient cognitive structure. The changes are followed by renewed testing; depending upon the outcome, action may be triggered, or further exploration and deliberation may result.

On the other hand, when an excessive amount of arousal is present, behavior will also be interrupted and exploration and deliberation will occur, but this time activity will be aimed at reducing the arousal potential, resulting again in a changed cognitive structure and renewed testing.

Altogether, this mechanism determines whether the individual will behave smoothly and uninterruptedly, by search for excitement and stimulation, or attempt to reduce situational and other arousal potentials.

A number of different routes may be taken in Figure 8.2. For example, the sequence 1-3-1-4 corresponds to a kind of "simple problem solving,"

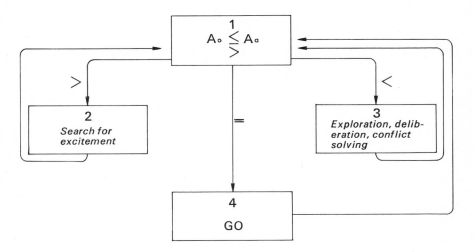

FIGURE 8.2. **The comparison between optimal (AO) and actual (AA) arousal.**

which can occur when an individual is interrupted in a behavioral response by environmental stimulation and when the modified cognitive structure contains a satisfactory response alternative. On the other hand, a sequence like 1-3-1-3- . . .-3-1-4 represents more complex problem solving. Here more than one step is needed in order to restore balance between actual and optimal arousal.

When the original discrepancy is one in which the arousal falls short of the optimal level (1-2-1-2), the first exploratory and deliberatory attempt can generate a cognitive structure that is conflicting to such an extent that the arousal now exceeds the optimal level (1-2-1-3- . . . -1-4). Alternatively, exploration may immediately generate a response alternative that is able to restore balance between actual and optimal arousal (1-2-1-4). It is difficult to tell which of these two patterns is the most common when the environment produces an insufficient amount of arousal potential. Considering purchases, the question really is whether "making the purchase" itself restores balance, or whether the balance is achieved by first generating a cognitive conflict and then solving it. This question can be illustrated by a consumer who suddenly changes brand: Does "picking up the new brand" supply the needed arousal potential, or is it provided by the self-generated problem that has to be solved before the new brand is chosen? Another problem will be dealt with subsequently: How does the consumer select responses so that in the long run correspondence between actual and optimal arousal is maintained.

1. Arousal and Conflict

The actual amount of arousal and the optimal arousal level are crucial variables. The actual amount of arousal can change as a result of changes in the situational, the cognitive, and the physiological arousal potential.

The cognitive arousal potential can change because of more or less random associations that make new concepts salient; but the cognitive arousal potential is not likely to be a major cause of disturbances. The physiological arousal potential can cause disturbances when some physiological process is "getting out of control," as will occur when too long a time elapses between meals, and the individual thereby gets "hungry". Attempts to induce "hunger" in shoppers in supermarkets by piping odors of freshly baked bread through the air-conditioning system may possibly have such effects. However, such interruptions are rare. Commonly, situational aspects will have directed the attention to the growing physiological imbalance long before it reaches such proportions that it generates a considerable amount of arousal. Most frequently, situational aspects will be the cause of conflicts.

When a conflict has been aroused, the picture changes. In the course of the choice process, the consumer's environment does not undergo important changes, and abrupt changes in the physiological arousal potential are unlikely. Under these conditions there will be limits to the extent that the situational arousal potential can be manipulated. Similarly, significant manipulation of physiological arousal potential is rare. Consequently, when the situational arousal potential has given rise to a more or less complex conflict, any attempt to bring the actual amount of arousal back to the optimal level is likely to involve manipulation of the cognitive arousal potential. Since the cognitive arousal potential first and foremost is reflected in the amount of cognitive conflict, it means that cognitive conflict is manipulated. Therefore, the typical choice process can be described as follows: Situational novelty, change, surprise, and complexity generate an orienting response and, depending upon the salient cognitive structure, the choice process will either terminate immediately or take the form of more or less complex problem-solving. Once the conflict has been aroused, the cognitive conflict is the crucial variable.

The optimal level of arousal depends upon the arousal level prevailing before the generation of the choice process and upon the overall nature of the situation. If the situation is one which by experience is judged to require a considerable amount of arousal, it is likely that a moderate upward adjustment in the optimal level will take place; and similarly if the individual has learned that in this situation a low level of arousal is ideal, then some downward adjustment in the optimal level will result. But these adjustments are minor and, whatever the optimal level, it is unlikely that the arousal can be brought back to optimum without some manipulation of the cognitive conflict. Consequently, the optimal level of arousal defines a preferred or *tolerable level of conflict*, which characterizes the specific situation in which the choice process occurs.

2. *The Model*

In the course of the choice process, response alternatives are compared. In essence, comparison means that the individual asks how much conflict he will face if he chooses the most attractive alternative. It may result in one or two outcomes: Either a response is selected or deliberation and exploration continue. The first will be the case if one of the response alternatives is able to reduce the aroused conflict, or if the possibility of extended exploration and deliberation is less attractive than the best response alternative.

If the exploration and deliberation activity is continued, it will modify the cognitive structure. New alternatives can be established, new values can become salient, and the perception of the available alternatives can change. When the cognitive structure changes, a new comparison process is performed which again can result in a choice or in continued deliberation and exploration. In this way the choice process may go on for some time. Sooner or later, however, it will terminate, either because a response is selected or because the possibilities for deliberation and exploration are exhausted. In extreme cases a considerable number of alternatives may be examined, and the response ultimately selected can be one far removed from the problem present in the original cognitive structure.

This description of the choice process raises several questions. First, in what order are the various possibilities for deliberation and exploration utilized? Second, in what order are response alternatives established and tested? Finally, what do "satisfactory alternatives" and "tolerable amount of conflict "mean?

1. The Search Order

In connection with problem solving, Simon (1958) and Cyert and March (1963) have suggested that information search follows a *least efforts* rule that implies that information sources are selected because of their availability and their ability to eliminate the need for further search. A similar principle is supposed to apply to consumers' exploration and deliberation.

The most easily accessible exploration or deliberation strategy will vary depending upon the nature of the situation.[1] However, the process will normally move through certain steps. First, the memory will be examined for relevant information. Although this can go on for some time, the return will be negligible after a number of attempts. The next possibility is to explore the environment through observation, picking up alternatives, looking for other possible alternatives, and so on. Along with these steps, memory search will be renewed, as the exploration will produce a changed cognitive structure that may suggest new ways of inquiry to be used in regaining information from the memory. However, sooner or later the possibilities for further exploration and deliberation vanish. When no new sensory input can be obtained from the evniroment, a point occurs where no further changes in the cognitive structure can be generated, and additional information can be obtained only if the consumer chooses to search for information elsewhere. If this extended search can be performed immediately, the selected response may be simply to go somewhere and look for the information. Otherwise, the response can be a combination, in which the search is postponed while something else is attended to.

As long as a satisfactory solution has not been established and as long as a deliberation and exploration is more attractive than any of the choice alternatives, the conflict will continue. The attractiveness of exploration and deliberation (as well as of the choice alternatives) depends upon the evaluative attributes of the salient concepts and upon the relationships between the exploration alternatives and the concepts. As the most attractive possibilities for deliberation and exploration are used first, the attractiveness of deliberation and exploration will decrease as the choice process proceeds, a development also suggested by the following considerations.

In the choice process one or more of the following values can become salient. First, a *time value* may be aroused. As the conflict continues the consumer will experience an increasing time pressure. Second, the *effort* associated with extended deliberation and exploration will become important. As the process goes on, more and more effort is needed in order to carry out the subsequent exploration. Finally, the *likelihood of successful exploration* will decrease. As the choice process proceeds, all three factors will cause deliberation and exploration to decrease in attractiveness.

Although these considerations predict an overall decrease in the attractiveness of deliberation and exploration, it is still possible that single upward shifts in attractiveness can occur as the value structure changes in the course of the choice process. Although the deliberation and exploration alternatives chosen early were the most attractive ones, the addition of new values and the elimination of others can make the remaining alternatives even more attractive than the original ones, and new possibilities may be revealed.

---

[1] Here and in the following the term "search" is reserved for those instances where the consumer terminates the immediate conflict in order to seek information elsewhere. The information acquisition which occurs in the course of the choice process is labeled "exploration". This distinction is described further in Chapter 9.

Such upward shifts are especially important when the possibility of external search is introduced. To go to search for more information in a new environment can be perceived as stimulating or in other ways rewarding. Nevertheless, the overall tendency will be that the attractiveness of information acquisition will decrease as the choice process proceeds. The upward shifts indicate only that the attractiveness does not necessarily decrease monotonously.

2. The Choice Alternatives

The order in which alternatives are established and examined depends upon the deliberation and exploration activity, but the specific situation also plays a role. Whether the choice process occurs in a store or at home will have considerable influence on the response alternatives that will be examined. Similarly, the factors that cause the choice process are important. When an interruption occurs, the stimuli accounting for the interruption will also present clues as to what the response alternatives are likely to be. However, in spite of these specific influences, it is still possible to suggest a general pattern which reflects the order in which alternatives are established.

What the individual will look for in the information acquisition process depends upon whether the excessive amount of conflict is caused by the absence of acceptable alternatives or by two or more alternatives being equally attractive. In the first case the search will be for better alternatives, whereas the second case will generate search for new values and undiscovered aspects of the alternatives. Normally both things will occur simultaneously, but it simplifies the description to consider each strategy separately.

When it comes to purchases and consumption it might be expected that the consumer has only a limited number of alternatives. After all, most products are available only in limited variety which cannot be changed by the consumer. However, a closer look reveals a number of ways the consumer can establish new alternatives.

First, simpler alternatives can be combined to create new ones involving commitments to future action, postponement, and external search. In many product areas the consumer can manipulate alternatives by specifying the product to varying degrees, as is the case with many services, cars, homes, and many items of clothing. For example, by specifying color, additional equipment, and the like for his car, the consumer has a large number of ways to manipulate the alternatives. In other product areas, the consumer may vary the quantity, either by choosing among different sizes or by purchasing multiple units at one time. Furthermore, the time and place of the purchase can always be varied, and the same is true of the purchase form. The consumer can choose to pay cash, make special arrangements for payment, use credit cards, order by telephone or mail, and so on.

For the choice process to terminate, two things are required. First, the excessive amount of conflict must be eliminated; second, some immediate action must be decided upon. When it happens that a behavioral response is available that can reduce the conflict sufficiently, it will be chosen and the choice process will terminate, either early in the choice process or after considerable exploration and deliberation. If, however, no immediate action is found to eliminate the conflict, various combined responses may be tried, consisting of some immediate action plus some kind of internal response that will eliminate the conflict (Abelson 1959).

Often the internal response does not eliminate the original cause of the conflict, but it allows the individual to escape the conflict situation. In consumer choice processes, such responses will occur where no adequate purchase, consumption, or communication responses are available. The nature of these internal responses will vary with the specific circumstances, as they will be more or less firm commitments stored in memory for execution at some later time (Chapter 6). For example, a consumer may be interrupted on his way to work by information telling him that his train is late. He may choose to take a taxi, to go home for the car, or to wait. None of these alternatives is very attractive, and exploration and deliberation will occur, which in turn may result in the establishing of a new alternative, namely, to wait for the train *and* to decide to take the car next morning.

In the example the commitment is associated with the future environmental circumstances, "next morning". This association conditions the behavior to which the commitment is made to a specific future situation. Whether the commitment really will result in future action depends partly on the strength of the commitment and partly on the occurrence of an appropriate future situational setting. For example, a consumer may have committed himself to buy a new car sometime in the future, but environmental circumstances may constantly force him to delay the action.

Several factors can influence the strength of commitments. The more involving the choice process is, the more likely the resulting commitment is to lead to action, but whether or not the commitment is outspoken is also important. If the consumer tells others about the commitment, this action may in itself increase the probability that the action will be undertaken (Cohen et al. 1959 and Janis 1959b).

The commitment can also be to search for more information. The consumer can restore a balanced state by choosing to go to a store or to perform another search response; and if it is not possible to perform the response immediately, the choice process may terminate with a commitment to perform the action whenever it becomes feasible. However, not all conflicts terminate with a commitment. Attempts may also be made to avoid the conflict, either by suppressing the problem or by deliberately postponing it. If the conflict is minor these strategies may easily be applied, but if the issue is involving, it may be difficult to avoid the problem. Also, if external factors keep reminding the individual of the problem, it will not be easily neglected; and moreover, the partially solved problem may result in a motivational set that can influence subsequent behavior.

To avoid the problem by simply postponing it can be considered an extreme case of low commitment. The commitment is not "to do something in the future," but rather "to consider sometime in the future whether to do anything." As with the more specific commitments just discussed, the unspecified ones result in the formation of motivational sets and can be conditioned more or less firmly to future events. For example, a consumer may postpone the purchase of a new car until next year's models are available, or the decision concerning a possible new dress until the available offerings have been examined.

Altogether, these response alternatives are those generally facing the consumer; however, in some instances all of these possibilities are blocked or none of them is sufficient to restore equilibrium. Normally, a situation in which the more straightforward response alternatives are insufficient is characterized by extreme amounts of tension, fear, or anxiety, and if it reappears frequently enough it can result in severe mental problems. In such cases the individual will try to escape the unpleasant state of affairs. Responses applied with this purpose have much in common with the responses already discussed, except that they take more extreme forms. Some of these are denial, repression, isolation, reaction formation, displacement, undoing, introjection, projection, regression, and sublimation. They are all aimed at bringing the individual out of the unpleasant choice situation, but they do so in very different ways (Dollard and Miller 1950 and Blum 1966). However, since most consumer conflicts are solved long before these alternatives are introduced, they will not be discussed further here.

3. Changes in the Attractiveness of Alternatives

Deliberation and exploration aimed at establishing better alternatives may result in activating new values and new perceived relationships, but the cognitive processes may also do this directly. When alternatives are equally attractive, or when it is not possible to find new alternatives, as is the case in many forced-choice situations, deliberation can be aimed directly at the available alternatives in an attempt to discover new aspects by which the alternatives can be evaluated. Exploration of given alternatives, however, is not likely to continue forever. If it does not bring about a solution that can terminate the conflict, the individual will look for other alternatives. Although it may lead to thinking about unavailable alternatives, sooner or later the extended deliberation and search is likely to suggest a way to solve or to avoid the aroused problem.

Only when strong external forces rule out alternative solutions will deliberation and exploration concerned with the same alternatives continue for some time. Generally, however, the choice process is characterized by manipulation of alternatives. External factors may limit the extent of manipulation and this limitation will result in more specific exploration of the given alternatives, but if this exploration does not solve the conflict, a search for new alternatives will begin again.

That the choice processes will result in more alternatives does not necessarily mean that the salient cognitive structure becomes more complex. When comparison processes are performed, the poorest alternatives drop out, and the salient cognitive structure remains within reasonable limits. Similarly new values are added—often as a byproduct of the introduction of new alternatives—and insignificant values are deleted.

The overall effect of the continued evaluation is a decrease in the perceived conflict. Although the number of salient concepts changes only slightly, the amount of conflict in the cognitive structure decreases because better alternatives are constantly being substituted for poorer ones, so that in contrast to the deliberation and exploration alternatives, the choice alternatives will tend to become more attractive.

4. Acceptable Conflict and Satisfactory Alternatives

It has been suggested that when a satisfactory alternative has been established, then it will be chosen. But how attractive should an alternative be before it is satisfactory ?

The overall situation defines an optimal level of arousal, which in turn corresponds to the preferable amount of conflict. Unattractive alternatives arouse considerable conflict, as do alternatives which are equal in attractiveness. Consequently, an alternative of a certain attractiveness is necessary to reduce conflict sufficiently, and it is required that the most attractive alternative differ somewhat from the remaining alternatives. Therefore, the amount of conflict facing an individual if he chooses a certain alternative depends upon the attractiveness of the chosen as well as upon the attractiveness of the rejected alternatives.

It has been discussed that the tolerable amount of conflict—and thereby the nature of the acceptable alternatives—depends upon the overall situation and upon the optimal level of arousal prevailing before the conflict was aroused. This has an interesting implication. If for a moment the attention is fixed on a problem, whether a solution will be found depends on the tolerable level of conflict. If this level is high, the choice process may terminate with a "commitment" to a solution that still is quite conflicting and does not resolve the complex cognitive structure by which the problem is represented. In such a case elements of the problem can be neglected and a semi-solution can be established, but the conflict is likely to be rearoused. If, however, the tolerable amount of conflict is low, a considerably higher degree of consistency is required before a solution is deemed acceptable, which increases the likelihood that the problem really is solved.

Some evidence concerning the preferred amount of conflict can be found in studies of conflict and choice and in research dealing with perceived risk, specific self-confidence, and uncertainty. In addition, some studies dealing with achievement motivation and adaption levels have bearing on the issue (Chapter 5).

Considerable variation has been found in the extent to which people are willing to face risk, and the factors accounting for these differences are likely to be the same as those that determine the preferred level of conflict. There are two broad classes of relevant factors:

1. Personality variables.
2. Situational variables (especially familiarity with the situation).

The Harvard Group (Cox, 1967a) has consistently found that individuals vary in their willingness to accept risk, a finding which also emerges from a study by Brim and Hoff (1957). But attempts to identify the traits that characterize the individuals who place large, medium, and little importance on risk have not been too successful. Willingness to face risk has been related to self-confidence, but only inconclusive findings have been published (Chapter 15).

A somewhat different line of research has related willingness to face conflict with achievement motivation. (Chapter 4 and Chapter 15.) Evidence of situational influence upon consumers' willingness to face risk can be found in the work of the Harvard Group (Cox 1967a) also. Similarly Brim and Hoff (1957) found that the "desire for certainty" depends upon situational conditions, and other researchers have suggested that the presence of other persons will increase the individual's willingness to face risk (Lamm 1967, see Chapter 16).

A relationship between aspiration level theory and the quest for an optimal arousal level was suggested previously (Chapter 5). Research concerned with aspiration levels has frequently found that familiarity with the situation influences these levels, a conclusion that has also emerged from studies of adaption levels (Helson 1964) and achievement motivation. For example, Feather (1967b and 1968) and Feather and Saville (1967) confirm that aspiration levels will be modified as a result of experiences.

In conclusion, both personality variables and situational factors influence the preferred level of conflict. Among the personality variables, achievement motivation and self-confidence have been suggested as important variables; and among the situational variables, familiarity with the situation stands out as the only clearly identified variable.

5. Termination of the Choice Process

It is now possible to show how the choice process will proceed and eventually terminate, and this is done in Figure 8.3.

In the figure, time is measured along the horizontal axis and the amount of perceived conflict along the vertical axis. The tolerable amount of conflict is illustrated by the horizontal line, and the amount of conflict associated with choosing the most attractive alternative available at the beginning of the choice process is denoted by C_1. Similarly, the perceived conflict associated with choosing to perform exploration and deliberation is indicated by E_1.

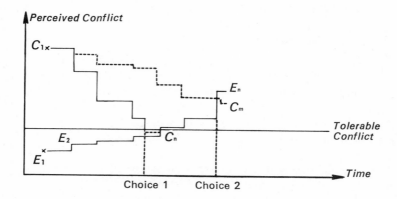

FIGURE 8.3. *Perceived conflict associated with choosing the most attractive alternative and with continued exploration as a function of choice time. (C_1: Perceived conflict associated with choosing best available alternative at the beginning of the choice process. C_n and C_m: Perceived conflict associated with chosen alternative. E_1: Perceived conflict associated with choosing exploration and deliberation at the beginning of the choice process. E_2, E_n: Perceived conflict associated with choosing subsequent exploration and deliberation alternatives.)*

As the choice proceeds, the attractiveness of subsequent exploration and deliberation alternatives will decrease; consequently, the amount of perceived conflict will increase (illustrated with the curve E_1-E_n). This follows from the *exploration order* described earlier.

For the response alternatives the opposite will occur. The perceived conflict associated with choosing the most preferable alternative will decrease as the alternatives become more attractive. As more attractive alternatives are more or less easily established, this decrease can occur more or less rapidly. If the curve marked C_1-C_n is taken as an example, it is suggested that the choice process will terminate when the curve intercepts the level corresponding to the tolerable amount of conflict.

The step-wise nature of the curve should be noted. It reflects that the choice process is a discrete one. How significant this is will depend upon how marked are the changes the salient cognitive structure undergoes between each comparison process. It is possible that in some instances both curves can be represented satisfactorily by continuous functions, but there is no doubt that under other circumstances the discrete nature of the curves reflects significant aspects of the choice process. This should be kept in mind throughout the following discussion, which uses continuous functions for the sake of simplicity.

If satisfactory alternatives are hard to find, the curve marked C_1-C_m may apply. In that case the choice process will terminate when the intersection with the exploration deliberation curve E_1-E_n is reached. This follows from the definition of attractiveness. As the most attractive alternative will always be chosen, deliberation and exploration activity will terminate when it becomes less attractive than the other choice alternatives.

In the second case the amount of conflict is not reduced to the tolerable level. Consequently the individual still experiences conflict after the choice has been made, but the choice was made because it was the most attractive strategy available. The post-choice conflict, however, shows that the acceptable level of conflict was not reached. The optimal arousal level probably is more accurately described as a tolerable range, so that the post-choice conflict must be of a certain magnitude before it has observable consequences (Chapter 5). If the discrepancy is more than can be tolerated, balance can be restored if the acceptable level or the perceived conflict can be changed.

Immediately after the choice, the consumer cannot apply the same conflict-reducing strategies he relied upon prior to the choice. The only additional reduction in the perceived conflict results from changes in values and in the way alternatives are related to the values (Chapter 9).

It is likely that the consumer who is repeatedly faced with a situation inducing post-choice conflict will learn to adjust the tolerable level of conflict; and as he repeats the choice, the process will become more and more like the one illustrated with the curves E_1-E_n and C_1-C_n. Moreover, elimination of the post-choice conflict can also be achieved because repeated exposure to similar conflicts results in increased ability to find attractive solutions. At least, when the consumer again is faced with the same conflict he will not accept a solution poorer than the one previously chosen.

The situation described in Figure 8.3 with the intersection of E_1-E_n and C_1-C_n is typical. Other cases can occur also but they are likely to elicit tendencies that eventually will make them look more like the case in Figure 8.3. For example, it is possible that, from the very beginning of the choice process, exploration and deliberation together with the best available alternative induces more conflict than is tolerable. In that case, if the best available alternatives are less attractive than continued deliberation and exploration then the latter will be performed; but when this activity becomes less attractive than the best alternative, a choice is made, and the consumer will be faced with a post-choice conflict. In general, if all choice processes were predictable and the consumer sufficiently familiar with them, they would be much like the typical case. However, the consumer's environment changes and so does the consumer himself. Consequently other cases, although unstable, are not uncommon.

6. Variations in Initial and Tolerable Level of Conflict

The difference between the initial and the acceptable level of conflict will determine the nature of the choice process. How variations in these levels will influence the choice process is shown in Figure 8.4a: with the tolerable level of conflict held constant, increases in the initial conflict will prolong the choice process and make post-choice conflict more probable.

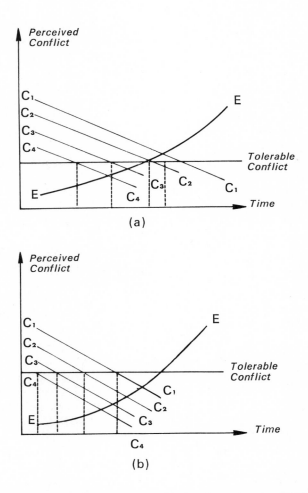

FIGURE 8.4.   *Choice processes with varying amounts of initial and tolerable conflict.*

Similarly, when graphs *a* and *b* of Figure 8.4 are compared, it appears that a decrease in the tolerable level of conflict will have the same effects.

Normally, both the initial and the tolerable levels of conflict will vary, depending upon the specific situation. If, for example, the amount of situational disturbance causing the conflict increases, it will increase the aroused conflict, but at the same time it may also cause some increase in the amount of tolerable conflict, depending upon the extent to which the situation is familiar and whether it had previously given rise to easily solved conflicts.

The most severe conflict occurs when initial arousal potential (and thereby the initial conflict) is large and the tolerable level of conflict is low. Very insignificant conflicts occur when the initial conflict is moderate and the tolerable amount of conflict is large.

In the course of the choice process, the amount of conflict associated with the most attractive alternative is modified. The tolerable amount of conflict, however, normally remains constant. Only when changes in salient cognitive structure result in changes in the overall nature of the problem, may the tolerable level of conflict change, as when exploration directs the attention to unexpected significant aspects of the environment. In such instances the new situation may be seen as a completely new choice process, or it can be studied as a sudden shift in the ongoing process.

7. Conflict, Tolerable Conflict, and the Complexity of Choice Processes

The overall nature of the choice process can be discussed in terms of its complexity, which in turn can be measured by the number of steps through which the process runs, the time it takes, the number of values involved in the evaluation of the alternatives, the importance of these values, the extensiveness of the exploration, the overall nature of cognitive activity, and like factors. The preceding discussion suggests a relationship between aroused conflict, tolerable conflict, and complexity of choice processes, as illustrated in Figure 8.5.

From the figure, it can be seen that perceived conflict exceeding the preferred level of conflict will cause choice processes of increasing complexity. If, however, the conflict is extreme, defensive reactions may take over, as can be seen in the extreme right part of the figure, where very large amounts of conflict correspond to moderately complex choice processes. Finally when the conflict falls short of the preferred level, exploratory behavior aimed at increasing stimulation will occur.

The relationship in Figure 8.5 will differ from person to person and vary with the specific situation studied. As suggested by Hebb (1966) and by Schroder et al. (1966), an individual can learn to deal with larger amounts of conflict, which will move the curve on the left side of the vertical axis upwards to the right (as indicated by the strippled curve). Future research may reveal more about the specific nature of these relationships, but the existence of an inverted U-shaped function is well documented (see, for example, Sieber and Lanzetta 1964, Hebb 1966, Berlyne 1967, and Schroder et al. 1966).

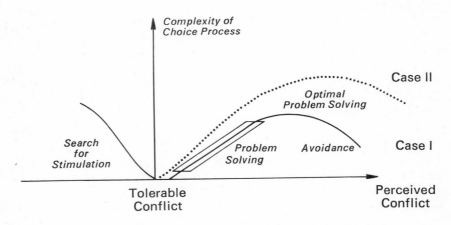

FIGURE 8.5.   *The relationship between perceived conflict and complexity of choice processes.*

In the present context it is particularly important to determine whether the kinds of problems which face consumers commonly arouse conflict to an extent that brings the consumer out in the extreme ends of Figure 8.5, or whether most consumer choice processes are found in the hatched area in the figure. If the latter is the case, a rather straightforward relationship between conflict and choice process behavior can be expected in studies of consumer behavior. The extent to which this is the case is explored in the experiments reported in Chapters 12 and 13.

3. *Maintenance of Tolerable Conflict*

So far we have discussed how the discrepancy between preferred and actual conflict will be eliminated, but not how the subsequent behavior will secure an appropriate amount of conflict. The question relates to the arousal potential the chosen behavioral response will bring about; it is difficult to answer, but a number of hypotheses can be suggested.

First, it is possible that responses are chosen with no regard to their ability to maintain a future appropriate level of arousal. In that case a chosen response will be performed undisturbed only if it "by chance" happens to secure a sufficient amount of arousal potential. Under other circumstances it will soon be interrupted, a new choice process will result, and this sequence will be repeated until the chosen response is satisfactory. This procedure seems to be too impractical to be the only explanation, although something like it may occasionally occur.

A second hypothesis is that as long as the chosen action is a well-established behavioral response, the performance of the response will automatically secure an appropriate arousal potential because the individual, while learning the behavioral response, becomes sufficienctly familiar with all its aspects and because the individual is able to predict what will be next and therefore can prepare for it. It is unlikely, however, that this explanation constitutes a complete answer. It would imply that the optimal arousal level always must remain constant and that all behavioral responses automatically result in the same arousal potential. If this were so, it would not be possible for any response to be sufficient in all situations. Nevertheless, the formulation has something to it. It rests on the assumption that extreme amounts of arousal potential are rare while the behavior is performed, which is likely to be true.

Third, the evaluative aspects associated with concepts may be learned in such a way that they tend to result in the selection of appropriate responses. This would be the case if instances in which a concept is associated with the selection of the appropriate response produce a positive evaluation of the concept, whereas instances in which the selected response turns out to be inappropriate reduce the evaluation of the concepts. This problem of the relationship between arousal and reinforcement (Berlyne 1967) has not yet found a definite answer.

Finally, it is possible that values such as *excitement, novelty, risk, conflict,* and *uncertainty* directly enter into the response selection. That risk can operate as a value has been proposed by Wallach and Wing (1968), and it seems obvious that variations in the extent to which alternatives are seen as exciting may influence the choice. This hypothesis would imply that the optimal arousal level is reflected in a salient *excitement* concept, in which the desired level of excitement is most positively evaluated. However, it is unlikely that the existence of *risk, excitement,* and similar values can provide the complete explanation. Such values would almost invariably contradict other salient values, and cases would occur in which it is not possible to find an alternative that both eliminates the aroused conflict and secures an appropriate subsequent arousal potential.

It seems likely that two or more of these hypotheses may be needed. Our own speculations suggest that the second hypothesis plays a major role, possibly in combination with the first and the third hypotheses. For one thing, behavioral responses do secure an intermediate level of arousal potential; the third hypothesis would explain how the selected response tends to be appropriate, and the first hypothesis would explain what happens when an inappropriate response is selected accidentally.

4. *Decision Processes*

Often single consumption acts occur in the course of a behavioral response; an explantion of these acts requires that the choice processes in which the particular behavioral response is chosen should be studied. However, the complete destruction of the product implied by consumption is rarely accomplished in a single response. For example, most food products are both prepared and consumed, and commonly they are purchased in such quantities as to suffice for a period of time. Similarly, purchases are normally preceded by several conflict situations so that the single purchase must be seen in relation to a number of choices occurring prior to the choice. Such sequences of choices will be labeled *decision processes*. So far, such more complex decisions have not been considered in the discussion of single choice processes. The reason is obvious. If single choice processes can be explained, then it is also possible to deal with behavior that results from a number of choice processes. In the present section, a few words will be said about the relationship among the several single choice processes that add up to a purchase, to consumption, or to the consumer's communication patterns.

It is possible to apply different criteria to all the choice processes that constitute the consumer's behavior and to select especially important choice processes for further study. One such selection criterion would be the following: consider all the choice processes that relate to a certain product or brand under study and analyze how the choice processes are linked together by means of commitments and classify them according to whether they occur in connection with purchase or consumption. Similarly a single purchase may be chosen for study, and it may be asked which choice process eventually led to that purchase. For different products, among different consumers, and even for the same consumer buying the same product at different times, different sequences of choices will be found.

Decision processes can be identified by looking at a specific purchase and asking what choice processes preceded the purchase. But it is also possible to ask, "Given a certain choice process in which a commitment is made, what will happen next?" The answer will reveal not only sequences that result in purchases, consumption, and communication, but also a number of sequences that are never completed, that is, the whole matter is dropped and a decision is avoided. The complexity and diversity of such sequences may be grasped from the following example. A consumer, working in his garden, sees a neighbor bringing home a new car. This sight interrupts his ongoing behavior, which is not continued until the aroused conflict is solved, perhaps by a decision to buy a new car sometime in the future. If no future situations revoke this commitment, the sequence of choices may stop here. However, it is unlikely that relevant situations would not occur in the future. The consumer may see a car in a showroom and obtain further information about it, only to realize that he cannot afford to buy a car; again the sequence of choices terminates. Later, new developments may rearouse the problem. For example, the consumer may see a TV commercial that provides new information about available credit terms, and this information in turn can result in an internal commitment to visit a bank. This sequence could continue ad infinitum, or it could terminate with a purchase, the important thing being that the commitment or the abandoned problem will work as a motivational set (Chapter 6) that insures that the consumer will attend to relevant information whenever it is available and that this information in turn will rearouse the conflict.

5. *The Consumer Choice Model*

A model of consumer choice-behavior has now been suggested. Arousal, optimal arousal, and arousal potential are crucial variables, and conflict and the attractiveness of salient alternatives are important factors in restoring and maintaining balance between the actual and the desired amount of arousal.

The consumer choice model describes how, in the single choice process, an individual attempts to modify available alternatives so that an acceptable one emerges. The extensiveness of the exploration and deliberation activity depends upon the amount of aroused conflict, the amount of conflict that can be tolerated in the specific situation, and upon the evaluation of the exploration and deliberation alternatives.

The nature of the choice process suggests a relationship between conflict and complexity of choices. An explanation of single choice processes will make it possible to study more complex decision chains involving a number of single conflicts.

Chapter 9

PRE-CHOICE AND POST-CHOICE PROCESSES

1. *Marketing Communication and the Consumer*

The present chapter deals with pre- and post-choice behavior in general, and with information acquisition in particular. The major elements of the theory of marketing communication are suggested in Figure 9.1.

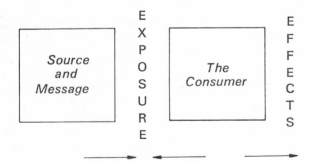

FIGURE 9.1. *Elements of marketing communication.*

This conceptualization differs somewhat from the classical "who says what to whom, through which channels and with what effect?" proposed by Smith et al. (1946). There are two major differences. The classical model, as is pointed out by Hovland (1954), deals with a communicator, a media, a

164

content, a receiver, and some effects. In the present formulation no distinctions are made among the communicator, the media, and the content. To the consumer this distinction does not exist. When he meets information, he is always faced with a message designed by a communicator and presented in a medium. That is, to the receiver the "who, what, and which" of the classical formula is one entity, although the distinctions may be important to the one who is planning the communication. As will be discussed, manipulating information along any of these dimensions will have impact upon the effects of the communication; however, communication occurs as an interaction between the consumer and the message (coming from a source and presented in a medium).

The classical formulation suggests a one-way flow from the source through the medium, the message, and the receiver, to a final effect. The present formulation rests upon the very different assumptions that communication occurs in exposure situations and that such situations may be generated by the receiver as well as by the information. This view is in line with most contemporary thinking. Klapper (1960) suggests that the communication process is much more complex than originally thought, and Bauer (1963 and 1964) and Cox (1965) point to the importance of the initiative of the audience.

1. Exposure Situations

An exposure situation occurs when the consumer is faced with marketing communication. To explain the effects of communication it is necessary to discuss how and when exposure occurs (i.e., attention is paid) and to analyze what happens when the consumer pays attention to the information.

Exposure may take place in three different ways, which in Chapter 3 were labeled: 1. experience formation, 2. forced learning, and 3. information acquisition.

Experience formation is especially important in connection with the use of products and services. Whenever consumption occurs it is possible that the product involved will perform above or below expectations. In both instances arousal will increase and a—possibly short and unimportant—conflict will result; in the process of dealing with the conflict perceived instrumentalities or values can change.

In *forced learning* situations the information itself must generate a sufficient amount of arousal. This is what happens when advertising influences the individual when he is not actively looking for information. Only to the extent that the advertisement is able to generate a minimum of conflict will a modification of concepts occur.[1]

---

[1] It might be argued that extrasensory perception does not fit this description. Two things should be pointed out; first, the extent to which ESP really *is* "extrasensory" is rather doubtful, and no firm proof of such a phenomenon has been presented. Second, even if such unconscious or extrasensory perception occurs, it is perfectly possible that it also involves a certain amount of conflict, that goes on without the individual's being aware of it (DeFleur and Petranoff 1959).

Information acquisition occurs when arousal has already been generated and a certain number of concepts are salient. The consumer is actively seeking out information, and the information to which he will attend depends upon the salient cognitive structure, the important thing being that the initiative is in the hands of the receiver.

Also, Chapter 3 discussed how most relevant consumer information can be classified into primary (product information), secondary (mass communication), tertiary (in-store communication), and personal communication. Assuming that a particular product is studied, information is further classified according to whether it is controlled by the company, by competitors, or by others. Finally, the information was classified in accordance with its contents.[2]

As was mentioned in Chapter 4, the consumer's *information acquisition* is not limited to exploration in the pre-choice situation. A choice process may be terminated by choosing an alternative that implies that the consumer will go out and search for more information. But again, when the *information search* is performed, a certain amount of conflict is aroused, and a new choice process is generated.

A word of caution should be said here. The distinction between information acquisition and forced learning suggests that either individual or situational factors alone explain how exposure is generated. Of course, all exposure situations depend on environmental as well as individual factors, but the relative importance of these factors varies. On the one hand, when a firm commitment to search for some specific information has been made and when the consumer subsequently addresses himself to that information, the importance of the internal factors is obvious, and the instance can easily be identified as information acquisition. On the other hand, when no intentions exist and when external information makes the consumer consider a product he would not otherwise have considered, a clear case of forced learning occurs. However, often vague intentions or motivational sets interact with favorable situational elements (for example, a particularly "good" advertisement) to create the exposure. Here it may be more questionable whether forced learning or information acquisition occurred, the essence being, of course, that forced learning and information acquisition represent extremes on a scale ranging from exposure situations in which situational factors dominate, to situations in which internal factors are the major determinants of choice.

Finally, a complete listing of the circumstances that modify consumers' values and beliefs should include the fact that changes in cognitive elements can occur after choices are made. Such a change does not necessarily involve any kind of information acquisition and may appear when post-choice conflict is present. These *post-choice processes* are dealt with separately in the last part of this chapter.

[2] Some of these categories may be empty. For example, secondary communication coming from competitors about the product in question is normally illegal.

2. Availability of Information Sources

Consumers can be exposed to many different kinds of information; but for the single consumer the narrow environment in which he lives limits the information he will face. The forced learning situations he will experience are biased to the extent that his environment is biased, and the same applies to the information to which he can attend in situations where he is actively acquiring information. Similarly, the consumer is not likely to have experiences with all possible products and brands.

In studies of selective exposure, many examples can be found to show how the availability of information in the individual's environment may bias the information he receives. A single example will suffice. In the studies of voting behavior by Lazarsfeld et al. (1948) and Berelson et al. (1954), it was found that Republicans tended to be exposed to more Republican propaganda and Democrats to more Democratic propaganda than would be expected by chance. There may be several reasons that Republican propaganda is more easily available to Republicans and Democratic propaganda to Democrats. For example, Republicans may tend to have Republican friends, read Republican papers, receive Republican brochures, and so on. Such findings have commonly been taken to indicate selective exposure, but when they are examined closely, they do not really prove that the individuals would have chosen the same information if they had other sources available. At best, the effect may be a secondary result following from the fact that the individuals have established certain life patterns whereby they create their own biased environments.

The environment may also affect in a more narrow sense which information sources the consumer will utilize. The alternatives to be considered depend upon the particular situation, and each situation has its own sources upon which the consumer must rely. Normally, if he wants to make use of other sources, he must choose an alternative that involves search outside the particular environment, and such an alternative will be chosen only when a certain amount of perceived conflict has been aroused and when no other sufficiently attractive alternatives are available.

Thus, when studying situations in which the consumer is exposed to information, it is necessary to consider the availability of different kinds of information.

3. Choice of Information

How the consumer will react to the information depends upon the relationship between the source and content of the message and the receiver's salient cognitive structure. A particular piece of information is chosen according to the individual's expectations with regard to that information.

However, when the consumer becomes exposed to the message, it may look completely different or it may turn out to be more or less in agreement with his expectations. This implies that the consumer's choice of information must be examined depending on his expectations, and that the effects of the information must be seen in relation to the actual content of the information.

For information to have any impact on the receiver, a certain amount of conflict must be present. What information the consumer will attend to depends upon how this conflict is aroused. When it is generated by information forced upon the individual or by a discrepancy between actual and expected product performance, the information is already there, and the only thing the consumer can do is to decide whether or not to address himself to it. The kind of information that can arouse the needed conflict in such a situation is likely to be novel, surprising, incongruent, or complex information.

Consumers' choice of information in information acquisition situations is more complex. We must know whether he will engage in exploration or not, and to what kinds of information he will pay attention.

Our previous chapters maintained that the amount of perceived conflict together with the attractiveness of the available information sources will determine the extensiveness of search. But these factors are also important determinants of what information the consumer will select. The attractiveness of the available information alternatives is particularly important, and in the specific situation, it can be influenced by a large number of factors. In most situations these factors are likely to appear: (1) the effort needed to obtain the information, (2) the time pressure resulting from postponing the choice, and (3) the likelihood that the information will prove useful (Chapter 8).

The effort needed to obtain the information can be a positive as well as negative factor. Increased effort may reduce the attractiveness of the information, but in some cases information acquisition is regarded as rewarding in its own right. For example, consumers may shop "for the fun of it," they may read advertisements because they like to, or they may discuss products because they are interested in them.

How much the information acquisition will postpone the choice may influence the attractiveness, positively or negatively. In some instances a choice of information not immediately available provides a way to avoid the conflict; in situations when the consumer prefers to postpone the choice, the fact that the information cannot immediately be obtained can add to its attractiveness. This, however, is the exception, rather than the rule. Immediately available information is usually preferred, and it therefore is important to study what information sources are available to the consumer in the particular situation.

How the usefulness of the information will influence the choice of sources depends upon the nature of the aroused conflict. The consumer's evaluation of the information relates to his expectations about the information's ability to help him reduce the conflict. Therefore the instrumentality of the information will depend upon how he expects the information to relate to his salient cognitive structure.

The usefulness of the information may also relate to the expected discrepancy between the information and the consumer's own stand. When the information is expected to be boring and uninteresting, the consumer will not seek it out. Similarly, when the message is expected to deviate too strongly to be incorporated into his salient cognitive structure, that is, when it is expected to be too complex, too new, or too difficult, it will be avoided. But when the message lies between these two extremes, the consumer will address himself to it. For example, a consumer who is evaluating alternative color television sets is aware of three possible information sources: (1) he can ask his wife her views, (2) he can turn to a friend who has recently bought a color television set, and (3) he can choose a highly technical and complex article describing problems associated with color television. Now, if the consumer is not technically oriented and if he does not expect his wife to say anything new, he may prefer to turn to his friend, who represents an alternative intermediate with regard to novelty, complexity, and the like.

Ideally the consumer would like to rely upon expectations with regard to the specific information, but often he does not know too much about the message. As he may have better clues about the source of the message, he then relies upon his perception of the source. Generally, he will prefer sources with high expertise and credibility and with low or no intentions to influence. The information source will be discussed in detail in connection with the consumer's reactions to the content of the message also.

4. Effects of Exposure

When the exposure has been generated, the consumer may attend more or less intensively to the particular information, and he may reject or accept it. What will happen depends upon the discrepancy between the perception of the actual information and the newly aroused cognitive structure. If the information is not sufficiently complex, new, and interesting, the consumer may still turn it down and return to whatever he was doing before the interruption. Similarly, if the information is too new, surprising, and complex, he may turn it down; but in that case somewhat more elaborate cognitive processes are likely to occur before the information is rejected.

How the information compares with the receiver's aroused cognitive structure can vary depending upon the nature of the exposure situation. When the initiative is not taken by the consumer (in instances of forced learning and experience formation), a discrepancy between the message and the receiver's beliefs is automatically generated, as the information or the product would not otherwise have been able to generate a conflict. The same is not necessarily the case when the consumer actively acquires the information. Here it is possible that the information turns out to be in perfect agreement with the beliefs and values of the receiver, in which case the question of effect is easily answered. Since the consumer's beliefs and expectations are confirmed, no change will occur. This does not necessarily mean that there is no effect, as the communication may reinforce the consumer's previous beliefs; but it does mean that some discrepancy between the message and the receiver's beliefs is a necessary condition for change to occur.[3]

More interesting, therefore, is the situation where there is disagreement between the information and the receiver's own position. What kind of changes will the information generate? Chapter 7 discussed these effects in terms of learning and modification of concepts; we must now relate that discussion to consumer exposure situations.

Just as the cognitions in choice processes vary from extremely complex to extremely simple, so the cognitions that relate to environmental information will vary. These variations depend on the aroused conflict.

As conflict depends upon uncertainty and involvement, it is expected that variations in either factor will result in variations in the cognitive processes involved in assimilating the information (Rosenbaum and Lewin 1969). Krugman (1965 and 1967) proposes such dependency in his high and low involvement advertising models.[4]

Both a high and a low conflict cognitive structure are illustrated in Figure 9.2. From the figure it appears that for both high and low conflict, the aroused cognitions can be grouped as *source perceptions, message perceptions* and *receiver's own stand*. This view has governed much Swedish research in marketing communication (Wärneryd and Nowak 1967), and a similar position is taken by Feather and Jeffries (1967). When the high and low conflict cognitions are compared, several differences can be seen. In the high conflict cognitions, the perception of the three basic elements is more detailed, and a number of related concepts may occur.

Analysis of effects of communication must consider the relationship between the receiver's own stand and the message together with the effects of the perception of the source. A framework for analysis of the message-receiver discrepancy is provided in the Hovland-Sherif assimilation-contrast model (Figure 7.7). The model predicts that the effect of the information reaches a maximum when the message is moderately discrepant with the receiver's own stand. Moreover, it predicts that the optimal distance between the message and the receiver decreases with increased involvement. The first prediction is well established (see Chapter 7), and it is in line with predictions derived from competing attitude models (Insko 1967). The involvement effect is less well documented. However, at an aggregated level, with the message held constant, the overall result of an increased involvement should

---

[3] One exception could occur where a negatively evaluated source communicates beliefs in agreement with the receiver's belief.

[4] The independent effects of uncertainty are less commonly discussed. It may be that they are not entirely parallel with the effects of variations in involvement. At the time of the writing no evidence is available, and any conclusion will have to await further research.

be a decrease in the effect of the exposure. This effect is found by Johnson and Scileppi (1969), and Barach (1969a and b) also provides data relating to this hypothesis. In an experimental setting, housewives' brand switching was

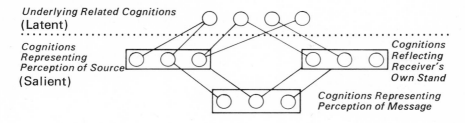

a) Cognitive Structure with High Conflict Exposure

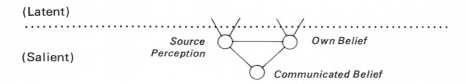

b) Cognitive Structure with Low Conflict Exposure

FIGURE 9.2.   *Varying cognitions depending upon aroused conflict.*

studied as a function of exposure to advertising. Among the major findings was a significant effect of the importance of the product upon the effect of the advertising messages: with products perceived to be less important, more effect was observed.

In relation to Figure 9.2, the involvement effect may be seen as a function of the salient related values. With more involvement (and conflict) more concepts are aroused, and the additional cognitions are likely to make the individual's beliefs and values more resistant to change.

5. Source Effects

The source to which the consumer ascribes a message is important for the choice of the information and for the effects of the message. Hovland et al. (1953) in their original work on the topic concluded that: "The reactions to a communication are significantly affected by cues as to the communicator's intentions, expertness, and trustworthiness" (p. 35).[5] Later studies have

---

[5] Later findings have suggested that this source effect is most important at the time when the message is received and that it may disappear after some time. For a disscusion of this *sleeper effect* see, for example, Cohen (1964).

largely supported this position, but Kelman (1958) proposes that in some situations the source's power and attractiveness may also be important. In a marketing context, Cox (1963) has shown that the trustworthiness (*confidence value*) and the expertise (*predictive value*) of the communicator are particularly important.

In marketing communication, the effect of the source plays a special role. In most ordinary communication the source is easily identified, but not in marketing. Whenever a company uses mass media or personal channels of communication such as salesmen, the receiver's perception of the source will depend partly upon the medium which brings the information and partly upon the company initiating the communication. The significance of these two components will vary from instance to instance. For example, when a nationally known manufacturer advertises in a large magazine, the source effects may be ascribed in large part to the company. In contrast, when an unknown company advertises almost anonymously in a more dubious publication, the evaluation of the publication may dominate the receiver's evaluation of the source. A study of this interaction effect is reported by Fuchs (1964). In a 3 × 3 design using three companies and three magazines of varying prestige as independent variables, he studied the amount of attitude change generated by each of the 9 company-magazine combinations. It was found that the attitude change varied significantly with magazine prestige as well as with company prestige.

How major categories of sources are evaluated, depending upon the character of the source, is reflected in a study of Udell (1966) of information acquisition preceding purchases of minor electrical appliances. He found that information obtained in the store was seen as by far the most useful. Approximately two thirds of the consumers preferred this source, as opposed to the one third preferring all other information sources combined. Moreover, among the latter the most useful source was past experience with the product, which was rated above personal communication sources and all secondary communication sources combined. This ordering is probably particular to the kind of product studied, and it seems to reflect a combined weighting of expertise and trustworthiness.

The combined source effect is further complicated by testimonials used in advertisements. In such instances, the source to which the consumer ascribes the message is a combination of the individual recommending the product, the medium bringing the advertisement, and the company whose product is being advertised.

Finally, that the magnitude of the source effect depends on the involvement is suggested by Johnson and Scileppi (1969), who found significantly more source effect in low involvement conditions than in high involvement conditions.

6. Selectivity in Information Acquisition

It is now possible to turn to an important topic in communication theory, namely, the problem of selectivity in response to information. That human beings are biased with regard to the information they obtain is probably the most frequently reported finding in sociology and in social psychology. Studies of media habits, advertising recognition, and recall have found selectivity in exposure to mass media, and studies dealing with personal influence have reported selectivity in exposure to personal communication. (Arndt 1967a). Selectivity in attention has been reviewed by Copland (1958) and Treisman (1969), and selective processes in reading and understanding have been reported by Edfelt (1960). Finally, selectivity in learning and retention is discussed in Greenwald and Sakumura (1967) and in Feather (1969).

Selectivity implies that people are biased in the material to which they become exposed and to which they attend, in what they read and understand, and in what they learn and remember. Bias, however, can have several different causes.

A review of studies of selectivity suggests that at least two kinds of selectivity occur. Many authors suggest that people are selective in that they seek out what they are interested in, while others suggest that people prefer information that supports whatever views they already hold. In some instances these two principles will make the same predictions, as when the supportive information happens to be the information in which the consumer is also interested.

Bias in the material to which persons are exposed may also result from limited availability of informational material, but this kind of selectivity does not reflect any tendency on the consumer's behalf to approach or to avoid particular kinds of information. Behavioral tendencies towards selectivity can be proven only to the extent that consumers can be shown to make biased choices among those information alternatives of which they are aware and to which they have access.

Selectivity may express itself in two ways. The consumer may avoid uninteresting and unsupporting information or he may approach interesting and supporting information. As discussed by Lowin (1967), the two kinds of selectivity are markedly different, and the available evidence concerning avoidance of unsupportive information is somewhat questionable. It may very well be that reported instances of selective avoidance are explainable by variations in the availability of the information and in terms of message distortion following the exposure.

Selectivity for supportive information and for interesting (useful) information will be discussed here with regard to aspects of particular importance in consumer behavior. The tendency to seek out supportive information has been widely discussed among sociologists and social psychologists. Very often familiarity cannot be isolated from selectivity, as in a study by Spence and Engel (1969), in which the authors attempt to show the existence of selectivity in brand recognition. The findings show a clear tendency to recognize preferred brands faster than less preferred brands. However, as the subject's preferred brand commonly is the brand he uses, it is also the brand with which he is most familiar; and consequently the faster recognition may have resulted because the respondent knew the preferred brand better than the unpreferred ones.

The generality of selectivity has repeatedly been questioned in recent years. After reviewing the literature, Sears and Freedman (1967) write: "Five studies showed some preference for supportive information . . . eight showed no preference . . . and five showed preference for non-supportive information . . . the conclusion seems clear. The available evidence fails to indicate the presence of a general preference for supportive information" (p. 208).

It can still be argued that there must be some principle by which individuals select supportive versus nonsupportive information. Cognitive dissonance has been suggested as such a principle. It is maintained that the more dissonance a certain situation arouses, the more likely it is that supportive information will be sought out and nonsupportive information avoided. Rhine (1967a and b), however, after reviewing the literature concludes that the relationship between dissonance and information selectivity is not a straightforward one.

Faced with the kind of problem encountered in studies of selectivity, one is tempted to point to the arousal principle (Chapter 5) as a mechanism explaining consumers' choices among supportive and nonsupportive information. This principle suggests that too-conflicting as well as too-trivial information will be avoided, whereas information between these extremes will be attended to. As supportive information generates only very low amounts of conflict, and too-nonsupportive information can generate considerable conflict, both will be avoided, whereas information that deviates moderately from the receiver's beliefs will be attended to. If so, the amount of arousal potential the individual expects to find in the information may produce either situation illustrated in Figure 9.3.

As nonsupportive information always will be more conflicting than supportive information, it will have a higher arousal potential. Now, if the supportive information has an arousal potential below the optimal level and the nonsupportive information is closer to the optimal level, then the latter will be chosen (Figure 9.3a). If, on the contrary, both the supportive and the nonsupportive information offer an arousal potential above the optimal level, then the supportive information will be chosen (Figure 9.3b). If this interpretation is correct, then the choice between nonsupportive and supportive information does not really reflect selectivity. Rather, it is a function of the aroused conflict and the perception of the available information alternatives.

Some evidence in support of this view comes from Rosen et al. (1963), who presented college students with a choice between more or less conflicting information and found that approximately 70% of the subjects preferred the more conflict-arousing information. As the test situation was dull and tedious, it may be assumed that the complexity of the situation was so far

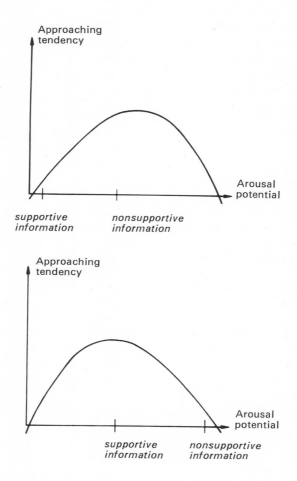

FIGURE 9.3. *Approach and avoidance of supportive information depending upon arousal potential.*

below the subject's normal experience that unfamiliar information was sought out in an attempt to increase arousal. This interpretation gains further support from the reasons the subjects gave for their choices. A significant proportion of those selecting unfamiliar information said that they did so because they expected the information to be *challenging, interesting,* and the like; whereas those who chose familiar information expressed preferences for easy and unchallenging material. Similar findings have appeared from experiments requiring subjects to learn balanced and unbalanced structures. Zajonc and Burnstein (1966) found no difference in the ease with which such structures were learned, a result which the authors suggest may be ascribable to variations in involvement among the subjects.

Selectivity governed by the individual's interest is less provocative and not really unexpected, as when a consumer seeks out information that is useful in connection with a choice. Selectivity of this kind is reported by Arndt (1968b), who finds support for the following two hypotheses: "(1) Persons who are predisposed to buy a new product are more likely to receive word-of-mouth communications about that product (Selective Exposure), and (2) more likely to be affected by the content of those communications (Selective Response)" (p. 19). As is evident from the formulation of the hypotheses, selectivity as defined here simply means that consumers interested in a particular product are also more interested than others in information about the product.

Waly and Cook (1966) and Greenwald and Sakumura (1967) report findings that support the hypotheses about selectivity for useful information, and Lowe and Steiner (1968) studied the effects of reversibility and the consequences of decisions in connection with information search, and they found that subjects preferred whichever information is useful. In line with this are the findings from Schyberger's (1965) study of readership patterns, which found a close relationship between interest in various issues and time spent reading material relating to the issues. Finally, usefulness of the information and "interest" are also pointed to as factors guiding the choice of information by Festinger (1964a), Feather (1967a), Sears and Freedman (1967), and Cerha (1967).

2. *The Nature of the Exposure*

1. Exposure in Forced Learning Situations

Forced learning occurs when environmental information generates a sufficient amount of conflict. Krugman (1967)[6] studied forced learning by observing the total time spent with magazine advertisements and TV commercials; from subjects' verbal reports, he computed the number of actual *connections* ("bits of information internalized"). He found that interaction depends upon environmental factors (such as whether the material is presented as editorial or as advertisements), the material that surrounds the

---

[6] Krugman does not deal with forced learning per se, but rather with what he calls "low involvement" exposure. The nature of the exposure situations, however, is such that it can be assumed that they closely resemble forced learning.

advertisement, and the nature of the medium. The data in Table 9.1 are reproduced as an example of his work.

TABLE 9.1

Number of connections, seconds per connection and exposure time for magazine and TV commercials, by editorial or advertising set, editorial environment, and product advertised.

| | | MAGAZINE | | | TV | |
	N	Seconds per Ad	Number of Connections	Seconds per Connection	N	Number of Connections
Set:						
Editorial	14	17.6	1.9	9.14	20	.75
Advertising	15	24.3	1.2	20.25	21	.43
Editorial environment:						
Serious (news)	15	21.9	1.8	12.14	26	.65
Light (entertainment)	14	19.6	1.3	15.23	15	.47
Product advertised:						
Airline	15	24.2	1.8	13.48	9	.67
Magazine	14	16.6	1.3	12.90	32	.56

(Reproduced with permission from Krugman, 1967, copyright by The Public Opinion Quarterly.)

Krugman's findings reflect variations in the way consumers react to advertising material forced upon them, and he suggests that these differences relate to the conflict (involvement) the message generates. Further evidence of such a relationship is provided by Wheatley and Oshikawa (1970) and by Lipstein (1968), who proposes that the more consumers perceive significant brand differences, the more likely they will be to perceive conflict (anxiety); consequently, the more frequently they will note advertisements. From data collected by the Advertising Research Foundation he finds a correlation coefficient of .7 between "belief of importance of brand differences" and "noting of ads by frequent users". Considering the number of other factors that can be expected to influence data of this kind, the correlation seems remarkable. Without presenting data, Lipstein further reports on a number of products for which relationships between conflict and reactions to exposure have been established.

Forced learning may be generated by secondary mass communication, by tertiary mass communication, and by personal communication. The various types of information will vary in their ability to create exposure situations. As for secondary mass communication, Krugman's data indicate differences between advertisements and editorial material and between TV and printed material. Furthermore, although studies of attention value have touched upon the subject, they have not made a distinction between forced learning and information acquisition. Nevertheless, it is worth mentioning that these studies (Copland 1958) have pointed at factors such as novelty, surprise, and complexity as important determinants of attention.

It is obvious that the frequency with which forced learning occurs will vary among different media. The nature of such situations as television viewing and movie-going, as compared with magazine reading, catalogue reading, and so on, suggests that media are able to force their messages upon the receiver to different degrees. The very low degree of control the receiver has over the information which he will meet in media such as television suggests that forced learning dominates the exposure situations this medium generates. That the conflict caused by television advertisements is often avoided by withdrawal is well known. Steiner (1966a) shows the process in his report that the percentage of viewers paying full attention to the screen drops from approximately 70% to less than 50% when commericals are shown. British findings reported by Nuttall (1962) suggest an even larger decrease in attention.

No available data throw light on forced learning caused by tertiary communication. No doubt considerable commercial research has been conducted in this area, but no findings have been published. If the principles established in studies of reading and seeing (Brandt 1944 and Edfelt 1960) apply to the store situation, factors such as surprise, interest, novelty, and complexity can be expected to generate forced learning in connection with tertiary communication.

Personal communication can result in forced learning both when the source is another consumer and when the communication comes from salesmen. The salesman can, and often will, force his information upon the receiver. Of course, the receiver can withdraw from the information, but that requires that he leave the situation or take other actions, a course often more difficult than to turn the page in a magazine, turn one's back to the television set, or move to the next rack in the supermarket.

Personal communication from other consumers may be forced upon the receiver, but often such a source will lack the motivation to do so, and the receiver can more easily influence the transmittal of information. Consequently, in such instances, forced learning is expected to be less frequent. However, within social psychology, it is generally agreed that overheard communication can be extremely efficient (Walster and Festinger 1962). When the receiver is aware of a source's persuasive intentions, he can prepare himself against the communication and consequently minimize its effect. This process, however, is not at work in connection with overheard communication (McGuire 1964). In marketing, the frequency and effects of such communication have never been studied, but future research may reveal that it constitutes a very important class of personal communication.

The kinds of information the consumer becomes exposed to in forced learning situations is limited by the information sources in the consumer's environment. The advertisements forced upon the consumer are in the papers he reads, in the television shows he views, and so on. The tertiary mass communication he will be exposed to is found in the stores he visits and at shows and fairs and exhibitions he goes to. Similarly, the personal communication he receives is received from those people he knows or otherwise gets in touch with.

Within the consumer's limited environment he can be selective in the sense that his primary interests will be more likely to arouse conflict and exposure. In this way, interest can act as a motivational set. A preference for supportive information is not likely to be found in forced learning situations.

It is difficult to tell how frequently forced learning occurs. In studies of the amount of advertising to which the consumer becomes exposed, no distinction has been made between forced learning situations and information acquisition. Future research will have to specify the frequency with which the different kinds of exposure situations occur. At the present time one may speculate that considerable differences can be found among products and among consumers. Forced learning probably dominates in minor nondurable product areas, whereas it is less significant among larger durable products.

2. Experience Formation

Experience formation, as defined here, will occur in connection with primary communication. Like forced learning, experience formation also is generated by environmental factors, but in contrast to forced learning, these factors are related to the product and its use. Surprise in the form of unexpectedly poor or unexpectedly good performance can generate experience formation as can the discovery of new aspects of the product.

In many product areas, experience formation will be the one most important way the consumer learns about the product. For example, a cigarette smoker may not be exposed to secondary, tertiary, or personal communication about his brand for days. However, if he is an average smoker, he will have the package in his hand and use the brand 15 to 20 times a day. In many product areas, this potential for exposure runs as high as 20, 30, or 50 times the potential for exposure to all other information sources combined. This fact has commonly been overlooked in studies of consumers and their information sources, which traditionally have centered around mass communication, personal communication, and in-store behavior.

Although the potential for experience formation is large, the effects of such exposures will depend upon how frequently a sufficient amount of conflict is aroused, which in turn depends upon the performance of the product relative to the consumer's expectations (aspirations). Discrepancies can result for two reasons. The consumer's expectations may increase after he has heard about or tried other alternatives, or simply as a result of repeated satisfaction (Katona 1963). Discrepancies can also be generated by the alternatives. However, traditionally, branding and product quality are areas where the manufacturer puts great emphasis on minimizing the amount of change. Even though product changes have become more frequent over the last two decades, the instances in which the consumer will meet changes in the product are rare compared with those in which he faces the same product in an unchanged package. This means that conflict will not often be aroused. The future may show increased use of this potential source of communication. As a curiosity, it can be mentioned that a major Danish brewery, in the early 1960's, introduced systematic changes in their labels. Small informational items attached to the main label were changed so frequently that the consumer rarely would meet the same piece of information more than once. No data have been published about the effects of this policy, but a considerable increase in number of efficient exposure situations was generated (although it is doubtful whether it had any impact on the perceived instrumentality of the brand).

The potential for exposure through experience formation is considerable; on the other hand, the frequency with which it occurs may be low. The total effect of experience formation cannot be judged without consideration as to the efficiency of the exposure situation when it occurs. Here it is important that it is the consumer himself who is "experiencing." The effect of the information will not be retarded by negative source effects, that is, satisfaction or dissatisfaction itself acts as a positive or a negative reward, as opposed to the indirect effects of symbolic communication. For this reason, these exposure situations can be extremely efficient. The overwhelming effects of such experiences can be seen in a study reported by Cohen and Goldberg (1969), who show how a product (coffee brands) that does not perform in accordance with the consumer's expectations will be detected and will not be chosen again. Similarly Cardozo (1965) found product experience to be an extremely important factor, and a related observation by Peterson (1969) found that promotion is the most efficient when it reaches the consumer at "the point of consumption".

Although there can be little doubt about the importance of experience formation, some caution should be taken. In his normal environment, the consumer can accept a relatively wide range of alternatives. That is, in a normal consumption situation the deviation between expectations and actual performance has to be of a certain magnitude in order to arouse conflict. In a test situation consumers may be perfectly able to discriminate among products; but when they meet the products under more normal circumstances they find no differences, or at least, they find no differences large enough to cause a change in their behavior (Banks 1950c).

3. Consumers' Information Acquisition

Once a conflict has been aroused, it may result in more or less extensive exploration. The individual will first apply the most attractive strategies in his attempt to solve the problem (Chapter 8). He will first draw upon his memory, and only if it does not provide a satisfactory alternative will exploration and eventually information search occur. Therefore, the more familiar the consumer is with the problem he faces, the less he will have to rely upon environmental information and the more he can use information already stored in memory. Data indicating such a relationship are presented by Wärneryd (1961).[7] For consumers who had recently purchased a car, he constructed an index reflecting the total amount of information they had acquired. He found that the information acquisition varied systematically among heavy, medium, and light car users, with the latter acquiring the most information. Similarly a comparison between consumers who were buying their first car and consumers who had previously bought other cars reveals a significant difference in the amount of information acquired. Among the repeat purchasers, those who changed brand (and consequently knew less about the chosen alternative) acquired more information than those who stayed with the same brand.

The tendency to acquire information also depends directly upon the amount of perceived conflict. The more conflict (or in the terminology of other authors: anxiety, risk, uncertainty, and so on), the more information will be acquired (for data see Chapter 5).

To acquire more information when faced with serious conflict seems very rational. However, it must be emphasized that although the amount of information varies with the amount of conflict, the information acquisition process is not entirely rational, at least, not in accordance with any traditional concept of rationality. The information acquisition stops when the perceived conflict has been reduced sufficiently, which will happen relatively independently of the price of information, the expected value of further search, and such. Consequently, as has been shown by Farley (1964a), a model like the one proposed by Stigler (1961), which assumes that the consumer continues search until the value of additional information becomes smaller than the costs involved in obtaining the information, is not a very good one.

Conflict-arousing factors shown to influence the extent of a consumer's information acquisition include the price of the product, the length of time the consumer will be committed to his choice, the reversibility of the choice, and the conspicuousness of the product (see Engel et al. 1968). Convincing data are also reported by Cox and Rich (1964) in their study of risk and telephone shopping (Chapter 5). Compared with in-store shopping, telephone shopping can be seen as less intensive information acquisition, and it was found to be most common with low risk products.

A few suggestive findings about different kinds of exposure situations throw light upon the consumer's choice among major groups of information sources. Wärneryd (1961) used his information acquisition index to illustrate the relative importance of personal communication, secondary communication, and particularly advertising. As his study deals with car purchases in

---

[7] This and a few studies referred to later do not relate to the single choice situation, but to the entire sequence of choices preceding a purchase, which limits the kind of conclusion which can be drawn. However, it has been attempted to apply these studies only where conclusions pertinent to the entire sequence can be applied to the single choices also. This approach is necessitated by the scarcity of data.

Sweden, where no commercial TV is available, it can be assumed that a good many of the exposures upon which his index is based reflect information acquisition. Brochures were the most frequently sought source; the index also shows how different communication sources can substitute for each other. For example, the consumer who does not know anybody who owns a car of the make he is considering relies more heavily upon secondary mass communication than the consumer who does have such a contact. Other authors have found limits to the extent to which information sources can substitute for each other. Engel et al. (1966) conducted a study that shows how the preferred source of information varies for different products for self-medication. With diseases of increasing seriousness (from dandruff to flu to heart disease), the preferred information source change from advertisements, to personal friends, to pharmacists and physicians. The findings also suggest that increased conflict makes sources with greater expertise and reliability more attractive, perhaps because reliable and better sources often are more difficult to get to, and only if considerable conflict is aroused will the consumer be willing to go to more trouble for information.

PRIMARY INFORMATION

Primary information is not the most important source when consumers are actively seeking information, because in order to utilize primary communication the consumer must have access to the product. As the upcoming purchase of same product is often the cause of the conflict, reliance on primary communication is normally ruled out. However, consumers faced with minor conflicts can acquire information by buying and trying the product, as was shown by Tucker (1964) in his study of brand loyalty for bread, in a later replication of the same study by Stafford (1966), by McConnell (1968) in his study of brand loyalty for beer, and by Sheth and Venkatesan (1968) in their study of women's choices of hairspray. All these researchers found that consumers who were offered choices among unknown alternatives used the first couple of choices to try out the various alternatives before they became loyal. Similarly, Kelly (1967a) in a study of store patronage found that many consumers went to the store once or twice to examine it before they decided whether or not to patronize it. In this connection it can also be mentioned that the manufacturer of non-durable products may try to force primary communication upon the consumer by the use of samples, coupons, gift certificates, and the like (Luick and Ziegler 1968).

Primary information in connection with more expensive durable products is not common, but it may occur if the consumer is able to arrange a trial period before he commits himself. Rogers (1962) reports that it is a very common phenomenon in his studies of farmers' adoption of new products, and findings from two other studies suggest that this method is also applied by consumers. Studying purchases of durable products such as radios, television sets, and vacuum cleaners, Wickström (1965) found that more than 20% of the consumers tried out one or more items at home before they made their purchase, and approximately one third of these consumers did not purchase the product they had tried at home. Similarly Wärneryd (1961) found that approximately 60% of all Swedish car purchasers tried one or more cars before purchasing.

SECONDARY (MASS) COMMUNICATION

The consumer can more or less easily acquire information from mass communication sources. On the one hand there are easily accessible sources such as magazines, newspapers, brochures, catalogues, and telephone books, while on the other hand there are sources such as television, radio, movies, and posters, which allow the consumer less control over the material to which he will be exposed. Much available literature discusses the effects of mass communication (Klapper 1960, Schramm 1960, Crane 1965, and Tannenbaum and Greenberg 1968). However, in the reported studies, no attempts have been made to distinguish between forced learning and information acquisition. To the extent that it deals with products about which information acquisition can be expected to be frequent, this material throws some light on consumers' choices among mass communication sources. As an example, Udell's (1966) study of preferences for different information sources in connection with purchases of minor electrical appliances found that among secondary information sources, mail-order catalogs, circulars, newspaper ads, television ads, consumer rating publications, magazine ads, and radio ads were rated as most useful in the order mentioned. Comparisons with similar studies of other products (discussed in Chapter 15) suggest that such evaluations vary among product categories and reflect the availability of information in different areas. Nevertheless, they can provide highly useful information for the planner of marketing communication.

The relatively moderate effect of exposure to mass communication is reflected in a comparison among studies of consumers' use of information made by Engel et al. (1968). They found that when exposure is used as criterion, mass communication is the most important source, but when effect measures are used, personal information dominates.

A large number of studies have dealt with variables that influence the way consumers respond to persuasive communication in print. Apart from the discrepancy effect and "the source effect" discussed previously, the effects of warning an individual about a possible attempt to influence his beliefs (*forewarning* effects) (McGuire and Papageorgis 1962), the effects of using fear-arousing appeals (Janis and Feshbach 1953, and McGuire 1963), the effects of giving pro- or con-arguments first (*order* effect) (Hovland 1957), and the effect of personality variables (Hovland and Janis, 1959) have been explored.

TERTIARY COMMUNICATION

The study of the way the consumer responds to tertiary communication must be approached in two steps. First, how does he decide to go to stores to inspect alternatives and obtain information? Second, how, when faced with a particular choice in the store, does the consumer go about acquiring information in his immediate environment?

Several studies throw light on consumers' use of shopping trips to acquire information. An increased propensity to shop for products that generate high perceived conflict appeared in the data from the Cox and Rich's (1964) study; and the same relationship shows up in a study by Bucklin (1966), who reports that shopping increases with the price of the product and lack of knowledge about product and store and that it decreases the more expensive the shopping becomes. In general, the extensiveness of shopping shows great variations among products. Research in connection with in-store behavior and impulse purchases is reviewed in Chapter 15.

PERSONAL COMMUNICATION

The consumer may acquire information from salesmen and other professional sources as well as from family members, neighbors, and friends. This kind of information acquisition raises two problems. First, it must be determined who initiates the interaction. Only when the consumer seeks out the personal source in an attempt to acquire information will it be considered information acquisition by the consumer. Second, the nature of the exposure must be considered. In the course of the interaction process, forced learning and information acquisition occur so closely together that it is often difficult to distinguish between the two types of exposure.

In studies of personal selling the main emphasis has been on factors influencing the final outcome of the selling situation (Ellsworth and Fraser 1953, Munn and Opdyke 1961, Farley and Swinth 1967, and Albaum 1967). No available data throw light upon who initiates the interaction. Of course the initiative can be expected to vary depending upon the type of the sales situation. The door-to-door salesman will have to take a great part of the initiative. The salesman in the store can take the initiative to varying degrees, and in the selling situation characterizing such service areas as banking, the consumer will normally take the initiative.

When the salesman is the source, he will be believed normally to have expertise, and the impact of the information will vary with the trustworthiness and intentions ascribed to him. Only in the case of such professional sources as physicians and lawyers are both expertise and trustworthiness high.

An attempt has been made to study how the interaction between the salesman and the customer proceeds. Willett and Pennington (1966) and Pennington (1968) used Bales' technique (Bales 1950) in an observational study of the interaction between customer and salesman.

Bales' technique rests upon the assumption that communications within a group can be classified as task-oriented (serving problem-solving goals) or oriented towards group maintenance (serving social and emotional goals). The approach also makes it possible to classify each act of communication depending upon who takes the initiative and whether it involves questions, answers, suggestions, or other activities.

In Willett and Pennington's (1966) study of household appliances the process of interaction is seen as a case of problem solving, in which the actors constantly provide feedback for each other. The customer engages in such activities as asking, answering, listening, and eventually interrupting or reacting to interruptions. The process can be seen as a continuous sequence of choices. In the study, the interaction process was broken down into basic units, classified according to their functions. It was found that on the average ten elements were completed per minute, and as the entire interaction was quite long (23 minutes on the average), the total process was highly complex. From the data, it appears that the information transmitted changes as the interaction moves toward completion. In early phases, the alternatives are established and clarified, whereas in later phases the information relates more closely to the evaluation of the alternatives. Furthermore, when transactions were not completed with a purchase, the consumers' total information acquisition declines towards the end of the process. Finally, when each act of interaction is classified in accordance with its content (task-oriented or socially and emotionally oriented) and with regard to who initiated the particular interaction, it appears that approximately 15% of the total number of interactions are task-oriented questions; and of these approximately four-fifths are raised by the customer.

Studies of personal influence from friends, neighbors, family members, and the like are difficult to relate to the present discussion because they rarely distinguish between forced learning and information acquisition. However, a few studies have more or less incidentally revealed who initiates the interaction. Cox (1963), reviewing older literature, and Cunningham (1966), studying three grocery products, both report that approximately 50% of the instances can be classified as exposure initiated by the receivers. Troldahl (1963) for horticultural products, Engel et al. (1966) for products for self-medication, and Feldman (1966) for choice of physician found somewhat larger percentages; but for coffee Arndt (1967b) reports a considerably smaller percentage, a finding he suggests can be ascribed to the special character of his study and to the nature of the product.

When personal information is sought out, the trustworthiness of the source and the absence of intentions to influence are important factors. Generally personal information sources will be rated high on both, and when the source to which the consumer addresses himself also is believed to have expertise, personal communication can be very efficient.

Across products there are considerable differences in the extent to which personal information sources are used. These differences have been found to relate to the consumer's interest in the issue (Cerha 1967, Myers and Robertson 1969) and to the amount of aroused conflict (risk) (Arndt 1967b and Perry and Hamm 1969).

Like mass communication, personal communication will not be analyzed further here. (Excellent sources are available in Katz and Lazarsfeld 1955 and Arndt 1967a.) Consumers' perception of personal information sources and the role of opinion leaders is discussed in Chapter 16, and in Chapter 18 aggregated effects of personal information are considered.

3. *Post-Choice Processes*

In principle, post-choice conflict can follow all choices, but it is most likely to be important when the choice has significant consequences, when it can not easily be reversed, and when the individual experiences a high degree of volition (Brehm and Cohen 1962). In consumer behavior such choices are most commonly found when a purchase is made, or to a lesser extent when consumption follows.

Reversibility is particularly important. When the choice can be reversed, the consumer can change his mind if he finds that the rejected alternative is more attractive than the one he chose. That this often occurs has been reported in many dissonance studies (see for example Brehm and Cohen 1962, and Festinger and Walster 1964). In such instances it is difficult to say whether a choice really has been made or whether the first "choice" should rather be seen as a step in the evaluation process. On the other hand, when the choice is irreversible, the consumer cannot suddenly decide that he would rather have the rejected alternative; consequently, if he is experiencing conflict after the choice, he will have to find other ways of reducing it.

What will happen after the choice depends upon whether or not conflict is present. Post-choice conflict can occur because the consumer had to decide upon an alternative that was not attractive enough (Chapter 8), but it can also occur even though a satisfactory alternative was found. Walster (1964), Festinger (1964a), and Brehm (personal communication) have found that immediately after the choice, the chosen alternative can become less attractive and rejected alternatives more attractive. At the present time very little is known about the conditions which will produce such a "regret" effect, but under some circumstances it can cause post-choice conflict of such a magnitude that some kind of cognitive processes are called for.

Post-choice processes may occur immediately after the choice, but the conflict may not be dealt with until some time later. Delay can occur if the consumer is able to neglect the conflict just after making the choice but later is reminded of it again. Just like unsolved pre-choice conflicts that are avoided, the delayed post-choice conflict can result in a motivational set that will make the conflict reappear at some later time.

Post-choice conflict-reducing strategies have been studied within dissonance theory. Dissonance is seen as a motivational state that occurs when the individual experiences cognitive conflict, and some of the most convincing studies of it have dealt with post-choice conflict. Whether dissonance really is a motivational state in its own right, and in what range of situations it can be expected to occur has been questioned by a number of authors (Jordan 1964, Maccoby and Maccoby 1961, Chapanis and Chapanis 1964, Weick 1965, Elm 1967, and Oshikawa 1969). Other authors have seen dissonance as a special case of a more general principle of balance (Osgood 1960 and Zajonc 1960). For the present discussion it is important that this line of research has dealt with a range of post-choice processes important to understanding consumer behavior and that these post-choice processes have been related to conflict in terms of problem importance and uncertainty (Greenwald, 1969).

The available evidence will be reviewed here in an attempt to answer the following questions: First, does post-choice conflict give rise to particular conflict-reducing strategies? Second, is the application of such strategies likely in consumer behavior? Third, when they occur, do they have lasting effects? Finally, when conflict-reducing strategies are applied after a choice, do they include information acquisition or are changes in salient cognitive elements more common?

Considerable evidence shows that conflict-reducing strategies are applied in post-choice situations. Early findings are reviewed by Cohen (1964); and later studies are reported by Wallace (1966), Gerard (1967a and b), Linder et al. (1967), Papageorgis (1967), Pallak and Brock (1967), and Epstein (1968). Most of these are confirmative, but occasional experiments have shown that these processes may not be as universal as originally believed. In a single study conducted under very realistic circumstances, Knox and Inkster (1968) found strong confirmation for post-choice adjustments in beliefs about chosen alternatives among gamblers on a horse track.

There can be little doubt that post-choice conflict occurs and that it can produce a number of different reactions. That such processes are common in consumer choices is evident from a number of social-psychological dissonance studies also. In this area, consumption and choices among consumer products have been a favorite object for research.

Among the studies dealing with consumption, reduction of post-choice conflict has been found by Brehm (1962) in research dealing with thirst and hunger, by Brehm (1959) in a study requiring subjects to eat liked and disliked dishes, and in a study (1960) of liked and disliked vegetables. Post-choice conflict is also reported in a study by Smith (1961) which had army reservists eating disliked food items, by Watts (1966) in a study dealing with the taste of drugs, and by Johnson (1968) in a study of smoking habits.

Purchase behavior has been studied by Brehm (1956) who used eight different products offered for choice; by Ehrlich et al. (1957), who studied dissonance-reducing strategies among new car purchasers; by Mills et al. (1959), who used a number of different consumer products; by Brehm and Cohen (1959), Brock (1963), Walster et al. (1967) and Aronson and Carl-smith (1963) who studied children's choices among toys. Similarly, Festinger (1964a) used choices among records, and Mills and Jellison (1968) in an experiment studied 22 different products. Finally, Brehm (oral communication) has conducted a number of studies in which female subjects made choices among luxury items. In all of these studies strategies aimed at reducing post-choice conflict have been found.

Also within marketing research, several studies have dealt with conflict-reducing strategies after the choice. Favorite subjects have been car purchases. Engel (1962), in an attempt to replicate the findings by Ehrlich et al. (1957), found no significant difference in readership of car advertisements among owners and non-owners of Chevrolets. Bell (1967), however, who limited his study to new car buyers, did find dissonance-reducing strategies applied. Other products studied are: men's suits (Mittelstaedt 1963); opinions towards the oil industry (Auster 1965); car batteries (Holloway 1967); cigarette smoking (Kassarjan and Cohen 1965); records (LeSciuto and Perloff 1967); brands of toothpaste, hair shampoo, and cigars (Sheth 1968b). Most of these studies have found some evidence of conflict-reducing strategies after the choice, but the findings also suggest that the phenomenon is not universal.

Even though post-choice processes do occur, they are of little interest if they have no lasting effects. The existence of such effects can be studied by testing whether subsequent choices are influenced by adjustments made after earlier choices, and whether the changes in the cognitive structure made in the post-choice process persist over time.

Several studies have used the latter approach (Aronson and Carlsmith 1966, Walster 1964, Freedman 1965, and LoSciuto and Perloff 1967). The findings have been rather inconclusive. Although the post-choice effects are not proved to persist, it cannot be concluded either that the effects deteriorate shortly after the choice is made. One major problem is that disturbing factors cannot be held constant when the application of conflict-reducing strategies is not measured until weeks or months later.

The first approach has been somewhat more successful. Studies by Brehm (1962), Brehm et al. (1964), and Zimbardo et al. (1966) dealing with thirst, hunger and pain motivation have shown that the post-choice conflict and attempts made to eliminate it do have impact on subsequent choices. Consider as an example Brehm's study of thirst: For a number of hours before the experiment the subjects voluntarily deprived themselves of water. Then varying amounts of post-choice conflict were generated by having some of the subjects commit themselves to extending the experiment for a couple of hours more. After this commitment, subjects rated how thirsty they felt they were, and they were then allowed to drink as much water as they wanted. It was found that the more post-choice conflict (dissonance) there was, the less thirsty they reported themselves to be and the less water they drank. Similar findings are reported by Brock and Grant (1963), Weick (1966), Behar (1967), Waterman and Katkin (1967), and Harris (1969).

It can be concluded that consumers do engage in post-choice processes and that the changes in the cognitive structure are significant to such an extent that they can have impact on subsequent choices.

The strategies which will be applied in attempts to reduce the post-choice conflict can be classified into two categories. The consumer can modify perceived instrumentality and value importance in such a way that conflict is reduced, or he can seek out information to help him arrive at a less conflicting cognitive structure.

When conflict is present after the choice, the salient cognitive structure is modified so that the chosen alternative becomes more attractive and the rejected alternatives less attractive. This is evident from most of the studies already mentioned. The changes that occur are likely to be those that are easiest to make, that is, cognitions closely tied in with other elements in the individual's conceptual structure are less frequently changed (Walster et al. 1967, and Burnstein 1967).

That post-choice adjustments are made does not necessarily mean that the individual also will acquire information after the choice. If the conflict can be reduced without the use of external information, there is no reason to believe that the consumer will engage in exploration and search. However, the more easily information can be obtained, the more likely it is to be attended to. Consequently, when information is easily available and the post-choice conflict cannot be easily solved, the consumer will be expected to search for information. In spite of this, studies have not been uniformly successful in showing that selective information search follows the choice.

A number of researchers have found a preference for consistent information after the choice. Several of these have already been mentioned, such as studies of car purchasers' post-choice information preferences. Other studies showing that information about the chosen alternative can be preferred after the choice are reported by Mills et al. (1959) and Rosen (1961). However, Festinger (1964a) suggests that none of these prove a preference for consistent information after the choice. It is just as likely that they reflect preferences held by subjects before the choice. It is possible that the supportive information is chosen for the very same reasons which made the subjects choose the alternative. This view gains support from experiments in which this disturbing effect is controlled (Jecker 1964 and Brock and Balloun 1967); they find only a slight preference for consistent information.

Another way of approaching the problem is to study differences in informational preferences before and after the choice. Such studies have been reported by Gerard (1967a), and by Lowe and Steiner (1968). These authors find that in the pre-choice period, people select information according to its usefulness, whereas in the post-choice situation, some preference for consistent information occurs.

In this connection a study by Mills and Jellison (1968) should be mentioned. Subjects were presented with two alternatives; in the first condition the alternatives were an el-shoe-shine kit and a considerably more attractive alternative. In the second condition, the more attractive alternative was the same as in the first condition but the el-shoe-shine kit was replaced by another alternative similar in attractiveness. Subjects were told that they could make their final choice a week later. Before leaving the session, they were asked to study an advertisement for the el-shoe-shine kit. It was found that subjects for whom the el-shoe-shine kit was not an alternative spent more time on the advertisement than subjects who had been offered the el-shoe-shine kit as an alternative. This is interpreted as evidence of avoidance of discrepant information prior to the choice, because the advertisement would favor the less attractive alternative. However, this interpretation may be questioned. As the difference between the two alternatives was considerable, it is likely that little conflict was aroused when subjects were told to make a choice; consequently, it is possible that they made their choices immediately. If so, and the choice was made before the information (the ad) was presented, then the findings indicate avoidance of discrepant information after, rather than before the choice.

The absence of a dominant preference for supportive information in the post-choice situation may have two possible explanations. Either the experiments studying information search have been such that they have not caused significant post-choice conflict, or the subjects have been able to reduce the aroused conflict without having to rely upon external information. However, most of these experiments—compared with other experiments that found dissonance reduction—are such that a considerable amount of post-choice conflict can be expected. This is also supported by several experiments in which the presence of post-choice conflict has been checked, as was done by Gerard (1967), who used a measure of blood pressure.

The following conclusion is proposed: When post-conflict is present, the consumer may seek supporting information. However, in most instances he is able to cope with the conflict without having to rely upon external information, so that selective information acquisition is the exception rather than the rule. The most common effects of the post-choice conflict are changes in the cognitive structure.

Chapter 10

PREDICTION OF CHOICE

In the present chapter choice predictions based upon the model outlined in Chapters 8 and 9 will be discussed. Depending upon the nature of the conflict aroused in the consumer, different choice principles are used. When considerable conflict is aroused, very elaborate choice principles may be applied, resulting in *rational choices*. With more moderate amounts of conflict somewhat less complex comparisons are made, resulting in *semi-complex choices*. Finally, when the aroused conflict is only minute, very simple choices, the *clue-directed choices* or *choices of reduced complexity*, are made.

1. *Environmental Problems and the Choice Process*

In Chapter 8 a relationship between perceived conflict and complexity of choice processes was illustrated (Figure 8.5). In consumer choice processes the conflict depends primarily upon the nature of the problem facing the consumer. When a consumer is choosing between two different shirts to wear, it is safe to conclude—regardless of the specific environment—that the conflict is limited. On the other hand, when the consumer is faced with the problem of whether to buy a new color television set or to send the old black-and-white set out for repair—regardless of the particular situation—the conflict may be considerable. This is not to say that the nature of the consumer's choice behavior depends entirely upon the problem he faces. In each example, different situational settings may generate somewhat larger or smaller conflicts.

191

In Chapter 8 it was argued that consumer choice processes are never very complex; yet we also make the somewhat contradictory observation that the consumer is faced with many problems more complex than he can handle in a single choice process. Seemingly, there is a discrepancy, and it is important to look at strategies that may reduce the complexity of the environmental problems. Several such strategies are available.

1. Larger problems can be broken down into minor ones, each of which is attended to separately. For example, the problem of selecting a new car may be dealt with in a number of separate choice processes, one that handles the problem of where to purchase the car, another dealing with the size of the car, a third dealing with special equipment, and so on. Furthermore, these choice processes may be spread out so that they occur over a considerable period of time.

2. Seemingly complex problems may not be so to the consumer, as he deals only with those aspects of the alternatives that are not identical. For example, in a choice between two airline companies a factor such as safety may be extremely important. But to the extent that the two companies are perceived as equally safe, the consumer can neglect this element in his choice process.

3. Problems may be complex because the number of alternatives is extremely large. In many product areas the total number of available brands, sizes, and varieties is considerable. Nevertheless, the choice process can be kept simple by eliminating alternatives.

4. When the problem is extremely complex, the consumer can reduce the complexity of the choice process by changing to less demanding evaluation procedures. For example, in a choice among different textiles, choices based upon evaluation of a number of very complicated technical aspects may be avoided simply by relying upon clues such as brand names or personal recommendations.

5. It is not always necessary for the consumer to deal with all the aspects of a problem each time he is faced with it. Often it will be possible to apply a solution arrived at in some earlier situation involving a similar problem. For example, when a consumer is faced with a new product such as freeze-dried coffee for the first time, a choice process of considerable complexity may be generated; it may even be necessary to break down the decision into several separate choice processes. However, when the same situation has occurred a number of times, it is possible that without much deliberation an earlier choice is repeated.

6. Finally, the consumer may attempt to avoid problems that are too complex. As was discussed in Chapters 6 and 8, the immediate conflict may be solved with a commitment to take the problem up again later, or by postponing the problem through the choice of an alternative involving a search for more information.

Some of these processes are illustrated by Kiesler (1966) and by Hendrick et al. (1968). In experiments disguised as product tests, subjects were offered choices among different neckties. Four conditions were applied. In the first condition, two equally attractive alternatives were offered and subjects were required to compare them along one dimension. In the second condition, two alternatives were offered again, but this time comparisons were to be made along several dimensions. In the third condition, four alternatives were compared along a single dimension, and in the fourth condition four alternatives were evaluated along several dimensions. According to reasoning very much in line with the model discussed here, the authors suggest that when the alternatives are compared along a single dimension, it will take longer to choose among the four alternatives than among the two alternatives. But when several dimensions are involved, the choice among four alternatives should be the faster, as the problem is now so complex that a shift in the choice principle will occur. The findings clearly confirm this hypothesis (Table 10.1).

TABLE 10.1

Mean choice time in four experimental conditions

Number of Dimensions	Choice Set	
	2 equal	4 equal
One	19.2	59.2
Many	42.2	32.4

Reproduced with permission from Hendrick et al., 1968, copyright by The American Psychological Association.

The four-alternative, multiple-dimension choice is made faster than either the two-alternative, multiple-dimension choice or the four-alternative, single-dimension choice.

The "learning to deal with the problem" effect is also illustrated in the study. A repetition of the choices with new alternatives but with the same subjects reduced the average decision time significantly. Moreover, the effect produced originally by the four-alternative, multiple-dimension condition was less marked in the second choice. This finding may indicate that subjects were better able to deal with the more complex problem the second time; consequently, they did not have to modify the choice procedure to the same extent.

The use of the kind of strategies discussed here makes the relationship between the environmental problem and the choice process somewhat less than straightforward. Only with relatively simple problems can it be expected that increased problem complexity results in increased choice complexity. When the complexity of the problem increases further, the described strategies may be applied; and the researcher will have to deal, not with one complex choice process, but rather with a sequence of choice processes of varying complexity.

2. *Choice Processes of Varying Complexity*

Even though extremely complex problems are simplified, the single choice process may still vary considerably in complexity (Katona 1953). At the same time evaluation procedures of different complexity are applied. Basically, alternatives are evaluated in accordance with their relationships with salient values; but, depending upon the nature of the cognitive structure, these relationships can be of several different kinds. In all cases, however, the choice principle specifies how the attractiveness of the alternatives (or the response strength) is determined.

Cognitive structures of varying complexity are shown in Figure 10.1. The most complex structures are composed of (1) the salient values, (2) the possible future outcomes, (3) the alternative actions, and (4) the beliefs that link these elements together. The beliefs are of two different kinds. Those relating future outcomes to values have much in common with perceived instrumentalities, i.e., they reflect the extent to which the future outcomes are likely to be instrumental to the aroused values. In contrast, beliefs connecting the alternatives with future outcomes reflect the individual's subjective probability that a certain event will result when a particular alternative is chosen. With a cognitive structure of this kind the comparison process will be highly complex and it may be questioned how frequently consumers actually engage in choices so complex. The choice processes which occur when conditions of this kind are aroused have been labeled *rational choices*. They are characterized by the number of alternatives, the nature of the evaluation process, and the type of cognitions which intervene between values and alternatives. There are several different models of rational choices, all of which assume highly complex cognitive processes, and they all have some similarity with normative decision models (Miller and Starr 1960, and Churchman 1961).

In less complex cognitive structures, alternatives are related directly to values, as is illustrated in Figure 10.1. Here the cognitive elements are (1) values, (2) beliefs (perceived instrumentalities), and (3) alternatives. Choice processes of this kind have been labeled *semi-complex choice processes*, and they will be dealt with in more detail.

When only little conflict is aroused, cognitive structures like the one illustrated in the lower part of Figure 10.1 may occur. Here there are no salient values, and only a single or a few concepts act as clues. Such clues owe their ability to direct the choice to their previous associations with values that otherwise might have occurred during the choice process. Choice processes of this kind, labeled *clue-guided choices*, would include an alternative chosen because of its reputation, quality judged by price, or a choice based entirely upon a recommendation by some known authority.

What choice process will occur in a particular situation depends upon the perceived conflict. With high amounts of conflict, rational choice behavior may be found, whereas small amounts of conflict will generate clue-guided choice processes. Whether the consumer perceives more or less conflict depends not only upon the nature of the problem, but also on how familiar he is with the situation. The first time a consumer is faced with a particular situation, he may apply a procedure much like the one described as rational choice; but as the situation reoccurs the choice will gradually become semi-complex, and it can finally end up as a choice process of reduced complexity.

Finally, it must be emphasized that the three prototypes introduced here,

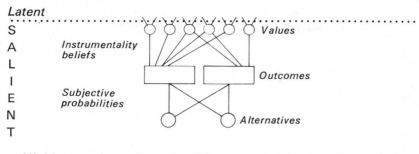

a. Highly complex salient cognitive structure (rational choice)

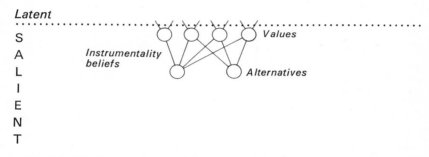

b. Semi-complex salient cognitive structure (semi-complex choice)

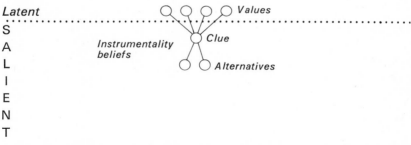

c. Simple salient cognitive structure (clue guided choice)

FIGURE 10.1. *Salient cognitive structures of varying complexity.*

rather than being the only three possibilities, represent points on a scale ranging from extremely complex to extremely simple choices. In the following, however, this scale will be exposed through a more detailed discussion of the three types.

3. *Models of Rational Choice*

1. A General Framework

Models of rational choice have ancestors in economic as well as psychological theory. Restle (1967) has suggested a general framework on which these models can be evaluated. The basic model consists of three independent systems, namely:

     1. A means-end schedule (A).
     2. An ends-goal schedule (C).
     3. A maintenance schedule (V).

The means-ends schedule rests upon the assumption that each individual's choice alternatives (means) may result in a number of different outcomes (ends). In a case with three means and three ends, the matrix, denoted (A_1) is as follows:

$$A_1 = \begin{array}{c|ccc} & E_1 & E_2 & E_3 \\ \hline M_1 & s_{11} & s_{12} & s_{13} \\ M_2 & s_{21} & s_{22} & s_{23} \\ M_3 & s_{31} & s_{32} & s_{33} \end{array}$$

The entries in the matrix represent the subjective probabilities with which the individual associates means and ends. For example, s_{11} is the subjective probability that M_1 will lead to E_1.

The end-goal matrix describes the relationships among the alternative outcomes (ends) and the individual's values (goals). Again if three possible outcomes and three relevant values are considered, the matrix, denoted C_1, is as follows:

$$C_1 = \begin{array}{c|ccc} & G_1 & G_2 & G_3 \\ \hline E_1 & b_{11} & b_{12} & b_{13} \\ E_2 & b_{21} & b_{22} & b_{23} \\ E_3 & b_{31} & b_{32} & b_{33} \end{array}$$

The entries in the matrix show to what extent the outcomes will result in satisfaction of the goals (i.e., be instrumental to the salient values).

The two matrixes A and C can be multiplied with each other. This gives a new matrix A, which Restle calls the belief-value matrix (B):[1]

---

[1] In this reduced form the matrix essentially is identical with the instrumentality-value model dealt with subsequently. In that case the means correspond to the choice alternatives;

$$B_1 = \begin{array}{c|ccc} & G_1 & G_2 & G_3 \\ \hline M_1 & a_{11} & a_{12} & a_{13} \\ M_2 & a_{21} & a_{22} & a_{23} \\ M_3 & a_{31} & a_{32} & a_{33} \end{array}$$

Here the a's can be seen as the instrumentality of the alternatives; for example, a_{11} is computed as $(s_{11} \times b_{11}) + (s_{12} \times b_{21}) + (s_{13} \times b_{31})$. However, Restle goes further, to suggest that the goals (values) gain their importance from their association with an underlying demand (need) system. This formulation is described in the maintenance schedule V. Again using an example with 3 goals and 3 underlying demands, the schedule is as follows:

$$V_1 = \begin{array}{c|ccc} & D_1 & D_2 & D_3 \\ \hline G_1 & v_{11} & v_{12} & v_{13} \\ G_2 & v_{21} & v_{22} & v_{23} \\ G_3 & v_{31} & v_{32} & v_{33} \end{array}$$

In this matrix the demands may represent such basic needs as hunger, thirst, and need for rest. The entries in the matrix represent the valences of the goal with regard to the underlying demands. These valences depend upon the history of the individual in a time interval immediately preceding the particular choice situation. If, for example, the individual has been deprived of water, the valence of dry food is reduced while the valence associated with water goes up. In this way the maintenance schedule determines which goals will become salient and how important they will be. However, it must be emphasized that, in the model here presented, salient values are functions of physiological states of the organism only, that is, they are entirely dependent upon the underlying demands and the past history with regard to their satisfaction. The possibility, which plays an important role for the present approach, that environmental factors may cause goals (values) to become salient is not discussed.

Now by multiplying the belief (B) matrix with the maintenance (V) matrix, the expected valence matrix is obtained:

$$BV = \begin{array}{c|ccc} M_1 & D_1 & D_2 & D_3 \\ \hline M_1 & d_{11} & d_{12} & d_{13} \\ M_2 & d_{21} & d_{22} & d_{23} \\ M_3 & d_{31} & d_{32} & d_{33} \end{array}$$

the goals to the salient values; and the entries in the matrix to the perceived instrumentality of the alternatives.

In this matrix the alternatives (means) are related directly to the underlying physiological needs (demands), and the entries reflect how well a particular mean will satisfy a certain demand.

It will be seen that the complexity of the cognitive processes will vary depending upon what one assumes about the nature of the choice. It may be described in terms of the BV matrix, the B matrix together with the V matrix, or in terms of the C, A, and B matrices existing independently of each other. Moreover, the choice process may be seen as even more complex since it is possible that several levels of outcomes (ends) are at work. Instead of the C matrix just described, it is possible to have two separate matrices, of which the first illustrates the relationship among immediately available ends and some more remote outcomes and the second illustrates the relationships among the more remote outcomes and the salient values (goals).

$$C_2 = \begin{array}{c|ccc} & E_1 & E_2 & E_3 \\ \hline E_4 & c_{41} & c_{42} & c_{43} \\ E_5 & c_{51} & c_{52} & c_{53} \\ E_6 & c_{61} & c_{62} & c_{63} \end{array}$$

and

$$C_3 = \begin{array}{c|ccc} & G_1 & G_2 & G_3 \\ \hline E_1 & b_{11} & b_{12} & b_{13} \\ E_2 & b_{21} & b_{22} & b_{23} \\ E_3 & b_{31} & b_{32} & b_{33} \end{array}$$

Various models of rational choice can be seen as special cases of the more general model. If it is assumed that the ends-goal matrix is deterministic, that is, that each end will result in the satisfaction of one particular goal and no goals can be satisfied by more than one outcome, then the end-goal matrix may look as follows:

$$C_4 = \begin{array}{c|ccc} & G_1 & G_2 & G_3 \\ \hline E_1 & 1 & 0 & 0 \\ E_2 & 0 & 1 & 0 \\ E_3 & 0 & 0 & 1 \end{array}$$

In this case the extent to which various possible outcomes (events) will result in satisfaction of the demands is completely determined, because in the maintenance schedule the goals can be substituted for the corresponding events. The choice process can then be illustrated as follows:

$$A_2 = \begin{array}{c|ccc} & E_1 & E_2 & E_3 \\ \hline M_1 & s_{11} & s_{12} & s_{13} \\ M_2 & s_{21} & s_{22} & s_{23} \\ M_3 & s_{31} & s_{32} & s_{33} \end{array}$$

where E_1, E_2, and E_3 are determined by:

$$C_5 = \begin{array}{c|ccc} & D_1 & D_2 & D_3 \\ \hline E_1 & t_{11} & t_{12} & t_{13} \\ E_2 & t_{21} & t_{22} & t_{23} \\ E_3 & t_{31} & t_{32} & t_{33} \end{array}$$

Here the entries in the first matrix reflect the subjective probability that various choice alternatives (means) will result in various outcomes (ends). In this version the demands can be seen as the different dimensions in a utility space, and the model thus described is the *multidimensional uncertainty utility* model.

If it is further assumed that only one demand is involved and if that is denoted *utility*, the C matrix becomes:

$$C_6 = \begin{array}{c|c} & D = U \\ \hline E_1 & t_1 \\ E_2 & t_2 \\ E_3 & t_3 \end{array}$$

and the well-known subjective expected utility model (SEU model) emerges. Findings that relate to variants of this model will be reviewed in a following section under the heading of *unidimensional uncertainty* models.

If one further assumption is added to those already introduced, the classical utility model results. If it is assumed that entries in the A_x matrix are either zero or one, as for example:

$$A_3 = \begin{array}{c|ccc} & E_1 & E_2 & E_3 \\ \hline M_1 & 1 & 0 & 0 \\ M_2 & 0 & 1 & 0 \\ M_3 & 0 & 0 & 1 \end{array}$$

the complexity of the problem is further reduced, and the choice can be described as a choice between alternatives with a known ability to satisfy the only single motivational factor that influences the choice (the utility).

In the following, this model will be reviewed under the heading of *uni-dimensional certainty* models.

If the unidimensional certainty version is modified slightly, a fourth type of choice model emerges. Assume that instead of only one demand dimension, two (or more) dimensions are involved. In the case of two alternatives and two demands the choice process can be described by the following means-end matrix:

$$
A_4 = \quad \begin{array}{c|cc} & E_1 & E_2 \\ \hline M_1 & 1 & 0 \\ M_2 & 0 & 1 \end{array}
$$

and a reduced maintenance schedule like:

$$
C_7 = \quad \begin{array}{c|cc} & D_1 & D_2 \\ \hline E_1 & t_{11} & t_{12} \\ E_2 & t_{21} & t_{22} \end{array}
$$

Because of the extreme simplicity of the means-end matrix the evaluation of the alternatives can here be described as follows:

$$
M_1 = (t_{11} \times D_1) + (t_{12} \times D_2)
$$
$$
M_2 = (t_{21} \times D_1) + (t_{22} \times D_2)
$$

This model will be dealt with under the heading of *multidimensional certainty* models. Over the last two decades different versions of these models have been tested. As excellent reviews are available, the following discussion will deal only with findings of significance for evaluating the model's ability to predict consumer choices. For detailed accounts, the reader may turn to Edwards (1954a and 1961), Arrow (1958), Clarkson (1963), Becker and McClintock (1967), and Simon (1967b).

2. The Unidimensional Certainty Choice Model

Unidimensional certainty models or models of riskless choice go several centuries back in history. A thorough analysis of their development is presented by Kauder (1965). Until the late 1940's they were the only models dealing with consumer choice behavior, and they still form a foundation for much contemporary economic thinking. They are popular for their simplicity and because they are easily incorporated into more complex economic models. However, as long as no device has been invented to measure the crucial variable, utility, the model remains useless when it comes to predicting actual choices.

   The traditional utility model rests upon a number of assumptions. In most theoretical applications of the model it is assumed that the consumer has complete information about his environment, that is, he knows all possible alternatives. Second, it is assumed that in making his choice he evaluates all the alternatives. Moreover, an important assumption relates to the rationality of the consumer. The existence of a stable utility curve is postulated, and the only changes in utility occur as a result of decreasing utility associated with additional units of each kind of product. (For example, the second overcoat will have a lower utility associated with it than the first.) The existence of the utility curve also implies that the utility of different products can be compared, that, for example, the satisfaction a consumer gets from a pair of shoes and the satisfaction he gets from a pound of roast beef can be measured along the same dimension. Second, it is assumed that the individual chooses among all the possible alternatives so as to maximize the total amount of utility he gets. That is, he will always compare all alternatives and choose the one which gives the highest utility. This implies that the consumer makes choices so that he ends up with equal marginal utilities in all product areas. One additional assumption is implied, namely, that all units of goods are so small that the consumer can adjust his consumption properly. If products are purchased in units that are too large, it would not be possible to secure equal marginal utilities in all product areas.

   In an attempt to subject the theory to empirical test, it has been shown (Edgeworth, 1881) that if indifference curves between alternative products can be established then the underlying utility functions can be derived. The indifference curve rests upon the simple assumption that consumers can judge what combinations of two products will give them equal satisfaction (utility). Consequently, it is extremely important for an evaluation of the theory to test whether such judgements can be made. Here the little evidence available will be reviewed.

   Thurstone (1931a) performed a very simple experiment. He presented a single subject with a number of choices among hats and overcoats. For example, the subject might be asked to decide whether he would choose 5 hats and 4 overcoats or 10 hats and 2 overcoats. Data was also obtained for hats and shoes and for shoes and overcoats. The main purpose of the experiment was to predict the indifference curves between shoes and overcoats based upon the indifference curves established between the two other products. The attempt was rather successful. Nevertheless, Thurstone's experiment has met with severe criticism on a number of points (Edwards, 1954a). First, the use of only one subject raises considerable doubt as to the generality of the findings. Second, the use of imaginary rather than real choices has been criticized. Finally, it has been maintained that, although it may be possible to establish indifference curves among closely related products such as overcoats, shoes, and hats, it may not be possible to do so when products are less alike, such as beef and shoes or education and a new home.

The same criticism has been raised against an experiment reported by Rousseas and Hart (1951). The authors were fairly successful in constructing indifference maps between bacon and eggs. From their experiment, however, it is not possible to conclude anything about the predictive value of the findings, as no attempts were made to predict subsequent choices.

A number of attempts have been made to modify the unidimensional certainty model so that some of these weaknesses would be overcome. Without making the same strict demands with regard to the transitivity of the preferences as the traditional formulation does, Wagner (1959) suggests a model based upon what he calls *revealed preferences*, which leads to the same conclusions as do models based upon the indifference formulation; Koo (1963) has reported positive results based upon the model. Similarly, Basmann (1956) has suggested a modification which drops the assumption that utility remains constant; and instead he suggests that the effect of advertising and other marketing variables should be dealt with in terms of changes in the marginal utility. Finally, Benson (1955) presents a model that attempts to derive utility from preference ratings.

It cannot be ruled out that the traditional utility model may reflect individual consumer choice behavior in some special situations, but it is very unlikely that it represents the kind of cognitive process consumers most commonly apply. This view will be further supported when some of the findings relating to other models of rational choice are reviewed.

A somewhat different matter is that at a highly aggregated level demand functions derived from the simple utility model have proven to be quite useful. In general, when working with broad commodity classes in sizeable market segments (see for example, Wold and Jureen 1953 and Court 1967) meaningful relationships can often be established. However, as the emphasis is shifted towards single products and brands, and from aggregated markets to individuals, difficulties arise. The problem seems to appear in several different contexts, and it will be identified again in connection with simple attitude models segmentation and studies: In marketing, aggregated predictions may often seem to be possible, even though the particular model does not work at the individual level. It is a fundamental question which still remains unanswered, whether one can have faith in predictions based on models in which the parameters have no relationship to identifiable variables at the level of the basic units with which the model works. In a sense, departure from the individual level, which characterizes the approach taken here, may be seen as an attempt to circumvent this problem.

3. Multidimensional Certainty Models

In the multidimensional certainty model, each alternative is represented by an n-tuple, where n represents the number of dimensions along which the alternative is evaluated. Such a model was prepared by Adams and Fagot (1959), who tested it in a two-dimensional case. Their findings, however, are not very encouraging, and the work has never been followed up. A somewhat more successful attempt has been reported by Jones (1959), who used preference ratings to measure utility for menu items and who was able to derive utility curves for money from comparisons between choices and ratings. It may, however, be questioned whether the preference ratings obtained do not include subjects' own estimates of the probabilities associated with getting satisfaction from the alternatives. If that is the case, the model should rather be considered a multidimensional uncertainty model.

It is a general problem with these models that predictions of choice can be made only if one alternative is superior along all utility dimensions or if some way of transforming the different dimensions into one single dimension can be found.[2] However, the first is rarely the case, and the second changes the nature of the model so that it becomes a unidimensional certainty model. The fact that it is hard to imagine situations where the certainty assumption can be realistically applied seems to severely limit the applicability of the multidimensional certainty model.

4. Unidimensional Uncertainty Models

Out of Von Neumann and Morgenstern's "Theories of Games and Economic Behavior" (1947) has grown a considerable interest in utility models. In early years the model was used for utility estimation within the framework of traditional utility models. These studies assumed that if subjects choose among alternatives related to outcomes by means of known probabilities, it is possible to estimate the utility associated with the alternatives. If, for example, a person is offered a choice between a certain $5 and a gamble where he may win $10 or nothing, it is possible to calculate the utility of the $5 if it is known at which probability of winning the $10 the individual is indifferent about the choice between the two alternatives. If, for example, a probability of winning the $10 equal to .4 makes the individual indifferent to whether he takes the $5 or the gamble, then the utility of the $5 can be calculated as follows: Ascribe 1 unit of utility to the $10 and zero units of utility to the zero dollars. Then the utility of the $5 is given by:

$$U(\$5) = 1 \times .4 + 0 \times .6 = .4$$

In these kinds of game situations different alternatives can be studied; consequently, it should be possible to estimate the utility associated with all possible goods. Several studies have been reported. Mosteller and Nogee (1951) studied utility for money, and within the experimental situation they were able to establish rather meaningful utility curves.[3] Experiments in line

[2] A third possibility would be to have subjects satisficing along the various dimensions, a possibility which is explored in a subsequent section.

[3] In this study it was also found that the choice time varied systematically with the nature of the choice. When one of the alternatives was either very good or very poor, the choice was easily made, whereas instances where the two alternatives were more alike took more time. This agrees with the position taken in previous chapters that an increasing amount of conflict will result in increasing choice time.

with theirs are reported by Davidson et al. (1957) and by Coombs and Komorita (1958); and other findings are reviewed by Edwards (1961).

The utility approach has also been used in a marketing content by Herrmann and Stewart (1957) and by Larzelere et al. (1965). The latter report findings from an experiment in which subjects were offered a choice between a branded turkey and an unbranded turkey with a certain cash prize added to it. From this study reasonable utility curves emerged, but unfortunately no attempt was made to predict actual choices based upon the estimated utilities, so that it is hard to judge the validity of the findings. Similarly, based upon the expected utility model, Pashigian et al. (1966) and Gould (1969) report contradictory findings concerning predictions of consumers' selection of an optimal deductible amount for a given insurance policy.

Out of the work with Von Neumann and Morgenstern's game, modified models of the unidimensional uncertainty type have emerged. Several such variants have been discussed (Georgescu-Roegen 1954, Suppes 1956, Quandt 1956, Luce 1959b, and Ramond 1964). Here we are primarily concerned with Edwards' (1962) subjective expected utility (SEU) model. The usefulness of the SEU model depends upon whether the utility and the subjective probabilities can be estimated. Whether utility can be determined depends upon the extent to which subjects make consistent choices. Consequently, by studying transitivity of choices, the validity of the assumption of an underlying stable unidimensional utility function can be checked.[4] A number of studies have attempted to do so and they have found varying amounts of consistency. Papandreou (1957), in a study offering subjects imaginative choices among tickets for recreational activities such as baseball games, football games, and concerts, found intransitivity in approximately 5% of the cases. Similarly Davidson and Marschak (1959) also found that the number of intransitive choices was smaller than one would expect by chance. In the same way Davis (1958) in a replication of an original experiment by Edwards (1953) found less intransitivity than Edwards originally did, a finding that he suggests may be explained by the fact that he obtained all his observations in the same experimental session, whereas Edwards obtained his observations in repeated sessions. Davis' interpretation points to situational influence on choice behavior: When the situation remains stable, subjects behave more consistently than when faced with different situations.

Less positive results are reported by Morrison (1963), Tversky (1969), and Dolbear and Lave (1967). The last found considerable inconsistency in 2,600 choices among lottery tickets, and they suggest that the subjects had difficulty perceiving their own utility functions and consequently made wrong decisions. Moreover, they found that the inconsistency varied with the difference between the alternatives, with the signs of the pay-off (whether subjects would win or lose), with the wealth of the subjects, and with the order of the choices.

---

[4] The transitivity assumption is crucial for the unidimensional certainty model as well. Consequently, the following discussion throws further light on these models also.

In an attempt to overcome problems associated with a less-than-perfect transitivity, the concept of stochastic transitivity has been introduced. As long as stochastic transitivity exists, it is possible to operate with stochastic versions of the unidimensional utility models. Stochastic transitivity may be either *weak* or *strong*. Strong stochastic transitivity implies that if the probability of preferring A to B and B to C are both equal to or greater than .5, then A should also be preferred to C with a probability greater than or equal to the largest of the other two probabilities. The weak stochastic transitivity only implies that A should be preferred to C with a probability larger than .5. In most studies at least the weak assumption has been found to hold. But as Dolbear and Lave (1967) argue, "The decision maker implicit in most stochastic models is a man with perfectly definite and perfectly well-known preferences. This decision maker does make errors at random, but there is no learning, no change in his basic preferences" (p. 24). Consequently, to the extent that systematic variations can be found in the occurrence of intransitivity, one should doubt the stability of utility curves. Such systematic variations are reported by Dolbear and Lave themselves and by Tversky (1969). The *learning effect* in particular is important. To the extent that subjects improve their behavior in repeated choice situations, the assumption of a stable underlying utility function does not hold. But such a learning effect is well documented. It appears in Dolbear and Lave's study, it is reported by Davidson and Marschak (1959), and it is reported by Rapaport (1966 and 1967a).

Another problem with the subjective expected utility model relates to the subjective probabilities. Early applications of the model have revealed that individuals' subjective probabilities are not identical with those that can be observed objectively. In the Von Neumann–Morgenstern game, one cannot assume that subjects expected the various outcomes with a probability identical to that stated in the description of the alternative (Edwards 1954b). Of course, the subjective probabilities can be estimated based on the Von Neumann–Morgenstern game if the utilities are known, or the utilities can be estimated if the subjective probabilities are known, but to attempt to estimate both from the same game situation is meaningless. Consequently, it is necessary to find ways in which either the utility or the subjective probability can be estimated outside the game situation. That this might be possible has been discussed by Stevens (1959), who suggests utility estimates based upon paired comparisons and who also proposes that utility may be estimated by means of physiological scaling methods normally used in experiments with perceptual thresholds.

Most of the studies dealing directly with the subjective expected utility model are reviewed by Becker and McClintock (1967), who conclude, "In general however, the data have shown that people often fluctuate in their response to the same stimulus (as currently defined by these models) even when there are no obvious changes in their information or resources" (p. 261).

Only Brim et al. (1962) have tried to predict the outcomes of choice situations by independent estimates of subjective probabilities and utility. In their study of choice behavior related to child rearing, they obtained ratings of the probabilities with which subjects associated success with the various strategies. Furthermore, the importance subjects ascribed to finding a right solution was rated for different situations. Using these ratings, it was possible to compute the subjective expected utility associated with each of the choice alternatives, and this enabled the authors to predict, although not perfectly, the strategies that were chosen. Several aspects of this experiment are worth noting. First, the choice problems facing the subjects were fairly complex and were probably more involving than most consumer choice processes. (For example, one of the situations asked parents what they would do if their child were cheating in school.) The relative success of the predictions should be evaluated against this background. It is likely that people really think about such important choice problems in terms of possible actions, the likelihood of future outcomes, and the desirability of these outcomes.

5. Multidimensional Uncertainty Models

In the multidimensional uncertainty model each alternative may result in two or more different events, and in turn these events satisfy different needs (utility dimensions). Like the multidimensional certainty model, these models require a mechanism to transform the different utility dimensions into a single dimension. Such transformations have been discussed within normative decision theory (Ackoff 1962) and in connection with consumer behavior (Nehnevajsa, 1963). However, no experimental studies of human decision-making have tested whether such transformations are made. Future research will have to show if and how this occurs in more complex choices. The SEU model can be said to rest upon such a transformation, but the problems involved are rarely discussed. Normally it is assumed that each event can be evaluated along one and the same dimension.

In spite of the evidence, it is possible that human choice behavior under some circumstances may approach the kind of choice behavior described in models of rational choice. Such choice processes are expected to occur when the perceived conflict is high.

4. *Semi-complex Choice Processes*

1. Attractiveness, Choice, and Utility

In semi-complex choice processes the relationship between alternatives is simpler, as alternatives are assocated directly with values. Until recently only little has been done to reveal the underlying cognitive structure in such choice processes. A few relevant approaches will be discussed here, and a fuller discussion will be found in Chapters 11–13.

In semi-complex choice processes the choice prediction can be approached in different ways. The overall evaluation of the alternatives may be studied in terms of attitudes towards, or preferences for the alternatives. Alternatively, attractiveness can be dealt with in terms of the salient values and their relationships with the alternatives; or the response strength associated with an alternative can be studied by means of various indirect approaches. Finally, the choice can be explained in terms of satisficing behavior. All of these approaches rely on different kinds of attractiveness or response strength variables. It is important to point out the relationship between these variables and the utility variable that appears in models of rational choice.

In traditional utility theory the individual knows all possible choice alternatives and is certain about his evaluation of them, that is, each possible alternative has a fixed *utility*. The attractiveness, however, depends completely upon the aroused values and the way the alternative is related to them. Only when the same—unchanged—values and relationships always occur in the cognitive structure will the attractiveness remain fixed. But even in similar choice situations, values and relationships may be different, and consequently the attractiveness rarely remains stable. Moreover, although the individual is supposed to be certain about the utility he will gain from choosing a certain alternative, the same is not true with attractiveness. Relationships among alternatives and salient values will vary in strength, reflecting variations in the degree to which the individual believes in the relationships. Finally, by its very nature, utility is a unidimensional concept, whereas attractiveness is an intervening variable that in a specified way reflects the evaluation of alternatives along a number of dimensions.

In spite of these differences, the recent modifications of utility models have reduced the discrepancy between the utility approach and the semi-complex choice models discussed here. That the three types of choice models dealt with here represent points on a continuum, ranging from extremely complex to very simple choices, also suggests that the difference is a matter of degree rather than inherent in the structure of the models. Also it should be recalled that the semi-complex choice models can be seen as special cases of the more general model underlying models of rational choice (p. 261).

2. Measuring Attractiveness; Preferences

In spite of the common use of response strength and other variables similar to attractiveness, only few attempts to measure such variables have been made. Most work has dealt with preference ratings or attitudes toward the alternatives. How well these measurements reflect the attractiveness of the alternatives can be judged from their ability to predict the outcomes of

choices. Most studies attempting to validate attitude and preference measures
have correlated them with measures of behavior (see for example, Banks
1950, Udell 1965, Achenbaum 1966, and Myers 1967) and many work at a
highly aggregated level (for a review see Day, 1970). Many such studies
report high correlation between ownership of a particular product and
attitudes towards that product, or between purchases of a product and
preference for that product. However, these studies are of little value when it
comes to answering the question of whether preference measures can predict
the outcome of individual choices. The major problem is that it is not known
whether the reported correlation reflects adjustments in preferences made
as a result of the choices, or whether the behavior was really chosen because
the preference existed before the choice process occurred. Somewhat more
confidence can be placed in studies where preferences have been measured
before any action took place. For example Stappel (1968) and Marder
(1967) have reported that attitudes towards new durable products are
significantly related to subsequent purchases. However, their study's level of
aggregation is high.

It is still questionable whether a change in attitudes is a necessary and
sufficient condition for a purchase to be made. To test an experimental design
like the following is required.

EXPERIMENTAL GROUP	CONTROL GROUP
1. Measurement of behavior	1. Measurement of behavior
2. Measurement of attitude	2. Measurement of attitude
3. Manipulation of attitude	3. NO manipulation of attitude
4. Measurement of attitude (before new behavior is possible)	4. Measurement of attitude (before new behavior is possible)
5. Measurement of behavior	5. Measurement of behavior

In this very complex experimental design, major problems are associated
with the repeated measures of behavior and attitudes, both of which are
likely to introduce bias into the experiment. Festinger (1964b) in a review of
the literature found only four studies of this kind, and from them he concludes that it is not at all established that behavioral change is functionally
related to attitude change. Moreover, Cohen (1964), Rokeach (1967), and
Bauer (1968) have made the same observations, and findings reported by
Appel (1966) agree. He conducted an elaborate field study of attitudes as a
function of different advertising campaigns and of behavior as a function of
the emerging attitudes. He was unable to establish any firm relationship
between attitudes and behavior, a result which Clement (1967) also obtains
in a similar study of dairy products and which is further supported by Haskins
(1964), Palda (1966), and Axelrod (1968). Axelrod tested the sensitivity,
stability, and predictive power of ten different preference, awareness,
attitude, and similar scales. Of particular interest are his findings concerning
the ability of the preference scales to predict changes in behavior (brand
switching). Axelrod reports that although measures obtained with a constant
sum scale and a *forced switching* measure did correlate with brand-switching

behavior, none of them were nearly so good predictors as a simple measure of brand awareness. More confirming evidence has been reported. Using aggregated data on brand share, attitude, and awareness, Assael and Day (1968) report somewhat more positive results for analgesics, deodorants, and instant coffee, and Day (1970) provides some insight into the conditions under which such measures may be applicable. By controlling disturbing environmental conditions such as deals and income constraints, he is able to improve predictions based upon simple attitude measures significantly. He also finds simple attitude measures to be better predictors for nondurable than for durable products, an observation that may be explained in terms of the longer purchase cycles characterizing durable products and the consequently greater opportunity for disturbing factors. Similarly, among durable products he finds that attitude measures perform better for minor than for major products.

Altogether the available evidence suggests that preference measures as predictors of behavior should be applied with care. Such measurements are not always worthless; future improvements in rating scales may overcome some of the present shortcomings, and this kind of prediction is more useful in some product areas than in others. For the time being, however, it is advisable to consider the total salient cognitive structure when trying to predict the outcome of choice processes, a position further strengthened when practical applications are also considered. Even though simple attitude measures may predict quite well in some product classes, they give few or no clues as to what marketing strategies might be successful in attempts to change them.

3. Measuring Attractiveness: Values and Instrumentalities

If, in a conflict situation, the importance of the salient values and the perceived instrumentalities of the alternatives are known, it is possible to predict the choice of response. How the two sets of variables interact may be illustrated by considering the following example: Picture a consumer faced with his regular brand and the same brand at a reduced price. If these are the only two alternatives, the choice is easily predicted. The consumer will choose the price offer, and the choice process can be interpreted as follows: Only one value—namely, a price value—influences the decision, and the premium offer is perceived as more instrumental to this value than the brand at the regular price. In this example it is important that only a single value is salient. As long as this is the case, the choice is simple. What is required for a choice to be made is (1) that the salient value has some importance, and (2) that the alternatives differ in instrumentality.

When more values are salient, the process is more complicated. The choice will then be governed by the differences in importance of the values and the differences in perceived instrumentalities. However, taken separately, each value operates much as just described.

Generally, when more values are salient, value importance and perceived instrumentality influence the choice as follows: Given the perceived instrumentality of the alternatives with regard to a salient value, the higher the importance of the value, the more likely it is that the alternative will be chosen that is most instrumental to that value. On the other hand, given that a salient value is important, the more instrumental an alternative is to this value, the more likely it is that this alternative will be chosen. This principle can be formulated in the following expression:[5]

$$A_i = \sum_{j=1}^{m} V_j I_{ji} \qquad (10.\text{I})$$

where A_i is the overall attractiveness of alternative i, V_j the value importance of the jth value, I_{ji} the perceived instrumentality of alternative i with regard to value j, and m the number of salient values. In this expression the sign of $V_j I_{ji}$ depends on the signs of V_j and I_{ji}. If they are both positive, the sign of the combined expression is also positive, as it is if they both are negative. If the value importance and the perceived instrumentality have opposite signs, the combined expression is negative. Altogether, the larger the A-measure, the more attractive the alternative in question, and if A-measures are computed for all the alternatives, the one with the highest A-measure will be chosen.[6] Especially if only two alternatives are considered, the difference between the two attractiveness scores (A_d) may be rewritten as follows:

$$A_d = A_1 - A_2 = \sum_{j=1}^{m} V_j I_{j1} - \sum_{j=1}^{m} V_j I_{j2} = \sum_{j=1}^{m} V_j (I_{j1} - I_{j2}) \qquad (10.\text{II})$$

This formulation has the advantage of making it possible to deal with the differences in perceived instrumentality instead of the absolute instrumentality of each of the alternatives. In many instances it will make applications easier.

Other authors have dealt with evaluation of alternatives along the lines suggested in Equation (10.I). The research tradition centered around Rosenberg's work (1956) uses an essentially identical relationship. However, until recently it has been applied only to computation of attitudes based on their related values (see for example Constatinoble, 1967). Similarly, Fishbein's (1965 and 1966) belief attitude model implies an equation like Equation (10.I), and Insko and Schopler (1967) in their analyses of affective-cognitive-conative consistency suggest that the overall evaluation of an alternative is a function of instrumentality and value importance.

Within marketing theory Swedish researchers have touched upon functional relationships of the type applied here. Ölander (1964) suggests an attractiveness score that can be separated into an "expected satisfaction from

---

[5] Other functional relationships could be suggested. Some of these will be discussed in the following.

[6] Strictly speaking, this applies only when positive conflict is present. However, as discussed in Chapter 8, negative conflict can often be reversed by the introduction of additional alternatives.

consumption" dimension and a "probability of obtaining the satisfaction" dimension. An application of a simplified version of this model is discussed in connection with price concepts in Chapter 16. Moreover, Nowak et al. (1966), Lundberg and Hulten (1967), and Seipel (1967) have discussed similar models in connection with consumers' reactions to mass communication. The same authors also present findings supporting the predictive power of these models.

Several authors have discussed functional relationships resembling Equation (10.I) (Andreasen 1965, Hansen 1967b, Kassarjian 1968, and Kotler 1968). Kotler's formulation is particularly interesting. In discussing a model by which brand-purchase probabilities are computed, he suggests that the probabilities depend upon: "(a) how attractive the relative brand characteristics are; and (b) how much weight the buyer attaches to the different characteristics."

Until recently only a few attempts to experimentally apply a measure like Equation (10.I) have been reported: Looking for variables which can predict whether a consumer will be a buyer of a new product or not, Pessemier et al. (1967) computed a preference score like (10.I), which turned out to be one of the most predictive variables in the study. Similarly, Rowan (1967) discusses an attractiveness measure used in connection with predictions of newspaper choices; and Tucker (1965) has reported a study testing which of the following two expressions would best predict choices:

$$\frac{P_1 \times R_1}{E_1} \underset{<}{>} \frac{P_2 \times R_2}{E_2}$$

or

$$(P_1 \times R_1) - E_1 \underset{<}{>} (P_2 \times R_2) - E_2 \qquad (10.\text{III})$$

Here the R's are the rewards associated with the alternatives, the P's are the (objective) probabilities associated with obtaining the reward, and the B's are the physical efforts required to obtain the reward. Both formulations are similar to (10.II). The reward can be seen as corresponding to the total value importance, and the probability of reward to the perceived instrumentality associated with it. Similarly, effort can be separated into a value and an instrumentality term.

In his experiment, Tucker manipulated the probability of reward and the effort needed to obtain the reward. His experimental situation is somewhat special (each subject was required to pull 15- to 60-pound handles more than 100 times), and the findings must be evaluated with this in mind. Basically Tucker found that both formulations predicted reasonably well, but that in the particular experimental conditions, the influence of the probability of reward is considerably more important than the influence of the effort. Whether this is ascribable to low importance associated with the effort or with low instrumentality (unpleasantness of effort) cannot be judged from the published findings. However, it is noteworthy that from his results Tucker suggests a choice model that substitutes a subjective measure of the probability of reward and a subjective measure of the importance of the reward for the actual probability and the actual rewards.

Since the experiments discussed in Chapters 11-13 were made, a couple of studies have been reported in which semi-complex choices have been approached much as suggested in (10.I) and (10.II). Though this research was not familiar to the author at the time of the experiments, it will be reviewed here.

Bither and Miller (1969) obtained measurements of value importance and perceived instrumentality of three automobile brands, with 98 students as subjects. They used Equation (10.I) to compute the attractiveness of the alternatives, and with this measurement they were able to make significant predictions of preferences for all the tested brands. Moreover, they found that both values and instrumentalities taken alone give significant predictions. A similar approach was used by Bass and Talarzyk (1969), who attempted also to predict preference rankings. Data on brands of frozen orange juice, mouthwash, toothpaste, toilet tissue, lipstick, and brassieres were obtained from a national sample with useable responses from approximately 1000 housewives in each product category. Significant predictions were made by using these data. The latter two studies differ in the samples used, the products studied, the types of values dealt with, and the rating techniques applied. It is noteworthy that they both provide highly significant findings.

4. Measuring Attractiveness: Maximizing or Satisficing?

So far it has been assumed that alternatives are compared along a single dimension, namely, the attractiveness of the alternatives. It should be emphasized that this attractiveness is not necessarily stable. From the previous discussion it follows that the attractiveness of an alternative can vary with the situation, and the attractiveness may vary in the course of the choice process. However, attractiveness and similar variables rest upon the assumption that some transformation of the different evaluative dimensions occurs. As with multidimensional models of rational choice, it is possible that consumers do not compare alternatives along a single dimension, but according to the following interpretation: For each salient value a certain acceptable region exists. As long as an alternative is sufficiently instrumental to the value in question (i.e., falls within its acceptable region), it is acceptable with regard to that particular value. Furthermore, when an alternative falls within the acceptable regions of all salient values then it will be chosen (Hansen 1967a). A choice principle of this kind implies that consumers are satisficing along as many dimensions as there are salient values. Such a satisficing procedure would mean that alternatives are examined until one has been found that is acceptable with regard to all salient values. These models relate to aspiration-level theories (Chapter 5), and they are discussed by Simon (1955 and 1956), March and Simon (1968), Cyert and March

(1963) and Starbuck (1963). However, most of the little evidence available relates to organizational behavior, about which Simon (1967b) concludes "there is some empirical evidence that business goals are in fact stated in satisficing terms" (p. 11).

The few studies that present data relevant to consumer behavior do not provide any clearcut conclusions; Dickins et al. (1954) conducted a study analyzing choices of menu items. In some instances they found that a single item could cause a whole menu to be chosen or rejected in spite of the fact that other menu alternatives were totally more attractive. This finding would indicate a satisficing choice principle, but the fact that the opposite effect occurred in a considerable number of cases makes it impossible to draw any firm conclusion. Similarly, Brim et al. (1962) were not able to improve their predictions by introducing a satisficing assumption, whereas Kerby (1969) found that in evaluating products consumers normally do not generalize several quality aspects into a single dimension. The evidence is inconclusive, but considering the extent to which "attractiveness-like" variables have successfully predicted choice behavior, it seems reasonable to start out assuming the existence of such a variable.

5. Measuring Attractiveness: Indirect Approaches

Before value importance and perceived instrumentality can be measured, the researcher must have some hypotheses regarding the values aroused in the choice processes. This requirement often constitutes a problem; consequently, approaches where this requirement is weakened have gained interest.

When behavioral or attitude data are available from a not-too-heterogeneous group of consumers, factor analysis may reveal a limited number of underlying value dimensions. This approach is particularly helpful when significant intercorrelations are thought to exist among the original variables. Several such studies have been reported; for example, when Mukherjee (1965) had consumers rate coffee along 14 different dimensions such as "hearty flavor" and "expensive taste", he was able to identify a limited number of underlying value dimensions. Similar attempts are reported by Banks (1967) and by Swanson (1967a and b), who searched for factors underlying differences in exposure to television and magazines, and by Becknell and Maher (1962), Farley (1968), and Myers and Nicosia (1968), who identified important factors in supermarket choices. Finally, Stoietzel (1961) analyzed French consumers' liquor preferences, and Reynolds and Wofford (1966) identified value factors underlying air-travel attitudes.

These approaches may use data reflecting consumers' perception of the alternatives, or they may rely upon behavioral, value, or attitude data. In all instances a number of underlying value dimensions emerge. However, the approach rests upon several assumptions. First, the relationship among the underlying values is normally assumed to be linear. Second, all the consumers in the study are assumed to rely upon the same values. The validity of the latter assumption in particular is relatively unexplored, and even though these assumptions may be valid, it is still difficult to interpret the meaning of the factors uncovered.

So far, no factor analytical studies have been reported in which the revealed value dimensions have been applied to choice predictions, nor have they been studied in relation to the perceived instrumentality of the alternatives.

As a substitute for factor analysis, latent structure analysis has been proposed. The approach was introduced by Lazarsfeld (1954), and a few applications to marketing problems have been reported (Myers and Nicosia 1967 and 1968). Also, a recently developed discrete measurement model of finite order (Andersen 1966) may prove useful in attempts to quantify simultaneously the effects of situational and individual differences on value importance. So far, however, none of these attempts have been applied to predict outcomes of choices.

Another approach starts in the consumers' perception of the alternatives. If the consumers' choices and their perception of the alternatives are known, it is possible to explain the choices in terms of the perceived attributes of the alternatives, the approach taken in a study reported by Sheth (1969). From data obtained from a panel of housewives, instrumentality beliefs about two brands of a food product were obtained. Value importance was not measured; rather, the relative importance of the different belief dimensions were established through correlation analysis. High correlations between beliefs and preferences were obtained, whereas somewhat smaller (although significant) correlations with subsequent purchases were reported, which suggests that the lack of information about value importance is unfortunate.

A somewhat similar study is reported by Perry (1969). For brands of dog food, perceived instrumentality was measured along ten dimensions, and from the same consumers information about recall, use of brand, and repurchase intentions was obtained. Using the latter as dependent variables, discriminant analyses were conducted and significant predictions made. Once again, however, there is no information included about value importance; and moreover, the causal relationships between the behavior and the instrumentality measures are not clear, as no information about subsequent purchases was obtained.

Recently a number of sources studied the consumer's perception of alternatives by means of nonmetric multidimensional scaling based upon similarities data (Green et al. 1968, Neidell 1969, and Beals et al. 1968). The underlying idea is simple. From a set of alternatives, the perceived similarity between each possible pair of alternatives is measured (for example, by asking subjects to rate how "alike" they perceive each pair of alternatives to be). These measures can be quite reliable when consumers' perception of alternatives is relatively homogeneous, which was found to be the case in some studies (Seffltre 1968 and Green and Carmone 1969); and if the number of dimensions can be specified in advance or if requirements as to goodness of fit can be established, it is possible from these data to estimate the perceptual space for both individuals and groups of respondents. Several procedures are available for this purpose (Shepard 1963, Kruskal 1964, and McGee 1966). As an example of a perceptual space, Figure 10.2 shows the perception of toothpaste brands along two dimensions. Such perceptual maps show how consumers perceive a set of alternatives. The importance of their perceptual differences for choices among the alternatives is introduced when the perceptual map is derived from preference data, as can be done by means of different unfolding models (Young and Torgerson 1967, Carroll and Chang 1967, and Kruskal 1968). In such a map it is possible to estimate the consumer's (or the group of consumers') ideal point (Coombs 1964), or a vector indicating the direction of the ideal point (Tucker and Messick 1963).[7] When maps derived in this way are compared with maps based upon similarities data, one important conclusion emerges. It seems that the relative importance of the attribute dimensions must be taken into account when the unfolded map is transformed to the similarity map. Green and Carmone (1969) write:

> Stimulus configurations obtained from the analysis of direct similarities judgements will not generally agree with the unfolded stimulus configuration obtained from preference data alone. Instead what seems to result is a transformed transfiguration that reflects DIFFERENTIAL WEIGHTING of the perceptual dimensions. (p. 338)

How this approach can be used in studies of consumer choices is shown by Neidell and Teach (1969). For brands of toothpaste they used Coombs' (1964) unfolding model in conjunction with Young and Torgerson's (1967) multidimensional scaling analysis. With this approach the authors were able to locate the six studied brands in a two-dimensional space, where the axes can be seen as value dimensions. Their aggregated data are illustrated in Figure 10.2, where the "ideal brand" is plotted also. In this diagram the distance from the actual brands to the ideal brand significantly predicts the market shares of the brands.

It is noteworthy that this approach does not require that the value-dimensions be identified in advance. Moreover, techniques are available not only to provide the axis, but also to give the weights to be assigned to the axis corresponding to the value importance. However, in its simple form the procedure rests upon the highly questionable assumption that practically all consumers rely upon the same values in all situations; and several

---

[7] Such a configuration can be seen as a multidimensional utility space with the ideal point identifying the maximum of the utility surface. It could therefore be argued that these models should be seen as a kind of multidimensional model of rational choice. The proper placement of the models, however, depends entirely on the assumptions as to the type of underlying cognitive processes. Practically no information is available on this, but judged from the type of issues which have been studied, it seems that the models apply well to choices of the semi-complex type.

studies have suggested that important intra-individual differences exist (Neidell and Teach 1969, and Green and Morris 1969). Moreover, as with factor analysis the interpretation of the axis may pose serious problems;

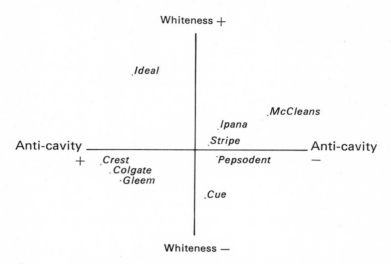

FIGURE 10.2.   A perceptual map for 6 brands of toothpaste. (Reproduced from Neidell and Teach, 1969, with the permission from The American Marketing Association.)

in addition the determination of the number of dimensions to apply can be quite arbitrary. Nevertheless, this approach may in the future develop into a valuable tool for analyzing the cognitive structures underlying choices.[8]

5. *Clue-guided Choice Processes*

Reduced-choice processes are extremely simple. Only one or a few concepts are salient at the time of the choice, and they are rarely important in themselves. Rather, they act as clues, gaining their ability to guide choices from previous experiences in which the alternatives have been related to both the clue and some underlying values. For example, in earlier choice processes alternatives associated with high quality may also have been related to high price. As similar choice processes reappear, the quality concept need not become salient, rather the choice is made with price as an indicator of quality. In this way, semi-complex choice processes gradually change to

[8] In a later study (Hansen and Balland, 1971) the hypothesis has been tested that dimensions revealed by nonmetric multidimensional scaling are identical with the more important among the salient value dimensions. The results confirm the hypothesis and Green (personal communication) has conducted studies which also support the proposition.

reduced-choice processes and may remain so as long as new choice processsses are not generated in which the perceived conflict is large enough to make a semi-complex choice process reappear. Factors which may cause such an increase in conflict are:

1. New, surprising, and complex elements in the situation in which the particular choice process occurs can generate sufficient arousal to produce a semi-complex choice process. Such new stimulation could, for example, be the observation of a new brand close to the one normally picked, or a price change of some significance.

2. The consumer may undergo experiences that oppose his previously established relationship between the clue and the underlying more important value concepts. When such a change in expectations occurs, it can result in an increased amount of arousal the next time the consumer is confronted with the particular choice process.

3. The cognitive structure represented by the clue and the alternatives may not be able to arouse the amount of conflict required to maintain an optimal level of arousal. In that case, the consumer will begin to explore the situation and a more conflicting choice process is likely to be generated, as the exploration will produce more alternatives and values.

In clue-guided choices, previous experiences with the same or similar conflicts are crucial, which suggests that studies of sequential decision making may improve our understanding of this kind of problem solving. Unfortunately research in this area is scarce and not easily applied to consumer behavior. However, in these studies it is a common observation that repeated choices result in reduced conflict (Schill 1966), and some researchers have studied the extent to which learning and improved performance result. For example, Edwards (1956) observed some learning in an experiment in which subjects gambled for prices.

Peterson and Beach (1967), after reviewing the literature on sequential decision-making, conclude that humans may be fairly good at estimating expected probabilities intuitively; and with a sequential sampling model, Becker (1958) was partially successful in predicting female undergraduates' information purchases in a dynamic decision-making task. However, Cangelosi and March (1966) found college professors to be only slightly successful in building models of binary choices, and Rapoport (1967b) as well as Becker (1958) found considerable deviation from "rational" behavior. Additional studies may give further insight into simple choice processes of the type dealt with here. The few attempts so far made to study consumer behavior as sequential decision making are discussed in connection with loyalty (Chapter 15). The evidence relating to clue-guided choices concerning the functioning of specific clues will be reviewed in Chapter 16.

6. *Attractiveness Factors*

1. Averaging versus adding

It is assumed that the total attractiveness is a simple additive function of the values salient in the choice situation. Rather than a sum of all the values, an averaging function like (9.IV) could be applied.

$$A_i = \sum_{j=1}^{m} \frac{V_j I_{ji}}{m} \qquad (10.IV)$$

Results of the methods may differ. Consider the following example: An alternative is very positively evaluated along two value dimensions; then a third value, which is positive but somewhat less positive than the first two, is added. If (10.I) is applied, the attractiveness will increase. In accordance with the averaging hypothesis (10.IV), however, the third, less important value will decrease the total attractiveness of the alternative.

When alternatives are compared along the same value dimensions, it makes no difference whether an additive or an averaging model is used. However, when alternatives are evaluated along different value dimensions, the choice of either (10.I) or (10.IV) is crucial. Such alternatives may appear in choice processes in which alternatives from different product areas are compared, as for example, "buying a new car" compared with "spending a large amount of money on a vacation." Similarly, when the attractiveness of continued deliberation and exploration is compared with other choice alternatives, it may be crucial whether averaging or adding is assumed.

This issue has never been raised explicitly in connection with consumer choice behavior, but it is important within attitude theory. Traditional formulations such as in Osgood et al. (1957) and Heider (1958) assume an averaging function (Chapter 6), by which the evaluation of an attitude object is seen as an average of the evaluation of two or more related objects. Recent formulations, however, have suggested an additive relationship (Triandis and Fishbein 1963, Fishbein and Hunter 1964, Anderson and Fishbein 1965, Anderson 1965, and Lampel and Anderson 1968). These authors present considerable evidence in favor of the additivity assumption. For example, Fishbein and Hunter (1964) show that when subjects are asked to evaluate a hypothetical character then the total evaluation increases almost proportionately with the amount of positive information given about the character.

Significant findings favoring the additivity assumption are also presented by Thurstone and Jones (1959). After having subjects evaluate single gift items such as brief cases, record players, fountain pens, desk lamps, and dictionaries, they asked the same subjects to evaluate various combinations of two items, in an attempt to estimate a true zero point for the applied rating scales. Of particular interest for the present discussion is the fact that the rating of the combined alternatives came out strongly in favor of the additivity assumption. Similarly, Ölander (1967) in his price experiment (Chapter 18) found that "subjects tend to combine the aspects of sacrifice and attractiveness in an additive way" (p. 46).

Later studies, however, raise some doubt as to the generality of the additivity assumption. Rosnow and Arms (1968), Brewer (1968), Wyer and Dermer (1968), and Schmidt (1969) all found that an additive model works better than an averaging model, but their findings also suggest that the number of elements in the cognitive structure has an effect separate from the composite effect of the single elements.

Altogether the additive model seems to give better predictions, and for the present time work with it is warranted. Future research may suggest how this simpler formulation will have to be modified.

2. The Number of Salient Values

The complexity of the salient cognitive structure is shown in the choice process by the number of salient values and alternatives. It is important, as the number of cognitive elements may be so large as to make application of the model very complicated, if not impossible.

The maximum number of values and alternatives which can enter into a choice process depends upon the data-processing capabilities of the human brain. There is some evidence that this capacity is quite limited. Miller (1956), after reviewing a considerable number of studies, suggests that humans normally only deal with "seven, plus-or-minus two" informational units at a time. He suggests that this limitation is explained by the individual's limited ability to receive and process information and to simultaneously make larger amounts of information available for immediate memory. Miller's suggestion has been supported by several later findings (see Kaplan 1966).

Furthermore, studies of consumer choice behavior have also suggested that in a choice process the number of salient values and alternatives is limited. Katona and Mueller (1954) in their study of purchasing processes for durable products found that one third of the consumers considered only the brand they eventually purchased. Similarly Dommermuth and Cundiff (1967) report for products such as refrigerators, television sets, washing machines, electric irons, and vacuum cleaners that the percentage of purchases for which only one brand is examined varies from approximately 40% to more than 70%; and Kollat (1966) reports even higher percentages for nondurable products such as beverages, food, paper products, and detergents. Finally, Campbell (1969) reports that for toothpaste and detergents consumers rarely consider more than 3 to 5 alternatives.

The number of features considered in connection with each purchase is limited. Katona and Mueller (1954) report that 27% of their subjects did not consider anything but price and brand; 34% considered only one additional feature, 18% considered 2 additional features, and only 17% considered three or more additional features. Similarly, Kelly (1967a) in a study of the patronage decision in connection with a new store found that almost 80% considered three or fewer factors, and no one considered more than six.

Most of the findings relate to the complete purchasing process which may involve a considerable number of single choice processes. The number of elements in each choice process can therefore be expected to be even smaller, a proposition in line with Sheth (1969), who in his study of cognitive aspects of choices found that 2 or 3 aspects often explained most of the variance, and with Neidell and Teach's (1969) ability to predict market shares based upon a similarity space with only two dimensions.

In conclusion, neither the number of alternatives considered nor the number of features (or values) entering into the process is very large. It therefore seems warranted to conclude that the single choice process is not too complex.[9]

3. The Time Dimension and Attractiveness

In consumer behavior an important distinction can be made between *instrumental* and *congenial* behavior (Alderson 1965). Congenial behavior is behavior regarded as "worthwhile in itself," that is, it is an *end* rather than a *mean*. For example, recreational activities are congenial behavior. Instrumental consumer behavior is undertaken in order to achieve some future goal. Much purchasing is instrumental in the sense that it is not the purchase itself that is rewarding, but the possibility of future consumption of the purchased goods.

In general, consumption behavior is congenial to a much larger extent than purchasing behavior. However, it is perfectly possible that purchasing behavior can be congenial also, as would be the case if the completion of the purchase is rewarding in its own right.

When consumers are faced with alternatives that all represent congenial behavior, the salient values relate to behavior that is immediately forthcoming. However, when the alternatives are instrumental, the salient values may relate to behavior that will be completed at some future time, and the question arises whether the time that will elapse until the reward is obtained will influence the choice process. That is, do consumers, when they evaluate alternatives, apply a discounting factor such that the most immediately available alternatives become relatively more attractive? If so, it may be necessary to add a discounting factor to each of the elements in Equation (10.I). Grusec (1968) and Mischel et al. (1969) have found that as the probability associated with obtaining the delayed outcome increases, subjects are more likely to choose the delayed reward, and when the amount of delayed reward increases, the probability of the delayed reward being chosen also increases. This result suggests that some kind of discounting factor can be applied. However, it is also possible that such a factor becomes reflected in the instrumentality relations or that the time element enters in as a value. There is some evidence that such a factor is of minor importance in consumer and similar behavior (Brim et al. 1962).

[9] Although most of the studies which have been cited include only factors the consumer himself is consciously aware of and can report, the number of factors reported is so low that even a considerable number of unconscious salient values do not change the conclusion.

4. The Dimensions of Attractiveness

An important question arises about the type of scales along which instrumentalities are normally measured. In many instances when a certain value is salient, the more closely the alternative is associated with the value, the more instrumental it is. When, for example, durability is a salient value in a car purchase, then the more durable a certain car is perceived to be, the more attractive it is. The instrumentality increases with the extent to which the alternative is associated with the value concept. Here the individual's ideal value lies at the end point of the value dimension. However, another situation occurs when an individual's ideal value lies somewhere in the middle of the scale. For example, when an individual is evaluating a product with regard to sweetness, both too much and too little sweetness can be negative. In such instances the instrumentality of an alternative depends not upon the amount of sweetness in a straightforward way, but rather upon the difference between the actual sweetness and the ideal sweetness. The issue has been dealt with by Guttman and Suchman (1947), Coombs (1950, 1959, and 1960), and Kerlinger (1967); and marketing implications are discussed by Kuehn and Day (1962), Benson (1963), and Taylor (1967 and 1968).

The perceived instrumentality of an alternative depends upon the difference between the extent to which the alternative possesses the quality in question and the ideal amount of that quality, as is illustrated in Figure 10.3, where it can be seen that the smaller the distance, the more instrumental the alternative is.

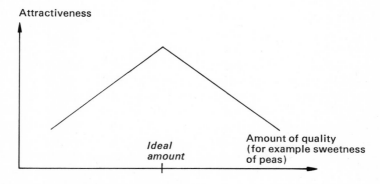

FIGURE 10.3.   *Relationship between attractiveness and bipolar value dimensions.*

Such bipolar values can be dealt with in various ways. The instrumentality can be measured directly. For example, if the dimension (as in Figure 10.3) is the sweetness of a food product, the preference for the alternative's sweetness can be measured directly. Or, the extent to which the alternative is perceived as sweet can be measured together with a measurement of the ideal amount of sweetness. The perceived instrumentality of the alternative can then be computed from the difference between the two measurements. For this purpose the previously mentioned multidimensional scaling techniques can be used to identify the ideal point and to locate the alternatives relative to it.

Finally, it should be mentioned that in a satisficing model like the one described a somewhat different approach can be applied. Along each value dimension, one can attempt to estimate the ideal point and the acceptable range surrounding it, eventually applying the Sherif et al. (1965) category procedure. For each alternative it would then have to be determined whether the alternative fell within or without the acceptable regions.

PART FOUR

*Research
and Findings*

Chapter 11

EXPERIMENTAL STUDIES OF CONSUMER CHOICES

The preceding chapters have dealt with three problems:

1. The overall nature of choice processes.
2. Prediction of the outcome of the choice process based upon the salient cognitive structure, particularly upon the salient values and the relationship between choice alternatives and values.
3. The use of an attractiveness variable as a summary measure of the relevant aspects of the salient cognitive structure.

In an attempt to verify the proposed model, seven experiments to study response selection situations have been conducted. The hypotheses that form the background for the experiments and the methods of conducting them are discussed here.

1. *Hypotheses*

The experiments dealt with two main issues in connection with the proposed model, testing whether choices can indeed be predicted from measures of the attractiveness of the alternatives and examining further the nature of the choice process. Each problem has given rise to a number of hypotheses.

1. Prediction of Choice

ATTRACTIVENESS AND CHOICE BEHAVIOR

The attractiveness of choice alternatives is computed from Equations

225

(10.I) and (10.II), which require measurements of value importance and perceived instrumentality.

In order to measure value importance two things are needed: (1) a technique by which value importance can be estimated and (2) some knowledge about the salient values.

Most techniques used in attitude studies are ultimately aimed at measuring the affective aspects associated with the attitude-object. Perhaps this purpose is most apparent in the evaluative dimension of the semantic differential (Osgood et al. 1957), but other techniques give essentially the same information. The procedure used by Rosenberg (1956) deserves special attention here. He asked respondents to rate the extent to which attainment of various values gave them satisfaction or dissatisfaction. From this information, he was highly successful in predicting overall evaluations.

It is extremely difficult to predict which values will be aroused in a given situation, a problem common to all research. No procedures directly answer this kind of "open question"[1]; but to the extent that hypotheses can be formulated, they can be confirmed or disproved. Consequently, to the extent that relevant consumer-decision situations can be specified and hypotheses formulated as to the values salient in them, it is possible to eliminate less important values and to concentrate on the highly significant ones.

Measuring perceived instrumentality is less complicated. For one thing, when values are defined, the dimensions along which perceived instrumentality should be measured are also defined. Further, what is being measured in much advertising and marketing research closely resembles perceived instrumentality. For example, image studies deal with perceived instrumentality of products and brands, and many techniques are available for measuring images. Often, it is possible to have respondents rate perceived instrumentality directly.

For the experiments presented here, a major task was to show that *with value importance and perceived instrumentality measured, it is possible to predict choices when using either Equation (10.I) or Equation (10.II).*

COMPARISON BETWEEN ATTRACTIVENESS AND ATTITUDES

The present model holds that choices can be predicted if the consumer's salient cognitive structure is known at the time of the choice. In an attempt to construct a variable that reveals significant aspects of this structure, attractiveness has been introduced. However, it might be argued that a traditional attitude or preference measurement may do the same job. Attitude measurements have not always been too successful in predicting choice behavior (see Chapter 10), but this does not necessarily mean that an attractiveness measure will do better. Consequently, it will be tested *whether*

---

[1] Nonmetric, multidimensional scaling models discussed in Chapter 10 could be said to do this. However, with these procedures, the interpretation of the dimensions becomes a very difficult question and the choice of stimuli for the study also influences the dimensions which will be found.

a traditional preference rating will make poorer predictions than the computed attractive-ness score.

When a consumer is faced with a device for measuring preferences, he is faced with a choice among a number of alternatives represented by the different ways he can respond to the test situation (i.e., check a number on the scale or express preference for one of two or more alternatives). If the consumer's salient cognitive structure is known at the time he is responding to the preference measure, his response can be predicted. Consequently, *an attractiveness score relevant to the test situation should predict the attitude measurement.*

The extent to which the attitude measurement will predict the choice depends upon the similarity between the choice process aroused in the situation in which the attitude is measured and the conflict when the choice is made. Whether the attractiveness measure from a situation similar to the one from which the attitude measurement is taken will also predict the subsequent choice depends upon whether the measured values and instrumentalities will be aroused in the choice process and upon how constant these variables remain from the time of the measurement to the time the choice is made. Consequently, the relationships illustrated in Figure 11.1 are suggested.

FIGURE 11.1. *The relationship among attractiveness score, attitude measure, and choice.*

THE RELATIONSHIP BETWEEN VALUE IMPORTANCE AND PERCEIVED INSTRUMENTALITIES

Even though the attractiveness score makes better predictions than a preference rating, the two components of the attractiveness score (i.e., value importance and perceived instrumentality) may be so closely related that either would make as good or better predictions than the combined expression. In order to test this, correlations between measurements of perceived instrumentalities and value importance measures have been studied. *It is suggested that the two variables are highly independent.*

THE ROLE OF VALUE IMPORTANCE AND PERCEIVED INSTRUMENTALITY IN PREDICTION OF CHOICE

Even though the two variables are not correlated, one of them may account for most of the predictions which can be made. If this is the case, that component might as well be used alone. In order to learn whether both components of the attractiveness score contribute significantly to the predictions, an attempt has been made to predict choices with each factor separately. *It is suggested that both value importance and perceived instrumentality add significantly to the quality of the predictions and that neither of them makes predictions as well as the computed attractiveness score.*

STABILITY OF VALUE IMPORTANCE AND INSTRUMENTALITY

For the attractiveness score to be of any practical value, it must be possible to obtain measurements of value importance and perceived instrumentality in situations other than those in which the choice is made. Even though it has been assumed that the values are known, the importance a consumer ascribes to a certain value may vary with the specific situation. Similarly, it is possible that the perceived instrumentality is situationally influenced to such an extent that choices cannot be predicted by measurements obtained in another situation.

Both questions have two aspects: Can the concepts which will be salient be predicted, and can the relevant measures be obtained independent of the particular choice situation?

In order to throw some light on this, attempts have been made to predict choices according to measurements from subjects who did not know the particular choices which would later face them. It is expected that *predictions can be made also when perceived instrumentality and value importance are measured in a situation in which the consumer is not aware of the choice he will face.*

The fact that an individual's concepts are related and form a total structure suggests that more easily measureable values may be substituted for others that are more difficult to quantify. Consider the following example. In connection with many products, durability is an important value. In some situations consumers may ascribe high importance to this value. However, a closer analysis reveals that durability is not rewarding in itself. Durability gains importance only to the extent that it reduces repair expenses and postpones repurchases. Consequently, the question is whether the value importance associated with durability should be measured or whether values at other levels in the consumer's value structure can be used instead. The question is important because almost all values can be measured at a number of levels. Therefore, it will be tested *whether the relationship between values at different levels is fixed and predictable to such an extent that values at one level can be substituted for values at another level of the consumer's conceptual structure, even though the values studied are not salient in the choice process, but are some underlying, more basic ones.*

SATISFICING OR WEIGHTING

The data make it possible to test *whether a prediction based upon the attractiveness score (which reflects weighting) or a prediction based upon satisficing behavior gives the better result* (Chapter 10).

AVERAGING OR ADDING

Based upon the variables used in computing the attractiveness score, an averaging formula can be used also. It is tested whether choice predictions based upon this averaging formula (10. IV) can substitute for predictions based upon an adding formula (10.I).

2. The Nature of the Choice Process

CHANGES IN THE SALIENT COGNITIVE STRUCTURE
DURING THE CHOICE PROCESS

As the choice proceeds, it is expected that less attractive alternatives will be deleted and that the consumer will concentrate his effort on the more attractive ones. In a natural setting, it is also expected that new alternatives will be established, either being thought up or resulting from exploration (Chapter 8). However, when the situation leaves little or no room for exploration and when the initial number of alternatives is considerable, the first tendencies are expected to dominate. Consequently, it has been attempted to show *how the number of alternatives considered decreases and how the attractiveness of the remaining alternatives increases as the choice proceeds.*

INITIAL CONFLICT AND OPTIMAL CONFLICT

The nature of the choice process depends upon the difference between the amount of initial conflict and the amount of conflict the consumer can tolerate (Chapter 8). It is important to study the extent to which these variables are related. If a considerable amount of initial conflict also causes the tolerable level of conflict to be high, it will simplify studies of consumer choice behavior considerably. Unfortunately, it is likely that, regardless of the amount of initial conflict, some situations require that the conflict be reduced considerably, whereas in other situations the consumer is willing to tolerate more conflict.

It is difficult to study the relationship between the amount of aroused conflict and the tolerable amount of conflict, because neither variable can be measured directly. However, in choices among fixed alternatives, it can be assumed that the involvement remains relatively constant during the choice process so that the conflict is reduced mainly through changes in the perceived uncertainty. Consequently, if *the amount of uncertainty in the beginning of the choice process does not correlate with the amount of uncertainty with which the consumer is left immediately after the choice, it can be concluded that the amount of initial conflict is not closely related to the tolerable level of conflict.*

INITIAL CONFLICT AND CHOICE TIME

The more conflict the consumer perceives, the more time he will need to eliminate the conflict (Chapter 8). As conflict is a function of involvement and perceived uncertainty, it is expected that *the time it will take to make the choice will increase with the involvement and the perceived uncertainty.* However, it should be kept in mind that the amount of perceived conflict can be so large that defensive strategies are applied; consequently, subjects who are extremely involved and who perceive a considerable amount of uncertainty may spend less time making their choices than other subjects.

NUMBER OF VALUES IN THE CHOICE PROCESS

The consumer's limited ability to manipulate information suggests that *the number of values salient in the choice process is limited* (Chapter 10). If in a choice process the consumer's attention is directed to a considerable number of possible values, he will neglect some of them. The larger the number of values to which the consumer's attention is brought, the stronger this tendency will be.

SEARCH BEHAVIOR

The consumer will search for more information when no sufficiently attractive alternatives are available, when a certain amount of perceived conflict is present, and when attractive search alternatives are within reach (Chapters 8 and 9). Consequently, it is predicted that *information search is more likely as the consumer perceives more conflict and as the available information alternatives become more attractive.*

EXPLORATION AND CONFLICT

The more conflict the consumer perceives at the beginning of the choice process, the more exploration and deliberation he will engage in (Chapters 8 and 9). Consequently, it is predicted that deliberation and exploration of the *situation will increase as the perceived conflict increases.*

POST-CHOICE CONFLICT

When post-choice conflict exists, the consumer will attempt to eliminate it, which can be accomplished by appropriate changes in the salient cognitive structure (Chapter 9). Particularly, it is predicted that *post-choice conflict will generate changes whereby the rejected alternatives become less attractive and the chosen alternative becomes more attractive.*

SITUATIONAL INFLUENCES

The consumer's choices should be studied in relation to the environment in which they are made. It has already been discussed (Chapter 3) that situational factors can significantly influence the choices consumers make and that the environment gains its importance through its influence upon the salient cognitive structure. Here, it is held that *the environment influences choices only to the extent that it determines the salient cognitive structure.* That is, it is predicted that only those factors that influence the salient cognitive structure significantly will also affect the choices.

2. *Summary of Hypotheses*

1. Prediction of Choice

1. Perceived instrumentality and value importance can be measured; and, given these measures, it is possible to predict consumer choices using Equations (10.I) and (10.II).

2a. The attractiveness score will make predictions superior to those made from a traditional attitude measurement.

2b. The attractiveness score will predict the attitude measurement.

3. Value importance and instrumentality are highly independent variables.

4. Both value importance and perceived instrumentality add significantly to the prediction of consumer choices.

5. Value importance and perceived instrumentality are stable to such an extent that (1) measurements obtained at times other than the choice situation can predict choices and (2) values can successfully be measured at different levels in the individual's total value structure.

6. The attractiveness score based upon a weighting process predicts choices better than a score based upon an assumption about satisficing.

7. The attractiveness score computed by an additive process makes better predictions than a score computed by averaging.

2. The Nature of the Choice Process

1. As the choice process proceeds the number of salient alternatives will decrease, and the least attractive alternatives will be deleted first.

2. The amount of perceived conflict at the beginning of the choice process is independent of the preferred level of conflict.

3. The more conflict the consumer perceives, the more time the choice will take.

4. The number of salient values in the cognitive structure will not be very large.

5. More information search occurs as the attractiveness of available search alternatives increases and as the consumer's uncertainty and involvement increase.

6. The tendency towards deliberation and exploration increases as the consumer perceives more conflict.

7. When conflict persists after the choice, changes in the cognitive structure will occur that will reduce this conflict.

8. The choice is dependent upon the environment only to the extent that the environment influences the salient cognitive structure.

3. *The Simulated Choice*

Preferably, consumer choices should be studied in real-life situations. However, the information obtainable from such studies leaves much to be desired. Perceived instrumentality and value importance are of special interest as they occur in the choice situation, but these variables cannot be measured in a real-life choice, because the time the choice is made is not definitely known.

If one wants to obtain measures that relate to the choice in a known way, it is necessary to manipulate the choice. Faced with such problems, experimenters have often turned to simulated choices (Rosenberg and Abelson 1960, Brehm & Cohen 1962, and Festinger 1964a). The same approach is used here. In all seven experiments, subjects were asked to simulate consumer choices. They were faced with situational descriptions presenting various alternatives, and they were then asked to react as they thought they would in such a situation.

Most studies conducted in social psychology and marketing with simulated behavior (or role playing) have resulted in valuable findings, but they have also pointed at difficulties with the approach. A review of most of the work in social psychology is provided by Greenberg (1967), who concludes that despite difficulties associated with the role-playing technique, the procedure is promising. Similarly, Holloway (1968) reviews work done in marketing and points out the advantage inherent in the approach.

The simulated choice experiment assumes that an individual can place himself in a described situation and behave realistically, but can he? Generally, when the situation is not familiar, a subject has trouble imagining what he would do in the situation. On the other hand, if the subject is too familiar with the situation, he may rely upon values and experience gained in previous situations. The range of problems which can be studied in role play experiments is therefore limited. On the one hand, subjects cannot be expected to react meaningfully to a situation dealing with a completely unknown product; on the other hand, subjects cannot be expected to apply rational or semi-complex choices to a problem they normally solve by a highly automatized choice procedure.

Another problem relates to the subject's degree of involvement in playing the role. Can the individual in an experimental environment produce a sufficient amount of involvement to simulate an important choice ? In such a case, there is a danger that subjects withdraw themselves from the role they are supposed to play and complete the experimental material only formally. In our experiments this possibility has specifically been checked.

A third problem in all experimental studies is related to the so-called evaluation apprehension phenomenon. As Orne (1962) points out, subjects may—consciously or unconsciously—want to please the experimenter. Consequently, depending upon the way they perceive the experiment, subjects form their own hypotheses about the purpose of the experiment and act accordingly. The hypotheses that subjects form depend upon the demand characteristics of the experiment, that is, the clues the subjects rely on in their interpretations of the experiment. When the experiment is planned, it is important to be aware of the demand characteristics inherent in the experimental procedure and to control the subjects' own interpretations of the situation. One way to deal with this problem is to check whether subjects are aware of the real hypothesis after the completion of the experiment and then discard those who were. It is generally agreed that only subjects who are able to explain the experimental hypothesis are significantly affected in their behavior (Orne 1962).

These dangers are opposed by a number of advantages. First, the simulated choice experiment makes it possible to test a number of hypotheses that could not otherwise be dealt with. This is particularly important in a marketing context, as a number of consumer choices are made in situations that cannot be replicated. For practical reasons, many problems are excluded from testing. For example, purchasing processes for most durable products cannot be studied experimentally because of the costs of offering the subject a choice among the real products. Furthermore, even where the cost of the product is not prohibitive, a simulated choice experiment has the advantages that it is less expensive and can usually be completed faster.

The simulated choice experiment is also advantageous because it permits the manipulation of price and other variables in the simulated buying situation. In a real situation these variables can be manipulated only with extremely high costs; but in the simulated choice, the flexibility of the procedure allows for variations in the situational description which make it possible to approach problems which could not otherwise be tested.

That the timing of the choice can be manipulated is also an advantage. In real-life studies, the experimenter must wait until the consumer makes the choice he wants to study, and even then it may be difficult to know exactly when the choice is made. Furthermore, as it cannot be known what choice the consumer will make until he has chosen, it may be necessary to study a very large number of choices in order to find a sufficient number of choices of the kind in which the experimenter is interested. In the simulated choice, however, the timing of the choice can be controlled.[2]

Finally, the simulated choice procedure offers one very important advantage. As the salient cognitive structure is closely dependent upon the overall situation and as the situation can easily be manipulated, it is possible to administer some control over the salient cognitive structures of the subjects. Although the experimenter does not acquire perfect control over what will become salient in the simulated choice process he is able to exert some influence and to bias the salient cognitive structure.

One reason that the role playing experiment is becoming popular in social psychology is that it provides a way to deal with situations in which the alternative (deception of the subjects) would have been extremely unpleasant for the subjects, or would at least have influenced them to such an extent that the propriety of the procedure could be questioned. In this connection, it can be mentioned that a recent study (Mann and Janis 1968) indicates that emotional role-playing experiments may have long-term effects similar to those of studies that deceive the experimental subjects into experiencing the

---

[2] Because subjects may predict that they will be faced with a choice and consequently make it before they are required to, one can only be sure of the approximate time the choice is made. However, although some subjects make their choices before they are required to do so, the pre- and the post-choice conditions will undoubtedly generate significant differences in the average time of the choice. For discussion of this see Festinger (1964a).

emotions. However, this is not a major problem in studies of consumer behavior, as in such studies subjects are required to simulate normal, everyday choices.

A number of successful applications of simulated choices have been reported (Banks 1950b, Greenberg 1956, Pessimies 1960, Aldenson and Sessions 1962, and Pessemier and Teach 1966 and 1968). Also, much work which applies indirect techniques such as sentence completion or picture interpretation, essentially relies upon role playing.

The simulated choice experiments may be conducted in two ways, each of which has certain advantages. The experimenter may describe both an individual and his situation to the subjects, who then are asked to behave as would the described individual (the method used by Rosenberg and Abelson 1960). Alternatively, the experimenter can describe the situation and ask the subjects to behave as they themselves would in a similar situation (the method used by Festinger 1964a). The first procedure has the advantage that it makes the subject less sensitive to tabooed topics that might otherwise influence his behavior in the experiment. On the other hand, this procedure requires a considerable amount of imagination from the subject; and if the situation is too unfamiliar, the subject may not be able to play the role or, if it is too familiar, it may be difficult for him to abstract from his own previous experiences. In the following, both procedures have been tried; but, for the reasons just discussed, in the later studies the simulation of the subject's own behavior has been preferred.

4. *Description of the Experiments*

A total of seven experiments have been conducted. Although they are built basically in the same way, there are some significant differences among them; therefore, each of the experiments will be briefly described. The first experiment will be dealt with in detail, but the following experiments will be described only as they differ from the first.

1. First Experiment: First Hairdryer Choice

In this experiment male subjects were asked to choose one of two hairdryers, which they were told was to be used as a gift. The hairdryer was chosen as the product because it was desirable to create a situation of which one could be reasonably sure that subjects had no previous experience. Thus, subjects could be expected to rely heavily on the material presented. The description of the hairdryers centered around their durability, efficiency, and price. A factorial design was used, and subjects (34 male junior and senior students at the Whittemore School of Business and Economics) were randomly assigned to the four experimental conditions, which were as follows: (1) situational description I, values and instrumentalities measured before the choice, (2) situational description I, values and instrumentalities measured after the choice, (3) situational description II, values and instrumentalities measured before the choice, and (4) situational description II, values and instrumentalities measured after the choice. The questionnaire and material pertinent to (1) are reproduced in the appendix.

Subjects were asked to act on behalf of an individual described to them in the situational description. The instructions directed them "to act as if they were in the situation of the described consumer." The situational descriptions were presented in two parts. The first part, preceding the first choice, gave a brief summary of the decision-makers' background: "Mr. Blomberg, an engineer, is about to buy an anniversary present for his wife." Mr. Blomberg has decided to buy her a hairdryer, and he was considering alternatives in the only appliance store in town. Blomberg had limited the choice to two alternative brands. One of these, Varig, was described as a not too expensive unit ($11.00), which was very durable but not too efficient. The other, Schnell, was described as a somewhat more expensive unit ($16.00), which was very efficient but not too durable.[3] At this point in time, the subjects were asked to place themselves in the position of Mr. Blomberg, and a questionnaire was administered to them. In the before-choice condition, values and instrumentalities were measured before the choice was made; whereas in the after-choice condition, the choice was made before measurements were obtained.

The rating-before-choice and choice-before-rating variation was introduced in order to make comparisons possible between post- and pre-decisional processes. To further delay subjects in making a choice before the rating was completed, they were told that more information was coming, a technique which has previously proven successful in postponing choices (Festinger 1964a).

The situational description was varied by introducing Mrs. Blomberg into the "Situational Description I" conditions by hinting that she had once mentioned that she considered the time a hairdryer took to dry her hair (efficiency) to be very important. The purpose of this hint was to make sure that sufficient differences in choice would be found among the subjects. As it was not known whether the experimental procedure would create a conflict resulting in different choices, this device was used to increase the likelihood of obtaining choices of both Varig and Schnell and to make it possible to study the effect of introducing an additional cognitive element into the subject's salient cognitive structure.

The second part of the situational description was presented to subjects after they had made the first choice. This material introduced the possibility of search by telling of a department store 11 miles away that might have a

---

[3] The actual descriptions are approximately 400 words in length.

better hairdryer. However, the trip there would take at least an hour; further, as Mr. Wintergarden, the owner of the store in which Blomberg presently was considering hairdryers, was a close friend of Blomberg, he might consider it impolite of Mr. Blomberg to go to the competitor.

The overall structure of the experiment is described in Table 11.1.

TABLE 11.1

Experimental plan for first hairdryer choice (Questionnaires are reproduced in the appendix)

	Rating Before Choice	Choice Before Rating
1st set of material	Pre-situation measures	Pre-situation measures
2nd set of material	1st situational description (a or b)	1st situational description (a or b)
3rd set of material	Post-situational ratings	1st choice and post-situational ratings
4th set of material	1st choice and 2nd situational description	2nd situational description
5th set of material	Ratings of search alternatives and 2nd choice	Rating of search alternative and 2nd choice
6th set of material	Post-experimental measures	Post-experimental measures

As will be seen, four questionnaires were administered during the experiment. In the first, before the situational description was introduced, subjects were asked to indicate how important they found various values often associated with purchases of minor durable items. Measurements were obtained on 11-point scales ranging from 0 to 100, with 100 meaning "the single most important" factor and 0 meaning "not important at all." The values rated were *durability, price* and *efficiency*, the values of importance in connection with the search-alternative, and a single item used for control.

After this first questionnaire was completed, the first situational description was given to subjects, and immediately thereafter the second questionnaire was administered. It again measured the importance of *price, durability* and *efficiency*. Further, it measured the perceived instrumentality of the two alternatives with regard to the three values, also on scales ranging from 0 to 100, where 0 meant "no difference" and 100 meant "Varig (Schnell) very much more durable (efficient, expensive) than Schnell (Varig)." On the other half of this questionnaire, subjects were asked to make their choices. This decision was required either before or after the ratings were made, according to the conditions to which the subjects were assigned.

After the second questionnaire, the second situational description was introduced; immediately after, the third questionnaire was administered, measuring the instrumentality of three aspects of the search alternative and obtaining the second (possibly revised) decision (*search, Schnell,* or *Varig*). The three aspects were "How likely does Mr. Blomberg consider it to be that he will find a better alternative at the department store?" "How boring does Mr. Blomberg find the extra trip to the department store?" and "How impolite does Mr. Blomberg consider it to be not to buy the hairdryer at Wintergarden's ?"

Given these measures, it is possible to compute the attractiveness of the search by using equation (10.I).

The fourth questionnaire was administered in order to check whether the various experimental treatments had been successful. First, subjects were asked to name any factor which they thought might have entered into their decision, in order to check whether values other than those suggested by the situational descriptions had been at work. Then the salient values were remeasured together with the extra item from the first questionnaire and various filler items, in order to check the stability of the value measures and to discover systematic changes in values applied in the choice.

Finally, subjects were presented with 35 brief statements concerning their feelings about the experiment. Subjects were supposed to tell whether they agreed, disagreed, or felt indifferent with regard to these statements, in order to identify subjects who did not take the task seriously. By means of the reactions to these 35 statements, it was also hoped to construct a measure of involvement in the experiment, simply by counting the number of statements on which the subject took a stand.

2. Second Experiment: Second Hairdryer Choice

This experiment was carried out with 80 male sophomore and junior students at the University of New Hampshire (all different from subjects in the first experiment), using a procedure almost identical with the one described above. The main differences were:

1. The situational description did not contain a detailed account of the fictional "Mr. Blomberg," and subjects were asked to make the choice on their own behalf.

2. The description of the two alternatives differed to the extent that the Varig alternative was described somewhat less favorably than in the first experiment, in order to secure an equal number of choices of each alternative. For the same reason, the search alternative was made more attractive in the second situational description.

3. In the experimental design four different price combinations were used, in order to study the influence of variations in price on value importance and perceived instrumentality. As four different price combinations were applied, and as half the subjects made their choices after rating perceived instrumentality and value importance and the other half made their choices before that rating, a total of 8 (2×4) experimental conditions were applied.

4. After the third questionnaire, a third situational description was presented, saying that Mr. Blomberg had decided to go to the Star Market. Here, he finds two additional alternatives. The first is less durable than Varig but more durable than Schnell and less efficient than Schnell but more efficient than Varig, thus representing a viable alternative compared with the two already known. The last alternative is described as clearly inferior compared with the other three. Mr. Blomberg is then offered the possibility of taking two of the four home to his wife for inspection. The purpose of this modified situation was to force an intermediate step in the choice process upon the subjects, in order to study how they would go about eliminating alternatives.

5. Finally, although ratings were basically the same as in the first experiment, a few minor improvements were introduced when the second experiment was carried out. The 35 statements were not given to these subjects.

3. Third Experiment: Restaurant Choice

Part of this restaurant-choice experiment, as well as the following two book-choice and travel-choice experiments, was aimed at testing the hypothesis that it is possible to predict a variety of choices from one set of value measures. Consequently, in these three and the related menu-choice experiment the same subjects were used, 90 undergraduate male and female students from the University of New Hampshire.

The sequence of these four experiments is given in Table 11.2.

TABLE 11.2

Experimental program for four related choices

1. Questionnaire 1. All pre-choice measures
2. Situational Description 1. (Travel choice)
3. Questionnaire 2. Travel choice
4. Situational Description 2. (Restaurant choice)
5. Questionnaire 3. Restaurant choice
6. Situational Description 3. (Menu choice)
7. Questionnaire 4. Menu choice
8. Situational Description 4. (Book choice)
9. Questionnaire 5. Book choice

For reasons hereafter discussed, it was preferable to have the book choice presented last and to have the menu choice follow the restaurant choice, which does not leave much room for reversal of the order of presentation. Nevertheless, it is possible to change the order of the first three choices to (1) restaurant choice, (2) menu choice, and (3) travel choice. This order was used in a pre-test in an attempt to reveal order effects. As none were found, the arrangement described in Table 11.2 was used in the entire study.

Subjects in this experiment were told that they were participating in a survey conducted by "The School of Hotel Administration" at the University of New Hampshire, and they were paid $4 each for their participation. The total experimental sessions took from one hour and a half to two hours. Two short breaks were given, but subjects were not allowed to contact other participants before all the material had been completed.

In the restaurant choice, the situational description told subjects that during a stay in a large city they were supposed to choose between two restaurants described in the material. Choice-before-rating and rating-before-choice conditions were applied.

Compared with the first two experiments, the restaurant one applied a considerably larger number of values. The two restaurants were described along as many as ten dimensions (expensiveness, intimacy, kind of food served, and so on). Consequently, both value importance and perceived instrumentality were rated on ten different scales. Value importance was measured in much the same way as in the first two experiments, but the measurement of perceived instrumentality differed somewhat. In the first two experiments, subjects were asked to rate the relative advantage of one of the alternatives. In this experiment subjects rated the absolute instrumentality of each of the two alternatives. That is, measures were obtained for each value on two 11-point scales ranging from "extremely expensive" (intimate, and so on) to "not expensive (intimate, and so on) at all." This gave two independent measures of perceived instrumentality, one for each of the alternatives; according to these measurements the overall attractiveness (A) was computed using equation (10.I). Values were measured both before and after the situational description. Instrumentalities were measured only after.

As in the first two experiments, the values are closely related to the specific choice situation. Except for a few values, such as the *price* value, it is not possible to apply the same values when very different decisions are studied. When the same values are to be used in connection with different products, more general values must be applied. One possible approach would be to use one or another personality schedule and to relate products to the values measured in it. However, such an approach is questionable. In general, studies relating consumer behavior to personality measures have not been too successful (Chapter 16), and when personality traits are used as values, the measurement of perceived instrumentality becomes extremely complicated. Consequently, a number of general values that could be applied to the situations studied were constructed as follows. First, a basic list of approximately two hundred value statements was constructed. The values were taken from *Edward's Personal Preference Schedule* (A. L. Edwards 1956), from Murray's list of values used in his *Exploration in Personality* (Murray 1938), from Allport, Vernon, and Lindzey's *Study of Values* (Allport et al. 1960) and from Rosenberg's previously mentioned study (Rosenberg 1956). Then, 24 values were selected from the basic list. This selection was made in such a way that all the values were applicable to the three choices and not too closely interrelated.[4] The values applied were such as "to be independent of others," "being with other people,—socializing," and "to have strict moral standards."

Before the situational descriptions were introduced, subjects were asked to rate the importance of the 24 values on 21-point scales (minus 10 to plus 10) ranging from "the attainment of this value gives me maximum satisfaction" to "the attainment of this value gives me maximum dissatisfaction" and with the zero point reading "gives me neither satisfaction nor

---

[4] As it turned out, some of the values actually were significantly correlated; however, since the correlation coefficients were small, all 24 values were retained in the subsequent tabulations.

dissatisfaction." After the introduction of the situational description—with material from the other choices acting as filler items—the values were restated, and subjects were asked to indicate how instrumental to the values they saw the alternatives to be. This again was done on 21-point scales of statements such as "this value is completely attained by going to (name of restaurant)," and with the zero point labeled "completely irrelevant." Using these measures, it is possible to compute a second set of attractiveness scores applying Equation (10.I).

After the choice, subjects were asked to rate (on an 11-point scale) how certain they felt about the choice they had just made and to write down any information they would have liked to have and to tell how they would have attempted to obtain it. The uncertainty rating was obtained in an attempt to measure the extent to which post-choice conflict was present. The question about the information wanted would make it possible to judge the application of factors not considered in the computation of attractiveness scores and to learn about exploration and search tendencies.

4. Fourth Experiment: Book Choice

In the book-choice experiment, subjects were the same as in the previous experiment, and a two-by-two factorial design was used. The conditions were choice-before-rating and rating-before-choice, and an experimental variation was introduced by telling half the subjects that they were allowed to keep the book they chose, an offer not made to the other half of the subjects. This was done in order to reveal differences, if any, between a simulated choice and a real choice. The situational description presented subjects with a choice between two books, both of which were handed out for inspection. None of the subjects were familiar with the alternatives before the experiment. The alternatives were recently published books retailing at approximately $5.00 (Simone de Beauvoir, *Les Belles Images*, Ronald Press 1967; and Ronald Clark, *Queen Victoria's Bomb*, William Morrow and Co., Inc. 1968). The alternatives selected were not too much alike. Value importance and instrumentality were measured only for the 24 values described earlier.

Finally, measurements were obtained of the choice time and of the extent to which subjects felt certain about the choice they had just made. The time measure was obtained in order to study the relationship between choice time and conflict. Because subjects participated in sections of 15–20 persons, an observational measure could not be obtained. However, it was hoped that the following crude measure would be sensitive enough. In each section, all subjects were started simultaneously; each subject was instructed to write on his paper the highest number written on the blackboard in the room immediately after he had completed his choice. Ascending numbers were written on the blackboard by an assistant at 5-second intervals.

5. Fifth Experiment: Travel Choice

In the travel-choice experiment subjects were told that in planning a vacation in Europe, they were to choose to go by boat or by plane. Subjects can be assumed to be familiar with both these alternatives without further description. Thus, it is possible to measure both value importance and perceived instrumentality before the introduction of the situational description.

Subjects were assigned to four conditions in a two-by-two factorial design. The conditions were choice-before-rating and rating-before-choice combined with two different situational descriptions. The first description simply described the situation and mentioned the alternatives. The second introduced copy from two advertisements for a major oceanliner taken from recent issues of the *Boston Herald Traveller* and *Time* and described the boat trip as very pleasant and fashionable. This experimental variation was introduced in order to study the effects of this kind of material upon value importance, perceived instrumentality, and choices.

Rating was carried out as in the third experiment, the only difference being that perceived instrumentality was measured both before and after the introduction of the situational description. To conceal the identity of the choice alternatives and to make computations of attractiveness for other alternatives possible, ratings were obtained before the situational description for car, bus, and train transportation also. Similarly, before the introduction of the situational description, preference ratings for all five alternatives were obtained to make it possible to test the predictive power of these ratings compared with the computed attractiveness scores.

6. Sixth Experiment: Menu Choice

The menu-choice experiment was carried out to test whether the model is able to predict choices among a considerable number of alternatives. Again subjects were the 90 male and female college students from the University of New Hampshire. Only two experimental conditions were used. Subjects were told that they were seated in a restaurant described to them in the material. Half the subjects were told that the restaurant was a popular steakhouse, whereas the other half were told that the restaurant was an intimate French restaurant. In both conditions the same nine menus were offered for choice.

In order to secure menu alternatives not too different in attractiveness, they were composed of items previously used in an experiment by Benson (1955). In this experiment, the attractiveness of the menu items had been rated, making it possible to compose menus in such a way that a certain amount of conflict would be aroused by each.

All rating was carried out before the introduction of the situational description. First, the 16 menu items were rated for "liking" on a 21-point scale ranging from "likes extremely well," to "dislikes extremely." At the same time, subjects were asked whether any of the items were ones they felt they would definitely not eat. Then, after a number of filler items, nine fixed menus were rated for overall liking, expensiveness, and heaviness. These menus were composed of items taken from the rated 16 items. Finally, value importance was rated in connection with liking, expensiveness, and heaviness. From these measures, Equation 10.I was used to compute overall attractiveness for each of the nine menus offered for choice.

In this experiment decision time and certainty about the choice was measured also. Further, subjects were asked to indicate which alternatives (if any) they immediately had deleted and which they had considered just before the choice had been made, making it possible to study the order in which alternatives were inspected and to follow how the choice had progressed.

This experiment also attempted to face the subjects with a choice that would reveal whether they used a weighting or a satisficing choice principle. A forced choice offered at the end of the experiment was designed so that one alternative was the most attractive, but at the same time contained at least one aspect which fell below the consumer's level of acceptance. The other alternative was then made slightly less attractive, but contained no aspects that were definitely rejectable.

From the measurements of subjects' liking of the menu items and the information about items they would definitely reject, it was possible to estimate the attractiveness of the nine menu alternatives as well as to identify those that contained rejectable (unsatisfactory) alternatives. After choosing among the nine menus, the subjects were offered the forced choice. The forced choices were constructed from the original ratings while the subjects went on with the experiment. However, as it turned out, it was difficult to find alternatives from the nine menus that met the required criterion. It was possible to offer only 26 of the 90 subjects a clearcut weighting-satisficing choice.

7. Seventh Experiment: Second Menu Choice

Experiments 3 through 6 were all completed with the same subjects. It can be questioned whether the participation in such a sequence of experiments influences subjects so that their behavior in the later experiments will be biased. To learn to what extent such an effect occurs, it was decided to replicate one of the experiments with new subjects. For this purpose the menu-choice experiment was selected. As the menu choice had been presented to subjects late in the sequence of experiments, the suspected influence could have occurred; it was also preferable as a test case because detailed information about the choice process had been obtained. Furthermore, a special problem had appeared in the first application of this choice. One purpose was to see whether the introduction of two very different situational descriptions (the two restaurants) would influence the choice behavior significantly. However, as will be discussed, the situational description was found to have only a moderate effect upon the choices and the choice processes.

The lack of situational influence in this experiment may be caused by one of two factors: Either the other simulated choices respondents made had a disturbing influence, or none of the choice alternatives were very closely associated with one of the two restaurants. In order to test whether either of these explanations applies, it was decided to repeat the experiment with two additional experimental conditions.

In this repetition, the subjects were 46 undergraduate students at the University of New Hampshire who were unfamiliar with the previous experiments. The first experimental condition was simply a replication of the experiment described above, carried out with other subjects. As in the original experiment the rating of menu items and complete menus was carried out early, with some of the other experiments acting as "filler items," it was not possible to replicate these ratings. A replication would have required other filler items, which would undoubtedly have introduced uncontrollable bias when compared with the original version. Consequently, it was decided to replicate only the section that dealt with the choice and the choice process. In this section the choice was made, information was obtained about the number of items considered at various stages in the choice process, and uncertainty about the choice and decision time was measured.

The second experimental condition was identical with the previous one except that nine new menu alternatives were constructed, some of which were closely associated with a French restaurant and others with a steak house. In this replication, it was not possible to manipulate choices as no ratings of menu items were obtained. Instead, in the first condition a forced choice between two items that were known from the first experiment to present many of the subjects with a satisficing-weighting conflict were used. In the second condition, the forced choice was between two alternatives, each closely associated with one of the two restaurants.

5. *Controls*

In these seven experiments, a number of controls were applied. An overview is given in Table 11.3.

In the two hairdryer experiments and in the menu choice experiments, subjects were asked to describe the criteria they applied in the choice process, to check whether subjects really applied the values introduced through the situational description and not others. Only to the extent that the values controlled in the experiment play a major role in the choice process can the

TABLE 11.3

Summary of controls applied in experiments

	Values applied in choice	Involve-ment	Relia-bility of value scales	Compari-son between real and simulated choice	Effects of repeated choices	Demand charac-teristics	Intercor-relations among values
First hairdryer choice	X	X	X			X	
Second hairdryer choice	X		X			X	
Restaurant choice	X					X	X
Travel choice						X	X
Book choice				X		X	X
First menu choice	X				X	X	
Second menu choice	X				X	X	

computed attractiveness score be expected to predict the outcome of the choices. Neither in the hairdryer nor in the menu choice experiments did subjects to any significant extent report values other than those measured in the experiment.

In the restaurant choice, a similar control was applied. Subjects were asked to indicate any additional information they would have liked to have. The extent to which information about values not considered in the computation of attractiveness is requested indicates that values other than those studied may have influenced the choice. A summary of the information subjects requested is presented in Table 11.4.

TABLE 11.4

Information requested in restaurant choice experiment (N =90; 19 subjects mentioned source of information only)

Type of information wanted	Number of subjects	Percentage
Type of restaurant	60	
Type of food	31	
Service	19	
Price	19	
Crowded	16	
Location/distance	13	
Total controlled in experiment	— 158	76.7%
Liquor, entertainment	20	
For single girl	11	
On situation	13	
Miscellaneous	4	
Total not controlled in experiment	— 48	23.3%
TOTAL	206	100%

It will be seen that most of the information wanted relates to the values that are measured by the experiment. However, two pieces of information requested suggest values that should have been included in the computation of the attractiveness score. Twenty subjects ask if the restaurants have liquor licenses and 11 subjects (all female) ask whether restaurants are places a single girl would go. Furthermore, 13 subjects ask for more information about the specific situation (How much money do I have, how tired am I, and so on). Altogether, it must be concluded that in this experiment, the possibility exists that uncontrolled values were applied by a number of the subjects; consequently, less than perfect predictions can be expected.

The simulated-choice situation is not likely to generate the same amount of involvement as a similar real situation. However, only if subjects at least to some extent involve themselves in the experiments, can it be expected that the findings have any applicability to real choices. Therefore, in the first hairdryer experiments 35 questions were asked regarding subjects' evaluation of the experimental procedure, their involvement, and the extent to which they had found the experiments worth-while and interesting. Replies to these questions revealed a surprisingly high degree of involvement in the simulated choice. The 35 statements to which respondents replied ranged from extremely positive to extremely negative. But almost all responses lie in the positive end of the scale. It can therefore safely be concluded that the subjects took the task sufficiently seriously.

In all the experiments, values were measured on various graphic scales, with the end points verbally defined. As the findings to be reported rely heavily upon the reliability of these scales, it was tested in the two hairdryer experiments. In each, a value irrelevant to the choice in question was measured at the beginning and at the end of the experiment. In the first experiment, the value was "design of the product" and in the second experiment, "the reputation of the manufacturer." As these values are irrelevant to the choices, the reliability of the procedure is reflected in the extent to which the second measure is predicted by the first. In both instances, it was found that the two measurements correlated closely. There were no significant differences between the two measurements, and for individual subjects only a few small changes occurred from the first to the second measurement.

A main purpose of the book-choice experiment was to test the extent to which the simulated-choice situation gives findings which replicate a real choice situation. In Table 11.5, data are presented from the simulated and the real book-choice conditions. The results vary depending upon whether the choice was made before the alternatives were rated or whether the rating was completed before the choice. Therefore, data are presented separately for the two conditions.

In the rating-before-choice condition there are only minor and insignificant differences between the real and the simulated choice.

In the choice-before-rating condition *Les Belles Images* was preferred to a significantly higher degree in the real choice than in the simulated choice. This change in preference is also reflected in the average attractiveness ratings of the two alternatives. The remaining measures do not differ significantly. It is difficult to tell why the difference in choice occurs in this experimental condition. However, one possible explanation suggests itself.

TABLE 11.5

The choice process in the simulated and real book choice

	RATING BEFORE CHOICE		CHOICE BEFORE RATING	
	Real choice N = 20	Simulated choice N = 24	Real choice N = 18	Simulated choice N = 25
Percentage of subjects choosing *Les Belles Images*	65.0%	60.0%	77.7%[a]	51.9%[a]
Attractiveness (Equation 10.II) of *Les Belles Images*	3.91	3.51	4.26[b]	3.09[b]
Number of salient values	16.90	18.15	16.89	17.57
Rated uncertainty about choice	0.76	0.76	0.62	0.70
Choice time (no. of 5-second intervals)	18.5	17.1	17.9	19.9

[a] Difference significant with $p \leq 01$ (x^2 test).
[b] Difference significant with $p \leq$ (0^2 x^2 test).
(3 subjects were deleted because of incomplete ratings.)

For reasons which could not be controlled, a relatively larger number of male subjects showed up in the simulated choice-before-rating condition than in the real condition. It is known from the rating-before-choice condition that male subjects are more likely to choose *Queen Victoria's Bomb*. This can explain the extraordinarily low percentage of subjects choosing the *Les Belles Images* and the differences in the attractiveness ratings. However, it cannot be ruled out that post-choice processes differ depending upon the nature of the choice. In the following, this will have to be kept in mind when the post-choice processes are analyzed.

Although neither the number of salient values, the choice time, nor the uncertainty differ significantly between real and simulated choice conditions, it is worth noting that they are all higher in the simulated choice. The fact that all three variables reflect the extent to which the individual has been involved in the choice supports the conclusion that the simulated-choice condition does generate a considerable amount of involvement.

The menu-choice experiment was repeated to test whether subjects become biased in their response from participating in several choices. In Table 11.6, data from the first menu choice experiment are compared with data from the first condition in the second menu choice.

There are no significant differences between the choices made in the two experiments. In both, the most, the second-most, the third-most, and the fourth-most preferred alternatives are the same. Neither the number of alternatives deleted immediately, the number of alternatives finally considered, nor the rating of uncertainty about the choice differ. However, the decision time differs significantly between the two experiments. A very plausible explanation is the following: In the original version of the experiments, subjects had already rated menus identical with those they were choosing among, whereas in the replication subjects had never seen the alternatives before they were presented with the choice alternatives. Therefore, subjects

TABLE 11.6

Choices and choice process variables from first and second menu choices

Menu chosen	ORIGINAL VERSION (N = 90) Percentage choosing	REPLICATION (N = 15) Percentage choosing
Menu L	29.2	33.3
Menu R	19.1	20.1
Menu T	19.1	13.3
Menu S	12.4	13.3
Menu M	12.4	0
Menu N	4.5	0
Menu P	2.1	0
Menu G	1.1	0
Menu H	0.0	0
Number of alternatives rejected	3.06	2.27
Number of alternatives considered	2.47	2.73
Rated uncertainty	.712	.800
Decision time (number of 5-second intervals)	7.60[a]	40.20[a]

[a] Difference significant with $p \leq 01$ (t-test).

were more familiar with the alternatives in the original version; consequently, they had to spend less time exploring them. This interpretation is also supported by the slight differences in the number of alternatives rejected in the very beginning of the choice processes. Although the difference is not significant, the subjects in the original version were immediately able to delete more alternatives than were the subjects in the replication. Altogether, the menu choice was not significantly influenced by the fact that subjects had previously made other choices, and there is no reason to believe that such an effect should have appeared in the other choices.

In those experiments studying a larger number of values, it is possible that significant correlations occur among the values. This would make the use of Equations (10.I) and (10.II) questionable, as both formulas assume independence among the values. As a check, intercorrelations among values were studied in the travel-choice, the restaurant-choice, and the book-choice experiments. It was found that the simple choice values were not significantly correlated, whereas some small but significant correlations appeared among the 24 basic values. Because the coefficients of correlation were small, all 24 values were retained in the date.

Finally, after each session a number of subjects were interviewed concerning their feelings about the experiment and what they thought the experiment dealt with, partly to check whether subjects had become frustrated or irritated and therefore had not involved themselves in the choices, and partly to reveal whether subjects had any idea of the hypotheses tested in the experiment. The impression gained from these conversations with subjects was that the experimental procedure had been accepted without difficulty and that subjects were not aware of the hypotheses being tested. In particular, no subjects had given thought to the relationship between the values and the choices that were made.

6. *Conclusions*

Although the experimental procedures applied in these seven experiments have proved to be rather successful, the findings to be reported are not representative for any major segment of the total population. The subjects studied are in no way representative of any group except perhaps University of New Hampshire students. Even if some kind of representative sample had been used, the findings would still have to be taken as merely suggestive. The author does not believe, nor does he want his readers to believe, that the choices made in these experiments would be found in a real situation.

All experimentation with human subjects—like the work reported here—rests upon the assumption that the cognitive, motivational, and other processes studied under these conditions resemble those found in "the real world." The validity of this assumption cannot be tested before the findings from such experimentation have been confronted with observation of behavior in a natural setting. Consumer behavior seems to be an area in which such confrontation eventually will be made. At the present stage of development, however, the possibilities for simplification which one obtains in the experiment makes experimentation the most promising approach.

Chapter 12

EXPERIMENTAL RESULTS

The present chapter presents the findings from the seven experiments described in Chapter 11. Because most of the experiments are relevant to several of the hypotheses, the experimental evidence is related to each hypothesis of Chapter 11, rather than separately discussing the findings from each experiment.[1]

1. *The Attractiveness Score and Prediction of Choice*

1. Prediction of Choice

In all but two of the experiments computations are possible of either the relative attractiveness or the attractiveness of each alternative.[2] The computed attractiveness scores should predict the choices. The extent to which they do can be tested by comparing the evaluations of the alternatives. The results are summarized in Table 12.1.

From inspection of the table, it can be seen that in all but one case the relative attractiveness scores differ significantly between the chosen alternatives, or the absolute score differs between chosen and rejected alternatives. As all but one of the results are based on measurements before the choice is made (in the first hairdryer choice, perceived instrumentality for half

[1] Part of the findings discussed in this section are presented in Hansen (1969a). Reprinted here with the permission of the American Marketing Association.

[2] In the second menu choice, values and instrumentalities were not measured, and in the book choice only the 24 basic values were measured. Predictions based upon these are discussed subsequently.

subjects is measured after the choice), it can be concluded that the attractiveness score does predict the outcome of the decisions.

TABLE 12.1

Attractiveness scores for chosen and rejected alternatives

	Chosen alternative	Rejected alternative	Percentage correct predictions
First hairdryer choice (N = 34)[c]			
1st alternative chosen	0.860[a]	not available	91.2
2nd alternative chosen	−0.153[a]	not available	
Second hairdryer choice (N = 41)[c]			
1st alternative chosen	0.456[a]	not available	76.3
2nd alternative chosen	0.287[a]	not available	
Restaurant choice (N = 43)			
1st alternative chosen[d]	1.110	0.326	71.1
2nd alternative chosen[e]	1.204	0.976	
Travel choice (N = 41)[c]			
1st alternative chosen	0.380[a]	not available	77.6
2nd alternative chosen	−0.554[a]	not available	
Menu choice (N = 90)[c]	0.386	−0.091[b]	63.3[f]

[a] Relative advantage of first alternative as compared with second alternative (Eq. 10.II used).
[b] Average for 8 rejected alternatives.
[c] Difference significant with $p \leq 0.001$ (t-test).
[d] Difference significant with $p \leq 0.01$ (t-test).
[e] Difference significant with $p \leq 0.15$ (t-test).
[f] Out of nine alternatives. In addition 12.2% of the subjects chose the alternative with the 2nd highest attractiveness score, 12.2% the alternative with the 3rd highest attractiveness score. A total of 94.4% of the choices fell upon the 4 most attractive alternatives.

Further inspection of Table 12.1 reveals that the quality of the predictions varies considerably. It is worth noting that the best predictions are made in the hairdryer experiments. These experiments were purposely designed with male subjects so that the subject would be extremely unlikely to apply previous experience from similar choice processes. Consequently, in these experiments the amount of control is higher than in the following ones. This, not unexpectedly, suggests that when the salient cognitive structure can be predicted, the attractiveness scores give very good predictions. In the latter experiments, in which subjects were allowed to draw upon previous experiences to a greater extent, perfect predictions cannot be expected. As it was seen in connection with the restaurant choice (Chapter 11), under such circumstances subjects may apply values that are not experimentally controlled.

2. Attractiveness and Attitude Measures

It may be argued that the results presented in Table 12.1 could have been obtained with a simple attitude-rating scale. In order to test this, preference ratings were obtained in the travel-choice experiment. "Going by boat" and "going by plane" were rated on two 11-point scales. As discussed earlier, it was possible to obtain these ratings before the introduction of the situational description.

It was found that the "plane trip" was the most positively evaluated alternative. In spite of this, the "boat trip" was preferred by a majority of the subjects, as is reflected in the rating of alternatives. On the average the chosen alternative received a rating of .769 as opposed to a rating of .685 for the rejected alternative, a difference which is not significant (t-test).

However, these ratings are not directly comparable with the results in Table 12.1. The data presented there are based on ratings completed after the situational description was introduced. Consequently, the comparison ought to be made with perceived instrumentality and value measures obtained before the introduction of the situational description. The average attractiveness computed from these scores for the chosen alternative becomes .417 as opposed to .240 for the rejected alternative. The difference is significant with $p \leq .10$ (t-test),[3] and it can be concluded that in predicting the outcome of the choice, the attractiveness score is superior to the preference ratings.

The second part of this hypothesis stated that the preference rating should be predicted by the attractiveness score measured under the same conditions as the rating. In the travel choice experiment ratings were obtained not only for plane and boat transportation, but also for three other means of transportation; consequently for five different alternatives it was possible to test in two ways whether the computed attractiveness score predicts the attitude measure. First, it was tested across alternatives. The average attitude score for all subjects for each of the alternatives was correlated with the corresponding attractiveness scores, yielding a correlation coefficient of .86. Second, for each alternative the attitude score for each subject was correlated with the attractiveness scores for the same subjects, giving correlation coefficients ranging from .82 to .94. These correlations are all significant, and it can safely be concluded that the attractiveness scores give reliable predictions of the attitude measure.

The fact that the attractiveness score predicts the choices and also predicts the preference rating (which does not predict the choices) suggests that the attractiveness score gives a better representation of the underlying cognitive structure.

3. The Relationship Between Value Importance and Perceived Instrumentality

From the data obtained in the first six experiments it is possible to analyze 175 different correlations between corresponding measures of value importance and perceived instrumentality. From a listing of these a random

---

[3] In most other tabulations subjects who made their choice before rating are not included in choice predictions. However, here the ratings are all obtained before the choice, and all subjects (N = 90) are included.

sample of approximately 10%, a total of 18 correlation coefficients, were computed. None of these were significant. It can safely be concluded that value importance and perceived instrumentality are highly independent variables.

4. Choices Predicted Based on Value Importance and Instrumentality Separately

The fourth hypothesis stated that both value importance and perceived instrumentality add significantly to the quality of the overall predictions. This can be tested with data from the two hairdryer experiments, from the restaurant-choice experiment, and from the travel-choice experiment. In order to test this hypothesis it is necessary to compute the total value importance and the total perceived instrumentality for each of the alternatives. These tabulations are illustrated in Table 12.2. The table is a typical summary sheet for a single subject in one of the hairdryer experiments.

TABLE 12.2

Sample of computational sheet from first hairdryer experiment

Subject no. N	Value importance (1)	Perceived instrumentality (2)	Attractiveness (1) × (2)
Efficiency	(−).3	−.3	−.09
Durability	.4	.2	.08
Price	.5	.6	.30
Total advantage of Varig over Schnell	.6[a]	.5	.29

[a] Sign applied from 2nd column.

(Note: Here, as in other computations, ratings obtained in scales ranging from 0 to 100 have been converted to values from 0 to 1.)

Consider perceived instrumentality first. In computing the total relative perceived instrumentality for this subject one simply adds the figures in the second column and arrives at a total of .5. Note the sign associated with the *efficiency* value. As the relative advantage of one of the alternatives (Varig) is being computed and as the other alternative (Schnell) is seen as more efficient, this aspect has a negative sign. By computing similar perceived instrumentality for all subjects and by comparing the averages among subjects choosing either one of the two alternatives, it can be tested whether perceived instrumentality predicts the choices. Results are presented in Table 12.3.

Inspection of the table makes it clear that perceived instrumentality does add to the overall prediction. Furthermore, by comparing the levels of significance in Table 12.1 with those in Table 12.3 it can be seen that the overall attractiveness score is a better predictor than perceived instrumentality taken alone.

Value importance has been treated in a similar fashion. However, in adding up the totals it is necessary to apply the sign of the value determined by the measure of perceived instrumentality (see Table 12.2). Results from these computations are also presented in Table 12.3. It can be seen that

TABLE 12.3

Perceived instrumentality and value importance for chosen alternatives

	RELATIVE PERCEIVED INSTRUMENTALITY		AVERAGE VALUE IMPORTANCE	
	1st alternative	2nd alternative	1st alternative	2nd alternative
Restaurant choice (n = 43)	1.755[c]	1.685[c]	1.348[c]	1.081[c]
Travel choice (n = 41)	0.093[c]	−0.323[c]	12.266[b]	−0.323[b]
First Hairdryer choice (n = 34)	1.041[a]	0.043[a]	0.646[b]	0.480[b]
Second Hairdryer choice (n = 41)	0.756[b]	0.496[b]	0.830[b]	0.393[b]

[a] Difference significant with $p \leq 0.001$ (t-test).
[b] Difference significant with $p \leq 0.01$ (t-test).
[c] Difference in predicted direction, but not significant.

value importance adds to the overall prediction also; and by comparing Table 12.3 with Table 12.1 it can be concluded that value importance taken alone is a poorer predictor than the overall attractiveness score.

In conclusion, both value importance and perceived instrumentality add to the predictive value of the overall attractiveness score, but neither of them taken separately is as good a predictor as the overall score.

5. Stability of Value Importance and Perceived Instrumentality

Are value importance and perceived instrumentality influenced by environmental and other factors to such an extent that reliable prediction cannot be made from measures obtained outside the situation in which the choice is made? In an attempt to throw some light on this, several approaches have been tried.

In the two hairdryer experiments and in the travel-choice and restaurant-choice experiments, value importance was measured both before and after the introduction of the situational description, making it possible to compute two different attractiveness scores. The more the value importance is influenced by the situation, the poorer the predictions should be that are obtained from the attractiveness score based on value importance measured before the situational description. Consequently, the two different attractiveness scores should be compared. As both scores are computed from the same measure of perceived instrumentality, any difference in the predictions can be ascribed to differences in value importance. Results are presented in Table 12.4.

From the table it can be seen that there is little difference between the two sets of predictions. Judged by the differences in attractiveness scores, three of the predictions are better when value measures obtained after the

TABLE 12.4

Attractiveness of alternatives computed from measures of value importance obtained before and after the introduction of the situational description

	Value importance measured before situation	Value importance measured after situation
First hairdryer choice (N = 34)		
Relative attractiveness among subjects choosing 1st alternative	.503[b]	.860[a]
Relative attractiveness among subjects choosing 2nd alternative	.042[b]	−.153[a]
Second hairdryer choice (N = 41)		
Relative attractiveness among subjects choosing 1st alternative	.456[a]	.644[a]
Relative attractiveness among subjects choosing 2nd alternative	.250[a]	.287[a]
Travel choice (N = 41)		
Relative attractiveness among subjects choosing 1st alternative	.492[c]	.380[a]
Relative attractiveness among subjects choosing 2nd alternative	.024[c]	−.554[a]
Restaurant choice (N = 43)		
Attractiveness of chosen alternative	1.014[c]	1.168[c]
Attractiveness of rejected alternative	.533[c]	.717[c]

[a] Difference significant with $p \leq 0.001$ (t-test).
[b] Difference significant with $p \leq 0.01$ (t-test).
[c] Difference significant with $p \leq 0.05$ (t-test).

situation are used; whereas in the last case the reverse is true. However, in all instances highly significant differences in the attractiveness scores are found.

Fewer data are available upon which the applicability of perceived instrumentality measured before the situation can be judged. But in the travel choice experiment both values and perceived instrumentality were measured before and after the situational description was introduced. Thus, it is possible to compare predictions based on (1) value importance and perceived instrumentality measured before the situation is described, (2) value importance measured before and perceived instrumentality measured after the situation, and (3) both variables measured before the introduction of the situational description.

In Table 12.5, the three sets of attractiveness scores are presented. It can be seen that the introduction of perceived instrumentality measures obtained independently of the situation decreases the difference between the attractiveness scores. However, one should not be led to the conclusion that choices cannot be predicted from measures of perceived instrumentality obtained independently of the choice situation. This can be seen from the highly significant predictions which were made in the menu-choice experiment, in which all measures were obtained before subjects had any information about the situation or the actual alternatives.

TABLE 12.5

Attractiveness scores in the travel choice based on measures before and after situation

	Among boat choosers	Among plane choosers	Difference in attractiveness score
Value importance and perceived instrumentality measured after situation (N = 41)	−0.554	0.380	.934[a]
Value importance measured before and perceived instrumentality measured after situation (N = 41)	0.024	0.492	.468[b]
Value importance and perceived instrumentality measured before situation (N = 90)	0.240	0.417	.177[c]
Choice-rating condition alone (N = 39)	(.142)	(.395)	(.253[b])

[a] Difference significant with $p \leq 0.001$ (t-test).
[b] Difference significant with $p \leq 0.05$ (t-test).
[c] Difference significant with $p \leq 0.10$ (t-test).

Another way of looking at the situational influence upon values and perceived instrumentalities is to compare measures of identical variables obtained before and after the introduction of the situational description. In several of the experiments, value importance was measured both before and after the introduction of this description. Thus it is possible to make 22 comparisons between value measures. All of these correlate closely (all correlation coefficients are larger than .85 and significant), but if the averages are compared it is found that ten of these changed significantly ($p \leq 0.05$, t-test). However, as these changes are systematic (as revealed by the high correlations) they have only limited influence on the overall predictions. Nevertheless, they indicate significant situational influence upon value importance.

In conclusion, perceived instrumentality and value importance are influenced by the actual situation. Even though predictions can still be made from measures obtained outside the choice situation, the findings suggest that the greater the similarity between the situation in which measurements are obtained and the one in which the choice is made, the better the predictions.

To test whether values at different levels of the consumers' conceptual structure can be used for predictions even though the values themselves are not necessarily salient in the choice process, data from the travel, restaurant, and book choice experiments can be used. In all three experiments the same 24 basic values were used. Based upon the importance and perceived instrumentalities, attractiveness scores have been computed. The results are presented in Table 12.6.

In evaluating these findings it should be remembered that value importance is measured completely independently of any of the choice situations; consequently, comparisons should be made with the figures in the first column of Table 12.4.

TABLE 12.6

Attractiveness scores based on 24 values

	Chosen alternative	Rejected alternative
Restaurant choice[a] (N = 41)	2.450[b]	1.726[b]
Travel choice[a] (N = 39)	3.305[b]	2.465[b]
Book choice (N = 44)	3.299[c]	3.075[c]

[a] With 2 subjects deleted because all questions were not completed.
[b] Difference significant with $p \leq 0.05$ (t-test).
[c] Difference not significant.

In all three experiments the attractiveness score is higher for the chosen than for the rejected alternative. However, compared with the corresponding figures in Table 12.4, results are somewhat poorer. This difference may be ascribed to the values chosen for study or to situational influence on value importance. In any event, although predictions can be made, it seems advisable to concentrate on the values that will become salient in the actual choice process.

6. Maximizing (Weighting) versus Satisficing?

It is extremely difficult to obtain information by which to judge what kind of an evaluation principle subjects have applied. Therefore in the menu-choice experiments subjects were offered a forced choice between two menus picked so that a choice of one would reflect weighting whereas a choice of the other would reflect satisficing. As it turned out, it was difficult to find alternatives among the nine menus which met the required criterion, and out of the total of ninety subjects it was possible to offer only 26 clearcut weighting-satisficing choices. Of these 26 subjects, 18 chose the alternative that indicated that they had applied a weighting choice principle, and 8 made a choice that indicated that they applied a satisficing principle. The difference is significant with $p \leq 0.01$ (χ^2 test). However, this does not necessarily mean that all subjects prefer a weighting choice principle all the time. The data may as well indicate that some people will weight the alternatives and others primarily satisfice. This interpretation gains support when the data are analyzed in more detail.

In the replication of the menu-choice experiment, a slightly modified procedure was used. It was not possible to construct choice alternatives in the same way as in the original version; consequently, two alternatives were chosen based upon the experience from the first experiment. The first alternative was known to be highly attractive but also to include an item that a large number of subjects had rejected. The second alternative did not include such an item and was somewhat less attractive.

These two alternatives were offered in a forced choice following the regular choice. To the extent that the first alternative was chosen it would indicate application of a maximizing procedure, whereas choice of the second alternative would suggest that a satisficing choice principle had been applied. Again approximately two thirds of the subjects chose the alternative that indicated that they applied a maximizing choice principle.

As suggested, these findings may indicate that people differ with regard to the choice principles they apply. It is possible that some consumers primarily apply a satisficing evaluation procedure and others tend to rely upon a maximizing procedure. It is also possible that most consumers have both evaluation procedures available and that they apply one under some circumstances, and under other circumstances prefer the other. In order to examine this possibility the subjects' own descriptions of their choice processes were analyzed. As information is available about both the alternatives deleted early in the choice process and the alternatives considered just before the choice was made, it is possible to analyze the application of different choice principles in different stages of the choice process. The subject's own descriptions can be classified in accordance with the step in the choice process to which they relate. Not all subjects gave information about all steps in the process; rather, some described how they deleted alternatives in the beginning of the process, whereas others provided detailed descriptions of how they evaluated the alternatives just before the choice was made. Still others gave information about intermediate steps in the choice process. Altogether, out of the 90 subjects, from 69 to 81 gave information about the various steps in the process. This information can be classified depending upon whether it reflects a maximizing or satisficing choice principle. A subject who applied a satisficing procedure would, for example, write that some of the menus were deleted because they contained an item which was definitely not liked. A statement reflecting application of a maximizing (or at least a weighting) principle would be one that explained how a certain alternative was rejected because it "on the average" looked less attractive. Of course, a number of the descriptions cannot be classified into either category. Altogether, the result of this content analysis is presented in Table 12.7.

When the table is inspected, an interesting picture emerges: In the final choice the percentage of subjects applying a maximizing procedure is in line with the findings already reported. However, satisficing behavior is much more frequent earlier in the choice process. This could indicate that the consumer can make use of both strategies and that he tends to apply a satisficing procedure early and then to change to a maximizing procedure later in the process. This finding was not expected, but it suggests a flexibility on behalf of the consumer that ought to be examined in future research.

One more suggestive finding emerged from these data. Application of a maximizing choice principle would be assumed to result in choices of

TABLE 12.7

Application of weighting and satisficing choice principles in the first menu-choice experiment (classification based upon content analysis of subjects' own descriptions)

		First deletion of alternatives	Intermediate steps	Final choice	"Quality" of choice[a]
Satisficing	(%)	79.5	18.8	21.0	1.00
Cannot be determined	(%)	17.8	66.7	17.3	1.43
Weighting	(%)	2.7	14.3	61.7	1.40
Total	(%)	100.0	100.0	100.0	1.25
	N	73	69	81	
No information available	N	17	21	9	

[a] A low score means "high quality".

alternatives more attractive than choices based upon a satisficing principle. In order to test this hypothesis, all subjects were assigned a value of 1 if they chose a menu that had the highest attractiveness or computed liking score.[4] All other subjects were assigned a value of 2. The scores presented in the last column of Table 12.7 have been computed from these figures. It can be seen that the subjects who applied a satisficing principle made significantly "better" choices than the remaining subjects. Although this may indicate that a satisficing choice principle is superior, another interpretation is possible. Those subjects who applied a satisficing procedure in the final choice may have been faced with much less conflict than those who turned to a maximizing procedure. If this is the case the data suggest that the shift from a satisficing to a maximizing procedure depends upon the complexity of the problem.

To test this hypothesis, the difference in rating between the chosen and the rejected alternatives was computed for all subjects. The more alike the alternatives are, the more conflict the subject is supposed to experience. For subjects applying a satisficing procedure it was found that the average difference in attractiveness between the chosen alternative and the second best of the alternatives finally considered was 3.39 as opposed to 1.67 for subjects who applied a maximizing procedure. The difference, significant with $p \leq .01$ (t-test), supports the view that the shift to maximizing choice procedures is more likely when considerable conflict is present.

[4] The computed liking is the total evaluation of the menu computed from the evaluation of the single menu items.

7. Averaging Versus Adding

When two or more alternatives are compared along the same dimensions it makes no difference for the choice prediction whether an averaging principle (10.IV) or an adding principle (10.I) is applied. Only when the alternatives are related to a different number of values will the two principles give different predictions. In most of the experiments the alternatives are compared along the same dimensions, and the predictions based upon the two principles are almost identical.[5] Only the predictions made with the attractiveness score computed from the 24 basic values vary with the computational procedure. Consquently, this hypothesis can be tested only with the attractiveness scores based upon these values, which means that data can be used from the book choice, the restaurant choice, and the travel choice experiments. In Table 12.8 the percentages of correct predictions based upon the two principles is given.

TABLE 12.8

Percentage of correct predictions based on adding or averaging 24 values and instrumentalities

	Percentage of correct predictions based upon "adding"	Percentage of correct predictions based upon "averaging"
Restaurant choice (N = 41)	63.3[c]	58.6[d]
Travel choice (N = 39)	74.4[a]	74.4[a]
Book choice (N = 44)	65.9[b]	56.8[d]

[a] Prediction significant with $p \leq .01$ (x^2 test).
[b] Prediction significant with $p \leq .05$ (x^2 test).
[c] Prediction significant with $p \leq .10$ (x^2 test).
[d] Prediction not significant.

In the travel choice the two principles predict equally well (in percentages), but in the two other experiments the additive attractiveness score is better. Although computations based upon adding do give slightly better predictions, the difference is not extreme. That this slight difference does not result because the alternatives are evaluated along the same dimensions is indicated by the fact that in more than one third of the cases, the two principles do not predict the same choices. The data do not allow any conclusion to be drawn with regard to what computational procedures are applied by the consumer. If the findings suggest anything, it is that neither method represents the underlying cognitive processes perfectly. The interaction between the number of values and the evaluation of the alternatives may be more complex than suggested by either formulation (Chapter 10).

[5] Differences may occur to the extent that some subjects disregard some of the values.

2. *The Nature of the Choice Process*

1. Changes in the Salient Cognitive Structure

It is expected that during the choice process the consumer will eliminate some alternatives and concentrate on the more attractive ones. In any study of this process, the number of immediately available alternatives must therefore be large. The menu-choice experiment was designed to meet this requirement. Faced with nine alternatives, the subjects were asked to tell which alternatives they immediately rejected and which they included in their final evaluation. Data from this experiment are presented in Table 12.9.

TABLE 12.9

Number of alternatives deleted and attractiveness of deleted alternatives in the menu-choice experiment

	NO. OF ALTERNATIVES DELETED	NO. OF ALTERNATIVES CONSIDERED	ATTRACTIVENESS[b]	PERCENT OF SUBJECTS USING A WEIGHTING PROCEDURE
	N = 90	N = 90	N = 90	N = 73, 69, and 81[c]
Rejected immediately	3.045	9	− 34.44	2.7%
Deleted in the course of the process[a]	3.435	5.955	3.28	14.5%
Finally considered	1.520	2.520	18.91	61.7%
Chosen	1	1	38.75	——

[a] Alternatives neither deleted immediately nor considered in the final evauation.
[b] All average attractiveness scores are significantly different with p≤.01 or more (t-test).
[c] For the remaining subjects the procedure cannot be determined.

It can be seen that the subjects gradually limited the number of alternatives considered. Just before making the choice, most consumers were considering only two or three alternatives. The same pattern is found in the replication of the experiment.

In the choice process the least attractive alternatives are deleted first. The average attractiveness for alternatives deleted immediately was – 34.44. The alternatives deleted next had an average attractiveness score of 3.28; the alternatives considered in the final choice had an average attractiveness score of 18.91. Finally, the chosen alternatives had an attractiveness score of 38.75.

In an analysis of systematic changes in the cognitive structures, the shift from a satisficing to a maximizing (weighting) choice principle should be remembered. The percentage of the subjects who applied a maximizing procedure is also given in Table 12.9. Altogether, these data illustrate the dynamics of the choice process.

It was previously suggested that human beings can simplify the problems

they face in a number of ways. One such strategy is to delete irrelevant alternatives, that is, alternatives which are poorer in all respects than other
salient alternatives. The data in Table 12.9 are clearly in line with this
strategy. In order to learn more about this process, subjects in the second
hairdryer experiment were asked to pick two of the four alternatives for
further inspection. Of these four, one was clearly poorer than all the others.
The extent to which this alternative was avoided suggests that the subjects
perceived it to be clearly inferior to the other alternatives. The number of
times each alternative was selected for further inspection is presented in
Table 12.10. In almost all instances the inferior alternative was turned down.

TABLE 12.10

Alternatives selected for inspection in second hairdryer choice

	Number of times selected (N = 80)	Percent
1st alternative (Varig)	30	18.8
2nd alternative (Schell)	51	31.8
3rd alternative (inferior)	6	3.8
4th alternative (new)	73	45.6
	160	100%

2. Initial Conflict and the Preferred Level of Conflict

To the extent that involvement varies only slightly among subjects
faced with the same choice, conflict is reflected in the perceived uncertainty.
The perceived uncertainty is supposed to relate to the attractiveness of the
alternatives. The larger the difference between the best and the second best
alternative, the less uncertainty the individual is expected to perceive;
consequently, initial uncertainty can be measured as the difference in
attractiveness between the best and the second best alternatives prior to
the choice.

The preferred level of conflict cannot be measured directly. However,
to the extent that the available alternatives are sufficiently attractive, the
amount of uncertainty subjects perceive after they make their choices will
reflect the preferred level of conflict. To the extent that post-choice conflict
exists, the amount of perceived uncertainty following the choice exceeds the
preferred level of conflict. Nevertheless, the rating of perceived uncertainty
after the choice is the best measure of the preferred level of conflict that can
be obtained here. Such ratings were obtained in the menu choice, the
restaurant choice, and the book choice.

To the extent that the preferred level of conflict is related to the amount
of initial conflict, the two measures should correlate. In order to test whether
they do, the subjects in the three experiments who rated the alternatives

before making a choice were divided into two groups. The first group is composed of those subjects who experienced considerable initial conflict. They
are identified by having rated the alternatives as being almost equal in
attractiveness. The second group consists of the remaining subjects. They
are supposed to have experienced less initial conflict, as their attractiveness
scores for the best and the second best alternatives differed considerably.
For these groups the average post-choice uncertainty is computed. Data
are presented in Table 12.11.

TABLE 12.11

Post-choice uncertainty among subjects with high and low initial conflict

	RESTAURANT CHOICE		MENU CHOICE		BOOK CHOICE	
	N	Average post-choice uncertainty	N	Average post-choice uncertainty	N	Average post-choice uncertainty
Low initial uncertainty	20	7.38[a]	39	8.20[a]	23	7.00[a]
High initial uncertainty	23	7.20[a]	51	7.66[a]	21	7.29[a]
Total	43	7.27	90	7.89	44	7.14

[a] Difference not significant.

It can be seen that the subjects with high initial uncertainty did not
perceive more uncertainty after the choice than did subjects who initially
perceived less uncertainty.[6] The data support the proposition that the preferred level of conflict is independent of the initially aroused conflict. That
is, regardless of the amount of uncertainty which subjects initially perceive,
they continue the choice process until a certain level of uncertainty is
reached.

3. Decision Time and Conflict

The menu-choice and book-choice experiments attempted to measure
the total time spent on the choice. Subjects who experienced high initial
conflict were expected to spend more time on the choice than the subjects
who perceived little initial conflict. The amount of initial conflict is assumed
to vary with the difference in attractiveness between the best and the
second best alternatives. In the first part of Table 12.12 the average time
measure for subjects who perceived high conflict is presented, along with
the average time measure for subjects perceiving little conflict. In both
experiments the differences are in the predicted direction, but in neither
is it significant. Two explanations are possible.

[6] This procedure was preferred to correlation analysis as there is no reason to believe
that a relationship between the two variables should be linear.

First, some subjects may have perceived so much conflict that they applied avoiding strategies and consequently spent less time on the choice than did subjects with moderately high conflict. In order to test this, the "high conflict" subjects have been divided into subjects with extremely high conflict and subjects with moderately high conflict. When that is done, the data in the lower part of Table 12.12 emerge.

TABLE 12.12

Choice time as a function of amount of initial conflict

| | FIRST MENU CHOICE | | BOOK CHOICE | |
	N	Measure of average time[b]	N	Measure of average time[b]
High initial conflict	51	8.55	21	20.7
Low initial conflict	39	8.04[a]	23	19.0[a]
Moderately high initial conflict	26	9.11[a]	13	22.8[a]
Extremely high initial conflict	25	7.95[a]	8	15.0[a]

[a] The probability of finding a difference of this magnitude is smaller than .15 (t-test).
[b] Number of five-second intervals.

It can be seen that in both experiments the subjects with very high initial conflict spent approximately the same time on the choices as did those with very low conflict, and in both experiments the subjects with moderately high conflict spent the most time on the choice. None of the differences are significant, but they all produce noticeable t-values.

Still another possibility may explain the lack of significant differences in the choice time between subjects with high and low conflict. Time measures were obtained simply by having subjects write down a number that indicated when they had completed their choice. The number changed at five-second intervals. This procedure is not very accurate, particularly not when choices are made relatively quickly. It is possible that this very primitive measure introduced such inaccuracies that real differences were overruled.

Altogether it is not possible to draw any conclusions with regard to the relationship between conflict and choice time. The relationship has not been confirmed, but because of possible inaccuracies in the measurements and the occurrence of an inverted U-shaped relationship, the hypothesis cannot be rejected, either.

4. Number of Salient Values

In most of the experiments the number of important aspects was limited to the extent that the situational descriptions provided information pertinent to a limited number of values. However, it is perfectly possible for subjects to reduce further the number of aspects taken into consideration. If either value importance or perceived instrumentality is rated with a zero, it implies that this aspect does not influence the attractiveness score. The first column in Table 12.13 shows the number of aspects actually entering into the attractiveness scores in the first six experiments. It appears that where a larger number of values are introduced experimentally, the tendency to reduce the number of salient values is stronger.

This problem can also be approached in a different way. In the travel-choice, the restaurant-choice, and the menu-choice experiments, 24 value dimensions were applied. How many of these values actually influenced the attractiveness score is also shown in Table 12.13.

TABLE 12.13

Number of salient values in choices

		CHOSEN FROM LIMITED NUMBER OF VALUES		CHOSEN FROM 24 VALUES	
		Maximum	Actual	Maximum	Actual
Restaurant choice	(N = 43)	10	8.39	24	12.14
Book choice	(N = 44)	a	a	24	17.16
Menu choice	(N = 90)	3	2.82	a	a
Travel choice	(N = 41)	6	4.54	24	12.91
First hairdryer choice	(N = 34)	3	2.95	a	a
Second hairdryer choice	(N = 41)	3	2.94	a	a

a Not available.

Even though the number of salient values is still large, a considerable number were eliminated. Moreover, when the raw data are inspected, it becomes clear that a very limited number of values account for most of the difference in the attractiveness scores. In an attempt to pursue this further, the three most important values were taken for each subject and used to compute attractiveness scores. From these scores, predictions could be made that were as good as those based on the total number of values (Table 12.5), which suggests that the number of values actually governing the choice is limited. Just how many one should consider is an open question that deserves further testing. Presently, it can be concluded that the number of salient values is not extremely large.

One further finding deserves mention. The most predictive of the 24 values seem to closely resemble the values significantly influencing the attractiveness scores presented in Table 12.1. For example, for one subject in the travel-choice experiment, the second attractiveness score (based on 24 values) depends largely on "to meet new people," "to be looked up to," and "favoring change and variety." The same subject decides to go by boat, and in his attractiveness score based on the six predetermined dimensions, *sociable* and *fashionable* overrule *price* in determining an overall positive evaluation of the boat trip. It has not been possible formally to test the hypothesis that essentially the same limited number of underlying values governs the response in rating on the two sets of scales, but inspection of the replies gives that impression strongly. Future research will throw more light on this problem, we hope.

5. Information Search

When the consumer is faced with conflict in a choice situation, he may temporarily solve the problem by making a commitment to seek more information. Whether such a solution will be chosen depends upon the attractiveness of the available search alternatives (relative to the attractiveness of other alternatives) and upon the amount of aroused conflict.

In the two hairdryer experiments, subjects were presented with a modified situational description in which information search was made available (Hansen 1968). Although certain disadvantages were associated with these search alternatives, search still might help to establish better alternatives. As the value importance and perceived instrumentality were also measured in connection with the search alternatives, it is possible to compute an attractiveness score for them also (using Equation 10.I).

It should be noted that the attractiveness scores from the two experiments cannot be compared because the scales applied in the second hairdryer experiment were modified versions of those used in the first. Moreover, in the second experiment the situational description was modified to make search more attractive, in order to induce a larger number of subjects to seek information.

In Table 12.14 the average attractiveness of the search alternative is computed for subjects who sought more information and for subjects who chose to make their choices right away.

In both experiments, subjects who sought more information also evaluated the information search alternative significantly higher than subjects who did not make use of this possibility.

As previously discussed, perceived uncertainty can be estimated from the difference in attractiveness between the chosen and the rejected alternatives.

TABLE 12.14

Information-seeking behavior and attractiveness of search in the two hairdryer choices

	ATTRACTIVENESS OF SEARCH ALTERNATIVE	
	First hairdryer choice	*Second hairdryer choice*
Subjects seeking more information	−.057 (N = 10)	−.289 (N = 54)
Subjects not seeking more information	−.451 (N = 24)	−.500 (N = 24)
Difference	.396[a] (N = 34)	.211[a] (N = 78)[b]

[a] Significant with $p \leq 0.01$ (t-test).
[b] Two subjects deleted because of incomplete information.

According to the perceived attractiveness at the beginning of the choice, subjects can be divided into those with high and those with low perceived uncertainty. From the hairdryer experiments, the data shown in Table 12.15 emerge.

TABLE 12.15

Information-seeking behavior among subjects with high and low initial conflict in the two hairdryer experiments

	FIRST HAIRDRYER CHOICE[b]			SECOND HAIRDRYER CHOICE[c]		
	High initial conflict	Low initial conflict	Total	High initial conflict	Low initial conflict	Total
Subjects seeking information	7	3	10	30	24	54
Subjects not seeking information	10	14	24	9	15	24
Total	17	17	34	39	39	78[a]

[a] Two subjects deleted because of incomplete ratings.
[b] Not significant (x^2=2.27 with one degree of freedom).
[c] Not significant (x^2=2.17 with one degree of freedom).

In both experiments there is a tendency for information search to be more frequent among subjects with high initial conflict. The differences, however, only approach significance.

Involvement is related to how central the applied values are. In an experiment of the present kind, involvement is generally low compared with similar real-life situations. Nevertheless, it can be expected that variations in involvement among subjects will have an impact on the decision.[7] In an attempt to show this, the figures in Table 12.16 were computed. In the first hairdryer experiment, subjects were divided into high and low involvement categories according to their scores on the evaluation questions on the last questionnaire (Chapter 11). The frequency of search was then computed for each of the categories. The observed differences are in the predicted direction but not significant.

TABLE 12.16

Search as a function of involvement in the first hairdryer experiment

	NUMBER OF SUBJECTS DECIDING		
	to search for more information	not to search for more information	Total
High involvement	6	10	16
Low involvement	4	14	18
Total	10	24	34[a]

[a] χ^2=1.0 with one degree of freedom.

[7] Although involvement is not expected to vary significantly as the choice proceeds, it is possible that some subjects are more involved than others. Consequently, it is possible to examine the extent to which highly involved subjects seek more information than less-involved subjects.

It was predicted that search would be a function of perceived conflict, and it has been shown that the propensity to search increases with involvement and with uncertainty. But none of the differences is significant. A possible explanation for this lack of significance is that a sufficient amount of perceived conflict occurs only when both involvement and uncertainty are high. In order to test this possibility the propensity to search information has been computed depending upon involvement and uncertainty simultaneously. These data are presented in Table 12.17.

TABLE 12.17

Percentage of subjects seeking information depending upon initial uncertainty and involvement (a χ^2-test based upon the underlying absolute figures gives $\chi^2 = 3.70$ with 1 d.f. This is significant with p = .06)

	Initial uncertainty high (N = 17)	Initial uncertainty low (N = 17)
Involvement high (N = 16)	67%	20%
Involvement low (N = 18)	27%	15%

The percentages have been computed as follows. The subjects who were high in both involvement and initial conflict were counted; the number of these who chose to search for information is expressed as a percentage of the total number of subjects. This procedure was repeated for the other three categories in the table. It can be seen that the propensity to seek information is considerably higher for people who are high in both involvement and uncertainty than in all other categories.

In the discussion of consumer's information acquisition (Chapter 10), it was suggested that the availability of information is an important factor. As in the hairdryer experiment only one search alternative was available, the preference for different sources could not be evaluated. In the restaurant experiment, however, subjects were asked what additional information they would like to have and what they would do to acquire this information. The data in Table 12.18 were computed from their replies.

The data, illustrative in nature, show two things. First, it can be judged that approximately two thirds of the suggested information sources would be obtainable in the immediate environment. Second, the data illustrate the wide variety of sources to which the consumer may turn. Secondary, tertiary, and personal sources all receive a considerable number of choices. Of course, the data are relevant only to the particular situation, but considering the limited number of subjects and the relatively simple nature of the choice, the diversity of information sources mentioned is remarkable.

6. Exploration

It is difficult to measure exploration in the choice process. Ideally such a measurement would be based upon observation of the subjects, but

TABLE 12.18

Suggested information sources in the restaurant-choice
experiment (N = 90)

	Number of replies	Replies by category	Percent by category
Personal sources			
Ask other people	26		
Ask friends	10		
Ask car driver	2		
Ask at hotel counter	19		
Ask bartender	1	58	42.9%
Secondary communication			
Newspaper	11		
Local guide	6		
Guidebooks	8		
Pamphlets	1	26	19.3
Tertiary communication			
Go and see (and see outside)	17		
Go and see menu	7		
Go inside	6		
Call	10	40	29.6
Primary			
"Try it"	2	2	1.5
Miscellaneous	9	9	6.7
		135	100%

observation was not possible with the present experimental procedure. Therefore, in the restaurant choice an attempt was made to obtain other information which would reflect the tendency to explore the situation. Subjects were asked to write down what information they would have liked to have. It is assumed that the amount of information subjects requested reflects the extent to which they would have explored the situation.

Like choice time and deliberation, exploration is expected to increase with increased conflict. Consequently, subjects who made their choice after rating value importance and perceived instrumentality were divided into two categories depending upon the amount of uncertainty they initially perceived, judged by the difference in attractiveness scores for the best and the second best alternatives. For low and high uncertainty subjects in both experiments, the average number of informational items required was computed. Results are presented in Table 12.19.

It can be seen that, although not significant, the difference is in the wrong direction. As with the relationship between choice time and uncertainty it is possible that some subjects with very high perceived conflict attempted to avoid the problem and consequently engaged in less exploration than subjects who perceived a moderately high amount of conflict. In order to test this, the "high-uncertainty" subjects were divided into two groups, those with extremely high uncertainty and those with moderately high uncertainty, resulting in the data in the lower part of Table 12.19. It

TABLE 12.19

Exploration (amount of information requested) and initial uncertainty

		RESTAURANT CHOICE
	N	Average number of information items
High initial uncertainty	23	2.09[a]
Low initial uncertainty	20	2.13[a]
Total	43	2.11
Extremely high initial conflict	11	1.90
Moderately high initial conflict	12	2.29
Low initial conflict	23	2.13

[a] Difference not significant.

appears that subjects with extremely high uncertainty required less information than those with low uncertainty, and subjects with a moderate amount of uncertainty required more information than subjects with either low or extremely high uncertainty. However, the difference is not significant.

As conflict is a function not of uncertainty alone, but of involvement also, it is possible that the introduction of involvement will improve the findings. However, as no direct measurement of involvement was available, an estimate of involvement was made, based upon the following considerations: In the restaurant-choice experiment ten values were applied, and Table 12.13 shows that a number of these values were eliminated in the choice. Furthermore, involvement is expected to be reflected in the complexity of the salient cognitive structure; consequently, it can be assumed that subjects who are highly involved also apply more values in their choices. Thus, involvement in the choice may be reflected in the number of salient values. Accordingly, subjects were divided into two categories. Subjects who employed nine or ten of the ten possible values were considered to be highly involved, and subjects who employed fewer were considered to be less involved. For each group the average number of informational items requested was computed. Data are presented in Table 12.20.

Again, the difference is in the predicted direction but not significant. Furthermore, a comparison between subjects who were high in both uncertainty and involvement and the remaining subjects does not give a significant difference.

It has not yet been shown that measurements reflecting the tendency to explore are significantly influenced by the amount of initial conflict. However, before the hypothesis is turned down one further consideration should

TABLE 12.20

Information acquisition and involvement in the restaurant-choice experiment

	N	Average number of informational items requested
High involvement	24	2.23[a]
Low involvement	19	1.94[a]
	43	2.11

[a] Difference not significant.

be made. As subjects were asked what information they wanted after making their choices, it is possible that the amount of information they requested is a function of the perceived conflict following the choice, rather than a function of the perceived conflict in the pre-choice period. If so, the amount of information requested should be related to the subject's uncertainty following the choice rather than to the uncertainty estimated from the difference in the attractiveness scores of the best and the second best alternatives. In order to test this interpretation, the average number of informational items requested by subjects with low post-choice uncertainty is compared with the average number of informational items required by subjects with high post-choice uncertainty. As in this case both dependent and independent variables were measured after the choice, subjects who made their choices before the rating are also included. From the results presented in Table 12.21, it appears that the highly uncertain subjects required more information than did the less uncertain ones. Furthermore, when the highly uncertain subjects are divided into subjects with extremely high uncertainty and subjects with intermediately high uncertainty, the subjects with intermediately high uncertainty request more information than either subjects with low or subjects with very high perceived uncertainty. Both the difference between the low and the high uncertainty groups and the difference that emerges from the three-way classification are significant. These findings suggest that the amount of information requested by the subject in this experiment is a function of post-choice conflict rather than of initially perceived conflict. Furthermore, the tendency to seek information increases with the amount of post-choice uncertainty, but extremely high amounts of post-choice uncertainty reverse the relationship. If this interpretation is correct, similar findings should be obtained when the number of informational sources mentioned are related to the post-choice uncertainty. These data are also presented in Table 12.21. It can be seen that these data also suggest a nonlinear relationship. The difference between the high and low un-

TABLE 12.21

Information acquisition and post-choice uncertainty in the restaurant choice

	N	Average number of informational items requested	Average number of informational sources mentioned
Low post-choice uncertainty	29	2.32[c]	1.36[d]
High post-choice uncertainty	59	2.98[c]	1.50[d]
Total	88[a]	2.81	1.45
Low post-choice uncertainty	29	2.32[c]	1.36[b]
Intermediate post-choice uncertainty	25	3.48[c]	2.00[b]
Extremely high post-choice uncertainty	34	2.75[c]	1.12[b]

[a] Two subjects deleted because of incomplete ratings.
[b] Difference significant with $p \leq 0.01$ (χ^2 test on underlying values).
[c] Difference significant with $p \leq 0.10$ (χ^2 test on underlying values).
[d] Difference not significant (χ^2 test on underlying values).

certainty categories is slightly smaller than in previous cases, but the results from the three-way classification are highly significant.

It must be concluded that no significant relationship between initially perceived conflict and exploration could be established. However, this failure can be ascribed to the measurement that was to reflect the subject's tendency to explore the environment during the choice process. Presumably, it reflects the post-choice tendency to seek information, and it relates in a meaningful way to the amount of post-choice uncertainty.

7. Post-Choice Processes

In the two hairdryer-choice experiments, in the book-choice, the travel-choice, and the restaurant-choice experiments, choice-before-rating and rating-before-choice conditions were applied. In the choice-before-rating condition the attractiveness score reflects the evaluation of the alternatives after the choice is made, whereas in the rating-before-choice conditions the attractiveness score predicts the choice. Data from these experiments are reported in Table 12.22.

In the hairdryer experiments and in the travel-choice experiment the relative attractiveness scores (10.II) can be computed according to what alternative was chosen. In the book-choice and in the restaurant-choice experiments, in which the perceived instrumentality of each of the alternatives was rated, the attractiveness of chosen and rejected alternatives can be computed. From inspection of the table it can be seen that in the hairdryer experiments highly significant post-choice changes occur. In the book choice and the travel choice experiments some changes in the predicted direction occurred, but in the restaurant choice no significant changes were found. These findings are in line with the overall expectation that consumers may adjust their perception of the alternatives after making a choice, but that they do not always do so.

The following considerations can be added. Post-choice changes in the evaluation of alternatives is most likely to occur when a significant amount of

TABLE 12.22

Attractiveness scores before and after the choice

	Attractiveness before choice	Attractiveness after choice	Difference	Percent difference	Significance (t test)
Book choice (N = 90)					
Chosen alternative	3.299	4.465	1.166	35.3	p ≤ .05
Rejected alternative	3.075	2.593	−.482	15.7	n.s.
Travel choice (N = 90)					
Plane chosen	0.380	0.497	.117	30.8	p ≤ .01
Boat chosen	−0.554	−0.597	.043	7.8	n.s.
Restaurant choice (N = 90)					
Chosen alternative	1.146	1.081	−.065	−5.7	n.s.[a]
Rejected alternative	0.712	0.683	−.039	5.5	n.s.
First hairdryer choice (N = 34)					
Varig chosen	0.860	1.170	0.310	36.0	p ≤ .01
Schnell chosen	−0.153	−0.333	−0.180	117.7	p ≤ .01
Second hairdryer choice (N = 80)					
Varig chosen	0.456	0.592	0.136	29.8	p ≤ .01
Schnell chosen	0.287	0.238	−0.049	17.1	p ≤ .01

[a] Difference in a direction opposite to prediction.

conflict is present after the choice. In a choice situation with a predetermined number of alternatives, the less attractive the available alternatives are, the more likely post-choice conflict is. With this in mind, the situational descriptions applied in the five experiments can be reviewed. In the book choice, the travel choice, and the restaurant choice the alternatives have no significant negative aspects associated with them. In all three experiments the subjects are presented with choices among relatively pleasant alternatives. In contrast, neither of the two alternatives in the hairdryer experiments is ideal. Either the subject will choose a highly efficient hairdryer, knowing that he is not getting the most durable product, or he will select a very solid item, knowing that he is not obtaining the most efficient one. Consequently, the alternatives in the hairdryer experiments are less satisfactory than those in the other experiments, and the most significant post-choice changes should be expected here.

The changes in the attractiveness of the alternative following the choice may be ascribable to changes in value importance, in perceived instrumentality, or in both. In an attempt to study this, the data from the hair-dryer experiments can be analyzed. (Data from these experiments are chosen because the most significant post-choice changes were found in them.) Results are presented in Table 12.23.

TABLE 12.23

Changes in total relative perceived instrumentality and value importance in the hairdryer experiments

	First hairdryer choice	*Second hairdryer choice*
Total perceived instrumentality[a]	$-.10$[b]	.39[c]
Total value importance[a]	.91[d]	.16[b]

[a] For computation see Table 12.2.
[b] Not significant.
[c] Significant with $p \leq 0.05$ (t-test).
[d] Significant with $p \leq 0.01$ (t-test).

In the first hairdryer experiment a significant change occurred in value importance, whereas in the second experiment significant change occurred in the perceived instrumentality. When single values and instrumentalities are analyzed, only two significant differences appear (out of 24 comparisons). Both of these are in value importance (for price and efficiency). Neverthe-less, an inspection of the 24 measurements of values and perceived instru-mentalities suggests that the adjustment in the total attractiveness score depends upon perceived instrumentality as well as value importance.

Finally, it can be mentioned (see Table 12.22) that in the book-choice and travel-choice experiments the significant changes were found to occur in the chosen alternatives. This result is opposite to what one would expect, as it seems that the rejected alternatives could more easily be changed. Nevertheless, the differences are small, and no conclusions will be attempted.

8. Situational Influence

Systematic variations in the descriptions of the situations were intro-duced in the two hairdryer choices, the travel choice, and the menu choice. In the first hairdryer choice half of the subjects were told that the wife (who was to receive the hairdryer as a gift) had mentioned that she considered the time a hairdryer took to dry the hair (efficiency) to be extremely im-portant. In the second hairdryer experiment four different price combina-tions were used, and in the travel-choice experiment half of the subjects were presented with material from an advertisement that described the boat trip as comfortable, sociable, and fashionable. Finally, in the menu-choice experiment, half of the subjects were told that they were in a French restaurant and the other half that they were in a steakhouse.

To the extent that these situational variations influence the salient cognitive structures, they are also expected to influence the choices. On the other hand, when cognitive elements are not influenced, choices should not be influenced either. In the first hairdryer experiment the effect should occur in the importance of efficiency and in the corresponding perceived instrumentality. From Table 12.24 it can be seen that subjects who were told about the wife's preferences placed more importance on the efficiency value and rated the Schnell hairdryer (the most efficient alternative) as relatively more efficient. Only the effect on the perceived instrumentality is significant.

The changed cognitive structure influenced the choice. In the condition in which the wife was introduced, ten out of eighteen subjects chose Schnell, but only three out of sixteen subjects chose this alternative when she was absent. This difference is significant with $p \leq .05$ (χ^2-test).

TABLE 12.24

Influence of wife's preference upon cognitive structure and choices in first hairdryer experiment

	Importance of efficiency	Perceived instrumentality of efficiency (Schnell over Varig)	Schnell chosen	Varig chosen
Wife introduced (N = 18)	.659[a]	.706[b]	10[c]	8[c]
Wife not introduced (N = 16)	.564[a]	.581[b]	3[c]	13[c]

[a] Not significant (t-test).
[b] Significant with $p \leq .10$ (t-test).
[c] Significant with $p \leq .05$ (χ^2 test).

In the second hairdryer experiment, price differences of $2, $4, and $6 were used. These variations can be expected to influence the importance of the price value and the perceived instrumentality of the alternatives with regard to price.[8] Data are presented in Table 12.25.

TABLE 12.25

Effects of price differences upon cognitive elements and choices in second hairdryer choice (N =41)

	Value importance of "price" (in favor of Varig)	Perceived instrumentality of price (in favor of Varig)	Schnell chosen	Varig chosen
Price difference $2	.34[a]	.63[b]	9[c]	1[c]
Price difference $4	.65[a]	.55[b]	11	10
Price difference $6	.67[a]	.61[b]	4	6

[a] Difference significant with $p \leq 0.01$ (t-test).
[b] Difference not significant.
[c] Choices in this condition differ significantly from choices made in all other conditions combined, $p \leq .05$ (χ^2 test).

[8] In this as in the previous experiment, no differences were found in other values or instrumentalities.

There are no differences in the perceived instrumentalities; but in the condition where the price difference was $2, the value importance associated with the price is significantly lower than in the remaining conditions. Consequently, it is expected that the price difference influenced the choices only in this condition. This effect is also reflected in the choices given in Table 12.25.[9]

In the travel-choice experiment the introduction of the advertisement should influence value importance and perceived instrumentality of comfort, sociability, and fashionableness. Data are presented in Table 12.26. The only significant difference occurs in connection with the value associated with comfort. This value becomes significantly more important after the advertisement is introduced. None of the other measures differ significantly, although all the differences are in a direction favoring a choice of the boat trip.

TABLE 12.26

Effects of advertising copy upon cognitive elements in travel-choice experiment (N = 41)

| | PERCEIVED INSTRUMENTALITY[a] | | VALUE IMPORTANCE | |
	with ad	without ad	with ad	without ad
Sociable	−.83	−.85	.75	.66
Fashionable	−.11	−.12	.37	.36
Comfortable	−.31	−.32	.71[b]	.56[b]

	with ad[c]	without ad[c]
Number of subjects choosing boat	17	8
Number of subjects choosing plane	7	9

[a] The negative signs associated with the perceived *instrumentality* reflect that it is the relative advantage of the plane trip as compared to the boat trip which is rated.
[b] Difference significant with $p \leq .10$ (t-test).
[c] Difference significant with $p \leq .10$ (χ^2-test).

The changes in values and instrumentality suggest that the boat trip should be chosen more frequently in the condition introducing the advertisement. This also occurred. Out of 24 subjects exposed to the advertising material, 17 decided to go by boat, whereas only 8 out of 17 subjects not exposed to the advertising material chose to go by boat.

In the menu-choice experiment the rating of the alternatives was completed before the introduction of the situational description, and only the effect of the situational variations upon the choices can be studied. In Table 12.27 the distribution of choices in the two conditions are presented. They do not differ significantly, although a slight tendency to prefer French menus in the French restaurant can be seen (menus 1, 3, 9).

[9] This finding may suggest that the $2 and the $4 price differences did not generate significantly different price perceptions, whereas the $6 difference (relative to the two minor ones) did so.

Even though the choices were not influenced, it is still possible that the choice process was. As a test, data relevant to the choice process are also given in Table 12.27, from which it can be seen that only slight differences occur, and none are significant.

It is possible that the limited situational influence results because the alternative (menus) were not closely associated with either kind of restaurant. To test whether this explanation applied, the second menu-choice experiment was conducted, in which the alternatives were modified so that some of them clearly belonged to a steak house and the others to a French restaurant. It was again found that the choices did not differ significantly (see Table 12.27).

In the replication, subjects were also offered a forced choice between alternative menus which could be expected to be associated with a particular restaurant. Under this condition a slight difference was found. Out of 15 subjects in the French restaurant, 12 chose the French menu, whereas 8 out of 17 in the steak house chose the French menu ($p=.06$, χ^2 test). The experimental variations in the menu choice did not influence the choice to the extent expected. The most likely conclusion seems to be that menu preferences, at least for the subjects in these experiments, are relatively stable across situations.

TABLE 12.27

Situational influence upon choices and choice process variables in first and second menu-choice experiments

	FIRST EXPERIMENT		SECOND EXPERIMENT[a]	
	French restaurant	Steak-house	French restaurant	Steak-house
Menu number 1	8	9	2	0
2	11	15	5	7
3	10	7	0	2
4	0	1	3	0
5	5	6	0	4
6	6	5	0	0
7	1	2	1	2
8	0	0	2	1
9	4	0	2	1
Total	45	45	15	17
Post-choice uncertainty	.786	.727	.772	.727
Choice time	7.42	7.58	31.3	29.9
Number of comments	3.44	3.83	4.13	4.17
Number of alternatives finally considered	2.52	2.39	2.93	2.73
Number of alternatives deleted immediately	2.89	3.20	2.60	1.94

[a] Includes only the new-menu condition.

Taken together with the data on post-choice changes, these results suggest that both value importance and perceived instrumentality are influenced by environmental conditions and that both may be modified in the course of the conflict. It might have been expected that value importance would be more stable than perceived instrumentality, as values are generally more closely tied in with the individual's total conceptual structure, but for the choice processes studied here, this was not the case. Nevertheless, some indication of the stabilizing effect that results when values are tied in with more central concepts is found in the first hairdryer experiment. Here the efficiency value was influenced by the introduction of the wife. In the condition which introduces the wife, the efficiency value is expected to be more stable because of its association with the more central concept, the wife. We therefore expect that among subjects in the "with wife" condition, post-decisional changes in the efficiency value will be less than in the "without wife" condition. As the direction of the predicted post-decisional change depends on the choice made, it is necessary to test this hypothesis separately for subjects choosing Varig and for subjects choosing Schnell, as in Table 12.28.

TABLE 12.28

Changes in importance of efficiency depending on presence of wife and choice made

	AMONG VARIG CHOOSERS (N = 21)			AMONG SCHNELL CHOOSERS (N = 13)		
	Before choice	After choice	Change	Before choice	After choice	Change
With wife (N = 18)	.54	.60	.06	.82	.84	.02
Without wife (N = 16)	.54	.38	−.16[a]	.93	.90	−.03

[a] Significant with $p \leq .10$ (t-test).

It can be seen that the only significant change occurs in the "without wife" condition among Varig-choosers. It is, however, surprising that no similar significant changes occur among the Schnell-choosers. This lack of change may be ascribed to the fact that the importance of efficiency is so high before the choice that no further increase is possible.

3. Conclusions

The findings in the first section of the present chapter suggest that choices can be predicted from a computed attractiveness score. As the values that will be salient in the choice process become better known, the overall predictions improve. The attractiveness score predicts not only the choice, but also how a consumer will rate on a preference scale. The attractiveness score gives a better choice prediction than the preference rating.

In the situations studied it was found that an attractiveness score based upon both value importance and perceived instrumentality is preferable to either measure taken alone. Both add significantly to the quality of the predictions, and they are highly independent. Predictions *can* be made from measurements obtained outside the choice situation; but the more the measurement situation resembles the choice situation, the better the predictions will be.

It is possible to use values at different levels of the individual's conceptual structure; but in the experiment reported here, the best results were obtained when the values applied came close to those the consumer himself relies upon when he makes his choices.

Finally, it was suggested that the comparison processes are more complex than follows from Equations (10.I) and (10.IV). Neither adding nor averaging give ideal results, and it is likely that the consumer relies upon computation procedures more complex than reflected in either formula. The findings concerning the consumer's application of a satisficing or a weighting evaluation procedure suggest that the consumer may have both choice principles available and that he will tend to rely more upon a weighting procedure when the choice becomes more complex.

The hypotheses concerning the nature of the choice process were largely confirmed. It was found that the number of salient alternatives decreases as the choice process proceeds. Furthermore, the alternatives to which the consumer directs his attention are the more attractive ones.

The comparison between initial uncertainty and doubt following the choice suggests that these two variables are not closely correlated. As the preferred level of conflict (reflected in the uncertainty remaining after the choice) is expected to be fairly stable, this finding is not unexpected.

The number of values the consumer applies in his choice is relatively limited. When many potential values are suggested by the environment, some of them will not be applied.

Whether the choice process will be temporarily solved by means of a commitment to carry out further information search depends upon the attractiveness of the available search alternatives and the amount of conflict aroused in the particular situation.

If conflict is present after the choice, adjustments in attractiveness may result. Such adjustments can occur in both value importance and perceived instrumentality. Similarly, situational variations influence not only the perception of the alternatives but also the importance associated with values.

When the salient cognitive structure is influenced, it will also influence the choices. On the other hand, in no instance did significant differences in choice occur without a preceding difference in the attractiveness of the alternatives.

Concerning the relationship, among the amount of aroused conflict, decision time, and exploration, no conclusive findings were reported. The data suggested a curvilinear relationship between conflict and decision time and similarly, in the post-choice situation, between information seeking and conflict. However, these aspects of the choice process need further study.

Chapter 13

EXPLORATION, DELIBERATION, AND CHOICE TIME

The experimental findings reported in the previous chapter did not uniformly confirm the experimenter's hypotheses concerning the relationships among exploration, deliberation, choice time, and conflict. It was suggested that the lack of support could be due to inadequacies in the measurements used in the experiments. The present chapter reports an additional experiment, conducted after the findings from the previous seven experiments were analyzed, to further explore the nature of choice processes.

1. *Hypothesis*

The hypothesis to be tested follows directly from the preceding experiments.

1. The tendency to explore the environment is a function of the conflict aroused by the situation. When the aroused conflict increases, the tendency to explore also increases; but extreme amounts of conflict may reverse this relationship.

2. The amount of cognitive activity (deliberation) is a function of the amount of conflict aroused by the situation. When the aroused conflict increases, the amount of deliberation also increases, but extreme amounts of conflict may reverse this relationship.

3. Choice time is a function of the amount of conflict aroused by the situation. When the aroused conflict increases, the choice time also increases. But extreme amounts of conflict may reverse the relationship.

The aroused conflict varies among individuals faced with the same situation because they perceive the situation differently, and it varies for the same individual between situations because he perceives different situations differently. Therefore, exploration, deliberation, and choice time may vary with situational differences as well as individual differences. Both will be studied.

2. *Experimental Procedure*

1. Dependent Variables

To study the effect of aroused conflict upon deliberation, exploration, and choice time, we must decide how to obtain measurements of these dependent variables. Deliberation reflects the amount of thought the in-individual gives to the particular problem, the extent of inquiry into memory, and the extent of comparison and evaluation processes. Deliberation is a completely internal process that cannot be observed; therefore, it is necessary to rely upon the subject's own reports. In a pilot study, the following question was used to measure deliberation: "When faced with this particular problem, how carefully would you say that you would consider the alternatives?" The question was accompanied by an 11-point scale ranging from 0 to 10, with 10 explained by: "Would engage in extremely careful deliberation and evaluation" and with 0 explained by: "Would not engage in deliberation at all." However, this question, introduced shortly after the situation was described, resulted in extremely high scores. Almost all subjects said that they would engage in a maximum amount of deliberation and evaluation, probably because the subjects want to think of themselves as very careful and deliberate decision-makers. Consequently, in the experiment the question was worded indirectly as follows: "When faced with a problem of this kind, how carefully would you think that most people would consider the alternatives?" The question was followed by the same scale used in the pilot study.

The tendency to explore the environment is an internal variable, but to the extent that it produces actual exploration, behavioral measures can be obtained. In the course of the experiment, subjects were given situational descriptions and asked to make choices. Following each choice, subjects were asked to indicate how many times they had read the situational description and whether they had been looking back into the situational description when making the choice. Subjects who read the description only once and who did not look back were assigned a value of 0, subjects who read the description more than once and also looked back were given a value of 2, and subjects who either read the description more than once or looked back were assigned a value of 1. It was hoped that this index would reflect actual exploration.

In addition a rating of the tendency toward exploration was obtained through the following question: "A situation like the one you just read can be described in more or less detail and more or less information can be made available. If you had a choice, would you have liked the description to be:

☐ As it was?
☐ A little more detailed (approximately twice as long)?
☐ Somewhat more detailed (approximately half a page)?
☐ More detailed (approximately one page)?
☐ Much more detailed (approximately two pages)?
☐ Extremely more detailed (approximately four pages)?"

As it was not possible to vary the amount of information to which subjects would attend, it was hoped that this measure would reflect the amount of exploration in which subjects would engage.

Choice time can be observed directly. However, as the experiment was conducted in one session with all subjects present, it was necessary to rely upon the subjects' own reports. To make it possible for subjects to record the time, a large clock was installed in the experimental room. The clock was located so that all in the room could read minutes and seconds accurately. Subjects were then asked to write down the precise time immediately after they had read the situational description, and again immediately after they had made their choices. The difference between the two time measures gives the choice time. Since subjects spent from one to six minutes on each choice, minor inaccuracies in the time measure should not overrule the total variation in the actual time. According to observations made by three observers during the experiment, the time measures seem to be fairly accurate.

2. Independent Variables

Perceived conflict is a function of involvement and uncertainty; consequently, it is possible to manipulate this independent variable by using situations that vary in involvement and in the uncertainty associated with their outcomes. Therefore, the experiment was constructed so that such variations could be created. How this was accomplished is described in a subsequent section.

In addition to producing experimental variations in conflict, it is desirable to measure each subject's perceived conflict. With such a measurement inter-subject comparisons can be made, and the extent to which the experimental manipulation has been successful can be observed. However, as the previous experiments have shown, perceived conflict is a difficult variable to measure. In the experiment to be reported here, three different attempts were made to measure it.

First, ratings reflecting subject's subjective evaluation of the uncertainty in the situation were obtained. Next, subjects were asked to indicate how important they thought the problem was by rating how serious they thought it would be to make a wrong decision. By multiplying these two measures, reflecting uncertainty and involvement respectively, a measure of perceived conflict was computed.[1]

Second, the subjects' perceived conflict was inferred from the subject's rating of the attractiveness of the alternatives; consequently, subjects were asked to indicate how attractive they thought the choice alternatives were. Subjects who considered one of the alternatives to be much better than the other were judged to experience little conflict, whereas subjects who perceived only little difference between the alternatives were considered to perceive more conflict.

Finally, an attempt was made to measure the arousal generated by the situations. For this purpose, an index of *motive arousal* developed by Byrne and Clore (1967) was applied. This measure consists of 5 five-point self-rating scales dealing with feelings of unreality, uneasiness, confusion, dreaming, and a desire to know the thoughts of others. These scales, which are presented together with four "filler" items, are each scored from 0 to 4, and thus the total motive arousal score can range from 0 to 20. The scale has previously been used successfully to study differences in the motive arousal generated by movies and by attitude-scale material. It was hoped that this measuring would reflect the amount of arousal generated by the situational description and also the arousal conflict, because perceived conflict is related to arousal.

3. Conflict Situations

It is possible to approach the problem of testing the three hypotheses in various ways. One approach would be to present all subjects with the same situation and then compare the choice processes for subjects who perceive high and low conflict. The major disadvantage with this procedure is that its success depends entirely upon the validity of the measurement of perceived conflict. Besides, this approach does not make it possible to study variations in choice processes generated by different situations, because all variations in the choice processes result from subjects' differential perceptions of the same situation.

Alternatively, it is possible to expose different groups of subjects to different situations. This approach makes comparisons among situations possible; but, if there are considerable individual differences, an extremely large sample is required.

Finally, the same subjects can be exposed to several different situations.

---

[1] As discussed in Chapter 4, Berlyne (1960) proposes a multiplicative relationship, and in risk studies (Cox 1967a) multiplication has been similarly applied. However, Lanzetta and Driscoll (1968) report findings from a study providing some confirmation of an additive function. When this study became known to the author some of the subsequent relationships were reanalyzed using an additive function. However, as this change did not result in any improvement of the established relationships, the multiplicative function was retained. The issue, however, is worthy of further exploration.

This approach allows for comparison within situations as well as across situations; and, as the same subjects are exposed to all situations, differences among situations can be ascribed to situational variations alone and differences within situations to individual differences. This approach has the disadvantage of introducing a possible order effect. However, by randomizing the order of presentation and by controlling the order effect, this disadvantage can to some extent be overcome. As it is desirable to explore individual as well as situational differences, this approach was chosen.

Preferably, the situational descriptions should not be too long, and they must vary in the extent to which they induce conflict. The situations used by Kogan and Wallach (1964) in their studies of risk-taking fit this description nicely. Their complete choice-dilemma instrument consists of twelve brief situational descriptions, each composed so that subjects are faced with a choice between a less preferable "sure thing" and a more preferable "risky" alternative. When the instrument is used to measure individuals' propensities to take risks, subjects are asked to indicate how certain they want to be before they will choose the more preferable, but less certain, alternative. In the present context, however, it is preferable to fix the uncertainty associated with the most preferable outcome. By assigning different probabilities to these outcomes, it is possible to vary the uncertainty associated with the choice.

Of the twelve situations, six were used in a pilot study, and from them three were selected which were believed to present problems of varying importance. In addition, one choice-dilemma situation was used for instructions. Consider the following example (hereafter named the "college choice" situation): "A college senior seeking a doctorate in chemistry must choose between graduate work at university X, whose rigid standards result in only a fraction of the graduate students receiving the Ph.D. degree, and university Y, which has much less prestige in chemistry, but where almost every graduate student receives the Ph.D. degree."

The two other situations present a choice involving a delicate medical operation ("surgery choice") and a choice between an important long-term research project versus a number of less significant, but easier, research problems ("research choice"). The complete wording of all situations is presented in the appendix.

The choice-dilemma situations do not present typical consumer choices, and the nature of the problems is such that they can be expected to be more important than most problems facing consumers. To secure an adequate range of problems and to allow for a test of the hypothesis in connection with consumer choice problems, six additional situations were constructed for the pilot study, and three were selected for use in the experiment. These situations follow the same lines as those used in the choice-dilemma instrument. The first deals with a choice between two makes of car ("car choice"), the second presents a choice between two makes of television set ("television choice"), and the last presents a choice between two brands of a headache remedy ("aspirin choice"). These situations are also presented in the appendix.

Six situations presenting problems differing in importance are used. Furthermore, each situation is presented in two versions, one with a high and one with a low probability associated with the most preferable outcome. For the first three situations, probabilities were chosen at intermediate levels so that choices of both alternatives can be expected to occur in both conditions. This is possible, according to the findings reported from earlier applications of the situations. In the three consumer-choice situations, probabilities were assigned in a similar fashion, but the choice of probabilities was based upon experience gained in the pilot study.

The choice of six situations represents a compromise. On the one hand, it was desirable to show variations in choice processes in as many different situations as possible. On the other hand, when too many situations are applied, subjects tend to become tired and lose concentration. In the pilot study, this fatigue occurred after seven or eight situations, and other researchers' experiences with similar situations also suggest that six is a reasonable number (Wallach and Wing 1968).

All subjects were exposed to six situations each; each situation was presented in a high and a low probability version, and half the subjects were exposed to the high and the other half to the low probability version; this was done in a random fashion so that every subject saw both high and low probability conditions.

Although the situational variations in importance are fairly obvious, it was decided to have subjects in the pilot study order the situations in accordance with their importance. The six situations selected for the final study were ordered relatively uniformly by the subjects as follows (in the order of increasing importance):

> Aspirin choice
> Television choice
> Car choice
> Research choice
> College choice
> Surgery choice

Although only 11 subjects participated in the pilot study, the ordering seems reasonable and agrees with the researcher's expectations. Only the ordering of the research and the college choice may require a few comments. The two situations are not too different (in studies of propensities to take risk, they elicit very similar responses, see for example Wallach and Wing 1968), but to an undergraduate student the college choice is likely to be more involving, as it is one which may soon face many of them.

4. Choice Predictions

The type of situations applied here differ from those used in the previous seven experiments. Therefore, it was desirable to test whether predictions can be made along the same lines. However, to include value importance and perceived instrumentality measures with all situations would increase the length of the experimental material to such an extent that several situations would have to be deleted. Therefore, predictions were made only in connection with a single choice. For that purpose, the car-purchase situation was chosen, and measures of value importance and perceived instrumentality from it were obtained along fifteen dimensions established in the pilot test. Values were measured before the introduction of the situational descriptions, but perceived instrumentality could be not measured until the alternatives were introduced. From these measures, an attractiveness measure was computed to check whether predictions of choices can be made in such situations.

5. Design and Experimental Material

Each of the six choices was structured in the same way, and an example is provided in the appendix. The first time measure is obtained after the situational description, then the index of motive arousal is applied, and then the remaining choice-process variables are measured. Only the car-choice situation follows a slightly different pattern. Here, the perceived instrumentality is measured immediately after the motive arousal index, and before the choice is made. These measurements were obtained as in the previous experiments.

Before beginning the experiment, subjects were told that they were evaluating different conflict situations to be used in subsequent experimentation. To ensure that all subjects understood the instructions, a sample situation was completed under the experimenter's supervision.

All situations are presented in a randomized order, with the single exception of the car-choice situation, which is presented to all subjects as the second situation. If this situation were the first, it would follow too closely upon the rating of the car values. The experimental material thus was presented in the following order:

1. Instructions.
2. Measurement of car values.
3. Situation 1, 3, 4, 5, or 6 in random order.
4. Car-choice situation.
5. Situation 1, 3, 4, 5, or 6 in random order.
6. Same as 5.
7. Same as 5.
8. Same as 5.

6. Subjects

Subjects were 101 undergraduate students in a basic marketing class at the University of New Hampshire. Three were subsequently deleted from the analysis, one because he had previously used the choice-dilemma instrument and two others because they completed only part of the questionnaire. From the remaining 98 subjects, a few incomplete questionnaires were received, but in no case was more than a single question omitted. Assuming that it had been overlooked, we decided not to exclude these subjects completely. Instead, data from these subjects were disregarded for any situation having incomplete information, and only the remaining five situations were retained in the tabulations. For that reason, the number of observations for each situation varies between 96 and 97.

3. *Predictions and Order Effects*

In the car-choice situation, perceived instrumentality was measured as the relative advantage of one alternative (new Volkswagen) compared with the other alternative (used Mustang). Consequently, based upon Equation (9.II) the relative attractiveness score for those who chose the Volkswagen (.291) can be compared with the same score for those who chose the Mustang (1.837), yielding a difference significant with $p \leq .001$ (t-test). The distribution of choices presented in Table 13.1 shows that in 79% of the cases correct predictions were made. Somewhat poorer but still significant predictions can be made from value importance and perceived instrumentality taken separately.

TABLE 13.1

Prediction of car choices based upon attractiveness scores ($p \leq 0.001$, χ^2 test)

	Relative attractiveness < .1	Score > .1	Total
Mustang chosen	33	12	45
Volkswagen chosen	9	43	52
Total	42	55	97

Each of the five situations, which were presented in random order, appeared approximately 20 times in each position. It is therefore possible to study variations in the different measurement depending upon whether the situation was presented first, third, fourth, fifth, or sixth. Data from the television-choice situation are presented in Table 13.2, and data from the other situations are omitted, as they follow a very similar pattern.

It can be seen that only the choice time varies systematically with the order of presentation. The choice takes significantly less time when the situation is presented last than when it is presented first. None of the other

TABLE 13.2

Effects of order of presentation in the television choice situation

Order	N		Arousal index	Impor-tance	Uncer-tainty	Conflict	Index of delibera-tion	Propen-sity to explore	Choice time	Second explora-tion measure
1	19	Mean	2.84	7.11	6.84	52.79	8.79	2.37	136.79	0.42
		Variation	5.19	10.09	5.71	911.64	1.22	2.55	2961.96	0.45
3	21	Mean	2.33	6.76	7.19	48.05	8.24	2.67	136.38	0.76
		Variation	4.41	3.42	3.77	367.28	1.90	2.13	3217.85	0.66
4	19	Mean	4.05	7.21	6.42	47.63	8.21	1.74	105.16	0.32
		Variation	16.58	6.06	5.82	692.34	2.48	1.56	1584.03	0.22
5	21	Mean	1.86	7.52	7.29	56.19	8.48	2.00	100.00	0.14
		Variation	4.79	3.68	2.87	475.49	1.58	3.52	2330.00	0.12
6	17	Mean	3.18	5.82	6.82	42.12	7.94	2.82	91.47	0.65
		Variation	9.20	5.79	3.67	481.40	2.64	2.62	1240.84	0.46

variables vary systematically. However, in the behavioral (second) exploration measure, some significant, although not systematic, changes are found.
These variations are difficult to explain, but suggest that this variable must
be taken with some care. The phenomenon is more apparent in the television choice situation than in any of the other situations.

Except for these two cases, order effects can be disregarded, which implies that the car choice, which always appeared as the second situation, can
be compared with the other situations except for the time measure and
possibly the behavioral (second) exploration measure.

4. *Situational Variations in Aroused Conflict*

In Table 13.3, the aroused conflict scores computed from measurements of
perceived uncertainty and importance (involvement) are presented.

TABLE 13.3

Aroused conflict as a function of situational involvement and uncertainty

Situation (involvement in increasing order)	UNCERTAINTY			t-test of differences
	Low probability	High probability	Total	
Aspirin choice (N = 97)	5.81	6.18	6.01 ⎫	
Television choice (N = 96)	22.76	23.57	23.18 ⎭	p ≤ .01
Car choice (N = 97)	23.37	23.96	23.63 ⎫	NS }
Research choice (N = 96)	43.33[b]	34.85[b]	38.62 ⎭	p ≤ .01
College choice (N = 97)	50.30	48.89	49.61 ⎫	} p ≤ .01
Surgery choice (N = 96)	82.66[a]	72.30[a]	77.60 ⎭	p ≤ .01

[a] Difference significant with p ≤ 0.01 (t-test).
[b] Difference significant with p ≤ 0.10 (t-test).

It can be seen that within both high and low uncertainty conditions, the amount of aroused conflict increases with the importance of the situation. The conflict aroused by the surgery choice situation is 13 times as high as the conflict aroused by the aspirin choice situation. The four other situations generate intermediate amounts of conflict. The variation in uncertainty, however, generates significant differences in the aroused conflict only in the surgery choice situation and differences that merely approach significance in the research choice situation only. The differences in aroused conflict resulting from the variation in uncertainty may be small because the variations in the probability associated with the outcomes are small (10 to 20 percentage points in each case). However, it is worth noting that the two predicted differences occur in two of the three most involving situations. It is possible that only when a certain amount of involvement is present do small differences in uncertainty have impact on the aroused conflict. Other findings also support this view: Significant differences in the attractiveness of the alternatives occur only in the three most-involving choice situations, and the variation in the probabilities does not influence the choices significantly in the aspirin choice situation or in the car choice situation.

In any event, Table 13.3 clearly shows how the different situations arouse different amounts of conflict; consequently, differences in the choice processes are expected in the different situations.

The performance of the index of arousal motive is evaluated in Table 13.4. Again, there are no significant differences between the two probability conditions; and, with only a single exception, the arousal measure varies across the situations in the same way as the conflict measure. Only in the aspirin choice situation is the index of arousal higher than expected.

TABLE 13.4

Situational variations in the "index of motive arousal"

Situation	Conflict	AROUSAL MOTIVE		
		Average probability	High probability	Low probability
Aspirin choice	6.01	2.06	2.18	1.91
Television choice	23.18	1.91	2.13	1.74
Car choice	23.63	2.02[a]	1.89	2.14[a]
Research choice	38.62	2.67[a]	2.17	3.09[a]
College choice	49.61	2.82[a]	2.34[a]	3.26
Surgery choice	77.60	3.01[a]	3.09[a]	2.94

[a] Difference significant with $p \leq .05$ (t-test).

The differences in the index of arousal motive are considerably smaller than the differences in the conflict measure (the largest arousal score is only 50% larger than the lowest arousal score, whereas the highest conflict score is approximately 13 times larger than the lowest conflict score). Moreover, within situations the conflict measure is significantly correlated with the arousal measure (R = .83) only in the surgery choice situation. Altogether, the index of arousal motive is only moderately sensitive to situational variations, and within situations it correlates poorly with the conflict measure. Consequently, the latter will be preferred, partly because of its higher sensitivity and partly because it agrees better with the situational variations.

The attempt to measure aroused conflict in terms of the similarity of the attractiveness of alternatives was only moderately successful. There was no tendency to perceive the alternatives as more alike in the more conflict-arousing situations. Furthermore, when subjects who rated either of the alternatives as very attractive are compared with those who perceive only little difference in the alternatives, the latter have significantly higher conflict scores in only four of the six situations. In the two remaining situations, the differences are opposite to what was predicted, although not significantly so.[2]

A comparison of the motive arousal for subjects who rated either but not both of the alternatives as very attractive with the arousal motive for those who perceived little difference between the alternatives gives similar results. In three of the six situations, the arousal index differed significantly in the predicted direction; but in two of the remaining three situations, the differences are in the opposite direction, and in one of these the difference is significant ($p \leq .05$).

Altogether, among the alternative measures, aroused conflict seems to be most appropriately reflected in the perceived uncertainty and involvement, and this estimate is applied in the following.

5. *Findings*

1. Situational Variations in Choice Processes

In Table 13.5, the average deliberation index, the average exploration indexes, and the average time measure are computed for each of the six situations. As there were only small differences in conflict between high and low uncertainty conditions, they are grouped together and comparisons made between situations only.

From the figures, it can be seen that both deliberation and exploration increase as the amount of situationally aroused conflict increases. The

---

[2] In Chapter 12, data were analyzed based upon the hypothesis that similarity in attractiveness corresponds to high initial uncertainty. The present conclusion may suggest that this hypothesis is less valid. However, even though the conflict measure does not relate perfectly to similarity in attractiveness, it is still possible that the latter relates to the uncertainty measures, but not to the involvement measure. To test this, an analysis similar to the one described above was completed for involvement and uncertainty taken separately. When that is done, the perceived uncertainty measure is significantly higher within all situations for subjects rating the alternatives as very similar, whereas no relationship can be observed between involvement and similarity.

measure of choice time, however, does not vary significantly across situations. As it will be recalled, the choice time was significantly influenced by the order of presentation. To reveal whether this overrules an underlying relationship between choice time and conflict, the average choice time was computed for each situation depending upon its order of presentation (Table 13.5). Again, no significant differences across situations were found.

TABLE 13.5

Variation in choice process variables between situations

Situation	Deliberation index	EXPLORATION First measure	Second measure	All data	Choice time situation presented first	Choice time situation presented last
Aspirin choice (Conflict: 6.01)	3.14	.50	.19	104.29	122.66	86.79
Television choice (Conflict: 23.18)	6.25	1.53	.20	101.83	134.44	91.47
Car choice (Conflict: 23.63)	7.16	1.65	.25			
Research choice (Conflict: 38.62)	7.74	2.14	.39	124.02	155.04	89.22
College choice (Conflict: 49.81)	8.34	2.31	.45	114.18	136.79	83.85
Surgery choice (Conflict: 77.60)	9.61	2.66	.47	108.77	144.16	96.15
Spearman's *rho* (Siegel 1956)	1.00 ($p \leq .01$)	1.00 ($p \leq .01$)	1.00 ($p \leq .01$)	.69 (N.S.)	.81 (N.S.)	.34 (N.S.)

Whereas the changes in deliberation and exploration strongly confirm the first two hypotheses with regard to the effect of situational variations, the data do not support the third hypothesis. Two possible explanations can be pointed to. First, subjects' own time ratings may not be accurate enough to reveal an underlying relationship. However, this does not seem likely when the very small differences across situations are compared with the considerable differences between subjects who spent the most and the least time on the choices. As mentioned, time measures vary from approximately one to more than six minutes, whereas the difference between the situation with the highest time measure and the situation with the lowest time measure is approximately twenty seconds. A second possible explanation is the following: In a naturalistic setting, differences in the amount of deliberation and exploration will automatically be translated into differences in time spent on the choice, as deliberation and exploration take time. In the experiments conducted here, however, there is no additional information on which time can be spent. Only to the extent that subjects return to the situational description in the process of making the choice will exploration tendencies be reflected in time differences. The small values of the behavioral (second) exploration measure suggest that such exploration was very limited. Furthermore, when no additional information can be generated, it is possible that the deliberation is reduced because subjects run short of information to process.[3] Finally, it should be recalled that the time measure includes the time spent checking the scales. Variations in individuals' ability to complete this task may overrule the differences in the time spent on the choice.

2. Within Situational Differences

In all six situations, subjects are divided equally into those perceiving high and those perceiving low conflict. By comparing these two groups, differences in choice processes within situations can be revealed. Figures are presented in Table 13.6.

TABLE 13.6

Variations in choice-process variables within situations, by subjects perceiving low conflict and subjects perceiving high conflict

Situation	DELIBERATION INDEX		FIRST EXPLORATION MEASURE		SECOND EXPLORATION MEASURE		CHOICE TIME	
	Low conflict	High conflict	Low conflict	High conflict	Low conflict	High conflict	Low conflict	High conflict
Aspirin choice	2.41[a]	3.87[a]	0.47	0.54	.08[b]	.31[b]	102.96	105.67
Television choice	5.69[b]	6.82[b]	1.06[a]	2.00[a]	.19	.20	95.02	107.45
Car choice	6.42[b]	7.81[b]	1.42[b]	1.83[b]	.22	.27	—	—
Research choice	7.15[b]	8.31[b]	1.94	2.18	.40	.37	118.40	130.33
College choice	7.55[a]	9.08[a]	1.85[b]	2.75[b]	.36[c]	.56[c]	111.53	117.48
Surgery choice	9.32[b]	9.88[b]	2.31	2.80	.51	.43	115.11	102.67

[a] Difference between low and high conflict groups significant with p ≤ .001 (t-test).
[b] Difference significant with p ≤ .01 (t-test).
[c] Difference significant with p ≤ .10 (t-test).

In all the situations, the deliberation index is significantly higher among subjects with high perceived conflict than among subjects with low perceived conflict. Similarly, in all situations the first exploration measure is higher among subjects perceiving high conflict than among those perceiving low conflict. However, only two of these differences are significant, and a third approaches significance. The behavioral exploration measure differs significantly in the aspirin choice situation, and differences approaching significance are found in the college choice situation. But, in two of the situations this measure shows insignificant differences opposite to what is predicted. Altogether, the exploration measures suggest variations within

---

[3] It should be recalled that the deliberation measure reflects the tendency to compare and evaluate the alternatives, not the actual amount of deliberation.

situations related to aroused conflict, but the evidence is less confirmative than the variations across situations.

None of the five time measures show significant differences, and one difference is in a direction opposite to that predicted, a fact in line with the findings concerning situational differences.

Altogether, the differences in the deliberation index confirm the first hypothesis with regard to inter-situational differences, whereas the exploration measures only provide moderate support for the second hypothesis. Again, the third hypothesis is not confirmed at all.

The less extensive variations within situations may have a very natural explanation. To the extent that variations in the aroused conflict are significantly higher across situations than within situations, smaller variations in choice-process variables should also be expected within situations. To test this, an analysis of variance has been conducted. In accordance with the previous results, it shows a highly significant effect of the situational variations ($p \leq .001$). At the same time, also significant individual differences appear ($p \leq .001$). However, when the mean squares are compared (Duncan 1959), it can be seen that the situational variations account for more than four times as much of the total variance as do the individual differences.

3. Curvilinear Relationships

The data in Table 13.4 did not suggest the existence of curvilinear relationships across situations, perhaps because when situations vary, not only will the actual amount of conflict differ, but also the amount of tolerable conflict.

To see whether curvilinear relationships may be found within situations, subjects in all situations were divided into those perceiving either high or low conflict and those perceiving moderate conflict. For both of these categories average deliberation, average exploration, and average time measures are computed. With these data, a curvilinear relationship will show up in terms of higher averages for subjects perceiving moderate conflict. Such a relationship appears only in the surgery choice situation, in which subjects perceiving a moderate amount of conflict show a significantly higher tendency to explore the situation and also spend significantly more time on the choice. It is worth noting that the surgery choice situation arouses the most conflict. Presumably, in this situation some subjects experience conflict to such an extent that it elicits avoiding tendencies.

6. *Conclusions*

Choice time measures presumably are complicated variables, and choice time may be influenced by several other factors than conflict. Other authors also suggest that this variable, particularly as a measure of choice process behavior, is difficult to apply. It should be noted that, even though the existence of a curvilinear relationship between conflict and the nature of choice processes is not entirely ruled out by the present findings (real choices as compared with simulated choices may arouse a sufficient amount of conflict), the findings do suggest that the phenomenon is not of major importance in consumer choice behavior. It seems that the straightforward relationship between conflict and the amount of energy available for solving the conflict is more significant. This relationship suggests that the more conflict a given advertising (or other message) can arouse, the more carefully it will be explored; and similarly, the more conflict a brand arouses, the more deliberate decision making will be generated. This basic relationship is given major attention in the subsequent chapters.

PART FIVE

Consumer Decisions and Market Behavior

Chapter 14

CONSUMER DECISION PROCESSES I

Consumer behavior should be studied not as single choices, but as sequences of choices. By bringing choice processes together from the consumer's total stream of action such sequences can be composed in many different ways. Particularly important are purchase sequences, or *decision processes*. Such sequences are composed of the choice processes that precede the purchase.

The present chapter suggests that the consumer may apply a wide variety of decision processes. Variations result because the consumer is not equally familiar with all of the products he buys. But decision processes vary also depending upon whether the product is for individual or collective use, whether it is a durable or nondurable product, whether it is frequently or infrequently purchased, and whether it represents a major or minor expenditure. Here major emphasis is placed upon the distinction between first purchases and repeat purchases and between major durable products and frequently purchases nondurable products.

1. *The Nature of Decision Processes*

1. The Purchase Sequences

The choice processes constituting a purchase sequence are those which precede the purchase and are necessary for an explanation of the final purchase. The conflicts preceding a particular purchase represent a relatively homogeneous subset of the large number of conflicts facing the consumer. In many instances these purchase-related conflicts will be tied closely together. The sequence may begin with a commitment; it is carried over to the next conflict, when a modified commitment is made which in turn is carried over to the following conflict, and so on, until the sequence ends, either with a purchase or with the abandoment of the problem.

In other instances, the ties from one conflict to another are less obvious. Consider a purchase sequence in which each single conflict is aroused solely by environmental factors. Here the choices have in common only that they are needed in order to explain the purchase. In such sequences the single conflicts may not appear to be related, but a closer inspection reveals that they are. All or most of them will center around the same alternatives, and the values and instrumentalities which are salient are, if not the same, at least closely related. Further inspection will also reveal that in addition to having alternatives and values in common, the choices will also be functionally related. In the earlier conflicts, information acquisition and adjustments in cognitive elements will occur, and as the same cognitive elements enter into later conflicts, the outcome of the latter depends upon the changes that occurred in the earlier conflicts.

In consumer behavior, however, the decision processes rarely look like either of these examples, but lie somewhere between the two extremes. Commonly, some conflicts are related by means of intentions and commitments; others are generated solely by environmental factors; and still others result from interaction between environmental factors and more or less firm commitments made in previous choices. An example of a decision process is illustrated in Figure 14.1.

FIGURE 14.1.   *A decision process described as a sequence of conflicts.*

Here each single choice may be studied in terms of:

1. The circumstances initiating the conflict.
2. The amount of perceived conflict aroused at the onset of the process.
3. The acceptable amount of conflict.
4. The alternatives that are considered.
5. The salient value structure.
6. The beliefs (instrumentalities) relating alternatives with values.
7. The information acquired.
8. The choice principle applied.
9. The alternative chosen.

10. The amount of conflict immediately following the choice.
11. The extensiveness and the nature of post-choice processes.
12. Behavioral consequences of the choice (action taken).
13. Cognitive consequences of the choice (information stored in memory, modification of values and beliefs, and the like).

The conflicts can vary along several or all of these dimensions, and systematic changes occur during the decision process. The amount of information acquisition will vary between early and late conflicts, the number and nature of alternatives considered will change, systematic changes in initial and acceptable amount of conflict occur and so on. Normally a motivational set governs the decision process. When an initial commitment has been made, or when a conflict has been aroused that has terminated without all conflicting cognitions being eliminated, then a determining tendency has been established that accounts for the reappearance of the problem. The determining tendency will influence behavior as long as a sufficient amount of (latent) conflicting cognitions exist, but gradually, as the decision process progresses, the latent conflict will be modified. In each single choice process a limited number of concepts are made salient, in the process of solving the aroused conflict, cognitions are changed, and over time the elements of the motivational set will be mutually adjusted. Eventually, when the latent conflict has been reduced sufficiently, the motivational set will cease to exist. Often this occurs when the purchase is made. Processes of this nature have been discussed by several authors. Lewin (1958) talks about a "general idea" and Alderson (1965) about a "vague motive" that gradually becomes specified and results in a purchase when a sufficient level of specification has been reached.

When the complete decision process is studied, it is important to look at its overall complexity as reflected by the number of conflicts of which it is composed and by its duration in time. The sequence may be completed within a couple of hours or less, or it may go on for years. As the single choice processes vary and can be combined in many ways, it is obvious that decision processes vary widely. A model that attempts to cover all possible cases is therefore not appropriate. Rather, the type of decision should be specified meaningfully and the sequence of choices studied according to the type.

2. Consumer Intentions

A consumer can be described in terms of a set of propensities that reflect the probability that he will respond to particular situational settings. As these propensities can be modified in choice processes, they depend upon the consumer's past history. If he has just bought a car, chances are very low that he will enter into a car-purchase situation in the immediate future. On the other hand, if he has just received very favorable information about a particular make of car, the probability increases that he will enter into a new situation where he acquires additional information about the car. In this way, after each choice, some probabilities increase and others decrease.

Of course, there is no such psychological variable as a "probability of entering into a situation," but the meaning of commitments and intentions and the effects of "being set" on something can operationally be quantified in terms of such probabilities. In this way a decision process may be characterized as a sequence of choices such that each subsequent choice situation has a high probability of being reached, provided the previous ones have been completed.

Variables of this nature have been dealt with in studies of purchase plans and intentions (Namias 1959, Tobin 1959, and National Bureau of Economic Research 1960), and Juster (1964) has tested seven different measures of intentions in connection with thirteen products and found that for all combinations of measures and products the purchase rate is higher among intenders than among nonintenders. Moreover, among the different measurements he finds that the consumers' own subjective purchasing probabilities are superior, and buying intentions based on these are now being reported regularly (Commercial Credit Company 1967–1969).

Most of such work has concentrated on durable products (Juster 1966, Ferber 1966, and Murray 1969). A few attempts with nondurable products have been less successful (Wells 1961 and Rothman 1964), perhaps because they have tried to predict brand purchases rather than purchase situations. With nondurable products specific brand purchase can be extremely difficult to predict from measures of pre-purchase plans because there are no intentions with regard to specific brands. But consumers may be perfectly able to predict specific purchase situations because such situations tend to reappear in certain patterns.

That purchase intentions reflect ongoing decision processes is evident from several studies. For example, in a study of purchases of new products Stapel (1968) found that Dutch consumers who stated positive intentions to buy a TV shortly after the introduction of television rediffusion actually went out and bought it to a significantly larger extent than did consumers with less firmly established intentions. Similarly, Granbois and Willett (1969) report that intention influences other prepurchase activities and Smith et al. (1963) and a later study by Smith (1965) found that consumers who intend to purchase certain products also are more likely to read advertisements about these products.

2. *Decision-Process Models*

1. Overview

Decision-process models have been suggested in a number of different areas, and in recent years they have gained popularity among students of consumer behavior. Most of these models have a number of concepts in common. They all deal with the individual's acquisition of information, and they describe how this information is related in order to reach a decision. Very few of them consider the time dimension explicitly. Rather, they assume that the decision process is one continuous process in time and usually hold that the process always follows a certain predetermined pattern. Finally, they describe the decision process as composed of a number of separate steps, such that each step always occurs and the steps are always found in the same order.

Most early versions of decision-process models dealt with decision-making in other areas than consumer behavior. For example Simon (1957) and March and Simon (1958) deal with decision-making in organizations. Beal and Bohlen (1957) and Johnson (1957) suggest models with major relevance to farm decision-making, and Parsons and Shills (1953), Gagne (1959) and Brim et al. (1962) discuss general frameworks for decision-process models.

Even though the different models relate to the specific areas in which they have been developed, they have much in common, as can be seen in Table 14.1, which shows that most of the models deal with five different steps in the decision process: problem identification, information search, evaluation of alternatives, choice, and post-choice processes. Most of the models cover all of these areas, and some even specify two or more steps within each class. Other models cover only three or four of the five steps. Some of the more important models will be discussed in the following section.

2. General Models

General models of consumer behavior fall into two categories. Some put the main emphasis on information acquisition and can be labeled *consumer information-processing* models. Others put greater emphasis upon the evaluation of alternatives and can be labeled *problem-solving* models. Of course, the distinction is not always easy to maintain as all models deal with both aspects of the decision process; but when the models are analyzed more closely, a marked difference in emphasis is evident.

TABLE 14.1

An overview of selected decision-process models

	Problem identification	*Information acquisition*	*Evaluation*	*Decision*	*Post-decision*
General models Gagne (1959)	1. Perception of stimulation		2. Concept formation 3. Determining causes of action	4. Decision-making	5. Verification
Brim et al. (1962)	1. Problem identification	2. Information search	3. Production of possible strategies 4. Evaluation	5. Selection of strategy	6. Actual performance

Table 14.1 contd.

General consumer models Granbois (1963)	1. Identification	2. Obtaining information	3. Recognition of alternative solutions 4. Evaluation of solutions	5. Selection of strategy	6. Actual performance and reinforcement
Howard & Sheth (1967)	1. Attention	2. Comprehension	3. Attitudes 4. Intentions	5. Purchase	
Nicosia (1966)	1. Attitude formation	2. Search	3. Evaluation	4. Purchase	5. Feedback
Engel et al. (1968)	1. Problem recognition	2. Search	3. Alternative evaluation	4. Purchase	5. Post-purchase behavior
Ås (1966)	1. Unconscious needs 2. Attention to unconscious needs 3. Availability of alternatives	4. Information search	5. Inspection of alternatives 6. Evaluation and choice	7. Purchase	8. Preparation, demonstration and use 9. Repair, return and scrapping 10. Total satisfaction 11. Re-purchase
Adoption models Rogers (1962)	1. Awareness	2. Interest	3. Evaluation	4. Trial	5. Adoption

Advertising models
  Lavidge &
  Steiner (1961)

awareness	knowledge

cognitive

liking	preference

affective

conviction	purchase

conative

Colley (1961)	1. Awareness		2. Comprehension 3. Conviction	4. Action	
"AIDA"	1. Attention	2. Interest	3. Desire	4. Action	
Cerha (1967)	1. Knowledge		2. Attitudes 3. Intentions	4. Behavior	
Income allocation models Pratt (1965a)	1. No intention to purchase 2. Preliminary allocation of household resources among major product categories	3. General shopping	4. Allocation to major categories 5. Product decision	6. Specific shopping 7. Purchase	8. Reactions to purchase 9. Post-purchase attitudes
Gredal (1959)	1. General purchasing decision	2. Concrete purchasing decision	3. Selection decision	4. Technical purchasing action	
Situational models Sandel (1969)	1. Environmental initiation of the purchase 2. Calculations	3. Product class choice	4. Search	5. Purchase	6. Use

One of the first models in the area of consumer behavior is presented by Nicosia (1966). Another early version is found in Kollat (1966), who discusses decision processes in connection with impulse purchases. Closely related is the family decision-making model discussed by Grandbois (1963) and the later and more elaborate versions presented by Engel et al. (1968) and by Howard and Sheth (1967 and 1969). Finally, a less general model is suggested by Wickström (1965), who deals with family decision processes for major individual purchases.

All of these models are concerned with consumer behavior in general, they put major emphasis on information search, and they predict more or less complex decision processes depending upon the specific circumstances. The models are described in the sources mentioned and a comparison is made in Engel et al. (1968).

An early model with its main emphasis upon the evaluation of alternatives is suggested by Kornhauser and Lazarsfeld (1955). Of the same nature is the Michigan Group's model explicitly formulated by Morgan (1961). Here a distinction between individual and household decision-making is made also, and the model is restricted to "decisions of major importance to the family." In this model the consumer's choices are explained as due to stable wants and needs which in the particular situation interact with the environmental factors (see Table 17.2). Within home economics similar models have been discussed by Burk (1969), and a model building upon the Michigan scheme is suggested by Ås (1966). This version is one of those which go furthest in an attempt to incorporate consumption behavior as an integrated part of the total decision process. Finally, Cox's (1967b) sorting-rule model should be mentioned. This model gives a very detailed description of the evaluation process and is closely related to psychological models of thinking and problem solving (Rimoldi 1955, Bruner et al. 1956, and Gagne 1959).

3. The Adoption Model

The acceptance of new products, ideas, and practices has been studied in a number of different areas. The approach originated in various branches of sociology, and early studies dealt with farmers' adoption of new farm practices (Ryan and Gross 1943, Wilkening 1958, and Lionberger 1959); school systems' acceptance of new practices (Mort and Cornell 1938); and physicians' acceptance of new drugs (Katz 1957). Several models have been proposed, but today the formulation presented by Rogers (1962) has gained general acceptance. This model suggests that the consumer moves from awareness, interest, evaluation, and trial to final adoption.

In contrast with most other decision-process models, the adoption model has given rise to considerable research, most of which is reviewed in Rogers (1962) and in Rogers and Stanfield (1968). In recent years consumers' acceptance of new products has been studied within the framework of the model.

In early applications the acceptance of radically new products and practices has been studied. Here it has normally been possible to identify the different steps in the adoption process (Rogers 1962). However, this is not always possible when the innovation is a new product that differs only slightly from products already in the market (Robertson 1968 and Sheth 1968a) or when the introduction of a new brand is studied (Arndt 1967b). In such instances the complete adoption process may occur very quickly, with no way to detect whether separate steps really existed. It is therefore not surprising that the model has been most successfully applied in studies of the adoption of major durable products.

Whereas the adoption process itself concerns individual behavior, the closely related innovation model deals with aggregated effects. This model describes how different consumers will adopt a new product in different time periods. The consumers are classified as (Rogers 1962):

innovators (the first 2.5%)
early adopters (the next 13.5%)
early majority (the next 34%)
late majority (the next 24%)
laggards (the last 16%)

In Figure 14.2 the relationship between the adoption and the innovation models is illustrated.

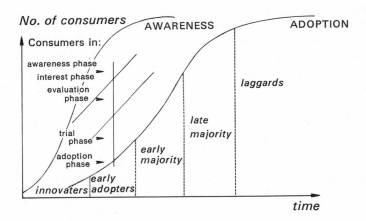

FIGURE 14.2.   *The innovation process. The figure shows how different consumers adopt the product at different times. At the same time it illustrates different consumers passing through different phases of the adoption process.*

Many discussions of the innovation model assume that a market can be defined so that all consumers will adopt the product. But it is also possible to study innovation processes resulting in less than 100% adoption by including an additional category of consumers, namely, those who do not adopt.

Related to innovation models are also fashion models (Nystrom 1928, King 1965, and Carman 1966b). The basic hypothesis underlying these models states that some consumers (*imitators*) will imitate other consumers, whereas other consumers (*differentiators*) will differentiate themselves through their product choices (Gold 1964). The differentiators will be less likely to purchase a certain product the more other consumers have bought it in the preceding period, whereas the imitators will be more likely to purchase the product as more consumers purchase it. More accurately, consumers can be seen as ranging from extreme imitators to extreme differentiators. Depending upon the consumer's location on such a scale, he can be classified by his tendency to adopt new fashions, and the lower this tendency, the later he will adopt.

It has been proposed that the tendency to adopt new fashions varies among social classes and with geographical location. However, in recent years it has been pointed out that the fashion adoption process does not have to be a trickle-down process by which new fashions move downwards through social classes and geographically from fashion centers to rural areas (Fallers 1954 and King 1963). Basically, in the fashion models the dependent variable is total acceptance in a given period, and the independent variable is the adoption in previous periods. The model particularly applies to products that are socially consumed and offer possibilities for expressing personal tastes (such as clothing, furniture, and art objects). However, special features such as trends in car design have also been studied as fashion processes (Reynolds 1965), and there is no general agreement as to what constitutes a fashion. Fashion cycles have been found in historical data covering a very long time period, but in recent years such cycles appear to be less easily identified (Carman 1966).

4. Models of the Hierarchy of Effects

Several models have been suggested that rest upon more or less intuitive conceptualizations of the advertising process. For decades the AIDA formula (*A*ttention, *I*nterest, *D*esire, *A*ction) has been a common ingredient in advertising textbooks, and recently related models have gained renewed interest. Lavidge and Steiner (1961) compare the stages in the advertising process with the components of an attitude as seen by many social psychologists. Awareness and knowledge are seen as corresponding to cognitive effects, preference and liking to affective effects, and changes in conviction and purchase to conative (behavioral) effects. One reason for the interest aroused by the Lavidge and Steiner formulation is that they also suggest different kinds of marketing communication that can be applied in the different stages of the process and that they propose measurements which can be used in attempts to control whether the expected changes occur.

The advertising control model proposed by Colley (1961) rests upon basically the same assumptions, as does the approach of Hughes (1963) to control with personal selling. However, later authors have criticized these models from several different points of view. Palda (1966), in particular, maintains that all the steps between initial awareness and final purchase need not always occur, and if they do, they need not occur in the same order, a position he supports with convincing evidence from a number of private and published studies.

In spite of this controversy, modified versions of the model are still in use. The knowledge, attitude, intention, behavior model applied by Cerha (1967) belongs to this category, and so do the models used by Assael and Day (1968) and by Montgomery and Armstrong (1968). However, in these models the assumptions about causal relationships among the variables are weakened.

5. Household Budgeting Models

Other researchers have approached consumer behavior from the point of view of income allocation. Basically, they maintain that consumer decision processes should be studied as processes by which the consumer allocates his disposable income, first to major product categories, then to different products, and finally to individual brands. Although not assuming that all consumers engage in such a budgeting procedure, they maintain that consumers' behavior can be described as if they did. An early version of these models was discussed by Schmidt (1941), and Lewin's (1958) "gate-keeper" model also belongs to this category, as do models proposed by Clarkson (1963), Gredal (1959), and Pratt (1965a). The latter two are interesting because they attempt to unify the traditional decision process approach with the income-allocation model. Both authors discuss information acquisition and deliberation activities as they relate to the allocation of income. Unfortunately, these models have given rise to little research. Only Bilkey (1965), in an attempt to relate psychological variables to the income allocation process, finds some relationship between a measure of the overall attractiveness of products in different categories and the amount of money spent on the category.

6. Situational Models

An interesting version of the decision-process model is proposed by Sandell (1969). This model describes the decision process as a number of steps: environmental initiation of the process, calculations, product-class choice, search, purchase, and use. However, Sandell is particularly interested in situational influences, not only in the beginning of the process but also in the various subsequent steps. He suggests that each single step in the process can be seen as a function of the previous steps and the environment in which the steps are performed. In this way he emphasizes that information acquisition occurs in all steps of the process, whereby the model comes close to the one that emerges when the decision process is seen as a sequence of conflicts.

3. Variations in Consumer Decision Processes

1. Classifying Decisions

Consumers differ along an infinite number of dimensions, among them income, sex, education, intelligence, personality, social interaction pattern, and group memberships. Most of them may influence the consumer's decision processes. In the present discussion, however, only two distinctions are made. First, a distinction is made between individual decisions and collective decisions. Individual decisions occur when the consumer chooses a product for his own use. Collective decisions occur when more than one individual actively takes part in the decision and shares the goals and risks associated with the purchase of the product (Matthews et al. 1964). The present chapter primarily concerns individual decision processes. Collective decision processes are dealt with in Chapter 17.

The second distinction is made between first purchases and repeat purchases and is important for several reasons. Basically, it reflects differences in the consumer's familiarity with the product. When the consumer makes a first purchase, he has no experience with the product; consequently, he must rely solely upon other information sources. In contrast, when the consumer makes a repeat purchase, he knows about the product from previous use and consequently may have learned something between purchases.

Studies of first purchases will have to put the main emphasis on the consumer's selection of information sources, and in many instances credibility and expertise will make personal information and, to some extent, shopping the most important factors. With repeat-purchases, in contrast, the one most important factor often is the experience the consumer has had with the product. If it has been negative, any combination of other information sources is unlikely to generate a repeat purchase, and if it has been positive, a repeat purchase may occur regardless of most information from other sources.

The distinction between first purchases and repeat purchases makes a few comments necessary regarding the nature of first purchases. Whether a purchase is a first purchase does not depend on the product but rather the consumer's experience with the product. A first purchase can occur when a new product is introduced or when a consumer for the first time purchases a product which has existed for some time. In the first case, the question is, how different should the new product be to be classified as really new and a cause of first purchases? In the second case the question is, how different should the product be from products already familiar to the consumer? In both instances the problem really is, how can products be meaningfully compared?

The question of comparison has been a major issue within economic theory, particularly within the theory of competition, and it has been discussed within adoption and innovation theory. In economic theory, the problem has been to determine the extent to which products are competing with each other. As the amount of competition depends on substitution, it also reflects similarly among products. On the one hand are products which are completely independent of all other products; their sellers can be said to have monopolies on their respective products. On the other hand are identical products, such that an infinitely small increase in the price for one product (assuming initially identical prices) causes the consumers to buy only the other products (a homogeneous market). Of course, between these two extremes any degree of competition may exist. Traditionally, analysis of competition has rested upon the relationship between the quantity demanded of one product and the prices charged for other products (Triffin 1940). To the extent that changes in the price of one product influence the quantity demanded of the other, competition is said to exist. More recently (Rasmussen 1955) it has been suggested that not only price relationships but also advertising and quality relationships should be considered. That is, for example, when a change in the advertising strategy of one product results in changes in the demand for another product, then the products are competing with each other.[1] This approach leads to a pair of definitions of what constitutes a new product. A new product can be defined either as one that will create a monopoly when it is introduced or as one that is not completely identical with existing products, that is, such that some, but not perfect, competition will result when the product is introduced. Although theoretically elegant, such definitions are of little practical value so long as they do not provide tools to determine whether a product is "new" or not.

Distinctions between repeat and first purchases will have to reflect whether the consumer has bought the product before and the extent to which he can apply experience from previous similar purchases. The first can normally be determined very easily. The latter underlies several suggestions made by students of innovations. Rogers (1962) suggests that an innovation may be characterized along the following dimensions:

1. Its relative advantage (i.e., the extent to which it is superior to alternatives already available).

[1] The analysis is more complicated because, in a broader sense, all products can be said to be competing with each other because they all compete for shares of the same limited income. This wider concept of competition, however, is not used here.

2. Its compatability (reflected in the extent to which it violates or is in agreement with social values in the society into which it is being introduced).

3. Its complexity (i.e., the extent to which the use of the innovation can be easily understood and requires only little learning).

4. Its divisibility (reflected in the extent to which it is possible to try out the innovation on a small scale before definitely adopting it).

5. Its communicability (reflected in the extent to which the innovation lends itself easily for communication, particularly the extent to which the use of the innovation is observable by others).

Of these dimensions, however, only the first and possibly the second have to do with whether the product is new or not. The three later ones relate to aspects of the product which affect the way consumers will react to it.[2] Moreover, the classification of a product as an innovation is not much more easily determined by these criteria than by the economists'. Part of the problem is that a given product may represent any degree of "newness" and that a two-way classification is likely not to be fine enough. Realizing this, Robertson (1967b) discusses three classes of innovations according to their effect upon the consumer:

1. Continuous innovation has the least disrupting influence on established patterns. Alterations of a product are involved rather than the establishment of new products. Examples: fluoride toothpaste; new model automobile change over; menthol cigarettes.

2. A dynamically continuous innovation has more disrupting effects than a continuous innovation, although it still does not generally alter established patterns. It may involve the creation of a new product, or the alteration of an existing product. Examples: electric toothbrushes; the Mustang automobiles; touch-tone telephones.

3. A discontinued innovation involves the establishment of a new product and the establishment of new behavior patterns. Examples: televisions, computers (pp. 15–16). (Reprinted from "The Process of Innovation and the Diffusion of Innovation," *Journal of Marketing* Jan. 1967 Vol. 31 No. 1 published by the American Marketing Association.)

The classification rests upon the product's total influence upon the consumer's behavioral pattern and in this respect is in line with Mueller's (1958) distinction between new products that merely replace products already in use (for example, nylon shirts) and new products that expand the total demand (for example, TV). New brands that differ only slightly from existing ones are not considered to be innovations, and minor changes in product quality or in advertising, merchandising, or packaging policies are not considered to be generating a new product. Although the following chapters rest upon Robertson's classification, most emphasis is placed on the last two types of innovations, partly because the most evidence is available for these groups and partly because the special behavioral patterns in connection with new products can most easily be identified for them.

[2] The divisibility factor seems to reflect aspects closely associated with the risk involved in adopting the product.

2. Environmental Differences

Choice processes will vary with the specific situation in which they occur, and similarly the entire decision process will depend upon environmental factors. However, often the single choices in the sequence are made in different environments, and therefore it is difficult to classify the process in accordance with a particular situation. Of course, in some instances the complete process is performed at once and the relevant situation can be identified easily. However, most commonly some steps in the decision process take place in one environment (for example, at home) and other steps are performed most commonly in other environments (for example, in the store). If a decision process cannot be classified systematically according to its environment, one must look for situational factors that remain constant throughout the process. The product under consideration is one such factor, and consequently the decision process can be classified according to the kind of product being examined.

Probably the most widely used product classification is the one proposed by Copeland (1925), which distinguishes among convenience, shopping, and specialty goods. As in definitions suggested by various other authors, the distinctions rest upon purchase patterns. The committee of Definitions of the American Marketing Association (1960) defines convenience goods as "those consumers' goods which the customer usually purchases frequently, immediately, and with a minimum of effort in comparison and buying" (p. 10); shopping goods are "those consumers' goods which the customer, in the process of selection and purchase, characteristically compares on such basis as suitability, quality, price and style" (p. 21). Finally, specialty goods are "those consumers' goods with unique characteristics and/or brand identification for which a significant group of buyers are habitually willing to make a special purchasing effort" (p. 22).

The nature of the classification is further explored by Groeneveld (1964), who suggests that, rather than making a distinction among three different kinds of products, the classification reflects a scale ranging from complete absence of forethought to a great deal of forethought. Furthermore, he suggests a rating procedure to place a particular product on this scale; the value assigned to a product is determined by its unit price, the frequency with which it is purchased, its size (cubic inches), its perishability (number of hours until spoilage), and the style of obsolescence (number of months until obsolescence).

Another interesting proposal has been made by Kaish (1967), who points out that the distinction among shopping, convenience, and specialty goods is basically a classification of decision processes. In an attempt to relate it to dissonance theory he suggests that convenience goods can be characterized as those which are unimportant to the consumer and cause only little dissonance (conflict). Shopping goods are those which are important but arouse dissonance (conflict) that can easily be reduced through information gathering, and finally specialty goods are those which are important and arouse dissonance (conflict) that is difficult to reduce because of the complexity of the evaluation of the products.

The major disadvantage with Copeland's classification is that it rests upon a mixture of characteristics, some inherent in the product and others that reflect the consumer's way of purchasing the product. The latter is particularly inconvenient, as a definition of this kind should make it possible to explain differences in consumers' purchase sequences.

Another important distinction is that between durable and nondurable products (Kjaer-Hansen 1960). Basically the distinction is simple. A durable product is one which is not destroyed in one or a few uses, whereas a nondurable product is consumed while it is being used. However, a couple of problems arise in practice. Many products that are technically durable have many things in common with nondurable goods, even such minor items as man's socks or pencils. In an attempt to reserve the term *durable* for larger products, several authors have suggested that only products that last for a number of years should be so classified. For example, Matthews et al. (1964) suggest that a serviceable life of three years be used as a minimum.

The most important aspect of the distinction between durable and nondurable goods is the fact that if a durable product is purchased, then it will be available to the consumer for some period of time, that is, it will represent a "stock" for the consumer and it will influence consumption, communication, and later repurchase sequences. The economically most significant aspect of stocks is that they make the product available in some later time period. Since a year is the most commonly used period in economic and business analysis, it is suggested here that a durable product is one which will last a year or longer.

Another problem exists in connection with services. Because of their nature, many services cannot be classified either as durable or nondurable. Some authors prefer to consider services as a completely separate group of products. Others (Kjaer-Hansen 1960) have attempted to classify services as durable or nondurable depending upon whether they are purchased as durable products or as nondurable products. Here the latter view is adhered to, because purchase sequences do not vary significantly between services and other products if the services are properly classified. Consequently, a service is classified as durable when its purchase will influence behavior in subsequent periods. For example, purchase of life insurance, major home repairs, education, and a major vacation trip will be considered as durable purchases, whereas purchases of a haircut, a minor trip, and a short-term bank loan will be classified as nondurable purchases.

Some authors have classified products according to consumer shopping habits. Dommermuth (1965) distinguishes among products depending upon the number of stores the consumer normally visits and the number of alternatives in each store. Such classifications are purely descriptive, because they rest entirely upon the variable to be explained, namely, the nature of the decision process.

Other authors have emphasized the importance of the consumption of the product. Gredal (1959), for example, distinguished among products for personal use and products for collective use. The consuming unit concept found in many contemporary textbooks also relies upon aspects of consumption (Matthews et al. 1964), as does a classification based upon data on food consumption which is proposed by Cerha (1967). The latter classifies products as (1) products frequently used by a high percentage of all households, (2) products infrequently used by a high percentage of all households, (3) products frequently used by a low percentage of all households, and (4) products infrequently used by a low percentage of all households. The frequency of consumption is particularly important because it reflects the consumer's familiarity with the product. Nondurable products will be classified herein as *frequently used* and *infrequently used* products. With durable products, however, there is no close relationship between the frequency of use and the frequency of purchase, and consequently for them the distinction is less important.

Finally, a number of product characteristics have been used for classification, such as the price of the product, the extent to which the decision is reversible, the importance of the product to the consumer, the extent to which the product can be stored, the amount of risk associated with the decision, and so on. Any one of these may be significant for some product classes, but the fundamental aspect underlying them all is reflected in the distinction between minor and major purchases. Because purchases of nondurable products almost always are purchases of minor products, the distinction is most important in connection with durable products and will be applied to them in the following discussion.

The consumer-oriented and the product-oriented criteria suggest a classification of decision processes like the one illustrated in Table 14.2.

TABLE 14.2

Classification of consumer decision processes

	DURABLE PRODUCTS		NONDURABLE PRODUCTS	
	Major	Minor	Infrequently used	Frequently used
First purchases	X	X	X	X
Repeat purchases	X	X	X	X

First purchases of major durable products and repeat purchases of frequently used nondurable products will now be discussed in detail, for a number of reasons. First, these cases include a significant proportion of all consumer decision processes. Second, they represent end points on a scale ranging from extremely complex to very simple decision processes. Finally, important evidence is available about them.

Among the remaining cases, first purchases of nondurable products and repeat purchases of major durables will be treated in most detail. With these extreme instances covered, the remaining cases may be evaluated through comparison.

Chapter 15

CONSUMER DECISION PROCESSES II

1. *Consumer Decision Processes for First Purchases*

1. First Purchases of Major Durable Products

Innovation studies may provide evidence relevant to decision processes in first purchase situations, but they seldom distinguish between major and minor products and between durable and nondurable products. As these studies also deal with both collectively and individually purchased products, the nature of the product must be carefully considered when their findings are evaluated.

Other studies of shopping and purchasing plans in connection with shopping and specialty goods deal with durable products and occasionally distinguish major and minor products, but almost always they combine first purchases with repeat purchases and individually with collectively used products.

Studies of innovations assume that the consumer moves from awareness through interest, evaluation, and trial to final adoption (Chapter 14), though it is doubtful whether all these steps can be identified for minor innovations. However, when it comes to first purchases of major durable products, the evidence suggests that by and large the model is appropriate (Robertson 1968), and in the following pages, it will be used to analyze the decision process for first purchases of major durables.

Studies of innovations have repeatedly found that the decision process may extend over a considerable amount of time. For example, Rogers' (1962) review, primarily of farm studies, finds average decision processes ranging from $\frac{1}{2}$ year for "miracle" fabrics to 9 years for hybrid seed corn.

Extensive consumer decision processes are found in connection with house purchases. Unfortunately, no specific evidence on first purchases is available, but it is reasonable to assume that a considerable number of the respondents in house-purchase studies are making a first purchase. For example, Norris (1954) reports that purchasers of new houses had engaged in serious search from less than one day to more than seven years, with the median time being two months. Fifteen per cent of the subjects searched more than a year and 30% for more than six months. Similarly, Hempel (1969) finds that 32% spent more than a year and 33% from two to twelve months on such decisions.

Decision processes in connection with purchases of major durables have been reported by Katona and Mueller[1] (1954) and by Ferber (1955a), including repeat purchases. Katona and Mueller found that approximately 20% of the decisions took more than a year and 50% more than two months. Similarly, Ferber, dealing with slightly smaller purchases, found that 10% of the decision processes lasted more than a year and 30% more than three months, and from Sweden decision processes of similar length have been reported by Wickström (1965).

As none of the studies listed were limited to first purchases, a number of their respondents had previous experience with the products, which would tend to reduce the complexity of the decision process; consequently, when only first purchases are considered, even longer planning periods may be found. On the other hand, in all of the studies a significant proportion of consumers appear to have extremely short decision processes, and it is not certain that all these represent repeat purchases. For example, Ferber (1955a) reports that 28% of the purchases were made without any significant amount of preplanning. Obviously, the length of first-purchase processes varies widely and both extremely long and very short processes may be found.

That preplanning goes on for a long period of time does not necessarily mean that a large number of conflicts occur. Unfortunately, no direct data are available, but some indication of the complexity of the decision processes can be found in Norris (1954) and in Kelley (1957). Norris reports that most consumers entered six houses, they inspected four additional houses without entering them, and they heard descriptions of four more houses they did not see. Great variability exists; for example, some consumers entered more than 100 houses. Katona and Mueller's (1954) deliberation index (Chapter 2) shows considerable variations among consumers and generally indicates highly complex decision processes. An interview report from their study illustrates the complexity of decision processes in first purchases. (Reprinted with permission of the publisher from *Consumer Behavior*, edited by Lincoln N. Clark © by New York University.)

---

[1] As these authors based their estimate of the length of the planning period upon information about how long a time consumers have been "thinking about buying", the data cannot be compared directly with those reported by Norris or Ferber.

A tool and die worker in a G.E. plant: The family bought its first television set for Christmas. There was a great deal of hesitation, both between spending and saving the money and between the television set and other durables, especially a car. The purchase was discussed at length in the family. The respondent was eligible for an employee discount on a General Electric set. He reports, "I wanted G.E. since I worked there and had heard quite a bit about them, although I did look at others. . . . I looked to see if they might be better without discount even. I looked at Philco and R.C.A. I read ads in the papers until I got to the dealers, and then I looked at the folders." He visited two or three stores, talked to the salesmen there, and also had some discussions with friends. This gave him a pretty general idea of prices, size of screen, picture tube, how easy to adapt to U.F. Respondent bought a G.E. set. (p. 41)

Major durable products will represent significant expenditures for the consumer. Therefore, cognitive elements related to price, income, and financing are expected to be common in the decision process. For major purchase plans Ferber (1955a) reports that 48% of plans counted on utilizing credit and 39% of the purchases were actually made with the use of credit. Purchase plans were more frequent in families who expected a better economic status. Similarly Wickström (1965) found that from 15 to 32% of the consumers (varying among products) reported that the length of the decision process had been significantly influenced by financial considerations, and up to 10% of the consumers indicated that they finally made the purchase after changes in their economic situation.

It can be hypothesized that, if "rational choices" ever are found in consumer decision-making, it is likely to be in connection with first purchases of major durable products. The nature of the problem is complex enough to arouse such processes, and broad classes of alternatives will have to be considered because their consumption will be influenced by the purchase decision. Because the satisfaction derived from the use of durable products is normally not realized immediately, one may expect choice processes to include future states of affairs as cognitive elements. This does not mean that all choices made in the course of the decision process are rational. Obviously many semicomplex choices will be found, but "clue-guided" choices are not likely to be frequent, as the consumer will not have many clues to rely on.

The most important characteristic of the first purchase is that the consumer does not have previous experience with the product. Consequently, the decision process must be generated by external information, and the subsequent evaluation rely upon external information. It is therefore not surprising that studies of innovation repeatedly have dealt with the use of secondary, tertiary, and personal information sources (Zaltman 1965). Particularly in the awareness phase, when the product represents an innovation, some external information is needed; or when the product is new to a particular consumer, some major change in this consumer's environment must have occurred to generate the decision process.

Whereas forced learning may occur in the awareness phase, information acquisition is the most likely activity in the interest and evaluation phases, during which a considerable number of alternatives may be considered and many different information sources be attended to, as reported in many studies of innovations and of purchases of major durable products.

Smith et al. (1963) and Smith (1965) found a relationship between purchase plan and advertisement reading. Prepurchase shopping and information acquisition from secondary and personal sources is reported by many authors—Katona and Mueller (1954), Norris (1954), Katz and Lazarsfeld (1955), Ferber (1955a), Wärneryd (1961), Rogers (1962), Wärneryd (1965), Wickström (1965), Udel (1966), Bucklin (1966), Kleimenhagen (1967), and Dommermuth and Cundiff (1967).

The very nature of the major durable product rules out the possibility that the consumer tries out the product on a small scale. However, Chapter 9 discussed a trial phase in which consumers frequently take durable products home for inspection or try them out in the store.

The amount of conflict aroused in the choices in the decision process has not been studied systematically, nor has the acceptable amount of conflict or the amount of conflict immediately following the choices. It is possible only to speculate that systematic changes do occur. The aroused cognitive structures will change systematically as the decision is approached, and the way the conflict is solved will vary from early to late in the sequence. In early choice processes, vague commitments are frequently made, whereas in later choices the conflicts are solved through more specific choice alternatives. Also, the extensiveness of information search will vary systematically, being expected to increase as the process goes on, but to start tapering off before the final decision is reached. However, little evidence is available.[2]

A number of studies have revealed that consumers may consider a number of different products simultaneously (Ferber 1955a, Wickström 1965, and Granbois and Willett 1968), but the interaction among simultaneous decision processes has never been studied. Only McFall (1969) has presented data which at an aggregated level show how different preference patterns may result in entirely different developments in the acceptance of major durables.

A couple of studies have dealt with decision processes that are discontinued before a purchase is made. Studies of consumer planning frequently find that even consumers with very definite purchase plans often do not carry out the purchase. For example, Ferber (1955a) reports that more than half of the subjects in his survey who had planned a major purchase did not carry out the purchase, and Juster (1961 and 1964) and Granbois and Willett (1968) report similar findings. Other findings illustrate the discontinuance of decision processes. Pratt (1965) found that, out of five thousand households, 56% of those who had stated intentions to buy a particular brand did not buy anything within the product category at all.

---

[2] Some evidence relating to durable products in general is reviewed in connection with repeat purchases of durable products.

Among those who did buy the product, one third bought another brand than the one they initially intended to purchase. Similarly, Wickström (1965) reports that, for major household appliances over a two-month period, approximately one third to one half had given up their plans. These findings suggest that only few of the decision processes underway at any given time will result in purchases.

The pattern found in the adoption of innovations seems to describe decision processes in first purchases of major durable products. When such purchase processes are studied for the introduction of new products, a pattern like that in Figure 14.2 is expected.

Many consumers apply extensive decision processes in first purchases of major durable products. A considerable number of single choice processes are involved, information is acquired from the environment, and all but primary information sources are used. Systematic changes in the cognitive structure are expected to occur as the decision proceeds. In comparisons with alternatives from other product classes as well as with other alternatives of the same type, income and price considerations are important. At any given time the consumer may have several purchase sequences going on, and many decision processes are never completed.

2. First Purchases of Nondurable Products

In first purchases of nondurable products the consumer has no experience with the product and must rely upon secondary, tertiary, and personal information sources. However, first purchases of minor nondurable products are not so consequential as first purchases of durable products, as the single item is less expensive and the consumer is committed to it only as long as the product lasts, by definition a short time. Moreover, in decision process in first purchases of nondurable products some transfer of learning from slightly similar previous situations may occur. These decision processes are expected to be less complex and shorter, the choices will frequently be semi-complex; and when learning from similar situations can be transferred, clue choices can also occur.

A few adoption studies have dealt with first purchases of nondurable products. Sheth (1968a) found in his study of the adoption of stainless steel razor blades that approximately half of the subjects adopted the product immediately after having heard about it, and of the remaining subjects, approximately 15% adopted it within three months and an additional 25% within a year. These figures support the suggestion that for nondurable products a large percentage of the consumers have extremely short first-purchase sequences. But the findings also show that relatively long decision processes can occur.

A similar picture emerges from a study of a new coffee brand reported by Arndt (1967b). In this study the consumers learned about the new product for the first time when they received a coupon in the mail. The length of the decision process was later measured when they adopted the product. It was found that 12% adopted within the first two days, an additional 18% within three to nine days, and an additional 12% within ten to sixteen days. Here again, there is some indication of decision processes considerably shorter than for durable products. However, it is noteworthy that only few consumers adopted the product immediately. An explanation may be found in the way the consumers initially became aware of the product. The mailed coupon could not be redeemed immediately, as the consumer had to go to a store. Under other circumstances, a number of consumers would accidentally have learned about the product in stores and immediate adoption would have been possible.

Attempts to identify innovators for nondurable products have been less successful than similar attempts with more important products. For example, Frank and Massy (1963) found that only few of the socio-economic characteristics that describe innovators in other areas (Chapter 16) applied to early purchasers of a newly introduced coffee brand.

There are no findings about the number of choices made in the purchase sequence for nondurables. From the evidence, however, it is suggested that the length of decision process is lower than in connection with first purchases of durable products.

TABLE 15.1

Awareness of stainless-steel razor blades generated by different sources (adapted from Sheth, 1968a)

	LEARNED FIRST ABOUT STAINLESS-STEEL BLADES FROM:		
	Mass communication	*In store*	*Personal communication*
Adopted immediately	127	56	177
Adopted later	210	22	17
Number of subjects	337	78	194

The consumer may learn about new products from mass media, observe them in stores, or be exposed to personal communication about them. Data from Sheth's study are presented in Table 15.1. For this product, mass communication is a more important source of awareness than tertiary and personal communication combined. It also appears that consumers with extremely short decision processes relied more heavily upon tertiary and personal communication than did other consumers. As Sheth points out, a possible explanation may be found in differences in the reliability of the sources. When a person learns about a new product from a personal source, he is more likely to adopt soon than when he learns about it through mass communication, in which case he may want to acquire other information to reduce the aroused conflict sufficiently before making a purchase.

The role of information sources later in the decision process is studied by Arndt (1968a), who found perceived risk to be an important factor. Basically his findings suggest that consumers who perceive high risk in connection with the product either avoid adopting it or, if they do adopt, engage in more extensive decision processes in which personal information sources become important.

Other studies that throw light upon consumers' use of information sources are reported by Haines (1966), who dealt with cereals, toothpaste, detergents, dog food, soap, and ready-made desserts, and by Myers (1966), who studied freeze-dried food. All these studies show that personal as well as mass communication is used. In all the studies, all information sources have been found to have some influence, and between the studies considerable disagreement exists as to the relative importance of the sources. This disagreement may be ascribable to differences in the procedures or to difference in the products studied. It should be possible to point to factors that predict the kind of information sources preferred in connection with different products. The availability of different information sources is important, and the studies reported by Cunningham (1966) and Arndt (1968a) also suggest that "high risk products" make the more credible sources such as personal information more important.

With nondurable products, the consumer only rarely can try the product before he purchases it. Unless store demonstrations or free samples are available, the consumer has to buy the product before he can use it. Consequently, for many consumers the first purchase of nondurable products serves the same functions as the trial does for major durable products, and there is some evidence that the first purchase may be seen as a step in the information acquisition process. For example, in the study of repeated choices of relatively unknown brands of hairspray by Sheth and Venkatesan (1968), it was found that in the first few choices subjects systematically shifted among products, presumably in an attempt to learn about them; a finding that also appeared in the studies by Tucker (1964) and McConnell (1968b).

Decision processes for first purchases of nondurable products deviate significantly from decision processes for first purchases of durable products. As they are frequently shorter, an interest phase and an evaluation phase often cannot be identified, and in general it is questionable whether a distinction between interest and evaluation is meaningful. Moreover, as the first purchase often acts as a trial, adoption should be defined as the second purchase or as regular use rather than as the first purchase.

2. *Consumer Decision Processes for Repeat Purchases*

1. Repeat Purchases of Frequently Used Nondurable Products

First purchases of a nondurable product may involve a decision process of some complexity, and the single choices will often be semi-complex.

However, as the purchase process is repeated, the consumer becomes more and more acquainted with it, and the amount of conflict aroused will decrease. Sooner or later several of the choice processes that made up the initial purchase sequence will disappear and others will be reduced in complexity. Eventually such purchase sequences could be:

1. a. Observe at home that the household is out of stock.
   b. Enter item on shopping list.
   c. Pick up item in store.
2. a. Make some related decision (for example, what dinner to serve).
   b. Pick up item in store.
3. Observe and pick up item in store.
4. a. Receive forced exposure to product in mass media.
   b. Make internal commitment to purchase.
   c. Pick up item in store.

Compared with the decision process in first purchases, several characteristics of the repeat purchase are important. Whereas the first purchase can be studied from the time of awareness, the repeat purchase is initiated when some kind of problem recognition occurs. This first phase only slightly resembles the awareness in first purchases. As suggested, the repeat purchase sequence may be initiated in the store by forced learning, at home when the household runs out of stock, or in connection with planning of meals or other activities; and in these and similar cases problem recognition has no relationship to brand or product awareness.

Following the problem recognition, the repeat purchase sequence will terminate with a purchase, but intervening conflicts may or may not occur. These intermediate steps, however, only vaguely resemble the intermediate step of the first purchase process. Trial rarely occurs, and the information acquisition and comparison that characterize interest and evaluation are not dominant features of the intervening conflicts.

In spite of the extreme simplicity of the single decision process, consumers' repeat purchases may be quite complex; often they follow so close after each other that an attempt to break them up into single decisions is questionable. Frequently consumption appears as an integrated part of the purchase process and at the same time consumption experiences initiate and influence subsequent purchases. Rather than a number of purchases, a continuous stream of decision and consumption sequences should be considered.

In the decision process for repeat purchases of minor nondurable products the last choice in the sequence is particularly important. Frequently this choice determines the brand taken. The first times the purchase is made, semi-complex choice processes will be applied. However, as the choice is repeated, choice processes of reduced complexity will become frequent; and if the choice is repeated over and over again in the same store, with the same brands available and with no interruptions occurring, the aroused conflict may fall short of the optimal level. When that occurs, the consumer can seek out additional conflict by choosing a different brand or by taking up the alternatives for renewed evaluation, which also may result in a new brand's being chosen.

In spite of the overall tendency towards choice processes of reduced complexity, there are significant variations in the ability of a frequently used nondurable product to arouse conflict, as is reflected in several studies of perceived risk (Cox 1967a). Similarly, Lewin (1958) had subjects rating the tension associated with the purchase of different food products and found large variations among different products and among different income groups.

As a choice process is repeated and as it changes from a semi-complex process to a process of reduced complexity, repeated choices of the same brand are likely to result. When the arousal potential falls short of the optimal level and strategies are applied in attempts to generate increased conflict, a new brand may be purchased; the same end may result when increased conflict is generated by the environment.

LOYALTY

The term *loyalty*, especially brand loyalty, has been used to name the commonly observed phenomenon that consumers do not distribute their choices randomly within a given product area. On the contrary, one or a few brands are picked more frequently than would be expected by chance. Various operational definitions of loyalty have been applied, and in Chapter 3 examples were mentioned.

The existence of brand loyalty has repeatedly been documented. Some of the earliest results were reported by Brown (1952–53) and by Cunningham (1956), and most later studies confirm these findings (Farley 1964b). Similar observations have been reported from England (Murray and Goodhardt 1963) and from Sweden (Wickström 1965). Most authors report considerable differences among brands, product categories, and consumers.

Brand loyalty may be seen as resulting from a psychological tendency to apply less and less complex choice processes and an opposing force resulting from a psychological tendency to avoid trivial situations and from environmental changes that interfere before the latter tendency ever goes to work (Chapter 5). Loyalty may also result for a completely different reason. Even where rational choice processes dominate, the same brand may repeatedly be chosen simply because it remains the most attractive. No studies have attempted to quantify the relative frequency of the two kinds of loyalty, and only little evidence is available about the relationship between brand preferences and repeat purchases of the same brand. However, Day (1969) proposes a definition of loyalty that takes the strength of the consumers' preference for the brand into consideration. His loyalty measure (L_i) is defined as:

$$L_i = \frac{P(B_i)}{kA_i^n} \tag{15.I}$$

where $P(B_i)$ is the proportion of all purchases devoted to brand i, A_i the strength of the preference[3] towards that brand, and k and n are constants. The advantage of the approach is that it largely neglects those consumers who happen to show a sequence of repeat purchases because of incomplete distribution of all brands or simply as a result of random choices.

Using the loyalty measure (15.I) in a study of purchase and preference data for a frequently used minor nondurable product, Day shows that it may lead to more meaningful results than traditional measures. He finds that more than 70% of the consumers have strong preferences for the product they most frequently purchase. Day's observation is in line with results reported by Peckham (1963), who asked consumers what they would do if the store were out of the brand they normally purchased. For the products studied, frequently used minor nondurables such as floor wax, detergents, salad oil, margarine, toilet soap, cake mix, juice, cereal, and crackers, he found that from one third to two thirds would refuse to buy a substitute brand. As the absence of the regular brand is likely to generate a more complex decision process, the findings indicate that a significant proportion of consumers may exhibit loyalty rooted in the perceived attractiveness of the alternatives. However, their refusal to change to a new brand does not prove that they had not developed choice procedures of reduced complexity, but only shows that the regularly purchased brand is also the most attractive one.

Systematic effects of repeated choices have been studied by Tucker (1964), who asked a number of housewives to make choices among four identical loaves of bread differentiated only by letter codes. Subjects were told that the study was meant to find out how people would choose a brand if they had moved to a new area and did not know the brands offered. Over a period of days they were offered choices in their homes, and with this procedure, Tucker found that after a period of trials, subjects began to become loyal to different brands. The strength of this loyalty was further tested by the following addition to the experiment: When a subject had chosen the same brand for three days in a row, a penny premium was added to one of the other brands, and if the choice did not change, an additional penny was added the following day. It was found that subjects tended to stay with their preferred brand in spite of the premium. In most cases from two to seven cents were needed before a brand change occurred. Furthermore, Tucker found that some subjects did not shift to the brand with the premium. It seems that the introduction of pennies regenerated conflict and semi-complex choices but did not automatically result in choices of the promoted brand. Tucker writes: "... the addition of a premium to any brand restructured the entire situation" (p. 35), and a little later: "the premium apparently was a signal to do something, but anything rather than the encouraged action" (p. 36).

It is also interesting to note that clear evidence of search in terms of

[3] A_i is defined so that a low value corresponds to a strong preference.

shifts among the brands occurred in the first of the choices: ". . . patterns from the entire group suggest that the first four choices were qualitatively different from the remaining selections. The evidence for a period of search or exploratory consumer behavior is clear" (p. 33).

Similar results have been reported by McConnell (1968b) in a study of beer brands and by Stafford (1965), who repeated Tucker's experiment with an additional feature. Stafford was interested in testing whether personal communication between subjects would influence the establishment of loyalty. He selected his subjects so that they represented small clusters of housewives known to be friends. Besides obtaining results confirming Tucker's, Stafford also found some influence from personal communication.

Sheth and Venkatesan (1968) studied how choice processes change as the same choice is being repeated. It was expected that repeated exposure to a choice situation would increase the individual's ability to cope with the situation and consequently decreasing amounts of conflict would be aroused. Furthermore, the less uncertain the situation is, the faster the decrease in arousal will be. Stated a little differently, these hypotheses were tested in the following experiment.

A "high-risk choice" and a "low-risk choice" were given to different groups of subjects. The low-risk choice was between nationally known brands of hairspray, whereas the high-risk choices was between less-well-known alternatives. Each of the two groups of subjects was offered the same choice for five consecutive weeks. In connection with each choice the following variables were measured: the time spent on deliberation, the extensiveness of information search, and the frequency of repeat choices (loyalty). The findings show that deliberation and information search decrease as the choice process is repeated, and this decrease occurred faster in the low-risk group than in the high-risk group. Loyalty also increased, but no difference was found between the two experimental conditions. At the end of the fifth choice, two-thirds of the subjects had become loyal. These findings are confirmed in a replication of the experiment with brands of shampoo (Sheth and Venkatesan 1969), in which a larger number of choices were studied and more than 80% of the subjects ended up being loyal. However, in this experiment a measure of perceived conflict in connection with each choice did not show any decrease as the choices were repeated, contrary to expectations.[4]

In line with these results were the findings discussed by Krugman (1965 and 1968), who studied choices of detergent packages as a function of the number of exposures, and the results reported by a group of researchers who have studied the formation of brand loyalty in a highly abstract way. Wells (1964), Wells and Chinsky (1965), and LoSciuto et al. (1967) have dealt

---

[4] Discussion with the authors suggests that this may have resulted because the risk measure did not reflect risk associated with the specific situations. Rather it measured the overall amount of risk which subjects associated with this type of product.

with the influence of recency and repetition on learning of responses. Their experiments had subjects make choices among different numbers, representing brands, to study how the choices changed as a result of changes in exposure. For example, Wells (1964) exposed subjects to different sequences of numbers and then asked them to choose a "brand". Results are presented in Table 15.2.

TABLE 15.2

Choices and number of exposures in simulated choices (Wells 1964)

Message number	Share of messages	Share of choices	Message number	Share of messages	Share of choices	Message number	Share of messages	Share of choices
	%	%		%	%		%	%
2	30	32	1	50	36	1	30	25
9	25	25	4	20	20	4	25	22
3	20	20	6	15	15	6[a]	20	30
7	15	14	2	10	10	2	15	12
4	10	9	3	5	19	3	10	11

[a] Message placed in last half of message stream.
Table reproduced with permission from the American Marketing Association.

From the first set of columns it can be seen that the relationship between the share of the messages and the share of the choices reflects a learning curve. Furthermore, in the last set of columns it can be seen that both the share of the messages and recency influence the learning. Finally, if the second set of columns is compared with the first set, it appears that increasing the frequency of a certain number above a certain level does not cause a proportional increase in the choices of that number.

Related findings are also reported by Becknell et al. (1963), who conducted a study offering female subjects a choice among boxes containing identical nylon stockings differentiated only by means of an artificial brand name. Prior to the choice, subjects were exposed to slides with the "brand names"; some subjects received more exposure to one brand name, others to other brand name. By comparing the actual choices, it was found that the most frequently exposed brands were preferred. Unfortunately the study did not increase the frequency of exposure to a level such that one would have expected a reverse effect. Nevertheless learning and the establishing of the brand name as a clue is clearly illustrated.

Similar learning effects occasionally also appear in studies of effects of repetition of advertising (Ray et al. 1971 and Indow 1971). In these studies the effects of forced learning are isolated and the parameters determining the shape of the response functions are typical learning parameters.

These experiments confirm that a tendency towards less complex choices relying upon clues can be found and that semi-complex choice processes may be generated by boredom or environmental changes. The evidence also shows clear effects of learning and suggests that in connection with repeat purchases of frequently used nondurable products a "mere exposure" hypothesis may apply (Chapter 7). The extent to which such a tendency occurs outside the experimental laboratory may be tested with data from studies of brand choices in the market place. As the dominant source of influence in connection with frequently used nondurable products is the experience with the product, such effects should show up in relationships between previous use (and purchases) and subsequent purchases. This kind of learning has been explored in several studies relating the observed probability of buying a given brand to the pattern of previous purchases. Such data have been studied by Kuehn (1962) for a brand of frozen orange juice, by Morrison (1965) for a coffee brand, by Wickström (1965) for brands within five grocery product areas, and by Carman (1966) for Crest toothpaste. Examples of these data are presented in Table 15.3.

TABLE 15.3

The probability of purchasing a given brand on the following occasion, given the previous purchase sequence (1 means that the same brand has been purchased, 0 that some other brand was purchased)

Purchase sequence	Orange Snowcrop (Kuehn 1962)	Coffee brand (Morrison 1965)	Purchase sequence	Coffee brand (Wickström 1965)	Toothpaste Crest (Carman 1966a)
1111	.81	.89			
0111	.69	.75	111	.96	.89
1011	.67	.75			
1101	.60	.70	011	.89	.60
1110	.49	.68			
0011	.55	.61	101	.57	
1001	.57	.61			.64
0101	.50	.58	110	.48	
1010	.41	.49			
0110	.47	.55	001	.15	
1100	.31	.48			.30
0001	.33	.59	010	.33	
0010	.19	.37			
0100	.13	.48	100	.26	.40
1000	.15	.38			
0000	.05		000	.04	.10

Theoretically, patterns like those in Table 15.3 could occur in a completely random process. That is, as one or another brand always will be purchased, it might as well be the same as the one bought previously. However, Frank (1962) has tested a similar set of data on instant coffee purchases with regard to this possibility and concludes that "there are too many families with an excess of long runs" (p. 389). Massy (1966), who specifically examined 800 individual purchasers, found only 33 heavy purchasers whose behavior could be explained in terms of random purchases and he reports that, when data are aggregated, significant deviations from a random process are found, a conclusion similar to one reached by Haines (1968), who tested different loyalty models on data for an unidentified frequently used nondurable product.

Another indication of learning is found in the so-called recency effect. From learning theory it will be predicted that the later the last purchase of a given brand, the higher the repurchase probability of that brand. For example, both Kuehn (1962) and Wickström (1965) find a decreasing repurchase probability with increasing time between purchases. However, it should be mentioned that Morrison (1966b) suggests that this effect is primarily ascribable to a difference between heavy and light users and not to a straightforward recency effect.

Evidence of loyalty and learning has also appeared in other kinds of studies. Winer (1967) reports that gasoline buyers will tend to be loyal towards a particular station, and for 15 different nondurable products Guest (1955 and 1964) reports brand loyalty among the same consumers over time periods as long as 12 and 20 years. Similarly, several studies have shown that the consumer will develop loyalty towards different kinds of stores. For example, Donnahoe (1956) reports on loyalty towards department stores, and Tate (1961), Cunningham (1961), Wickström (1965), Farley (1968), Carmen (1970), and Aaker and Jones (1971) all present evidence in favor of considerable supermarket loyalty. Finally, Kelly (1966 and 1967b) reports on the development of store loyalty towards a dairy product store. As with brands, consumers rarely become 100% loyal to single stores, as is evident in most of the above studies. The "Better Homes and Gardens Consumer Questionnaire" (1968) reports that only 10% of the respondents were completely loyal to one grocery store and that one third of the consumers pay weekly visits to more than one store. However, it is still possible to find a fairly well established pattern in the consumer's choice of stores even though he shops in a number of different stores. How such a pattern emerges is studied by Bell (1969), who analyzed how people who move to a new area establish their new store preferences. Data from the study are presented in Table 15.4, where it can be seen that quite extensive decision processes are applied before a favorite store is identified. Several stores may be visited, different information sources are used, and the average time to the choice of the store varies from three to seven weeks.

It can also be mentioned that marked changes in consumers' shopping behavior have been observed over the last decade. Schapker (1966) reports that in 1954 41% of all supermarket shoppers shopped only in one store as opposed to only 17% in 1965. Other evidence of a shift away from habitual store choices is also evident in the observation that 57% of the supermarket shoppers read an average of 1.7 store ads a week in 1954 as opposed to 72% reading an average of 2.8 ads in 1965.

Finally, the significance of learning processes in the market is also illustrated by the success of various forecasting models based on different types of learning curves (Fourt and Woodcock 1960, Parfitt and Collins 1968).

Evidence that changes in the environment may interact with the formation of loyalty is found in several studies, including Tucker's (1964) study as well as other experimental work. Similarly Wickström (1965) and Rao (1969a) find considerable evidence that a change of store also results in a change in brand, and Carman (1970) reports findings from a special

TABLE 15.4

Favorite store choice by mobile consumers (Bell, 1969)

Purchase category	Information sources used		Mean weeks between arrival and supplier selection	Number of potential suppliers visited prior to choosing favorites
1. Supermarkets	38.6%	Personal	3.4 weeks	3.4
	56.1%	Searching		
	5.3%	Impersonal		
2. Beauty parlors	57.3%	Personal	7.0 weeks	2.0
	37.5%	Searching		
	5.2%	Impersonal		
3. Drycleaners	57.3%	Personal	5.5 weeks	2.0
	37.5%	Searching		
	5.2%	Impersonal		
4. Banks	51.0%	Personal	1.7 weeks	1.0
	43.0%	Searching		
	6.0%	Impersonal		
5. Furniture stores	48.2%	Personal	6.2 weeks	3.0
	21.7%	Searching		
	30.1%	Impersonal		
6. Appliance stores	62.0%	Personal	5.3 weeks	2.0
	17.7%	Searching		
	20.3%	Impersonal		
	N = 79			
7. Clothing purchases				
a. Women	56.8%	Personal	8.6 weeks	3.2
	29.7%	Searching		
	13.5%	Impersonal		
	N = 37			
b. Men	65.0%	Personal	8.3 weeks	2.2
	30.2%	Searching		
	4.8%	Impersonal		
	N = 43			

Berkeley panel suggesting that 60% of the loyalty for coffee brands can be explained in terms of store loyalty. In line with this are findings by Kuehn et al. (1966), who report success with a model in which price, advertising, and quality changes influence brand loyalty and sales. Similarly, Montgomery (1968), who studied loyalty among toothpaste consumers just before and just after a major change in promotion, reports that a model considering environmental influence is superior to a learning model in the period after the promotional change. Finally Claycamp (1966) shows that price changes for gasoline interfere with loyalty and Farley (1964c) reports that loyalty decreases with price activity and increases with wide distribution.

Perhaps the most convincing evidence of the importance of situational factors as a major determinant of loyalty behavior is provided by Wind and Frank (1969). In a study of 38 different products they found that the fact that a consumer is loyal to a brand in one product area does not mean that he is likely to be loyal to brands in other product areas, a finding that suggests that it will not be easy to identify individual characteristics that explain brand loyalty.

The effects of major environmental changes can be studied with consumers who have moved to a new area. Besides Bell's (1968) study, Andreasen and Durkson (1968) and Sheth (1968d) have dealt with the issue. Although it is not possible to identify changes in single choice processes, the studies do present findings in line with the view proposed here.

With regard to frequently used nondurable products, a consumer who moves to a new area can apply three different strategies. He can stay with a brand he is already using if it is available, he can imitate what other consumers are doing, and he can examine the available alternatives himself. That is, he can begin to resolve the new conflict that the new alternatives present to him.

That the consumer does not automatically choose the brand he has been using when he is faced with new alternatives is evident from the studies reported by Sheth (1968d) and by Andreasen and Durkson (1968), but whether imitative behavior or more complex processes occur is not quite clear. Andreasen and Durkson suggest that the new consumers will automatically change their brand choices to resemble those of the previous consumers. But for frequently used nondurables Sheth (1968d) finds imitative behavior to be relatively infrequent, a result which also appears in Hansen (1969b). Both suggest that, when it comes to establishing consumption and purchase patterns, the consumer's own problem solving is highly significant. Moreover, a closer inspection of the Andreason and Durkson data suggests that this hypothesis is not necessarily in conflict with their findings. It is possible that the consumers in this study end up with the same purchase pattern as the previous consumers not because of imitative behavior, but rather because of the nature of the available alternatives and the way they are perceived. That the newcomers actually explore the alternatives available in the new area is reported by Andreasen and Durkson, who found that newcomers shifted among brands significantly more than the settled residents.

These findings suggest that major environmental changes may regenerate conflict to such an extent that more elaborate choice processes are applied, which may lead to adoption of new alternatives. Not until the decisions have been repeated a number of times will choice processes of reduced complexity dominate the behavior, an equilibrium be established, and a stable purchase pattern emerge.

STOCHASTIC MODELS OF REPEAT PURCHASES OF FREQUENTLY USED NONDURABLE PRODUCTS

Because repeat purchases of frequently used minor nondurables are heavily influenced by experiences with the previous purchases, models of such purchases have dealt not with the single decision processes, but with sequences of purchases. Several stochastic models have been proposed to describe patterns of such choices. Some of these are concerned with the distribution of choices in subsequent time periods (brand-share models), others deal with the single consumer's distribution of purchases over time (interpurchase-time models, Montgomery and Urban 1969). It is the purpose here to relate only the main features of these models to the present approach. Excellent reviews are available in Kuehn and Day (1964), Farley and Kuehn (1965), May (1965), Lawrence (1966), and Massy et al. (1970).

Interpurchase-time models (Ehrenberg 1959, Goodhardt and Ehrenberg 1967, Massy 1968 and 1969, and Grahn 1969) rest upon the assumption that within a certain product category or with regard to a certain brand, the consumer will distribute his purchases randomly over time. Often purchases are assumed to be exponentially distributed and, consequently, the number of purchases a certain consumer will make in a given time interval is described by the Poisson distribution. In these models the consumers may have different purchase probabilities, but it is required that the probabilities remain constant for the period of analysis. Consequently no learning can take place.[5] In spite of this the model has provided reasonably good predictions in several product classes (Ehrenberg and Goodhart 1968).

Brand-share models focus on the distribution of purchases among several alternatives. Depending upon the assumptions with regard to the effects of previous purchases, zero-order, Markov, or learning models emerge.

In zero-order models (Frank 1962 and Massy 1966) each consumer is assumed to have a constant probability. Typically a Bernoulli or a multi-nominal distribution is assumed. Massy and Frank (1964) report that these models have performed reasonably well in some product areas (coffee and tea) but have been less successful in others (beer). Similarly Chatfield et al. (1966) report some success with the negative binominal distribution.

Compared with most of the following models, the zero-order models have the advantage of allowing for the application of different probabilities to the single consumer, giving the models a flexibility which may overrule the disadvantage inherent in not considering effects of previous experiences with the brands.

In more elaborate versions past purchases influence subsequent brand choices; in Markov models (Maffei 1960, Harary and Lipstein 1962, R. Howard 1963, Massy and Morrison 1968) the purchase depends upon the immediately preceding purchase, and the basic assumptions of the model are contained in the brand-switching matrix illustrated in Table 15.5.

The matrix shows the probability that a consumer will purchase different brands, depending upon the brand he has purchased last. The model is dynamic in the sense that it makes it possible to follow changes in brand share over time, provided that the brand-switching matrix remains constant.

---

[5] Of course, the purchase parameters may have resulted from learning in the first place, so that the only requirement is that no additional learning or forgetting takes place.

However, when major changes in marketing strategies occur this assumption is likely to be violated (Ehrenberg 1965, and Massy and Morrison 1968). In its basic form the model assumes that the same probabilities apply to all consumers, but for the case of only two brands, models that allow for variations among consumers have been proposed by Morrison (1966a).

TABLE 15.5

Brand-switching matrix (the entries in the matrix show the probability with which a consumer who in the last period purchased a certain brand will purchase either of the different brands available)

Purchase in period 1	Purchase in period 2			
	A	B	C	
A	.70	.20	.10	1.00
B	.30	.60	.10	1.00
C	.10	.40	.50	1.00

Independent of the intitial market shares, the Markov models define equilibrium market shares that will be reached if the brand-switching matrix remains constant for a sufficient number of periods.

Major problems with the model may arise from variations in the length of the periods studied. If periods are too short, many consumers will not have time to make purchases in all periods; and if periods are too long, some consumers will make more than one purchase. In both instances the model cannot be applied in its simple form.

In learning models (Kuehn 1962, Haines 1964 and 1969, and Carman 1966a) one further dynamic aspect is introduced. Product use is assumed to result in predominantly positive consumption experiences which work as rewards, reinforcing repeat purchases of whatever brand was bought last. That is, purchasing probabilities change depending upon the immediately preceding purchase, so that the probability of purchasing a given brand will increase if the brand has just been purchased; if some other brand has been purchased, it will decrease. Findings from studies using this type of model were reviewed previously (Table 15.4), and frequently applications have been quite successful. However, a number of authors have recently pointed to weaknesses of the model; McConnel (1968c) was unable to estimate meaningful parameters using Kuehn's version of the model; Montgomery (1968), comparing the model with a model that allows for the influence of other factors than previous purchases, found the learning model to be inferior; and Lawrence (1969), studying toothpaste brand purchases, found that the switching pattern does not fit the traditional linear learning models.

At the present time it seems that learning models may reflect important patterns of consumer choices; but the facts that they rarely have allowed for the inclusion of other factors than experience formation and that individual differences are not included limit their applicability. However, further development of these models, overcoming these problems and distinguishing between random choices and loyalty based upon preferences, may prove to be the most useful approach to studies of repeat purchases of frequently used nondurable products.

2. Repeat Purchases of Major Durable Products

Repeat purchases of major durable products have aspects in common with both first purchases of durables and repeat purchases of frequently used nondurables, but they differ from them in several ways. First, experience from previous purchases are important. Second, because they are purchases of major durable products, they will have important consequences for some time, and the decision process may be quite elaborate. Third, because they are durable products, considerable time has passed since the last purchase was made. Finally, because the purchase is a replacement, the beginning of the purchase sequence should be studied in relation to the use of the unit already owned, and rather than being characterized as awareness it should be viewed as a kind of problem recognition.

Mueller (1966) reports findings that illustrate how the initiation of repeat purchases relates to the use of the old unit. Based upon a national probability sample she studied purchase plans for refrigerators and found that the occurrence of purchase plans was related to the age of and the satisfaction with the old unit in interaction with awareness of new features in new models.

Most evidence suggests that repeat purchases of major durable products have most in common with first purchases of the same durable products. In the present section the first purchase will be taken as a model; starting from that base, emphasis is placed on differences between the first and the repeat purchase of major durables. The concern is primarily with information acquisition, evaluation, and trial.

Although most of the studies reviewed in connection with first purchases also dealt with repeat purchases, a few findings highlight the differences between the two kinds of purchases. Wärneryd (1961), in studying first purchases of automobiles, found that 73% tried one or more cars before making their purchase, whereas only 51% of the repurchasers did so. Similarly, with regard to information acquisition he found that first purchasers engaged in somewhat more extensive information search than repurchasers. Although these findings suggest that differences exist, they also show that the repurchase is a fairly complex decision process.

Other evidence that highlights the systematic differences between first purchases and repurchases is reported by May (1969). He studied automobile purchasers' decision processes and, in line with the usual findings in studies of loyalty, he found that the probability of purchasing a certain brand is positively correlated with the frequency with which the brand has been purchased earlier. His findings are presented in Table 15.6.

The decision process is also influenced by the brands the consumer has previously owned; most commonly, the first brand to be considered seriously is one previously owned. Moreover, consumers who in an early

TABLE 15.6

Effects of previous car ownership upon subsequent purchases
(C is currently owned make; O is other makes)

Make bought	CCC	OCC	COC	OOC	All buyers
Currently owned	73%	64%	57%	43%	56%
Other make	27%	36%	43%	57%	44%
Total	100%	100%	100%	100%	100%
N	30	28	14	60	132

(Reproduced from F. E. May, "Adoptive Behavior in Automobile Board Choices," *Journal of Marketing Research*, Vol. 6, No. 1, Feb. 1969, with permission from The American Marketing Association).

phase consider other brands than the one they currently own are more likely to engage in extensive search than are consumers who started out considering their currently owned brand (May 1969).

Similar findings are reported by Bennett and Mandell (1969), who also studied repeat purchases of automobiles and found that the amount of pre-purchase information acquisition is smaller, the more frequently the consumer has purchased the same brand in the past and the more times the consumer has repeated purchases of (been loyal to) the same brand. However, it is noteworthy that the authors do not find information acquisition to decrease as a simple function of the total number of previous purchases, a finding which suggests that there are limits to the extent of learning transfer from previous situations and that repeat purchases are capable of arousing as much conflict as first purchases. More evidence is required before this proposition is documented fully, but it is definitely worthy of further exploration. It may be that subsequent studies will show that repeat purchases, rather than "on the average" being less complex than first purchases, are either about as complex or very much simpler. The first would occur when factors such as dissatisfaction with the old item suggest a change in brand, the latter when a repeat purchase is made.

Katona and Mueller (1954) present similar findings for buyers of television sets, refrigerators, washing machines, and stoves. Their deliberation index (see Chapter 1) is approximately 20% higher for first purchases than for repeat purchases. Moreover, their finding that the deliberation index is significantly higher for consumers who were dissatisfied with their previously owned brand than for consumers who were satisfied also suggests that the consumer's experience with previously owned products influences the decision process.

Another effect of familiarity is suggested by the difference between first purchasers who had the possibility of using the product regularly, as compared with first purchasers who did not. The deliberation index for the latter group is considerably higher.

Also, the individual elements of the Katona–Mueller deliberation index suggest some, but not dramatic, differences in the decision process. In the first purchases slightly more extensive decision processes are found. This is reflected in extensiveness of search, in careful choosing, and in consideration of price and brands. Only one exception is found. The number of features considered is higher among repurchasers who were satisfied with their previous brand than among all other consumers. Although these findings suggest differences between first purchases and repeat purchases, they also indicate that repeat purchases may be quite complex.

Finally, evidence of extensive decision processes preceding repurchases of major durable products is reported in studies dealing with consumers' anticipations and plans. Particularly interesting are findings reported by Granbois and Willett (1968 and 1969). Although their study is not restricted to repeat purchases (judged from the products studied, a majority of the purchases must have been repeats), the findings are interesting because they show how data about the decision process can improve predictions and because they indirectly reveal important aspects of this process. The authors attempted to predict whether households would purchase major durable products and when the purchase would be carried out. Two classes of independent variables were used. The first group consisted of the subject's own ratings of the probability that he will carry out a purchase within a certain time period; the probability that he will purchase a specific brand; and the probability that he will carry out the purchase in a specific store. Of these measures, the subjective probability of a purchase of a particular product within six months gave fair predictions of the actual purchases and of the timing of the purchase. However, neither the brand nor the store where the purchase would be carried out could be predicted, which suggests the following interpretation: The consumer's subjective probability of carrying out a purchase reveals how far along he is in the decision process leading to the purchase. Although not all the consumers with high probabilities carry out a purchase, and although some consumers who have low purchase probabilities at the time of interview eventually will purchase within the time limit of the study, the occurrence of decision processes which will result in a purchase is frequent enough to enable predictions of products purchased. However, when it comes to brand and stores, the predictive power is lower, as the selection of a brand and a store will be made so late in the process that the majority of the consumers have not yet reached that stage at the time of the interview.

The second class of independent variables consisted of an index of deliberation (like the index used by Katona and Mueller 1954), a measure of information sources utilized, the number of stores considered, the number of stores visited, the number of brands considered, and a measure of the time from the initial intention to the final purchase. Of these, the deliberation index and the number of information sources used were positively correlated with the purchases and with the timing of the purchase, which suggests that the greater the amount of deliberation and information search completed, the sooner the purchase will be made. Similarly, the number of stores visited and the number of brands considered also were positively correlated with the actual purchases made, which suggests that these variables also reveal how far the decision has progressed.

Based upon the four most predictive variables (two subjective probabilities, the deliberation index, and the number of brands considered), highly successful predictions were made. A linear discriminant analysis was 95% successful in classifying purchasers, and 87% of those classified as nonpurchasers did not purchase. Although an attempt to predict purchase timing was somewhat less successful, the findings do suggest that for major durable products meaningful predictions of purchases can be made based upon relevant measures of aspects of the decision process.

Thus, although repeat purchases of major durables follow a pattern like that of first purchases of major durables, information acquisition, deliberation, and trial are less extensive, and considerable variations are found. The initiation of the decision process and the variations in the complexity of the process are also dependent upon the previous experiences the consumers have with the product.

In general, the adoption model provides a framework for analysis of first purchases of major durables, and various models of loyalty and purchase sequences may develop into applicable models of repeat purchases of frequently used nondurable products. Repeat purchases of major durables and first purchases of nondurables are less complex than prescribed by the adoption model, but still too elaborate to be studied within the framework of loyalty models. So far, the available evidence suggests that several modifications in the adoption model are required before it can be applied to these cases and that considerable variation exists in the decision processes within each category. Future research may improve our understanding of these processes.

3. *Other Purchase Sequences*

1. Minor Durable Products and Infrequently Used Nondurable Products

The decision processes not yet discussed, that is, first and repeat purchases of minor durables and repeat purchases of infrequently used nondurables, have much in common with the cases already described. The purchase sequences in first and repeat purchases of minor durable products are less complex than the corresponding decision processes in purchases of major durables and more complex than in purchases of frequently used minor nondurable products. Repeat purchases of infrequently used nondurable products fall between the repeat purchases of durables and of frequently used nondurables.

Carefully designed studies will undoubtedly reveal important differences among the three types of purchase sequences not yet discussed, but unfortunately the available evidence does not distinguish among them. In the present section they will be studied as one group.

Bucklin (1966) studied shopping behavior in first and repeat purchases of products costing more than $5. As approximately 60% of the purchases amounted to less than $14 and 80% amounted to less than $50, it can safely be assumed that the majority of the products were either minor durable or infrequently purchased nondurable products. A majority (56%) of the consumers made only one trip to one store to make the purchase, which shows that considerably less extensive shopping occurs than for major durables. A relationship between the importance of the product and shopping behavior is reflected in a comparison between low-priced and high-priced items also. For items that cost less than $15, 61% shopped in only one store, whereas for items that cost more than $100, only 37% shopped in just one store. An effect of familiarity with the product also appears in the findings. Consumers who at the beginning of the shopping had no knowledge of the brand they eventually bought engaged in more extensive shopping than did consumers who knew the brand. Of the latter, only 15% made more than one shopping trip, in contrast to approximately 28% in the first group.

Similar findings are reported by Udell (1966), Dommermuth and Cundiff (1967), and Kleimenhagen (1967). Udell studied shopping behavior in connection with purchases of minor electrical appliances ranging in price up to $75 and found that 60% of the respondents shopped in only one store. Also, a close relationship between the price of the item and the extensiveness of shopping is reported. Only 28% of those who purchased inexpensive appliances ($7.50 or less) shopped in more than one store as opposed to 63% of those who bought items costing $50 or more. Udell also found the length of the decision processes to be shorter than in connection with major durables, as 83% reported that they bought within one month, 50% within two weeks and 22% on the day they first thought about it. On the other hand it was also found that these decision processes are more elaborate than in repeat purchases of frequently used nondurable products, as 73% reported that they had planned their purchase prior to entering the store and only 13% made their final decision during their first visit to a store.

Further, Katona and Mueller (1954) report findings in connection with purchases of sport shirts which are very much in line with those just reviewed. The decision process in purchases of sport shirts (which practically always can be classified as repeat purchases of a minor durable product) is less extensive than the decision process in purchases of major durables. The planning period is considerably shorter, the number of stores visited smaller

(70% of the consumers visited only the store in which they bought the shirt), knowledge about brands is less common, and information acquisition is less extensive (more than 60% acquired no information prior to the purchases, in contrast to approximately 30% of the consumers buying major durable products). Surprisingly, however, the number of features for which the consumers are looking is not smaller among the sport shirt purchasers than among the durable goods purchasers. This may, however, be a feature peculiar to the sport shirt, whose style, collar, and pattern are important aspects.

The study also illustrated effects of familiarity with the purchase situation. Consumers who showed some evidence of routine behavior (consumers who bought where they always or usually buy or who bought the brand they always or usually buy) engaged in less information seeking and deliberation than other consumers. The price effect previously reported is also found in this study. Consumers who bought more expensive sport shirts made more careful choices, engaged in more information search, and considered price and brand more carefully.

From the Katona–Mueller study it was found that consumers who employed careful deliberation when they bought major durables were not the same as those who had a high deliberation index in connection with the purchase of sport shirts, a finding which suggests that personality factors cannot be expected to explain major differences in consumers' purchase sequences.

Also, Ferber (1954 and 1955a) reports findings very much in line with those reviewed here. By comparing purchase plans for major and minor products (minor items of clothing, small appliances) he found shorter planning periods, less frequent plans, and less deliberation in connection with minor products. Similarly Bell's (1969) study of the formation of store preferences suggests more elaborate processes when suppliers of major durable products are chosen (Table 15.4), and other effects of learning are reported by Swan (1969). In an experiment dealing with purchases of shirts he found search to decline faster when choices among the same alternatives were repeated than when new alternatives were introduced. However, some evidence in favor of the adoption model in purchases of minor durables is provided by Beal and Rogers (1957), who in a study of the use of information sources in the adoption of new man-made fibers found a pattern closely resembling that which characterizes the acceptance of new major durable products.

2. Impulse Purchases

Impulse purchases and in-store behavior are characterized neither by the products purchased nor by the consumers buying. Nevertheless, they constitute important special types of purchase sequences; and reviewing the findings concerning these purchases will throw further light on the nature of consumer processes.

Systematic studies of impulse buying have been conducted since the early fifties. During that time the term *impulse buying* was meant to explain the observation that consumers make unplanned purchases and that in doing so they are influenced by such factors as product display, point-of-purchase material, and in-store advertising. Since then, many more definitions have been used in studies of "impulse purchases." In recent years the tendency has been toward a more diversified conceptualization, and impulse buying is commonly seen as a number of distinctive kinds of buying behavior (Stern 1962 and Kollat 1966).

Many studies have dealt with such purchases. Most of these find impulse purchases to be quite frequent (Clover 1950 and West 1951); and for grocery purchases Kollat and Willett (1967) found that 50% were not planned when the consumer entered the store, and Engel et al. (1968) report that the percentage of unplanned purchases in drugstores amounts to 22% and in liquor stores to 80%.

Different types of impulse purchases are discussed by Stern (1962), who suggests that unplanned purchases constitute four completely different types of decision processes. He first talks about *pure impulse purchases*, which he characterizes as purchases such that in-store stimuli actively—and without much involvement—cause purchases of a not-previously purchased product or brand. Such instances can be seen as decision processes with only one choice involved, as in the first purchase of a new, slightly different kind of bread.

Second, he deals with *reminder impulse purchases*. In these instances the sight of the product is the important aspect that reminds the consumer that he is out of stock or that he previously decided to buy this product. Here, in-store stimuli work as clues for a rather uncomplicated choice. The purchase is made through decision processes composed of only a few choices. Examples of such decision processes may be found in all grocery product categories.

Stern's third category, *suggestion impulse buying*, is a little difficult to distinguish from pure impulse buying. Stern suggests that the categories differ in the amount of deliberation involved; in pure impulse buying it is almost nil, whereas a good deal of consideration may occur in suggestion impulse buying. However, in both cases, the consumer is making a first purchase, and the decision process is completed immediately.

Finally, the fourth category, *planned impulse buying*, consists of purchases made when the consumer has made a general commitment to carry out the purchase decision in the store. Stern writes: "The shopper enters the store . . . with the expectation and intention to make . . . purchases that depend on price specials, coupon offers and the like" (p. 60). Here special stimuli in the store are decisive, and examples may be found in all product classes. These decision processes may be composed of many different kinds of choices, and the situational aspects applying here are highly important.

Decision processes for unplanned purchases are studied by Kollatt and Willett (1967). In their study, plans and intentions were measured when the consumer entered the store, and actual purchases were recorded when he left it. A home interview supplied information concerning brands and products stocked at home. Kollat and Willett found a considerable number of consumers with shopping lists, which can be taken as an indication of purchase sequences started before the actual shopping trip. Also, shoppers without a written list who indicated various buying plans must have been faced with purchase-related choices before shopping. Approximately 50% of the purchases were classified as completely unplanned purchases, but there is some indication that the decision process had started before the consumer entered the store. In approximately 70% of these cases, the household was out of stock of the item when it was purchased (the study dealt with frequently used grocery items).

Kollatt and Willett's results indicate that even with minor grocery items some decision-related activity occurs before the consumer enters the store. Furthermore, some evidence suggests that even the completely unplanned purchase may be seen as an element in a well-established behavior pattern; of all unplanned purchases, 87% acquired the same brand as the one bought last time.

3. In-store Behavior

Most studies of shopping behavior have been based on interviews. Only Wells and LoSciuto (1966) studied shopping behavior by means of direct observation. Their findings, although highly tentative, are very interesting. Evidence of exploration in terms of inspection of packaging and price was found. On package inspection, the authors write:

People spend a lot of time handling packages—picking them up, putting them down, fondling them, reading them, dropping them, picking them up and putting them back in the wrong place, etc. Sometimes they are looking at the weight and price, sometimes to see what premiums are being offered on the package back, and sometimes just reading the fine print. (p. 233)

Moreover, data presented show how decision processes can be initiated in the store by shopping companions and King (1969), using a protocol technique, reports findings that give a very similar picture of the shopping procedure.

The effects of changes in aspects of the situational setting the store provides have repeatedly been studied. Havas and Smith (1960) report that sales of food products are highly influenced by their location in the store, a finding which Hvelskamp et al. (1955) confirm. However, Harris (1958) showed that increasing the display width for well-known soap brands did not significantly influence sales; and Cox (1964) found that the sale of only one (hominy) of four products (Tang, baking soda, hominy, and powdered coffee cream) was significantly influenced by variations in shelf space. Similarly Krueckenberg (1969) finds for dairy products that doubling the number of facings does not increase sales sufficiently to warrant the added cost, and Kotzan and Evanson (1969), Cox (1970), and Frank and Massy (1970) find that as long as the product is located properly in the store, the amount of space assigned to it is not very important.

McKenna (1966) finds considerable influence of store displays, as do Kelly (1965) and a number of studies released by the Point of Purchase Advertising Institute (reviewed by Engel et al. 1968). On the other hand, Farrell (1965) finds that the sale of cantaloupes is only little influenced by store display, and similarly Banks (1961) finds correlation between in-store promotional activities and sales for cleanser, but not for coffee brands. It can be added that a number of studies attempting to explain variations in brand loyalty agree on the importance of availability but fail to find any significant influence of store display (Farley 1964c, Frank 1967a). It seems that the influence of store display is not a general phenomenon but depends on the specific circumstances.

The influence of special deals, multiple units, and price changes is fairly well established (Farley 1964c and Claycamp 1966), although it should be mentioned that Stockman (1957) found only limited effects of price deals for five frequently used food products.

These findings show that the phases of the purchase sequence that occur in the store are influenced by environmental factors in the store and that this influence varies among products.

4. *Total Consumer Behavior*

1. Consumption Sequences

The choice processes that must be considered to explain consumption behavior are those in which different consumption alternatives are considered. Such choice processes may result in the product's being consumed, as is the case with nondurable products; or the products may be left essentially unchanged, as is the case with most durable products. Moreover, consumption may involve the use of services or relate to the maintenance and repair of the product; it may result in the product's being discarded. Frequently choices among consumption alternatives arouse only little conflict, and consumption may become an integrated part of more complex behavioral responses. For example, the use of a product like dishwashing liquid will probably have to be studied in relation to the entire behavioral repertoire that relates to doing dishes.

We have discussed the importance of frequency of consumption of nondurables for the nature of subsequent purchases, and we have emphasized that the consumer's experience with durable products is extremely important for an understanding of repeat purchases of durables. Nevertheless, very little research has dealt with these relations. Cerha (1967) studies the frequency of use of 43 different food products in Swedish households and proposes that frequency of use is a major determinant of the consumers' information acquisition patterns, but so far no data have been reported that explore this relationship.

Another approach to the study of consumption patterns is emerging in the so-called backwards segmentation studies (Wells 1968). Future developments in this area may provide valuable insights into patterns of substitution and complementarity in consumption (Bass et al. 1969, see also Chapter 16).

Few existing studies are of any value for the study of consumption behavior. Most of them deal with consumption in a very broad sense and give only little information about the choice processes involved. Some of the more interesting describe the consumption pattern of a specific segment of the population. Typical for this category are studies of "mobile-home owners" (Moore 1963), "the Negro-market" (Bauer et al. 1965), "working-wife families" (Duker 1965), and "elder consumers" (Goldstein 1968). Others deal with consumption of specific products (Brown 1953; Bandeen 1957, Wax 1957, Allison et al. 1958, and Stone and Rowe 1960) but when it comes to behavioral aspects of consumption almost none are left. One area is an exception. In recent years, a number of media studies have focused on consumption patterns related to media use (Schyberger 1965, Swanson 1967a and 1967b, and Banks 1967). A main conclusion has been that people have very stable media habits and behave in a quite predictable way; their loyalty tends to develop in much the same way as for frequently purchased nondurable products.

Following the purchase, two processes are important for subsequent choices: the changes in the evaluation of the alternatives in response to post-choice conflict (Chapter 10) and the experiences the consumer has with the product. When the latter are positive, the effect will be to increase the probability of repeat purchase of the same brand; but when the experiences oppose the consumer's expectations, the two factors will draw in opposite directions. It is important to ask what the net effect will be. Cardozo (1965) has approached this problem in a study dealing with ballpoint pens, which found that the effects of disconfirmation of expectations overruled the post-choice adjustments in the evaluation of the alternatives, even though both tendencies were present. Similarly, in their study of coffee brands Cohen and Goldberg (1969) found the effect of negative product experiences to dominate dissonance-reducing responses.

However, in both studies the discrepancies between product performance and expectations are of a magnitude the consumer will rarely encounter in real situations, and it is possible that post-choice changes in the evaluation of the alternatives can overrule minor negative product experiences. Some evidence of the latter is present in a study reported by Mittelstaedt (1963 and 1969). He had subjects evaluate bathing suits and subsequently presented them with choices between two of the alternatives they had just rated. One group (the high-dissonance condition) was offered a choice between the alternative they had rated third and the alternative they had rated fourth. The other group (the low-dissonance condition) was offered a choice between the alternative they had rated third and the alternative they had rated fifth. In both conditions all subjects first chose the highest-rated alternative, but when they subsequently were asked to chose between their second and third rated alternatives the majority of the subjects in the low-dissonance condition chose the second-rated alternative, but a majority of the subjects in the high-dissonance condition did not change their choice of the third-rated alternative.

The nature of the consumer's experiences does not depend only upon the performance of the product. Axelrod (1963) and later Dommermuth and Millard (1967) have shown that the overall nature of the situation significantly influences the evaluation of the product. For example, Dommermuth and Millard found that a soft drink consumed while the subject watched a pleasant movie became more positively evaluated than when it was consumed while he watched an unpleasnt movie.

Occasionally adoptive behavior in a broader sense has been documented. Demsetz (1962), using panel data for orange juice, found changes over a seven-year period which he interprets as "learning about the market." Brown (1952), using aggregated data, explains major variations in consumption based on habit formation. Similarly, it has been found that elderly people have more stable consumption patterns than younger ones (Miller 1955). Altogether, the little evidence which exists indicates that consumers tend to form habits—much as they do in connection with repeat purchases of minor nondurable products. On this background it is tempting to suggest that in consumption sequences choice processes of reduced complexity are common, that semi-complex choices may occur, and that rational choices are rare.

2. Communication Sequences

Communication sequences in the choice process may take place when the consumer transmits information to others. Several studies have dealt with such communication or at least have shown that it occurs (Katz and Lazarsfeld 1955; Wärneryd 1965; Dichter 1966; Arndt 1967a). The main interest in personal communication has been in studies of it as a factor influencing other consumers, and few have looked at it from the point of view of the source. Arndt (1967a) touches upon the subject, in a review of the available evidence which suggests that the consumer may choose to transmit information for a variety of reasons, such as (1) altruism (the consumer tells a friend about a superior new product), (2) to prove himself well-informed (he reads and talks about advertisements as a conversational gambit), (3) to project frustrations and dissatisfactions (he blames his car for a minor accident), (4) special interest (a sports fisherman does not miss a chance to generate conversation about lures and other equipment), (5) to establish clarity (he reacts negatively in a conversation to positive information about a product he dislikes), and (6) an attempt to reduce dissonance (he attempts to convince others of the superiority of the product he has just purchased). To this it probably has to be added that a consumer may choose to transmit information for the sole purpose of communicating with others or to influence others' perception of himself.

Arndt's last three reasons in particular suggest that consumers communicate about products in attempts to reduce conflict. Similarly, Engel et al. (1969) observed that early users of a new automotive service "talk a lot about their experience" in an attempt to reduce post-purchase conflict. It seems that the selection of communication response has much in common with other conflict-reducing responses.

Besides volunteering oral information in a more or less planned attempt to influence, the consumer may demonstrate the product and may act as a source of overheard communication. Some of the same reasons which explain the consumer's oral communication also apply to his demonstration of products, especially in cases of conspicuous consumption. However, the consumer's involuntary demonstration of products and instances where he acts as a source of overheard communication are more difficult to explain. The communication may be provided for an indefinite number of reasons, and the extent to which it results in information perceived by other consumers must be studied in relation to the receiver also.

3. Interaction Among Purchase, Consumption, and Communication

The consumer's total behavior is one complete system in which every single choice is more or less dependent upon all other choices; consequently any attempt to define particular sequences of choices will always meet with the problem that some more-or-less closely related choice processes will have to be left out. However, as it is never possible to deal with the complete system of choices which constitutes the consumer's total behavior, how successfully consumer behavior can be studied depends upon whether meaningful sequences can be defined.

Communication responses occur as more or less integrated parts of purchase and consumption behavior, and consumption and purchase sequences often are closely related, as has been discussed. Particularly in connection with frequently used nondurable products, the consumption experience will constantly act as a feedback to influence subsequent purchases.

That all purchase sequences are related to the extent that they all involve use of the same limited financial resources is particularly important. Very little is known about the procedures consumers apply when they allocate their available income, but the area seems promising for future research. One could fruitfully study how consumers perceive their disposable income, what kinds of formal or informal budgeting procedures they apply, what budgeting periods they use, the extent to which budgets hold, what strategies are applied when they do not hold, how frequently they are revised, and what principles are applied when revisions are made.

That consumers do engage in budgeting to an extent that warrants further exploration is suggested by "Better Homes and Gardens Consumer Questionnaire" (1968), which reports that 22% of all consumers budget total family expenses and that an additional 46% of the respondents have some kind of budget for family expenses. Furthermore, 80% of the respondents report that they regularly or occasionally save with specific purposes in mind.

Consumers' priority patterns for major durables is an important area for further research. Paroush (1965) and McFall (1969) show that meaningful patterns can be established that reflect the order in which major durables are acquired. This line of research may gain significantly from being related to studies of consumer budgeting and preference patterns.

Purchase and consumption sequences related to different products influence each other because products can substitute for each other in use. Similarly, products that are complementary to each other will have related decision processes. For example, the purchase of a car gives rise to a number of closely related purchases of products such as gas, oil, and repair services. Certain purchase sequences influence each other to the extent that the final purchases are carried out together. As the consumer visits relatively few stores, the alternatives he sees are limited, and when a new store is chosen in connection with one purchase, it may influence other purchases as well. Consequently, it is important to study the consumer's overall shopping patterns. In this area, research can be conducted with methodologies already available (see for example Krugman 1960). It is important to gain knowledge about the different stores the consumer knows, the stores he visits, the stores in which he usually shops, and the products he expects to find in different stores.

Finally, the purchases made determine the consumption that subsequently can occur. Accordingly the availability of alternatives as reflected in the consumer's stocks of durable and nondurable products becomes the one most important factor in explaining consumption behavior. In traditional societies each household has only a few consumption alternatives available. Before consumption can occur a purchase must be made. Consequently only small discrepancies exist between demand and consumption In modern Western societies, however, the average household has a wide range of consumption alternatives available. The refrigerator and the freezer have provided the household with an almost unlimited food storage capacity, rising incomes have made large stocks of clothing possible and the consumer owns a large number of major durable products. These stocks represent available consumption alternatives. Therefore, today there is no straight-forward relationship between purchases and consumption. As in industry, stocks act as a buffer between the two. In one period the household may cut down on spending without changing its consumption, and in other periods it may change consumption without changing spending; the consumer's stocks are therefore crucial, and study of them may explain part of the in-teraction between purchases and consumption. This study, together with studies of income allocation processes and shopping patterns, may con-stitute some of the most promising areas for future research in consumer behavior.[6]

All told, this description of the consumer's behavior suggests that it can be seen as constantly approaching an equilibrium state. An equilibrium may be seen as a state towards which a system is moving, and a stable equilibrium is one which the system will attempt to maintain when that state is reached. It is questionable whether any kind of stable equilibrium can be identified in individual consumer behavior. The affect of boredom with its subsequent rises in arousal would seem to rule this out,[7] but it does not make sense to talk about an individual equilibrium as a state towards which the single consumer is moving. It is possible to analyze this state in terms of the con-sumer's purchase, consumption, and information acquisition behavior. For a given product, such an equilibrium would be a state in which repeat purchases are made in the form of clue-guided choices, consumption has become part of integrated behavioral responses, and information acquisition and search are nonexistent.

The definition of such an equilibrium is worthwhile, not so much be-cause of the equilibrium state itself (which hardly ever is reached), but because it provides a framework for looking at individual consumer be-havior. The individual's behavior can be thought of as constantly approach-ing the equilibrium state, and when environmental factors influencing the consumer are considered, they can be thought of as influences which inter-fere with this process.

[6] In a predominantly rural society with a large number of self-supplying farm households, a similar problem may exist. In such societies, the application of economic models developed in Western societies may, for that reason, be highly questionable.

[7] If the arousal effects are included in the equilibrium definition one might talk about a kind of stable dynamic equilibrium.

Chapter 16

CONSUMER VALUES AND INSTRUMENTALITIES

It has become evident that an understanding of consumer choice behavior requires knowledge of the values held by the consumer and the relationships among values and alternatives.

It was suggested that memory can be seen as a large system of latent concepts: the conceptual system (Chapter 6). In choice processes elements from this system are aroused. It is the purpose of this chapter to study consumers' conceptual systems with a special emphasis on the values that are important in consumer choices.

1. *The Conceptual System*

The molecular view of motivation and cognitive elements inherent in the present approach calls for some kind of systemization of the individual's many concepts. Such an attempt can build upon the relationships among concepts. Either similar concepts can be grouped together, or concepts can be classified according to their relationship to other concepts. One such classification groups concepts according to whether they primarily operate as *actors*, *means*, or *ends*, a distinction used by many authors (Simon 1957 and Abelson and Rosenberg 1958). In accordance with this classification an *actor* may be "the household," "the family," "the retailer," or "the manufacturer." The actor can be represented by a simple or a highly complex concept. Of special interest is the actor "I", which is usually referred to as the individual's *self-image*. *Means* may be "a purchase," "a mail-order catalogue," "a request for information," or "to go to a store." Means are strategies that can be applied in attempts to achieve ends. Choice alternatives especially will occur as means, i.e., purchase responses, commitments to future behavior, and the like. *Ends* may be "to save money on weekly food purchases," "to acquire a reliable means of transportation," or "to be looked up to by friends." That is, they are future states towards which the individual strives. They can be very concrete goals, such as a new house in a nice area or one additional car for the family; but they can also be less specific, taking the form of general values such as the "durability" and "efficiency" of a television set, "good taste" in food, and so on. Eventually, actors, means, and ends can form complex structures in which one end gains its significance only because it acts as a means towards more remote goals. In different contexts the same concept may operate as an actor, a means or an end.

Another classification rests upon differences in the level of generalization (Chapter 6). The classification of marketing communication proposed by Cerha (1967) is based upon this criterion (Chapter 3). By working with the "type of product level," "assortment level," "manufacturer level" and "brand level" Cerha maintains: "We thereby expect to always cover the level whose concepts the consumers utilize when attempting to orientate themselves in a market with excessive differentiation of symbols" (p. 80).

To study what concepts a consumer classifies as belonging to different levels may give insight into the way he looks at his world. For example, to study the consumer's classification of different products in different retail assortments may make it possible to understand his choices among stores, and similarly knowing the brands the consumer groups together as a *product class* (his "evoked net", Howard and Smith 1967) is important for understanding what alternatives he considers in a particular situation.

Other classifications of potential relevance for studies of consumer behavior are proposed by Janis (1959a) and by Rokeach (1960 and 1968a). Janis classifies values as (1) anticipated utilitarian gains for self, (2) anticipated utilitarian gains for others, (3) anticipated approval and disapproval from others, and (4) anticipated approval and disapproval from self. It seems that the kind of values salient in consumer choice processes lend themselves easily to classification into these four categories. However, no studies have been made to attempt to quantify the relative importance of these different classes of values.

Rokeach's belief structure model (Chapter 7), distinguishing among beliefs of different centrality, describes important aspects of the total conceptual structure and is highly relevant to consumer choice behavior. Generally, clues will be inconsequential or peripheral beliefs, whereas the concepts entering into more complex choice processes can include authority and personal beliefs. In a discussion of the model and its relationship to advertising decision making, Rokeach (1968b) observes that the more competition there is in a market, the less will consequential beliefs be attacked through advertising. The observation is interesting, because it agrees with a proposition common in the theory of competition: In a highly competitive market (with few sellers) price competition will be neutralized, as no single company will dare to decrease its prices because it fears that its competitors will immediately do the same. Similarly, in connection with advertising budgets and quality competition a related neutralizing tendency can occur (Rasmussen 1955). Rokeach's observation suggests that the same mechanism is at work in connection with advertising content: When competition is severe, the company can choose only advertising messages which attack inconsequential beliefs. Attempts to influence more central beliefs are unlikely, because they would be counteracted immediately and because they would require underlying product differentiation, which cannot be attained because that too would be counteracted by competitors.

In his later work, Rokeach (1968a and 1969) has concentrated on attitudes and particularly on values, which he defines as "an enduring belief that a particular mode of conduct or a particular end-state of existence is personally and socially preferable to alternative modes of conduct or end-states of existence" (1969, p. 550).[1] Rokeach sees the value structure as a subset within the belief structure composed of terminal values (for example, "a comfortable life," "a world of peace," "freedom" (and instrumental values (for example, ambitious, cheerful, helpful). Rokeach further suggests that as values are related, it is possible to identify a relatively limited number of basic values that can explain large parts of the individual's behavior. Rokeach (1969) presents 36 such terminal and instrumental values that have been found to differ significantly among different groups such as "hippies" and "nonhippies," "hawks" and "doves," men and women, policemen and unemployed Negroes, or good students and bad students. It will be interesting to apply these values in studies of consumer behavior. Future research will show whether they represent a possibility for segmentation of consumers and whether they can be used to predict choices.[2]

In spite of the extreme complexity of the conceptual structure, it can be studied meaningfully. Perhaps this is most clearly seen in cross-cultural studies of subjective values (Dubois 1955, Osgood 1967, and Triandis et al. 1968). Although these studies have been aimed primarily at general cultural values, the approach seems feasible also with more consumption-oriented values and perceptions. Moreover, it should be possible with this kind of study to reveal important differences in market segments at lower than national levels.

[1] It will be seen that Rokeach's definition of values is more restrictive than the one applied here. A major reason for the wider concept applied in the present approach is to be found in the different types of behavior with which Rokeach and the present author deal. Rokeach is interested in such activities as church-going and political opinions.

[2] This particular set of values was not known to the author when the experiments in Chapter 12 were conducted. It would have been interesting to substitute these values for the 24 used in these experiments.

Altogether, systematic analyses of conceptual structures (belief-value systems) are only beginning. Presently, there is no single approach that is particularly suitable for studies of consumer behavior. In the following discussion of the concepts common in consumer choices, we hope to reveal aspects that must be considered when consumers' conceptual systems are studied.

2. *Perception of Product Attributes and Related Values*

Study of consumer behavior must deal with the values to which alternatives are related and the beliefs which tie values to alternatives. Motivation research studies report findings which might give some insight into the kind of valued concepts on which consumers rely. Unfortunately, most of these studies are difficult to evaluate, since results often are presented without description of the procedures applied and because the studies are so heterogeneous that it is almost impossible to make meaningful comparisons between findings derived from different studies. However, from some of the more systematic reports (Cheskin 1962, Dichter 1964, and the Chicago Tribune studies), it seems that the number of values different consumers may apply in different situations is extremely large.

Rather than attempting to systemize the findings from motivation research studies, the following discussion will rely heavily upon two other sources. First, findings will be reviewed that are derived in experiments in which subjects make choices after they are presented with different stimuli. This design makes it possible to infer the concepts that were salient in the choice processes. Second, findings from survey studies in which consumers directly or indirectly report the concepts they relied on will be discussed.

In choice processes consumers' salient cognitive structures are composed of (1) alternatives, (2) valued concepts, and (3) instrumentalities relating alternatives to values.

What alternatives are perceived depends upon the specific situation. For an alternative to become salient, it must either be present in the immediate environment or be otherwise known to the consumer, that is, it must be present in his conceptual system. The latter case is reflected in measures of awareness. Brand awareness can be interpreted as a measure of the chance that a certain alternative will be considered next time the consumer is making a choice. As awareness measures can be varied by changing the amount of aid given to the respondent, it is also possible to obtain measurements that reveal the order in which the alternatives are likely to be aroused. The relative success of *first-brand awareness* measures as predictors of brand shares, reported by Axelrod (1968), Assael and Day (1968), and Gruber (1969), supports this view.

1. Income as a Cognitive Element

In spite of its importance, very little is known about income as a cognitive element and about how it operates in consumer choice processes. It is therefore possible only to present a few findings and to suggest problems for future study.

The income the consumer perceives as relevant in a particular choice can be anything from the amount of cash he has at hand to an estimate of his potential buying power. In a particular situation the relevant income concept may be current income, disposable income, discretionary income or expected income. To the economist all thes econcepts are related in a well-defined way. For example, disposable income is identical with the current income less fixed expenditures (taxes, rent, and so on), and discretionary income is identical with disposable income less an amount corresponding to the minimum expenses for necessary variable expenditures (Katona 1960). However, the consumer's perception of income may be significantly different from these theoretical income concepts. For example, his perception of his buying power can vary depending upon the assets and credit possibilities he considers. Since assets vary from highly liquid to completely nonliquid, his buying power will be determined differently depending upon how far he goes in including less liquid assets. Similarly, the consumer's credit possibilities are many and varied, and his perception of his buying power will vary according to which of them he includes. The problem appears even more complex when it is realized that the consumer most likely will also consider some form of expected income and that he can make choices based upon expected disposable or expected discretionary income as well as upon expected buying power.

In economics, where income plays a major role, it has been attempted to define *the* income concept that will explain consumer behavior at a highly aggregated level. In its simplest form the absolute income hypothesis (Keynes 1936) maintains that consumption will increase as income increases, but less rapidly. Here the consumer is assumed to perceive and act upon his actual income at the time of the purchase decision. However, even at very high levels of aggregation this income concept has proven to be an oversimplification (Ferber 1967); consequently other concepts, considering aspects of the consumer's perception of his buying power, have been proposed. Among these the *relative income hypothesis* (Dusenberry 1949) suggests that the proportion of total income spent should be explained in terms of the household's income relative to the income of other households; thus the way the consumer perceives his income relative to the income of other consumers is the important factor. However, attempts to explain the consumer's total spending by means of the relative income concept have met with difficulties also (Ferber 1967). Finally, it has been suggested that income is determined not by the actual income, but by the average expected income in the long run (Friedman 1957), an explanation which leads to a decomposition of income into a permanent and a transitory component and to a similar decomposition of consumption. In this version the hypothesis is that (permanent) consumption is a constant fraction of permanent income, where the permanent income results when the consumer's income is adjusted for short-term fluctuations. Aspects of the consumer's perception of his long-term income are considered to be crucial, but again, with this income concept it has not been possible to establish highly predictive relationships. It is noteworthy that all these attempts assume that most aspects of consumer behavior can be explained in terms of a single income concept, but the preceding discussion of consumer choices suggests that this is an oversimplification. Rather, under different circumstances consumers perceive income differently.

A few studies have explored factors that may cause variations in the income concepts consumers apply. Lansing and Morgan (1955) show that consumer finances vary not only with actual income but also with available assets, credit possibilities, and the amount of fixed outlays. Similarly Ferber (1955a), Kreinin (1959), and Katona and Mueller (1954) found that expectations with regard to future income as well as income change and liquid assets were important.

How the perceived income influences choices can be expected to depend upon the phase in the decision process in which the income factor is considered. Early in the process income considerations may take the form of budgeting decisions, that is, sometimes early in the purchase sequence a choice is made which acts as both a constraint on action and a commitment to further action. However, when income is not considered until late in the decision process it may act as a kind of "go"—"no go" factor; that is, after the preferred alternative has been identified the question is raised, "Can I afford it?" The answer determines whether the purchase is to be made. The same consumer may in some cases use the first approach, in others the second. Budgeting can occur in connection with some products, although in connection with others income is not considered until just before the purchase. Similarly, some consumers may tend to consider income early, whereas others rarely pay attention to it until just before the final purchase.

Income considerations may occur in several different phases of the same purchase sequence, and they can result in criteria which guide the evaluation of alternatives and the selection of information sources. Such a process occurs when the perceived income suggests an acceptable price interval so that subsequent search and evaluation concentrate on alternatives within this interval, a phenomenon illustrated by findings reported by Katona and Mueller (1954). In connection with purchases of major durables they found that 57% of the consumers considered only alternatives within a limited price range. Similarly, Norris (1954) reports that a majority of the consumers in their search for a house ruled out alternatives by using such criteria as the size of the house, the number of bedrooms, and the price of the house compared with a previously established cost ceiling. The latter criterion alone was applied by 80% of the consumers. Moreover, Shaffer (1960) reports that, although impulse purchases are frequent in food purchases, they have only little influence on the total spending, an observation which suggests that income acts as a restraint here also.

Financial considerations can influence the length of the decision process. Ferber (1955a) and Wickström (1965) found that changing economic conditions can postpone purchases as well as trigger purchases that had been planned over longer periods (see Chapter 16).

However income is perceived, its importance depends upon how frequently it is aroused in consumer choices. No evidence is available, but it is natural to expect that income is considered more frequently the more expensive the product is. Although only little is known about the consumer's perception of income and its role in consumer choice processes, it is obvious that income-related values are among the most important concepts in consumer choices.

2. Credit and Saving as a Cognitive Element

The consumer is able to modify his perception of his buying power, which makes income a complex factor in cognitive processes. As a result of early conflicts a consumer may attempt to increase his liquid assets, and in the long run this can involve realization of nonliquid assets or a search for ways to ensure additional income. In the short run, however, it is likely to involve the use of credit or savings.

Credit, as contrasted to income, has given rise to research directly dealing with cognitive aspects of consumer choice processes. Wärneryd (1965) reports that a considerable number of Swedish consumers have attitudes opposing the use of installment credit, and negative values associated with extensive use of credit are reported in the "Better Homes and Gardens Consumer Questionnaire" (1968). On the other hand, Ferber (1955a) reports that availability of credit is an important factor in purchases of major durable products, and several other studies have supported this finding.

In evaluating credit offers, consumers may pay more or less attention to amount of down payment, size of monthly payments, total interest, or interest rates. Juster and Shay (1964) report that although borrowing decisions, particularly those made by older people, may be influenced by the real cost, the size of the monthly payment is the most commonly considered factor. Similarly, Venkatesan and Hancock (1967), in a study of consumer's perception of credit, found that for both charge accounts and installment credit, the monthly payments were the most important factor. The same study also found that consumers perceive revolving charge accounts and installment credit very differently. With charge accounts, a considerably larger number of the consumers pay major attention to the price of the purchase as compared with installment purchases, in which the down payment, the size of the monthly payment, and the number of installments are the most important factors.

Several authors have dealt with consumers' saving behavior (Goble 1966 and 1969, Ölander and Seipel 1967, and Myers and Alpert 1968). Most of them, however, do not show how saving decisions interact with purchase decisions. Only the "Better Homes and Gardens Consumer Questionnaire" presents a few suggestive findings. Twenty-seven per cent of the respondents reported that they follow a consistent program of saving before bills are paid. Such behavior will undoubtedly influence decision processes for major products. How different approaches may be followed when major expenses occur is also suggested in findings related to vacation travelling. Sixteen per cent reported that they have a special savings program for this purpose, 25% start saving just before vacation, 56% take from general savings, and 27% use credit cards or other forms of credit.

3. Price as a Cognitive Element

That price is an important cognitive variable is obvious from a large number of demand analyses (see for example Schultz 1938). Nevertheless, a number of studies have reported price to be less important than traditionally believed. Early findings were reported by Brown (1950), Markstein (1953), and Katona and Mueller (1954), and many later studies have arrived at a similar conclusion. On the other hand, McClure and Ryans (1968) report that in connection with major durables consumers ascribe considerably more importance to price than retailers believe, and Wärneryd (1965) reports that Swedish consumers firmly believe that "one should carry out price comparisons."

There is little agreement as to the exact role of price in consumer decision processes, but we will review the available evidence now. A number of studies have dealt with the consumer's perception of price. Zabel (1963) reports that test shoppers in a supermarket were only moderately successful in locating "best buys," and for household products such as soap and detergent Haines (1966) found that many consumers do not perceive the price correctly.

Similarly Gabor and Granger (1964) found for different grocery products that from 65% to approximately 20% of the consumers did not know the correct prices. Similarly for detergents and cereals Wells and LoSciuto (1966) report significant differences in the extent to which consumers were concerned with prices, and Anderson et al. (1966) found concern with prices to vary with the number of alternatives considered. Finally, it can be mentioned that differences in consumers' price consciousness are evident in the findings reported by Stone (1954), who was able to identify highly price-sensitive consumers as a special market segment. In reviewing the evidence on the accuracy of price perception, Shapiro (1968) finds variations depending upon social class, stores, and products.

Another observation related to the consumer's perception of price is presented by Oxenfeldt (1968). He suggests that most consumers, instead of perceiving prices of single products, tend to rely upon perception of the price ranges offered in different stores. Thereby the price factor becomes more important in choosing a store than in selection of products within the store. However, consumers perceive prices imperfectly in evaluating stores. In an extensive study Brown (1969) found considerable inaccuracies in consumers' perceptions of price levels for retail stores.

Consumer decision processses are influenced not only by current prices, but also by expectations with regard to future prices. This has repeatedly been reported by Katona (1960 and 1964), who has shown that major purchases may be postponed or hastened according to what price changes consumers expect. Moreover, consumers' price perceptions depend on their expectations with regard to the pricing strategies applied by the marketers. For example, Gabor and Granger (1964) find the effectiveness of "psychological prices" to be dependent upon the frequency with which they are used in a particular product area. For a product for which they are common, the authors find positive price elasticities just below the psychological prices, but for another product for which the psychological price is not used a similar effect does not occur. The use of stamps, deals, coupons, and "two-for-one" prices, will influence price perceptions also. On the one hand such special arrangements can be expected to draw the attention to the price (Nielsen 1965); on the other hand they may make it more difficult for the consumer to perceive price levels accurately. It would seem worthwhile to study how the accuracy of consumers' price perceptions is related to the amount of deals and pricing activity for the product, but little research—to this time, only a single exploratory study (Seipel 1971)—has been reported. A special problem is represented by trading stamps. Much evidence is available on their effects upon demand and price levels (Kroeger 1953, Ellsworth 1957, and Fox 1968), but little is known about the way they influence consumers' perceptions of price levels for stores.

Other problems relate to consumers' perceptions of price changes. Engel et al. (1968) propose that a form of Weber's perceptual law (Chapter 3) should apply, so that the higher the initial price, the larger the price change must be before it is noticed. Kamen and Toman (1970), however, testing the hypothesis for gasoline brands, find that a "fair price" type of model agrees with their data. That is, consumers tend to accept prices as long as they stay below a certain level they consider fair.

Further complications result because consumers frequently judge quality by price. Cole et al. (1955) and Morris and Bronson (1969) show that this may or may not be a rational practice. By comparing Consumers' Union product ratings for 48 products over a number of years, Morris and

Bronson found some correlations between quality and price in some product areas, but for others even negative relationships appeared. However, whatever the rationale of the practice, it has important implications for traditional economic models of consumers' reactions to prices (Scitovsky 1945). Several studies have revealed "judging quality by price" effects of varying magnitude. For example, Leavitt (1954) found subjects' choices among brands of floor wax to be influenced by price; moreover, subjects choosing the more expensive alternative also judged it to be of higher quality, an observation also made by Tull et al. (1964), Schreiber (1965), McConnell (1968), Smith and Broome (1967), and Ölander (1968).

Some difficulties encountered in attempts to establish price-quality relationships from experimental observations are related to judging quality by price also (Pessimier 1960, Abrams 1964, Pessimier and Teach 1966, and Stout 1969). In these studies, the established price-quality relationships have rarely compared well with actual sales tests. Presumably in an experimental environment the "judging quality by price" tendency is relatively stronger than the more straightforward economic considerations. Shapiro (1968) in his review concludes that the "judging quality by price" phenomenon is well established and that it occurs more or less frequently in different areas. He finds the following factors to be important:

1. The more easily products can be evaluated, the less important the phenomenon will be.
2. The less expensive the product, compared with the psychological costs associated with seeking more information, the more the consumer will tend to judge quality by price.
3. The more prestigious the product, the more its quality will be judged by price.

In an attempt to integrate the effects of different factors upon price perception Adam (1958) and Fouilhe (1960) have introduced the concept of the maximum and minimum prices that define an acceptable price range, and Gabor and Granger (1966) and Monroe (1969) have shown such price ranges to exist. When the product becomes too expensive, it is rejected for economic considerations, and when it is too inexpensive the consumer rejects it because he assumes that the quality is too low.

However, it is questionable whether the complete effect of prices can be described within such a framework. For example, when several alternatives fall within the acceptable price range, it is possible that their attractiveness will be influenced by their prices. Under such circumstances the effect of price upon the overall attractiveness of the alternative can be very complex. The less expensive alternatives will not always be the most attractive ones. Because of the "judging quality by price" effect, it is possible that the most attractive alternatives are found somewhere in the middle of the region of acceptable prices and that more or less expensive alternatives are seen as less attractive. Findings which suggest such a relationship are reported by Ölander (1968), who in line with Bilkey (1953) suggests that consumer choices should be studied as a function of the *attractiveness* of the alternatives (here used as a summary measure of the positive aspects of the product) and the sacrifice associated with obtaining the product (a summary measure of negative aspects of the product, including the price). To explore the independent affects of the positive aspects (attractiveness) and the negative aspects (price), Ölander conducted several experiments. The effect of judging quality by price is evident in findings from a study in which subjects made choices from pairs of towels. As different prices were randomly assigned to the alternatives, it is possible to observe the extent to which the same towel was chosen more frequently when labelled with a higher price. From this experiment highly significant results emerged; and when scale values of subjects' preferences for the alternatives were constructed, it was found that the preferences showed a very high linear correlation with the prices. As the subjects did not pay for the towels (to secure involvement, subjects were given two of the towels they had chosen) the sacrifice factor was neutralized, and the data illustrate the isolated effect of judging quality by price.

In a real purchase, the judging quality by price effect can be expected to be offset by the monetary offer. How this interaction works can be studied if the attractiveness of the alternative (with no regard to price) is compared with the attractiveness of the purchase offer (composed of the alternative at a certain price). Such an experiment was conducted with curtain textiles as choice alternatives, and the findings suggest that consumers are willing to substitute attractiveness for price. For example, a purchase offer with an attractiveness of "1" and a price of S.kr. 13 was rated equally attractive as a purchase offer with an attractiveness of "5" and a price of S.kr. 20.

Related evidence is reported by Stafford and Enis (1969). These authors had subjects evaluating rug samples while their information about prices and stores was varied systematically. Here, as all subjects rated the same samples, the interaction occurred between store and price information, and the expected price effect was established together with a significant interaction effect with the stores.

The extent to which the consumers' differentiated price perceptions lead to different distributions of purchases over the relevant price ranges is shown by Koenig (1971), who uses panel data for textiles, meat, and food products to illustrate the phenomenon, and who also shows how changes occur over time.

The highly complex nature of consumers' price perceptions is also illustrated by Doob et al. (1969), who studied the effect of different initial selling prices for new products in supermarkets. The authors hypothesized that an initial low price might retard subsequent sales, as it would make the consumers perceive the product as relatively inferior, and they analyzed sales developments for new brands of mouthwash, toothpaste, aluminum foil, light bulbs, and cookies. Using matched samples of stores they found that when the product was introduced at a reduced price, it would sell better as long as the price was kept low, but that the sales after restoration of the higher price became significantly lower than sales of the same brand introduced at the higher price. Moreover, this effect remained for the entire period under study, which is noteworthy because consumers could not have stored the new brand in excessive amounts in the period of low prices, because of the length and nature of the study. As only private brands were studied it is not possible to know how general such an effect is, but even if it is peculiar to private brands the phenomenon warrants further research.

Altogether, the available evidence suggests that consumers' perception of price is a much more complex phenomenon than traditionally believed and that straightforward predictions of effects of price changes may very well be misleading. So far the findings do not allow for specification of the conditions under which different perceptual processes will occur, and research on the relative magnitude of the various effects is badly needed. Similarly, the relationship between the consumer's income perception and his acceptable price ranges needs further exploration. It is a tempting suggestion that, contrary to economic tradition, the effects of prices and income upon consumers' choices should be dealt with simultaneously and that *relative price*, defined as price divided by income, may be a highly explanatory variable.

4. Time and Effort as Cognitive Elements

In Chapter 9, *time* and *effort* were discussed as factors influencing the extensiveness of information acquisition. These factors may also be thought of as cognitive elements aroused in choice processes. Like the price element they may be part of the sacrifice associated with the purchase or with information acquisition. However, shopping may be an activity that is rewarding in its own right despite the time and effort spent; and consequently it can also appear as a positive factor.

Except for consumers' choices of retail outlets, in which convenience has been shown to be important, these factors have rarely been studied, but time and effort may be the most important attributes of the alternatives in connection with many services such as restaurant meals and transportation, and in connection with other products they may be important when alternatives are compared which differ in availability. In a sense they represent the "price" for increasing the selection of available alternatives, and particularly in connection with consumption they may determine whether an immediately available or a more suitable but also more remote alternative is chosen.

A general framework for studying the role of time in consumer behavior is prescribed by Schary (1971), but so far research has not been reported.

5. Functional and Semi-Functional Attributes of the Product as Cognitive Elements

Different products are evaluated along an infinite number of dimensions, and it makes little sense to try to systemize them across products. The cognitive elements aroused in a conflict concerning home purchases are entirely different from those aroused in choices among items of clothing, and different again from those found in food purchases (Gottlieb 1958).

Generally product attributes can be classified as functional and semi-functional, the first group consisting of attributes related to the performance of the product and the second category consisting of those reflecting style and appearance. The relative importance of functional and semi-functional quality aspects varies among products. Rizzo and Naylor (1964), who had subjects rate the importance of different consumer choice parameters (Table 16.1), found style and comfort to be the most important factor for clothing, whereas performance was the most important single factor for all other products studied.

TABLE 16.1

Mean importance ratings for selected consumer choice parameters

Dimension	Clothing	Car	Appliance	Home	Food
Comfort	7.64	7.19	7.68	8.09	6.23
Style	7.42	6.84	5.33	7.30	6.04
Performance	6.96	8.36	8.40	8.22	8.11
Cost	6.65	7.47	7.28	7.61	6.80
Manufacturer	4.69	6.76	6.53	6.85	5.88
Place of purchase	4.67	5.39	5.28	7.84	6.16

(Reproduced with permission from Rizzo and Naylor, 1964, Copyright American Psychological Association.)

Even for one product a large number of different quality attributes can be identified (Trier et al. 1960, LcGrand and Udell 1964, Payne 1966, and McClure and Ryans 1968). Very often, the number exceeds what the consumer is able to deal with in a single choice process, a problem previously discussed which the consumer may solve by disregarding some aspects, evaluating the overall "quality" of the product, relying upon clues such as price, brand name, or market standing, or not considering all aspects in a single choice process.

In the discussion of perception (Chapter 3) the consumer's limited ability to detect product differences was discussed. Moreover, in connection with unconscious processes (Chapter 6) it was shown how consumers could rely upon cognitive elements they were unable to verbalize. Both phenomena complicate the relationship between the marketer's product strategies and the consumer's choices. Not all product change can be assumed to influence behavior, and consumers cannot be expected to report accurately about the factors they rely upon. On the other hand mere knowledge of product quality factors may influence choices. At least for food products, Henell (1953) finds that the extent to which consumers are familiar with product attributes such as nutritional value influences their choices.

Perceptual limitations in connection with taste are discussed by Yensen

(1959); while Ramond et al. (1950), Fleishman (1951), and Allison and Uhl (1964) report on consumers' limited ability to discriminate among brands of cigarettes and beer. The Ramond study is particularly interesting because it reveals large differences in the discriminating ability of consumers related to familiarity with the product. It was found that heavy smokers were more than twice as good in identifying their own brand as compared with other smokers.

Evidence of more or less conscious perceptual processes appears in Laird's (1932) study of women's stockings, in Quenon's (1951) study of housewives' evaluations of children's shorts, in studies by Eastlack (1964) and by Taylor (1967) dealing with the perception of taste in coffee, and in Gridgeman's study (1966) of the taste of jam. Significant influences upon choices resulting from more or less consciously perceived product differences can be inferred in all these studies.

6. Brand Name, Market Standings, and Other Clues

A major function of brand names may be to act as clues. Larzelere et al. (1965) found that consumers were willing to pay a higher price for a brand-name turkey than for an identical non-brand turkey. Presumably the brand name was taken as a clue to higher quality. Similar findings are reported by Smith and Broome (1967), and other evidence of brand names as clues in consumer choice processes appears in studies of private and national brands. For example, Myers (1967) found a general tendency among consumers to perceive private brands as being of inferior quality. Interesting in this connection is also Rao's (1969b) finding that the success of any given private brand is positively associated with the success of similar private brands carried by other stores, a finding which suggests that the extent to which private brands are seen as having lower quality varies systematically among products.

Other evidence of the use of clues is provided by Brown (1958), who reports that housewives evaluating freshness of bread rely upon the nature of the packaging material rather than upon the freshness of the bread itself, and by Cox (1963), who reports that scent has been shown to act as a clue in choices among stockings, by Hall (1958), Britt (1960), and Cox (1967b), who show how color in food products such as jam, syrup, margarine, and butter can act as a clue, and by Froman (1953) with regard to suds in detergents.

Interesting findings are also reported by Smith and Broome (1967), who found that besides price and brand name, consumers may use knowledge of the producer's market standing as a clue. Finally, although it is commonly found that the name of the manufacturer may act as a clue (see Table 16.1), Uhl (1962) found that share-owners were not significantly influenced in their product choices. Presumably the way a cognitive element becomes established as a clue is not a straightforward function of familiarity with the concept; the nature of previous experiences plays a significant role also.

7. Perceptions Related to Product Use

Often it can be expected that consumers, rather than rely upon the features of the product itself, will concern themselves with how the product will perform in use. In this connection a distinction between "consumers' criteria" and "producers' criteria" has been prepared (Brems 1950), but no research has been reported showing how consumers perceive products in relation to all the situations in which they are used.

8. Packaging and Other Product-related Cognitive Elements

Packaging acts as a means of communication (Lincoln 1965 and Gardner 1967), it has an important influence on the perception of semi-functional aspects of the product, and it may have an impact of its own, for example, if the package is reusable. Being almost a part of the product, the packaging may also interact closely with the evaluation of the product itself. Brown (1958) showed that the wrapper influences the perception of freshness in bread, and a somewhat similar finding is reported by Banks (1950c).

In many product areas the experiences the consumer has with the product may depend as much upon the packaging as upon the product. However, that product perception may also occur relatively independently of the packaging, for example, is shown by Naylor (1962), who found that consumers were able to distinguish among identical packages with different amounts of potato chips.

To complete the list of cognitive elements which may occur in choice processes, a number of aspects of products and other alternatives should be mentioned, such as availability of service, delivery arrangements, gifts, coupons, premiums, lottery tickets, and other features which are not part of the product itself but which may be part of the alternative the consumer perceives.

9. Mass Media and Other People as Concepts in Cognitive Structures

Information sources occur as cognitive elements in the consumer's choices. They influence the way information is received (see Chapter 9), and they act as *value concepts*. Another individual may act as a value concept for example: Person *A* is positively evaluated; person *A* is known to use product X (is positively related to product X); the attractiveness of X is increased because of this relationship. That is, whether A acts as an information source or not, the fact that he represents a positively evaluated concept associated with an alternative may influence the choice. In this way both mass media and personal information sources may more or less directly act as value concepts.

The information source represented in the choice process as an evaluated concept may be a known person or medium. Here the consumer relies upon the other's judgment, and such choice processes will often be of reduced complexity, with the information source acting as a clue.

A personal information source can be an agent for the marketer (for example, a salesman) or personal friends or relatives. Cox (1963) has shown that the evaluation of the salesman affects the way he influences the consumer; and Whyte (1954), Katz and Lazarsfeld (1955), Feldman and Spencer (1965), and Gilkison (1965) show that other personal sources of information can influence choices. Related evidence is also provided by Lindhoff and Naukhoff (1966). In a study of unknown brands associated with either positive or negative persons, it was found that the total evaluation of the brands was significantly influenced by the products with which they were associated. Similarly, where individuals were associated with positively or negatively evaluated brands, the evaluations of the individuals changed accordingly (Stålberg and Säve-Söderberg 1965).

The mass media may also act as clues in choice processes. The consumer may choose a product which he perceives as frequently advertised, that is, he uses the "amount of advertising" as a clue to judge functional and semi-functional aspects of the alternative. Similarly, approval from particular mass media such as Consumers Union reports, or Good Housekeeping magazine may act as clues (Sargent 1959 and Hempel 1966).

That various consumers evaluate media in different ways is a common observation that can be seen in a study such as Schyberger's (1965), and that advertising in general is evaluated variously can be seen from the AAAA study of consumers' judgment of advertising (Kanter 1964).

Less directly, other people become positively or negatively evaluated concepts when the product is seen as associated with special types of consumers. Many image studies have shown how different products can be perceived as for example "primarily for high-class consumers," "primarily for females," "primarily for the young." Here the value concept is a certain type of person, and it gains its importance because the consumer believes that he, by choosing a particular product, associates himself with that type.

Findings which show how consumers perceive different products as related to different types of people are provided by Haire (1950), Westfall et al. (1957), Sommers (1963), Carlson (1964), and Hamm et al. (1969). Similarly, Weale (1961) and Rich and Portis (1964) have shown that consumers perceive stores in terms of who is likely to shop there.

Alternatives are not always related directly to a well-defined category of people. As can be seen from many image studies (to be reviewed subsequently) they are frequently only vaguely perceived as "modern," "masculine," "active," "aggressive," "passive," and so on. Such relationships, however, often gain their importance through the consumer's relationship with his environment. For example, "active" is important as a value only to the extent that the consumer values active people or wants other people to perceive him as active.

Where the relationship among alternatives and categories of people is less direct, it is often difficult to decide whether the value concepts derive their importance from association with particularly valued social groups or whether they relate to functional and semi-functional aspects of the product. When, for example, as Bennett et al. (1957) report, air and rail transportation are perceived differently along such dimensions as "slowness," "helplessness," "pleasurableness," and "fearfulness," then the related values are important for social as well as functional reasons.

3. *Perception of Alternatives*

1. The Consumer's Image

The dimensions along which consumers perceive products, brands, and other alternatives may be classified into three main categories, namely, *price and income aspects*, *functional aspects*, and *social aspects*. Taken together they constitute the consumer's image of the product.

The price image is not necessarily identical with the price of the product. Consumers do not perceive prices accurately, and in different product areas the perception of price is related differently to the perception of income. Moreover aspects such as credit availability, deals, trade-ins, and needed effort also appear in the consumer's price image.

The functional image of the product reflects the way the consumer perceives the product along performance and appearance dimensions. They may reflect aspects of the products themself or they may relate to the consumers expected satisfaction from use. The consumer may apply a large number of such dimensions, or he may summarize his evaluation in terms of clues or possibly a generalized quality dimension.

Finally, the social image is the consumer's perception of who uses the product, what kind of personality he will express about himself by using it, and the like.

A similar definition of brand images is proposed by Rasmussen (1968): "The set of emotional conceptions which the users of a product have of individual brands, their functional and nonfunctional properties, the people who use them and the sort of person the user will demonstrate himself to be by using one of the brands" (p. 151).

An image composed of a price image, a functional and semi-functional image, and a social image is highly complex and multidimensional. As consumers frequently make choices based upon only a few values, this complete image is not always aroused in choice processes. Rather, in one particular situation some aspects are considered, and in another situation other elements are aroused. Besides, the consumer does not carry a complete image of all possible choice alternatives around with him, but stores some aspects in memory and forms others at the time of the choice.

Although the previous discussion has primarily dealt with brand and product values and perceptions, the corporate, institutional (Bolger 1959, Clevenger et al. 1965, and Easton 1966), and store images (Kunkel and Berry 1968) can be defined along the same lines. The perception of information sources in exploration and search processes, however, deviates somewhat, and such factors as expertise, credibility, and availability are important (Chapter 9).

For a detailed study of image, the consumer's perception of stores has been chosen, partly because it deviates somewhat from other images and partly because it represents an area in which a considerable number of findings have been published.

2. Consumer's Perception of Stores

One of the more detailed studies of store images is reported by Kunkel and Berry (1968), who classified aspects of store images into twelve different categories.

Unstructured responses were received from 744 department store customers, who provided nearly 4,000 statements describing their perception of the stores. Of those, approximately 99% could be classified into the twelve categories shown in Table 16.2. Of the image dimensions in Table 16.2, several reflect aspects of the price image (01, 08a, 09a, 09b, 12a, 12b), others are primarily functional image aspects (02, 03, 06, 07), others are semi-functional aspects (04, 08b, 08c, 08d, 10, 11a, 11b, 11c, 11f, 12c), and still others are social aspects of the store's image (05, 11d, 11e, and 11g). Although Kunkel and Berry's study dealt with department stores only, corresponding images can be found for other stores as well. For example, for food stores similar, but less detailed classifications have been published by Fisk (1961) and by Becknell and Maher (1962).

The large number of dimensions along which stores are perceived emphasizes that only a minor part of the total image can be salient in a particular choice process. Consequently, studies that will explain store choices cannot restrict themselves to a measure of the "average consumer's" perception of the store along all possible dimensions. It is necessary to know what values will be aroused, how important they are, and what environmental and other factors govern them. Answers to these questions may make it possible to predict store choices. Studies that rely solely upon differences in the overall perception of stores can only explain gross differences in such choices. Nevertheless, the importance of the consumer's

TABLE 16.2

Aspects of store images

01 Price of Merchandise
  a. low prices
  b. fair or competitive prices
  c. high or non-competitive prices
  d. values, except with specific regard to premiums, such as stamps, or quality of merchandise

02 Quality of Merchandise
  a. good or poor quality of merchandise
  b. good or poor department(s), except with respect to assortment, fashion, etc.
  c. stock brand names

03 Assortment of Merchandise
  a. breadth of merchandise
  b. depth of merchandise
  c. carries a brand I like

04 Fashion of Merchandise

05 Sales Personnel
  a. attitude of sales personnel
  b. knowledgeability of sales personnel
  c. number of sales personnel
  d. good or poor service

06 Locational Convenience
  a. location from home
  b. location from work
  c. access
  d. good or poor location

07 Other Convenience Factors
  a. parking
  b. hours store is open
  c. convenience with regard to other stores

  d. store layout with respect to convenience
  e. convenience (in general)

08 Services
  a. credit
  b. delivery
  c. restaurant facilities
  d. other services (gift consultants, layaway plans, baby strollers, escalators, etc.)

09 Sales Promotions
  a. special sales, including quality or assortment of sales merchandise
  b. stamps and other promotions
  c. fashion shows and other special events

10 Advertising
  a. style and quality of advertising
  b. media and vehicles used
  c. reliability of advertising

11 Store Atmosphere
  a. layout of store without respect to convenience
  b. external and internal decor of store
  c. merchandise display
  d. customer type
  e. congestion
  f. good for gifts, except with respect to quality, assortment or fashion of merchandise
  g. "prestige" store

12 Reputation on Adjustments
  a. returns
  b. exchange
  c. reputation for fairness

Reproduced with permission from Kunkel and Berry, *Journal of Marketing 1968* Vol. 32 No. 4 by permission from the American Marketing Association.

image of the store is evident in studies reporting a relatively uniform ranking of store attributes by regular patrons of different stores (Martineau 1957, and Meyer 1965).

A few authors have studied the relative importance of different image aspects. For example, Ellsworth et al. (1958), Moore (1966), Winer (1967), and Brunner and Mason (1968) have shown that distance is a major factor in connection with store choices, and Becknell and Maher (1962), who conducted a factor analysis of image items for food stores, found that the five most important factors explain more than 50% of the total variance. These factors were food quality, cleanliness, pricing, service, and unique features.

Similar findings are reported by Comish (1958) and by Kelley (1967a), who in a study of store patronage for a dairy product store reports the most important factor to be product quality, economy, convenience of location, courteous employees, special milk containers, and cleanliness.

4. *Consumer Value Systems : Segmentation*

Some studies have attempted to classify consumers into different categories, by focussing on differences among consumers rather than among products. That is, their concern is with the values that characterize consumers.

The concepts in a consumer's conceptual system are closely related. It may be possible to explain consumer behavior by means of more or less central values—or by basic values never or rarely salient in actual choice processes (Chapter 11). For example, a consumer who places high importance upon values such as "for the young," "aggressive," and "sporty" may be characterized by some underlying central value to which the less central concepts are related; and if this underlying value can be determined, the researcher can try to relate it to choice behavior. When such central values can be identified, they can be expected to be more stable than less central ones, and they will make it easier to predict choices. Many personality tests attempt to quantify such central values (often in terms of motives).

Systematic differences in consumer behavior based upon socioeconomic and demographic variables may also be studied. It is possible that consumers of different ages or consumers belonging to different social classes differ in their conceptual structures to such an extent that segmentation by means of these criteria is more useful than any kind of segmentation based upon personality tests. Consumer types such as innovators and opinion leaders are also important.

A particularly interesting subset of the consumer's conceptual structure is composed of those concepts that the individual believes describe himself. This subset constitutes the consumer's self-image, and may explain important aspects of consumer behavior, as may studies of the relationship between self-image and product images (image congruence).

The differences in consumers' value structures that are of interest are those which explain variations in choice behavior. These values may be inferred from observation of behavioral differences, that is, underlying differences in conceptual structures may be revealed by systematic differences observed in consumer behavior.

Finally, it may be possible to learn about consumer values simply by asking about the interests, likes, and favored occupations of the consumer, and in this connection studies of consumer interests seem promising.

1. The Use of Personality Inventories

Within psychological theory a large number of personality inventories have been developed. A discussion of the more commonly used ones is available in Freeman (1962), and recent research is reviewed in Klein et al. (1967). In studies of consumer behavior, the most commonly applied personality inventory is Edwards' (1954) Personal Preference Schedule (EPPS). This inventory, which builds upon Murray's (1938) study of personality and motivation, is a forced-choice, paper-and-pencil test classifying individuals along 15 personality dimensions. The classical study is reported by Evans (1959), and a confirming replication is reported in Evans (1968). Evans administered selected items from the EPPS to Ford and Chevrolet owners and found only few and slightly significant personality differences among them. He also attempted to predict brand choices by a discriminant analysis using the personality scores as independent variables. This method classified 62.9% of the owners correctly, a prediction only slightly improved (to 63.6%) when 8 demographic variables were added to the personality variables.[3] Moreover, an attempt to distinguish among car purchasers with different shopping patterns was only a little more successful (Evans 1962).

Other authors (Kuehn 1963 and Marcus 1965) have reanalyzed the data and improved the predictions slightly. However, when the procedures developed by these authors are applied to the data from the 1968 replication, they give even poorer predictions than the linear discriminant function used by Evans. It is evident that EPPS does not discriminate between Ford owners and Chevrolet owners.

Other applications of EPPS reported by Koponen 1960 and by The Advertising Research Foundation (1964) attempt to predict brand choice, brand loyalty, quantity purchased, and other aspects of consumer grocery choices. Neither study was very successful. Koponen found some significant personality differences, but when the data were used for predictions based upon regression equations the results were not impressive. However, Brody and Cunningham (1968), concentrating on the most loyal consumers (assumed to be high-risk perceivers), were able to improve the predictions somewhat, although it should be mentioned that their procedure implies that more than three-fourths of the original data are discarded. Massy, Frank, and Lodahl (1968) applied the EPPS to try to explain differences in a number of consumer purchase variables. As in the previous studies, only slightly significant predictions were obtained, and the addition of demographic variables did not help much. Only Claycamp (1965) reports moderately successful results with the EPPS, from his study of thrift deposit owners in commercial banks and in savings-and-loan associations.

Many other personality inventories have been applied. Westfall (1962)

---

[3] It is noteworthy that with demographic data alone 69.9% of the consumers were classified correctly.

was moderately successful with "Thurnstone's Temperament Schedule" (Thurnstone 1953) in a study comparing owners of compact cars, convertible cars, and standard cars; but he too found no differences between Ford and Chevrolet owners. Wiseman (1971) found the same instrument to be of little use in a study of differences among the first buyers of a new season's car models compared with those buying later. Similarly, applications of the "Gordon Personal Profile" (Gordon 1963) have not been too convincing. With this inventory, Kernan (1968) was moderately successful in predicting differences in consumers' choice criteria, and Tucker and Painter (1961) found some, mostly small, correlations between the four personality types revealed by the test and data on use of seven of the nine products studied (headache remedies, vitamins, mouthwash, cigarettes, chewing gum, alcoholic drinks, fashions, deodorants, and automobiles). It should be mentioned, however, that this instrument, in combination with canonical correlation analysis (Sparks and Tucker, 1971), has been used in a study revealing significant but extremely complex discriminations.

Other studies are reported by Wicks and Nelson (1967), who used the "Guilford-Zimmerman Temperament Survey" (Sheridan Supply Company, 1955) and found some relationship between personality scores and marginal propensities to consume; and Ruch (1966) in a study where he compared differences among heavy and light users, and loyal and nonloyal users of grocery products but had only little success with "McCloskey Personality Inventory." Similarly Myers (1967) found that consumers' attitudes towards private brands are not significantly related to their score on "Cattell's 16 Personality Factor Inventory" (Cattell and Stice 1957), and Brim et al. (1962) were unable to explain differences in choice process behavior with personality scores obtained with "Taylor's Manifest Anxiety Scale" (Taylor 1953), 12 general personality traits (French 1953), and a number of tests related to family interaction patterns. In line with the results are also those reported by Robertson and Myers (1969), who found no correlations between, on the one hand measures of opinion leadership and innovative buying behavior and on the other hand personality scores obtained with the "California Psychological Inventory" (Consulting Psychologists, Inc. 1957). Similarly, Rizzo and Naylor (1964), who applied Allport et al.'s (1960) "Study of Values" found only little correlation between their consumer choice parameters and the value dimensions, and Scott (1957) who applied the "Minnesota Multiphasic Personality Inventory" (Welsh and Dahlstrom 1956) in a study of motion picture preference found significant, but not very meaningful correlations.

Altogether, personality inventories have not proven very useful in studies of consumer choice behavior. Wells (1966b) summarizes the results nicely: "The findings of these studies have been very consistent. Almost always they have resulted in statistically significant correlations that have been too small to be of much practical value" (p. 187). It would be tempting to conclude that systematic differences in the value consumers hold do not relate to the choice they make. However, before this view can be adopted, two alternative explanations must be rejected. First, personality tests are highly complex and difficult to construct, and those available may not be ideal. Second, the tests which have been applied have been developed for clinical and other uses, and it is questionable whether they can be expected to explain differences in a completely unrelated area such as consumer choice behavior. The last explanation seems the most plausible. As Steiner (1966b) suggests, "I do not blame psychologists for the failure reported here in attempts to explain behavior by using certain tests of personality—you cannot take just any tool off the shelf simply because it happens to be there and expect that it will be the best tool for your job" (p. 208).

2. Individual Personality Traits

Some authors have tried to relate consumer behavior to individual personality traits rather than general personality inventories. Some of the more promising attempts have dealt with inner-other directedness, self-esteem and self-confidence, propensity to take risks, achievement motivation, and measures of cognitive style.

Inner-other directedness reflects the individual's tendency to rely upon others (other-directedness) in decision making and evaluation of information, as opposed to a tendency to rely upon his own judgment and values (inner-directedness). The dimension is related to Riesman's (1961) distinction among traditional-, inner-, and other-directedness, and it has usually been measured by means of a 36-item social preference scale constructed by W. Kassarjian (1962). Using this scale, H. Kassarjian (1965) found inner- and other-directedness to be related to consumers' preferences for persuasive communication, and similarly, Arndt (1968c) and Donally (1970) found it related to innovativeness. However, Gruen (1960), who used several different measures of conformity, found no relationship between these factors and preferences for new products.

Self-esteem or *generalized self-confidence* (Cox and Bauer 1964) is a personality dimension that reflects the individual's feelings of social adequacy and of confidence in his own ability to cope with problems and aggressions.[4] Generalized self-confidence has frequently been measured with some or all of 23 items constructed by Janis and Field (in Hovland and Janis 1959) as a measure of feelings of inadequacy. Generally it has been related to individuals' susceptibility to persuasive communication.

Some of the earlier work is reported by Hovland and Janis (1959), who

[4] The variable should not be confused with *specific self-confidence*, which reflects the individual's confidence in his ability to cope with a specific problem he faces (for a discussion see Cox and Bauer 1964). The latter variable, rather than being a personality trait, seems to relate to the amount of conflict with which a person can cope in a particular situation. As to the general effects of specific self-confidence there is general agreement that it is inversely related to persuadability (Schuchman and Perry 1969).

found male subjects with low self-esteem to be more susceptible to persuasive communication than subjects with high self-esteem. Similarly, Canon (1964) reported that choice of information source is dependent upon self-esteem. He found that men with high self-confidence tended to prefer dissonant information following a choice, as opposed to men with low self-confidence, who showed a significant preference for consonant information. However, Venkatesan (1968) found only a weak relationship between male subjects' generalized self-confidence and responsiveness to group influence.

For female subjects Cox and Bauer (1964) have proposed a curvilinear relationship between the two factors. Their hypothesis (for which they supply some evidence) suggests that subjects with an intermediate amount of generalized self-confidence are more influenced by persuasive communication than subjects who are either high or low in generalized self-confidence. Further support is reported by Gergen and Bauer (1967), Bell (1967a), and Barach (1967 and 1969b). However, Schuchman and Perry (1969) question the validity of several of these findings, and only slight support is presented by Arndt (1967b); and Arndt (1968c) and Ostlund (1969) were unable to establish any significant relation between generalized self-confidence and innovativeness. Altogether it seems that an inverse relationship between self-esteem and persuadability holds for men whereas the existence of a curvilinear relationship for women is less certain, and a relationship between generalized self-confidence and innovativeness is questionable.

Propensity to perceive risk may be related to the amount of aroused conflict in the specific choice situation and to individual differences in the way conflicts are dealt with. Only the latter aspect is of interest here.

Individual differences in willingness to accept risk are reported by Brim and Hoff (1957) and by Cunningham (1967b). The latter found that subjects who tend to perceive high risk in one product area also tend to perceive high risk in other product areas and that subjects who perceive little risk in one product area also are more likely to perceive little risk in other product areas.

Several studies confirm the importance of perceived risk as a personality variable. Arndt (1967b and 1968a and c) report that low-risk perceivers are more likely to be innovative, and Cunningham (1964) reports that the extent to which consumers engage in personal communication in connection with grocery products is related to their tendency to perceive risk. Furthermore, a number of studies have indicated relationships between loyalty and perceived risk (Cunningham 1967a, Arndt 1967b, and Brody and Cunningham 1968), and between innovativeness and a propensity to perceive risk (Arndt 1968c and Ostlund 1969).

Achievement motivation (see Chapter 5) has been measured in several different ways. Normally, however, it is inferred from projective measures, most commonly the Thematic Apperception Test (TAT). Attempts to apply measures based upon self-reports have not been too successful (Atkinson and Feather 1966).

A basic proposition in the theory of the achievement motive is that economic activity is related to achievement. Morgan (1966) reports significant differences in income and spending behavior depending upon achievement motivation. Similarly, Boulding (1960) relates differences in consumer behavior to two personality types characterized as "integrated achievers" and "satisfied securers." Moreover, a number of studies have found need achievement to be related to risk-taking propensities. For example, Scodel et al. (1959) studied a large number of personality variables but found only achievement motivation to be significantly related to risk taking. In this study intelligence was found not to influence risk taking, although it did influence the variability in taking risks. Similarly, Feather (1967b) applied four different personality variables and found that only achievement motivation significantly influenced responses in aspiration tasks.

In other studies the nature of the relationship has been explored. Atkinson and Feather (1966) hypothesize a curvilinear function, predicting that individuals high in need achievement will prefer intermediate amounts of risk. Several studies have confirmed this (see Morris 1966); and Weinstein (1969), who reviewed 18 published studies, found that 16 support the hypothesis. However, a major problem with this research has been that the different need-achievement measures do not correlate very well, and somewhat less confirmative results are reported by Raynor (1966) and Maehr and Videbeck (1968).

Although no attempts have been made to relate achievement motivation to consumer choices, the available evidence suggests that this variable may prove highly useful in attempts to understand consumer choice behavior, in spite of certain problems of measurement.

Cognitive style reflects the way the individual approaches problems: whether he applies more or less wide categories, whether he places major emphasis on problem-solving goals or upon social goals, and whether he strives for cognitive clarity or simplicity. A test of category width is proposed by Pettigrew (1956), and a test which reflects a "need for cognitive clarity" is proposed by Cox (1967b).

Several studies have used these variables. Popielarz (1967) reports that consumers who use wide conceptual categories (supposed to reflect willingness to face risk) are more willing to accept new brands, and Phares and Davis (1966) found such subjects made larger adjustments in expectations following disconfirming experiences. Similarly, Cox (1967b) found that subjects with a high need for cognitive clarity are more susceptible to persuasion than subjects with a low need for cognitive clarity, and in the same study it appeared that subjects who could be characterized as clarifiers (those who tend to clarify an issue) as opposed to simplifiers (those who tend to simplify an issue) respond differently to persuasive communication. Finally, Wilding and Bauer (1968) found subjects with predominantly social goals to react significantly differently to communication than subjects with predominantly problem-solving goals.

The findings suggest that cognitive style may be an important variable, but so far the interrelations among the different measures are completely unexplored; and not until we have a better understanding of the nature of cognitive styles can more general hypotheses be formulated.

Other studies, less directly associated with consumer behavior, have related personality types to choices of dissonance-reducing strategies. They have shown that subjects characterized as *concrete* and *abstract* behave differently (Harvey and Ware 1967), and that subjects classified as highly anal (a category supposed to reflect orderliness and clarity in thinking) respond differently in dissonance-producing situations (Bishop 1967). Similarly, studies using the orientation inventory (Bass 1967) have explored differences in the extent to which individuals are task-, social-, or self-oriented. So far none of this work has been related to consumer behavior, but future studies may reveal to what extent differences in consumer choice behavior are related to these aspects of cognitive style.

3. Socio-economic and Demographic Variables

Although personality variables have not yet proven to be highly useful for the purpose of market segmentation, investigators have asked if segmentation could be accomplished with socio-economic and demographic variables. To some extent these variables are useful, particularly when aggregated market segments rather than individual consumers are dealt with (Bass et al. 1968) or when differences among product classes are studied (Ferber 1962). Homeowners are likely to purchase outdoor paint, households with babies are likely to purchase baby food, and so on. Such socio-economic and demographic variables can define that segment of the total population which can demand a certain product. Often the *consuming unit* (Rasmussen 1955) and the *decision-making unit* (Matthews et al. 1964) concepts reflect such segments. Even though some marked differences may exist among the users of different brands and certain retail stores may attract certain consumers, it has often been found that the ability of socio-economic and demographic criteria to discriminate among consumers is relatively limited. Evans (1959) only slightly improved the discriminative power of the regression equation he used to predict ownership of Chevrolets and Fords by introducing demographic variables, and Frank et al. (1967) found only slight socio-economic and demographic differences among consumers who purchased more or less expensive grocery items. Similarly, Frank and Boyd (1965) and Myers (1967) found no differences between consumers who prefer private brands and those who prefer manufacturers' brands, and Kuehn (1966), Frank (1967a), and Massy et al. (1968) report that loyal consumers cannot be identified by means of demographic and socio-economic characteristics. Finally, Frank (1967b) reports that heavy versus light buyers of a grocery product do not have different socio-economic characteristics. The evidence warrants this conclusion by Frank (1968): "For the most part socio-economic characteristics are not particularly effective bases for segmentation" (p. 53).

4. Social Class

An individual's social class reflects the way he is perceived by others in the society. Warner and Lunt (1941) suggest that a social class consists "of people who are believed to be, and are accordingly ranked by the members of the community, in socially superior and inferior positions" (p. 82). Defined in this way, members of different social classes can be expected to have different value systems.

Warner proposes a social class system composed of an upper, a middle, and a lower social class, each of which is divided into an upper and a lower segment. Other social class systems are discussed by Kahl (1957), and an evaluation of the concept in connection with consumer behavior is available in Engel et al. (1968). Generally, social class is inferred from characteristics such as income, occupation, and geographical location; Himmelfarb and Senn (1969) show how individuals are able to infer social classes from information about a person's income, job, and education.

Several studies have attempted to relate social class to consumer behavior. Graham (1956) found different adoption patterns in different social classes for products such as television, canasta, supermarkets, and medical services. Similarly, Martineau (1958) reports that many aspects of spending behavior and store choices are related to social class. However, Brim et al. (1962) found social class to have only little influence upon decision-process variables, and with regard to consumer behavior Rotzoll (1967) suggests that finer distinctions among social classes are of doubtful value. It is rarely possible to identify more than two separate classes. In the early sixties Martineau (1963) found many social class differences in shopping behavior to be disappearing; and Rich and Jain (1968), after reviewing the literature, suggest that with the rapid changes in income, leisure time, and education, and the movement to suburbia, social class differences which have existed earlier are likely to disappear in the future. Supporting this view, the authors present findings from an extensive study of shopping behavior in Cleveland and New York which shows only slight social class differences.

5. Family Life Cycle

The "Family Life Cycle" concept was discussed in Chapter 3. Consumers in different stages of the family life cycle are expected to behave differently, and they may have differing value structures. Studies of differences in consumer behavior according to stages in the family life cycle are reviewed in

Clark (1955) and B. Madsen (1964). Often significant differences in spending behavior, savings, and possession of different durable products have been reported. However, no studies have found important variations in brand choices or in purchases of most nondurable products.

With regard to choice process behavior, Miller (1955) found that, in later stages of the life cycle, consumers rely more extensively upon habitual choice behavior (see Chapter 15). They recall fewer brand names; they become more brand loyal, and they engage in less discussion in connection with frequently used nondurable products.

Rich and Jain (1968) suggest that many differences traditionally associated with the family life cycle tend to be ruled out by other changing factors in contemporary societies. Nevertheless, as in different phases of the life cycle consumers are faced with different problems, they behave differently. How this behavior is reflected in their value structures, however, is completely unexplored.

6. Innovators and Early Adopters

Much effort has been expended in attempts to identify consumers who are likely to accept new products early. These consumers have in different contexts been treated as either dependent or independent variables. To the extent that such consumers can be defined as a special market segment, they are a group of particular importance, the *innovators*. Innovators have been defined in several ways. Researchers have observed who adopts new products first, and in certain product areas consumers have been asked directly whether they consider themselves to be more or less innovative. Other researchers have tried to identify innovators by variables believed to be correlated with innovativeness. For example, Andreasen (1966) suggests that mobile consumers are more willing to face risk and to try new products and brands.

Two questions must be raised about innovators as a special market segment. Do those who adopt a particular product early differ from those who adopt it later? Are those consumers who adopt early in one product area also likely to be innovators for other products? Considerable evidence shows that early adopters differ from late adopters. Findings from several areas of research are reviewed by Rogers (1962) and by Rogers and Stanfield (1968); and several studies of marketing innovators have found such differences. It has been reported that innovators are exposed to more personal and mass communication (Sheth 1968a and Summers and King 1969); they are more willing to face risk (Cunningham 1966 and Arndt 1968a and 1968c); they have above-average incomes (Bell 1963, Robertson 1967a and Kegerreis and Engel 1969); they have smaller families (Uhl et al. 1970); they are more socially integrated (King 1965 and Robertson 1967a); they are more venturesome and cosmopolitan (Rogers 1962, Robertson 1967a, and Gorman 1968); (in some product areas) they have higher social status (Graham 1956, Bell 1963, and Kegerreis and Engel 1969); and they have been found to be more socially mobile (Pessemier et al. 1967 and Robertson 1967a). However, most of these predispositional, demographic, and socio-economic variables produce only weak relationships. Other authors have disconfirmed several of them (Frank et al. 1964, Pessemier et al. 1967, and Ostlund 1969), and it seems that none of them apply uniformly to all products.

It has been reported that innovators perceive innovations differently. Rogers (1962) suggests that innovations should be studied in terms of their relative advantage, compatibility, divisibility, communicability, complexity and risk; and for each of six different products Ostlund (1969) found the first four factors to be positively correlated and the last two negatively correlated with innovativeness; moreover, these relationships are considerably stronger than relationships with demographic, socio-economic, and personality variables examined in the same study. King and Summers (1967) report also that innovators differ from followers in their perception of new products.

The observation that innovators of various products often are described as being different from each other suggests that innovativeness in one area does not automatically imply innovativeness in other areas. In this context the findings by Graham (1956) speak out clearly: Whereas the early acceptor of canasta was found in higher social classes, a completely opposite characterization was found to apply to television innovators. Surprisingly enough, only few studies have directly explored the amount of overlap between innovativeness in different areas. However, Wärneryd (1965), in studying products such as synthetic curtains, frozen food, and home appliances, found few and slight relationships; and Robertson and Myers (1969), for appliances, clothing, and food products, and Arndt (1968), for soft margarines, electric dishwashers, and electric toothbrushes, found practically no overlap among innovativeness. There is little support for the concept of innovators as a special personality type; and to the extent that overlap exists, it may be governed by overlap in interests (Myers and Robertson 1969).

7. Opinion Leaders

It is a common assumption in communication research that some people act primarily as *opinion leaders* (sources of communication) and others primarily as *followers* (or receivers) (Katz and Lazarsfeld 1955, Katz 1957, Rogers 1962, and Mancuso 1969). The influentials can be assumed to constitute a special market segment composed of consumers with special values and perceptions; and, as with innovators, much concern with opinion leaders has centred around their influence upon other consumers. It has been a generally held belief that market communication directed to this segment will be more efficient than communication directed to consumers in general. However, for the belief to have practical implications, it must be possible to identify opinion leaders, and they must be at least as susceptible to marketing communication as their followers. The latter requirement is normally held to be the case, and it is known that opinion leaders tend to be exposed to more mass communication (King and Summer 1969, and Myers and Robertson 1969), but identification of opinion leaders has caused some controversy. However, it is generally agreed that self-designation is a relatively reliable procedure (Silk 1966 and Robertson and Myers 1969), and sociometric procedures have also been applied (Katz and Larzarsfeld 1955).

Opinion leadership does not correlate closely with socio-economic and demographic variables. Illustrative findings are reported by Myers and Robertson (1969). In an extensive study of 12 products, they found only small correlations with demographic variables, and no single variable was significant for all products. For example, education was positively correlated with opinion leadership for home entertainment and politics, mobility was negatively correlated with opinion leadership for home upkeep, travel, medical and personal care only.

With regard to personality variables even fewer relationships have been found (King and Summers 1967 and Myers and Robertson 1969). There is, however, some consensus regarding a few variables. Several authors (Rogers 1962, Myers and Robertson 1969, and Summers and King 1969) suggest that opinion leaders are relatively more nonconforming than their followers, that they use more impersonal information sources, that they are more cosmopolitan, that they are better informed and have slightly higher status than their followers, and that they are socially more active. It has also been found that they adopt new products before the average consumer, and that they are more interested in new products. Although these characteristics suggest that opinion leaders have much in common with innovators, they are normally not innovators or very early adopters (Rogers 1962, and Robertson and Myers 1969).

Several researchers have studied the amount of overlap among opinion leaders in different product areas. Katz and Lazarsfelt (1955) found only little overlap, as did studies reported by Wärneryd (1965), Silk (1966), Cerha (1967), and Myers and Robertson (1969). Other authors have found some overlap among related products (Summers and King 1969 and Montgomery and Silk 1969).

The concept *opinion leaders* rests upon the assumption that some consumers act primarily as sources of personal communication whereas others are primarily receivers. However, few studies have been concerned with the extent to which opinion leadership results in communication between "leaders" and "followers," and recent studies have suggested that people who act primarily as receivers are rare (Wärneryd 1965, and Cerha 1967).

Working from completely different data, both authors suggest that in most product areas from 60% to 80% of all consumers can be characterized either as *frequent* receivers and initiators of communication or as *infrequent* receivers and initiators of communication. When this finding is taken together with some of the more consistent characteristics of opinion leaders—their interest in innovations, their better knowledge, and their more frequent exposure to mass communication—it appears that one should distinguish between consumers engaging in more or less personal communication rather than between opinion leaders and followers. Basically, those who are interested in a given product also are those who talk about it, and in the process they provide information for others as well as acquiring additional information for themselves. Such a view is supported by the data reported by Summers and King (1969), who found a close relationship between opinion leadership, exposure to personal communication, and interest in the area. Similarly, within the different product areas the highest correlations appear among opinion leadership, amount of talk, knowledge, interest, and influence from others. Supportive also are findings reported by Montgomery and Silk (1969), who studied associations among opinion leaders in 7 different product areas and found that the amount of overlap decreases drastically as the product areas become less related. For example, only slightly more individuals than would be expected by chance were opinion leaders in all 7 areas, whereas those who were opinion leaders with regard to food purchases also were very likely to be so with regard to preparation of food.

8. Purchase Characteristics

Several authors have studied relationships among different aspects of the same consumer's behavior. For example, there is some evidence that brand loyalty is positively related to the market share of the brand (Schuchman 1968), that "deal-proneness" is related to the number of different brands purchased, to the number of units purchased, and to the brand loyalty (Webster 1965). Similarly Kollat and Willet (1967) found impulse purchases to be related to the number of items purchased, to the number of members in the shopping party, and to variables reflecting the structure of the transaction (major or minor purchasing trip); Frank et al. (1964) showed relationships between innovative behavior and purchase characteristics; and Rao (1969b) found brand loyalty and private-brand proneness to be related to store loyalty.

Relationships of this kind may be useful in some attempts to identify special market segments, but consumers with special purchase patterns can rarely be identified in other ways than through their purchase behavior. For example it is of limited use to know that heavy users tend to be more loyal than light users if neither loyal nor heavy users can be identified. But it is a common observation that neither loyal, deal-prone, private-brand loyal, heavy users, or innovative consumers are easily identified (Frank 1968).

9. Image Congruence Theories

Consumers' perceptions of purchase alternatives are reflected in the cognitive relationships between brands, products, and stores, on the one hand, and aroused values on the other. Similarly, the consumer's perception of himself can be described in terms of the perceived relationships between the concept of the self and valued concepts.

Several authors have suggested that the consumer's self-image is reflected in his life style, and studies of life styles in relation to consumer behavior have been proposed (Boyd and Levy 1963, Levy 1963, and King 1964). Other researchers maintain that the consumer tends to select products that he perceives as congruent with his self-image. A statement of the underlying theory can be found in Rogers (1965); Martineau (1957) discusses how the consumer chooses products and stores that have images corresponding to his perception of himself, and similar hypotheses are explored by Birdwell (1964), Kernan and Sommers (1967) and Grubb and Grathwohl (1967). Most of the earlier research is evaluated by Myers (1968).

The image congruence hypothesis can be seen as a special case of the more general choice principle tested in Chapter 12. When the values aroused in a choice process are those to which the perception of the self relates, the most attractive alternative will be the one most congruent with the perception of the self. This implies that image congruence should predict choices when two conditions are met. First, there must be a significant overlap between the values to which the self-concept relates and those by which the choice alternatives are evaluated. That is, image congruence can be expected to predict choices only when brands, products, or stores can be associated with important values which are also aspects of the self-image. Second, image congruence will predict choices only if those values common to both the self-concept and the alternatives are the values aroused in the choice process. If, in a majority of the choices, only few or none of the values related to the self are aroused, there is no reason that the chosen alternative should reflect the consumer's perception of himself.

These two limitations suggest that the image-congruence hypothesis may apply somewhat less generally than has commonly been assumed. However, when the two conditions are met, the self-image and the product image are the dominant aspects of the salient cognitive structures, and the hypothesis should predict choices well. Unfortunately, most of the available evidence has appeared in studies for which it is not possible to decide to what extent the two conditions are met. How likely it is that product image and self-images overlap depends on the complexity of the latent self-image.

The more values there are related to the concept of the self, the more likely it is that in a certain choice process values will be aroused which relate to the self.

That the concept of the self can be related to a large number of value terms is suggested by Anderson (1968), who identified 555 personality trait words that could meaningfully be rated with regard to likeableness. Even though all consumers hardly perceive themselves along all these dimensions, the number of latent relationships between the concept of the self and value concepts is likely to be large. Eventually, the Anderson study is a useful source of information on possible dimensions to consider in image-congruence studies.

A number of studies have attempted to validate the image-congruence hypothesis. Most of them have tested one or both of the following propositions that (1) there are significant differences in the ways products are perceived and (2) those products the consumer owns or prefers have images that deviate less from his self-image than the images of the products he does not own or does not prefer. From several studies of automobile brands, supportive evidence is reported by Jacobsen and Kossoff (1963), Birdwell (1964), Grubb and Hupp (1968), and Ito (1967); however, Evans (1959) found only small differences between the ways Ford and Chevrolet owners perceive their brands. Other products have been studied by Grubb (1965), who reports supportive evidence in connection with beer brands, and by Dolich (1969), who presents confirmative results from a study of four different grocery products. Studies of consumers' choice of retail outlets (Rich and Portis 1964 and Tillman 1967) have generally shown that consumers evaluate stores differently and that they tend to choose stores which correspond to their own images.

Altogether, there is ample evidence that the perception of preferred or owned brands is congruent with the perception of the self. However, it may be questioned whether this evidence really proves that consumers choose the products that are most congruent with their self-images. It is possible that the consumer's choice is governed primarily by other factors, but that after the choice he changes the evaluation of the chosen alternatives so that congruence emerges (see Chapter 9).

To test whether knowledge of the consumer's perception of himself and of his images of brands makes it possible to predict his choices, both images should be measured before the choice. This has never been tried. What comes closest is the study reported by Ito (1967), in which a nationwide probability sample of car owners, 577 Ford and Chevrolet owners who were planning to purchase a new Ford or Chevrolet, were identified. From measures of self-image and product images, it was possible to predict from 51% to 66% of the purchase intentions correctly. Although these percentages are not very high, from 82% to 96% of those who intended to switch brand were classified correctly. Unfortunately, subsequent measures of the actual purchases were not obtained, and it can be argued that a majority of the respondents at the time of the survey had already chosen their brand and had started modifying their perceptions accordingly. The same applies to the findings reported by Birdwell (1968), who studied car buyers who had bought a new car within four months prior to the interview. He also found correlation between self-image and the image of the chosen brand. However, here again it is possible that the perception of the alternatives was changed in the period between the purchase and the interview.

Post-choice adjustment in the perception of the alternatives can be ruled out, if it can be shown that the alternatives are perceived uniformly also after the choice, that is, if the perception of the alternatives does not vary among consumers who have chosen different alternatives. This, of course, would imply that the choices are explained through differences in self-concepts alone. However, it has repeatedly been found that the perception of the alternatives varies depending upon what has been chosen.

Another attempt to prove the significance of the self-image rests upon the following reasoning: As the consumer is not likely to change his perception of himself after a purchase decision, significant differences in the self-images of consumers who have chosen different brands can be presumed to have existed before the brand was chosen. Such differences have been identified by Grubb and Hupp (1968) in a study comparing Pontiac owners and Volkswagen owners. They found that Pontiac owners rated themselves significantly higher on dimensions that were positively associated with the Pontiac, whereas the Volkswagen owners rated themselves significantly higher on dimensions that were positively associated with the Volkswagen.

Somewhat contrary to most of the above findings are Rothman's (1964) results. In a test of different preference rating methods he obtained different ratings for two brands of toilet soap and for two brands of cereal. Based upon these ratings he attempted to predict subsequent choices among the same brands. The *overall distance* between the ideal image of the brand and the actual image of the brand was used as one of the measures, and with it only the very poorest predictions were obtained. Although the relationship between the ideal image of the brand and the self-image may be questioned, the findings still suggest a somewhat limited applicability of the congruence hypothesis.

As some positive evidence has been reported, measurement techniques may be improved if values are selected which are known to be related both to the self-concept and to the choice alternatives and if research is concentrated on products where such values are many and important. Moreover, improved studies would ensure that the values selected are actually aroused in the choice processes studied.

That improvements along these lines may result in better predictions is suggested by Dolich's (1969) study. As the self-image also reflects how the individual likes others to perceive him, it would be expected that predictions for products which are consumed publicly should be more successful. Dolich, who dealt with two publicly consumed products (beer and cigarettes) and two privately consumed products (bar soap and toothpaste), found considerably closer agreement between self- and brand-image for the socially consumed products than for the privately consumed ones.

The individual may perceive himself as he would like to be (his ideal self) or as he is (his real self). Most studies do not distinguish between real and ideal self-images or they deal with only one of the two. This would not be a problem if there were only little difference between them, but White (1966), Hamm (1967), and Dolich (1969) all show that the ideal self-image may deviate significantly from the real self-image. Therefore it is important which self-image is studied. Only Dolich (1969) has compared predictions based upon the two images. For female subjects he found no differences, but for male subjects the real self-image was most closely associated with the preferred alternatives.

It has been suggested that the difference between the real and the ideal self-image may reveal aspects of importance for consumer choice behavior. Hamm (1967) and Hamm and Cundiff (1969) report that product perception is significantly influenced by the congruity between the two self-images, and White (1966) found that subjects with a moderate discrepancy between ideal and real self-images are less dependent upon others in their evaluation of products and are more likely to be innovators.

10. Backwards Segmentation

Classification of consumers according to their consumption and purchase patterns and their product interests and attitudes has been tried. Large-scale factor analysis made possible through the availability of computers has normally been the technique used. The approach agrees with previous findings: Attempts with personality inventories have suggested that identification of consumer types should start in analysis of the behavior of consumers; attempts to make predictions of different purchase and consumption variables according to socio-economic and demographic studies have shown that many of them are correlated; and finally the proposal that significant aspects of consumers' conceptual structures may be reflected in their life styles suggests that more systematic utilization of information about consumer behavior may lead to meaningful classifications.

Several studies have been reported. Wilson (1966) used factor analysis to identify 20 different variables reflecting aspects of the respondent's values and interests. His data were responses to 57 self-descriptive items dealing with everyday behavior, such as "I like to organize community projects," "I dress for comfort not for fashion," "I go bowling often," and "I really enjoy cleaning my house." Similar findings are reported by Pessemier and Tigert (1966) who also factor-analyzed data on consumer interests, market-oriented activities, purchase patterns, media exposure, and the like. In this research 14 interest factors and 8 personality factors were identified, many of which closely resemble those identified in the

Wilson study. Later the same authors (Bass, Pessemier, and Tigert 1969) worked with purchase data, from which 14 product-oriented factors emerged, closely resembling those reported by Wells (1967 and 1968), who in factor analysis of data on product use found 16 family factors and 7 female personal factors. Similarly, Alpert and Gatty (1969), from a study of male consumers alone, report 16 different male factors.

All of these studies suggest that it is possible to characterize consumers meaningfully according to information about their consumption and purchase patterns and their interests in different product areas. In spite of considerable differences in the samples and the type of data used, many almost identical factors have been identified. For example, Wilson (1966) found a "special shopper" factor characterized by positive loadings on questions such as "I shop for specials," "I study the food ads each week," "When I find a coupon in the paper, I usually clip it. . . ." Similarly, Pessemier and Tigert (1966) found a factor which they describe as "careful shopper, price conscious, shops for specials." Another example is the "dieter" factor of Wells (1968), which corresponds to a "weight-watcher" factor identified both by Pessemier and Tigert (1966) and by Wilson (1966).

Another approach to backwards segmentation uses different forms of cluster analysis (Green and Frank 1968), grouping consumers according to differences in the characteristics which are to be explained. At the present time a number of techniques have been developed, but the implications of the resulting classifications are not fully understood. It is hoped that systematic research will reveal which types of problems can be approached with what kinds of techniques. As an example of this research a study by Carman (1970) can serve. From panel observations it was possible to identify consumers with different loyalty characteristics, but because of the number of observations involved, meaningful tests of significance were not possible.

So far no studies have been reported which attempt to predict consumer choices from these personality factors, but the consistency of the findings suggests that future work may provide useful classifications that reflect differences in consumers' conceptual and value structures.

11. Interests

In several ways the research reviewed in the previous pages has pointed to the importance of interests as factors governing consumer behavior. Chapter 9 suggested that selectivity may be related to interest in the information and that the frequency with which personal and other information sources are attended to may vary with interest in the issue. In Chapter 14 interest was seen as a factor determining the extent to which consumers will volunteer as information sources. Earlier in this chapter it was suggested that innovativeness relates to interest and that the opinion-leader-follower distinction might be replaced by a distinction between consumers who are more or less interested in particular products. Finally, backward segmentation has often relied upon consumers' own ratings of interests.

Interest in an issue implies that the consumer has a number of important and positive values in relation to the topic. It is surprising that very little research has been concerned with this variable. Except for the findings reviewed in connection with backwards segmentation only few studies have been reported.[5] Among these Cerha (1967) obtained interest scores for 91 products on simple seven-point scales and found considerable variations among products, as well as close relationships between interest and exposure to mass and personal communication. Moreover, he found relatively small intercorrelations among the different product areas, and with factor analysis he was able to identify seven highly independent interest factors. In another study Pennington and Peterson (1969) used the "Strong Vocational Interest Blank" (Cambell 1966). Constructed primarily for purposes of counselling and personal selection, this interest questionnaire would be expected to have the same shortcomings as general personality inventories. Nevertheless, using the most predictive items in the test for a discriminant analysis, the authors were able to make correct predictions of choices among vacation trips and savings forms in 72% to 80% of the cases. Unfortunately, the products chosen were rather special, but further research with this or similar interest-test batteries seems promising. Particularly if tests are developed which are especially relevant to consumer behavior, our ability to predict consumer choices may improve significantly. In this connection exploration of the relationship between value structures and interests and between interests and involvement is badly needed. That the latter relationship may be important is suggested by Barach (1969b), who found that reactions to advertising are dependent upon subject importance, which was measured with scales closely resembling interest scales, and by Wolfe et al. (1969), who have found interest to be related to measures of advertising readership also.

5. *Competitive Strategies and Consumer Values and Perceptions*

The way the consumer perceives products and prices and his knowledge about availability of alternatives depends upon the products and prices offered by the marketers, and the way the marketer informs him about them. Similarly, the values consumers apply in choice processes are not independent of the strategies used by the marketers. However, several of the findings

---

[5] Myers and Robertson's study (1969) and Summers and King's study (1969) both apply "interest" variables, but they do so in an attempt to explain variations in personal influence only.

reviewed suggest that a kind of second-order relationship may exist between the marketers' choices of strategies and the consumers' responses; the consumers' handling of information and their choice process behavior may vary among products depending upon the marketing strategies applied. Gabor and Granger (1964) also observe that consumers' responses to pyschological prices vary depending upon the kind of pricing strategies applied and that the extent to which consumers perceive prices correctly may relate to the stability and uniformity of prices. Support for the hypothesis is also provided by Demsetz's (1962) finding that over a period of years consumers learn about a product area (orange juice), change their clues, and become less dependent upon higher-priced, nationally advertised brands.

In the same way, consumers' judgment of quality by price may depend upon the way prices and quality normally are related, and the frequency with which consumers project social values into products may be related to the kind of information marketers provide about the products. Similarly, the extent to which brand names are used as clues may depend upon the number and market-standing of the leading brands, just as the acceptance of one private brand depends upon the acceptance of private brands in other stores (Rao 1969b).

Related is also the following speculation: It is a common practice in advertising to exaggerate the product description, i.e., to make the product look much better than it is. An analysis based upon aspiration levels would suggest that this technique might be dangerous, as it will tend to establish expectations which eventually will be disconfirmed. The common and repeated use of the practice, however, suggests that this prediction may not be valid. The explanation could be that because consumers have experience with advertising they expect "large words," and while internalizing the message they perform the appropriate decoding. For example, a consumer may know that a detergent advertised as making clothes look "shining white" is one which is "quite good at making the laundry look white." The important thing being, of course, that consumers develop appropriate decoding techniques as a kind of defense.

Finally, differences in the amount of risk associated with different products (Cunningham 1964), in the perceived importance of products (Barach 1969b), and in the amount of personal communication about products (Myers and Robertson 1969) may be related to the kind of marketing practices applied. Presently, most of these relationships are highly hypothetical, and more research in the area is needed. However, there are several reasons that this kind of research is complicated. Exploring relationships of this nature calls for comparisons among different markets. For that purpose it is necessary to define markets operationally.[6] Such definitions would have to consider how the consumer perceives products as substituting and complementary to each other.

[6] Here the problems discussed in connection with the definition of first purchases are involved again.

Further, studies of consumers' reactions to various product classes call for aggregated measures of the applied marketing strategies. Whereas the practices of the single campaign can be defined in terms of the strategies chosen, aggregated marketing practices will have to be studied in the marketplace in terms of the kind and the amount of marketing information provided, the price structure at the retail level, and the nature of the product assortment facing the consumer.

The most complex problem may be the following. While the hypothesis discussed here maintains that consumers adapt their decision-making behavior to the marketing practices of the sellers, it is at the very heart of the economic system that marketers adapt to the behavior of consumers. Just as competition involves studies of choices of strategies and counter-strategies, the study of consumer behavior may force the researcher to deal with changing behavior patterns in a dynamic system.

Chapter 17

COLLECTIVE
DECISION-MAKING

In many instances, purchases and consumption result from decisions made by groups of individuals. Commonly, those involved in a particular consumer decision belong to the same family or household; consequently, when consumers' collective decision-making is discussed, the concern is with households and families, as economic entities. The study of different types of decision processes is crucial for an understanding of a household's behavior and overall differences among families' decision-making patterns.

Extensive studies of decision-making within families have been conducted by sociologists. For a review see Kephart 1966.

1. *The Nuclear Family as an Economic Unit*

Collective decision-making occurs when two or more individuals are engaged in making a decision. However, participation is more than just taking part in discussions. It is necessary to distinguish among instances involving only an exchange of information and instances in which individuals are both exchanging information and actively engaged in the decision-making. The latter occurs when the decision has consequences for all of the participants, that is, when the goals satisfied by the decision are common to the decision makers and when the risk and expenses are shared (Matthews et al. 1964). In consumer behavior, these conditions are met when the participants in the decision process belong to the same family and live in the same household. The nuclear family is the group in which collective consumer decisions are most frequently made. It should be emphasized that occasionally other groups of consumers may be the relevant unit, but they will not be discussed separately, as their decision processes are much like those found in the nuclear family.

The nuclear family is tied together in a number of different ways. The family relationship, of course, is fundamental, and it explains a number of the goals common to the members of the family. Furthermore, collective consumption results because the individuals live together. All family members have access to collectively owned durable goods (for example, television), many nondurable products are acquired and prepared collectively, although individually consumed (for example, food), and others are used collectively (for example, bar soap). Finally, the family is tied together through economic relationships which make it possible to study the nuclear family as a unit disposing of a certain amount of income.

In the nuclear family, consumption and purchases can be described in terms of a number of related variables shown in Table 17.1.

At a certain point in time (t_1), the nuclear family is described in terms of the variables in the left part of the figure. The variables will be discussed briefly:

Stock of durable and nondurable products: The family has a certain number of durable products available together with a stock of nondurable products. All consumption must either come out of these stocks or be preceded by purchases.

Fixed commitments: The family also has a certain number of fixed commitments to be met in each period. Such commitments can be rent or mortgage payments, insurance premiums, savings plans which have to be fulfilled, or loans to be repaid.

Essential consumption: Normally the family will have established a certain consumption pattern. Certain products are repeatedly used; and, like Katona's (1960) "essential outlays," they can be said to represent a certain minimum consumption necessary to keep the family intact. This consumption includes only nondurable products such as food, beverages, other household products, and items necessary for the regular use of durable products, such as gas for the car. Essential consumption includes items for which the consumption can be predicted easily; operationally, they can be defined as those products consumed in a number of consecutive periods, whereby they become identical with products for which continuous repeat purchase cycles are found.

Ongoing purchasing plans: At any point in time there will be a number of decision processes going on within the family. As decision processes for durable products normally last longer than for nondurable products and involve more expensive items, the most important plans will involve such products.

Important aspects of family decision-making may be studied in terms of what and how many purchasing plans different families have. Such studies should relate the plans to the total income of the family, and they should study how new processes are started, how old ones are deleted, and how purchases are made.

TABLE 17.1

Economic and consumption transactions within the household

Beginning of period	Change during period	End of period
Stock of durable products	+ addition of durables − discarded durables	new stock of durable products
Stock of non-durable products	+ purchase of nondurables − consumption of nondurables	new stock of nondurables
Fixed commitments	+ new fixed commitments − terminated commitments	new fixed commitments
Essential consumption	+ new essential consumption − deleted essential consumption	new essential consumption
Ongoing durable purchase plans	+ new durable purchase plans − completed durable purchasing plans − deleted nondurable purchase plans	new ongoing durable purchase plans
Ongoing non-durable purchase plans	+ new nondurable purchase plans − completed nondurable purchase plans − deleted nondurable purchase plans	new ongoing nondurable purchase plans
Liquid assets	+ income + realised nonliquid assets and obtained loans − expenditures on fixed commitments − completed purchasing plans	new liquid assets
Nonliquid assets	+ addition to nonliquid assets − use of nonliquid assets	new nonliquid assets
Loan possibilities	+ new loan possibilities − used loan possibilities − deleted loan possibilities	new loan possibilities

Liquid and other assets: The family will have a certain buying power, which depends upon its liquid and nonliquid assets and upon its loan possibilities. Liquid assets are the money the family has available for immediate use in the form of cash or in checking accounts. Nonliquid assets represent funds that can be made available for use but are normally held for other purposes than immediate use, which range from bonds and life-insurance policies to such major products as cars and homes. The transfer of nonliquid assets to liquid assets will normally involve more extensive decision processes. Loan possibilities, although often difficult to quantify, exist in terms of unused charge accounts, credit cards, and other financing possibilities.

All these variables describe the family's situation at a certain time. Some time later, some or all will have changed. Often, the student of consumer behavior is most interested in these changes. In Table 17.1 some of the more important changes are suggested. Together with the dynamic variables, each of the static variables defines an equation by which the new value of the static variable can be determined. Furthermore, as several of the variables are related, all the relationships form a total system which describes the family's consumption and purchase behavior. It is possible to measure either the static or the dynamic variables or any combination of them. Therefore, different models of household behavior can be formulated.

The dynamic (change) variables may also be described briefly:

The durable products in stock at the end of a period consist of those available at the beginning of the period plus those purchases during the period, less those discarded. Acquisition of new durable products is related to purchasing plans for durable products. Durable products that are discarded can be studied through the age distribution for existing durable products and in relation to repurchase plans for durable products.

Nondurable products can be dealt with in much the same way. Purchases can be seen as a function of completed nondurable purchase plans and repeat purchase cycles, and consumption as a function of essential consumption and other nondurable purchases. As with durable products, the crucial variables are the ongoing and completed decision processes.

Fixed commitments are also changed through decision processes. Completed durable purchasing plans may result in new fixed commitments, or commitments related to previously completed durable purchasing plans can terminate. Furthermore, decisions directly related to saving will result in new commitments.

If *essential consumption* is defined as consumption of products used in n consecutive periods, then products which have been adopted and used in a sufficient number of periods should be added as new essential consumption. Similarly, the products which are no longer used regularly should be deleted. These changes relate to the decision processes for nondurable products.

Purchasing plans may be studied directly or in relation to the variables influencing decision processes. The beginning of new plans, the deletion of old plans, and the execution of other plans underlie the changes in most other variables. Any attempt to explain family consumption and purchase patterns will have to begin with an explanation of such processes.

The family's buying power changes if the liquid assets change, as when new income is received and when money is spent on completed purchasing plans and fixed commitments. Furthermore, liquid assets can change when nonliquid assets are made liquid or when loans are obtained.

Nonliquid assets change as they deteriorate, when they are used, or when new assets are acquired. Changes in loan possibilities result when debts are made or repaid and when changes occur in the conditions for obtaining loans.

Additional relationships among the variables described make it possible to study the family over time. For example, total spending is equal to payments for additions to the stock of durables, payment for purchases of nondurables, and payment of fixed commitments. Saving results from saving commitments plus the difference between income and expenditures on fixed commitments and on completed purchasing plans. Changes in nonliquid assets result from saving commitments and purchases of durable products which are resaleable.

2. *Interaction within the Family*

Some of the decision processes within the family are concerned with individually purchased goods for personal use. These processes may occasionally cause interaction, particularly in connection with general budgeting decisions, but in the short run the single individuals carry out such purchases relatively independently of other family members. At the most, other members may act as information sources much like personal information sources outside the family. Here the interaction processes are of minor interest, as the decision processes follow the same pattern as the previously discussed individual purchase sequences.

Other decision processes are concerned with products that are collectively consumed or not consumed by the one who purchases them. Here the family may apply two completely opposite strategies. Authority can be delegated to a particular family member who then is in charge of purchasing the product; he can be labeled the *purchasing agent*. Alternatively, two or more individuals can be engaged in the decision process and reach the final decision through one or another kind of bargaining. This is true collective decision-making.

A particular purchase sequence may be anywhere between the two extremes. As all purchases have to be paid out of the same limited financial resources, it is likely that most decision processes at some point in time have involved collective decision-making. However, in the short run many frequently repeated decisions never reach the level of collective decision-making.

Collective decision processes are most common in connection with general budgeting decisions and the less frequent and more important single purchase. However, there are considerable differences among families in the extent to which they rely upon purchasing agents or collective decision-making.

1. Bargaining and Conflict Solving in Collective Decision-making

An assumption that underlies this chapter is that the study of collective decision-making can be based upon studies of the single family members' decision processes. This view is supported by findings reported by Clarkson (1968) and in line with the position taken by Morgan (1961) and Clawson (1961).

The nature of the collective decision process will depend upon how each of the participants perceives the alternatives. In many instances the family members involved in the decision may consider the same alternative to be the most attractive. In such instances there is no important conflict, and the outcome can be predicted from knowledge about the decision processes of each of the participants. Sometimes the participants do not initially agree upon what alternative is the most attractive, but an exchange of factual information can be sufficient to establish consensus among the family members. Here it is also possible to study each decision-maker relatively independently of the other family members.

However, even after exchange of information, agreement may not be reached. If influence is defined as the ability to make other family members agree with one's own position, the question is, who will influence whom, and what is the nature of the cognitive and interaction processes which make it possible to reach a final conclusion To answer this, values other than those occurring in individual decision-making must be studied. Perhaps one family member may place a value upon exerting power, and he may have the ability to do so. Another family member may want to give in to other members of the family; he may be guided by altruism or by a need for affiliation, both values which may conflict with dominance-oriented values. Morgan (1961) illustrates how these factors interact with the individual's own evaluation of the alternative. His model is outlined in Table 17.2.

TABLE 17.2

The individual *X* contributes to a family decision about alternative *A*

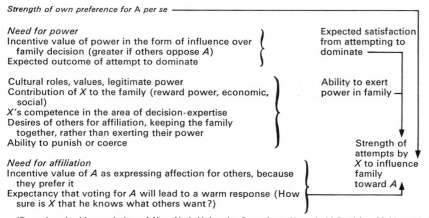

(Reproduced with permission of New York University Press from *Household Decision Making*, ed. by Nelson N. Foote, Copyright 1961 by New York University.)

Morgan suggests that the two types of cognitions should be added to the individual decision-maker's salient cognitive structure, namely, a *need for power* and a *need for affiliation*. Each of these elements is decomposed into a value term (incentive value) and an instrumentality term (expected outcome). Moreover, the individual's perception of his ability to influence the choice affects the evaluation. The overall attractiveness of the alternative then depends upon a total salient cognitive structure that includes values reflecting the individual's relationships with the group. To the extent that these additional factors bring about modifications in the attractiveness of the alternatives so that consensus emerges, the collective conflict is solved. Otherwise, each family member will attempt to influence the decision in the direction of his own most positively evaluated alternative, and his ability to do so will depend upon his ability to exert power within the family.

2. Solving Open Conflicts

Open conflict can be extremely unpleasant to the family members; consequently, they may try to avoid as many conflicts as possible. This may not be possible the first time a conflict appears, but eventually the family may learn to deal with the problem without open conflict.

How open conflicts are handled can be studied in different ways. Several authors have presented subjects with game-like situations and have observed the responses chosen (Rapoport and Minas 1965, Gamson 1964, Gallo and McClintock 1965, and Komorita and Brenner 1968). Few of these studies have dealt explicitly with family decision-making, but several of the approaches could be applied in such a context. For example, the so-called prisoners' dilemma creates a situation which closely resembles many family conflicts. Here subjects are presented with a non-zero-sum game in which both players can maximize their combined gains by choosing a competitive strategy, but in the long run they can maximize their combined gains by choosing a cooperative strategy (Rapoport 1967a and Guyer 1968).

So far, these game-oriented approaches have not been applied directly to family behavior, and in this context the findings of other studies are of questionable value. However, future applications of game theory may provide insight into family bargaining processes.

Alternatively, studies of conflict-solving within the family can rely on observation of the decision process. Here Bales' (1950) technique has been applied (see Chapter 9) in a study reported by Kenkel (1961a), in which husbands and wives were presented with a simulated decision-making task and their decision-process behavior was studied. The findings are of an illustrative character, but it can be mentioned that wives were found to engage more in group maintenance tasks and that husbands tend to dominate task-oriented communication. The findings also suggest an identity of the one who is the most influential with the one who does most of the talking. However, a detailed understanding of how families solve open conflict requires many more extensive studies.

3. Handling Recurring Conflicts

In a particular situation considerable conflict may occur. When the situation repeats itself, however, norms can be established which prescribe how to deal with the problem. A simple norm would be a rule that every second time a conflict occurs one family member is allowed to have his choice. How norms help the family avoid severe conflict is discussed by Thibault and Kelley (1959). In discussing husband-wife interaction, they suggest that a norm can be defined as "A behavioral rule that is accepted, at least to some degree, by both members of the dyad" (p. 30). Such norms tend to be self-confirming because all the members of the group will adhere to them most of the time, and if they don't, other family members will apply power in an attempt to produce conformity. Norms within the family make it easier for the members to deal with collective decision problems and help to eliminate unpleasant effects of open conflicts.

The extent to which norms become established and the kind of norms that emerge depend upon the individual member's relationships with the group. Homans (1961) suggests that the norms within the group define an equilibrium established through the exchange of costs and rewards. Each group member gets different kinds of satisfaction (rewards) from his membership in the group, but the membership also has certain costs to him. Often the costs to one individual are more or less directly the rewards for other individuals, and the norms are such that, in the long run, all members receive a sufficient amount of reward to be willing to remain within the group.

The interaction within the family also varies to the extent to which the wife or the husband dominates the decision-making. Furthermore, it may depend upon whether the decison-making is largely automatic or whether a majority of decisions are made collectively (Herbst 1954).

Two summary hypotheses have been proposed to explain the overall pattern of interaction in family groups. Blood and Wolfe (1960) suggest that the role structures within the family depend upon the relative contributions (in terms of income, work, decision-making ability, and so on) of the family members. The more an individual contributes, the more influential he will be. Other authors have suggested that one who is the least dependent on the group is the one who has the most influence (Engel et al. 1968).

4. Determinants of Family Interaction Patterns

The frequency of collective decision-making within the family has been related to the stage in the life cycle and to the social class of the family. Several studies have found collective decision-making to decrease as the family gets older (Blood and Wolfe 1960; and Granbois 1963), a phenomenon frequently ascribed to the establishing of more and firmer norms with the increased duration of the marriage.

Kenkel (1961b) and Komarovsky (1961) suggest that class and status are important determinants of collective decision-making. The latter proposes a curvilinear relationship implying that collective decision-making is less frequent in upper and lower social classes, a suggestion supported by findings by Wolgast (1958), by Bartel and Gross (1954), and by Sharp and Mott (1956). The less frequent collective decision-making in lower-class families should be ascribable to difficulties in expressing and dealing with problems. In higher social classes the same effect occurs because of a less pressing need for finding the best solution and because of better and more firmly established norms.

The life-cycle and the social-class hypotheses point to a problem that underlies all studies of family decision processes. Infrequent collective decision-making may occur either because norms become established and are adhered to or because families are maladjusted and each family member tends to go his own way. Alderson (1965) in his discussion of a household model suggests that the latter aspect is a particularly important determinant of family decision-making patterns. He proposes a variable defined as the amount of time spent by the family members on collectively acceptable tasks relative to the amount of time spent in ways on which there is no consensus among the family members. This variable is meant to reflect how well or how poorly the family is adjusted, and it should be a determinant of family decision-making behavior. However, no research has been reported which can confirm or reject the hypothesis.

Other studies have suggested important factors to be geographical location, income, education, wives' occupation, and church affiliation. These findings are reviewed by Kenkel (1961b) and by Granbois (1963).

Generally, attempts to explain differences in family decision processes by means of personality variables have not been too successful (Brim et al. 1962). However, it is possible that differences in personality between the husband and the wife may be an explanatory variable, rather than personality variables per se. For example, Cattell and Nesselroade (1967) report higher correlation between 16 personality factor measures among stable than among unstable married couples, and Levinger and Breedlove (1966) report that more agreement exist on values and goals in well-balanced than in unbalanced families.

3. *Patterns of Interaction in Collective Decision Processes*

Individual decision processes were described as sequences of choices through which the individual moves from problem recognition to the selection of a final alternative. Such processes vary in length and complexity. Some sequences may be of considerable length, and phases such as attention, interest, evaluation, trial, and adoption can be identified. In other rather uninvolving processes, the complete sequence consists of only one or a few choices. It is our purpose in the present section to examine whether collective decision processes follow a pattern similar to that of individual decision processes, and, if differences exist, to identify them. Do the single events of which collective decision processes are composed correspond to the single choices in the individual decision process? How do collective decision processes compare with individual decision-making? Finally, the changes that occur as collective decision processes are repeated will be examined.

1. Collective Choice Processes

Individual decision processes are composed of single choices made at different times. Part of the decision problem is attended to at one time, and other parts are dealt with later. Similarly, a collective decision process consists of a number of separate events, and only part of the problem is considered in each. Each instance may or may not involve interaction among family members. When interaction does not occur, the event can be seen as an individual choice process; and just as choice processes early in the individual purchase sequence influence later choice processes, these instances will have impact upon how the individual will behave next time he interacts with other family members concerning the particular problem.

When interaction occurs in collective decision processes, the question is how such instances compare with the single choice processes in individual decision processes. Here the participants will have to select several responses —at least as many as the number of comments they contribute to the inter-action. Therefore such instances will consist of several choice processes on behalf of each single individual. The study by Willett and Pennington (1966) of interaction between salesman and customer illustrates how such interaction processes can be decomposed into a number of choice processes on behalf of each of the participants. It is possible that each such instance of interaction can be described along the same lines as the individual choice process and can be seen as a "collective choice process." It is the purpose here to examine whether available evidence supports this concept.

Several findings suggest that considerable similarities exist between individual and collective choice processes. Brim et al. (1962) presented groups of parents and individual parents with the same problems and found that collective and individual choices follow similar patterns, and only a few differences were identified.

Other findings are presented by Schroder et al. (1966), who studied human information processing and decision-making in small groups. They presented their subjects with various versions of a war game and studied how the groups arrived at decisions. Unfortunately, the findings cannot be compared with individual decision-making in similar situations because such sessions were not conducted, but the nature of the findings suggests that the collective choice process follows a pattern much like individual choices. The collective choice process was studied in terms of variables such as decision time, complexity of selected strategies, and amount of information processing. The independent variable was environmental complexity, which was manipulated through variations in the games. The findings, presented in Figure 17.1, suggest a relationship between environmental complexity and the nature of the collective choice process much like that discussed in connection with individual choice processes.

Other suggestive evidence is provided by Moore and Anderson (1954). In a study of individual and group problem-solving they found no significant differences in the amount of search, the efficiency of search, or the amount of time spent on information search. Findings in line with this are also reported by Granbois (1963), but he also found a slight tendency towards more extensive search in collective decision-making than in individual decision-making.

Findings which suggest that collective choice processes are relatively independent of the nature of the group are provided by Morrisette (1966). He reports that group performance varied only slightly as a function of different group settings and group size, but that variations in the complexity of the problem generated considerable variations in performance. Similarly, Harnett (1967) and Zander and Newcomb (1967) were able to study group aspiration levels along the same lines as individual aspiration levels.

Several studies have dealt with risk-taking in individual and group choices (Lamm 1967, Wallach and Wing 1968, Blank 1968, and Vinokur 1969). Generally, it has been found that group discussion and collective decision-making make individuals more willing to take risks. The choice-dilemma instrument discussed in Chapter 13 is frequently used, and risk is seen as a willingness to gamble on a highly valued uncertain outcome rather than a certain, but less valued outcome. The more certain individuals want to be of obtaining the highly valued outcome before they will choose it, the less risk they are said to be willing to face.[1] The propensity to take risks may increase either because the willingness to face conflict increases in a group as a result of shared responsibility or because the group discussion tends to make salient those values which favor more risky choices. Recent findings favor the latter interpretation.[2]

The available evidence suggests that collective choice processes have much in common with individual choices. This, of course, does not mean that it makes no difference whether the choice is made by a single individual or by individuals in a group. The alternative chosen may be different when more than one individual is involved, as the presence of other individuals will influence which values become salient and the perception of the alternatives. However, in both instances, the choice processes themselves are much alike.

[1] It is questionable how this concept of risk compares to concepts of uncertainty and risk used here and in other studies of consumer behavior.

[2] A recent study (Clark and Willems 1969) reports the phenomenon to be highly dependent upon type of instructions given to subjects.

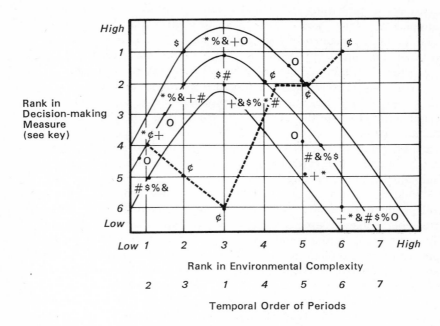

FIGURE 17.1.   *Decision-making qualities as a function of informational complexity load in a tactical game (reproduced with permission from Shroeder,et al. Holt, Rinehart and Winston,1966). (# mean integration rank [omitting decision frequency], $ integration frequency, % multiplexity, & total time span, * time span/decision, + time-weighted multiplexity, O high-level integration quality, ¢ decision frequency)*

2. Methodological Problems in Studies of Collective Decision Processes

Collective decision processes may seem easier to study than individual ones, in that most aspects of individual decision processes cannot be observed, whereas in a collective decision process personal communication occurs which can be more easily studied. In studies of collective decision processes the researcher must either rely upon observations or use reports from one or more of the participants in the decision process, but with both approaches inaccuracies have been found.

Kenkel (1961b), who used Bales' technique in his study of family decision-making, found that the presence of an observer influences the behavior of the participants in the decision process; in line with this are the observations of O'Rourke (1963) and Brim et al. (1962) of situational influence upon family decision-making.

When direct questioning is used, often there is only little agreement among the responses obtained from different family members. Ferber (1955b) found considerable discrepancies between husbands' and wives' reports about previous purchases; Levinger and Breedlove (1966) have found considerably less agreement between family members than the husbands and wives themselves believed. Similarly, in a study conducted by LIFE (1965) it was found that family members have different perceptions of their roles in decision processes, and Haberman and Elinson (1967) found that husbands and wives differ significantly in their estimates of family income. Finally, Granbois and Willett (1969) in their study of purchase intentions found that for some products the purchase probabilities obtained from the wife were superior whereas in other cases the husband provided the most reliable probabilities. These findings raise questions about what member of the family should be interviewed, or if several members are interviewed, how their answers can be combined. These methodological problems should be kept in mind in evaluating evidence, but when similar results emerge from studies using different approaches, some validity can be ascribed to the conclusions.

3. The Frequency of Collective Decision-Making

The frequency of collective decision-making varies considerably among products. Katona and Mueller (1954) found evidence of collective decision-making in 70% of the purchases of major durables, and in one third of these cases the purchase was preceded by extensive family discussions. In connection with purchases of men's shirts, on the contrary, only little collective decision-making was found. Similarly, in Sweden, Wickström (1965) found that approximately 70% to 80% of the purchases of major durable products were preceded by collective decision-making and that important variations occurred among products; Kelly and Egan (1969), who studied husband and wife interaction in different task areas and for different family activities, found major expenditures to be planned collectively in approximately two thirds of the households, whereas household tasks were dealt with collectively in less than a quarter of the cases; and other evidence of considerable variations among products are provided by Converse and Crawford (1949), by Sharp and Mott (1956), and by Blood and Wolfe (1960). Using a slightly different approach than applied in the previous studies, Jaffee and Senft (1966) found collective decision processes in connection with 75% to 85% of the purchases of refrigerators and vacuum cleaners and in approximately 65% of the purchases of rugs and paint, but they report very low percentages for coffee and toothpaste.

A general impression from these studies is that the frequency of collective decision-making varies along several dimensions. Collective decision-making becomes more common, the more important the purchase is and the less frequently it is made. Further, some decisions are so closely associated with either the wife's or the husband's role that, whatever their importance, very little interaction occurs. These differences can also be seen when the roles of the different family members in the various phases of decision processes are reviewed.

4. The Roles of Family Members Early in the Decision Process

Early phases of decision processes are characterized by awareness, problem recognition, decision about whether to buy or not, initiating conversations, and initial suggestions. Here, the initiative usually lies with one of the family members, and collective behavior is less frequent than later in the purchase sequence. For example, Wickström (1965) reports that for major durables, only from 10% to 40% of the purchases were initiated collectively. Similarly, for cars Brown (1961) found that in approximately 85% of the cases purchase discussions were initiated by a single family member, usually the husband.

That the importance of the purchase is a crucial factor is suggested by Wickström's (1965) finding that collective problem identification is more frequent for television sets than for radios and record players and by the data from the LIFE study (1965), which show that it occurs more frequently for refrigerators, vacuum cleaners, and automobiles than for pet foods, coffee, and toothpaste.

The different roles of husbands and wives are also reflected in available evidence. For example, in the LIFE study (1965) it was found that collective problem recognition is less frequent for the husband-dominated automobiles than for rugs and carpets, and less frequent for the wife-dominated washing machines than for television sets.

The same pattern is also reflected in the distribution of initiative among husbands and wives. Several studies have suggested that early in the purchase sequences for cars, the husband is from 7 to 10 times as important as the wife (Alderson and Sessions 1957, Wolgast 1958, Brown 1961, and LIFE 1965). Similarly, it has been found that the husband dominates early phases of such purchases as radios, record players, and photographic equipment. On the other hand, the wife dominates the early phases of decision processes in connection with washing machines, vacuum cleaners, sewing machines (Wickström 1965), pet foods, frozen orange juice, and toothpaste (LIFE 1965).

5. The Roles of Family Members in the Interest and Evaluation Phases

The interest and evaluation phases are characterized by information search, comparisons, and discussions about product and brand choices. Collective decision-making is more frequent in these phases than earlier ones, as can be seen from the information-seeking behavior of husbands and wives. For refrigerators, for example, 92% of the husbands and 85% of the wives require information from personal sources and 59% of the husbands and 55% of the wives obtain additional information from non-personal sources (LIFE 1965). In general, the family member who is the most passive early in the decision process becomes more active when it comes to information acquisition.

With regard to product choices, timing of the purchase, and the like, the data also suggest an increased amount of interaction. For cars, Brown (1961) reports that purchase discussions were initiated mutually in only 11% of the cases, but that model-make decisions were arrived at collectively in 25% of the households. Similarly, Wickström's (1965) data suggest that general purchase decisions are frequently influenced by more family members than earlier stages in the purchase process, and the Better Homes and Gardens' Consumer Questionnaire (1968) reports that brand choice decisions are made collectively in 60% to 70% of the cases for refrigerators, furniture, and other home equipment. The same study also finds considerable variation between products. For example, for automobile tires, the final purchase decision was made collectively in only 6% of the households. Similar variations among products are reported in the LIFE study and by Blood and Wolfe (1960), who found that general purchase decisions are made collectively in 25% of the households in connection with car purchases, in 41% of the households in connection with life insurance, in 68% of the households in connection with vacation sites, and in 58% of the households in connection with home purchases.

The relative importance of husband and wife in the interest and evaluation phases also varies among products. Blood and Wolfe (1960) found that some decisions are dominated by the wife, others by the husband, and still others are shared. The LIFE study (1965) reports that decisions concerning refrigerators, vacuum cleaners, and rugs and carpets were dominated by the wife, whereas the husband dominated decisions about automobiles. Similarly, Wickström (1965) finds that radios, television sets, and photographic equipment are husband-dominated products, whereas the wife dominates decisions concerning washing machines, vacuum cleaners, and sewing machines. Finally, Alderson and Sessions (1957) found that for different products husbands and wives acquire different information.

Again, in these phases of the decision process the amount of interaction seems to depend upon the importance of the decision, familiarity with the product and the roles of husband and wife within the family. The latter particularly influences who will dominate the decision process.

Often the roles of husband and wife depend upon who uses the product, as is exemplified by the husband's role in car purchases and the wife's in connection with products such as refrigerators and vacuum cleaners. Jaffe and Senft (1966), in an analysis of data from the LIFE study (1965), find correlation between who most frequently uses the product and who dominates the product evaluation.

It is not quite clear whether the amount of collective behavior increases or decreases in later phases of the evaluation process. Findings reported by Wickström (1965) suggest a slight increase in the amount of collective decision-making, but on the other hand, the LIFE study (1965) found less interaction in connection with brand choices than in connection with decisions concerning type and style of products.

6. The Roles of Family Members in Shopping and Purchasing

Last in the decision process, the purchase is made. Often it is preceded by more or less extensive shopping, and again collective behavior occurs. Alderson and Sessions (1957) found that most commonly the final purchase of a car is made by the husband and wife together, and similar findings are reported by Jaffe and Senft (1966). Even for minor nondurable products, collective shopping is common. Wells and LoSciuto (1966) report that from 40% to 50% of the purchases of products such as cereals, candy, and detergent are made by family groups of more than one individual, and DuPont's Consumer Buying Habit Study (1959) finds that from 30% to 40% of the shopping in supermarkets is done by groups consisting of more than one family member.

There is some evidence suggesting that the amount of collective behavior decreases in these phases, as can be seen when the frequency with which both husband and wife are involved in preliminary shopping is compared with the frequency with which they both participate in the final purchase trip. For example, for rugs and carpets, preliminary shopping is made collectively in connection with 70% of the purchases, whereas the final purchase is made by two or more family members in only 50% of the cases (LIFE 1965). Similarly, Wickström (1965) reports that final purchases are carried out collectively less frequently than any other activity in the purchase sequence.

There are also considerable differences in who dominates the shopping and purchasing for different products. The wife is the most important for grocery products, vacuum cleaners, and sewing machines; and the husband dominates in areas such as automobiles, radios, and photographic equipment (LIFE 1965 and Wickström 1965). Bells' data on choice of favorite store (1969) show that the choice of supermarkets was made by the wife alone in 66% of the cases, the choice of automobile insurance agents by the husband in 80% of the cases, and the favorite appliance store was chosen jointly in 55% of the cases.

7. The Roles of Husband and Wife in Income and Price Decisions

Income and price decisions, which may be made at any time in the purchase sequence, can involve more or less interaction among family members, and they can be dominated by either the wife or the husband. Income and price decisions are most easily observed in connection with saving plans, overall budgeting, determination of price levels, and handling of bills. Some of these decisions are dominated by the husband (see, for life insurance, Blood and Wolfe 1960; and for family budgeting, Kelly and Egan 1969); others are wife-dominated (see, for decisions about food budgets and payment of bills, Blood and Wolfe 1960). There are marked differences between products. For automobiles, budgetary decisions are dominated by the husband, whereas for rugs and carpets the wife is the most important (Jaffe and Senft 1966). Collective budgeting is common also. Blood and Wolfe (1960) find that it occurs in areas such as saving decisions, purchase of life insurance, food budgets, and administration of bills from 30% to 50% of the time, and similar findings are reported by Kelly and Egan (1969).

8. Patterns of Collective Decision Processes

The available evidence does not make it possible to specify in much detail the family role structures in different product areas. However, the findings do suggest that collective decision processes are structured much like individual ones. They also suggest a curvilinear relationship with the most intensive interaction in intermediate steps of the purchase sequence, and they point at considerable differences in the roles of husbands and wives in different product areas.

Collective decision-making occurs most frequently in connection with more important decisions, such as those for major durable products, and most findings concern such products. The little evidence available concerning nondurable products suggests that when collective decision-making occurs, the nature of the interaction is not markedly different from collective decision-making in other product areas.

9. The Influence of Other Family Members

A few researchers have dealt with the roles of other family members in collective decision processes, but most of these studies have dealt exclusively with children and teenagers. The children's role as consumers has three aspects. Individually, they act as consumers and purchasers for a number of products, for other products they are information sources for the family members who act as purchasing agents, and for some products they engage actively in the collective decision-making (McNeal 1965 and Wells 1966a).

For major durable products such as radios, television sets, record players, and photographic equipment, children are most influential early in the purchase sequence. Wickström (1965) found that children initiate purchase sequences in 19% of the cases, that their influence in the general purchasing phase decreased to 12%, that 5% make the final brand choice, and that only 3% carry out purchases.

The role of children in supermarket shopping is larger. Wells and LoSciuto (1966) found that 20% to 25% of shopping trips are made by family groups including one or more children. In such trips the child's role is not limited to passive participation. It was found that they actively influence the purchases, make suggestions, and make brand choices.

There is considerable variation in the influence children have in different product areas. For grocery products, Wells and LoSciuto (1966) found that children influence twice as many cereal purchases as detergent purchases. For major durable products, Wickström (1965) reports that children are three times more important for record players than for radios.

The influence of children in purchase sequences increases with the age of the child. In connection with care purchases, it has frequently been found that teenagers play an important role, and a study conducted by Printers Ink (1965) shows that they have considerable influence upon purchases of many different major durable products such as furniture. The importance of children in the family consumption process increases with age also. The same study found that 40% of the female teenagers engage actively in baking, preparation of meals, and home cleaning.

4. *Family Purchasing Agents*

Besides individual purchases for individual use and collective purchases for collective use, purchases are made by single individuals for collective use or for use by other members of the family. That is, for some products and in some situations, single family members are given authority to perform purchases and to make choices on behalf of the family. Such family members are *purchasing agents*, or to use Lewin's (1958) concept, they act as "gate-keepers" for the household. The specification of the purchasing agent's role may imply that he (or she) is in charge of complete decision processes or parts of such processes. Purchasing agents may be found more or less frequently in different product areas, and for a particular product the agent may be more or less important in different phases of the decision process. Furthermore, variations can occur among families.

1. Establishing Roles and Norms in the Family

Purchasing agents emerge in the process through which roles and norms are established within the family. If two people who did not know each other were asked to spend annually six to fifteen thousand dollars together, it is likely that considerable conflict would result. To solve this, extensive interaction would be required. However, as the problems which initially caused conflicts begin to reappear, many of the solutions agreed upon earlier can be repeated. Eventually, many decisions can be made without any preceding conflict or interaction. That is, norms about what to do will be established, and roles emerge that prescribe who will be doing what.

Essentially, this is what happens in a family, although at the time of the marriage the partners are not completely unknown to each other, and the problems they face do not remain unchanged. Thus several decisions do not cause conflict even the first time they are made, as the family members can apply norms and role prescriptions upon which they agree and which they learned before they entered the family (from parents, among friends, and so on). New decisions can occur late in the family's life cycle. The income to be allocated does not remain constant, and the problems which have to be dealt with do not remain the same. Particularly after changes such as moving to a new home, a new job, the arrival of children, the wife's entering or leaving the labor force, children leaving home, or retirement, new problems will be generated and the amount of collective decision-making increase.

This description applies to family decision-making in general, but a similar pattern is found in connection with single products. When first purchases are made—either of products recently introduced or of products in which the family has recently become interested—collective decision-making is common. But when the same product is purchased repeatedly, previous solutions can be transferred and delegation of authority can be made.

The establishment of norms and roles within the family serves the same purpose as the decrease in complexity in individual choice and decision processes as they are repeated. It minimizes the required effort, and it eliminates wearisome conflicts. But, exactly as the reduced complexity of individual decision processes is not irreversible, the role prescriptions of the purchasing agents are not final. Only as long as they provide reasonable solutions to the problems the family faces will they be reinforced. When that is not the case the role can be modified; either adjustments can be made as family members express satisfaction or dissatisfaction with the behavior of the agent, or the authority can be withdrawn. The latter is particularly likely if the agent violates the norms established for this role. When that occurs family conflict will reappear, just as changing environmental conditions can cause increased conflict in individual choice processes.

The decision process within the family is a constantly changing mixture of individual decision-making, collective decision-making, and decision processes performed by purchasing agents.

2. The Role of the Purchasing Agent

The purchasing agent's decision process looks much like individual decision processes. However, as the agent is not concerned only with his own use of the product, an important additional class of cognitive elements must be considered. The agent will have knowledge about, and be more or less inclined to adhere to preferences of other family members. Furthermore, as first purchases and more unfamiliar problems often are dealt with collectively, the purchasing agent will more commonly deal with relatively shorter and simpler decision processes.

Variations in the total amount of interaction within families have already been discussed, and the findings suggest that the purchasing agent is more frequent in higher- and lower-class families and in later phases of the family life cycle. Moreover, the use of purchasing agents varies with the norms of the particular culture to which the family belongs, and factors such as church affiliation and geographical location are important. Finally, the effects of familiarity with the product show up in the more extensive use of purchasing agents for more frequently used products.

Differences in the choice of the particular family member who will act as an agent are reflected in the findings already presented. Some families are husband-dominated and others are wife-dominated. Moreover, families may be more or less child-oriented and more or less oriented towards delegating authority to older children and teenagers.

The family member who will become the purchasing agent also varies across products. Some product areas are traditionally the husband's responsibility, whereas others are assigned to the wife. Traditionally, the wife is the purchasing agent for many frequently used nondurable products, but in recent years this role structure has changed somewhat. Moreover, particular tasks in the purchase sequence may be more or less frequently delegated to different family members.

It was suggested that the amount of collective decision-making reaches its peak in intermediate steps of the purchase sequence. When that is the case, variations in the amount of authority delegated will also be found. However, it is possible that early in the decision process individual initiative occurs for which less firmly established norms exist. Then at intermediate steps, more or less extensive bargaining takes place, and when an acceptable solution has been outlined, the remaining action is delegated to the appropriate agent. There is no evidence available to validate this hypothesis, but it fits most of the findings reported and deserves further testing.

3. Decision Processes of Purchasing Agents

The decision process of the purchasing agent differs first and foremost from the individual decision process to the extent that the preferences of other family members are constantly observed. The observation of other family members' preferences serves an important purpose. It makes it possible for the agent gradually to modify his behavior to avoid conflicts that otherwise would have threatened his authority. By gradually modifying his strategies in accordance with changing wants and preferences of other family members, the purchasing agent maintains his authority in spite of developments that would otherwise have called for collective decision-making.

Only a few studies have dealt with other family members' influence upon the purchasing agent. Based upon depth interviews, Alderson and Sessions (1957) found that the housewife, in her role as purchasing agent, tries to select items that will please other family members and that other family members more or less knowingly attempt to influence her behavior. But the study also reveals that the housewife considers factors to which she herself ascribes importance, but which are not necessarily important to other family members. Other findings are provided by Wells (1966a). In his study of children as consumers, he found that the child can influence the purchasing behavior of other family members directly or by "passive dictation," where the mother buys several different brands, but purchases certain ones more frequently after observing which the child likes and consumes.

An interesting study of the influence of other family members upon the housewife as a purchasing agent is reported by Coulson (1966). In a small sample from the Chicago area he examined the extent of housewives' knowledge of other family members' preferences and the frequency with which they are taken into consideration. For the 10 grocery products studied, 80% of the housewives knew other family members' preferences, and 80% of those who knew regularly considered these preferences. It was also found that housewives were more familiar with preferences of other family members and more likely to take them into consideration when the brand was visible in use and when the product was only slightly changed in the process of preparation. Furthermore, more influence appeared for adult products (beer, cigarettes, deodorants) than for children's products (cereals, candy, chewing gum), although, as indicated, the influence was considerable in both areas.

Finally, Berey, and Pollay (1968) have reported findings from a study of children's influence upon mother's choice of brands of cereal. Somewhat contrary to expectations, they found yielding on the part of the mother to be negatively related to her child-centeredness, and they found only a slight correlation between the child's assertiveness and its influence upon brand choices. In spite of the study's moderate success, it is interesting because it points to a type of variable which may be necessary in future studies of influence processes within the family.

PART SIX

Integrated Models of Markets

Chapter 18

SOCIAL INTERACTION AND AGGREGATED CONSUMER BEHAVIOR

The present chapter is concerned with the problems which arise from the study of the behavior of total markets, because total markets cannot be described only through summarized measures of the behavior of single individuals or households. A market is more than a number of individual consumers—it is a system in its own right, in which interactions among consumers generate aggregated responses different from the sum of the responses of the single consumers.

Different aggregated models emerge from the various ways single choices are summarized. The discussion of a very simple case which rests upon a number of highly simplifying assumptions will aid in understanding the models that emerge when the simplifying assumptions are dropped.

When a system is left to itself, it will usually end up behaving in a predictable fashion. That is, an equilibrium will be established, and as long as the system is not disturbed, no further changes occur. Markets are rarely "left to themselves"; consequently, a state of equilibrium is rarely reached. However, a discussion of the kind of equilibria established under different conditions provides insight into the mechanism of markets.

1. *Interaction Among Consumers*

To go from individual behavior to total markets would raise only minor problems if consumers did not interact. Of course, the move would add data-handling problems, because, instead of one individual and his cognitive structures, a large number of such structures would have to be considered. In the process of aggregating data that reflect the cognitive processes of several consumers, information can get lost. For example, average attractiveness scores and average values may have less meaning than attractiveness scores and values of single individuals.

Interaction among consumers implies that information is exchanged. This communication does not have to be directly related to particular products, and it does not have to be oral, but it must take place with consumers acting as sources as well as receivers. (See Chapter 9 for the individual consumer's information acquisition, Chapter 15 for the consumer's role as an information source, and Chapter 16 for the perception of information sources and the role of opinion leaders.)

There can be two types of aggregated effects of such communication. Other consumers represent a class of information sources that can be utilized; in addition, they may appear as cognitive elements that influence what alternatives are considered and how they are evaluated. The first type of communication is rather obvious, the latter requires a few comments. The presence of other individuals may make the consumer consider their reactions to his behavior, and may thereby cause him to choose alternatives he would not otherwise have considered. For example, the way a consumer evaluates different brands can depend upon how he expects others to react to his choices, and the way a woman evaluates alternative dresses to wear can depend upon by whom she expects to be seen.

The consumer is most likely to receive impressions from and to attend to individuals who belong to his own social environment. Particularly important are primary groups such as the family, the work group, neighbors, friends, and members of his clubs and associations. Of course, the consumer may be influenced by other individuals through conversations or observation, but most frequently the influence comes from members of the consumer's own primary groups (Katz and Lazarsfeld 1955).

Social interaction may also have two types of effects. First, the individual may adopt beliefs and values held by other consumers not directly related to any particular products. Such influences are not particularly related to the individual's role as a consumer, and they are difficult to trace. For example, between making two similar choices, the consumer may adopt new values and beliefs that result from communication that is completely unrelated to the particular product but will eventually influence the second choice. Second, consumers may receive influences directly related to products. Influence of this kind will have impact upon the consumer's perception of products or the values associated with them. Because such direct influence can more easily be traced than general influences, most studies deal with it.

1. Informational Effects and Imitative Behavior

Two types of processes may account for the effects of product-related communication in primary groups. Often, other group members act as information sources for the consumer. This is a general effect of *personal communication*, and that it occurs within a primary group does not necessarily mean that the receiver is conforming to group norms. The effect may result simply because this information, like any other information, helps the receiver to arrive at a decision, one which may or may not conform to the norms within the group.

In other instances, group influence works more directly. Conformity may result because individuals adopt attitudes or behavior required by their roles in the group. This phenomenon can be labeled *imitative behavior.*

It is difficult to distinguish between the effects of personal communication and imitative behavior. Imitative behavior is normally preceded by some kind of communication within the group, and observable personal communication may result in behavior changes that can be interpreted as changes toward conformity.

In consumer behavior, three research traditions have dealt with personal influence. First, a number of studies such as Katona and Mueller (1954), Summers and King (1969), and Myers and Robertsen (1969) have shown that personal communication occurs among consumers and that it may be more important than any other form of communication. These studies, however, do not tell anything about imitative behavior.

Other studies more or less explicitly assume that imitative behavior occurs. This is true of most of the innovation studies reviewed by Rogers (1962) and by King (1966), and it is true of a number of studies dealing with the "two-step flow of communication" (Whyte 1954), Katz and Lazarsfeld 1955, and Haines 1966). Although these studies show effects following from personal communication, they do not present their findings in such a way that it is possible to conclude that imitative behavior is a major factor.

Finally, a few studies have more directly examined the nature of influence processes in small groups. Early findings are reported by Bourne (1957), who found that the extent to which a product is used by an individual's reference group significantly influences the persons's own acceptance of the product. Furthermore, in many instances this influence overrules economic, technical, and other considerations. Bourne's findings are difficult to evaluate because a detailed report is available for only one product, and the nature of this product is not known. Moreover, one aspect of the study raises some doubt as to the validity of the findings. Subjects were asked to rate not only their own evaluation of the product but also the popularity of the product among reference group members. The validity of the latter rating is highly questionable, as it is possible that rationalizations like those frequently found in dissonance studies have occurred (see, for example, Brehm and Cohen 1962).

Other findings are reported by Myers (1966). In a study of the acceptance of freeze-dried food he found some, although not impressive, tendencies towards conformity with the group leader. However, his experimental procedure does not allow a conclusion concerning the nature of the influence. As both group leaders and non-leaders were asked to distribute the food samples to other members of their groups, it cannot be known to what extent the factual information alone explains the established relationship. That is, the group leaders may simply have been more efficient information transmitters.

Among other researchers, Venkatesan (1966), dealing with choices among identical men's suits, found a slight tendency toward conformity when an intermediate group pressure was applied, but with strong group pressure there was no such tendency. Stafford (1966) also found some group influence in a study of consumers' choices among brands of bread. The influence, however, is only slight, and no relationship was established between group cohesiveness and conformity. Only group leaders had some influence upon brand choices and loyalty. Similarly, Cook (1967) conducted a study of car makes to test whether a homogeneous group would demonstrate more changes in attitudes following group discussions than a heterogeneous group, but he found no differences; and similarly, Sheth (1968d) found only slight evidence of imitative behavior in a study of brand preferences. Finally, Witt (1969) found only a weak correlation between measures of group cohesiveness and similarity of brand choices in small primary groups of male students.

Altogether, the reported studies either do not make it possible to identify imitative behavior or report findings which, although slightly significant, suggest that the phenomenon is only of little practical importance. However, as several of the studies have been conducted under highly artificial conditions, they do not indicate whether more or less imitative behavior will be found in a more realistic environment. A study reported by Hansen (1969b) attempts to answer this question.

In this study, attitude changes, changes in brand choices, and changes in product use were studied within 19 primary groups composed of 10 to 15 female students at a secretarial school. The groups were studied at the time of their formation and eight months later, and they consist of young persons with far from fixed habits for whom the groups became highly significant in the course of the study; consequently, significant tendencies toward conformity would be expected.

Ten different product areas and ten specific brand choices were studied together with attitudes related to these products. On the whole, considerable stability in brand choices, product use, and attitudes was found, and the changes which did occur could not be ascribed to imitative behavior. They were not in the direction of increased conformity, and they were not closely related either to group cohesiveness or to the role of group leaders.

Faced with the dilemma that personal influence within groups occurs, but does not always take the form of imitative behavior, the question arises: What are the processes which govern interaction among consumers in small groups? There seem to be three possible answers to this question. Alone or together they may explain the dilemma. First, it is possible that primary group members act as important information sources for the consumer, but that the information received can favor as well as oppose group conformity. The receiver may evaluate the information in its own right and not automatically copy other people's behavior.

Second, it is possible that products play an important role in small groups, but that some of them act as means of differentiation rather than as means by which the individual can identify himself with the group. Such a phenomenon is well known in connection with fashions (Chapter 14), and it may also occur with products such as cosmetics and cigarettes. It may even be true that in connection with a particular product some consumers identify themselves with the group through their product choices, whereas other consumers attempt to differentiate themselves. If so, an aggregate tendency towards conformity cannot be expected.

Finally, it is possible that a "reactance" mechanism is at work (Brehm 1966), which would imply that moderate group pressure would generate conformity but that increased pressure would generate the opposite reaction. Something like this may account for Venkatesan's (1966) findings in his study of choices among men's suits, and several curvilinear relationships between group cohesiveness and conformity in the Hansen (1969b) study also fit this interpretation.

Presently, it is not possible to decide among these hypotheses, but it seems to be a worthwhile task for future studies to attempt to reveal the nature of group influence processes in consumer behavior. The evidence now suggests that the consumer does not react automatically to the impulses he receives from peers and friends, but that in one way or another he manipulates them before he makes his decisions.

2. Interaction in the Market

The nature of social interaction is illustrated in Figure 18.1. The figure shows how interaction is most intense among individuals belonging to the same groups, but it also shows how information can be transmitted when the same individual belongs to more than one primary group.[1] Unfortunately, most available evidence relates to communication within groups. Only studies of innovation processes have been concerned with communication patterns in larger segments of society, and such studies have shown that innovators are likely to be those group members who have the most extensive interaction with persons outside the group (see Chapter 16).

---

[1] Information may also be transmitted indirectly between groups through overheard conversations, observations of strangers, and so on.

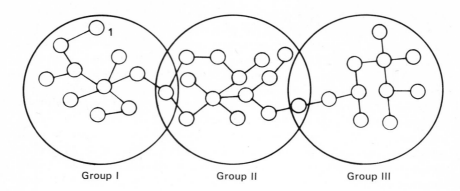

Group I   Group II   Group III

FIGURE 18.1.   *Interaction patterns in three related groups.*

Interaction effects following from personal communications are not equally important in all product areas. Personal information sources are less used in connection with nondurable products, and personal communication is more important when the product is used publicly than when it is used privately (Chapters 10 and 15). Moreover, several studies have revealed considerable differences in the amount of personal communication in different product areas. For example, Myers and Robertsen (1969) found five times as much personal communication for packed food products than for cosmetics and personal grooming aids.

Besides being influenced by personal communication, consumers also receive information from primary, secondary, and tertiary communication sources. To the extent that these sources dominate, consumer behavior can be studied as directly related to the amount and content of this communication. However, when personal information sources dominate, a two-step flow of information will also be found (Katz 1957), much like that illustrated in Figure 18.1. In its extreme form a single impulse (for example, from a TV commercial) is received by a single individual (for example, "1" in Figure 18.1); and from him, the information is spread.

Most frequently, however, neither personal nor primary, secondary, or tertiary communication dominates. With varying frequency, the consumer will be exposed to information from different sources, and only rarely will the consumer depend entirely upon a single type of information source.

2. From Individual to Aggregated Consumer Behavior

1. Consumer Behavior in a Static Market

Normally, consumers do not respond immediately to the information and other influences they receive. Some time will elapse between the time

the communication is received and the time a purchase is made. The interaction among consumers takes time; consequently, if a market is viewed at a
fixed point in time, the observed effects of personal influence are minor.
Alternatively, if the consumers' values and beliefs are constant, either because of a lack of new influence or because influences tend to counteract
each other so that there is no net effect, interaction processes can be disregarded.

Assume that the task is to explain consumer choices under either of these
circumstances. The choices may be among information sources, among
products to use in preparation of a meal, or among brands to purchase. The
choices must be defined in terms of the situations in which they occur, but
there are no further limitations to the choices which can be studied. For the
sake of illustration, consider a situation requiring a choice among brands of
canned peas in a supermarket. Further, assume that there are only two
alternatives, that they are equally priced, that they are identical in every
aspect but the size of the peas, that all consumers perceive the differences in
size of peas perfectly, that they all consider size of peas to be equally important, and that they know what size of peas they prefer. Under these
simplifying assumptions, each consumer's choice can easily be predicted.
He will choose the brand offering peas closest in size to what he considers
ideal, that is, the brand which is most instrumental to him. By comparing
ideal and actual size of peas, the observer can predict the choices; the aggregated behavior of the market results from summation of the individual
choices.

Such aggregated choices can also be studied a little differently (Benson
1962, 1963, and 1966; Kuehn and Day 1962; and Day 1965). The consumers' ideal sizes of peas can be illustrated in a diagram which shows how
many consumers will prefer peas of varying sizes (Figure 18.2).

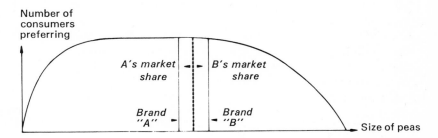

FIGURE 18.2. *Theoretical preference distribution for peas of varying sizes.*

In this diagram the two available alternatives are shown by vertical lines
indicating the size of the peas of the two brands. It is now obvious that all
consumers with preferences for peas smaller than those offered by brand A

will choose brand A, that all consumers with preferences for peas larger than those offered by brand B will choose brand B, and that those with preference for peas of a size between A and B will choose the brand which comes closest to their ideal. Eventually, a dividing line can be drawn between A and B.

Under these highly simplifying assumptions, the relationship between the marketing strategies and consumer behavior is also very simple. If the marketers are free to manipulate the size of their peas, manufacturer "A" should increase the size of his peas so that they are only a little smaller than those of "B." Thereby, he maximizes his share of the market. "B," however, can act in a similar manner; if "A" makes his peas too large, "B" can decide to make his own peas smaller than those of "A," whereby he will get a larger share of the market. Eventually, such strategy changes could continue, until the two competitors each have half of the market. When that occurs, neither can make any change which will improve his situation.

If the marketers cannot freely manipulate the size of their peas, the situation is a little different. If there are costs involved, the situation can be stabilized somewhat earlier, since the gain from each single move must cover the costs associated with changing the size of the peas. Consequently, the more expensive the change in strategy, the more stability in the market.

Now consider a third marketer who is planning to enter the market. If he assumes that "A" and "B" will not change their strategies as a result of his entry into the market, his problem is simple. He will choose the size of his peas so that a maximum number of consumers will prefer his size. In Figure 18.2, he will decide to make peas a little smaller than those of "A." In that case, however, "A" is not likely to keep his product unchanged. He may decide to make his peas a little smaller than those of the newcomer, which in turn may induce the latter to reconsider his strategy. With three or more companies there are no stable solutions. But regardless of the strategies the consumers will again be distributed—this time among three brands— according to the instrumentality of the brands relative to the consumers' ideal sizes of peas.

This analysis is simple because of the assumptions made. By eliminating the assumptions we make the problem more complex, but also more realistic. At the same time a number of problems will become evident with which aggregated models must deal.

In the above analysis, the most important assumptions were:

1. The consumers perceive the actual differences in the alternatives perfectly.
2. Consumers know their own preferences.
3. The alternatives differ along only a single dimension.
4. The consumers ascribe equal importance to the dimensions along which the alternatives are evaluated.
5. A choice must be made among a fixed number of alternatives.
6. The choice takes place in a particular point in time, that is, the model is static.

What if, one by one, these assumptions are dropped?

2. Perceived Differences in Alternatives

Normally consumers do not perceive choice alternatives perfectly. Even with identical alternatives, consumers may perceive differences (Chapter 16); and when the alternatives vary, they may be perceived imperfectly. Rather than dealing with actual differences, an aggregated model must consider the consumer's perception of the alternatives. In terms of the example in Figure 18.2, the *perceived* sweetness of the peas must be measured along the horizontal axis, rather than the actual sweetness.

This adjustment has several implications: First, the consumer's perception of sweetness must be measured. Second, the locations of the two alternatives in the figure may be changed. Consumers can perceive the brands as more or less alike than they really are. Third, the perceived sweetness of the alternatives cannot be represented by a single line, but it must be represented by a distribution (Figure 18.3).

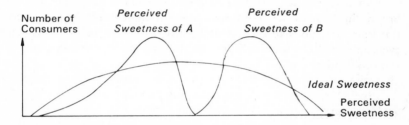

FIGURE 18.3. *Preferences for peas of varying sweetness and the perception of two alternatives.*

It is still possible to determine the share which each brand will obtain, but more complex computations are necessary. If it could be assumed that the perception of the alternatives is independent of the consumer's ideal choice and that the brands are represented by symmetrical distributions, the problem could be solved easily. In that case, the share each brand gets can be predicted from the average perceived sweetness of the alternatives, and the predicted brand shares would deviate from those predicted in Figure 18.2 only to the extent that the means of the distributions differ from the actual sweetness of the two brands. However, there is no reason to believe that ideal and actual perceptions are not correlated, as would be the case if the consumers perceive the brand they used previously more favorably than other brands, a tendency found to be common (Chapter 9). Similarly, it is questionable whether the distributions are symmetrical. If alternatives are only slightly different, there may be a tendency on the part of some consumers to perceive them as identical, and if they are very different, an opposite tendency may occur (Chapter 7). For these reasons, prediction of choices must be based upon the individual consumer's perception of ideal and perceived sweetness. Moreover, it requires estimates of the ideal sweetness on a scale comparable with the scale on which the perceived sweetness is measured, a problem which will be dealt with later.

The shift from actual to perceived sweetness of the alternatives also has implications for marketing strategies. As long as the consumer perceives the alternatives correctly, the marketer can only apply basic strategies in attempts to influence the consumer's choice. That is, for the present example, he will have to change the sweetness of the peas. However, when the concern is with perceived aspects, it may be possible to change the perception of the alternatives without actually having to change the products. This could be accomplished by communication strategies, and it is particularly likely to be successful when misperceptions of the alternatives already exist. That is, if consumers perceive the brand as more or less sweet than it actually is, information about the actual sweetness of the brand can be enough to change these perceptions.

Of course, it may also be possible to influence consumers' perception of brands in ways which contradict the actual features of the alternatives. But there are limits to the extent to which this can be done, as consumers eventually will learn about the product's real features through primary communications.

3. Perfect Knowledge of Preferences

Normally, the researcher will not have perfect knowledge about the consumers' preferences. This is not an important problem when the consumers prefer either a maximum or a minimum of the attribute in question. For example, if the choice depends on the amount of potato chips in otherwise identical packages, the alternative will be preferred which has the most chips. However, in some instances there may be too much as well as too little of the attribute. Similarly, when an attribute reflects variations in the product along more than one dimension, problems may arise. Price is such an attribute. The product is rejected not only if it is too expensive, but also if it is too cheap, the latter because the lower price suggests inferior quality (Chapter 16).

In such instances, it may be possible to learn consumers' ideal preferences through direct questioning, particularly when the dimensions can be meaningfully specified to the consumer and when the consumer is aware of his ideal. For example, a female consumer may be perfectly able to tell what the ideal length for a cocktail dress is for her, and an experienced golfer may know very accurately what the ideal weight of a golf club is for him.

In other instances, the dimensions along which the attributes are measured can be well defined, but the consumer is not able to express his preferences meaningfully or is not aware of them. The sweetness of peas is a point in case. Sweetness can be quantified operationally in terms of the percentage of glucose in the product, but the consumer is unable to express his preferences in such terms. In such cases a relationship must be established between the consumer's verbally expressed preferences and the objectively defined scales.

The problem is even more complicated when there is no objective dimension along which measurements can be made. With a dimension like *prestige*, the scales must be derived from the consumers' own judgments. Here (as in the previous case), nonmetric multidimensional scaling techniques may prove useful. Techniques are available which provide estimates of ideal points and the perception of the alternatives (Chapter 9). However, to be meaningful these techniques require a reasonable number of alternatives relative to the number of perceptual dimensions.

It is also possible that the consumers have, not ideal points, but rather acceptable ranges of alternatives. Here, the "own category" of Sherif et al. (1965) may prove useful, but so far its application has been reported only in connection with price perceptions (Chapter 16).

Presently, considerable difficulties arise when it cannot be assumed that the consumer knows and can express his ideal preferences. Fortunately, however, neither the ideal preferences nor the absolute perception of the alternatives are important in their own right. Rather, the differences between the two govern the choice. Therefore, as suggested in Chapter 9, the perceived instrumentalities of the alternatives may be a useful substitute. The less instrumental an alternative is perceived to be, the larger the differences between the ideal point and the perception of the alternative. The introduction of this variable greatly simplifies the required computations, and it also makes measurements easier. To return to the present example, instead of having to establish the ideal sweetness and the perceived sweetness of the peas, predictions can be based upon the perceived instrumentality of the brands.

4. Alternatives Differing in Several Attributes

The discussion of choices among alternatives which differ along only a single dimension illuminates some basic problems of aggregation, but it does not apply to very many practical cases. Commonly, alternatives will be evaluated along several different dimensions, and further problems arise.

Again, for the sake of simplicity, let it be assumed that the consumers know their ideal preferences and that their perception of the alternatives is perfect. Then consider the pea example. This time, the peas also differ in price. The two attributes can be illustrated as in Figure 18.4.

For those consumers who initially chose A, the introduction of a price

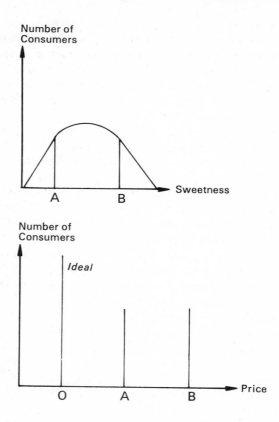

FIGURE 18.4. *Preference distributions for alternatives evaluated along two dimensions, sweetness and price.*

difference will cause no troubles as A is less expensive.[2] However, some of the consumers who originally chose B may now switch to A. The larger the price difference between the two brands, the more will do so. The consumers who prefer peas sweeter than B and those who prefer peas less sweet than B will behave differently. As it is assumed that all attributes are equally important, the absolute difference in sweetness compared with the absolute price difference will determine whether those with a preference for very sweet peas will switch to A or not. If the price difference is larger than the difference in sweetness, they will all switch to A, and if it is smaller, none of them will do so. For consumers with sweetness preferences between A and B the situation is different. Here, even a slight difference in price may make some switch from B to A; and the larger the difference, the more will switch. When the price difference becomes larger than the difference in sweetness, eventually all of B's consumers will change to A.

[2] Assuming that the consumers do not judge quality by price.

This case is still fairly simple because all consumers can be assumed to have the same preference for low price. With other attributes the situation may appear as in Figure 18.5. Here, the peas are assumed to vary with regard

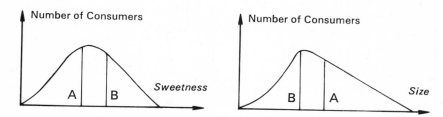

FIGURE 18.5. *Preference distribution for alternatives evaluated along two dimensions, sweetness and size.*

to both sweetness and size. Imagine a marketer who is planning to introduce a third brand of peas. If he considers the preference distribution for sweetness and size separately, he will choose a product a little less sweet than A and smaller than B. Thereby, he cuts off significant proportions of both distributions. Whether this is an optimal strategy, however, depends upon the way the consumers' preferences for sweetness and for size are related. Only if they are positively correlated or not related at all, will the strategy be the best possible. If it happens that those consumers who prefer sweet peas also are those who prefer small peas, a strategy like the one suggested may be very poor. The problem is that the preference distribution cannot be dealt with separately. One way to overcome this would be to look at a three-dimensional preference distribution instead of two independent two-dimensional ones. However, when the number of dimensions increases, this approach becomes extremely complex. The similarity concept as it underlies contemporary work with nonmetric multidimensional scaling is a relevant concept in this context (Green and Carmone 1971), and, eventually, further work with these models may result in valuable estimation procedures for the kind of model discussed here.

Alternatively, each consumer can be dealt with separately. For each individual a total preference for each alternative can be computed. Essentially, this is what the attractiveness score does. In the present example, as long as all dimensions are equally important, the brand will be chosen which deviates the least from the consumer's ideal sweetness *and* size. Also, the complications which follow when the assumption about perfect perception of the alternative is dropped are considered in the *perceived* instrumentality, which is used rather than the actual differences in the alternatives.

When the assumption is dropped that all attributes are equally important, it must be considered that the different attributes vary in importance so that some of them have more influence upon the choice than others. The attractiveness score reflects this factor through the variations in value importance. Moreover, as an extreme case, when the dimensions vary in importance, it is also possible that consumers will evaluate the alternatives along completely different dimensions if some consumers ascribe zero importance to some values. For example, in Figure 18.5, one consumer may consider size to be unimportant, and consequently he will base his choice upon sweetness alone. Similarly, other consumers may disregard sweetness and choose by size alone. Also, in connection with this problem, nonmetric scaling combined with unfolding of preference data may provide useful insights. Presently, programs are available which estimate the different importance of the dimensions revealed by nonmetric multidimensional scaling (Green and Carmone 1971).

When several dimensions vary in importance, the information with which the marketer must be concerned can be summarized as follows:

1. Specification of choice situations.
2. Number of consumers in different choice situations.
3. Values aroused in choice situations.
4. Importance associated with values.
5. Perception of alternatives relative to values.

As the choices increase in complexity, the marketer's strategy decisions get more complicated. He must consider the frequency with which particular situations occur, the possibilities for changing the perception of alternatives through changes in product and in communication strategies, and the possibilities for influencing the values aroused. Each of these decision problems has two aspects. First, provided consumers' cognitive variables can be modified, what changes should be aimed at? Second, what kind of strategies can bring about the desired changes? Answers to these questions require a detailed understanding of the choice situation under study.

5. Definition of Situations

Exploration, deliberation, and response-choice situations were discussed in Chapter 3. So far, only simple and easily defined situations have been dealt with, but often it is difficult to specify the appropriate situations. Preferably, they should be defined so that within each situation the consumers will choose among a few clear alternatives, but rarely can situations be defined with such precision. For example, in purchase situations the consumer may reject all of the brand or product alternatives and decide to seek more information; he may drop the whole matter; or he may just postpone the choice. These possibilities make it difficult to specify the alternatives considered in each situation.

The more precisely situations can be defined, the fewer will be the alternatives to be dealt with in each, but also the more will be the different situations to be studied. On the one hand, it is possible to study a particular product in terms of a few purchase situations in which consumers are faced with the product. These situations will be very heterogeneous, and at an aggregated level a considerable number of values and alternatives must be dealt with. Similarly, extreme variations in the choice processes will be found. On the other hand, it is possible to define situations so that a single aggregated situation consists of relatively homogeneous choices. But then the number of situations will be large. There is no easy way out of this dilemma. In the particular case, the advantages associated with having to deal with only a limited number of situations must be weighed against the disadvantages associated with extemely heterogeneous aggregated choice situations.

To identify the situations required for studies of market behavior, the purchase sequences for the particular product must be studied. In such studies, the more easily defined exposure and purchase situations can act as fix-points. Where cognitive elements after an exposure situation deviate significantly from those that enter into a subsequent purchase situation, significant deliberation must have taken place. A wide range of situations can be studied, and depending upon the particular problem, few or many of these may have to be considered.

In general, a choice process can be generated by particular environmental circumstances, it can result from a previously made, more or less specific commitment, or a combination of the two can arouse the required conflict. Therefore, a particular situation must be explained in relation to environmental factors and to intentions reflecting individual motivations.

3. *Aggregated Consumer Behavior over Time*

When consumer choices are studied over time, two things will have to be considered. What a particular consumer does at one time depends upon what he has done previously; and interaction among consumers may occur when more than one time period is studied. To simplify the problem, the case of no social interaction will first be considered. The time periods discussed are so short that the consumers can make only one choice in each period.

1. Outline of a Dynamic Model Without Interaction Among Consumers

In a static model, the relationship between environmental variables and responses is straightforward. The response is the dependent variable;

the values and perceptions the consumers bring into the situation and the stimulation that acts upon him in the choice process are the independent variables. Together, the individual and environmental variables determine the behavior in the particular period of time, and they also affect the beliefs, values, and intentions with which the individual will enter the subsequent period. When only one kind of choice process is involved, this interaction can be illustrated with the choice process as a "system" for which the different variables act as input and output (Ackoff 1962), as is done in Figure 18.6a, which illustrates a purchase situation. Similarly Figures 18.6 b and c illustrate consumption and exposure situations. In principle these instances differ only in the environmental factors and the behavioral responses (if any). For example, the consumption situation will have two results. The stocks of available consumption alternatives will be changed; and beliefs, values, and intentions may become modified as a function of satisfaction or dissatisfaction.

This framework can be extended into a dynamic model in which the environmental influence occurs in one time period and the effect upon choices occurs in a later period. This dynamic model can be illustrated with a case involving more choice situations. Imagine a product studied during two time periods in terms of two exposure situations, one deliberation situation, two purchase situations, and one consumption situation. This means that in each time period six different situations will have to be dealt with. Each can be seen as a static case as described in Figure 18.6, but the fact that the same consumers appear in both time periods makes it necessary to study how the responses in the two periods are related. As no interaction occurs among consumers, relationships between the first and second periods exist only to the extent that the same consumers make choices in both. A consumer who makes a purchase in the second period may have performed some preliminary step in the preceding period. When several consumers are considered, the relationships may appear as in Figure 18.7.

The illustration shows how the consumers engaged in different choice processes in the first time period move to other conflicts in the following period. If all consumers had identical decision processes, the heavy arrows in Figure 18.7 would illustrate the entire model. But as different consumers apply different decision processes, there will be several arriving and departing arrows associated with each conflict situation (see Chapter 15). Generally, the more variations in the decision process, the more complex the network becomes. With sufficient data-handling capabilities, however, the process is not hard to follow; and as no interaction occurs among consumers, the complete pattern can be decomposed into a smaller or larger number of independent decision processes, each following a different pattern.

In such a system, the outcome of a particular type of choice situation depends upon the number of consumers entering the situation, the factors that influence consumers in the situation, and the values and perceptions

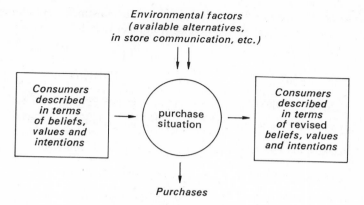

(a): purchase situation

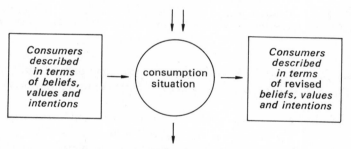

(b): consumption situation

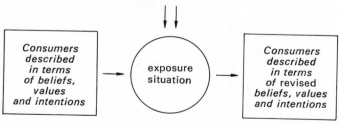

(c): exposure situation

FIGURE 18.6. *Interaction among variables in a market model composed of one choice situation in a single time period: (a) purchase situation, (b) consumption situation, (c) exposure situation.*

that consumers bring into the situation. How the consumers are changed in the choice processes must be studied with choice models like that proposed

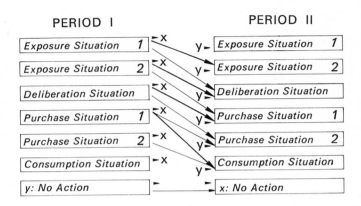

FIGURE 18.7. *Relationships among choice situations in two subsequent periods (x: to "no action" in period 2; y: from "no action" in period 1).*

in the previous chapters. A specification of the aggregated factors that influence the choices is needed to predict the outcome of the particular situations.

The number of consumers who at a given time will enter a particular choice situation depends upon the nature of the situation in that time period and the number of consumers who have completed preceding steps in purchase sequences in previous time periods. Consequently, the state of the system at the end of each period (which is identical with the state of the system at the beginning of the following period) must be described in terms of the number of consumers who have completed different steps in decision processes and the intentions, values, and perceptions these consumers have.

It is important to note that the latter statement does not necessitate a description of the individual's entire latent conceptual system. It is possible, and desirable, to concentrate on those alternatives among which the consumer normally chooses and upon the values and perceptions related to them. That is, the consumer should be described in terms of a subset of his latent cognitive system.

Knowing the state of the system at the beginning of a period and the factors which act upon the system makes it possible to predict the state of the system at the end of the period; consequently, when several time periods are considered, the total system can be studied as a flow which is being directed by external factors influencing the system in different time periods. This can be described as follows: When the state of the system at the end of one period is determined, the changes which occur in the following period are explained by the factors influencing the system in that period. These changes in turn determine the system at the beginning of the following period. The total system progresses step-wise, with the changes occurring in each step determined by the external factors.

2. Aggregated Situational Variables

Each aggregated choice situation is composed of a number of more or less heterogeneous single choices. In each type of situation the factors which influence the consumer are the environmental stimuli which determine the amount of perceived conflict and to which the consumer can attend in the course of the choice. In general terms these variables were discussed in Chapter 3, but they must also be dealt with at an aggregated level. Variables such as novelty, surprise, and change and the information available in the situations must be considered. In purchase situations, the concern will be with the availability of different products and brands, the obtainable information, and the changes occurring during the situation. In exploration situations, the concern will be with the information affecting the consumer, in terms of its novelty and complexity and in terms of its specific content. Similarly, in deliberation situations the concern will be with those overall aspects of the situation which influence the consumer's response to the conflict.

Attempts to quantify the total amount of primary, secondary, and tertiary information concerning particular products (Cerha 1967) represent a first step in this direction; but further specifications are required of the types of situation in which the information reaches the consumers.

3. Interaction Among Consumers

Because consumers interact, that is, they provide information to each other, communication situations will have to be dealt with. These situations are special in several ways. Both individuals engaged in the exchange of information may be changed during the process; and in such situations, the most important stimulation acting upon the consumer is provided, not by outside sources, but by the system itself, that is, by other consumers.

Both the amount and the nature of this stimulation are important. When the information transmitted is predominantly positive and interaction occurs frequently, it is possible for the system to continue changing even though external stimulation is provided only in a single period. For example, the number of purchases could increase because the necessary influence in subsequent periods is provided by the consumers themselves. Although such instances are of little practical significance, it can be mentioned that the process through which rumors spread follows such a pattern (Festinger et al. 1948).

When it comes to actual products, however, there will always be some stimulation from the outside, and as long as some personal communication occurs, the product may obtain a considerable amount of acceptance even with a minimum of communication from the marketer. Of course, the use of other information sources may accelerate the process, but the underlying communication pattern is extremely important. At the other extreme, if no personal communication occurs, only those who learned about the product from external information sources will purchase it; and after they have done so, all further effects disappear.

A special case occurs when considerable, but predominantly negative communication occurs. When that is the case, it may not be possible to generate sales at all, even with extremely heavy marketing communication. The personal communication may be so strong that it overrules all other communication sources; and furthermore, if the marketer increases his communication, it is possible that it will generate a reaction in terms of increased negative personal communication.

As discussed, the interaction among consumers may be more or less dominant. In many instances, it occurs relatively infrequently, in which case the need for information from other channels is considerable. However, as some personal information will almost always be found, an understanding of the market can be gained only by considering how the market's own communication pattern interacts with other attempts to influence the choice processes.

4. Outline of a Dynamic Model with Interaction Among Consumers

It is now possible to sketch a dynamic model of consumer behavior that considers interaction among consumers. The model is outlined in Figure 18.8. Here, as in Figure 18.7, a number of single conflict situations must be imagined, some of which are communication/exposure situations. For the sake of simplicity only a single situation is illustrated in each period.

From the figure, it can be seen that the ultimate dependent variables are the responses determined in the successive time periods and that the independent variables are the external stimulations. Consumer intentions, values, perceptions, and the like, when first fed into the system, act as intervening variables in the dynamic system.

In such a model the state of the system must be specified in terms of the consumers' (individuals or families) values, perceptions, and intentions at the beginning of each time period. The changes which occur during the period then follow from the choice situations the consumers enter. Moreover, the choice situations to which a certain consumer is assigned depend upon his values, perceptions, and intentions at the beginning of the period together with the personal and impersonal communication that occurs during the period.

Each consumer never appears in more than one choice situation in each period, and he may not enter into any. In the latter case, he can be left unchanged at the end of the period. But it is also possible that intentions, values, and perceptions should also be modified when the consumer passes

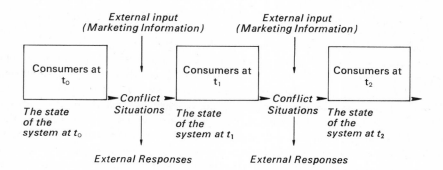

FIGURE 18.8. *Outline of a dynamic choice model.*

through a period without engaging in any choice processes. For example, it is possible that intentions deteriorate if they are not reinforced. Such modification can be allowed for in the model if a special "situation" is added through which those consumers pass who do not engage in regular choice processes. In this particular situation the intentions, values, and perceptions are modified properly.

For each consumer who enters into choice situations, his perceptions and intentions are changed, particularly in the purchase situations, as purchases are made.

The variables which determine the outcome of a particular choice situation (see Figure 18.6) are:

1. The values, perceptions, and intentions with which the consumer enters the situation.
2. The external influences (information) which act in the particular situation (particularly the primary, secondary, and tertiary communication).
3. The influences from other consumers (personal communication).

Finally the values, perceptions, and intentions determined in the choice situations become those with which the consumer begins the next period.

5. Market Equilibrium

As it is possible to think of a state of equilibrium in connection with individual consumers (Chapter 15), it is possible to apply the concept of a *market equilibrium*. It is hardly possible to imagine a market that remains in such a stage for a very long time, but the concept facilitates a distinction between factors which tend to move the system towards equilibrium and factors which retard this process. A couple of examples will make this clear.

First, assume a market system in equilibrium. That is, it receives the same external stimulation and provides the same responses in each time period. Then, if additional external communication is received in a single period and if personal communication does not occur, the system will behave as follows: A number of decision processes will be started in the time period when the communication is received. After a varying number of time periods, some of these processes will have been interrupted and others will have been completed. Then, if no repeat purchases are made, the effect of the initial information will deteriorate. As long as there is no personal communication, no new decision processes are generated by the system, and eventually it will approach the equilibrium which prevailed before the external information was provided, or a new equilibrium will be established.

A different case emerges when the same additional information is also provided in all subsequent periods. Here the system will again approach an equilibrium, but one different from the equilibrium that existed before the new communication was introduced.

If personal communication occurs, the system will behave very differently. Depending upon the frequency and the efficiency of the interaction among consumers, more or less extreme effects may be observed. The more there is of personal communication and the greater its effects are, the more consumers will eventually purchase the product and the sooner they will do so. If the personal communication retards the process, no acceleration occurs. After a certain number of periods, the system will have absorbed the disturbance, and the old or a new equilibrium will be established.

Another characteristic of the system can be illustrated if a number of consumers use a certain product regularly. Purchases will still occur even though no personal or external communication occurs, because each consumer passes through not only a purchasing sequence but also a consumption sequence, at the end of which a new purchasing sequence is generated. Again, under these circumstances, the system will reach an equilibrium of repeated purchases.

These simple cases illustrate the behavior of a system like the one outlined here. The extent to which such models will behave like actual markets depends upon how well conflict situations can be defined, whether it can be predicted which consumers will enter into what situations and whether it can be predicted what the outcome of the situations will be. The preceding chapters have presented insight into the problems these questions arouse and have shown that our understanding of these crucial processes is still limited.

The formulation of quantitative models of market systems has not been attempted here. At the present state of knowledge the attempt would be premature, but an idea of the type of models which could emerge can be found in the so-called "sprinter models" (Urban and Karash, 1971). However, in order to relate different research traditions and to construct a method for evaluating future achievements, the concluding chapter will discuss the problems inherent in attempts to formulate aggregated market models.

Consumer behavior is highly complex; so far, models have had to rest upon simplifying assumptions, which made the problems manageable but removed the models somewhat from reality. The models discussed in preceding pages can be seen as special cases of the more general model discussed in this chapter, cases which result when certain assumptions are made. An overview of some of the more important models is provided in the following chapter.

Chapter 19

MODELS OF CONSUMER BEHAVIOR: AN OVERVIEW

In this chapter, 28 models of consumer behavior are reviewed. The selection covers a wide range of models underlying contemporary research. To avoid overlap, only basic models are dealt with, those which state relationships among a few dependent and a few independent variables. Often, basic models are combined so that more complex structures emerge, but these more elaborate versions are not discussed here.

It is not our purpose to describe the models in detail nor to review the findings published in connection with each. Such reviews are available in Anastasi (1964), Twedt (1965), and Sheth (1967). Rather, the structure of each model is pointed out and the underlying assumptions are reviewed to emphasize the limitations of the particular models and suggest their relationship to more general models like those discussed in Chapter 18. Neither is it the purpose to promote any single model. In the view of the present author, they all have advantages as well as disadvantages. By analyzing the nature and the assumptions of the models we intend simply to improve the understanding of these models.

1. Classification of Models

Table 19.1 provides a summary of the 28 models. In the figure and in the subsequent discussion, distinctions are made in connection with each model. These will be discussed briefly. To help the reader, a few references are provided in connection with each model. Preferably, references are made to sources where the concern is with the basic model. Moreover, reference is also made to those previous chapters where the models or findings relating to the models have been discussed.

Each model can be described as a relationship between some *dependent* and some *independent variables*. For each of the models the *structure* is described in terms of these variables and in terms of the *hypothesis* concerning the relationship among the variables.

Models may deal with consumer behavior at an *individual* level or at a *household* level (Chapter 17). For each model, the kind of variables used is indicated. The models may be *dynamic* or *static*, and they may or may not consider effects of interaction among consumers (Chapter 18). Moreover, static models may be applied as comparative dynamic models when they are used to explain behavior in several time periods. The extent to which static models have been used in this way is discussed also.

The models deal with behavior in different *types of consumer choice situations* such as exposure, deliberation, and response choice situations; and among the latter, a distinction is made between consumption and communication situations (Chapter 3). Moreover, the models concerned with exposure situations can be more or less oriented towards forced learnings or information acquisition (Chapter 9). For some of the models, it is fairly obvious what kind of situations are studied. In other instances, it can be deduced only from the specifications of the dependent and independent variables with which the models work.

The different models apply more or less explicitly formulated choice principles. They are all concerned with how alternatives are matched with consumers; and in explaining this, they can either specify the alternatives in terms of one or more *product attributes* and/or the consumers can be described in terms of one or more *personality dimensions* such as values, motives, or traits (Chapter 16). The models also vary in the extent to which they primarily deal with *rational, semi-complex* or *clue-guided* choices (Chapter 10). These aspects of the models are considered also.

Consumer models may be *more or less aggregated* in terms of the variables upon which they build (Chapters 2 and 18). The variables in aggregated models may be of different kinds. Sometimes variables are used which have no counterparts at the individual level, whereas other models use aggregated variables which are measured at an individual level. Finally, the least aggregated models treat each single consumer individually.

Different models are more or less applicable to different types of decision processes (Chapters 14 and 15). Some models deal with all types of products in all types of situations; others are limited to particular products in particular situations. Similarly, some models are especially concerned with processes at a brand level, others deal with the manufacturers' level, some with the assortment level (for example, store choices), and others with product class choices (Chapter 2).

TABLE 19.1

An overview of the 28 basic models of consumer behavior. The classifications apply to the models in their most basic form. Information in parentheses concerns slightly less frequently used versions of the models.

1. Exp.—Exposure Situations   Com.—Communication Situations
   Del.—Deliberation Situations   Con.—Consumption Situations
   Pur.—Purchase Situations

2. Low—variables measured and applied at individual level.
   Intermediate—variables measured at individual level and applied aggregated.
   High—variables have no counterparts at individual level.

3. I—Rational choice processes assumed.
   II—Semi-complex choice processes assumed.
   III—Clue-guided choice processes assumed.
   IV—Type of choice process cannot be determined.

4. 1a—Choice depends upon uni-dimensional product attribute.
   1b—Choice depends upon multi-dimensional product attribute.
   2a—Choice depends upon uni-dimensional consumer attribute.
   2b—Choice depends upon multi-dimensional consumer attributes.
   3a—Choice explained in terms of interaction among single consumer and single product attributes.
   3b—Choice explained in terms of interaction among several consumer and several product attributes.
   4—Not specified.

Basic model	Dependent variables	Independent variables	Household or individual behavior	Static or dynamic	Choices processes underlying model (1)	Level of aggregation (2)	Type of personality and/or attribute variables explaining choice (3, 4)	Products most frequently applied to
1. Utility models	Purchases	Utility of alternatives	Individual	Static	Pur.	Low	I, 2, a	All
2. Perceived-risk models	Purchases, information acquisition	Perceived risk	Individual	Static	Exp., Pur., and Del.	Low (intermediate)	IV, 3, a	All products brands with some importance and uncertainy (often first purchases)
3. Dissonance models	Purchases, information acquisition, and post-choice attitudes	Dissonance	Individual	Static	Exp., Del., Pur., Com., and Con.	Low (intermediate)	IV, 3, a	All (conflict products of some importance)
4. Attitude and preference models I	Brand, product and store choices, occasionally information sources	Preferences and attitudes towards brands, products, etc.	Individual	Static (or comparative static)	Exp., Pur., and Con.	Low (to intermediate)	II, 1, a	All (with a tendency towards nondurables)
5. Attitudes and preference models II	Discretionary spending	Attitudes towards price and income changes and income	Household	Dynamic	Exp. and Pur.	Intermediate to high	II, 2, a	Major durables
6. Interest and value models	Purchases (consumption)	Values, interests	Individual	Static	Pur. and Con.	Low to intermediate	II, 2, b	All
7. Image models	Brand choices	Perception of brands	Individual	Static (dynamic)	Pur. and Exp.	Intermediate	II, 1, b	Frequently used nondurable products

TABLE 19.1 [*continued*]

Basic model	Dependent variables	Independent variables	Household or individual behavior	Static or dynamic	Choices processes underlying model (1)	Level of aggregation (2)	Type of personality and/or attribute variables explaining choice (3, 4)	Products most frequently applied to
8. Perceptual preference models	Brand choices	Perception of brands	Individual	Static	Pur.	Intermediate to high	II, 1, b	Not known
9. Lewinfield models	Purchases	Approaching and avoiding forces	Individual (household)	Static (dynamic)	Pur. (Exp., Del., Con.)	Low	II, III, 3, b	All (mostly applied to product level choices)
10. Hierarchy of effects models	Purchases	Mass communication	Individual	Dynamic	Pur., Del., Exp.	Intermediate	II, III, 1, a (1, b)	Frequently used nondurable brands
11. Situational-learning models	Response choice	Situational aspects	Individual	Static (dynamic)	Pur. (Com.) (Con.)	Low	III, IV, 3, b	All (most frequently brand choices)
12. Personality and motivational models	Purchases and choices of information sources	Motives and personality traits	Individual	Static	Pur., Exp.	Low	IV, 2, b	All (mostly applied at brand level)
13. Personal influence models	Purchases, preferences	Personal communication	Individual	Static (dynamic)	Com. (Exp.), Pur.	(Low to) intermediate	II, 4	All (conspicuous products and brands which arouse some interest)
14. Media exposure models	Exposure (purchases)	Descriptive con var media and message var.	Individual	Static (dynamic)	Exp., Pur.	Intermediate	IV, 4	Frequently advertised products and brands
15. Decision process models	Steps from problem identification to purchase	Information, previous experiences	Individual	Dynamic	Exp., Del., Pur. (con.)	Low (to intermediate)	I–II, 4 (often 3, b)	All (most frequently major durables)
16. Satisficing models	Purchases and information acquisition	Satisfaction levels (goals) and information	Individual (household)	Dynamic	Exp.	Low	II, 1, b	All
17. Innovation models	Awareness to adoption Adoption	Individual and mass communication	Individual and household	Dynamic	Exp., Del., Pur.	Intermediate to high	II, 3, b	First purchases

Model	Behavior modeled	Explanatory variables	Unit	Time	Stages	Aggregation/level	Classification	Product applicability
18. Fashion models	Fashion adoption (purchase and use)	Previous adoption, personal communication	Individual	Dynamic	Exp., Pur., Com., Con.	High	IV, 4	Fashion products
19. Household budgeting models	Income allocation	Income, household characteristics, preferences	Household	Static	Del., Pur.	Intermediate (high)	I (II), IV, 4	Larger single purchases and major product classes
20. Plans and intentions	Purchases	Plans, intentions	Household	Dynamic	Del., Pur.	Intermediate	II, IV, 4	Major durable products
21. Simple probability models	Purchases	Purchasing probabilities	Individual and household	Static	Pur.	Intermediate (to high)	IV, 4	All
22. Brand share models	Brand choices	Preferences (loyalty), previous purchases, and distribution	Individual and household	Comparative static and dynamic	Pur.	(Low to) intermediate	III, 4	Frequently purchase nondurables
23. Segmentation models	Purchases	Socio-economic, purchase and personality variables	Individual and household	Static	Pur.	Intermediate to high	IV, 2, b	All brands
24. Life cycle models	Major purchases and saving	Stages in family life cycle	Household	Comparative static	Pur.	Intermediate	IV, 2, a	Major durable products
25. Social class models	Purchases, store choices, choice of information sources, consumption	Social class	Household	Static	Exp., Pur., Con.	Intermediate	IV, 2, a	Store, brand, and product choices
26. Income hypotheses models	Total spending and saving	Income	Household	Comparative static	Pur.	High	IV, 4	Total spending
27. Demand function models	Product (and brand) purchases	Price, quality, promotion, etc.	Household and individual	Comparative static	Pur.	High	IV, 4	Product class choices (less applicable to brand choices)
28. Cultural-anthropological models	Exposure, consumption, and purchases	Cultural variables	Household and individual	Static	Exp., Pur., Con.	High	2, b	All

The models are not discussed in any particular order, but it has been tried to arrange them so that related models are dealt with in connection with each other. It has also been attempted to cover the less aggregated models first. However, the latter arrangement is difficult to follow strictly, as several models can operate at two or more different levels of aggregation.

2. *28 Consumer Behavior Models*

1. Utility Models

Utility models were discussed in Chapters 5 and 10. A history of utility theory is available in Kauder (1965), and a brief review is found in Edwards (1954a). Recent findings are discussed by Becker and McClintosh (1966). The basic model can be described as:

$$E_i = f(U_i)$$
$$E_i = \text{maximum}$$

which says that the evaluation (E_i) of alternative i is a function of the utility (U_i) of the alternative. The basic hypothesis states that the alternative which is evaluated as highest will be chosen. The model can be seen as a special case of the more general model outlined in Chapter 18, which emerges if all alternatives are evaluated along one dimension, if there is only one type of purchase situation into which all (individual) consumers enter, and if the consumers evaluate all available alternatives before each single choice. In its simple version, the model does not allow for influence from mass or personal communication, and thus it is static, although some authors have suggested comparative static versions. The model is illustrated in Figure 19.1 in terms of the schema used in Chapter 18.

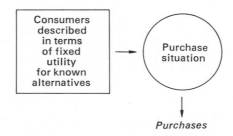

FIGURE 19.1.   **The basic structure of utility models.**

Attempts to apply the model directly or in terms of indifference curves have not been very successful. Also, applications of more complex versions derived from the basic model have had a limited success (Chapter 10).

2. Perceived Risk Models

A detailed account of the perceived-risk model is available in Cox (1967a), and it has been discussed in Chapters 5, 8, 9, 15, and 16. This model can be stated as:

$$E_i = f(PR_i)$$
$$E_i = \text{minimum}$$

which says that the evaluation of alternative E_i depends upon the perceived risk (PR_i) associated with the alternative. The main hypothesis states that the consumer will minimize perceived risk. The dependent variables are choices of information sources, brands and product alternatives. The independent variable, perceived risk, is related to problem importance and uncertainty, and it may vary among products as well as among consumers. Formalized in terms of the model described in Chapter 18, the model looks as shown in Figure 19.2.

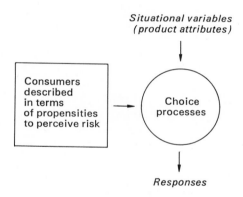

FIGURE 19.2. *The structure of perceived-risk models.*

Basically, the model is static, although some applications, particularly in connection with brand loyalty, have dealt with choices as a function of perceived risk in previous choice situations. The model deals with deliberation, purchase, and exploration situations. It also deals with interaction among consumers, as choices of other consumers as information sources are allowed for. The model is concerned with individuals rather than households, and choices are studied at an individual level (although findings are often presented summarized for groups of consumers so that it is not possible to follow the single consumers).

In principle the model is general, but so far it has been applied to relatively few product areas, where considerable uncertainty about the alternatives exists. There has been a tendency to apply the model to first purchases, and several of the attempts have been promising, although it is obvious that considerably improved predictions can be obtained when the model is combined with other models which allow for evaluation of alternatives along other dimensions.

3. Dissonance Models

The basic dissonance model is outlined by Festinger (1957) and elaborated upon by Brehm and Cohen (1962). A brief discussion of applications of the model to consumer choice behavior is provided by Engel and Light (1968) and by Oshikawa (1969). The dissonance model has been discussed in Chapter 9. Its basic structure can be described as follows:

$$E_i = f(D_i)$$
$$E_i = \text{minimum}$$

which says that the evaluation of alternative E_i depends upon the dissonance the alternative will arouse, the basic hypothesis being that individuals tend to minimize dissonance. In turn, the independent variable, dissonance, is a function of cognitive conflict which again is related to such variables as importance, volition, and commitment. In its basic form the model is uni-dimensional, and it explains choices among alternatives which vary in their ability to arouse dissonance. These alternatives may be information sources, products, or cognitive variables. The model deals with deliberation, purchase, exploration, and consumption situations. Formally, the dissonance model looks much like the risk model in Figure 19.2, but in this model the consumer variable is the propensity to perceive dissonance. The fact that dissonance will occur only when an individual perceives conflict after having committed himself to an important alternative suggests that post-purchase situations are the most important, and most empirical work has dealt with such situations.

In most applications the model is static, it deals with individuals rather than households, and it operates at a very low level of aggregation, although findings are frequently summarized to form data at an intermediate level. The model does not consider interaction among consumers, although choice of personal information sources may be among the independent variables.

As discussed in Chapter 9, the application of this model to consumer behavior has not been overly successful.

4. Attitude and Preference Models I

Attitude and preference models have been dealt with in the most detail in Chapters 6, 7, and 10. Different hypotheses are evaluated by Insko

(1968), and they are discussed in a marketing context by Crespi (1965) and Day (1970).

There are many versions of attitude and preference models. Here, the discussion is limited to those in which alternatives are evaluated along a single dimension. (Models where several dimensions are considered will be dealt with subsequently.) The unidimensional attribute is frequently referred to as the *preference*. The model states:

$$E_i = f(P_i)$$
$$P_i = f(C_i)$$
$$E_i = \text{maximum}$$

which says that the evaluation (E_i) of alternative i is a function of the preference (P) for i, which in turn is a function of communication (C_i) received previously. The basic hypothesis says that the consumer will choose the most preferred alternative.

Much research with the model deals with the relationship between communication and preferences. Here, the concern is with the prediction of choice based upon preferences only. With this limitation, the model is unidimensional, the dependent variables being brand and product preferences reflecting the consumer's overall perception of the alternatives' attributes. With preferences substituted for utility, Figure 19.1 illustrates the structure of the model.

Preference models deal with individuals rather than households. They are static, but when preferences are related to previous communication they can be characterized as semi-dynamic or comparative static. They deal with purchase, and to some extent, with consumption situations. They operate at a low to intermediate level of aggregation in the sense that the basic variable, preference, is defined at an individual level but most studies deal with average preferences for segments of consumers. Preference models do not specifically consider interaction effects among consumers, although such effects are possible because preferences are studied as depending upon communication, including personal communication.

Of the considerable research which has been reported, only little has dealt with the prediction of choices. A discussion of the inconclusive findings is found in Chapter 9.

5. Attitude and Preference Models II

A highly aggregated attitude concept is discussed by Katona (1956 and 1964) and by Katona and Mueller (1953). The following relationship is studied:

$$C_{t2} = f(A_{t1} Y_{t2})$$

where the dependent variable is consumption in time period 2 (C_{t2}), the independent variables are current income (Y_{t2}) and attitudes towards spending, income changes, and price developments in period 1 (A_{t1}). The basic hypothesis states that (discretionary) spending increases faster when consumers have positive attitudes towards spending.

In this model the attitude variable itself is an aggregated measure of several individual attitudes towards particular aspects of income and price developments. The model is dynamic, in that spending is related to attitudes in previous periods, and it allows for interaction among consumers, in that the attitudes towards spending are influenced by personal communication. The model can be illustrated as in Figure 19.3.

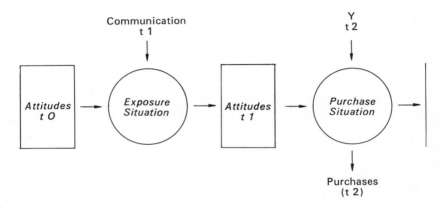

FIGURE 19.3.   *Outline of aggregated attitude model.*

The attitude variable and income and spending are measured at the household level. The model deals with exposure and purchase situations and is applied at a highly aggregated level. The income and the discretionary spending in particular do not have corresponding variables at the individual level. The model is concerned with major durable products primarily.

Attempts to use the model have been successful to the extent that the introduction of the attitude variable has resulted in an improved forecast of aggregated spending.

6. Value and Interest Models

In value and interest models the alternatives are evaluated in terms of two or more values or attitudes; different versions are discussed by Janis (1959a) and Rokeach (1969). The models dealt with in Chapters 9, 11, and 12 have some of the qualities of these models, and interest models in general were discussed in Chapter 16. Basically, the model can be described as:

$$E_i = f(V_i, \ldots, V_n)$$
$$E_i = \text{maximum}$$

that is, the evaluation of alternatives depends upon a number of different values $(V_i, \ldots, V_n)$, and the basic hypothesis states that the alternative with the most positive evaluation will be chosen. These models relate closely to preference models, to Lewin field models, and to image models. In application, it is often difficult to judge to which category a certain model belongs. They are grouped here because they all view the alternatives as related to a number of value dimensions, reflecting predispositional differences among the consumers. (When the model reflects perception of the alternatives along a multitude of product attribute dimensions, it is considered an image model.)

The dependent variables are choices or overall preferences for the alternatives. The independent variables vary considerably, and they may differ particularly in the kind of individual values applied.

Figure 19.2 illustrates the structure of this type of model, if the individuals are described in terms of values or interests. The model is static, and it deals with individuals rather than households. In its basic form, it does not allow for interaction among consumers, but in modified versions in which values are studied as a function of communication, interaction effects are considered. The model deals primarily with purchase situations although applications to consumption choices seem natural.

The model is general and should relate to all products, but only limited applied research has been reported. The attempts so far made with the model are promising.

7. Image Models

Image models were discussed in Chapter 16. Recent reviews of these models are provided by Rasmussen (1968) and Myers (1968). Formally, the model says:

$$E_i = f(\mathcal{J}_1, \ldots, \mathcal{J}_n)$$
$$or\ E_i = f(\mathcal{J}_1 - S_1, \ldots, \mathcal{J}_n - S_n)$$
$$\mathcal{J}_i = f(\text{Communication})$$

where the independent variable, the image, is the perceived aspects $(\mathcal{J}_1, \ldots, \mathcal{J}_n)$ of the alternatives. In turn, the image is seen as a function of primary, secondary, tertiary, and personal communication. The underlying assumption suggests that the alternative with the most positive image will be chosen; alternatively, the image-congruence hypothesis holds that the alternative most congruent with the consumer's self-image $(S_1, \ldots, S_n)$ will be chosen. The model is outlined in Figure 19.4.

The image is multi-dimensional and the model is static, although the inclusion of the relationship between image and communication suggests dynamic aspects. It deals with individuals rather than households, and it does not consider aggregated effects of interaction among consumers, although important aspects of the image may reflect the consumer's perception of others' evaluation of the alternatives. The model is mainly concerned with purchase situations, but the study of images as a function of

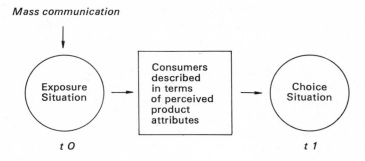

Mass communication

Exposure Situation

Consumers described in terms of perceived product attributes

Choice Situation

t 0   *t 1*

FIGURE 19.4.   *The structure of image models.*

communication incorporates exposure situations. In principle the model is aggregated to a low level only, but it is used in terms of average images on behalf of different categories of consumers, and in this sense it can be classified as at an intermediate level. In principle the model applied to all purchase situations, but it has most commonly been used in connection with frequently used nondurable products and store choices. As was reviewed in Chapter 16, attempts with the model have been moderately successful.

8. Perceptual Preference Models

Preference models are discussed in Chapters 10 and 18. Versions of these models are discussed by Benson (1962), Green and Carmore (1969), Neidell (1969), and Johnson (1971). Basically, the models propose:

$$E_i = f(\mathfrak{J}_1 - I_1, \ldots, \mathfrak{J}_n - I_n)$$
$$E_i = \text{minimum}$$

that is, the evaluation (choice) of alternatives depends upon $(\mathfrak{J}_1, \ldots, \mathfrak{J}_n)$, which are two or more perceptual dimensions, and I, which is the location of the consumer's ideal product in the n-dimensional space. Although the structure of the model is very similar to that of the image-congruence model, the dimensions differ and in particular the interpretation of the ideal point is different. Formally the models can be illustrated as in Figure 19.1.

Perceptual preference models deal with individuals rather than households, they are static, and they are concerned with consumer behavior in purchase situations. Basically, they rest upon individual perceptions, but the emerging perceptual space can be highly aggregated, and at the individual level the meaning of the perceptual dimensions is not always clear.

Research with these kinds of models is one of the fastest growing areas in marketing. An excellent review of its present standing is provided in Green and Carmone (1971). As discussed in Chapters 10 and 18, different versions of these models which are computerized may give valuable insights into consumers' perceptual and preference structures.

9. Lewin Field Model

In its structure, the Lewin field model has much in common with the perceptual preference models. However, it deviates somewhat in its application. The model is discussed by Bilkey (1953 and 1965) and by Lewin (1958). A special version is proposed by Ölander (1964). Aspects of the model are dealt with in Chapter 4. The model can be described as:

$$E_i = f(F_{i1} - F_{i2})$$
$$E_i = \text{maximum}$$

which says that the evaluation of an alternative (E_i) depends upon the difference between forces opposing the alternative (F_{i2}) and forces drawing the individual towards the alternative (F_{i1}). In turn, the forces depend upon product attributes and individual values, whereby the model combines aspects of image and preference models with aspects of value-interest models. The basic hypothesis states that the individual will choose the alternative towards which the net force is strongest. In principle the model is multi-dimensional, but in many applications the use of the net force concept makes it uni-dimensional. Formally the model looks like Figure 19.2.

In its basic form the model is static, but through a number of modifications it has been applied as dynamic. It has been assumed that the individual will repeat his behavior from period to period and that changes will occur when the net force towards a particular alternative exceeds a certain level. This mechanism is discussed as the freezing-unfreezing effect. Normally, behavior is "frozen" in a certain pattern, and considerable force is required before a change occurs. Subsequently, when the change has been made, the behavior will stabilize ("freeze") in a new pattern.

The model does not directly consider interaction among consumers, and no aggregated interaction effects are incorporated. However, the forces acting upon the individual may depend upon the individual's relationship with other individuals. Although the model deals with individual behavior, through the introduction of the gate-keeper concept (the purchasing agent), the model has been applied to household behavior. Conceptually, the model is at a low level of aggregation, but in applications aggregated consumer behavior has been dealt with.

In its basic form the model deals primarily with the purchase situation, but in extended versions it also incorporates exposure, deliberation, and consumation situations. In most applications the model deals with product class choices, but its use has also been suggested in connection with household-income allocation (Bilkey 1966) and brand choices (Ölander 1967).

10. Hierarchy of Effect Models

Some aspects of hierarchy of effect models were dealt with in Chapter 14, and they are discussed by Lavidge and Steiner (1961) and Palda (1966). The model can be described as follows:

$$\text{Purchase}_{i,t5} = f(\text{conviction}_{i,t4}, \text{communication}_{i,t5})$$
$$\text{Conviction}_{i,t4} = f(\text{preference}_{i,t3}, \text{communication}_{i,t4})$$
$$\text{Preference}_{i,t3} = f(\text{liking}_{i,t2}, \text{communication}_{i,t3})$$
$$\text{Liking}_{i,t2} = f(\text{knowledge}_{i,t1}, \text{communication}_{i,t2})$$
$$\text{Knowledge}_{i,t1} = f(\text{awareness}_{i,t0}, \text{communication}_{i,t1})$$
$$\text{Awareness}_{i,t0} = f(\text{communication}_{t0})$$

The dependent variables are purchases, and the independent variable, communication. Intervening between these are awareness, knowledge, liking, preference, and conviction. In its original form, the model is unidimensional, although in some applications preferences and liking have been measured in terms of multi-dimensional images. The model assumes that a purchase will be made only when all the steps in the hierarchy of effects have been completed. The model is dynamic in that each single step in the sequence depends upon the preceding step. The model does not explicitly deal with interaction among consumers—most frequently communication is seen as identical with advertising—but it allows for incorporation of these effects.

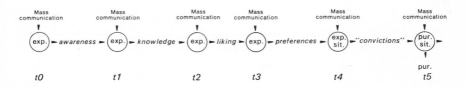

FIGURE 19.5.   *The structure of hierarchy of effect models.*

This model, illustrated in Figure 19.5, deals with individuals rather than households; it is concerned with exposure, deliberation, and purchase situations; and it is aggregated at an intermediate level in that the variables relate conceptually to the individual consumer but are applied to larger segments of consumers. Although applications to durable brands have been reported (Smith 1965), the model is primarily used for frequently purchased and heavily advertised nondurable brands. The basic model and related versions have been used in attempts to evaluate advertising campaigns, but only few findings have been published. A major problem with this model is to identify all the single steps in the process, and it is questionable whether the assumption is valid that all consumers pass through all steps.

11. Situational Learning Models

Learning models are dealt with in Chapter 7, and they are discussed by Krugman (1968) and by Sandell (1967). A good presentation of the underlying model is available in Restle (1961). Functionally, the model states:

$$E_i = f(S_1, \ldots, S_n)$$

The consumer brings a repertoire of possible responses with him into each choice situation. Of these, the one will be chosen which is most closely associated with the particular situation. In principle, the dependent variable can be any response, but so far only purchases have been dealt with. The independent variables, situational aspects $(S_1, \ldots S_n)$, are multi-dimensional although some authors talk about the association with a specific situation. How alternatives are associated with the situation is a function of learning in previous similar situations.

The model is static, but it acquires dynamic aspects when learning of associations are incorporated. The structure of the model is illustrated in Figure 19.6.

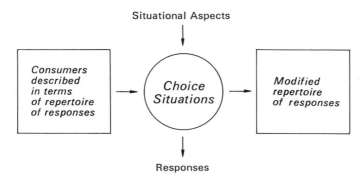

FIGURE 19.6. *The structure of situational learning models.*

There is no interaction with other consumers, but as associations can depend upon previous personal communication, it is possible to extend the model along these lines. The model deals with individuals, and both dependent and independent variables are defined at a very low level of aggregation. Some of the major problems with the model emerge when it is applied to aggregated choice behavior.

In principle, the model applies to all product classes and all situations, but so far it has mainly been used in studies of brand choices.

12. Personality and Motivational Models

A good review of some of these models is provided by Brody and Cunningham (1968), and they are discussed in some detail in Chapter 16. Formally, the model suggests that:

$$E_i = f(PT_1, \ldots, PT_n)$$

where the dependent variable is the evaluation or choice of alternative (E_i) and the independent variables are different personality traits or motives (PT_j). The basic hypothesis states that the alternative will be chosen which agrees most closely with the individual's personality. The model is multi-dimensional, and the dimensions relate to the consumer rather than to the alternatives; it is static, and it does not consider aggregated effects of interaction among consumers, although, depending upon the personality traits applied, the consumer's relationship with other individuals may be reflected in the model. The structure of the model is outlined in Figure 19.7.

The model has been applied to purchase situations mostly, but a few attempts to explain exposure to communication have been reported.

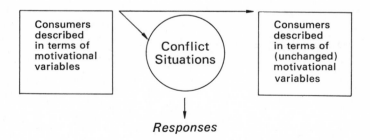

FIGURE 19.7.   *The structure of motivational models.*

It is concerned with individuals rather than with households and conceptually the variables are defined at an individual level. The models should apply to all types of products, but so far, most research has been with brands.

13. Personal Influence Models

A classical study of personal influence in marketing is found in Katz and Lazarsfelt (1955). A more recent review is available in Arndt (1967a), and findings have been discussed in Chapters 9, 15, 16, and 18. The personal influence model can be formalized as:

$$E_i = f(PC_i)$$
$$E_i = \text{maximum}$$

where the dependent variable is the evaluation or choice of brands and products and the independent variable the amount and type of personal communication received about these products or brands. The basic hypothesis states that the alternative for which the positive difference between positive and negative communication is largest will be chosen. The model is uni-dimensional in the sense that it deals with overall evaluation of the alternatives, but, as different information can be received from several sources, multi-dimensionality is introduced.

The model operates at an individual rather than a household level, and formally it is static although the related two-step flow hypothesis introduces dynamics into the model (Chapter 18). Nevertheless, the model is conceptually confined to the individual level, and it includes only aggregated interaction effects when it is combined with the innovation model.

The model is primarily concerned with communication situations, although exposure and purchase situations are also considered. The structure of the model is illustrated in Figure 19.8.

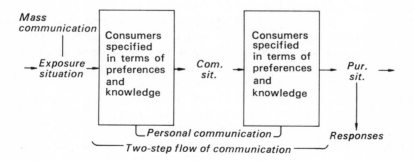

FIGURE 19.8 *The structure of personal communication models.*

The model applies where consumption is conspicuous or where consumers are highly interested in the products. Attempts with the model have been successful in the sense that the significance of personal influence has been repeatedly established, but the nature of the relationship with subsequent purchases is not fully understood.

14. Media Exposure

Media exposure models are reviewed by Schyberger (1965) and by Cerha (1967), and Reeves (1961) provides a provocative statement of the underlying hypothesis. Findings relating to the model have been discussed in Chapters 9 and 14. The model can be described as follows:

$$E_i = f(\text{Exp}_i)$$
$$\text{Exp}_i = f(\text{Socio-economic variables, media and content variables.})$$
$$E_i = \text{maximum}$$

That is, the evaluation of alternative i is a function of the exposure (Exp_i) to the alternative; and, in turn, exposure depends upon socio-economic variables, the content of the advertising, and the marketer's choice of media. Underlying the model is the assumption that the alternative is chosen for which the consumer receives most positive exposures.

Many researchers have contented themselves with exposure as the ultimate dependent variable, but here the concern is with those applications having evaluation and choice of alternatives as the dependent variable. In this formulation, exposure operates as an intervening variable between consumer responses and media characteristics and content variables.

In principle, the exposure variable is uni-dimensional, although multi-dimensional aspects are introduced through the exposure to several media and to quantitatively different messages. In most versions the model is static, although attempts have been made to relate purchases to exposure in preceding time periods. Formally, the model looks as illustrated in Figure 19.9. Operationally, it deals with individuals, but often it is applied at household levels. Interaction effects play little or no role as the model is primarily concerned with mass communication. It deals with exposure and purchase situations, and the effects of exposure are often measured at an individual level, in terms of recall, recognition, and the like.

In principle the model applies to all products, but it is especially relevant for products which are heavily advertised in mass media. In applying the model, it has often been a major difficulty that too many variables intervene between exposure and purchase, so that no simple relationship is established. However, in special cases such as coupon advertising, it may be possible to quantify the relationship postulated in the model.

15. Decision Process Models

Decision process models were discussed in Chapter 14. Elaborate versions are found in Engel et al. (1968), Nicosia (1966), and Howard and Sheth

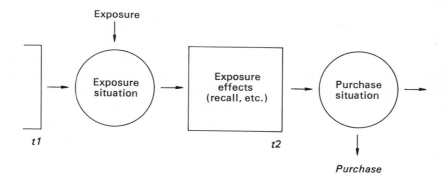

FIGURE 19.9. *The structure of media exposure models.*

(1967). The formal structure of the models varies depending upon the specific formulation, but, for example, Engel et al. (1968) proposed the following version:

Purchase$_{it3}$ = f(comparison processes$_{t2}$)
Comparison processes$_{t2}$ = f(search$_{t1}$)
Search$_{t1}$ = f(problem recognition$_{t0}$, available information$_{ti}$)
Problem recognition$_{t0}$ = f(situational variables$_{t0}$, communication$_{t0}$)

The purchase, or any preceding step in the sequence, can be studied as the dependent variable; and the independent variables are earlier steps in the sequence. In structure the model looks much like Figure 19.5, but the possibility of feedback loops makes it somewhat more flexible. The model allows for evaluation of the alternatives along several dimensions, and the basic hypothesis states that, provided the decision process is not disrupted before the purchase, the most attractive alternative will be chosen. The model is dynamic in the sense that it describes decision process behavior over time, and it deals with individuals rather than households. In principle, the model allows for interaction effects among consumers, but so far aggregated effects of this interaction have not been studied within the framework of the model. The model operates at a low level of aggregation, but its subscribers maintain that it can be applied to segments of consumers as well.

By the very nature of the model, it deals with all kinds of exposure, deliberation, and purchase situations. However, consumption is frequently dealt with briefly. In its basic version, the model applies where purchases are preceded by elaborate decision processes; but through appropriate elimination of steps in the process, the model is adaptable to less complex instances of consumer behavior also. So far, applications of the model have been promising.

16. Satisficing Models

A special group of decision process models can be characterized as satisficing models. Such models are discussed by Simon (1967a and 1967b), and the choice principle underlying them was discussed in Chapter 9. Often these models are referred to as information processing models, and they follow the same pattern as decision process models. Only the specification of the choice principle differs. It is assumed that alternatives are evaluated along a number of dimensions, and that an alternative must be satisfactory along all dimensions in order to be accepted. The basic hypothesis states that the consumer will continue to acquire information until an alternative has been established which meets these requirements. Consequently, the dependent variables are information acquisition and choice, and the independent variables are the satisfaction levels and the information which is acquired.

The model is dynamic, and, although in principle it applies to individuals, attempts to apply the model to problem solving in groups suggests that it may also be used to study family and household decision making.

The model deals with exposure, deliberation, and purchase situations; and, to the extent that adjustments in satisfaction levels result from use, consumption is also considered.

The model allows for interaction among consumers, as goals and satisfaction levels are influenced by other individuals, but so far aggregated effects of such interaction have not been studied. The model is not limited to any particular product area. The somewhat inconclusive evidence concerning application of the choice principle to consumer behavior was discussed in Chapters 10 and 12. One of the main problems with the model relates to aggregated application of the choice principle.

17. Innovation Models

At the individual level the innovation model rests upon the adoption model, which is a special case of the decision process models. As such, it is discussed by Rogers (1962). A brief discussion of the application of the adoption model to consumer behavior is available in Robertson (1967b). This model was also discussed in some detail in Chapters 14 and 15. It can be formulated as follows:

$$\text{Adoption}_{t4} = f(\text{trial}_{t3}, \text{communication}_{t4})$$
$$\text{Trial}_{t3} = f(\text{evaluation}_{t2}, \text{communication}_{t3})$$
$$\text{Evaluation}_{t2} = f(\text{interest}_{t1}, \text{communication}_{t2})$$
$$\text{Interest}_{t1} = f(\text{awareness}_{t0}, \text{communication}_{t1})$$
$$\text{Awareness}_{t0} = f(\text{communication}_{t0})$$

The model is multi-dimensional, although intervening attribute and personality variables are not always specified. The dependent variable is adoption, and the independent variables are the preceding steps in the adoption process together with personal and mass communication. Formally the model looks like Figure 19.5, and only the nature of the steps differs. It deals with exposure, deliberation, and purchase situations. Consumption behavior is normally not studied. The model relates particularly to new products with which consumers have little or no experience.

At an aggregated level, the model takes the form of the innovation model discussed in Chapter 14, and with this version, highly aggregated variables have been applied in attempts to explain different innovation patterns. As the innovation process is studied as a function of personal communication in interaction with mass communication, great emphasis has been placed upon the aggregated effects of interaction among consumers. Much of the work with hypotheses derived from the model was reviewed in Chapter 15.

18. Fashion Models

Fashion models were discussed in Chapter 14, and they are discussed by Nystrom (1928) and by Gold (1964). Formally, the model suggests that:

$$(\text{number of purchases})_{t1} = f(\text{purchases}_{t0})$$

The fashion model deals with fashion products. Basically, the model's dependent variable is the total product acceptance in a given period, and the independent variable is the adoption in previous periods.

Fashion models are dynamic and operate at a high level of aggregation. Most frequently, they deal with individual rather than household behavior. In spite of its high level of aggregation, the model rests upon behavior in exposure, purchase, and consumption situations. Formally, the model can be illustrated as in Figure 19.10.

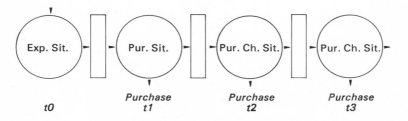

| Exp. Sit. | | Pur. Sit. | | Pur. Ch. Sit. | | Pur. Ch. Sit. |

| | Purchase | Purchase | Purchase |
| t0 | t1 | t2 | t3 |

FIGURE 19.10. *The structure underlying fashion processes.*

19. Household Budgeting Models

The household budgeting model is a special version of the decision process models. They are discussed by Gredal (1959) and by Pratt (1965a). Aspects of the model were discussed in Chapters 14 and 17. Formally, the model states:

(purchases of product class *j*) = *f*(budgeted spending for *j*)
(budgeted spending for *j*)   = *f*(income, preferences, family
                      structure)

The dependent variable is the amount of money spent on product classes and major purchases, and the independent variables are the income, the preferences for different kinds of consumption, and the nature and amount of interaction within the household. The structure of the model is shown in Figure 19.11.

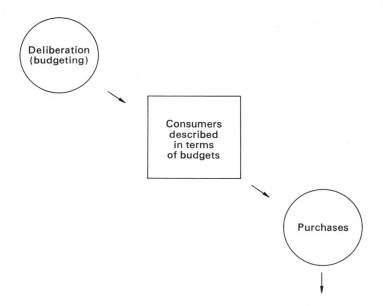

FIGURE 19.11.   **The structure of household budgeting models.**

In its basic form the model is static, but it becomes dynamic when combined with decision process models. It operates at the household level and applies variables describing individual households which can be aggregated to deal with segments of households. In its simple form, it deals with deliberation and purchase situations, and it is most applicable in connection with major durable purchases and with larger product classes. The model does not consider interaction among households.

20. Consumer Plans and Intentions

Consumer plans and intentions models can be seen as another special case of the decision process model. They were discussed in Chapter 14, and a detailed analysis is available in Juster (1964). Formally, the model states:

$$(\text{Purchases})_{t1} = f(\text{Plans and Intentions})_{t0}$$

The dependent variable is purchases, and the independent variables are plans and intentions which can be measured in a number of different ways.

The model is dynamic in that it studies purchases in one period as a function of plans and intentions in previous periods. It deals with households, but measurements are frequently obtained at individual levels. It covers purchase and deliberation situations, and it does not specifically consider interaction among consumers. Although independent variables are measured at an individual level, the model is normally applied to larger market segments. The model is illustrated in Figure 19.12.

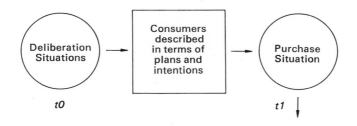

FIGURE 19.12. *The structure of models of consumer intentions.*

The model has first and foremost proven useful in connection with major durable products and other purchases where extensive pre-planning occurs.

21. Probability Models

Most of the models discussed can be given a probabilistic as well as a deterministic formulation. Commonly, however, they are deterministic. In the present section, a group of models which rest upon probability assumptions will be discussed, and only very simple versions will be dealt with. A thorough discussion is available in Montgomery and Urban (1969), and a brief discussion of basic aspects of the models is available in Howard (1968). Formally, the probability models can be written as:

$$q_{ti} = \Pr(x)$$

saying that the amount purchased in a period can be described as a probability function of some other variables. The probability distribution may be theoretical (as the Poisson distribution applied in many queuing models), or it may be observed. A simple example of such a model could look like this table:

q	P
1	.1
2	.2
3	.3
4	.3
5	.1

It says that there is a probability of .1 that one unit will be purchased, that there is a probability of .2 that two units will be purchased, and so on. When observed probability distributions are applied, the distribution of purchases in some previous time periods are assumed to describe the expected number of purchases in a following period. When a theoretical distribution is used, the parameters of the distribution will normally reflect one or another characteristic of the consumer's purchasing behavior (for example, the average purchasing rate).

In these models, the dependent variable can be the number of consumers purchasing, the number of purchases, purchase sizes, or another similar variable. The independent variables are the parameters of the probability distribution or some observed purchase distribution. The models are static, they most frequently describe behavior which occurs in purchase situations, and they do not consider interaction among consumers. Normally, they are highly aggregated, although they may rest upon assumptions about individual customers' purchasing behavior in a particular time period. They can apply to household as well as to individual behavior. The simple structure of the models can be seen from Figure 19.13.

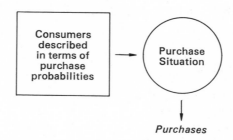

FIGURE 19.13.   *The structure of simple probability models.*

Models of this nature are frequently used in connection with queuing models, lot-size models, and other operations-research models. Their success depends entirely upon the underlying assumptions concerning the applied probability distribution. When an observed probability distribution is used, the factors explaining the demand in the time periods when the probabilities were observed must be the same in the period for which the demand is explained. Similarly, when theoretical distributions are applied, the assumptions about the underlying parameters must apply in the period for which predictions are made.

22. Brand Share Models

Probability models have been applied in connection with frequently purchased nondurable products, in attempts to explain market shares of different brands. These models were discussed in Chapter 15, and reviews can be found in Ehrenberg (1965) and Massy et al. (1970). Formally, the model states that:

$$E_i = P \text{ (propensity to buy brand } i\text{)}$$

In a given market consumers have a certain propensity to buy particular brands, and their actual purchases exhibit random fluctuations around a mean determined by this propensity. In their most simple formulation, brand-share models are probability models in which all consumers have the same constant probability of purchasing certain brands. In more elaborate versions, the propensity to buy the brand can vary among consumers and can be studied relative to other variables.

Simple brand share models are static or comparatively static, and, with a few exceptions, they are all aggregated. They deal with individual as well as household purchases; they are concerned with behavior in a purchase situation; and they do not allow for interaction among consumers. They are most common in connection with frequently purchased minor nondurable products.

In more elaborate versions of these models past purchases influence subsequent brand choices. These models are either Markov or learning models (Haines 1969), and like simple versions, they deal with individual as well as household behavior, and they are applied to aggregated panel data. They do not consider interaction among consumers, as little as they allow for influences from mass communication. Simple models are illustrated by Figure 19.13. The structure of the more elaborate brand-switching models is shown in Figure 19.14.

23. Market Segmentation

Market segmentation is characterized by its approach rather than the variables upon which it rests. The researcher tries to divide markets into segments composed of consumers who behave differently and, preferably, also respond differently to marketing strategies. A discussion of segmentation is found in Chapter 16, and a review is provided by Frank (1968).

Purchases

FIGURE 19.14.   The structure of Markov and learning brand-switching models.

In spite of the diversity of variables which can enter into such models, it is generally possible to formalize the model as follows:

$$E_i = f(\text{socio-economic variables, purchasing variables,}$$
$$\text{personality characteristics})$$

Here the response (E_i), the dependent variable, can be purchases of different brands, different purchasing sizes, brand loyalty, deal-proneness, and the like. The independent variables characterize the consumer, and the number of such variables may be considerable. Socio-economic variables are such as family size, occupation, or age. Purchasing characteristics are frequency of shopping, size of grocery bill, number of items purchased, and so on. As personality variables were discussed previously, they are mentioned here only because they have often been used with these other variables.

Often, these models do not rest upon a formalized hypothesis, but rather they study the relationship between responses and independent variables by means of correlation or similar analysis.

The model is static, and it deals with individual as well as household behavior. The behavior which is explained occurs in purchase situations, and interaction among consumers is rarely considered. Normally, these models are highly aggregated, and their structure is illustrated in Figure 19.7.

24. Life-Cycle Models

The family life-cycle concept is one of the more prominent variables frequently used in segmentation studies. Aspects of the model were discussed in Chapter 15, and they are dealt with in Clark (1955) and Madsen (1964). Formally, the model states:

$$E_i = f(\text{stage in the life cycle})$$

The dependent variables (E_i) are purchases of brand and products. The independent variables are stages in the family life cycle. The structure of the model is shown in Figure 19.7.

The model deals with households and is primarily concerned with behavior in purchase situations. Even though the model compares purchasing behavior in different stages of the life cycle, it is static (comparative static). It rests upon variables measured at an individual level, but generally, they are applied to segments of consumers so that the model is aggregated at an intermediate level. Formally, the model does not allow for interaction among consumers, although some of the differences found during the life cycle are explained in terms of different social relationships in different stages of the life cycle. The model has been most successfully applied in connection with major durable products and total spending and saving.

25. Social Class

Like the family life-cycle concept, social class is a specification of a particular variable which can be used in market segmentation studies. Social class is dealt with in Chapter 16, and the classical discussion of social class and consumer behavior is provided by Martineau (1958). Formally, the model states that:

$$E_i = f(\text{social class})$$

where the evaluation or choice of alternative i (E_i) is the dependent variable. The structure of the model corresponds to Figure 19.8. Frequently, the independent variable (social class) is inferred from such variables as income, occupation, and geographical location. There is no single basic hypothesis concerning the relationship between social class and consumer behavior. Significant differences among social classes have been found in such areas as shopping, possession and use of products, and family interaction. The model deals with households rather than individuals, and it is static. The model deals mostly with behavior occurring in purchase, exposure, and consumption situations. As the model is static, it does not allow for interaction among consumers. Nevertheless, a major factor explaining the similarity in behavior within social classes is the personal communication among individuals belonging to the same social class.

26. Income Hypotheses Models

Aspects of income hypotheses models are discussed in Chapter 16, and a review of the different formulations is available in Ferber (1967). Basically, the model suggests:

$$\text{Consumption} = f(\text{income})$$

The dependent variable is total household spending, and it is seen as identical with purchases (for an exception, see Friedman 1957). Depending upon how the independent variable, income, is defined, various hypotheses concerning the relationship between income and consumption result (Chapter 16). The models are unidimensional and deal with total consumption. They explain behavior in purchase situations, and they deal with household behavior. The absolute and the relative income hypotheses are static or comparative static, whereas the permanent income hypothesis is dynamic to the extent that permanent income is a function of past income experiences and expectations with regard to future income. The basic model is illustrated in Figure 19.15.

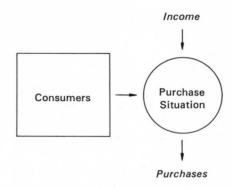

FIGURE 19.15.   *The structure of the basic income model.*

The models operate at a very high level of aggregation, and often the income and consumption variables studied do not have counterparts at the individual level. The model is especially used in studies of total consumption and saving.

The absolute and the permanent income hypotheses do not consider interaction among consumers, whereas it is a major assumption of the relative income hypothesis that the proportion of income which is spent depends upon the income of other households.

27. Demand Functions Models

Demand functions models were mentioned in Chapter 1, and extensive discussions can be found in Schultz (1938), Wold and Juren (1953), and Palda (1969). Recent applications of the model are presented by Banks (1961), Buzzel (1964), Palda (1965), and Bass (1969). Formally, the model says:

$$E_i = f(y, p, s, q, \ldots)$$

That is, evaluation or purchase of alternatives is studied as a function of income (y), prices (p), sales effort (s), product quality (q), and other variables. In simple versions all but one variable are held constant and, for example, the relationship between price and quantity can thus be studied. The underlying assumption states that the amount of a product which will be demanded depends upon the independent marketing variables. The model may be applied to individual as well as household levels; and normally it is static or comparative static, although some attempts with dynamic models have been made in studies of the carryover effect of advertising (Zeilske 1959, Williams 1963, and Tull 1965).

The model is aggregated, and frequently no variables at the individual level correspond to the independent variables (such as distribution or amount of advertising). It does not allow for interaction among consumers, and it deals with behavior in purchase situations only. It can be illustrated like the income models in Figure 19.15. Some successful results have been obtained at product level. At brand level it has often been difficult to quantify the postulated relationships.

28. Cultural Anthropological Models

An excellent discussion of these models is available in Engel et al. (1968). They were briefly touched upon in Chapter 16. Basically, the model states:

$$E_i = f(\text{cultural variables})$$

where the basic hypothesis says that the way an individual evaluates and chooses alternatives is dependent upon cultural variables such as economic values, religion, orientation towards achievement, and the like. In principle all kinds of responses can enter as dependent variables; however, exposure, purchase, and consumption behavior are studied most frequently.

The model is static, and it can be applied to individuals as well as to households. The model is highly aggregated, and many of the independent variables do not have counterparts at the individual level. Interaction among consumers is not explicitly accounted for, but the independent cultural values are presumed to be established through personal communication. The model can be illustrated as in Figure 19.7, and it is primarily applicable when societies with markedly different cultures are compared or when clearly different subcultures can be identified. Application of the model has frequently pointed at marked differences in consumer behavior among individuals belonging to different cultures.

Chapter 20

FUTURE PROBLEMS IN STUDIES OF CONSUMER BEHAVIOR

Some major problems facing students of consumer behavior can be summarized in a discussion of how to formalize an aggregated model like that proposed in Chapter 18. The model rests upon specifications of consumer choice situations. As discussed here, it represents a general framework for more specific models; such models will take on different forms depending upon the products studied.

Aggregated market models call for a considerable amount of information about each choice situation: the nature of the aroused conflict, the alternatives to be considered, the salient values, and the relationship of these values to the alternatives. Furthermore, some mechanism is required to explain which consumers will enter what situations. The use of this information raises three questions: First, how can the data-handling problems be solved? Second, what variables must be quantified and how? Third, how can the functional relationships of the model be specified?

1. *Data-Handling Problems*

The data-handling capabilities of large-scale computers suggest solutions to the problems associated with the complexity of the model. Simulation is an attractive method. The flexibility of this technique offers great advantages when models are in a stage of development such that many relationships are still to be specified. Furthermore, the present model can be broken down into a number of sub-models which can be handled separately. The overall model is thus well suited to formulation within the framework of a simulation model.

Several previous attempts with simulation suggest that the approach may prove applicable to large-scale market systems. Newell et al. (1958) and Reitman et al. (1964) have proposed computer-oriented information-processing models of thinking and problem solving. Ashby (1962) and Dennett (1968) discuss simulation of the brain. Hovland (1960), Abelson and Caroll (1965), and Colby (1967) have discussed simulation of individual belief systems, and Simon and Barenfeld (1969) deal with simulation of perceptual attention processes. Various aspects of simulation of consumer behavior are discussed by Wells (1963) and Alderson and Shapiro (1963), and Amstutz (1969) reviews the present standing of integrated marketing information systems. Finally, large-scale simulations of population systems are presented by Orcutt et al. (1961) and by Pool and Abelson (1961).

1. Situational Sub-Models

The core of a simulation model of a large-scale market system will be a number of sub-models, each handling a specific situation. For each sub-model, the independent variables will be the latent values and perceptions of the consumers entering into the situation and the stimulation acting upon them. The dependent variables will be the latent values and beliefs of the consumers leaving the situation (including more or less firm commitments to enter into future situations), and the behavior in the situation (purchases, consumption). The situational sub-models will follow a pattern like that discussed in Chapters 8–13.

2. Assigning Consumers to Situations

The single situational models should be connected at the beginning of each period by a mechanism which assigns each consumer to a particular situation. The independent variables for this mechanism would be the values, beliefs, and intentions of the consumers at the beginning of the period, together with the aspects characterizing the different situations in the particular period. These variables will be explained further on. In order to enter into a choice situation, the consumer must be present in the physical environment that specifies the situation, and aspects of the situation must be able to arouse conflict in him. Where the consumer "will go" and the conflict he will experience depend upon how his values, his beliefs, and particularly his intentions at the beginning of the period interact with the nature of the situation. An example will clarify this. A consumer may intend to acquire more information about a particular product as soon as it is available, but if no such information is made available in the period, he cannot enter into a situation where the information can be acquired. In contrast, the consumer may have no intention of attending to a particular advertisement, but the message may be forced upon him in such a way that sufficient conflict is aroused.

In addition to situational sub-models and the mechanism assigning consumers to situations, a complete market model will include two more features, a way to specify the aspects of the situations and a record of each single consumer.

3. Specifications of Situational Aspects

It is possible to let the situational aspects be determined externally for each single period. In that case, the stimuli acting upon the consumers must be specified and fed into the model. As it is often the effects of environmental variations which are to be studied, such an approach may be acceptable.[1] However, many situational aspects do not change from period to period, and others change in a way determined by the system; therefore, external specification of situational aspects may result in unnecessarily large inputs to the model in each period. Instead, situational aspects that do not change can be introduced as constants, and situational aspects that are changed by the system can be built into the model so that adjustments are made automatically. Examples of features that can be dealt with this way are the consumers' stocks of goods which change through consumption, durable products which deteriorate over time, the amount of products available in stores which decreases with purchases, and the consumers' liquid assets which change with expenditures.

The mechanisms governing these automatic changes may be more or less complex and, in early versions of the model, it may be preferable not to incorporate them, but ultimately models of markets will be improved by their inclusion.

4. The Consumer's Record

The record of each single consumer in the sample universe for which behavior is simulated must, of course, include the relevant latent values, beliefs, and intentions of the consumer. Several of the mechanisms just mentioned can be dealt with through more or less complete records of the consumer's past history. In its most extensive forms, such a record could

---

[1] When the model is extended to deal with complete markets (see Chapter 1), some or all of these variables may be generated by the system.

follow an outline such as scheduled in Table 17.1, but the stored information can also be less extensive. For example, a record of the consumer's liquid assets and available durable and nondurable products could be kept. Similarly, aspects of the consumer's past behavior of importance for the situations the consumer will enter later can be stored. These factors may include reading habits, television viewing habits, and shopping habits (to the extent that they are not determined by the model). The more extensive the records which are kept, the greater the information that can be generated by the system. With only a minimum of the consumer's past history recorded, it is possible to generate only the total behavior of the system from period to period. With information about the past history of each single consumer, the type of decision processes he applies can be reproduced, and the different decision patterns can be studied.

This review suggests that it is feasible to formalize such a model in terms of a simulation model. Only one additional problem should be mentioned. It has been assumed that each consumer makes only one choice in each period. Although this assumption is not strictly necessary, it simplifies the model considerably. However, it also introduces a problem. A consumer may go directly from one choice process to the next. If he can make only one choice in each period, periods will have to be extremely short. Furthermore, single choices will not generate very many changes in such consumer (household) variables as those suggested in Table 17.1.

Formally, a solution to the problem is simple, as it is possible to apply the model to a large number of consecutive periods. If this is done, however, many consumers will pass through single periods without making any choices, and it may be necessary to have the models generate outputs for a number of subsequent periods taken together, rather than for each single period.

2. *The Measurement of Variables*

There have been several reviews of the different problems of measurement associated with studies of consumer behavior. Stevens (1959) and Coombs (1960) discuss the relationship between the type of measurement and the kind of summary statistics that can be applied. Lucas and Britt (1963) and Robinson et al. (1968) all discuss methods applicable to studies of consumers' responses to mass communication. Torgerson (1958) provides an excellent review of problems related to scale construction, and Freeman (1962) discusses different approaches to the measurement of values and beliefs. Finally, Perloff (1968) reviews methods applied in studies of consumer behavior.

Many of the variables crucial for the models described in these pages can be quantified by means of existing techniques, but others suggest a need for future methodological developments.

Measurement problems relate to the consumer and to the attributes of the choice situations. In looking at the consumer, the researcher is concerned with his values, his perception of alternatives, his intentions and decision-process behavior, and with variables describing his income, available durables, and similar factors. In the following pages, methods are suggested which can be used to measure these variables.

1. Consumer Alternatives, Values, and Perceptions

It has been suggested (Chapter 16) that measurements of brand awareness may predict which alternatives are likely to become salient. Discussions of such measurements and their relationships to consumer responses can be found in Lucas and Britt (1963).

A major problem concerns the identification of the relevant consumer values (Chapters 11 and 16). Future developments of factor analysis, multidimensional analysis of similarity and preference judgments, latent structure, and cluster analysis may prove useful.

After the relevant values are identified, it is necessary to quantify them. Traditional scaling methods are available for this quantification (Thurstone 1928, and 1931b, Likert 1967, and Guttman 1944), and other applicable scales may be derived from the semantic differential (Osgood et al. 1957 and Brinton 1961). A large number of techniques can be used for indirect assessment of values (for a review see Campbell 1950). Several multivariate approaches indirectly provide estimates that reflect the differences in importance of the values (Green and Carmone 1971).

Other problems relate to the assimilation and contrast effects discussed previously (Chapter 6). These effects are likely to show up in connection with more involving values and may make it difficult to quantify even the relative importance of such values. Although the use of subjects' own scales as suggested by Sherif et al. (1965) may overcome some of the problems, the values measured in this way are difficult to aggregate.

After the possible alternatives and values are identified, the measurement of the perception of alternatives relative to the values is a less complex problem. Techniques used in image analysis are applicable, and perceptual mapping based upon similarities judgments may prove useful.

2. Consumer Intentions

The model outlined in Chapter 18 requires that, at the beginning of each period, the consumers be described in terms of probabilities which reflect how likely they are to enter into particular choice situations (Chapter 14). To quantify these propensities, it is necessary to study intentions, ongoing decision processes, and commitments, and also motivational sets.[2]

Studies of purchase plans and intentions were discussed in Chapter 14, but longitudinal studies of decision processes may also be helpful. Methodological problems of such studies are discussed by Johnsen (1957), and findings from a single study were reported by Pratt (1965b). By observing the different phases in decision processes and the order in which they occur the researcher can learn how to modify the probability that a consumer will enter into a particular situation. For example, Montgomery and Armstrong (1968) show how the probability of entering into subsequent situations is related to what previous steps have been completed.

3. Other Consumer Variables

Other consumer variables are stocks of durable and nondurable products, the age of durable products, liquid assets, income, fixed commitments, and the like (see Chapter 16). They are commonly dealt with in marketing research, and the problems related to their measurements are discussed in most textbooks (see for example Crisp 1963 or Green & Tull 1966). They are not always easy to quantify; but the problems of measurement are common to all marketing research and will not be dealt with here.

4. Measuring Situational Variables

The situational variables to be quantified are those of importance for the definition of situations, those which influence the consumer, and those which reflect the choice processes aroused in the particular situations.

The situations that occur can be studied through longitudinal research. The characteristics of these situations were discussed in Chapter 3; because nominal classification is sufficient, their measurement is not too complex a job. Rather the problem is what and how many situations to define, an issue dealt with in Chapters 3 and 18.

Among the situational aspects which act upon the consumer, the primary, secondary, tertiary, and personal communications are particularly important. This communication must be classified relative to the particular situations. It is not enough to know the total amount of information available in a certain time period; one must also know when and how the consumers come into situations where they can be exposed to this information. That is, the total information must be specified in terms of aspects of particular situations. In this way the effects of marketing communication can be dealt with in terms of: (1) what information will become available, (2)

---

[2] As previously indicated, the situations into which the consumer actually enters also depend upon the situational variables. Here the concern is only with the intentions that interact with the situational aspects.

of this information, what the consumer will respond to (i.e., what causes exposure), and (3) how the consumer internalizes the information to which he is exposed.

Of these three important variables, the problem of availability is the one for which traditional marketing research can offer most help. It has been studied within media research and in studies of personal communication, where circulation and similar data quantify the amount of information and where content analysis may attempt to quantify the meaning of the information. However, most commonly it is studied with no specification of the particular situations in which the information becomes available so that the techniques used must be modified. Only in connection with purchase situations has the study of specific situations been attempted. Here the distribution and availability of products and brands have been of concern to marketers.

Studies of what information consumers will perceive raise two problems: what stimuli will the consumer attend to, and when will he attend to it? A measure of the qualitative variations in attention must be applied, which makes measurement complex. Nevertheless, studies in several areas suggest approaches which may be useful. For example, measurements of attention value and exposure to advertisement may be developed into useful techniques.

Whether the consumer will attend to the stimuli does not depend only upon the stimulus itself and the nature of the choice process. The particular stimulus must be seen in relation to other aspects of the environment. For example, the availability of the product in the store is not the only important aspect of distribution. Qualitative aspects of the availability should also be considered, that is, whether the product is located in the rear or the front of the store, whether it is located on a top or a bottom shelf, and so on. Similarly, the context of the advertisements influences the way the consumers react to them.

How the consumer internalizes information was discussed in Chapter 9. The process relates to the situation's ability to arouse conflict, which in turn can be studied in terms of variables such as the novelty, surprise, complexity, and change in the situation.

5. Studying the Choice Process

Studies of the choice process behavior cannot be limited to the responses the consumers choose. Choice process behavior must be dealt with directly because only then is it possible to predict the responses. In Chapter 11 the use of the experimental approach was discussed. Within the framework of the experiment, the situation can be specified and manipulated, which gives flexibility to studies of particular situations. The use of experiments, however, does not do away with the problems of measurement. In the experimental setting, as well as in a naturalistic setting, measurements must be obtained. In Chapters 12 and 13 several verbal responses were applied which reveal aspects of choice process behavior. Observational procedures may also prove useful, and in Chapter 15 several attempts with such approaches were reviewed.

In this connection a number of psychophysiological measures, which are gradually becoming accepted within marketing research, may also be applicable. In Chapter 4 the use of measurements of eye movements (Edfelt 1960), changes in heart rate (Bockhout 1966), galvanic skin responses (Montagu and Coles 1966), measurement of pupil sizes (Hess 1965), and brain waves (Krugman 1971) were discussed. Future applications of these techniques may improve our understanding of consumer choice behavior.

A solution of all the measurement problems which accompany attempts to build aggregated models of markets has not been attempted. It has been shown, however, that many of these problems resemble those in other areas of marketing research and that some existing measurements may be improved for use in studies of consumer choice behavior.

3. *Future Exploration of Relationships Among Consumer Variables*

Knowledge about consumer behavior is derived from both experimental and survey research. Future studies will also have to rely upon these techniques. However, it has been a major problem that their findings frequently have conflicted. Some such differences in studies of mass communication have been reviewed by Hovland (1959), who points out that this controversy is a result of the different nature of the two approaches. The discrepancy disappears when the limitations of the approaches are considered. However, as this comparison is not frequently made and as the survey study deals with behavior in a naturalistic setting, the discrepancies have been taken to indicate that consumer behavior cannot be studied experimentally. This is a dangerous position because, if adhered to strictly, it implies that important problems in consumer behavior simply cannot be studied. It has repeatedly been pointed out that many aspects of consumer behavior cannot be dealt with in a naturalistic setting, either because the relevant variables cannot be controlled or because costs would be prohibitive.

On the other hand, when experimental findings are utilized, their severe limitations should be recognized. They can improve our understanding of consumer behavior only if this is kept in mind. The nature of the experimental response can be understood if it is realized that in the experiment the consumer is faced with a conflict, just as he is in a real situation. His reactions, however, will predict his behavior in a naturalistic setting only if the experimental conflict resembles the conflict aroused in the naturalistic setting. Many inconsistencies found when findings derived in different types of surveys and experiments are compared can be explained by the lack of such similarity. The difference in price elasticities that resulted when Baker and Berry (1953) used cross-sectional data, time series data, controlled experimentation, and direct questioning exemplifies this. The different sets of data are derived under completely different conditions, and simple conclusions based upon these cannot be expected to resemble each other to any significant extent. Similarly, the inconsistencies reported by Smith and Marke (1958), Bengston and Brenner (1964), and Stout (1969) can be explained in the same way.

The limitations discussed here imply that behavior in the marketplace can rarely be predicted from behavior in an experimental setting. Only to the extent that hypotheses derived from a model can be confirmed in an experiment is there reason to believe that the model will also apply to invididual behavior under conditions where the researcher has no control over the environment. As Homans (1961) puts it: "The laws of human behavior are not repealed when a man leaves the field and enters the laboratory. Naturally, the same laws working in different circumstances lead to different results: but not, once the circumstances are taken into account, to inconsistent results" (p. 15).

Another problem is that of the representativeness of studies, a problem not only with experiments but also relevant to many survey studies of consumer behavior as well. Ideally, all aspects of consumer behavior should be studied using sufficiently large representative samples of the total population. For several reasons, studies deviate in many ways from this ideal. Only selected products are studied, and for these only partial problems are dealt with. Moreover, basic research in consumer behavior has often relied upon a sampling principle which can be characterized as "the principle of the available nails." This is true of most experimental studies with students, faculty wives, and other selected respondents, and it is also true of many survey studies in local supermarkets, "representative" towns, and so on. These studies are valuable to the extent that they confirm properly derived hypotheses, and when several such studies agree with each other the underlying model gains support. Market models, however, do not require only confirmation of hypotheses. If they are to be used as decision-making tools they require representative data with which the relationships can be filled. It is one of the most important tasks for future research in consumer behavior to provide more and better data on which models can be built, a task which requires not only a redirection of research efforts, but also a complete restructuring of the funding of research in consumer behavior.

4. *Management-Oriented Information Systems*

Most companies dealing with consumer products invest considerable sums in market information. Often management is not aware of the amount of money involved because the information is obtained and handled in many different ways. Some data come from accounting departments, sales statistics, inventory management systems, and production departments. Others are obtained through market-research departments, service departments, from the sales force, and from the advertising departments and advertising agencies. Still other information is obtained through market-research companies and consulting firms. However, few companies control whether they get the right information in the right quantities, partly because many different individuals make independent decisions, and partly because few companies have explicitly formulated models of their markets which can guide them in selecting the appropriate information. Models like those discussed in the preceding pages may fill this gap.

With large-scale computers available, the problems associated with handling large amounts of information have become manageable. However, to secure efficient utilization of this data-handling capability, questions must be answered as to what data to obtain, how to manipulate them, and what output to produce to what levels of the organization. To answer these questions it is necessary to know who makes what decisions and what information they need; choices among alternative data collection methods must be made; and the necessary computations must be decided upon and programmed. When these problems are approached, more or less complex management information systems emerge (Amstutz 1969). It is not the purpose here to discuss all the organizational problems involved in the building of such systems, but only to point to the role of market models in this context.

Not only does the choice of what computations to make follow directly from the market model one decides upon, but also problems relating to the system's input and output may be approached from a market model. As discussed above, the market model specifies what information is needed; the decision-makers' information needs must be analyzed in relation to the independent variables of the system. Eventually in building the model the decision-making pattern of the organization must be considered. Who makes what decisions must be studied, and the frequency and the implications of these decisions must be analyzed.

The coordination of the model and the decision-making pattern may be approached in two ways. It is possible to outline the model from studies of the market and then to ask whether the model can provide the information required by the organization, or whether the organization would be improved if it were altered to handle the decision problems suggested by the model. If neither of these questions can be answered in the affirmative, the next step must be to go back and revise the model.

Alternatively, the model-building may start from analyses of the decision-making pattern of the organization, and this approach may result in meaningful models of the market. But regardless of the approach, model building implies a process of adjustment between the organization and its way of looking at its market, the latter being represented by the model.

To build information systems based upon market models may be said to be extremely complex. However, the fact remains that decisions are made and will be made, and models of markets only make explicit the assumptions upon which these decisions are made. If, in the process of formalizing the model, weaknesses in the present decision-making pattern are discovered, this result only makes the model and the work with it more valuable to the organization.

Appendixes

Appendix I

EXPERIMENTAL MATERIAL: HAIRDRYER CHOICE

The following material was used in the first hairdryer experiment (with-wife, rating-before-choice condition) in the fall of 1967. The second hairdryer choice, the first and second menu choices, the restaurant choice, the book choice, and the travel choice experiments were structured in a similar manner.

Role-Play Experiment M1.   November, 1967

The Whittemore School of Business and Economics

First we would like to have your opinion on various subjects related to purchases of minor durable items such as electric-shavers, wrist-watches, lighters, etc. Now, imagine that you were about to buy such an item. How important would you consider the following factors to be? You may give your answer by indicating on the printed scales the degree to which you regard the factors' importance.

QUESTION	ANSWER IN THIS COLUMN BY CHECKING SCALE
How important do you consider DESIGN?	———100 The single most important factor
	———90
	———80
	———70
	———60
	———50

————40
————30
————20
————10
————0 Not important at all

How important do you   ————100 The single most important factor
consider PRICE?   ————90
                              ————80
                              ————70
                              ————60
                              ————50
                              ————40
                              ————30
                              ————20
                              ————10
                              ————0 Not important at all

QUESTION   ANSWER IN THIS COLUMN BY CHECKING SCALE

How important do you   ————100 The single most important factor
consider DURABILITY?   ————90
(i.e. how long the item is   ————80
expected to last)   ————70
                              ————60
                              ————50
                              ————40
                              ————30
                              ————20
                              ————10
                              ————0 Not important at all

How important do you   ————100 The single most important factor
consider EFFICIENCY?   ————90
(i.e. accuracy of watch,   ————80
reliability of lighter, quality ————70
of shaving, etc.)   ————60
                              ————50
                              ————40
                              ————30
                              ————20
                              ————10
                              ————0   Not important at all

| When buying such a
minor durable item, how
do you consider the
shopping involved? | ——100
——90
——80
——70
——60
——50
——40
——30
——20
——10
——0 | Great fun, enjoy that kind of shopping
very much

Very boring, should be limited as
much as possible |

QUESTION	ANSWER	IN THIS COLUMN BY CHECKING SCALE
If you were about to buy such a minor durable item as a gift, and you knew about some features which the gift-receiver considered of some importance, how much shopping would you—if necessary—engage in?	——100 ——90 ——80 ——70 ——60 ——50 ——40 ——20 ——10 ——0	Continue shopping until all features were found Visit up to 5 stores in order to find item with preferred features Not care about the information at all

| Imagine that a close friend
of yours runs a small
grocery store. How obliged
would you feel to shop
there instead of in a large
near-by supermarket? | ——100
——90
——80
——70
——60
——50
——40
——30
——20
——10
——0 | Would feel obliged to do all my
grocery shopping there

Would feel obliged to do some shop-
ping there now and then

Would not feel obliged at all to shop
there |

Situational Description

INSTRUCTION: Read the following description carefully. Try to imagine what kind of person the described Heinrich Blomberg is, and when you have finished reading try to put yourself in his place. It is important that you pay attention to the kinds of thoughts Herr Blomberg has concerning the problem in question, and when you are answering the following questions, try as hard as possible to put yourself in his situation.

Role-description

A. BACKGROUND

Heinrich Blomberg is a chemical engineer. He is 33 years old and lives in Rotenburg, a little town between Hamburg and Bremen in the northern part of West Germany. In 1948 his family came from Magdeburg in East Germany and in 1949 his father, who is a school teacher, got a job at a gymnasium (high school) in the northern part of Hamburg. At that time Heinrich was 15 years old and in 1953 he joined the School of Engineering at the University of Hamburg. After having received his degree in 1959, he got a job at an average sized concrete factory in Rotenburg. At that time he had a second hand Volkswagen and since he still lived with his family in Hamburg, he commuted the 65 kilometers (app. 40 miles) to and from Rotenburg.

In 1961, however, he got married and soon after he bought a little house in the southern part of Rotenburg. His wife Lillian was 23 at the time of their marriage. They had met each other at the University in Hamburg, where Lillian had had a job as a secretary for one of his professors. They had known each other for three years when they married, and originally they had planned to get married as soon as Heinrich had finished his education. However, it was very difficult to get an apartment and consequently the marriage was postponed until they had enough money to buy the house in Rotenburg.

The first years of their marriage were a little difficult since the house was more expensive than they could really afford and Lillian had to get a job as a secretary at the town hall in Rotenburg. However, things soon became better. Heinrich was promoted and he now is the chief engineer at the factory and is in charge of one of the more important production departments. In 1964 their child was born, and Peter, who is now 3 years old, takes up a considerable part of Lillian's time.

B. SITUATIONAL DESCRIPTION

Today it is July 19th and the day before their sixth year wedding anniversary. Although they had not celebrated their previous wedding anniversaries, Heinrich decided to buy Lillian a gift this year. She had occasionally mentioned that she would make good use of a hairdryer and after thinking it over, Heinrich decided that this would be the thing to buy. On his way home, he therefore stopped in Burgstrasse at the local appliance dealer to purchase the dryer. Mr. Wintergarten who owns the appliance store, is there and since Heinrich knows Mr. Wintergarten very well (the

Wintergartens live out near the Blombergs), he asks for his advice. They soon narrow the choice to two models:

VARIG, which is a very durable model costing DM 45 (app. $11) and SCHNELL, which is known to be very efficient and which sells at DM 65 (app. $16).

Mr. Wintergarten points out that he has sold VARIG hairdryers for more than five years and he has only had repair work on very few items, which presumably had been treated very badly. He also mentions that the engine, the air-channel and the helmet are known to be very durable, and that it is likely that Mrs. Blomberg will be able to use this model for a good many years. In reply to Mr. Blomberg's question, however, he admits that to the best of his knowledge the drying capacity could be better. Especially with very heavy hair, it does take quite a while to dry the hair completely. Although Mrs. Blomberg does not have especially heavy hair this concerns Mr. Blomberg a little since a few days ago his wife mentioned that a friend of hers that had just purchased a hairdryer commented about the inconvenience associated with "just sitting there waiting for her hair to dry."

Mr. Wintergarten describes the other model—SCHNELL—as somewhat less durable than the VARIG, but with a better drying capacity. He admits that he recently has had some incidents where the engine burned out only after a few years of regular use. He has also had repair work on quite a few of these dryers since he took up the line a few years ago, but on the other hand, he points out that the model is very popular with many women since the drying capacity is so good.

At this time, Mr. Wintergarten is called to the telephone and Mr. Blomberg considers which one of the two makes to buy.

Comments

Now that you have read the brief description of Heinrich Blomberg and his problem, try to place yourself in his situation. He is now considering the two alternatives. Try to imagine what he thinks about the problem. If necessary, take another look at the above description.

Role-Play-Experiment M2A   November, 1967

The Whittemore School of Business and Economics

Although there will be more information coming you should do this based upon your present perception of the problem. We will now ask you to evaluate a number of factors of importance for the problem.

Try and put yourself in the position of Heinrich Blomberg, how would he rate the importance of the following factors?

How important is the durability of the hairdryer ?		*How important is the amount of time required to dry the hair ?*		*How important is the price of the hairdryer ?*
——100	The very most	——100	The very most	——100 The very most
——90	important	——90	important	——90 important
——80	factor	——80	factor	——80 factor
——70		——70		——70
——60		——60		——60
——50		——50		——50
——40		——40		——40
——30		——30		——30
——20		——20		——20
——10		——10		——10
——0	Not important at all	——0	Not important at all	——0 Not important at all

Still on behalf of Heinrich Blomberg, how do you think he would answer the following questions?

How is the durability of VARIG as compared with the durability of SCHNELL?	——100	Very much more durable
	——90	
	——80	
	——70	
	——60	
	——50	
	——40	
	——30	
	——20	
	——10	
	——0	No difference

How much more efficient is SCHNELL as compared to VARIG when it comes to hair-drying?	——100	Very much more efficient
	——90	
	——80	
	——70	
	——60	
	——50	
	——40	
	——30	
	——20	
	——10	
	——0	No difference

How much higher does ——100 Very much higher
Heinrich Blomberg ——90
consider the price of ——80
SCHNELL to be as compared ——70
to the price of VARIG? ——60
——50
——40
——30
——20
——10
——0 No difference

Role-Play-Experiment M2B

The Whittemore School of Business and Economics

IMPORTANT : *Before turning this page answer the following question :*

If you were to make a decision now, which one of the two hairdryers would you choose?

VARIG ☐
SCHNELL ☐

Revised Situation

When thinking about the problem, it suddenly comes to the mind of Mr. Blomberg that it may be possible to find a third alternative at the STAR MARKET 18 kilometers (app. 11 miles) out of town on the main route to Bremen.

The STAR MARKET is a large department store which was opened two years ago, and Mr. Blomberg knows that they are carrying a wide line in household appliances, and it is very likely that they will have a model which would be preferable to VARIG and SCHNELL. But on the other hand it is late in the afternoon and it will take him at least an hour to go there and pick up another dryer, and further if they do not have a satisfactory model he will have to go back to town to get the hairdryer from Wintergarten and this would take him at least half an hour more.

Secondly, he wouldn't like to walk out of Wintergarten's store in order to go to the STAR MARKET, which he knows Wintergarten considers an important competitor. After all, Wintergarten is a rather close friend and he has been very helpful.

Now Wintergarten returns. After a few comments about VARIG and SCHNELL Wintergarten suggests that the STAR MARKET may have other models. Mr. Blomberg could go there and have a look. He does not know which makes they are carrying, but since they are doing quite a bit in household appliances he suggests that they may also have something different in hairdryers.

Comments

Again, try to imagine the situation. What would you think about the possibility of going to the STAR MARKET? Take a look at the text again if necessary.

Role-Play-Experiment M3A   November, 1967

The Whittemore School of Business and Economics

How would you, in the	——100	Be sure to find a better alternative
role of Heinrich Blomberg,	——90	
evaluate the likelihood of	——80	
finding a better alternative	——70	
at the STAR MARKET?	——60	
	——50	
	——40	
	——30	
	——20	
	——10	
	——0	Be sure not to find a better alternative

How would you, as	——100	Very boring and troublesome
Heinrich Blomberg,	——90	
evaluate the extra trip to	——80	
the STAR MARKET?	——70	
	——60	
	——50	
	——40	
	——30	
	——20	
	——10	
	——0	Not boring or troublesome at all

In the situation of	——100	Feel very much obliged
Heinrich Blomberg, to	——90	
what extent would you	——80	
find yourself obliged to buy	——70	
the hairdryer at	——60	
Wintergartens?	——50	
	——40	
	——30	

——20
——10
——0   Feel not at all obliged

Role-Play-Experiment M3B   November, 1967

The Whittemore School of Business and Economics

IMPORTANT: *Before turning this page answer the following question:*

Which of the following three alternatives would you prefer?
Go to the STAR MARKET   ☐
Choose VARIG   ☐
Choose SCHNELL   ☐

Now considering the above decisions, can you give a brief statement of all the factors that you feel have had impact on the decision. It is very important that you try to account for all the factors you have considered, so try to remember as much as possible.

  1. ....
  2. ....
  3. ....
  4. ....
  5. ....
  6. ....
  7. ....
  8. ....
  9. ....
 10. ....
 11. ....
    (USE THE BACK OF THE SHEET IF MORE SPACE IS NECESSARY)

Finally, we would like to have your personal opinion concerning various factors relating to buying decisions for minor durable items. As before, you can answer these questions by marking the adjoining scales.

How important do you   ——100   The single most important factor
consider the directions for   ——90
use usually on the package?   ——80
                              ——70
                              ——60
                              ——50
                              ——40
                              ——30
                              ——20
                              ——10
                              ——0   Not important at all

How important do you   ——100   The single most important factor
consider the REPUTATION of ——90
THE MANUFACTURER?   ——80
                            ——70
                            ——60
                            ——50
                            ——40
                            ——30
                            ——20
                            ——10
                            ——0   Not important at all

How important do you   ——100   The single most important factor
consider the DURABILITY   ——90
of such product?   ——80
                            ——70
                            ——60
                            ——50
                            ——40
                            ——30
                            ——20
                            ——10
                            ——0   Not important at all

How important do you   ——100   The single most important factor
consider the DESIGN of   ——90
such products?   ——80
                            ——70
                            ——60
                            ——50
                            ——40
                            ——30
                            ——20
                            ——10
                            ——0   Not important at all

How important do you   ——100   The single most important factor
consider availability of   ——90
REPAIR SERVICE   ——80
                            ——70
                            ——60
                            ——50
                            ——40
                            ——30
                            ——20
                            ——10
                            ——0   Not important at all

How important do you ——100 The single most important factor
consider PRICE? ——90
——80
——70
——60
——50
——40
——30
——20
——10
——0 Not important at all

Now having participated in this role-playing experiment, we would like to have your opinion on various aspects concerning this kind of experimentation. Will you therefore, on the last page indicate for each of the statements given whether you agree, disagree or feel indifferent about it.

IMPORTANT: You are perfectly free to use the "do not know" column if you feel indifferent concerning the statement. You should only mark X in the "agree" or "disagree" columns if you really feel that you are either agreeing or disagreeing. Actually, "do not know" is just as valuable an answer to us as is agreement or disagreement.

Also, do not hesitate to give your real opinion. For one thing, no one can identify your answers since they are turned in anonymously. Secondly, what we really are interested in is your opinion.

	Agree	*Disagree*	*Do not know*
Role-play experiments are boring	....	....	....
Role-play experiments are valuable	....	....	....
Role-play experiments are interesting	....	....	....
Role-play experiments may reveal important aspects of consumer behavior	....	....	....
The story involved in the experiment was convincing	....	....	....
The questionnaires involved in this kind of testing are measuring reliable attitudes	....	....	....
Role-play experiments are fun	....	....	....
Role-play experiments are hardly worth the effort	....	....	....
It is impossible in this kind of experiment to play the role of another individual	....	....	....

	Agree	Disagree	Do not know
One will always bring some of one's own values into experiments of this kind	....	....	....
The questionnaires in this kind of experiment are not measuring anything of importance	....	....	....
This kind of experiment can not reveal anything about decision making	....	....	....
This kind of experimentation is important for the advancement of knowledge	....	....	....
Role-playing is just as good and just as bad as other kinds of behavioral analysis	....	....	....
Given a brief background concerning an individual, it is always possible to some extent to put oneself in his situation	....	....	....
It is doubtful whether the participants in role-play experiments take the task seriously	....	....	....
The description of Heinrich Blomberg is sufficiently detailed	....	....	....
The evaluation of the experiment (the questions on this and the following page) is more fun than the experiment itself	....	....	....
When participating in scientific experiments one should always try to take the task seriously	....	....	....
Making decisions on behalf of individuals which one only knows from a brief description is mere guessing	....	....	....
In experiments of this kind, one is more concerned with what those making the experiment expect one to answer than with playing the role	....	....	....
Although this kind of experimentation may have some value it is doubtful whether the results are reliable	....	....	....

	Agree	Disagree	Do not know
Giving answers in form of scales is a very precise way of stating one's opinion	....	....	....
The problem Heinrich Blomberg faces is a very typical consumer decision problem	....	....	....
In real-life situations many more factors occur than those described in the "role-description"	....	....	....
It is interesting to be faced with the same questions in different contexts	....	....	....
If anybody thinks that they will get anything from this kind of experiment, they better revise their thinking	....	....	....
Better understanding of what is happening in connection with buying decisions can be studied in role-play experiments	....	....	....
Most participants in this kind of experiment do not seriously try to play the prescribed role	....	....	....
The presence of the experimenter in the experimental situation disturbs the role playing	....	....	....
It shall be interesting to see the results of the experiment	....	....	....
I would like to attend a session where the background for this kind of experimentation is explained	....	....	....
Role-play experiments are not too interesting, but one ought to do one's best when participating	....	....	....
Role-play experiments are a waste of time	....	....	....
Role-play experiments are not uninteresting, but it is a little doubtful what kind of information they will give	....	....	....

Appendix II

EXPERIMENTAL MATERIAL: CONFLICT CHOICE SITUATIONS

University of New Hampshire
Evaluation of Conflict Situation
Code D

Situational Description

Mr. Johnson has decided to buy a color TV and after some exploration he has narrowed the choice down to either an R.C.A. model ($595) or an imported brand which can be obtained at $395. Mr. Johnson has looked into a good deal of information and he judges that chances are 7 in 10 that the imported brand will perform just as well or better than the R.C.A. model. (Do not make a choice now since you will learn more about the situation later.)

Look at the clock in the front of the room and write down the accurate time.

.... minutes   .... seconds

Feelings about situation:

How did you feel when you read the material (about the situation) just presented?

1. Entertained (check one)
☐ not at all entertained
☐ slightly entertained
☐ moderately entertained
☐ entertained
☐ quite entertained

2. Disgusted (check one)
☐ not at all disgusted
☐ slightly disgusted
☐ moderately disgusted
☐ disgusted
☐ extremely disgusted

3. Unreality (check one)
☐ strong feelings of unreality
☐ feelings of unreality
☐ moderate feelings of
    unreality
☐ slight feelings of unreality
☐ no feelings of unreality at all

4. Anxious (check one)
☐ not at all anxious
☐ slightly anxious
☐ moderately anxious

☐ anxious
☐ extremely anxious

5. Dreaming (check one)
☐ very similar to feelings I have
    when I am dreaming
☐ similar to feelings I have
    when I am dreaming
☐ moderately similar to feelings
    I have when I am dreaming
☐ slightly similar to feelings I
    have when I am dreaming
☐ not at all similar to feelings I
    have when I am dreaming

6. Bored (check one)
☐ extremely bored

☐ bored

☐ moderately bored

☐ slightly bored

☐ not at all bored

7. Uneasy (check one)
☐ not at all uneasy
☐ slightly uneasy
☐ moderately uneasy
☐ quite uneasy
☐ extremely uneasy

8. Confused (check one)
☐ not at all confused
☐ slightly confused
☐ moderately confused
☐ quite confused
☐ extremely confused

9. Others' thoughts
☐ strong desire to know what others thought
☐ desire to know what others thought
☐ moderate desire to know what others thought
☐ slight desire to know what others thought
☐ no desire to know what others thought at all

10. Looking at the two possibilities described in the situational description, all things considered, how attractive would you say they are to you?

—— 5 the imported brand is extremely
—— more attractive
——
——
—— 0 equally attractive
——
——
——
—— 5 the R.C.A. is extremely more
attractive

11. Considering the situation, how serious would you say that it would be to make a wrong decision?

—— 10 disastrous
——
——
——
——
—— 5
——
——
——
——
—— 0 not serious at all

12. When faced with a problem of this kind, how carefully would you think that most people would consider the alternatives?

—— 10 would engage in
—— extremely careful
—— deliberation and
—— evaluation
——
—— 5
——
——
——
—— 0 would not engage
in deliberation at
all

13. A situation like the one you just read can be described more or less detailed and more or less information can be made available. If you had a choice, how would you have liked the description to be? (Check One Box)

☐ like it was
☐ a little more detailed (approx. twice as long)
☐ somewhat more detailed (approx. half a page)
☐ more detailed (approx. one page)
☐ much more detailed (approx. two pages)
☐ extremely more detailed (approx. four pages)

14. Considering the problem, how uncertain would you think that most people would be about what to do? (Indicate your answer on the scale.)

    —— 10   extremely uncertain

    ——

    ——

    ——

    ——

    —— 5

    ——

    ——

    ——

    —— 0   not uncertain at all

15. Now think about the problem and imagine that you, in a similar situation, were about to make a final decision; which of the two alternatives would you choose?

☐ The R.C.A. model
☐ The imported brand

16. Now look at the clock again and write down the time:
……… minutes   ……… seconds

17. How did you study the situation?
☐ Read it once.
☐ Read it more than once

18. While answering the questions and making your choice did you look back at the description of the situation?
☐ Yes
☐ No

Situational Description L

A college senior seeking a doctorate in chemistry must choose between graduate work at university X, whose rigid standards result in only a fraction of the graduate students receiving the Ph.D. degree, and university Y which has much less prestige in chemistry but where almost every graduate student received the Ph.D. degree. He judges that the chances that he will succeed at university X are 6 out of 10.

Situational Description G

A man with a serious heart ailment must significantly curtail his customary way of life if he does not undergo a delicate medical operation which might completely cure him, or, on the other hand, might prove fatal. He judges that chances are 5 in 10 that the operation will be successful.

Situational Description S

Miss Arlberg is catching a cold for which she usually takes Anacin, which she has at home. However, she has just learned about a new brand, Delux, which a couple of friends have recommended. Her regular brand doesn't normally cure her cold but it does make her feel less uncomfortable. Delux, however, she has heard, might cure the cold. In the drug store where Miss Arlberg inspects the new brand, she judges that chances are 2 in 10 that the new brand can be expected to perform a little better than her regular one.

Situational Description R

A college junior has just decided to buy a car. After having gathered some information he has reduced the possible alternatives to the following two: from another student he can buy a little less than a two-year-old Ford Mustang (with a mileage of approx. 30,000) or at the same price he can buy a new Volkswagen. The Mustang is in good condition, but realizing that it is not a new car, it may cause major repair expenses within a not too distant future. He judges that chances are 8 in 10 that the Mustang will perform perfectly for a number of years.

Situational Description T

A research physicist, beginning a five-year appointment at a university, must choose between working on a series of short-term problems which admit easier solutions, but are of lesser importance, and working on a more important but also more difficult long-term problem with a risk of nothing to show for his five years of effort. He judges that the chances are 4 in 10 that the long-term project will prove successful.

Appendix III

BIBLIOGRAPHY

Aaker, D. A., and Jones, J. M., "Modelling Store Choice Behavior." *Journal of Marketing Research*, Vol. 8, No. 1, 1971, pp. 38–42.

Abelson, R. P., "Modes of Resolution of Belief Dilemmas." *Journal of Conflict Resolution*, Vol. 3, 1959, pp. 343–52.

Abelson, R. P., and Caroll, D., "Computer Simulation of Individual Belief Systems." *The American Behavioral Scientist*, Vol. 8, 1965, pp. 24–30.

Abelson, R. P., and Rosenberg, M. J., "Symbolic Psychologic: A Model for Attitudinal Cognition." *Behavioral Science*, Vol. 3, 1958, pp. 1–13.

Abrams, J., "A New Method for Testing Pricing Decision." *Journal of Marketing*, Vol. 28, 1964, pp. 6–9.

Achenbaum, A. A., "Knowledge is a Thing Called Measurement." In L. Adler, and I. Crespi (eds.): *Attitude Research at Sea*. Chicago: American Marketing Association, 1966.

Ackoff, R. L., *Scientific Method—Optimizing Applied Research Decisions*. New York: John Wiley and Sons, Inc., 1962.

Adam, D., *Les Reactions du Consommateur Devant le Prix*. Paris: Société d'Édition d'Enseignment Supérieur, 1958.

Adams, E. W., and Fagot, R., "A Model of Riskless Choice." *Behavioral Science*, Vol. 4, 1959, pp. 1–10.

Adams, J. K., "Laboratory Studies of Behavior Without Awareness." *Psychological Bulletin*, Vol. 46, 1957, pp. 383–405.

Advertising Research Foundation, *Tachistoscope Tests and Recall and Recognition Techniques in the Study of Memory*. New York: Advertising Research Foundation, 1957.

Advertising Research Foundation, *Are There Consumer Types?* New York: Advertising Research Foundation, 1964.

Agostini, J. M., "How to Estimate Unduplicated Audiences." *Journal of Advertising Research*, Vol. 1, No. 3, 1961, pp. 11–14.

Albaum, Gerald, "Exploring Interaction in a Marketing Situation." *Journal of Marketing Research*, Vol. 4, 1967, pp. 168–72.

Alderson, W., *Dynamic Marketing Behavior*. Homewood, Ill.: Richard D. Irwin, Inc., 1965.

Alderson, W., and Sessions, R. E., *Basic Research Report on Consumer Behavior*. Pennsylvania: Alderson and Sessions, 1957.

Alderson, W., and Sessions, R. E., "Report on a Study of Shopping Behavior and Methods for its Investigation." In R. E. Frank, A. E. Kuehn, and W. F. Massy (eds.): *Quantitative Techniques in Marketing Analysis*. Homewood, Ill.: Richard D. Irwin, Inc., 1962.

Alderson, W., and Shapiro, S. J., *Marketing and the Computer*. Englewood Cliffs, N.J.: Prentice-Hall, Inc., 1963.

Alexis, M., Haines, G. H., and Simon, L., "Consumer Information Processing: The Case of Women's Clothing." In R. L. King (ed.): *Marketing and the New Science of Planning*. Chicago: American Marketing Association, 1968.

Allison, R. I., and Uhl, K. P., "Influence of Beer Brand Identification on Taste." *Journal of Marketing Research*, Vol. 1, 1964, pp. 36–39.

Allison, H. E., Zwick, C. J., and Brinser, A., "Menu Data and Their Contribution to Food Consumption Studies." *Journal of Farm Economics*, Vol. 40, 1958, pp. 1–20.

Allport, F. H., *Theories of Perception and the Concept of Structure*, New York: John Wiley and Sons, Inc., 1955.

Allport, F. H., "Attitudes." In C. Murchison (ed.): *Handbook of Social Psychology*. Worchester, Mass.: Clark University Press, 1935.

Allport, G. W., Vernon, P. E., and Lindzey, G., *Study of Values*. Boston, Mass.: Houghton-Mifflin Company, 1960.

Alpert, L., and Gatty, R., "Product Positioning by Behavioral Life Styles." *Journal of Marketing*, Vol. 33, April, 1969, pp. 65–69.

Alpert, R., *Perceptual Determinants of Effect*. Middletown, Conn.: Wesleyan University, 1953.

Amstutz, A. E., "Management Oriented Marketing Systems: The Current Status." *Journal of Marketing Research*, Vol. 6, 1969, pp. 81–96.

Anastasi, A., *Fields of Applied Psychology*. New York: McGraw-Hill, 1964.

Andersen, E. B., *Den diskrete målings model af endelig orden*. Copenhagen: Copenhagen University, 1966.

Anderson, L. K., Taylor, J. R., and Holloway, R. J., "The Consumer and His Alternatives, an Experimental Approach." *Journal of Marketing Research*, 1966, pp. 62–67.

Anderson, L. R., and Fishbein, M., "Prediction of Attitudes from Number, Strength and Evaluative Aspects of Beliefs About the Attitude Object." *Journal of Personality and Social Psychology*, Vol. 3, 1965, pp. 437–83.

Anderson, N. H., "Averaging Versus Adding as a Stimulus Combination Rule in Impression Formation." *Journal of Experimental Psychology*, Vol. 70, 1965, pp. 394–400.

Anderson, N. H., "Likeableness Ratings of 555 Personality-Trait Words." *Journal of Personality and Social Psychology*, Vol. 9, 1968, pp. 272–79.

Andreasen, A. R., "Attitudes and Customer Behavior—A Decision Model." In L. Preston (ed.): *New Research in Marketing*. California: University of California at Berkeley, Institute for Business and Economic Research, 1965.

Andreasen, A. R., "Geographic Mobility and Market Segmentation." *Journal of Marketing Research*, Vol. 3, 1966, pp. 1–7.

Andreasen, A. R., "Leisure, Mobility and Life Style Patterns." In R. Moyer (ed.): *Changing Marketing Systems*. Chicago: American Marketing Association, 1967.

Andreasen, A. R., and Durkson, P. G., "Market Learning of New Residents." *Journal of Marketing Research*, Vol. 5, 1968, pp. 166–76.

Appel, V., "Attitude Change, Another Dubious Method for Measuring Advertising Effectiveness." In L. Adler and I. Crispi (eds.): *Attitude Research at Sea*. Chicago: American Marketing Association, 1966.

Arndt, J., "Word of Mouth Advertising." *Advertising Research Foundation*, New York, 1967a.

Arndt, J., "A Study of Word of Mouth Advertising." *Markedskommunikation*, Vol. 4, 1967b, No. 2, pp. 94–117.

Arndt, J., "New Product Diffusion: The Interplay of Innovativeness, Opinion Leadership, Learning, Perceived Risk and Product Characteristics." *Markedskommunikation*, 1968a, Vol. 5, No. 1, pp. 1–9.

Arndt, J., "Selective Processes in Word of Mouth." *Journal of Advertising Research*, Vol. 8, No. 3, 1968b, pp. 19–24.

Arndt, J., "Profiling Consumer Innovators." In J. Arndt (ed.): *Insights Into Consumer Behavior*. Boston: Allyn and Bacon, 1968c.

Aronson, E., and Carlsmith, J. M., "Effect of the Severity of Threat on the Devaluation of Forbidden Behavior." *Journal of Abnormal and Social Psychology*, Vol. 66, 1963, pp. 584–88.

Arrow, H. J., "Utilities, Attitudes, Choices." *Econometrica*, Vol. 26, 1958, pp. 1–23.

Ås, B., *Forbrukeren, idet moderne samfunn*. Oslo, Norway: Universiteds forlaget, 1966.

Ashby, W. R., "Simulation of a Brain." In H. Borko (ed.): *Computer Applications in the Behavioral Sciences*. Englewood Cliffs, N.J.: Prentice-Hall, Inc., 1962.

Assael, J., and Day, G. S., "Attitudes and Awareness as Predictors of Market Share." *Journal of Advertising Research*, Vol. 8, No. 4, 1968, pp. 3–12.

Atkins, A. L., Deaux, K. K., and Bieri, T., "Latitude of Acceptance and Attitude Change." *Journal of Personality and Social Psychology*, Vol. 6, 1967, pp. 47–56.

Atkinson, J. W., *An Introduction to Motivation*. Princeton, N.J.: Van Nostrand, 1964.

Atkinson, J. W., and Feather, N. T., *A Theory of Achievement Motivation*. New York: John Wiley and Sons, Inc., 1966.

Auster, D., "Attitude Change and Cognitive Dissonance." *Journal of Marketing Research*, 1965, pp. 401–5.

Axelrod, J. N., "Induced Moods and Attitudes Toward Products." *Journal of Advertising Research*, Vol. 3, No. 2, 1963, pp. 19–24.

Axelrod, J. N., "Attitude Measures that Predict Purchases." *Journal of Advertising Research*, Vol. 8, No. 1, 1968, pp. 3–18

Baker, D. J., and Berry, C. H., "The Price Elasticity of Demand for Fluid Skim Milk." *Journal of Farm Economics*, Vol. 35, 1953, pp. 124–29.

Bales, R. F., *Interaction Process Analysis: A Method for the Study of Small Groups*. Cambridge, Mass.: Addison-Wesley, 1950.

Bandeen, R. A., "Automobile Consumption 1940–1950." *Econometrica*, Vol. 25, 1957, pp. 239–48.

Banks, S., "The Relationship Between Preference and Purchase of Brands." *Journal of Marketing*, Vol. 15, 1950a, pp. 145–57.

Banks, S., "The Prediction of Dress Purchases for a Mail-Order House." *Journal of Business*, Vol. 23, 1950b, pp. 48–57.

Banks, S., "The Measurement of the Effect of a New Packaging Material Upon Preference and Sales." *Journal of Business*, Vol. 23, 1950c, pp. 71–80.

Banks, S., "Some Correlates of Coffee and Cleanser Brand Share." *Journal of Advertising Research*, Vol. 1, No. 4, 1961, pp. 22–28.

Banks, S., "Patterns of Daytime Viewing Behavior." In M. S. Moyer and R. E. Vosburgh (eds.): *Marketing for Tomorrow . . . Today*. Chicago: American Marketing Association, 1967.

Barach, J. A., "Self Confidence and Reactions to Television Commercials." In D. F. Cox: *Risk-Taking and Information-Handling in Consumer Behavior*. Cambridge, Mass.: Harvard Graduate School of Business, 1967.

Barach, J. A., "Advertising Effectiveness and Risk in Consumer Decision Processes." *Journal of Marketing Research*, Vol. 6, 1969a, pp. 314–20.

Barach, J. A., "Self-Confidence, Risk Handling, and Mass Communications." Paper presented at American Marketing Association's Fall Conference, Cincinnati, Ohio, August, 1969b.

Barker, R. G., "On the Nature of Environment." *Journal of Social Issues*, Vol. 19, 1963, pp. 17–38.

Barker, R. G., and Wright, H. F., *Midwest and Its Children*. New York: Harper and Row, 1955.

Barker, R. G., Wright, H. F., Barker, L. S., Schoggen, M. R., *Specimen Records of American and English Children*. Lawrence, Kansas: University of Kansas Press, 1961.

Basmann, R. L., "A Theory of Demand with Variable Consumer Preferences." *Econometrica*, Vol. 24, 1956, pp. 47–58.

Bass, B. M., "Social Behavior and the Orientation Inventory." *Psychological Bulletin*, Vol. 68, 1967, pp. 260–92.

Bass, F. M., "A Simultaneous Equation Regression Study of Advertising and Sales of Cigarettes." *Journal of Marketing Research*, Vol. 6, 1969, pp. 291–300.

Bass, F. M., Pessemier, E. A., and Tigert, D. J., "Complementary and Substitute Pattern of Purchasing and Use." *Journal of Advertising Research*, Vol. 9, No. 2, 1969, pp. 19–28.

Bass, F. M., and Talarzyk, W., "A Study of Attitude Theory and Brand Preference." Unpublished Working Paper, Krannert Graduate School of Industrial Administration, Purdue University, Indiana, 1969.

Bass, F. M., Tigert, D. J., and Lonsdale, R. T., "Market Segmentation: Group Versus Individual Behavior." *Journal of Marketing Research*, Vol. 5, 1968, pp. 264–70.

Bauer, R. A., "Consumer Behavior as Risk Taking." In R. S. Hancock (ed.): *Dynamic Marketing for a Changing World*. Chicago: American Marketing Association, 1960.

Bauer, R. A., "Risk-Handling in Drug Adoption." *Public Opinion Quarterly*, Vol. 25, 1961, pp. 546–59.

Bauer, R. A., "The Initiative of the Audience." *Journal of Advertising Research*, Vol. 3, No. 2, 1963, pp. 2–7.

Bauer, R. A., "The Obstinate Audience: The Influence Process from the Point of View of Social Communication." *American Psychologist*, Vol. 19, 1964, pp. 319–28.

Bauer, R. A., "Does Attitude Change Take Place Before or After Behavior Change?" In L. Adler and I. Crispi (eds.): *Attitude Research on the Rocks*. Chicago: American Marketing Association, 1968.

Bauer, R. A., Cunningham, S. M., and Wortzel, L. A., "The Marketing Dilemma of Negroes." *Journal of Marketing*, Vol. 29, No. 2, 1965, pp. 1–6.

Beal, G. M., and Bohlen, J. M., "The Diffusion Process." Special Report, No. 18, Agricultural Extension Service, Ames, Iowa, Iowa State College, March, 1957.

Beal, G. M., and Rogers, E. M., "Information Sources in the Adoption Process of New Fabrics." *Journal of Home Economics*, Vol. 49, 1957, pp. 630–34.

Beals, R., Krantz, D. H., and Tversky, A., "Foundations of Multi-Dimensional Scaling." *Psychological Review*, Vol. 75, 1968, pp. 127–42.

Becker, G. M., "Sequential Decision Making: Wald's Model and Estimation of Parameters." *Journal of Experimental Psychology*, Vol. 55, 1958, pp. 628–36.

Becker, G. M., and McClintock, C., "Value: Behavioral Decision Theory." *Annual Review of Psychology*, Vol. 18, Palo Alto, Calif.: Annual Reviews, Inc., 1967.

Becknell, J. C., and Maher, H., "Utilization of Factor Analysis for Image Clarification and Analysis." *Public Opinion Quarterly*, Vol. 26, 1962, pp. 658–63.

Becknell, J. C., Wilson, W. R., and Baird, J. C., "The Effect of Frequency of Presentation on the Choice of Nonsense Syllables." *Journal of Psychology*, Vol. 56, 1965, pp. 165–70.

Behar, B., "The Effect of Cognitive Dissonance or Inappropriate Emotional Reactions." *Journal of Personality*, Vol. 35, 1967, pp. 305–19.

Beier, E. G., and Griffin, M. C., "Influence of Subliminal Clues in an Incidental Choice Task." *Journal of General Psychology*, Vol. 69, 1963, pp. 187–92.

Bell, G. D., "Self-Confidence and Persuasion in Car Buying." *Journal of Marketing Research*, Vol. 4, 1967a, pp. 46–52.

Bell, G. D., "The Automobile Buyer After the Purchase." *Journal of Marketing*, Vol. 31, No. 3, 1967b, pp. 12–16.

Bell, J. E., "Mobiles, A Neglected Market Segment," *Journal of Marketing*, Vol. 33, No. 2, 1969, pp. 37–44.

Bell, W. E., "Consumer Innovators; A Unique Market for Newness." In S. A. Gryeser (ed.): *Toward Scientific Marketing*. Chicago: American Marketing Association, 1963.

Bem, D. J., "An Experimental Analysis of Self Persuasion." *Journal of Experimental Social Psychology*, Vol. 1, 1965, pp. 199–218.

Bem, D. J., "Self Perception: An Alternative Interpretation of Cognitive Dissonance Phenomena." *Psychological Review*, Vol. 74, 1967, pp. 183–200.

Bengston, R., and Brenner, H., "Product Test Results Using Three Different Methodologies." *Journal of Marketing Research*, Vol. 7, No. 4, 1964, pp. 49–52.

Bennett, G. M., Kemler, D., and Levin, B. T., "Emotional Associations with Air and Rail Transportations." *Journal of Psychology*, Vol. 43, 1957, pp. 65–75.

Bennett, P. D., and Mandell, R. M., "Prepurchase Information Seeking Behavior of New Car Purchasers—the Learning Hypothesis." *Journal of Marketing Research*, Vol. 6, 1969, pp. 430–33.

Benson, P. H., "A Model for the Analysis of Consumer Preferences." *Journal of Applied Psychology*, Vol. 39, 1955, pp. 375–81.

Benson, P. H., "Consumer Preference Distributions in the Analysis of Market Segmentation." In W. S. Decker (ed.): *Emerging Concepts in Marketing*. Chicago: American Marketing Association, 1962.

Benson, P. H., "Psychometric Procedures in the Analysis of Market Segmentation." In H. Comez (ed.): *Innovation—Key to Marketing Progress*. Chicago: American Marketing Association, 1963.

Benson, P. H., "Analysis of Irregular Two-Dimensional Distributions of Consumer Buying Choices." *Journal of Marketing Research*, Vol. 3, 1966, pp. 279–88.

Berelson, B. R., Lazarsfeld, P. F., and McPhee, W. N., *Voting: A Study of Opinion Formation in a Presidential Election*. Chicago: University of Chicago Press, 1954.

Berelson, B. R., and Steiner, G. A., *Human Behavior*. New York: Harcourt, Brace and World, Inc., 1964.

Berey, L. A., and Pollay, R. W., "The Influencing Role of the Child in Family Decision-Making." *Journal of Marketing Research*, Vol. 5, 1968, pp. 70–72.

Berlyne, D. E., "The influence of Complexity and Novelty in Visual Figures on Orienting Responses." *Journal of Experimental Psychology*, Vol. 55, 1958, pp. 289–96.

Berlyne, D. E., *Conflict, Arousal and Curiosity*. New York: McGraw-Hill, 1960.

Berlyne, D. E., "Arousal and Reinforcement." In D. Levine (ed.): *Nebraska Symposium on Motivation*. Lincoln, Nebraska: University of Nebraska Press, 1967.

Bernbach, H. A., "Decision Processes in Memory." *Psychological Review*, Vol. 74, 1967, pp. 462–80.

Better Homes and Gardens Consumer Questionnaire, New York: Meredith Corporation, 1968.

Bilkey, W. J., "The Vector Hypothesis of Consumer Behavior." *Journal of Marketing*, Vol. 16, No. 2, 1951, pp. 137–51.

Bilkey, W. J., "A Psychological Approach to Consumer Behavior Analysis." *Journal of Marketing*, Vol. 18, No. 3, 1953, pp. 18–25.

Bilkey, W. J., "Consistency Test of Psychic Tension Rating Involved in Consumer Purchase Behavior." *Journal of Social Psychology*, Vol. 45, 1957, pp. 81–91.

Bilkey, W. J., "Consumer Behavior: Disbursement and Welfare." In G. Schwartz (ed.): *Science in Marketing*. New York: John Wiley and Sons, Inc., 1965.

Bindra, Dalbin, "Neuropsychological Interpretation of the Effects of Drive and Incentive—Motivation on General Activity and Instrumental Behavior." *Psychological Review*, Vol. 75, 1968, pp. 1–22.

Birdwell, E. A., "Influence of Image Congruence on Consumer Choice." L. G. Smith (ed.): *Reflections on Progress in Marketing*. Chicago: American Marketing Association, 1964.

Birdwell, E. A., "A Study of the Influence of Image Congruence on Consumer Choice." *Journal of Business*, Vol. 41, 1968, pp. 76–85.

Birdwell, E. A., Stafford, J. E., and Van Tassel, C., "Verbal versus Non-Verbal Measures of Attitude: Use of the Pupillograph." Paper presented at Workshop on Experimental Research in Consumer Behavior. Ohio State University, 1969.

Bishop, F. V., "The Anal Character: A Rebel in the Dissonance Family." *Journal of Personality and Social Psychology*, Vol. 6, 1967, pp. 23–36.

Bither, W., and Miller, S. J., "A Cognitive Theory View of Brand Preference." Paper presented at American Marketing Association Fall Conference, Cincinnati, Ohio, 1969.

Bjuvman, A., and Schött, M., "En studie av hur behov påverkar identificering och urval av behovsrelaterede märkesnamn." Studior i ekonomisk psychologi, No. 30, Stockholm School of Economics, 1966 (stencil).

Blank, A., "Effects of Group and Individual Conditions on Choice Behavior." *Journal of Personality and Social Psychology*, Vol. 8, 1968, pp. 294–98.

Blood, R. D., and Wolfe, D. M., *Husbands and Wives.* Glencoe, Ill.: The Free Press, 1960.

Blum, G. S., *A Model of the Mind.* New York: John Wiley and Sons, Inc., 1961.

Blum, G. S., *Psychodynamics: The Science of Unconscious Mental Forces.* California: Wadsworth Publishing Company, Inc., 1966.

Blum, G. S., Geiwitz, P. I., and Stewart, C. O., "Cognitive Arousal: The Evaluation of a Model." *Journal of Personality and Social Psychology*, Vol. 5, 1967, pp. 138–52.

Bockhout, R., "Changes in Heart Rate Accompanying Attitude Change." *Journal of Personality and Social Psychology*, Vol. 4, 1966, pp. 695–99.

Bolger, J. F., Jr., "How to Evaluate Your Company Image." *Journal of Marketing*, Vol. 24, No. 2, 1959, pp. 7–10.

Bortel, D. G., Van, and Gross, I. H., "A Comparison of Home Management in Two Socio-economic Groups." Technical Bulletin 240, East Lansing, Michigan: State Agricultural Experiment Station, 1954.

Boulding, E., "Orientation Toward Achievement or Security in Relation to Consumer Behavior." *Human Relations*, Vol. 13, 1960, pp. 365–82.

Bourne, F. S., "Group Influence in Marketing and Public Relation." In Likert and Hayes, Jr., (eds.): *Some Applications of Behavioral Research.* Paris: UNESCO, 1957.

Boyd, H. W., and Levy, S. J., "New Dimensions in Consumer Analysis." *Harvard Business Review*, Vol. 41, 1963, pp. 129–40.

Brandt, H. F., *The Science of Seeing.* New York: Philosophical Library, 1944.

Brehm, J. W., "Post-Decision Changes in the Desirability of Alternatives." *Journal of Abnormal and Social Psychology*, Vol. 52, 1956, pp. 384–89.

Brehm, J. W., "Increasing Cognitive Dissonance by a *Fait Accompli*." *Journal of Abnormal and Social Psychology*, Vol. 58, 1959, pp. 379–82.

Brehm, J. W., "A Dissonance Analysis of Attitude-Discrepant Behavior." In M. S. Rosenberg, C. I. Hovland, et al.: *Attitude Organization and Change.* New Haven, Conn.: Yale University Press, 1960.

Brehm, J. W., "Motivational Effects of Cognitive Dissonance." In M. R. Jones (ed.): *Nebraska Symposium on Motivation.* Lincoln, Nebraska: Nebraska University Press, 1962.

Brehm, J. W., *A Theory of Psychological Reactance.* New York: John Wiley and Sons, Inc., 1966.

Brehm, J. W., Back, K. V., and Bogdonoff, M. D., "A Physiological Effect of Cognitive Dissonance Under Stress and Deprivation." *Journal of Abnormal and Social Psychology*, Vol. 69, 1964, pp. 303–10.

Brehm, J. W., and Cohen, A. R., "Reevaluation of Choice Alternatives." *Journal of Abnormal and Social Psychology*, Vol. 58, 1959b, pp. 393–98.

Brehm, J. W., and Cohen, A. R., "Choice and Chance Relative Deprivation as Determinants of Cognition Dissonance." *Journal of Abnormal and Social Psychology*, Vol. 58, 1959a, pp. 383–87.

Brehm, J. W., and Cohen, A. R., *Explorations in Cognitive Dissonance.* New York: John Wiley and Sons, Inc., 1962.

Brehm, J. W., Cohen, A. R., and Sears, D., "Persistance of Post-Choice Dissonance Reduction Effects." Unpublished Study (reported in Festinger, 1964a).

Brehm, J. W., and Sensening, J., "Social Influence as a Function of Attempted and Implied Usurpation of Choice." *Journal of Personality and Social Psychology*, Vol. 4, 1966, pp. 703–7.

Brems, H., *Product Equilibrium under Monopolistic Competition.* Cambridge, Mass.: Harvard University Press, 1950.

Brewer, M. B., "Averaging versus Summation in Composite Ratings of Complex Social Stimuli." *Journal of Personality and Social Psychology*, Vol. 8, 1968, pp. 20–26.

Brim, O. G., Glass, D. G., Lavin, D. E., and Goodman, N., *Personality and Decision Processes*, Stanford, Calif.: Stanford University Press, 1962.

Brim, O. G., and Hoff, D. B., "Individual and Situational Differences in Desire for Certainty." *Journal of Abnormal and Social Psychology*, Vol. 54, 1957, pp. 225–29.

Brinton, E., "Deriving an Attitude Scale From Semantic Differential Data." *Public Opinion Quarterly*, Vol. 25, 1961, pp. 289–95.

Britt, S. H., *The Spenders*. New York: McGraw-Hill Book Co., Inc., 1960.

Broadbent, S., "Regularity of Reading." *Journal of Marketing Research*, Vol. 1, No. 3, 1964, pp. 50–58.

Brock, T. C., "Effects of Prior Dishonesty on Post-Decisional Dissonance." *Journal of Abnormal and Social Psychology*, Vol. 66, 1963, pp. 325–31.

Brock, T. C., and Balloun, J. L., "Behavioral Receptivity to Dissonant Information." *Journal of Personality and Social Psychology*, Vol. 6, 1967, pp. 413–25.

Brock, T. C., and Grant, L. D., "Dissonance, Awareness and Motivation." *Journal of Abnormal and Social Psychology*, Vol. 67, 1963, pp. 53–60.

Brody, R. P., and Cunningham, S. M., "Personality Variables and the Consumer Decision Process." *Journal of Marketing Research*, Vol. 5, 1968, pp. 50–57.

Brown, F. E., "Price Image versus Price Reality." *Journal of Marketing Research*, Vol. 6, 1969, pp. 185–91.

Brown, G. H., "Brand Loyalty—Fact or Fiction?" *Advertising Age*, 1952–53 (Vol. 23, p. 952; Jun. 9, pp. 53–55; Jun. 30, pp. 45–57; Jul. 14, pp. 54–56; Jul. 28, pp. 46–48; Aug. 11, 56–58; Sept. 1, pp. 44–48; Sept. 22, pp. 80–82; Oct. 6, pp. 82–86; Dec. 1, pp. 76–77; Vol. 24, 1953: Jan. 26, pp. 75–76).

Brown, G. H., "The Automobile Buying Decision Within the Family." In N. F. Foote (ed.): *Household Decision-Making*. New York: New York University Press, 1961.

Brown, R., *Social Psychology*, New York: The Free Press, 1965.

Brown, R. L., "Wrapper Influence on the Perception of Freshness in Bread." *Journal of Applied Psychology*, Vol. 42, 1958, pp. 257–60.

Brown, T. M., "Habit Persistence and Lags in Consumer Behavior." *Econometrica*, Vol. 20, 1952, pp. 355–71.

Brown, W. F., "The Determination of Factors Influencing Brand Choice." *Journal of Marketing*, Vol. 14, 1950, pp. 699–706.

Brunner, J. A., and Mason, J. L., "The Influence of Driving Time Upon Shopping Center Preferences." *Journal of Marketing*, Vol. 32, No. 2, 1968, pp. 57–61.

Bruner, J. S., "The Course of Cognitive Growth," *American Psychologist*, Vol. 19, 1964. pp. 1–15.

Bruner, J. S., Goodnow, J. T., and Austin, G. A., *A Study of Thinking*. New York: John Wiley and Sons, Inc., 1956.

Bryan, W. L., and Harter, N., "Studies in the Physiology and Psychology of Language." *Psychological Review*, Vol. 4, 1967, pp. 27–53.

Bucklin, L. P., "Testing Propensities to Shop." *Journal of Marketing*, Vol. 30, No. 1, 1966, pp. 22–26.

Burk, M., *Consumption Economies*. New York: John Wiley and Sons, Inc., 1968.

Burnstein, E., "Source of Cognitive Bias in the Representation of Simple Social Structures." *Journal of Personality and Social Psychology*, Vol. 7, 1967, pp. 36–48.

Bush, R. R., and Estes, W. K. (eds.): *Studies in Mathematical Learning Theory*. Stanford, Calif.: Stanford University Press, 1959.

Bush, R. R., and Mosteller, F., *Stochastic Models for Learning*. New York: John Wiley and Sons, Inc., 1955.

Buzzel, R. D., "Prediction of Short-Term Changes in Market Share as a Function of Advertising Strategy." *Journal of Marketing Research*, Vol. 1, No. 3, 1964, pp. 27–31.

Byrne, D., and Clore, G. L., Jr., "Effectance Arousal and Attraction." *Journal of Personality and Social Psychology*. Monograph, Vol. 6, No. 4, Part 2, 1967.

Cambell, D. P., *Manual for the Strong Vocation Interest Blank*. Palo Alto, Calif.: Stanford University Press, 1966.

Campbell, B. M., "The Existence and Determinants of Evoked Set in Brand Choice Behavior," unpublished dissertation, Columbia University, 1967.

Campbell, D. T., "The Indirect Assessment of Social Attitudes," *Psychological Bulletin*, Vol. 47, 1950, pp. 15–38.

Cangelosi, V. E., and March, J. G., "On Experiment in Model Building." *Behavioral Science*, Vol. 11, 1966, pp. 71–75.

Canon, L. K., "Self-Confidence and Selective Exposure to Information." In L. Festinger (ed.): *Conflict Decision and Dissonance*. Stanford, University Press, 1964.

Cardozo, R. N., "An Experimental Study of Consumer Effort, Expectation, and Satisfaction." *Journal of Marketing Research*, Vol. 2, 1965, pp. 244–49.

Carlman, B., "Katagorisering of Meddelanden. Tre experiment." *Studier i Economisk Psykologi*, No. 26, Institute for Economic Research, The Stockholm School of Economics, Stockholm, Sweden, 1966 (stencil).

Carlson, E. R., "Attitude Change Through Modification of Attitude Structure." *Journal of Abnormal and Social Psychology*, Vol. 52, 1956, pp. 256–61.

Carlson, R., "Produktets Sociale Anseende." *Studier i Ekonomisk Psychologi*, No. 18, Institute for Economic Research, The Stockholm School of Economics, Stockholm, Sweden, 1964.

Cardozo, R. N., "An Experimental Study of Consumer Effort, Expectation, and Satisfaction." *Journal of Marketing Research*, Vol. 2, 1965, pp. 244–49.

Carman, J. M., "Brand Switching and Linear Learning Models." *Journal of Advertising Research*, No. 2, 1966a, pp. 23–31.

Carman, J. M., "The Fate of Fashion Cycles in Our Modern Society." In R. M. Haas (ed.): *Science Technology and Marketing*. Chicago: American Marketing Association, 1966b.

Carman, J. M., "Some Insight Into Reasonable Grocery Shopping Strategies." *Journal of Marketing*, Vol. 33, No. 4, 1969, pp. 69–71.

Carman, J. M., "Correlates of Brand Loyalty: Some Positive Results." *Journal of Marketing Research*, Vol. 7, 1970, pp. 67–76.

Carroll, J. D., and Chang, J. J., *Relating Preferences Data to Multidimensional Scaling Solutions via a Generalization of Coombs Unfolding Model*. Murray Hill, N.J.: Bell Telephones Laboratories, 1967.

Cartwright, D., and Harary, F., "Structural Balance: A Generalization of Heiders' Theory." *Psychological Review*, Vol. 63, 1956, pp. 277–93.

Cartwright, D., and Festinger, L., "Quantitative Theory of Decision." *Psychological Review*, Vol. 50, 1943, pp. 595–621.

Cattell, R. B., and Nesselroade, J. R., "Likeness and Completeness Theories Examined by Sixteen Personality Factor Measures on Stably and Unstably Married Couples." *Journal of Personality and Social Psychology*, Vol. 7. 1967, pp. 351–61.

Cattell, R. B., and Stice, G. F., *Handbook for the Sixteen Personality Factor Questionnaire: The 16 PF Test, Forms A, B, and C*. Champaign, Ill.: The Institute for Personality and Ability Testing, 1957.

Cerha, J., *Selective Mass Communication*, Stockholm: P. A. Norstedt and Soner, 1967.

Chalmers, D. K., "Meanings, Impressions, and Attitudes. A Model of the Evaluation Process." *Psychological Review*, Vol. 76, 1969, pp. 450–60.

Chapanis, N., and Chapanis, A., "Cognitive Dissonance: Five Years Later." *Psychological Bulletin*, Vol. 61, 1964, pp. 1–22.

Chatfield, C., Ehrenberg, S. C., Goodhardt, G. J., "Progress on a Simplified Model of Stationary Purchasing Behavior." *Journal of the Royal Statistical Society*, Vol. 129, Pt. 3, 1966, pp. 317–67.

Cheskin, Louis, *Basis for Marketing Decisions*. New York: Liveright, 1962 (p. 282).

The Chicago Tribune, "*Cigarettes, Their Role and Function*." Chicago: Chicago Tribune, no date

Churchman, C., *Prediction and Optimal Decisions*, Englewood Cliffs, N.J.: Prentice Hall, Inc., 1961.

Claeys, W., "Zeigarnik Effect, 'Revised Zeigarnik Effect,' and Personality." *Journal of Personality and Social Psychology*, Vol. 12, 1969, pp. 320–27.

Clark, L. H. (ed.): *Consumer Behavior*, Vol. II, New York City; University Press, 1955.

Clark, R. D., III, and Willems, E. P., "Where is the Risky Shift? Dependence on Instructions." *Journal of Personality and Social Psychology*, Vol. 13, 1969, pp. 215–21.

Clarkson, G. P. E., *The Theory of Consumer Demand; A Critical Appraisal*. Princeton, N.J.: Princeton University Press, 1963.

Clarkson, G. P. E., "Decision Making in Small Groups: A Simulation Study." *Behavioral Science*, Vol. 13, 1968, pp. 288–305.

Clawson, C. J., "Family Composition, Motivation and Buying Decisions." In N. F. Foote (ed.): *Household Decision-Making*. New York: New York University Press, 1961.

Claycamp, J. H., "Characteristics of Thrift Deposit Owners." *Journal of Marketing Research*, Vol. 2, 1965, pp. 163–70.

Claycamp, J. H., "Dynamic Effects of Short Duration Price Differentials on Gasoline Sales." *Journal of Marketing Research*, Vol. 3, 1966, pp. 175–78.

Clement, W. E., "An Analysis of the Advertising Process and Its Influence on Consumer Behavior." In R. Moyer (ed.); *Changing Marketing Systems*, Chicago: American Marketing Association, 1967.

Clevenger, T., Lazier, T., Clark, G. A., and Clark, M. L., "Measurement of Corporate Images by Semantic Differential." *Journal of Marketing Research*, Vol. 2, 1965, pp. 80–82.

Clover, T., "Relative Importance of Impulse Buying in Retail Stores." *Journal of Marketing*, Vol. 15, 1950, pp. 66–70.

Cohen, A. R., *Attitude Change and Social Influence*. New York: Basic Books, 1964.

Cohen, A. R., Brehm, J. W., and Latane, B., "Choice of Strategy and Voluntary Exposure to Information Under Public and Private Conditions." *Journal of Personality*, Vol. 27, 1959, pp. 63–73.

Cohen, J., and Goldberg, M. E., "The Effects of Brand Familiarity and Performance Upon Post-Decision Product Evaluation." Paper presented at the American Marketing Association's Workshop on Experimental Research in Consumer Behavior, Ohio State University, 1969.

Colby, K. C., "Computer Simulation of Changes in Personal Belief Systems." *Behavioral Science*, Vol. 12, 1967, pp. 248–53.

Cole, R. H., DeBoer, L. M., Millican, R. D., and Wedding, N., *Manufacturer and Distributor Brands*. Urbana, Illinois, University of Illinois Bureau of Economic and Business Research, Bulletin No. 80, 1955.

Collaza, C. J., Jr., "Effects of Income Upon Shopping Attitudes and Frustrations." *Journal of Research*, Vol. 41, 1966, pp. 1–7.

Colley, R. H., "Defining Advertising Goals for Measured Advertising Results." *Association of National Advertisers*, New York, 1961.

Comish, N. W., "What Influences Customers' Choice of a Food Store?" *Journal of Research*, Vol. 34, 1958, pp. 90–100.

Commercial Credit Company, *Consumer Buying Prospects, A Quarterly Survey*, Vol. I, Baltimore, Md.: Commercial Credit Company, 1967–68–69.

Committee of Definitions of the American Marketing Association, "Marketing Definitions." *American Marketing Association*, Chicago, 1960.

Conners, C. K., "Visual and Verbal Approach Motives as a Function of Discrepancy from Expectancy Level." *Perceptual and Motor Skills*, Vol. 18, 1964, pp. 457–64.

Constantinople A., "Perceived Instrumentality of the College as a Measure of Attitudes Towards Colleges." *Journal of Personality and Social Psychology*, Vol. 5, 1967, pp. 196–201.

Consulting Psychologist, Inc., *California Psychological Inventory Manual*. Pala Alto, Calif.: Consulting Psychologists Press, 1957.

Converse, P. D., and Crawford, C. M., "Family Buying: Who Does It? Who Influences It?" *Current Economic Comments*, Vol. 11, 1949, pp. 38–50.

Cook, V. J., "Group Decision, Social Comparison, and Persuasion in Changing Attitudes." *Journal of Advertising Research*, Vol. 7, No. 2, 1967, pp. 31–37.

Coombs, C. H., "Psychological Scaling Without a Unit of Measurement." *Psychological Review*, Vol. 57, 1950, pp. 145–58.

Coombs, C. H., "Inconsistency of Preferences as Measure of Psychological Distance." In C. W. Churchman and P. Ratoosh (eds.): *Measurement, Definitions and Theories*. New York: John Wiley and Sons, Inc., 1959.

Coombs, C. H., "A Theory of DATA." *Psychological Review*, Vol. 67, 1960, pp. 143–59.

Coombs, C. H., *A Theory of Data*. New York: John Wiley and Sons, Inc., 1964.

Coombs, C. H., and Komorita, S. S., "Measuring Utility of Money Through Decisions." *American Journal of Psychology*, Vol. 711, 1958, pp. 383–89.

Copeland, M. T., *Principles of Merchandising*. New York: Shaw, 1925.

Copland, B. O., *The Study of Attention Value*. London: Business Publications Limited, 1958.

Coulson, J. S., "Buying Decision Within the Family and the Consumer-Brand Relationship." In J. W. Newman (ed.): *On Knowing the Consumer*. New York: John Wiley and Sons, Inc., 1966.

Court, R. H., "Utility Maximization and the Demand for New Zealand Meats," *Econometrica*, Vol. 35, No. 3–4, 1967.

Cox, D. F., "The Measurement of Information Value: A Study in Consumer Decision-Making." In W. S. Deckers (ed.): *Emerging Concepts in Marketing*. Chicago, Ill.: American Marketing Association, 1963.

Cox, D. F., "The Audience as Communicators." In S. A. Gneyser (ed.): *Toward Scientific Marketing*. Chicago: American Marketing Association, 1965.

Cox, D. F. (ed.): *Risk Taking and Information Handling in Consumer Behavior*. Boston: Graduate School of Business Administration, Harvard University, 1967a.

Cox, D. F., "The Influence of Cognitive Needs and Styles on Information Handling in Making Product Evaluations." In D. F. Cox (ed.): *Risk Taking and Information Handling in Consumer Behavior*. Boston: Grad. School of Business Administration, Harvard University, 1967b, pp. 370–73.

Cox, D. F., and Bauer, R. A., "Self Confidence and Persuadability in Women." *Public Opinion Quarterly*, Vol. 28, 1964, pp. 453–66.

Cox, D. F., and Rich, S., "Perceived Risk and Consumer Decision-making." *Journal of Marketing Research*, Vol. 1, No. 4, 1964, pp. 32–39.

Cox, K. K., "The Responsiveness of Food Sales to Supermarket Shelf Space Changes." *Journal of Marketing Research*, Vol. 1, No. 2, 1964, pp. 63–67.

Cox, K. K., "The Effect of Shelf Space Upon Sales of Branded Products," *Journal of Marketing Research*, Vol. 7, 1970, pp. 55–58.

Crane, E., *Marketing Communication*. New York: John Wiley and Sons, Inc., 1965.

Crespi, I., *Attitude Research*. Chicago: American Marketing Association, 1965.

Crisp, R. D., *Marketing Research*. New York: McGraw-Hill Book Co., 1963.

Cunningham, R. M., "Brand Loyalty, What, Where, How Much." *Harvard Business Review*, Vol. 24, 1956, pp. 116–28.

Cunningham, R. M., "Customer Loyalty to Store and Brand." *Harvard Business Review*, Vol. 39, 1961, pp. 127–37.

Cunningham, S. M., "Perceived Risk as a Factor in Product-Oriented Word-of-Mouth. Behavior: A First Step." In L. G. Smith (ed.): *Reflections on Progress in Marketing*. Chicago: American Marketing Association, 1964.

Cunningham, S. M., "Perceived Risk as a Factor in the Diffusion of New Product Information." In R. M. Hass (ed.): *Science, Technology and Marketing*. Chicago: American Marketing Association, 1966.

Cunningham, S. M., "Perceived Risk and Brand Loyalty." In D. F. Cox (ed.): *Risk Taking and Information Handling in Consumer Behavior*. Boston: Graduate School of Business Administration, Harvard University Press, 1967a.

Cunningham, S. M., "The Major Dimensions of Perceived Risk." In D. F. Cox (ed.): *Risk Taking and Information Handling in Consumer Behavior*. Boston: Graduate School of Business Adminstration, Harvard University, 1967b.

Cyert, R. M., and March, J. G., *A Behavioral Theory of the Firm*. New Jersey: Prentice Hall, Inc., 1963.

Davidson, D., and Marschak, J., "Experimental Tests of Stochastic Decision Theory." In C. W. Churchman and P. Ratoosh (eds.): *Measurement: Definitions and Theories*. New York: John Wiley and Sons, Inc.

Davidson, D., Suppes, P., and Siegel, S., *Decision Making: An Experimental Approach*. Stanford, Calif.: Stanford University Press, 1957.

Davis, J. M., "The Transitivity of Preferences." *Behavioral Science*, Vol. 3, 1958, pp. 26–37.

Day, G. S., "A Two-Dimensional Concept of Brand Loyalty." *Journal of Advertising Research*, Vol. 9, No. 3, 1969, pp. 29–36.

Day, G. S., *Buyer Attitudes and Brand Choice Behavior*. New York: The Free Press, 1970.

Day, R. L., "Simulation of Consumer Preferences." *Journal of Advertising Research*, Vol. 5, 1965, No. 3, pp. 6–10.

Deering, G., "Affective Stimuli and Disturbance of Thought Processes." *Journal of Consulting Psychology*, Vol. 27, 1963, pp. 338–43.

Deese, J., *General Psychology*. Boston: Allyn and Bacon, Inc., 1967.

DeFleur, M. L., and Westie, F. R., "Verbal Attitudes and Quantitative Act: An Experiment on the Salience of an Attitude." *American Sociological Review*, Vol. 23, 1958, pp. 667–73.

DeFleur, M. L., and Petranoff, R. M., "A Televised Test of Subliminal Persuasion." *Public Opinion Quarterly*, Vol. 23, 1959, pp. 168–80.

Dember, W. N., *The Psychology of Perception*. New York: Holt, Rinehart and Winston, 1960.

Dember, W. N., and Earl, R. W., *Analysis of Exploratory, Manipulatory and Curiosity Behaviors*. Psychological Review, Vol. 64, 1957, pp. 91–96.

Demsetz, H., "The Effect of Consumer Experience on Brand Loyalty and the Structure of Market Demand." *Econometrica*, Vol. 30, 1962, pp. 22–33.

Dennett, D. C., "Machine Traces and Protocol Statements." *Behavioral Science*, Vol. 13, 1968, pp. 155–61.

Dichter, C., *The Strategy of Desire*. New York: Doubleday, 1960.

Dichter, E., *Handbook of Consumer Motivations*. New York: McGraw-Hill Book Co., 1964.

Dichter, E., "How Word-of-Mouth Advertising Works." *Harvard Business Review*, Vol. 44, 1966, pp. 147–66.

Dickins, D., Fanelli, A., and Ferguson, V., "Attractive Menu Items." *Journal of the American Dietetic Association*, Vol. 30, 1954, pp. 881–85.

Dickman, H., "The Perception of Behavioral Units." In R. Baker (ed.): *The Stream of Behavior*. New York: Appleton-Century-Crofts, 1963.

Dillehay, R. C., and Insko, C. H., "Logical Consistency and Attitude Change." *Journal of Personality and Social Psychology*, Vol. 3, 1966, pp. 646–54.

Dolbear, F. T., Jr., and Lave, L. B., "Inconsistent Behavior in Lottery Choice Experiments." *Behavioral Science*, Vol. 12, 1967, pp. 14–24.

Dolich, I. J., "Congruence Relationships Between Self Images and Products Brand.' *Journal of Marketing Research*, Vol. VI, 1969, pp. 80–85.

Dollard, J., and Miller, N. E., *Personality and Psychotherapy*. New York: McGraw-Hill Book Co., Inc., 1950.

Dommermuth, W. P., "The Shopping Matrix and Marketing Strategy." *Journal of Marketing Research*, Vol. 2, 1965, pp. 128–32.

Dommermuth, W. P., and Cundiff, E. W., "Shopping Goods, Shopping Centers, and Selling Strategies," *Journal of Marketing*, Vol. 4, No. 4, 1967, pp. 32–36.

Dommermuth, W. P., Jr., and Millard, W. J., Jr., "Consumption Coincidence in Product Evaluation." *Journal of Marketing Research*, Vol. 4, 1967, pp. 388–90.

Donnahoe, A. S., "Research Study of Consumer Loyalty." *Journal of Research*, Vol. 32, 1956, pp. 14–16.

Donnelly, Jr., J. H., "Social Character and Acceptance of New Products." *Journal of Marketing Research*, Vol. 7, 1970, pp. 111–13.

Doob, A. N., Carlsmith, J. M., Freedman, J. L., Landauer, T. K., and Tom, S., Jr., "Effects of Initial Selling Price on Subsequent Sales." *Journal of Personality and Social Psychology*, Vol. 11, 1969, pp. 345–50.

Douglas, T., Field, G. A., and Tarpey, L. X., *Human Behavior in Marketing*. Columbus, Ohio; Charles E. Merrill Books, Inc., 1967.

Driscoll, J. M., and Lanzetta, J. T., "Subjective Uncertainty and Prior Arousal or Predecisional Information Search." *Journal of Psychological Reports*, Vol. 14, 1964, pp. 975–88.

Driscoll, J. M., and Lanzetta, J. T., "Effect of Two Sources of Uncertainty on Decision-Making." *Psychological Report*, Vol. 17, 1965, pp. 635–48.

Driscoll, J. M., Tognolli, J. J., and Lanzetta, J. T., "Choice Conflict and Subjective Uncertainty in Decision Making." *Psychological Reports*, Vol. 18, 1966, pp. 427–32.

Dubois, "The Dominant Value Profile of American Culture." *American Anthropologist*, Vol. 57, 1955, pp. 1232–39.

Duesenberry, J. S., *Income, Saving and the Theory of Consumer Behavior*. Cambridge, Mass.: Harvard University Press, 1949.

Duker, J. M., "Some Aspects of Consumer Behavior of Working Wife Families." In L. G. Smith (ed.): *Reflections on Progress in Marketing*. Chicago: American Marketing Association, 1965.

Duncan, A. J., *Quality Control and Industrial Statistics*. Homewood, Ill.; R. D. Irwin, Inc., 1959.

duPont de Nemours and Co., E. I., *Consumer Buying Habit Studies*, E. I. duPont de Nemour and Co., 1945, 1949, 1954, and 1959.

Eagly, A. H., "Involvement as a Determinant of Response to Favorable and Unfavorable Information." *Journal of Personality and Social Psychology*, Vol. 7, Part 2, Monograph, 1967.

Eastlack, J. O., Jr., "Consumer Flavor Preference Factors in Food Product Design." *Journal of Marketing Research*, Vol. 1, No. 1, 1964, pp. 38–42.

Easton, Allan, "Corporate Style vs. Corporate Image." *Journal of Marketing Research*, Vol. 3, 1966, pp. 168–74.

Edfelt, A. W., *Silent Speech and Silent Reading*. Chicago: University of Chicago Press, 1960.

Edgeworth, F. Y., *Mathematical Psychics*. London: Kegan Paul, 1881.

Edwards, A. L., *Personal Preference Schedule: Manual*. New York: The Psychological Corporation, 1954.

Edwards, W., "Probability Preferences in Gambling." *American Journal of Psychology*, Vol. 66, 1953, pp. 56–67.

Edwards, W., "The Theory of Decision Making." *Psychological Bulletin*, Vol. 51, 1954a, pp. 380–417.

Edwards, W., "Probability Preferences Among Bets with Differing Expected Value." *American Journal of Psychology*, Vol. 67, 1954b, pp. 56–67.

Edwards, W., "Rural Probability, Amount of Information as Determinants of Sequential Two Alternative Decision." *Journal of Experimental Psychology*, Vol. 72, 1956, pp. 177–88.

Edwards, W., "Behavioral Decision Theory." *Annual Review of Psychology*, Vol. 12, 1961, pp. 473–98, Palo Alto, California: Annual Reviews, Inc.

Edwards, W., "Subjective Probabilities Inferred from Decisions." *Journal of Psychological Review*, Vol. 69, 1962, pp. 109–35.

Ehrenberg, A. S. C., "The Pattern of Consumer Purchases." *Applied Statistics*, Vol. VIII, No. 1, 1959, pp. 26–41. Also in R. E. Frank, A. A. Kuehn, and W. F. Massy (eds.): *Quantitative Techniques in Marketing Anlaysis*. Homewood, Ill.: Irwin, 1962.

Ehrenberg, A. S. C., "An Appraisal of Markov Brand-Switching Models." *Journal of Marketing Research*, Vol. 2, 1965, pp. 347–63.

Ehrenberg, A. S. C., and Goodhardt, G. J., "A Comparison of American and British Repeat Buying Habits." *Journal of Marketing Research*, Vol. 5, 1968, pp. 29–33.

Ehrlich, H. J., "Attitudes, Behavior, and the Intervening Variables." *The American Sociologist*, Vol. 4, No. 1, Feb. 1969, pp. 29–34.

Ehrlich, D., Guttman, L., Schonback, P., and Mills, J., "Postdecision Exposure to Relevant Information." *Journal of Personality and Social Psychology*, Vol. 54, 1957, pp. 98–102.

Ellsworth, T. D., Benjamin, D., and Radolf, H., "Customer Response to Trading Stamps." *Journal of Retailing*, Vol. 33, 1957, pp. 165–69.

Ellsworth, T. D., Benjamin, D., and Radolf, H., "Changing Trends in Regional Shopping Centers." *Journal of Retailing*, Vol. 34, 1958, pp. 177–94.

Ellsworth, T. D., and Fraser, E. D., "Salespeople: An Undeveloped Sales Potential." *Journal of Retailing*, Vol. 29, 1953, pp. 149–56.

Elms, A. C., "Role Playing, Incentive and Dissonance." *Psychological Bulletin*, Vol. 69, 1967, pp. 932–48.

Endler, W. S., and Hunt, J. M., "S-R Inventories of Hostility and Comparisons of the Proportions of Variance from Persons, Responses, and Situations for Hostility and Anxiousness." *Journal of Personality and Social Psychology*, Vol. 9, 1968, pp. 309–15.

Endler, N. S., Hunt, J. M., and Rosenstein, A. J., "An S-R Inventory of Anxiousness." *Psychological Monograph*, 1962, Vol. 76, No. 17, pp. 1–33.

Engel, J. F., "The Psychological Consequences of a Major Purchase Decision." In W. F. Decker (ed.): *Emerging Concepts in Marketing*. Chicago: American Marketing Association, 1962.

Engel, J. F., Kegerreis, R. J., and Blackwell, R. D., "Word of Mouth Communication by the Innovator." *Journal of Marketing*, Vol. 33, No. 3, 1969, pp. 15–19.

Engel, J. F., Knapp, D. A., and Knapp, D. E., "Source of Influence in the Acceptance of New Products for Self Medicating." In R. M. Hass (ed.): *Science, Technology and Marketing*. Chicago: American Marketing Association, 1966, pp. 776–80.

Engel, J. F., Kollat, D. T., and Blackwell, R. D., *Consumer Behavior*, New York: Holt, Rinehart and Winston, 1968.

Engel, J. F., and Light, M. L., "The Role of Psychological Commitment in Consumer Behavior: An Evaluation of The Theory of Cognitive Dissonance." In F. M. Bass, C. W. King, and E. A. Pessemier (eds.): *Applications of the Sciences in Marketing Management*. New York: John Wiley and Sons, Inc., 1968.

Epstein, R., "Effects on Commitment of Social Isolation under Children's Imitative Behavior." *Journal of Personality and Social Psychology*, Vol. 9, 1968, pp. 90–95.

Evans, F. B., "Psychological and Objective Factors in the Prediction of Brand Choice. Ford versus Chevrolet." *Journal of Business*, Vol. 32, 1959, pp. 340–69.

Evans, F. B., "Correlates of Automobile Shopping Behavior." *Journal of Marketing*, Vol. 26, No. 4, 1962, pp. 74–77.

Evans, F. B., "Ford versus Chevrolet: Park Forest Revisited." *Journal of Business*, Vol. 41, 1968, pp. 445–59.

Fallers, L. A., "A Note on the 'Trickle Effect'." *Public Opinion Quarterly*, Vol. 5, 1954, pp. 314–21.

Farley, J. U., "Testing a Theory of Brand Loyalty." In S. A. Greyser (ed.): *Towards Scientific Marketing*. Chicago: American Marketing Association, 1964a.

Farley, J. U., "Intensive and Extensive Margins as Summary Measures of Consumers' Brand Choice Patterns." Smith (ed.): *Reflections on Progress in Marketing*. Chicago: American Marketing Association, 1964b.

Farley, J. U., "Why Does Brand Loyalty Vary Over Products?" *Journal of Marketing Research*, Vol. 1, No. 4, 1964c, pp. 9–14.

Farley, J. U., "Dimensions of Supermarket Choice Patterns." *Journal of Marketing Research*, Vol. 5, 1968, pp. 206–8.

Farley, J. U., and Kuehn, A. A., "Stochastic Models of Brand Switching." In G. Schwartz (ed.): *"Science in Marketing."* New York: John Wiley and Sons, Inc., 1965.

Farley, J. U., and Swinth, R. L., "Effects of Choice and Sales Message on Customer-Salesman Interaction." *Journal of Applied Psychology*, Vol. 51, 1967, pp. 107–10.

Farrell, R. R., "Effects of Point of Sales Promotional Material on Sales of Cantaloupes."
    Journal of Advertising Research, Vol. 5, No. 4, 1965, pp. 8–12.
Feather, N. T., "An Expectancy Value Model of Information Seeking Behavior." *Psycho-
    logical Review*, Vol. 74, 1967a, pp. 342–60.
Feather, N. T., "Level of Aspiration and Performance Variability." *Journal of Personality and
    Social Psychology*, Vol. 6, 1967b, pp. 37–46.
Feather, N. T., "Change in Confidence Following Success and Failure as a Predictor of
    Subsequent Performance." *Journal of Personality and Social Psychology*, Vol. 9, 1968, pp.
    38–46.
Feather, N. T., "Attitudes and Selective Recall." *Journal of Personality and Social Psychology*,
    Vol. 12, 1969, pp. 310–19.
Feather, N. T., and Jeffries, D. G., "Balancing and Extremity Effects in Reactions of Receiver
    to Source and Content of Communication." *Journal of Personality*, Vol. 35, 1967, pp.
    194–213.
Feather, N. T., and Saville, M. R., "Effects of Amount of Prior Success and Failure on
    Expectations of Success and Subsequent Task Performance." *Journal of Personality and
    Social Psychology*, Vol. 5, 1967, pp. 226–32.
Feldman, S. (ed.): *Cognitive Consistency*. New York: Academic Press, 1966a.
Feldman, S., "Motivational Aspects of Attitudinal Elements and Their Place in Cognitive
    Interaction." In S. Feldman (ed.): *Cognitive Consistency*, New York: Academic Press,
    1966b.
Feldman, S. P., "Some Dyadic Relationships Associated with Consumer Choice." In R. M.
    Haas (ed.): *Science, Technology and Marketing*. Chicago: American Marketing Association,
    1966.
Feldman, S. P., and Spencer, M. C., "The Effect of Personal Influence in the Selection of
    Consumer Services." In P. D. Bennett (ed.): *Marketing and Economic Development*,
    Chicago: American Marketing Association, 1965.
Ferber, R., "The Role of Planning in Consumer Purchases of Durable Goods." *American
    Economic Review*, Vol. 44, 1954, pp. 854–76.
Ferber, R., "Factors Influencing Durable Goods Purchases." In L. H. Clark (ed.): *Consumer
    Behavior*, Vol. 2, New York: New York University Press, 1955a.
Ferber, R., "On the Reliability of Purchase Influence Studies." *Journal of Marketing*, Vol. 19,
    1955b, pp. 225–32.
Ferber, R., "Brand Choice and Social Stratification." *Quarterly Review of Economics and
    Business*, Vol. 2, 1962, pp. 71–78.
Ferber, R., "Anticipation Statistics and Consumer Behavior." *American Statistician*, Vol. 20,
    1966, pp. 20–24.
Ferber, R., "Research on Household Behavior." In *Surveys in Economic Theory, Vol. III, The
    Royal Economic Society*. New York: Macmillan, 1967.
Ferber, R., and Wales, H. G. (eds.): *Motivation and Market Behavior*, Homewood, Ill., P. D.
    Irwin, Inc., 1958.
Festinger, L., "Wish Expectation and Group Standards as Factors Influencing Level of
    Aspiration." *Journal of Abnormal and Social Psychology*, Vol. 37, 1942, pp. 184–200.
Festinger, L., *A Theory of Cognitive Dissonance*. Stanford, Calif: Stanford University Press, 1957.
Festinger, L., *Conflict Decision and Dissonance*. Stanford, Calif.: Stanford University Press, 1964a.
Festinger, L., "Behavioral Support for Opinion Change." *Public Opinion Quarterly*, Vol. 28,
    1964b, pp. 404–17.
Festinger, L., and Maccoby, N., "On Resistance to Persuasive Communication." *Journal of
    Abnormal and Social Psychology*, Vol. 68, 1964, pp. 359–66.
Festinger, L., and Cartwright, D., et al., "A Study of Rumor: Its Origin and Spread."
    Human Relations, Vol. 4, 1948, pp. 468–86.
Festinger, L., and Walster, E., "Post-Decision Regret and Decisional Reversal." In L.
    Festinger: *Conflict, Decision and Dissonance*. Stanford, Calif.: Stanford University Press,
    1964.

Fishbein, M., "An Investigation of the Relationships Between Beliefs About an Object and the Attitude Towards That Object." *Human Relations*, Vol. 16, 1963, pp. 233–39.

Fishbein, M., "A Consideration of Beliefs, Attitudes and Their Relationships." In J. Steiner, and M. Fishbein (eds.): *Current Studies in Social Psychology*. New York: Holt, Rinehart, and Winston, 1965.

Fishbein, M., "The Relationship Between Beliefs, Attitudes and Behavior." In S. Feldman (ed.): *Cognitive Consistency*. New York: Academic Press, 1966.

Fishbein, M., *Readings in Attitude Theory and Measurement*. New York: John Wiley and Sons, Inc., 1967.

Fishbein, M., and Hunter, R., "Summation Versus Balance in Attitude Organization and Change." *Journal of Abnormal and Social Psychology*, Vol. 69, 1964, pp. 505–10.

Fishbein, M., and Raven, B. H., "The AB-Scales." *Human Relations*, Vol. 15, 1962, pp. 35–44.

Fisk, G., "A Conceptual Model for Studying Customer Images." *Journal of Retailing*, Vol. 37, 1961, No. 4, pp. 9–16.

Fleishman, F. A., "An Experimental-Consumer Panel Technique." *Journal of Applied Psychology*, Vol. 35, 1951, pp. 133–35.

Foote, N. F., "The Time Dimension and Consumer Behavior." In J. W. Newman (ed.): *On Knowing the Consumer*, New York: John Wiley and Sons, Inc., 1966.

Fouilhe, P., "Evaluation Subjective des prix." *Revue française de sociologie*, Vol. 1, 1960, pp. 163–72.

Fourt, A., and Woodlock, J. W., "Early Prediction of Market Success for New Grocery Products." *Journal of Marketing*, Vol. 25, No. 4, 1960, pp. 31–38.

Fox, H. W., *The Economics of Trading Stamps*. Washington, D.C.: Public Affairs Press, 1968.

Frank, R. E., "Brand Choice as a Probability Model." *Journal of Business*, Vol. 35, 1962, pp. 43–56.

Frank, R. E., "Is Brand Loyalty a Useful Basis for Market Segmentation?" *Journal of Advertising Research*, Vol. 7, No. 2, 1967a, pp. 27–33.

Frank, R. E., "Correlates of Buying Behavior for Grocery Products." *Journal of Marketing*, Vol. 31, No. 4, 1967b, pp. 48–53.

Frank, R. E., "Market Segmentation Research: Findings and Implications." In F. M. Bass, C. W. King, and E. A. Pessemier (eds.): *Applications of the Sciences in Marketing Management*. New York: John Wiley and Sons, Inc., 1968.

Frank, R. E., and Boyd, H. W., "Are Private Brand Prone Grocery Customers Really Different?" *Journal of Advertising Research*, Vol. 5, No. 4, 1965, pp. 27–35.

Frank, R. E., Green, R. E., and Sieber, H. F., "Household Correlates of Purchase Price for Grocery Products." *Journal of Marketing Research*, Vol. 4, 1967, pp. 54–58.

Frank, E., and Massy, F., "Innovation and Brand Choice: The Folger's Invasion." In S. A. Greyser (ed.): *Toward Scientific Marketing*. Chicago: American Marketing Association, 1963.

Frank, R. E., and Massy, W. F., "Market Segmentation and the Effectiveness of a Brand Price and Dealing Policy." *Journal of Business*, Vol. 38, 1965, pp. 186–200.

Frank, R. E., and Massy, W. F., "Shelf Position and Space Effects on Sales," *Journal of Marketing Research*, Vol. 7, 1970, pp. 59–66.

Frank, R. E., Massy, W. F., and Morrison, D. G., "The Determinants of Innovative Behavior with Respect to a Branded, Frequently Purchased Food Product." In G. Smith (ed.): *Reflections on Progress in Marketing*. Chicago: American Marketing Association, 1964, pp. 312–23.

Freedman, J. L., "Long-Term Behavioral Effects of Cognitive Dissonance." *Journal of Experimental Social Psychology*, Vol. 1, 1965, pp. 145–55.

Freedman, J. L., "Role Playing. Psychology by Consensus." *Journal of Personality and Social Psychology*, Vol. 13, 1969, pp. 107–14.

Freeman, F. S., *Theory and Practice of Psychological Testing*. New York: Holt, Rinehart and Winston, 1962.

French, J. W., *The Description of Personality Measurements in Terms of Rotated Factors.* Princeton, N.J.: Educational Testing Service, 1953.

Freud, S., "The Interpretation of Dreams." In A. A. Bill (ed.): *The Basic Writings of Sigmund Freud.* New York: Modern Library, 1938a.

Freud, S., "Psychoanalysis." In A. A. Bill (ed.): *The Basic Writings of Sigmund Freud.* New York: Modern Library, 1938b.

Friedman, M., "A Theory of the Consumption Function." National Bureau of Economic Research, Princeton University Press, Princeton, N.J., 1957.

Froman, R., "Marketing Research, You Get What You Want." In J. H. Westing (ed.): *Reading in Marketing.* New York: Prentice Hall, Inc., 1953.

Fuchs, D. A., "Two Source Effects in Magazine Advertising." *Journal of Marketing Research*, Vol. 1, No. 3, 1964, pp. 59–62.

Furth, H. G., "Piaget's Theory of Knowledge." *Psychological Review*, Vol. 75, 1968, pp. 143–54.

Gabor, A., and Granger, C. W. J. "Price Sensitivity of the Consumer." *Journal of Advertising Research*, Vol. 4, No. 4, 1964, pp. 40–44.

Gabor, A., and Granger, C. W. J., "Price as an Indicator of Quality." *Economica*, Vol. 33, 1966, pp. 43–70.

Gagne, R. M., "Problem Solving and Thinking." *Annual Review of Psychology*, Palo Alto, Calif.: Annuals Review, Inc., 1959.

Galbraith, J. K., *The Affluent Society.* Boston: Houghton Mifflin Co., 1958.

Gallo, P. S., and McClintock, C. G., "Cooperative and Competitive Behavior in Mixed Motives Games." *Journal of Conflict Resolution*, Vol. 9, 1965, pp. 68–98.

Gamson, W. A., "Experimental Studies of Coalition Formation." In Leonard Berkowitz (ed.): *Advances in Experimental Psychology*, Vol. 1, New York: Academic Press, 1964.

Gardner, B. B., "The Package as a Communication." In M. S. Moyer and R. E. Vosburgh (eds.): *Marketing for Tomorrow—Today.* Chicago: American Marketing Association, 1967.

Geer, J. H., "A Test of the Classical Conditioning Model of Emotion. The Use of Nonpainful Aversive Stimuli as Unconditioned Stimuli in a Conditioning Procedure." *Journal of Personality and Social Psychology*, Vol. 10, 1968, pp. 149–56.

Geer, J. P., Van de, and Jaspars, J. F. M., "Cognitive Functions." *Annual Review of Psychology*, Palo Alto, Calif.: Annual Review, Inc., 1966.

Georgescu, Rogger, N. "Choice, Expectations and Measurability." *The Quarterly Journal of Economics*, Vol. 58, 1964, pp. 503–34.

Gerard, H. B., "Choice Difficulty, Dissonance and the Decision Sequence." *Journal of Personality and Social Psychology*, Vol. 35, 1967a, pp. 91–108.

Gerard, H. B., "Compliance, Expectation of Reward and Opinion Change." *Journal of Personality and Social Psychology*, Vol. 6, 1967b, pp. 360–64.

Gerard, H. B., and Fleischer, L., "Recall and Pleasantness of Balanced and Unbalanced Cognitive Structures." *Journal of Personality and Social Psychology*, Vol. 7, 1967, pp. 332–37.

Gergen, J. J., and Bauer, R. A., "The Interactive Effects of Self-Esteem and Task Difficulty on Social Conformity." In D. E. Cox (ed.): *Risk Taking and Information Handling in Consumer Behavior.* Boston: Harvard Graduate School of Business, 1967.

Gilkison, P., "What Influences the Buying Decision of Teenagers?" *Journal of Retailing*, Vol. 41, 1965, pp. 33–41.

Glickman, S. E., and Schiff, B. B., "A Biological Theory of Reinforcement." *Psychological Review*, Vol. 74, 1967, pp. 81–109.

Goble, R. L., "An Exploratory Study of Socio-psychological Determinants of Consumer Credit Behavior—Phase I. In J. S. Wright and J. L. Goldstucker (eds.): *New Ideas for Successful Marketing.* Chicago: American Marketing Association, 1966.

Goffman, E., *Behavior in Public Places*, New York: The Free Press of Glencoe, 1963.

Gold, R. L., " 'Fashion'." In J. Gould and W. M. Kolb (eds.): *A Dictionary of the Social Sciences.* New York: The Free Press of Glencoe, 1964.

Goldstein, S., "The Aged Segment of the Market, 1950 and 1960." *Journal of Marketing*, Vol. 32, No. 2, 1968, pp. 62–68.

Goodhardt, G. J., and Ehrenberg, A. S. C., "Conditional Trend Analysis: A Breakdown by Initial Purchasing Level." *Journal of Marketing Research*, Vol. 4, 1967, pp. 155–61.

Gordon, L. V., *Gordon Personal Profile*. New York: Harcourt, Brace, and World, Inc., 1963.

Gorman, W. P., "The Diffusion of Color Television Sets in a Metropolitan Fringe Area Market." *The Southern Journal of Business*, July 1968, pp. 50–57.

Gottlieb, M. J., "Segmentation by Personality Types." In L. H. Stockman (ed.): *Advancing Marketing Efficiency*. Chicago: American Marketing Association, 1958, pp. 148–58.

Gould, J. P., "The Expected Utility Hypothesis and the Selection of Optimal Deductibles for a Given Insurance Policy." *Journal of Business*, Vol. 12, 1969, pp. 143–51.

Graham, S., "Class and Conservatism in the Adoption of Innovation." *Human Relations*, Vol. 9, 1956, pp. 91–100.

Grahn, G. L., "N.B.D. Model of Repeat Purchase Loyalty: An Empirical Investigation." *Journal of Marketing Research*, Vol. VI, 1969, pp. 72–79.

Granbois, D. H., "The Role of Communication in the Family Decision-Making Process." In S. A. Greyser (ed.): *Toward Scientific Marketing*. Chicago: American Marketing Association, 1963, pp. 44–57.

Granbois, D. H., "Improving the Study of Customer In-store Behavior." *Journal of Marketing*, Vol. 32, No. 4, 1968, pp. 28–33.

Granbois, D. H., and Willet, R. P., "An Empirical Test of Probabilistic Intentions and Preference Models for Consumer Durables Purchasing." In R. L. King (ed.): *Marketing and the New Science of Planning*. Chicago: American Marketing Association, 1968.

Granbois, D. H., and Willett, R. P., "Correlates of Fulfillment of Brand and Store Intentions for Durable Goods." Paper presented at the Workshop on Experimental Research in Consumer Behavior, Ohio State University, Columbus, Ohio, 1969.

Grass, R. C., and Wallace, W. H., "Satiation Effects of TV Commercials." *Journal of Advertising Research*, Vol. 9, No. 3, 1969, pp. 3–8.

Gredal, K., *Moderne forbrugeres motiver og adfærd*. Copenhagen: E. Harchs Forlag, 1959. [Abbreviated version available in English in M. Kjär-Hansen (ed.): Readings in Danish Theory in Marketing. Copenhagen: E. Harchs Forlag, 1966.]

Green, P. E., "Consumer Use of Information." In J. W. Newman (ed.): *On Knowing the Consumer*. New York: John Wiley and Sons, Inc., 1966.

Green, P. E., and Carmone, F. J., "Multidimensional Scaling. An Introduction and Comparison of Nonmetric Unfolding Techniques." *Journal of Marketing Research*, Vol. 6, 1969, pp. 320–41.

Green, P. E., and Carmone, F. J., "Multidimensional Scaling in Marketing." Boston: Allyn and Bacon, 1971.

Green, P. E., Fitzroy, P. T., and Robinson, P. J., "Experimental Gaming in the Economics of Information." In P. M. Bass, C. W. King, and E. A. Pessemier (eds.): *Applications of the Sciences in Marketing Management*. New York: John Wiley and Sons, 1968.

Green, P. E., and Frank, R. E., "Taxonomic Classification Procedures." In J. Arndt (ed.): *Insights into Consumer Behavior*. Boston: Allyn and Bacon, 1968.

Green, P. E., Halbert, M. H., and Minas, J. S., "An Experiment in Information Buying." *Journal of Advertising Research*, Vol. 4, No. 3, 1964, pp. 17–23.

Green, P. E., Halbert, M. H., and Robinson, P. J., "A Behavioral Experiment in Sales Effort Allocation." *Journal of Marketing Research*, Vol. III, 1966, pp. 261–68.

Green, P. E., Halbert, M. H., and Robinson, P. J., "Perception and Preference Mapping in the Analysis of Marketing Behavior." In L. Adler and I. Crispi, (eds.): *Marketing Research on the Rocks*. Chicago: American Marketing Association, 1968.

Green, P. E., and Morris, T., "Individual Differences Models in Multi-Dimensional Scaling: An Empirical Comparison." Paper presented at the Workshop on Experimental Research in Consumer Behavior, Ohio State University, Columbus, Ohio, August, 1969.

Green, P. E., and Tull, D. S., *Research for Marketing Decisions*, Englewood Cliffs, N.J.: Prentice Hall, Inc., 1966.

Greenberg, A. L., "Respondent Ego-Involvement in Large-Scale Surveys." *Journal of Marketing*, Vol. 20, 1956, pp. 390–93.

Greenberg, M. S., "Role-Playing: An Alternative to Deception?" *Journal of Personality and Social Psychology*, Vol. 7, 1967, pp. 152–57.

Greenwald, A. G., and Sakumura, J. S., "Attitude and Selective Learning." *Journal of Personality and Social Psychology*, Vol. 7, 1967, pp. 387–97.

Greenwald, J. H., "Dissonance and Relative versus Absolute Attractiveness of Decision Alternatives." *Journal of Personality and Social Psychology*, Vol. 11, 1969, pp. 328–30.

Gridgeman, T. N., "A Tasting Experiment." *Applied Statistics*, Vol. 5, 1966, pp. 106–12.

Groeneveld, L., "A New Theory of Consumer Buying Intent." *Journal of Marketing*, Vol. 28, No. 3, 1964, pp. 23–28.

Grubb, E. L., "Consumer Perception of 'Self Concept' and Its Relation to Brand Choice of Selected Product Types." In P. D. Bennett: *Marketing and Economic Development.* Chicago: American Marketing Association, 1965, pp. 419–22.

Grubb, E. L., and Grathwohl, H. L., "Consumer Self Concept, Symbolism and Market Behavior: A Theoretical Approach." *Journal of Marketing*, Vol. 31, No. 4, 1967, pp. 22–27.

Grubb, E. L., and Hupp, G., "Perception of Self, Generalized Stereotypes and Brand Selection." *Journal of Marketing Research*, Vol. 5, 1968, pp. 58–63.

Gruber, A., "Top-of-Mind Awareness and Share of Families: An Observation." *Journal of Marketing Research*, Vol. 6, 1969, pp. 227–31.

Gruen, W., "Preference for New Products and its Relationship to Different Measures of Conformity." *Journal of Applied Psychology*, Vol. 44, 1960, pp. 361–64.

Grusec, J. E., "Waiting for Rewards and Punishments: Effects of Reinforcement Value on Choice." *Journal of Personality and Social Psychology*, Vol. 9, 1968, pp. 85–94.

Guest, L., "Brand Loyalty—Twelve Years Later." *Journal of Applied Psychology*, Vol. 39, 1955, pp. 405–8.

Guest, L., "Brand Loyalty Revisited: A Twenty Years Report." *Journal of Applied Psychology*, Vol. 48, 1964, pp. 93–97.

Gump, P. S., Schoggen, P., and Redl, F., "The Behavior of the Same Child in Different Milieus." In R. Barker (ed.): *The Stream of Behavior.* New York: Appleton-Century-Crofts, 1963.

Guthrie, G., and Wiener, M., "Subliminal Perception of Partial Cue with Pictorial Stimuli." *Journal of Personality and Social Psychology*, Vol. 3, 1966, pp. 619–28.

Guttman, L., "A Basis for Scaling Qualitative Data." *American Sociological Review*, Vol. 9, 1944, pp. 139–50.

Guttman, L., and Suchman, E. A., "Intensity and Zero Point for Attitude Analysis." *American Sociological Review*, Vol. 12, 1947, pp. 55–67.

Guyer, M., "Response-Dependent Parameter Changes in the Prisoner's Dilemma." *Behavioral Science*, Vol. 13, 1968, pp. 205–19.

Gyr, J. W., Brown, J. S., and Cafagna, A. C., "Quasi-formal Models of Inductive Behavior and Their Relation to Piaget's Theory of Cognitive Stages." *Psychological Review*, Vol. 74, 1967, pp. 272–89.

Haaland, G. A., and Venkatesan, M., "Resistance to Persuasive Communication, An Examination of the Distraction Hypothesis." *Journal of Personality and Social Psychology*, Vol. 9, 1968, pp. 167–70.

Haber, R. N., "Discrepancy from Adaption Level as a Source of Affect," *Journal of Experimental Psychology*, Vol. 56, 1958, pp. 370–75.

Haberman, P. W., and Elinson, J., "Family Income Reported in Surveys: Husbands vs. Wives." *Journal of Marketing Research*, Vol. 4, 1967, pp. 191–94.

Hahn, F. H., and Matthews, R. C. O., "The Theory of Economic Growth," The Royal Economic Theory, *Surveys of Economic Theory*, Macmillan, London, 1967.

Haines, G. H., Jr., "A Theory of Market Behavior After Innovation." *Management Science*, Vol. 10, 1964, pp. 634–58.

Haines, G. H., Jr., "A Study of Why People Purchase New Products." In R. M. Haas (ed.): *Science, Technology and Marketing*. Chicago: American Marketing Association, 1966.

Haines, G. H., Jr., "The Use of Alternative Models on a Set of Consumer Data." Working Paper Series #68–05, June, 1968, College of Business Administration, University of Rochester, Rochester, N.Y.

Haines, G. H., Jr., *Consumer Behavior, Learning Models of Purchasing*. New York: The Free Press, 1969.

Haire, M., "Projective Techniques in Marketing Research." *Journal of Marketing*, Vol. 14, 1950, pp. 649–56.

Halbert, M. H., "A Study About How New Families Learn About the Market." In J. W. Newman (ed.): *On Knowing the Consumer*. New York: J. Wiley and Sons, 1966.

Hall, R. D., "Flavor Study Approaches at McCormich and Co., Inc." In A. D. Little (ed.): *Flavor Research and Food Acceptance*. New York: Reinhold, 1958.

Hamm, B. C., "A Study of the Difference Between Self-Actualization Scores and Product Perceptions Among Female Consumers." In R. Moyer (ed.): *Changing Marketing Systems*. Chicago: American Marketing Association, 1967, pp. 275–284.

Hamm, B. C., and Cundiff, E. W., "Self-Actualization and Product Perception." *Journal of Marketing Research*, Vol. 6, 1967, pp. 470–72.

Hamm, B. L., Perry, M., and Wynn, H. F., "The Effect of a Free Sample on Image and Attitude." *Journal of Advertising Research*, Vol. 9, No. 4, 1969, pp. 35–38.

Hammock, T., and Brehm, J. W., "The Attractiveness of Choice Alternatives When Freedom to Choose is Eliminated by a Social Agent." *Journal of Personality and Social Psychology*, Vol. 34, 1966, pp. 546–54.

Hansen, B., *Finanpolitikens Ekonomiska Teori*. Uppsala, Sweden: Almquist and Wiksell, AB, 1955.

Hansen, F., "Konsumentadfärdens Placering i Ökonomiske Modeller." *Det Danske Marked*, Vol. 25, 1966a, pp. 207–20.

Hansen, F., "Attituder og Konsumentadfärd." *Markedskommunikation*, Vol. 3, No. 2, 1966b, pp. 1–16.

Hansen, F., "Varebilleder og Köbsbeslutninger." *Markedsökonomi*, Vol. 1, 1967a, pp. 97–110.

Hansen, F., "An Attitude Model for Analyzing Consumer Behavior." Paper presented at American Marketing Association Conference, Puerto Rico, Nov. 1967b. [Also in L. Adler and I. Crispi (eds.): *Attitude Research on the Rocks*. Chicago: American Marketing Association, 1968.]

Hansen, F., "An Experimental Test of a Consumer Choice Model." In R. L. King (ed.): *Marketing and the New Science of Planning*. Chicago: American Marketing Association, 1968.

Hansen, F., "Consumer Choice Behavior: An Experimental Approach." *Journal of Marketing Research*, Vol. 6, 1969a, pp. 436–43.

Hansen, F., "Primary Group Influence and Consumer Conformity." In P. R. McDonald (ed.): *Marketing Involvement in Society and the Economy*. Chicago: American Marketing Association, 1969b.

Hansen, F., and Bolland, T., "The Relationship between Cognitive Models of Choice and Non-Metric Multidimensional Scaling." Proceedings from the 2nd annual Conference of the Association of Consumer Research, University of Maryland, 1971.

Harary, F., "On Measurement of Structural Balance." *Behavioral Science*, Vol. 4, 1959, pp. 316–23.

Harary, F., and Lipstein, B., "The Dynamics of Brand Loyalty: A Markov Approach." *Operations Research*, Vol. 10, 1962, pp. 19–40.

Harris, D. H., "The Effect of Display Width in Merchandising Soap." *Journal of Applied Psychology*, Vol. 42, 1958, pp. 283–84.

Harris, R. J., "Dissonance or Sour Grapes?" *Journal of Personality and Social Psychology*, Vol. 11, 1969, pp. 334–44.

Harlow, H. F., "The Formation of Learning Sets." *Psychological Review*, Vol. 56, 1949, pp. 51–65.

Harnett, D. L., "A Level of Aspiration Model for Group Decision Making." *Journal of Personality and Social Psychology*, Vol. 5, 1967, pp. 58–66.

Harrison, A. A., "Response Competition, Frequency, Exploratory Behavior, and Liking." *Journal of Personality and Social Psychology*, Vol. 9, 1968, pp. 363–68.

Harvey, O. J., and Sherif, M., "Level of Aspiration as a Case of Judgmental Activity in Which Ego-Involvements Operate as Factors." *Sociometry*, 1951, Vol. 14, pp. 121–47.

Harvey, O. J., and Ware R., "Personality Differences in Dissonance Resolutions." *Journal of Personality and Social Psychology*, Vol. 7, 1967, pp. 227–30.

Haskins, J. B., "Factual Recall as a Measure of Advertising Effectiveness." *Journal of Advertising Research*, Vol. 4, No. 2, 1964, pp. 2–8.

Havas, N., and Smith, H. H., "Customers' Shopping Patterns in Retail Food Stores." Washington: U.S. Dept. of Agriculture, Agricultural Marketing Service, August, 1960.

Hebb, D. O., *The Organization of Behavior*. New York: John Wiley and Sons, Inc., 1949.

Hebb, D. O., *A Textbook of Psychology*, 2nd ed. Philadelphia: Saunders, 1966.

Hebb, D. O., "Concerning Imagery." *Psychological Review*, Vol. 75, 1968, pp. 466–77.

Heider, F., "Attitudes and Cognitive Organizations." *Journal of Psychology*, Vol. 21, 1946, pp. 107–12.

Heider, F., *The Psychology of Interpersonal Relations*. New York: John Wiley and Sons, Inc., 1958.

Heise, D. R., "Affectual Dynamics in Simple Sentences." *Journal of Personality and Social Psychology*, Vol. 11, 1969, pp. 204–13.

Helson, H., "Adaption Level Theory." In S. Koch (ed.): *Psychology: A Study of Science*, Vol. 1. New York: McGraw-Hill Book Co., 1959.

Helson, H., "Current Trends and Issues in Adaption-Level Theory." *American Psychologist*, Vol. 19, 1964, pp. 26–38.

Helson, H., "Some Problems in Motivation from the Point of View of the Theory of Adaption Level." In D. Levine (ed.): Nebraska Symposium on Motivation, Lincoln, Nebraska, Nebraska University Press, 1966.

Hempel, D. J., "An Experimental Study of the Effects of Information on Consumer Product Evaluation." In R. M. Haas (ed.): *Science, Technology and Marketing*. Chicago: American Marketing Association, 1966.

Hempel, D. J., "Search Behavior and Information Utilization in the Home Buying Process." Paper Presented at American Marketing Association Fall Conference, Cincinnati, Ohio, Aug., 1969.

Hendrick, C., Mills, J., and Kiesler, C. A., "Decision Time as a Function of the Number and Complexity of Equal Attractive Alternatives." *Journal of Personality and Social Psychology*, Vol. 8, 1968, pp. 313–18.

Henell, O., *Marketing Aspects of Housewives' Knowledge of Goods*. Gothenburg, Sweden: Institute for Marketing and Management Research, 1953.

Herbst, P. G., "Conceptual Framework for Studying the Family." In A. A. Oeser and S. B. Hammond (ed.): *Social Structure and Personality In a City*. London: Routledge and Kegan Paul, 1954.

Herrmann, C. C., and Stewart, J. B., "The Experimental Game." *Journal of Marketing*, Vol. 22, 1957, pp. 12–20.

Heron, W., "Cognitive and Physiological Effects of Perceptual Isolation." In P. Solomon et al. (eds.): *Sensory Deprivation*. Cambridge: Harvard University Press, 1961.

Hess, E. H., "Attitude and Pupil Size." *Scientific American*, Vol. 214, April, 1965, pp. 46–54.

Hess, E. H., "Pupillometrics." In F. M. Bass, E. A. Pessemier, and C. W. King (eds.): *Applications of the Sciences in Marketing Management*. New York: John Wiley and Sons, Inc., 1968.

Hilgard, E. R., and Bower, G. H., *Theories of Learning*. New York: Appleton-Century-Crofts, 1966.

Himmelfarb, S., and Senn, D. J., "Forming Impression of Social Class: Two Tests of an Averaging Model." *Journal of Personality and Social Psychology*, Vol. 12, 1969, pp. 38–51.

Holloway, R. J., "An Experiment on Consumer Dissonance." *Journal of Marketing*, Vol. 31, No. 4, 1967, pp. 39–43.

Holloway, R. J., "Experimental Work in Marketing: Current Research and New Developments." In F. M. Bass, C. W. King, and E. A. Pessemier (eds.): *Applications of The Sciences in Marketing Management*." New York: John Wiley and Sons, Inc., 1968.

Holman, P. A., "Validation of an Attitude Scale as Device for Predicting Behavior." *Journal of Applied Psychology*, Vol. 40, 1956, pp. 347–49.

Holt, L. E., and Watts, W. A., "Salience of Logical Relationships among Beliefs as a Factor in Persuasion." *Journal of Personality and Social Psychology*, Vol. 11, 1969, pp. 193–203.

Holzman, M., "Theories of Choice and Conflict in Psychology and Economics." *The Journal of Conflict Resolution*, Vol. 2, 1958, esp. pp. 310–20.

Homans, G. C., *Social Behavior*. London: Routledge and Kegan Paul, 1961.

Horowitz, I. A., "Effect of Choice and Focus of Dependence on Helping Behavior." *Journal of Personality and Social Psychology*, Vol. 8, 1968, pp. 373–76.

Hovland, C. I., "Effects of the Mass Media of Communication." In Lindsey, G. (ed.): *Handbook in Social Psychology*, Vol. 88. Cambridge, Mass.: Addison-Wesley, 1954.

Hovland, C. I., (ed.): *The Order of Presentation in Persuasion*. New Haven: Yale University Press, 1957.

Hovland, C. I., "Reconciling Conflicting Results Derived from Experimental and Survey Studies of Attitude Change." *American Psychologist*, Vol. 14, 1959, pp. 8–17.

Hovland, C. I., "Computer Simulation of Thinking." *American Psychologist*, Vol. 15, 1960, pp. 687–93.

Hovland, C. I., Harvey, O. J., and Sherif, M., "Assimilation and Contrast Effects in Reaction to Communication and Attitude Change." *Journal of Abnormal and Social Psychology*, Vol. 55, 1957, pp. 244–52.

Hovland, C. I., and Janis, I. L., (eds.): *Personality and Persuadability*. New Haven: Yale University Press, 1959.

Hovland, C. I., Janis, I. L., and Kelley, H. H., *Communication and Persuasion*. New Haven: Yale University Press, 1953.

Howard, J. A., *Marketing Executive and Buyer Behavior*. New York: Columbia University Press, 1963.

Howard, J. A., and Sheth, J. N., "Theory of Buyer Behavior." In R. Moyer (ed.): *Changing Marketing Systems*. Chicago: American Marketing Association, 1967, pp. 253–69.

Howard, J. A., and Sheth, J., *A Theory of Buyer Behavior*. New York: John Wiley and Sons, Inc., 1969.

Howard, R. A., "Stochastic Process Models of Consumer Behavior." *Journal of Advertising Research*, Vol. 3, No. 3, 1963, pp. 35–42.

Howard, R. A., "Stochastic Models on Consumer Behavior." In F. M. Bass, E. A. Pessemier, and C. W. King (eds.): *Applications of the Sciences in Marketing Management*. New York: John Wiley and Sons, Inc., 1968.

Huelskamp, H. J., Hoofnagle, W. S., and Myers, M., *Effects of Specific Merchandising Practices on Retail Sale of Butter*. Washington, D.C., U.S. Government Printing Office, 1955.

Hughes, D. G., "The Measurement of Changes in Attitude Induced by Personal Selling." In S. A. Greyser: *Toward Scientfic Marketing*. Chicago: American Marketing Association, 1963.

Hughes, D. G., Tinic, S. M., and Naert, P. A., "Analyzing Consumer Information Processing." Paper delivered at the fall meeting of the American Marketing Association, Cincinnati, Ohio, Aug., 1969.

Hull, C. L., *A Behavior System*. New York: John Wiley and Sons, Inc., 1952.

Humphrey, G., *Thinking: An Introduction to Its Experimental Psychology*. New York: Wiley and Sons, Inc. (Science Editions), 1963.

Hunt, J. M., "Traditional Personality Theory in the Light of Recent Evidence." *American Scientist*, 1965, Vol. 53, pp. 80–96.

Hunt, M. F., Jr., Miller, G. R., "Open and Closed Mindedness, Belief Discrepant Communication Behavior, and Tolerance for Cognitive Inconsistency." *Journal of Personality and Social Psychology*, Vol. 8, 1968, pp. 35–37.

Indow, T., "Models for Responses of Customers with a Varying Rate." *Journal of Marketing Research*, Vol. 8, No. 1, 1971, pp. 78–86.

Inhelder, B., and Piaget, J., *The Early Growth of Logic in the Child*. New York: Harper and Row, 1964.

Insko, L., *Theories of Attitude Change*. New York: Appleton-Century-Crofts, 1967.

Insko, C. A., and Oakes, W. F., "Awareness and the 'Conditioning' of the Attitudes." *Journal of Personality and Social Psychology*, Vol. 4, 1966, pp. 487–96.

Insko, C. A., and Schopler, J., "Triadic Consistency: A Statement of Affective-Cognitive-Conative Consistency." *Psychological Review*, Vol. 74, 1967, pp. 361–76.

Irwin, F. W., and Smith, W. A. S., "Further Tests of Theories of Decision in an 'Expanded Judgement' Situation." *Journal of Experimental Psychology*, Vol. 52, 1956, pp. 345–48.

Irwin, F. W., and Smith, W. A. S., "Value, Cost and Information As Determiners of Decision." *Journal of Experimental Psychology*, Vol. 54, 1957, pp. 229–32.

Irwin, F. W., Smith, W. A. S., and Mayfield, J. F., "Tests of Two Theories of Decision in an Expanded Judgemental Situation." *Journal of Experimental Psychology*, Vol. 51, 1956, pp. 261–68.

Ito, Pikuma, "Differential Attitude of New Car Buyers." *Journal of Advertising Research*, Vol. 7, No. 1, 1967, pp. 38–42.

Jacobsen, E., and Kossoff, J., "Self Percept and Consumer Attitudes Toward Small Cars." *Journal of Applied Psychology*, Vol. 47, pp. 242–45, 1963.

Jacobovitz, L. A., "Effects of Mere Exposure: A Comment." *Journal of Personality and Social Psychology*, Vol. 19, No. 2, Monograph, Part 2, pp. 30–32, June, 1968.

Jaffe, I. J., and Senft, H., "The Role of Husbands and Wives in Purchasing Decisions." In L. Adler and I. Crispi (eds.): *Attitude Research at Sea*. Chicago: American Marketing Association, 1966.

Janis, I. L., "Motivational Factors in the Resolution of Decisional Conflict." In R. Jones (ed.): *Nebraska Symposium on Motivation*. Lincoln, Nebraska: Nebraska University Press, 1959a.

Janis, I. L., "Decisional Conflicts: A Theoretical Analysis." *Journal of Conflict Resolution*, Vol. 3, 1959b, pp. 6–27.

Janis, I. L., and Feshbach, S., "Effects of Fear Arousing Communication." *Journal of Abnormal and Social Psychology*, Vol. 48, 1953, pp. 78–92.

Jecker, J. D., "Selective Exposure to New Information." In L. Festinger: *Conflict, Decision and Dissonance*. Stanford, Calif.: Stanford University Press, 1964.

Johnson, H. H., and Scileppi, J. A., "Effects of Ego-Involvement Conditions on Attitude Change to High and Low Credibility Communicators." *Journal of Personality and Social Psychology*, Vol. 13, 1969, pp. 31–36.

Johnson, G. L., "Methodology for Studying Decision Making." *Journal of Farm Economics*, Vol. 39, 1957, pp. 215–26.

Johnson, R. F., "Smoking and the Reduction of Cognitive Dissonance." *Journal of Personality and Social Psychology*, Vol. 9, 1968, pp. 260–65.

Johnson, R. M., "Market Segmentation as a Strategic Management Tool." *Journal of Marketing Research*, Vol. 8, No. 1, pp. 13–17.

Jones, A., Wilkinson, J. J., and Braden, I., "Information Deprivation as Motivational Variable." *Journal of Experimental Psychology*, Vol. 62, 1960, pp. 126–37.

Jones, L. V., "Prediction of Consumer Purchase and the Utility of Money." *Journal of Applied Psychology*, Vol. 43, 1959, pp. 334–37.

Jordan, N., "The Mythology of the Non-Obvious: Autism or Fact?" *Contemporary Psychology*, Vol. 9, 1964, pp. 141–42.

Juster, F. T., "Durable Goods, Purchase Intentions, Purchases and Consumer Planning Horizon." In N. F. Foote (ed.): *Consumer Decision-Making*. New York: New York University Press, 1961.

Juster, F. T., *Anticipations and Purchases: An Analysis of Consumer Behavior*. Princeton, N.J.: Princeton University Press, 1964.

Juster, F. T., "Consumer Buying Intentions and Purchase Probability: An Experiment in Survey Design." *Journal of the American Statistical Association*, Vol. 51, 1966, pp. 658–96.

Juster, F. T., and Shay, R. P., *Consumer Sensitivity to Finance Rates: An Empirical and Analytical Investigation*. Princeton, N.J.: Princeton University Press, National Bureau of Economic Research, 1964.

Kahl, J. A., *The American Class Structure*. New York: Holt, Rinehart, and Winston, Inc., 1957.

Kaish, S., "Cognitive Dissonance and the Classification of Consumer Goods." *Journal of Marketing*, No. 4, pp. 28–31.

Kamen, J. M., and Eindhoven, J., "Instructions Affecting Food Preferences." *Journal of Advertising Research*, Vol. 3, No. 2, 1963, pp. 35–38.

Kamen, J. M., and Toman, R. J., "Psychophysics of Prices." *Journal of Marketing Research*, Vol. 7, 1970, pp. 27–35.

Kanter, D. L., "The AAAA Study on Consumer Judgment of Advertising." In P. M. Kaplan (ed.): *The Marketing Concept in Action*. Chicago: American Marketing Association, 1964, pp. 216–30.

Kaplan, K. J., "A Methodological Comparison of Two Techniques of Attitude Measurement." Unpublished Master's thesis, University of Illinois, 1966.

Kassarjian, H. H., "Social Character and Differential Preference for Mass Communication." *Journal of Marketing Research*, Vol. 2, 1965, pp. 146–53.

Kassarjian, H. H., "Consumer Behavior: A Field Theoretical Approach." In R. King (ed.): *Marketing and the New Science of Planning*. Chicago: American Marketing Association, 1968.

Kassarjian, H. H., and Cohen, J. B., "Cognitive Dissonance and Consumer Behavior." *California Management Review*, Vol. 8, 1965, pp. 55–64.

Kassarjian, W. M., "A Study of Riesman's Theory of Social Character." *Sociometry*, Vol. 25, 1962, pp. 213–30.

Katona, G., "Rational Behavior and Economic Behavior." *Psychological Review*, Vol. 60, 1953, pp. 307–18.

Katona, G., "The Predictive Value of Consumer Attitudes." In L. H. Clark (ed.): *Consumer Behavior*, Vol. 2. New York: New York University Press, 1955.

Katona, G., *The Powerful Consumer*. New York: McGraw-Hill Book Co., 1960.

Katona, G., *The Mass Consumption Society*. New York: McGraw-Hill Book Co., 1964.

Katona, G., and Mueller, E., *Consumer Attitudes and Demand 1952*. Ann Arbor, Michigan: Survey Research Center, 1953.

Katona, G., and Mueller, Eva, "A Study of Purchase Decision." In L. H. Clark (ed.): *Consumer Behavior*, Vol. 1. New York: New York University Press, 1954.

Katona, G., and Mueller, E., *Consumer Expectations, 1953–63*. Ann Arbor, Michigan: Institute for Social Research, 1964.

Katz, "The Two-Step Flow of Communication: An Up-To-Date Report on an Hypothesis." *Public Opinion Quarterly*, Vol. 21, 1957, pp. 61–78.

Katz, E., and Lazarsfeld, P. F., *Personal Influence*. New York: The Free Press, 1955.

Katz, D., "The Functional Approach to the Study of Attitude Change." *Public Opinion Quarterly*, 1960, pp. 163–204.

Kauder, E., *A History of Marginal Utility Theory*. Princeton, N.J.: Princeton University Press, 1965.

Kegerreis, J., and Engel J. F., "The Innovative Consumer: Characteristics of the Earliest Adopters of a New Automobile Service." Paper presented at the American Marketing Association Fall Conference in Cincinnati, Ohio, 1969.

Keller, F. S., *Learning—Reinforcement Theory*. New York: Random House, 1954.

Keller, F. S., "The Phantom Plateau." *Journal of Experimental Animal Behavior*, Vol. 7, 1958, pp. 1–13.

Kelley, W. T., "How Buyers Shop for a New Home." *The Appraisal Journal*, Vol. 25, 1957, pp. 209–14.

Kelly, R. F., "An Evaluation of Selected Variable of End Display Effectiveness." In P. D. Bennett (ed.): *Marketing and Economic Development*. Chicago: American Marketing Association, 1965, pp. 622–23.

Kelly, R. F., "The Diffusion Model as a Predictor of Ultimate Patronage Levels in New Retail Outlets." In R. M. Haas (ed.): *Science, Technology and Marketing*. Chicago: American Marketing Association, 1966.

Kelly, R. F., "The Role of Information in the Patronage Decision: A Diffusion Phenomenon." In M. S. Moyer and R. E. Vosburg (eds.): *Marketing for Tomorrow—Today*. Chicago: American Marketing Association, 1967a.

Kelly, R. F., "Estimating Ultimate Performance Levels of New Retail Outlets." *Journal of Marketing Research*, Vol. 4, 1967b, pp. 13–20.

Kelly, R. F., and Egan, M. B., "Husband and Wife Interaction In a Consumer Decision Process." Paper presented at American Marketing Association Fall Conference in Cincinnati, Ohio, 1969.

Kelman, H. C., "Compliance, Identification and Internationalization: Three Processes of Attitude Change." *Journal of Conflict Resolution*, Vol. 2, 1958, pp. 51–60.

Kenkel, W. F., "Decision-Making and the Life Cycle: Husband-Wife Interactions in Decision-Making and Decision Changes." *Journal of Social Psychology*, Vol. 54, 1961a, pp. 255–62.

Kenkel, W. F., "Family Interaction in Decision-Making and Spending." In N. F. Foote (ed.): *Household-Decision-Making*. New York: New York University Press, 1961b.

Kephart, W. M., *The Family, Society, and the Individual*, 2nd ed., Boston, Mass.: Houghton Mifflin Company, 1966.

Kerby, J. K., "Borrowing From the Behavioral Sciences." *Journal of Business*, Vol. 42, 1969, pp. 152–61.

Kerlinger, F. N., "Social Attitudes and Their Critical Referents: A Structural Theory." *Psychological Review*, Vol. 74, 1967, pp. 110–22.

Kernan, J. B., "Choice Criteria, Decision Behavior, and Personality." *Journal of Marketing Research*, Vol. 5, 1968, pp. 155–64.

Kernan, J. B., and Sommers, M. S., "Dimensions of Product Perception." *Southern Journal of Business*, April 1967, pp. 94–102.

Keynes, J. M., *The General Theory of Employment, Interests and Money*. New York: Harcourt, Brace and Company, Inc., 1936.

Kiesler, C. A., "Conflict and Number of Choice Alternatives," *Psychological Reports*, Vol. 18, 1966, pp. 603–10.

King, C. W., "Fashion Adoption: A Rebuttal to the Trickle Down Theory." In S. A. Greyser (ed.): *Towards Scientific Marketing*, Chicago: American Marketing Association, 1963.

King, C. W., "Communicating with the Innovation in the Fashion Adoption Process." In P. D. Bennett (ed.): *Marketing and Economic Development*. Chicago: American Marketing Association, 1965, pp. 425–39.

King, R. H., "A Study of the Problem of Building a Model to Simulate the Cognitive Processes of a Shopper in a Supermarket." In G. H. Haines, Jr.: *Consumer Behavior: Learning Models of Purchasing*. New York: The Free Press, 1969.

King, C. W., "Adoption and Diffusion Research in Marketing: An Overview." In R. M. Haas (ed.): *Science, Technology, and Marketing*. Chicago: American Marketing Association, 1966, pp. 665–84.

King, C. W., and Summers, J. O., "Technology, Innovation and Consumer Decision Making." In R. Moyer (ed.): *Changing Marketing Systems*. Chicago: American Marketing Association, 1967, pp. 63–68.

King, R. L., "Life Styles Research and Consumer Behavior." In L. G. Smith (ed.): *Reflections on Progress in Marketing*. Chicago: American Marketing Association, 1964, pp. 266–76.

Kjaer-Hansen, M., *A Discussion of Market Classifications*. Det Danske Marked, 1960. (Also in M. Kjaer-Hansen (ed.): Readings in Danish Marketing Theory. Copenhagen: F. Harcks Forlag, 1966.)

Klapper, J. T., *The Effects of Mass Communication*. Glencoe, Ill.: The Free Press, 1960.

Kleimenhagen, A. K. "Shopping, Specialty, or Convenience Goods?" *Journal of Retailing*, Winter 1966–1967, pp. 32–39.

Klein, G. S., Barr, H. L., and Nditzky, D. L., "Personality." *Annual Review of Psychology*, Vol. 18. Palo Alto, Calif.: Annual Reviews, Inc., 1967.

Knox, R. E., and Inkster, J. A., "Post-Decision Dissonance at Post Time." *Journal of Personality and Social Psychology*, Vol. 8, pp. 319–25, 1968.

Koenig, C. J. de, "The Relationship between Price and Demand." Unpublished paper. Attwood, Nederlands, 1971.

Kogan, N., and Wallach, M. A., *Risk Taking: A Study in Cognition and Personality*. New York: Holt, Rinehart and Winston, 1964.

Kollat, D. T., "A Decision Process Approach to Impulse Purchases." In R. M. Haas (ed.): *Science Technology and Marketing*. Chicago: American Marketing Association, 1966.

Kollat, D. T., and Willett, R. T., "Customer Impulse Purchasing Behavior." *Journal of Marketing Research*, Vol. 14, 1967, pp. 21–31.

Komorita, S. S., and Bass, A. R., "Attitude Differentiation and Evaluative Scales of the Semantic Differential." *Journal of Personality and Social Psychology*, Vol. 6, 1967, pp. 241–44.

Komorita, S. S., and Brenner, A. R., "Bargaining and Concession Making Under Bilateral Monopoly." *Journal of Personality and Social Psychology*, Vol. 19, 1968, pp. 15–20.

Komarovsky, M., "Class Differences in Family Decision Making on Expenditures." In N. F. Foote (ed.): *Household Decision-Making*. New York: New York University Press, 1961.

Koo, Y. C., "An Empirical Test of a Revealed Preference Theory." *Econometrica*, Vol. 31, No. 4, 1963.

Koponen, A., "Personality Characteristics of Purchasers." *Journal of American Research*, Vol. 1, No. 3, 1960, pp. 6–12.

Kornhauser, A. W., and Lazarsfeld, P. F., "The Analysis of Consumer Actions." 1935, reprinted in P. F. Lazarsfeld and M. Rosenberg (eds.): *The Language of Social Research*. New York: The Free Press of Glencoe, 1955.

Kotler, P., *Marketing Management, Analysis, Planning and Control*. Englewood Cliffs, N.J.: Prentice-Hall, Inc., 1967.

Kotler, P., "Mathematical Models of Individual Buyer Behavior." *Behavioral Science*, Vol. 13, 1968, pp. 274–87.

Kotzan, J. A., and Evanson, R. V., "Responsiveness of Drugstore Sales to Shelf Space Allocations." *Journal of Marketing Research*, Vol. 6, 1969, pp. 459–64.

Kreinin, M. E., "Analysis of Used Car Purchases." *Review of Economic and Statistics*, Vol. 41, 1959, pp. 419–25.

Kroeger, A., "The Response to Trading Stamp Plans." *Journal of Research*, Vol. 29, Winter 1953, pp. 191–95.

Krueckebery, H. F., "The Significance of Consumer Response to Display Space Reallocation." Paper presented at American Marketing Association Fall Conference in Cincinnati, Ohio, 1969.

Krugman, H. E., "The 'Draw a Supermarket' Technique." *Public Opinion Quarterly*, Vol. 24, 1960b, pp. 148–53.

Krugman, H. E., "The Learning of Consumer Preferences." *Journal of Marketing*, Vol. 26, No. 2, 1962, pp. 31–33.

Krugman, H. E., "Some Applications of Pupil Measurement." *Journal of Marketing Research*. Vol. 1, No. 4, 1964, pp. 15–19.

Krugman, H. E., "The Impact of Television Advertising: Learning without Involvement." *Public Opinion Quarterly*, Vol. 29, 1965, pp. 349–56.

Krugman, H. E., "White and Negro Responses to Package Designs." *Journal of Marketing Research*, Vol. 3, 1966, pp. 199–201.

Krugman, H. E., "The Measurement of Advertising Involvement." *Public Opinion Quarterly*, Vol. 30, 1967, pp. 583–96.

Krugman, H. E., "The Learning of Consumer Likes, Preferences and Choices." In F. M. Bass, E. A. Pessemier, and C. W. King (eds.): *Applications of the Sciences in Marketing Management*. New York: John Wiley and Sons, Inc., 1968.

Krugman, H. E., "Brain Wave Measures of Media Involvement." *Journal of Advertising Research*, Vol. 11, No. 1, 1971, pp. 3–10.

Krugman, H. E., and Hartley, E. L., "The Learning of Tastes." *Public Opinion Quarterly*, Vol. 23, 1960, pp. 621–31.

Kruskal, J. B., "Multidimensional Scaling by Optimizing Goodness of Fit to a Nonmetric Hypothesis." *Psychometrica*, Vol. 29, 1964, pp. 1–27.

Kruskal, J. B., "How to use M-D-Scale, A Program to do Multi-dimensional Scaling and Multidimensional Unfolding." (Version 4 and 4M of MDSCAL), Bell Telephone Laboratories, Murray Hill, N.J., March, 1968, mimeographed.

Kubzansky, P. E., and Leiderman, P. H., "Sensory Deprivation; An Overview." In P. Solomon et al. (eds.): *Sensory Deprivation*. Boston: Harvard University Press, 1961.

Kuehn, A. A., "Consumer Brand Choice—A Learning Process?" In R. E. Frank, A. A. Kuehn, and W. F. Massy: *Quantitative Techniques in Marketing Anlaysis*. Homewood, Ill.: R. D. Irwin, 1962.

Kuehn, A. A., "Demonstration of a Relationship Between Psychological Factors and Brand Choice." *Journal of Business*, Vol. 36, 1963, pp. 237–41.

Kuehn, A. A., "Mathematical Models of Consumer Behavior." In J. W. Newman (ed.): *On Knowing the Consumer*. New York: John Wiley and Sons, Inc., 1966.

Kuehn, A. A., and Day, R. L., "Strategy of Product Quality." *Harvard Business Review*, Vol. 40, 1962, pp. 100–10.

Kuehn, A. A., and Day, R. L., "Probabilistic Models of Consumer Buying Behavior.' *Journal of Marketing*, Vol. 28, 1964, pp. 27–31.

Kuehn, A. A., McGuire, T. W., and Weiss, D. L., "Measuring the Effectiveness of Advertising." In R. M. Haas (ed.): *Science, Technology, and Marketing*. Chicago: American Marketing Association, 1966.

Kunkel, J. H., and Berry, L. L., "A Behavioral Conception of Retail Image." *Journal of Marketing*, Vol. 32, No. 4, pp. 21–27.

Laird, D. A., "How the Consumer Estimates Quality by Subconscious Sensory Impressions." *Journal of Applied Psychology*, Vol. 16, 1932, pp. 241–46.

Lambert, R. M., "An Examination of the Consistency Characteristics of Abelson & Rosenberg's Symbolic Psychologic." *Behavioral Science*, Vol. 11, 1966, pp. 126–29.

Lamm, H., "Will an Observer Advise Higher Risk Taking After Hearing a Discussion of the Decision-Problem?" *Journal of Personality and Social Psychology*, Vol. 6, 1967, pp. 467–71.

Lampel, A. K., and Anderson, N. H., "Combining Visual and Verbal Information in an Impression Formation Task." *Journal of Personality and Social Psychology*, Vol. 9, 1968, pp. 1–6.

Lansing, J. B., and Morgan, J. N., *Consumer Finances Over the Life Cycle*. New York: New York University Press, 1955.

Lanzetta, J. T., "Information Acquisition in Decision Making." In A. J. Harvey: *Motivation and Social Interaction*. New York: Ronald Press, 1963.

Lanzetta, J. T., and Driscoll, J. M., "Preference for Information About an Uncertain but Unavoidable Outcome." *Journal of Personality and Social Psychology*, Vol. 3, 1966, pp. 96–102.

Lanzetta, J. T., and Driscoll, J. N., "Effects of Uncertainty and Importance of Information Search in Decision Making." *Journal of Personality and Social Psychology*, Vol. 10, 1968, pp. 479–86.

LaPiere, R. T., "Attitudes Versus Action." *Social Forces*, Vol. 13, 1934, pp. 230–37.

Larzelere, H., Makens, T., and Marquardt, R. "Measuring the Utility Added by Branding and Grading." *Journal of Marketing Research*, Vol. 2, 1965, pp. 45–55.

Lavidge, R. J., "The 'Cotton Candy' Concept: Intraindividual Variability." In L. Adler and I. Crespi (eds.): *Attitude Research at Sea*. Chicago: American Marketing Association, 1966.

Lavidge, R. J., and Steiner, G. A., "A Model For Predictive Measurement of Advertising Effectiveness." *Journal of Marketing*, Vol. 25, No. 4, 1961, pp. 59–62.

Lawrence, R. I., "Models of Consumer Purchasing Behavior." *Applied Statistics*, Vol. 15, 1966, pp. 216–33.

Lawrence, R. I., "Patterns of Buyer Behavior: Time for a New Approach." *Journal of Marketing*, Vol. 6, 1969, pp. 137–45.

Lazarsfeld, P. F., "A Conceptual Introduction to Latent Structure Analysis." In P. Lazarsfeld (ed.): *Mathematical Thinking in the Social Sciences*. Glencoe, Ill.: Free Press, 1954.

Lazarsfeld, P. F., Berelson, B., and Gaudet, H., *The People's Choice*. New York: Columbia University Press, 1948.

Leavitt, H. J., "A Note on Some Experimental Factors About the Meaning of Price." *Journal of Business*, Vol. 27, 1954, pp. 205–10.

LeGrand, B., and Udell, J. G., "Consumer Behavior in the Marketplace." *Journal of Retailing*, Fall 1964, pp. 32–47.

Levinger, G., and Breedlove, J., "Interpersonal Attraction and Agreement: A Study of Marriage Partners." *Journal of Personality and Social Psychology*, Vol. 3, 1966, pp. 367–74.

Levy, S. J., "Symbolism and Life Style." In S. A. Greyser (ed.): *Towards Scientific Marketing*, American Marketing Association, 1963.

Lewin, K., *A Dynamic Theory of Personality*. New York: McGraw-Hill Book Company, 1935.

Lewin, K., "Group Decision and Social Change." In E. E. Maccoby, T. M. Newcomb, and E. L. Hartley (eds.): *Readings in Social Psychology*, 3rd ed. New York: Holt, Rinehart and Winston, 1958.

Lewin, K., Dembo, T., Festinger, L., and Sears, P. S., "Level of Aspirations." In J. McV. Hunt (ed.): *Personality and the Behavior Disorders*. New York: Ronald Press, 1944.

LIFE, "A Pilot Study of the Roles of Husbands and Wives in Purchasing Decisions," New York: LIFE, 1965.

Likert, R., "The Method of Constructing an Attitude Scale." In M. Fishbein (ed.): *Readings in Attitude Theory and Measurement*. New York: John Wiley and Sons, Inc. 1967.

Lincoln, C. W., "Total Brand Identification Through Packaging." In F. E. Webster (ed.): *New Directions in Marketing*. Chicago: American Marketing Association, 1965.

Linder, D. E., Cooper, J. and Jones, E. E., "Decision Freedom as a Determinant of the Role of Incentive Magnitude in Attitude Change." *Journal of Personality and Social Psychology*, Vol. 6, 1967, pp. 245–54.

Lindhoff, H., and Naukhoff, F., "Bedöms Produkter Efter de Manniskor Som Anvander Dem?" Stockholm School of Economics, 1966 (stencil).

Lionberger, H. F., "Community Prestige and the Choice of Sources of Farm Information." *Public Opinion Quarterly*, Vol. 23, 1959, pp. 110–18.

Lipstein, B., "Risk and Uncertainty in Advertising Effectiveness Meaurements." In L. Adler and I. Crespi (eds.): *Attitude Research on the Rocks*. Chicago: American Marketing Association, 1968.

Locke, E. A., "Relationship of Success and Expectation to Affect on Goal-Seeking Tasks." *Journal of Personality and Social Psychology*, Vol. 7, 1967, pp. 125–34.

Longman, K. A., "Promises, Promises." In L. Adler and I. Crespi (eds.): *Attitude Research on the Rocks*. American Marketing Association, 1968.

LoSciuto, L. A., and Perloff, R., "Influence of Product Preference on Dissonance Reduction." *Journal of Marketing Research*, Vol. 4, 1967, pp. 286–90.

LoSciuto, L. A., Strassman, L. H., and Wells, W. D., "Advertising Weight and the Reward Value of the Brand." *Journal of Advertising Research*, Vol. 7, No. 2, 1967, pp. 34–38.

Lowe, R. H., and Steiner, I. D., "Some Effects of the Reversibility and Consequences of Decisions on Postdecision Information Preferences." *Journal of Personality and Social Psychology*, Vol. 8, 1968, pp. 172–79.

Lowin, A., "Approach and Avoidance: Alternative Modes of Selective Exposure to Information," *Journal of Personality and Social Psychology*, Vol. 6, 1967, pp. 1–10.

Lucas, D. B., and Britt, S. H., *Measuring Advertising Effectiveness*. New York: McGraw-Hill Book Co., 1963.

Luce, R. D., *Individual Choice Behavior*. New York: John Wiley and Sons, Inc., 1959.

Luce, R. D., "A Probabilistic Theory of Utility and Its Relationship to Fechnerian Scaling." In C. W. Churchman and P. Ratoosh (eds.): *Measurement, Definitions and Theories*. New York: John Wiley and Sons, Inc., 1959.

Luick, J. F., and Ziegler, W. L., *Sales Promotion and Modern Merchandizing*. New York: McGraw-Hill Book Company, 1968.

Lundberg, D., and Hulten, O., "En Model for Studiet av Media använding," *Markeds Kommunikation*, Vol. 4, No. 2, 1967, pp. 46–60.

Lundberg, G. A., Komarovski, M., and McInerny, M. A., *A Suburban Study*. New York: Columbia University Press, 1934.

Maccoby, N., and Maccoby, E., "Homeostatic Theory in Attitude Change." *Public Opinion Quarterly*, Vol. 25, 1961, pp. 538–45.

Maddi, S. R., "Meaning, Novelty and Affect: Comments on Zajonc's Paper." *Journal of Personality and Social Psychology*, Vol. 9, No. 2, Monograph, 1968, pp. 28–29.

Madsen, B. O., *Familiens Ökonomiske Livslöb*. Copenhagen, Denmark: E. Harch's Forlag, 1964.

Madsen, K. B., *Moderne Psykologiske Teorier*. Copenhagen, Denmark: E. Munksgard Forlag, 1960.

Madsen, K. B., *Theories of Motivation*. Copenhagen, Denmark: Munksgaard, 1964.

Madsen, K. B., "Theories of Motivation, An Overview and Synthesis." In M. R. Jones (ed.): *Human Motivation*. Lincoln, Nebraska: Nebraska University Press, 1965.

Madsen, K. B., *Almen Psykologi*, Vols. I and II. Copenhagen, Denmark: Gyldendal, 1966.

Maehr, M. L., and Videbeck, R., "Predisposition to Risk and Persistence Under Varying Reinforcement Success Schedules." *Journal of Personality and Social Psychology*, Vol. 9, 1968, pp. 96–100.

Maffei, R. B., "Brand Preferences and Simple Markov Processes." *Operations Research*, Vol. 8, 1960, pp. 210–18.

Maier, N. R. F., "Reasoning in Humans." *Journal of Comparative Psychology*, Vol. 12, 1931, pp. 181–94.

Mancuso, J. R., "Why Not Create Opinion Leaders for New Product Introductions?" *Journal of Marketing*, Vol. 33, No. 2, 1969, pp. 20–25.

Mandler, G., "The Interruption of Behavior." In B. Levine (ed.): *Nebraska Symposium on Motivation*. Lincoln, Nebraska: Nebraska University Press, 1964.

Manis, M., and Ruppe, J., "The Carryover Phenomenon," *Journal of Personality and Social Psychology*, Vol. 11, 1969, pp. 397–407.

Mann, L., and Janis, J. L., "A Follow-Up Study of the Long-Term Effects of Emotional Role-Playing." *Journal of Personality and Social Psychology*, Vol. 18, 1968, pp. 339–49.

March, J. G., and Simon, H. A., *Organizations*. New York: John Wiley and Sons, Inc., 1958.

Marder, E. M., "Attitude as a Predictor of Purchasing Behavior." *Public Opinion Quarterly*, Vol. 31, 1967, pp. 445–46.

Marcus, A. S., "Obtaining Group Measures from Personality Tests Scores: Auto Brand Choice Predicted From the Edwards Personal Preference Schedule." *Psychological Reports*, Vol. 17, 1965, pp. 523–31.

Markin, R. J., *The Psychology of Consumer Behavior*, Englewood Cliffs, New Jersey: Prentice-Hall, Inc., 1969.

Markstein, D., "Why Price is 10th in Buyer Preference." *Sales Management*, Vol. 70, Feb. 15, 1953, pp. 110–12.

Martineau, P. D., *Motivation in Advertising*. New York: McGraw-Hill Book Co., 1957.

Martineau, P. D., "Social Class and Spending Behavior." *Journal of Marketing*, 1958, pp. 121–30.

Martineau, P. D., "Customers Shopping Center Habits Change Retailing." *Editor and Publisher*, Oct. 26, 1963, p. 11.

Massy, W. F., "Order and Homogeneity of Family Specific Brand Switching Processes," *Journal of Marketing Research*, Vol. 3, 1966, pp. 48–55.

Massy, W. F., 'Stochastic Models for Monitoring New Product Introductions." In F. M. Bass, E. A. Pessemier, and C. W. King (eds.): *Applications of the Sciences in Marketing Management*. New York: John Wiley and Sons, Inc., 1968.

Massy, W. F., "Forecasting the Demand for New Convenience Products." *Journal of Marketing Research*, Vol. 6, 1969, pp. 405–10.

Massy, W. F., and Frank, R. E., "The Study of Consumer Purchase Sequences Using Factor Analyses and Simulation." *Proceedings of The Business and Economics Section of the American Statistical Association*, 1964.

Massy, W. F., Frank, R. E., and Lodahl, T., *Purchasing Behavior and Personal Attributes*. Philadelphia: University of Pennsylvania Press, 1968.

Massy, W. F., Montgomery, D. B., and Morrison, D. G., *Stochastic Models of Buying Behavior*. Boston: The MIT Press, 1970.

Massy, W. F., and Morrison, D. G., "Comments on Ehrenberg's Appraisal of Brand Switching Models," *Journal of Marketing Research*, Vol. 5, 1968.

Matthews, J. B., Jr., Buzzell, R. D., Levitt, T., and Frank, R. E., *Marketing, An Introductory Analysis*. New York: McGraw-Hill Book Company, 1964.

May, F. E., "Adaptive Behavior in Automobile Brand Choices." *Journal of Marketing Research*, Vol. 6, 1969, pp. 62–65.

May, F. E., "Buying Behavior: Some Research Findings." *The Journal of Business*, Vol. 38, 1965, pp. 379–96.

McClelland, D. C., Atkinson, J. W., Clark, R. A., and Lowell, E. L., *The Achievement Motive*. New York: Appleton-Century-Crofts, 1953.

McClure, P. J., and Ryans, Jr., J. K., "Differences Between Retailers and Consumers Perceptions." *Journal of Marketing Research*, Vol. 5, 1968, pp. 35–40.

McConnell, J. D., "The Price-Quality Relationship in An Experimental Setting." *Journal of Marketing Research*, Vol. 5, 1968a, pp. 300–3.

McConnell, J. D., "The Development of Brand Loyalty: An Experimental Study." *Journal of Marketing Research*, Vol. 5, 1968b, pp. 13–19.

McConnell, J. D., "Repeat Purchase Estimation and the Linear Learning Model." *Journal of Marketing Research*, Vol. 5, 1968, pp. 304–6.

McFall, J., "Priority Patterns and Consumer Behavior." *Journal of Marketing*, Vol. 33, No. 4, 1969, pp. 50–55.

McGee, V. E., "The Multidimensional Analysis of Elastic Distances." *British Journal of Mathematical and Statistical Psychology*, Vol. 19, 1966, pp. 181–96.

McGuire, W. J., "A Syllogistic Analysis." In M. J. Rosenberg, C. I. Hovland et al.: *Attitude Organization and Change*. New Haven: Yale University Press, 1960a.

McGuire, W. J., "Cognitive Consistency and Attitude Change." *Journal of Abnormal and Social Psychology*, Vol. 60, 1960b, pp. 345–53.

McGuire, W. J., *Effectiveness of Fear Appeals in Advertising*. New York: Advertising Research Foundation, 1963.

McGuire, W. J., "Inducing Resistance to Persuasion." In L. Berkowitz (ed.): *Advances in Experimental Social Psychology*, Vol. 1, New York: Academic Press, 1964.

McGuire, W. J., "The Current Status of Cognitive Consistency Theories." In S. Feldman (ed.): *Cognitive Consistency*. New York: Academic Press, 1966a.

McGuire, W. J., "Attitudes and Opinions." *Annual Review of Psychology*, Vol. 17, Palo Alto, Calif.: Annual Review Press, Inc., 1966.

McGuire, W. J., and Papageorgis, D., "Effectiveness of Prewarning in Developing Resistance to Persuasion." *Public Opinion Quarterly*, Vol. 26, 1962, pp. 24–34.

McKenna, M. L., "The Influence of In-Store Advertising." In J. W. Newman (ed.): *On Knowing the Consumer*. New York: John Wiley and Sons, 1966.

McNeal, J. U., "An Exploratory Study of the Consumer Behavior of Children." In J. U. McNeal (ed.): *Dimensions of Consumer Behavior*. New York: Appleton-Century-Crofts, 1965.

Melton, A. W., "Implications of Short-term Memory for a General Theory of Memory." *Journal of Verbal Learning and Verbal Behavior*, Vol. 2, 1963, pp. 1–21.

Mendelsohn, G. A., and Griswold, B. B., "Assessed Creative Potential, Vocabulary Level and Sex as Predictors of the Use of Incidental Cues in Verbal Problem Solving." *Journal of Personality and Social Psychology*, Vol. 4, 1966, pp. 423–31.

Mendelsohn, G. A., and Griswold, B. B., "Anxiety and Repression as Predictors of the Use of Incidental Cues in Problem Solving." *Journal of Personality and Social Psychology*, Vol. 6, 1967, pp. 353–59.

Meyer, G., "Psychologische Aspekte der Gesch-äfts-wahl." In R. Bergler (ed.): *Psychologische Markt-analyse*. Stuttgart, W. Germany: Verlag Hans Huber, 1965.

Miller, D. L., "The Life Cycle and the Impact of Advertising." In L. H. Clark (ed.): *Consumer Behavior*, Vol. 2, New York: New York University Press, 1955.

Miller, D. W., and Starr, M. K., *Executive Decisions and Operations Research*. New Jersey: Prentice-Hall, Inc., 1960.

Miller, D. W., and Starr, M. K., *The Structure of Human Decisions*. Englewood Cliffs, New Jersey: Prentice-Hall, Inc., 1967.

Miller, G. A., "The Magic Number Seven, Plus and Minus Two: Some Limits on Our Capacity for Processing Information." *Psychological Review*, Vol. 63, 1956, pp. 81–97.

Miller, G. A., "Junk Box Theories of Memory." In W. H. Bantz (ed.): *Readings in General Psychology*. Boston: Allyn and Bacon, 1968.

Miller, N., "Involvement and Dogmatism as Inhibitors of Attitude Change." *Journal of Experimental Psychology*, Vol. 1, 1965, pp. 121–32.

Miller, N. E., "Experimental Studies of Conflict." In J. M. Hunt, *Personality and the Behavior Disorders*. New York: Ronald Press, 1944.

Mills, J., "Comments on Bem's 'Self Perception: An Alternative Interpretation of Cognitive Dissonance Phenomena'." *Psychological Review*, Vol. 74, 1967, p. 535.

Mills, J., Aronson, E., and Robinson, H., "Selectivity in Exposure to Information." *Journal of Abnormal and Social Psychology*, Vol. 59, 1959, pp. 250–53.

Mills, J., and Jellison, J. M., "Avoidance of Discrepant Information Prior to Commitment." *Journal of Personality and Social Psychology*, Vol. 8, 1968, pp. 59–62.

Mindak, W. A., "Fitting the Semantic Differential to the Marketing Problem." *Journal of Marketing*, Vol. 25, No. 2, 1961, pp. 28–33.

Mischel, W., Grusec, J., and Masters, J. C., "Effects of Expected Delay Time on the Subjective Value of Rewards and Punishments." *Journal of Personality and Social Psychology*, Vol. 11, 1969, pp. 463–73.

Mittelstaedt, R., "An Experimental Study of the Effects of Experience on Consumer Decision Making." In S. A. Greyser (ed.): *Toward Scientific Marketing*. Chicago: American Marketing Association, 1963.

Mittelstaedt, R., "A Dissonance Approach to Repeat Purchasing Behavior." *Journal of Marketing Research*, Vol. 6, 1969, pp. 440–43.

Monroe, K., and Venkatesan, M., "The Concept of Price Limits and Psychophysical Measurements." Paper presented at the Fall Conference, American Marketing Association, Cincinnati, Ohio, 1969.

Montagu, J. D., and Cloes, E. M., "Mechanism and Measurement of the Galvanic Skin Response." *Psychological Bulletin*, Vol. 66, 1966, pp. 261–79.

Montgomery, D. B., "Stochastic Consumer Models: Some Comparative Results." In R. L. King (ed.): *Marketing and the New Science of Planning*. Chicago: American Marketing Association, 1968.

Montgomery, D. B., and Armstrong, J. S., "Consumer Response to a Legitimated Brand

Appeal." In J. Arndt (ed.): *Insights Into Consumer Behavior*. Boston: Allyn and Bacon, 1968.

Montgomery, D. B., and Silk, J., "Patterns of Overlap in Opinion Leadership and Interest for Selected Categories of Purchasing Activity." Boston: A Working Paper of Massachusetts Institute of Technology, 1969.

Montgomery, D. B., and Urban, G. L., *Management Science in Marketing*. Englewood Cliffs, N.J.: Prentice-Hall, Inc., 1969.

Moore, C. T., "Consumer Travel Behavior—A Spatial Analysis." *Southern Journal of Business*, Apr. 1966, pp. 150–59.

Moore, D. G., "Life Styles in Mobile Suburbia." In S. A. Greyser (ed.): *Toward Scientific Marketing*. Chicago: American Marketing Association, 1963.

Moore, O. K., and Anderson, B. S., "Search Behavior in Individual and Group Problem Solving." *American Sociological Review*, Vol. 19, 1954, pp. 702–14.

Morgan, J. N., "Household Decision Making." In N. F. Foote (ed.): *Household Decision-Making*. New York: New York University Press, 1961.

Morgan, J. N., "The Achievement Motive and Economic Behavior." In J. W. Atkinson and N. T. Feather (eds.): *A Theory of Achievement Motivation*. New York: John Wiley and Sons, Inc., 1966.

Morlock, H., "The Effect of Outcome Desirability on Information Required for Decision." *Behavioral Science*, Vol. 12, 1967, pp. 296–300.

Morris, J. L., "Propensity For Risk Taking as a Determinant of Vocational Choice." *Journal of Personality and Social Psychology*, Vol. 3, 1966, p. 328.

Morris, R. T., and Bronson, C. S., "The Case of Competition Indicated by Consumer Reports." *Journal of Marketing*, Vol. 33, No. 2, 1969, pp. 26–34.

Morrisette, J. O., "Group Performance as a Function of Task Difficulty And Size And Structure of Group." *Journal of Personality and Social Psychology*, Vol. 3, 1966, pp. 357–59.

Morrison, D. G., "Models of Consumer Loyalty Behavior: Aids to Setting And Evaluating Marketing Plans." In P. D. Bennett (ed.): *Marketing and Economic Development*. Chicago: American Marketing Association, 1965.

Morrison, D. G., "Testing Brand Switching Models." *Journal of Marketing Research*, Vol. 3, 1966a, pp. 401–9.

Morrison, D. G., "Interpurchase Time and Brand Loyalty." *Journal of Marketing Research*, Vol. 3, 1966b, pp. 289–92.

Morrison, H. W., "Testable Conditions for Triads of Paired Comparison Choices." *Psychometriks*, Vol. 28, 1963, pp. 369–90.

Mort, P. R., and Cornell, F. G., *Adaptability of Public School Systems*. New York: Columbia University Teachers College Bureau of Publications, 1938.

Mosteiler, F., and Nogee, P., "An Experimental Measurement of Utility." *Journal of Political Economy*, Vol. 59, 1951, pp. 371–464.

Mueller, E., "The Desire for Innovation in Household Goods." In L. H. Clark (ed.): *Consumer Behavior*, Vol. 3. New York: New York University Press, 1958.

Mueller, E., "A Look at the American Consumer." In J. W. Newman (ed.): *On Knowing the Consumer*. New York: John Wiley and Sons, Inc. 1966.

Mukherjee, B. N., "A Factor Analysis of Some Qualitative Attributes of Coffee." *Journal of Advertising Research*, Vol. 5, No. 1, 1965, pp. 35–38.

Munn, H. L., and Opdyke, W. K., "Group Interviews Reveal Consumer Buying Behavior." *Journal of Retailing*, Vol. 37, 1961, pp. 30–31.

Murray, A. D., and Goodhardt, G. J., "Habit Buying Among Housewives." In Market Research Society: *New Developments in Research*. London: Oakwood Press, 1963.

Murray, H. A., *Explorations in Personality*. New York: Oxford University Press, 1938.

Murray, J. A., "Canadian Consumer Expectational Data: An Evaluation." *Journal of Marketing Research*, Vol. 6, 1969, pp. 54–61.

Myers, J. G., "Patterns of Interpersonal Influence in the Adoption of New Products." In R. M. Haas (ed.): *Science Technology and Marketing*. Chicago: American Marketing Association, 1966.

Myers, J. G., "Determinants of Private Brand Attitudes." *Journal of Marketing Research*, Vol. 4, 1967, pp. 73–81.

Myers, J. G., *Consumer Image and Attitude.* Berkeley: Iber Special Publications, University of California, 1968.

Myers, J. G., and Nicosia, F. M., "New Empirical Directions in Market Segmentation: Latent Structure Models." In R. Moyer (ed.): *Changing Marketing Systems.* Chicago: American Marketing Association, 1967.

Myers, J. G., and Nicosia, F. M., "On the Study of Consumer Typologies." *Journal of Marketing Research*, Vol. 5, 1968, pp. 182–93.

Myers, J. G. and Robertson, T. R., "Dimensions of Opinion Leadership." Paper presented at the Workshop on Experimental Research, Ohio State University, 1969.

Myers, J. H., and Alpert, M. I., "Determinant Buying Attitudes: Meaning and Measurement." *Journal of Marketing*, Vol. 32, No. 4, 1968, pp. 13–20.

Namias, J., "Intentions to Purchase Related to Consumer Characteristics." *Journal of Marketing*, Vol. 25, 1959, pp. 32–36.

National Bureau of Economic Research, *The Quality and Economic Significance of Anticipations Data.* Princeton, N.J.: Princeton University Press, 1960.

Naylor, J. C., "Deceptive Packaging: Are the Deceivers Being Deceived?" *Journal of Applied Psychology*, Vol. 46, 1962, pp. 393–98.

Nehnevajsa, J., "How Anticipation of Outcomes Affects Personal Decision Making." Paper delivered at American Association of Advertising Agencies Annual Conference, New York, 1963. Reprinted in S. H. Britt: *Consumer Behavior.* New York: John Wiley and Sons, Inc., 1966.

Neidell, L. A., "The Use of Nonmetric Multidimensional Scaling in Marketing Analyses." *Journal of Marketing*, Vol. 33, 1969, pp. 37–43.

Neidell, L. A., and Teach, R. D., "Conceptual Mapping of Convenience Goods." Paper presented at American Marketing Association Fall Conference, Cincinnati, Ohio, 1969.

Newcomb, T. M., "The Prediction of Interpersonal Attraction." *American Psychologist*, Vol. 11, 1956, pp. 575–87.

Newcomb, T. M., "An Approach to the Study of Communicative Acts." *Psychological Review*, Vol. 60, 1953, pp. 393–404.

Newell, A., Shaw, J. C., and Simon, H. A., "Elements of a Theory of Human Problem Solving." *Psychological Review*, Vol. 65, 1958, pp. 151–62.

Nicosia, F. M., *Consumer Decision Processes.* Englewood Cliffs, N.J.: Prentice-Hall, Inc., 1966.

Niebel, B. W., *Motion and Time Study*, 4th ed. Homewood, Ill.: Richard D. Irwin, Inc., 1967.

Nielsen, Jr., A. C., "The Impact of Retail Coupons." *Journal of Marketing*, Vol. 29, No. 4, 1965, pp. 11–15.

Nisbett, R. E., and Kaneuse, D. E., "Obesity, Food Deprivation and Supermarket Shopping Behavior." *Journal of Personality and Social Psychology*, Vol. 12, 1969, pp. 289–94.

Norman, D. A., "Toward a Theory of Memory and Attention." *Psychological Review*, Vol. 75, 1968, pp. 522–36.

Norris, R. T., "Processes and Objectives of House Purchasing in the New London Area." In L. H. Clark (ed.): *Consumer Behavior*, Vol. 1. New York: New York University Press, 1954.

Nowak, K., Carlman, B., and Wärneryd, K. E., "Masse-kommunikation och Åsikts förandringar." Stockholm, Sweden: Institute for Economic Research, The Stockholm School of Economics, 1966.

Nuttall, C. G. F., "TV Commercial Audiences in the United Kingdom." *Journal of Advertising Research*, Vol. 2, No. 3, 1962, pp. 19–28.

Nystrom, P. H., *Economics of Fashion.* New York: Ronald Press, 1928.

Ölander, F., "Preferensteori och preferensmätning." FFI, Stockholm: The Economic Research Institute of the Stockholm School of Economics, 1962.

Ölander, F., "A Conceptual Scheme for the Description of Consumer Choice Behavior. A Preliminary Draft." Stockholm: The Economic Research Institute of the Stockholm School of Economics, 1964.

Ölander, F., "The Influence of Price on the Consumer's Evaluation of Products and Purchases." Stockholm: The Economic Research Institute of the Stockholm School of Economics, 1968 (stencil).

Ölander, F., and Seipel, C. M., "Sparbeteandet yr Psychologisk Synsvinkel." Stockholm: The Economic Research Institute of the Stockholm School of Economics, 1967 (stencil).

Orcutt, G. H., Greenberger, M., Korbel, J., and Rivlin, A. M., *Microanalysis of Socioeconomic Systems: A Simulation Study.* New York: Harper Bros., 1961.

Orne, M. T., "On the Social Psychology of the Psychological Experiment: With Particular Reference to Demand Characteristics and Their Implications." *American Psychologist,* Vol. 17, 1962, pp. 776–83.

O'Rourke, J. F., "Field and Laboratory: The Decision-Making Behavior of Family Groups in Two Experimental Conditions." *Sociometry,* Vol. 26, 1963, pp. 422–35.

Osgood, C. E., "A Behavioristic Analysis of Perception and Language as Cognitive Phenomena." In *Contemporary Approaches to Cognition.* Cambridge, Mass.: Harvard University Press, 1957.

Osgood, C. E., "Cognitive Dynamics in the Conduct of Human Affairs." *Public Opinion Quarterly,* Vol. 24, 1960, pp. 341–65.

Osgood, C. E., "Cross-Cultural Comparability in Attitude Measurement via Multilingual Semantic Differential." In M. Fishbein (ed.): *Readings in Attitude Theory and Attitude Measurement.* New York: John Wiley and Sons, Inc., 1967.

Osgood, C. E., Suci, G. J., and Tannenbaum, P. H., *The Measurement of Meaning.* Urbana, Ill.: University of Illinois Press, 1957.

Osgood, C. E., and Tannenbaum, P. H., "The Principles of Congruity in the Prediction of Attitude Change." *Psychological Review,* Vol. 62, 1955, pp. 42–55.

Oshikawa, S., "Can Cognitive Dissonance Theory Explain Consumer Behavior?" *Journal of Marketing,* Vol. 33, No. 4, 1969, pp. 44–49.

Ostlund, L. E., "The Role of Product Perceptions in Innovative Behavior." Paper presented at Fall Conference of American Marketing Association, Cincinnati, Ohio, 1969.

Ottesen, O., *Problem, Midler og beslutninger i Foretakets Markeds-Kommunikasjon bind I.* Oslo, Norway: Instituttet For Markedsforskning, 1969.

Oxenfeldt, A. R., "How Housewives Form Price Impressions." *Journal of Advertising Research,* Vol. 8, No. 3, 1968, pp. 9–17.

Packard, V., *The Hidden Persuaders.* New York: David McKay Company, 1957.

Palda, K. S., "The Measurement of Cumulative Advertising Effect." *Journal of Business,* Vol. 38, 1965, pp. 162–79.

Palda, K. S., "The Hypothesis of A Hierarchy of Effects: A Partial Evaluation." *Journal of Marketing Research,* Vol. 3, 1966, pp. 13–25.

Palda, K. S., *Economic Analysis For Marketing Decisions.* Englewood Cliffs, N.J.: Prentice-Hall, Inc., 1969.

Pallak, M. S., and Brock, T. C., "Dissonance Arousal and Task Performance in an Incidental Learning Paradigm." *Journal of Personality and Social Psychology,* Vol. 7, 1967, pp. 11–20.

Papageorgis, D., "Anticipation of Exposure to Persuasive Messages and Belief Change." *Journal of Personality and Social Psychology,* Vol. 5, 1967, pp. 490–96.

Papandreou, A. G., "A Test of a Stochastic Theory of Choices." University of California Publications in *Economics,* Vol. 16, Berkeley: University of California Press, 1957.

Parfitt, J. H., and Collins, B. J. K., "Use of Consumer Panels for Brand-Share Predictions." *Journal of Marketing Research,* Vol. 5, 1968, pp. 131–45.

Parson, T., and Shills, E. A., (eds.): *Toward A General Theory of Action.* Cambridge, Mass.: Harvard University Press, 1953.

Parsons, T., and Smelser, N. J., *Economy and Society.* New York: The Free Press, 1956.

Paroush, J., "The Order of Acquisition of Consumer Durables." *Econometrica,* Vol. 33, 1965, pp. 225–35.

Pashigian, B. P., Schkade, L. L., and Menefer, G. H., "The Selection of an Optimal Deductible For a Given Insurance Policy." *Journal of Business,* Vol. 39, 1966, pp. 35–44.

Paul, C., and Paul, H., "Transfer-Activated Response Sets in Verbal Learning and Transfer." *Psychological Review*, Vol. 75, No. 6, 1968, pp. 537–49.

Pavlov, I. P., *Conditioned Reflexes*. London: Oxford University Press, 1927.

Payne, D. E., "Jet Set, Pseudo Store, and New Product Testing." *Journal of Marketing Research*, Vol. 3, 1966, pp. 372–77.

Peak, H., "Psychological Structure and Psychological Activity." *Psychological Review*, Vol. 65, 1958, pp. 325–47.

Peak, H., "The Effect of Aroused Motivation on Attitudes." *Journal of Abnormal and Social Psychology*, Vol. 61, 1960, pp. 463–68.

Peckham, J. D., "The Consumer Speaks." *Journal of Marketing*, Vol. 27, No. 4, 1963, pp. 21–26.

Penfield, W., and Roberts, L., *Speech and Brain Mechanisms*. Princeton, N.J.: Princeton University Press, 1959.

Pennington, A. L., "Customer-Salesman Bargaining Behavior in Retail Transactions." *Journal of Marketing Research*, Vol. 5, 1968, pp. 255–62.

Pennington, A. L., and Peterson, R. A., "Interest Patterns and Product Preferences: An Exploratory Analysis." *Journal of Marketing Research*, Vol. 6, 1969, pp. 284–90.

Perloff, R., "Consumer Analysis." *Annual Review of Psychology*, Vol. 19, Palo Alto, Calif.: Annual Reviews, Inc., 1968.

Perry, M., "Discriminant Analysis of Relations Between Consumers' Attitudes, Behavior and Intentions." *Journal of Advertising Research*, Vol. 9, No. 2, 1969, pp. 34–39.

Perry, M., and Hamm, G. C., "Canonical Analyses of Relations Between Socioeconomic Risk and Personal Influence in Purchase Decisions." *Journal of Marketing Research*, Vol. 6, 1969, pp. 351–54.

Pessemier, E. A., "An Experimental Method for Estimating Demand." *Journal of Business*, Vol. 33, 1960, pp. 373–83.

Pessemier, E. A., *Experimental Methods of Analysing Demand for Branded Consumer Goods with Applications to Problems in Marketing Strategy*. Pullman, Washington: Washington State University Press, 1963.

Pessemier, E. A., Burger, P. C., and Tigert, D. J., "Can New Product Buyers Be Identified?" *Journal of Marketing Research*, Vol. 4, 1967, pp. 349–55.

Pessemier, E. A., and Teach, R. D., "Pricing Experiments, Scaling Consumer Preferences, and Predicting Purchase Behavior." In R. M. Haas (ed.): *Science, Technology and Marketing*, American Marketing Association, 1966.

Pessemier, E. A., and Teach, R. D., "Simulation, Scaling and Predicting Brand Purchase Behavior." In R. L. King (ed.): *Marketing and the New Science of Planning*. Chicago: American Marketing Association, 1968.

Pessemier, E. A., and Tigert, D. J., "Personality, Activity and Attitude Predictors of Consumer Behavior." In T. S. Wright and T. L. Goldstocker (eds.): *New Views for Successful Marketing*. Chicago: American Marketing Association, 1966.

Peterson, C. R., and Beach, L. R., "Man as an Intuitive Statistician." *Psychological Bulletin*, Vol. 68, 1967, pp. 29–48.

Peterson, R. T., "Experimental Analysis of Theory of Promotion at Point of Consumption." *Journal of Marketing Research*, Vol. 6, 1969, pp. 347–50.

Peterson, P. D., and Koulack, D., "Attitude Change as a Function of Latitudes of Acceptance and Rejectance." *Journal of Personality and Social Psychology*, Vol. 11, 1969, pp. 309–11.

Pettigrew, T. F., "The Measurement and Correlates of Category Width as a Cognitive Variable." *Journal of Personality*, Vol. 26, 1956, pp. 532–66.

Pfaff, D., "Parsimonious Biological Models of Memory Reinforcement." *Psychology Review*, Vol. 76, 1969, pp. 70–81.

Phares, E. J., and Davis, W. L., "Breadth of Categorization and the Generalization of Expectancies." *Journal of Personality and Social Psychology*, Vol. 4, 1966, pp. 461–63.

Phillips, J. B., "A Model for Cognitive Balance." *Psychological Review*, Vol. 74, 1967, pp. 481–95.

Pool, I., de Sola, and Abelson, R. P., "The Simulmatic Project." *Public Opinion Quarterly,* Vol. 25, 1961, pp. 167–83.

Popielarz, B. T. "An Exploration of Perceived Risk and Willingness to Try a New Product." *Journal of Marketing Research,* Vol. 4, 1967, pp. 368–73.

Powell, F. A., "Latitude of Acceptance and Rejection and the Belief–Disbelief Dimension." *Journal of Personality and Social Psychology,* Vol. 4, 1966, pp. 453–56.

Pratt, R. W., "Consumer Behavior: Some Psychological Aspects." In G. Schwartz (ed.): *Science in Marketing.* New York: John Wiley and Sons, Inc., 1965a.

Pratt, R. W., "Understanding the Decision Process for Consumer Durable Goods: An Example of the Application of Longitudinal Analysis." In P. D. Bennett (ed.): *Marketing and Economic Development.* Chicago: American Marketing Association, 1965b.

Printers' Ink Staff, "Do Ad Men Understand Teenagers?" In T. U. McNeal (ed.): *Dimensions of Consumer Behavior.* New York: Appleton-Century-Crofts, 1965.

Quenon, E. L., "A Method for Pre-Evaluation of Merchandise Offerings." *Journal of Marketing,* Vol. 15, 1951, pp. 158–71.

Quandt, R. E., "A Probabilistic Theory of Consumer Behavior." *The Quarterly Journal of Economics,* Vol. 70, 1956, pp. 507–36.

Ramond, C. K., "Theories of Choice in Business." In G. Fisk (ed.): *The Frontiers of Management Psychology.* New York: 1964.

Ramond, C. K., Rachal, L. H., and Marks, M. R., "Brand Discrimination Among Cigarette Smokers." *Journal of Applied Psychology,* Vol. 34, 1950, pp. 282–84.

Rao, T. R., "Consumer's Purchase Decision Process: Stochastic Models." *Journal of Marketing Research,* Vol. 6, 1969a, pp. 321–29.

Rao, T. R., "Are Some Consumers More Prone to Purchase Private Brands?" *Journal of Marketing Research,* Vol. 6, 1969b, pp. 447–50.

Rapoport, A., "A Study of Human Control in a Stochastic Multistage Decision Task." *Behavioral Science,* Vol. II, 1966, pp. 18–32.

Rapoport, A., "Optimal Policies for the Prisoner's Dilemma." *Psychological Review,* Vol. 74, 1967a, pp. 136–48.

Rapoport, A., "Variables Affecting Decisions in a Multistage Inventory Task." *Behavioral Science,* Vol. 12, 1967b, pp. 194–204.

Rapoport, A., and Minas, J. S., "Experimental Games: A Review." *Behavioral Science,* Vol. 7, 1965, pp. 1–37.

Rasmussen, B., *Image-Begrebet og Salget.* Copenhagen, Denmark: E. Harcks Forlag, 1968.

Rasmussen, A., *Pristeori eller Parameterteori ?* Copenhagen, Denmark: E. Harcks Forlag, 1955.

Raush, H. L., Dittman, A. T., and Taylor, T. J., "Person, Setting, and Change in Social Interaction." *Human Relations,* Vol. 12, 1959, pp. 361–78.

Ray, M. L., Sawyer, A. G., and Strong, E. C., "Frequency Effects Revisited." *Journal of Advertising Research,* Vol. 11, No. 1, pp. 14–20.

Raynor, J. O., "Achievement-related Motives and Risk Taking in Games of Skill and Chance." *Journal of Personality,* Vol. 34, 1966, pp. 35–54.

Reeves, R., *Reality in Advertising.* New York: Knopf, 1961.

Reitman, W. R., Grove, R. B., and Shoup, R. G., "Argus: An Information Processing Model of Thinking." *Behavioral Science,* Vol. 9, 1964, pp. 270–81.

Restle, F., *The Psychology of Judgement and Choice.* New York: John Wiley and Sons, Inc. 1961.

Restle, F., "Linear Theory of Performance." *Psychological Review,* Vol. 74, 1967, pp. 63–69.

Reynolds, W. H., "The Wide C-post and the Fashion Process." *Journal of Marketing,* Vol. 29, No. 7, 1965, pp. 49–54.

Reynolds, W. H., and Wofford, G. T., "A Factor Analysis of Air Travel Attitudes." In J. S. Wright and J. L. Goldstucker (eds.): *New Ideas for Successful Marketing.* Chicago: American Marketing Association, 1966.

Rhine, R. J., "A Concept Formation Approach to Attitude Acquisition." *Psychological Review,* Vol. 45, 1958, pp. 362–70.

Rhine, R. J., "Some Problems in Dissonance Theory Research on Information Selectivity." *Psychological Bulletin*, Vol. 68, 1967a, pp. 21–28.

Rhine, R. J., "The 1964 Presidential Election and Curves of Information Seeking and Avoidance." *Journal of Personality and Social Psychology*, Vol. 5, 1967b, pp. 416–23.

Rhine, R. J., and Silun, B. J., "Acquisition and Change of a Concept Attitude as a Function of Consistency of Reinforcement." *Journal of Experimental Psychology*, Vol. 55, 1958, pp. 524–29.

Rich, S. U., and Jain, S. L., "Social Class and Life Cycle Predictions of Shopping Behavior." *Journal of Marketing Research*, Vol. 5, 1968, pp. 41–49.

Rich, S. U., and Portis, B. D., "The 'Imageries' of Department Stores." *Journal of Marketing*, Vol. 28, No. 2, 1964, pp. 10–15.

Riesman, D., *The Lonely Crowd*. New Haven: Yale University Press, 1961.

Rimoldi, H. J. A., "A Technique for the Study of Problem Solving." *Educational and Psychological Measurements*, Vol. 15, 1955, pp. 450–61.

Rizzo, J. R., and Naylor, J. C., "The Factorial Structure of Selected Consumer Choice Parameters and Their Relationship to Personal Values." *Journal of Applied Psychology*, Vol. 48, 1964, pp. 241–48.

Robertson, T. S., "Determinants of Innovative Behavior." In R. Moyer (ed.): *Changing Marketing Systems*. Chicago: American Marketing Association, 1967a.

Robertson, T. S., "The Process of Innovation and the Diffusion of Innovation." *Journal of Marketing*, Vol. 31, No. 1, 1967b, pp. 14–19.

Robertson, T. S., "Purchase Sequence Response: Innovations vs. Non-Innovations." *Journal of Advertising Research*, Vol. 8, 1968, pp. 47–54.

Robertson, T. R., and Myers, J. G., "Personality Correlates of Opinion Leadership and Innovative Buying Behavior." *Journal of Marketing Research*, Vol. 6, 1969, pp. 164–68.

Robinson, P. J., and Converse, P. E., *Summary of United States Time Use Survey*. Ann Arbor, Michigan: Survey Research Center, Institute for Social Research, University of Michigan, 1966.

Robinson, P. J., Dalbey, H. M., Gross, J., and Wind, Y., *Advertising Measurement and Decision Making*. Marketing Science Institute. Boston: Allyn and Bacon Inc., 1968.

Rodriques, A., "Effects of Balance, Positivity and Agreement in Triadic Social Relations." *Journal of Personality and Social Psychology*, Vol. 5, 1967, pp. 472–75.

Rogers, C. R., *Client Centered Therapy*. Boston: Houghton-Mifflin Company, 1965.

Rogers, E. M., *Diffusion of Innovations*. New York: The Free Press, 1962.

Rogers, E. M., and Stanfield, J. D., "Adoption and Diffusion of New Products: Emerging Generalizations and Hypotheses." In F. M. Bass, E. A. Pessemier, and C. W. King (eds.): *Applications of the Sciences in Marketing Management*. New York: John Wiley and Sons, Inc., 1968.

Rokeach, M., *The Open and the Closed Mind*. New York: Basic Books, 1960.

Rokeach, M., "The Organization and Modification of Beliefs." *Centennial Review*, Vol. 7, 1963, pp. 375–95.

Rokeach, M., "Attitude Change and Behavioral Change." *Public Opinion Quarterly*, Vol. 30, 1967, pp. 529–50.

Rokeach, M., *Beliefs, Attitudes and Values*. San Francisco: Jossey-Bass Inc., 1968a.

Rokeach, M., "The Consumer's Changing Image." In P. Bliss (ed.): *Marketing and the Behavioral Sciences*. Boston: Allyn and Bacon, 1968b.

Rokeach, M., "The Role of Values in Public Opinion Research." *Public Opinion Quarterly*, Vol. 32, Winter 1969, pp. 547–59.

Rokeach, M., and Rothman, G., "The Principle of Belief Congruence and the Congruity Principle as Models of Cognitive Interaction." *Psychological Review*, Vol. 72, 1965, pp. 128–42.

Roman, H. S., "Semantic Generalization in Formation of Consumer Attitudes." *Journal of Marketing*, Vol. 6, 1969, pp. 369–73.

Rosen, E., Siegelman, E., and Teeter, B., "A Dimension of Cognitive Motivation: Need to Know the Known vs. the Unknown." *Psychological Reports*, Vol. 13, 1963, pp. 703–6.

Rosen, S., "Post-decision Affinity for Incompatible Information." *Journal of Abnormal and Social Psychology*, Vol. 63, 1961, pp. 188–90.

Rosenbaum, M. E., and Lewin, J. P., "Impression Formation as a Function of Credibility of Source and Polarity of Information." *Journal of Personality and Social Psychology*, Vol. 12, 1969, pp. 34–37.

Rosenberg, M. J., "Cognitive Structure and Attitudinal Effect." *Journal of Abnormal and Social Psychology*, Vol. 53, 1956, pp. 367–72.

Rosenberg, M. J., "An Analysis of Affective Cognitive Consistency." In M. J. Rosenberg, C. I. Hovland, et al.: *Attitude Organization and Change*. New Haven: Yale University Press, 1960a.

Rosenberg, M. J., "A Structural Theory of Attitude Dynamics." *Public Opinion Quarterly*, Vol. 24, 1960b, pp. 319–40.

Rosenberg, M. J., "When Dissonance Fails: On Eliminating Evaluation Apprehension from Attitude Measurement." *Journal of Personality and Social Psychology*, Vol. 7, 1965a, pp. 28–42.

Rosenberg, M. J., "Inconsistency Arousal and Reduction in Attitude Change." In I. D. Steiner and M. Fishbein (eds.): *Current Studies in Social Psychology*. New York: Holt, Rinehart and Winston, Inc., 1965b.

Rosenberg, M. J., and Abelson, R. P., "An Analysis of Cognitive Balancing." In M. J. Rosenberg and C. I. Hovland, et. al.: *Attitude Organization and Change*. New Haven: Yale University Press, 1960.

Rosenberg, M. J., and Hovland, C. I. (eds.): *Attitude Organization and Change*. New Haven: Yale University Press, 1960.

Rosenzweig, M. R., "Environmental Complexity, Cerebral Change, and Behavior." *American Psychologist*, Vol. 21, 1966, pp. 321–32.

Rosenzweig, M. R., and Leiman, A. L., "Brain Functions." *Annual Review of Psychology*. Palo Alto, Calif.: Annual Reviews, Inc., 1968.

Rosnow, R. L., and Arms, R. L., "Adding Versus Averaging as a Stimulus Combination Rule in Forming Impressions of Groups." *Journal of Personality and Social Psychology*, Vol. 10, Dec. 1968, pp. 363–69.

Rothman, J., "Formation of an Index of Propensity to Buy." *Journal of Marketing Research*, Vol. 1, No. 2, 1964, pp. 21–25.

Rotzoll, K. B., "The Effect of Social Stratification on Market Behavior." *Journal of Advertising Research*, Vol. 7, No. 1, 1967, pp. 22–27.

Rousseas, S. W., and Hart, A. G., "Empirical Verification of a Composite Indifference Map." *Journal of Political Economy*, Vol. 59, 1951, pp. 288–318.

Routtenberg, A., "The Two-Arousal Hypothesis: Reticular Formation and Limbic System." *Psychological Review*, Vol. 75, 1968, pp. 51–80.

Rowan, J., "Decision Theory in Consumer Research." *British Journal of Marketing*, Spring 1967, pp. 35–41.

Ruch, D. M., "Limitations of Current Approaches to Understanding Brand Buying Behavior." In J. W. Newman (ed.): *On Knowing the Consumer*. New York: John Wiley and Sons, Inc., 1966.

Ryan, B., and Gross, N. C., "The Diffusion of Hybrid Seed Corn in Two Iowa Communities." *Rural Sociology*, Vol. 8, 1943, pp. 15–29.

Sandell, R. G., "Situations Inflytande på konsumentens Märksval." *Markedskommunikation*, Vol. 4, No. 2, 1967, pp. 67–84.

Sandell, R. G., "Effects of Attitudinal and Situational Factors on Reported Choice Behavior." *Journal of Marketing Research*, Vol. 5, 1968a, pp. 405–08.

Sandell, R. G., "The Effects of Attitude Influence and Representational Conditioning on Choice Behavior." *The Economic Research Institute at the Stockholm School of Economics*, Stockholm, 1968b.

Sandell, R. G., *Att Förstå Konsumenten*. Stockholm, Sweden: F. A. Norstedt and Söners forlag, 1969.

Sargent, H. W., *Consumer-Product Rating Publications and Buying Behavior*. Champaign, Ill.: University of Illinois, Bureau of Economic and Business Research, 1959.

Sarnoff, J., "Psychoanalytic Theory and Social Attitudes." *Public Opinion Quarterly*, Vol. 24, 1961, pp. 251–79.

Schachter, S., *The Psychology of Affiliation*. Stanford, Calif.: Stanford University Press, 1959.

Schachter, S., and Singer, J. E., "Cognitive, Social and Psychological Determinants of Emotional States." *Psychological Review*, Vol. 69, 1962, pp. 379–99.

Shaffer, J. O., "The Influence of 'Impulse Buying' or in the Store Decisions on Consumers' Food Purchases." *Journal of Farm Economics*, Vol. 42, 1960, pp. 317–24.

Schapker, B. L., "Behavior Pattern of Supermarket Shoppers." *Journal of Marketing*, Vol. 30 No. 4, 1966, pp. 48–50.

Schary, P. B., "Consumption and the Problem of Time." *Journal of Marketing*, Vol. 35, No. 2, 1971, pp. 50–55.

Schill, T., "The effect of Type and Strength of Induced Conflict and Confliet Generalization and later Preference for Conflict Stimuli." *Journal of Personality and Social Psychology*, Vol. 34, 1966, pp. 35–54.

Schmidt, C. F., "Personality Impression Formation as a Function of Relatedness of Information and Length of Set." *Journal of Personality and Social Psychology*, Vol. 12, 1969, pp. 6–11,

Schmidt, E. I., "Behovenes og Forbrugets Psykologi." *Nationalökonomisk Tidsskrift*, 1941, pp. 246ff.

Schneider, A. M., "Control of Memory by Spreading Cortical Depression: A Case for Stimulus Control." *Psychological Review*, Vol. 74, 1967, pp. 201–15.

Schramm, W. (ed.): *Mass Communication*. Urbana, Illinois: University of Illinois Press, 1960.

Schreiber, K., *Kaufverhalten der Verbraucher*. Wiesbaden: Betrickswirtschaftlicher Verlag, 1965.

Schroder, H. M., Driver, M. J., and Strevfert, S., *Human Information Processing*. New York: Holt, Rinehart and Winston, 1966.

Schuchman, A., "Are There Laws of Consumer Behavior?" *Journal of Advertising Research*, Vol. 8, No. 1, 1968, pp. 19–28.

Schuchman, A., and Perry, M., "Self Confidence and Persuadability in Marketing." *Journal of Marketing Research*, Vol. 6, 1969, pp. 146–55.

Schultz, H., *The Theory and Measurement of Demand*. Chicago: The University of Chicago Press, 1938.

Schwartz, H., "The Consumer in Focus: Packaging Innovations and Buyer Behavior." In R. M. Kaplan (ed.): *The Marketing Concept in Action*. Chicago: American Marketing Association, 1964, pp. 299–313.

Schyberger, B., W: son, *Methods of Readership Research*. Lund, Sweden: Lund Business Studies, 1965.

Scitovssky, T., "Some Consequences of the Habit of Judging Quality by Price." *The Review of Economic Studies*, Vol. 12, 1945, pp. 100–05.

Scodel, A., Ratoosh, P., and Minas, J. S., "Some Personality Correlates of Decision Making Under Conditions of Risk." *Behavioral Sciemce*, Vol. 4, 1959, pp. 19–28.

Scott, E. M., "Personality and Movie Preferences." *Psychological Reports*, 1957, No. 3, pp. 17–18.

Sears, D. D., and Freedman, J. L., "Selective Exposure to Communication: A Critical Review." *Public Opinion Quarterly*, 1967, Vol. 31, pp. 194–213.

Seipel, C. M., *Kommunikations effecter och meddelandets argumentering*. Stockholm, Sweden: Institute of Economic Research, Stockholm School of Economics, 1967.

Seipel, C. M., "Premiums—Forgotten by Theory." *Journal of Marketing*, Vol. 35, No. 2, 1971, pp. 26–34.

Sells, S. B., "The Atmosphere Effect: An Experimental Study of Reasoning." *Arch. Psychol.*, No. 200, 1936.

Sensening, J., and Brehm, J. W., "Attitude Change from an Implied Threat to Attitudinal Freedom." *Journal of Personality and Social Psychology*, Vol. 8, 1968, pp. 324–30.

Shannon, C. E., and Weaver, W., *Mathematical Theory of Communication*. Urbana, Ill.: University of Illinois Press, 1949.

Shapiro, B. P., "Psychology of Pricing." *Harvard Business Review*, Vol. 46, No. 4, 1968, pp. 14–25.

Sharp, H., and Mott, P., "Consumer Decisions in the Metropolitan Family." *Journal of Marketing*, Vol. 21, 1956, pp. 149–56.

Shepard, R. N., "Analysis of Proximities as a Technique for the Study of Information Processing in Man." *Human Factors*, Feb. 1963, pp. 33–48.

Sheridan Supply Company, *Guilford-Zimmerman Temperament Survey*. Beverly Hills, Calif.: Sheridan Supply Company, 1955.

Sherif, M., and Hovland, C. I., *Social Judgement: Assimilation and Contrast Effects in Communication and Attitude Change*. New Haven: Yale University Press, 1961.

Sherif, C. W., Sherif, M., and Nebergall, R. E., *Attitude and Attitude Change: The Social Judgement-Involvement Approach*. Philadelphia: Saunders, 1965.

Sherif, M., Taub, D., and Hovland, C. I., "Assimilation and Contrast Effects of Anchoring Stimuli on Judgements." *Journal of Experimental Psychology*, Vol. 55, 1958, pp. 150–55.

Sheth, J. N., "A Review of Buyer Behavior." *Management Science*, Vol. 13, 1967, pp. 718–56.

Sheth, J. N., "Perceived Risk and Diffusion of Innovations." In J. Arndt (ed.): *Insights into Consumer Behavior*. Boston: Allyn and Bacon, 1968a.

Sheth, J. N., "Cognitive Dissonance, Brand Preference and Product Familiarity." In J. Arndt (ed.): *Insights Into Consumer Behavior*. Boston: Allyn and Bacon, 1968b.

Sheth, J. N., "A Factor Analytical Model of Brand Loyalty." *Journal of Marketing Research*, Vol. 5, 1968c, pp. 395–404.

Sheth, J. N., "How Adults Learn Brand Preference." *Journal of Marketing Research*, Vol. 8, No. 3, 1968d, pp. 25–36.

Sheth, J. N., "Attitudes as a Function of Evaluative Beliefs." Paper presented at the Workshop on Experimental Research in Consumer Behavior, Ohio State University, 1969.

Sheth, J. N., and Venkatesan, M., "Risk-Reduction Processes in Repetitive Consumer Behavior." *Journal of Marketing Research*, Vol. 5, 1968, pp. 307–10.

Shiffrin, R. M., and Atkinson, R. C., "Storage and Retrieval Processes in Long Term Memory." *Psychological Review*, Vol. 76, 1969, pp. 179–93.

Sieber, J. E., and Lanzetta, J. T., "Conflict and Conceptual Structure as Determinants of Decision Making Behavior." *Journal of Personality*, Vol. 32, 1964, pp. 622–41.

Sieber, J. E., and Lanzetta, J. T., "Some Determinants of Individual Differences in Predecision Information-Processing Behavior." *Journal of Personality and Social Psychology*, Vol. 4, 1966, pp. 561–71.

Siegel, S., *Non-Parametric Statistics for the Behavioral Sciences*. New York: McGraw-Hill Book Co., 1956.

Siegel, S., and Goldstein, P. A., "Decision-Making Behavior in a Two-Choice Uncertain Outcome Situation." *Journal of Experimental Psychology*, Vol. 57, 1959, pp. 37–42.

Silk, A. J., "Overlap Among Self-Designated Opinion Leaders." *Journal of Marketing Research*, Vol. 3, 1966, pp. 255–60.

Simon, H. A., "A Behavioral Model of Rational Choice." *Quarterly Journal of Economics*, Vol. 69, 1955, pp. 99–118.

Simon, H. A., "Rational Choice and the Structure of the Environment." *Psychological Review*, Vol. 63, 1956, pp. 129–38.

Simon, H. A., *Administrative Behavior*, 2nd ed. New York: Macmillan, 1957.

Simon, H. A., *Models of Man*. New York: Wiley and Sons, Inc., 1958.

Simon, H. E., "Motivational and Emotional Controls of Cognition." *Psychological Review*, Vol. 74, 1967a, pp. 29–39.

Simon, H., "Theories of Decision-Making in Economics and the Behavioral Sciences." In *Surveys of Economic Theory*, Vol. III, *The Royal Economic Society*. New York: Macmillan, 1967b.

Simon, H. A., and Barenfeld, M., "Information on Processing Analysis of Perceptional Processes in Problem Solving." *Psychological Review*, Vol. 76, 1969, pp. 473–83.

Skinner, B. F., *Science and Human Behavior*. New York: The Free Press, 1953.

Smith, B. L., Laswell, H. D., and Casey, R. D., *Propaganda, Communication and Public Opinion*. Princeton, N.J.: Princeton University Press, 1946.

Smith, E. E., "The Power of Dissonance Techniques to Change Attitudes." *Public Opinion Quarterly*, Vol. 25, 1961, pp. 626–39.

Smith, E. L., and Broome, C. L., "A Laboratory Study of Consumers' Brand Preferences for Brands of Low Cost Consumer Goods." *Southern Journal of Business*, Apr. 1967, pp. 77–89.

Smith, G., "How GM Measures Add Effectiveness." *Printers' Ink*, May 14, 1965, pp. 19–29.

Smith, G., and Marke, S., "The Influence on the Results of A Conventional Personality Inventory by Changes in the Test Situation: A Study of the Humm-Wadsworth Temperament Scale." *Journal of Applied Psychology*, Vol. 42, 1958, pp. 227–40.

Smith, S. A., "Factors Influencing the Relationship Between Buying Plans and Ad Readership." *Journal of Marketing Research*, Vol. 2, 1965, pp. 40–44.

Smith, S. A., Parker, E., and Davenport, S. J., "Advertising Readership and Buying Plans." *Journal of American Research*, Vol. 3, No. 2, 1963, pp. 25–29.

Sokolov, E. N., *Perception and the Conditioned Reflex* (in Russian). University of Moscow Press, 1958. (Based upon Berlyne, 1960, pp. 80–94.)

Sommers, M. S., "Product Symbolism and the Perception of Social Strata." In S. A. Greyser: *Toward Scientific Marketing*. Chicago: American Marketing Association, 1963, pp. 200–16.

Sorokin, P., and Berger, C., *Time-Budgets of Human Behavior*. Cambridge, Mass.: Harvard University Press, 1939.

Soskin, W. T., and John, V. P., "The Study of Spontaneous Talk." In R. Barker (ed.): *The Stream of Behavior*. New York: Appleton-Century-Crofts, 1963.

Spence, H. E., and Engel, J. F., "The Impact of Brand Preference on the Perception of Brand Names: A Laboratory Analysis." Paper presented at the Fall Conference of the American Marketing Association, Cincinnati, Ohio, 1969.

Spence, D. P., "Subliminal Perception and Perceptual Defence: Two Sides of a Single Problem." *Behavioral Science*, Vol. 12, 1967, pp. 183–93.

Staats, A. W., "An Outline of an Integrated Learning Theory of Attitude Formation and Function." In M. Fishbein (ed.): *Readings in Attitude Measurement*. New York: John Wiley and Sons, Inc., 1967.

Staats, C., and Staats, A. W., "Meaning Established by Classical Conditioning." *Journal of Experimental Psychology*, Vol. 54, 1957, pp. 74–80.

Staats, C., and Staats, A. W., "Attitudes Established by Classical Conditioning." *Journal of Abnormal and Social Psychology*, Vol. 57, 1958, pp. 37–40.

Staats, C., Staats, A. W., and Heard, W. W., "Attitude Development and Ratio of Reinforcement." *Sociometry*, Vol. 3, 1960, pp. 338–49.

Stafford, J. E., "A Sociometric Analysis of Group Influence on Consumer Brand Preferences." In P. D. Bennett (ed.): *Marketing and Economic Development*. Chicago: American Marketing Association, Vol. 65, pp. 459–60.

Stafford, J. E., "Effects of Group Influences on Consumer Brand Preferences." *Journal of Marketing Research*, Vol. 3, 1966, pp. 68–75.

Stafford, J. E., and Enis, B. M., "The Price-Quality Relationship: An Extension." *Journal of Marketing Research*, Vol. 6, 1969, pp. 456–58.

Stålberg, L., and Säve-Söderberg, B., "Hur bedöms Hr. P." (published in) *Studier i Ekonomisk Psykologi*. Stockholm, Sweden: Stockholm School of Economics, 1965 (stencil).

Stapel, Jan, "Predictive Attitudes." In L. Adler and I. Crespi (eds.): *Attitude Research on the Rocks*. Chicago: American Marketing Association, 1968.

Starbuck, W. H., "Level of Aspiration." *Psychological Review*, Vol. 70, 1963, pp. 51–60.

Starch, D., "Relating Ad Dollars to Dollar Sales." *Printers' Ink*, Vol. 286(9), pp. 25–29; Vol. 287(1), pp. 29–33; (3), pp. 25–28; (7), pp. 25–28, 1964.

Stefflre, V., "Market Structure Studies: New Products for Old Markets and New Markets (Foreign) for Old Products." In F. M. Bass, E. A. Pessemier, and C. W. King (eds.): *Applications of the Sciences in Marketing Management.* New York: John Wiley and Sons, Inc., 1968.

Stein, D. A., "The Influence of Belief Systems on Interpersonal Preference." *Psychological Monographs*, Vol. 80, No. 8, 1966.

Steiner, G. A., "The People Look at Commercials: A Study of Audience Behavior." *Journal of Business*, Vol. 29, pp. 272–304, 1966a.

Steiner, G. A., "Consumer Behavior: Where do We Stand? A Psychologist's Appraisal." In J. W. Newman (ed.): *On Knowing the Consumer.* New York: John Wiley and Sons, Inc., 1966b.

Stern, H., "The Significance of Impulse Buying Today." *Journal of Marketing*, Vol. 26, No. 2, 1962.

Stevens, S. S., "Measurement, Psychophysics and Utility." In C. W. Churchman and P. Ratoosh (eds.): *Measurement, Definitions and Theories.* New York: John Wiley and Sons, Inc., 1959.

Stoetzel, J., "A Factor Analysis of the Liqueur Preference of French Consumers." *Journal of Advertising Research*, Vol. 1, No. 2, 1961, pp. 7–11.

Stigler, G. J., "The Economics of Information." *The Journal of Political Economy*, Vol. 69, 1961, pp. 213–25.

Stockman, L. H., "The Influence of Consumer Deals on Urban HH Purchases of Butter, Margarine, Veg. Shortening, and Salad and Cooking Oils in Metropolitan Chicago." In F. M. Bass (ed.): *The Frontiers of Marketing Thought and Science.* Chicago: American Marketing Association, 1957.

Stone, G. P., "City Shoppers and Urban Identification: The Social Psychology of City Life." *The American Journal of Sociology*, Vol. 60, 1954, pp. 36–45.

Stone, R., and Rowe, D. A., "The Durability of Consumers' Durable Goods." *Econometrica*, Vol. 28, 1960, pp. 407–16.

Stout, R. G., "Developing DATA To Estimate Price-Quantity Relationships." *Journal of Marketing*, Vol. 33, No. 2, 1969, pp. 34–38.

Summers, J. O., and King, C. W., "Interpersonal Communication and New Product Attitude." A paper presented at the Fall Conference of the American Marketing Association in Cincinnati, Ohio, 1969.

Suppes, P., "The Role of Subjective Probabilities and Utility in Decision-Making." In J. Neman (ed.): *Proceedings of the Third Berkeley Symposium on Mathematical Statistics and Probability.* Berkeley, Calif.: University of California Press at Berkeley, 1956.

Swan, J. E., "Experimental Analysis of Predecision Information Seeking." *Journal of Marketing Research*, Vol. 6, 1969, pp. 192–97.

Swanson, C. E., "The Frequency Structure of T.V. and Magazines." *Journal of Advertising Research*, Vol. 7, No. 3, 1967a.

Swanson, C. E., "Patterns of Night-time Television Viewing." In M. S. Moyer and R. E. Vosburgh (eds.): *Marketing for Tomorrow—Today.* Chicago: American Marketing Association, 1967b, pp. 143–47.

Tannenbaum, P. H., "Mediated Generalization of Attitude Change via the Principle of Congruity." *Journal of Personality and Social Psychology*, Vol. 3, 1966, pp. 493–99.

Tannenbaum, P. H., McCaviay, J. R., and Norris, E. L., "Principle of Congruity and Reduction of Persuasion." *Journal of Personality and Social Psychology*, Vol. 3, 1966, pp. 233–37.

Tannenbaum, P. H., and Greenberg, B. S., "Mass Communication." *Annual Review of Psychology*, Vol. 19. Palo Alto, Calif.: Annual Reviews, Inc., 1968.

Tate, R. S., "The Supermarket Battle for Store Loyalty." *Journal of Marketing*, Vol. 25, No. 4, 1961, pp. 8–13.

Taylor, J. R., "An Empirical Evaluation of the Application of Unfolding Theory to Market Segmentation." In R. Moyer (ed.): *Changing Marketing Systems.* Chicago: American Marketing Association, 1967, pp. 288–93.

Taylor, J. A., "A Personality Test of Manifest Anxiety." *Journal of Abnormal and Social Psychology*, Vol. 48, 1953, pp. 285–90.

Taylor, J. R., "Reevaluation of Preference Distribution Analysis." *Journal of Marketing Research*, Vol. 5, 1968, pp. 434–37.

Taylor, J. R., "Unfolding Theory Applied to Market Segmentation," *Journal of Advertising Research*, Vol. 9, No. 4, 1969, pp. 39–46.

Thibaut, J. W., and Kelley, H. H., *The Social Psychology of Groups*. New York: John Wiley and Sons, Inc., 1959.

Thorndike, E. L., "Animal Intelligence, An Experimental Study of the Associative Process in Animals." *Psychological Review*, Monograph Supplement, Vol. 2, No. 8, 1898.

Thurstone, L. L., "Attitudes Can be Measured." *American Journal of Sociology*, Vol. 33, 1928, pp. 529–54.

Thurstone, L. L., "The Indifference Function." *Journal of Social Psychology*, Vol. 2, 1931a, pp. 139–67.

Thurstone, L. L., "The Measurement of Social Attitudes." *Journal of Abnormal and Social Psychology*, Vol. 26, 1931b, pp. 249–69.

Thurstone, L. L., *Examiner Manual for the Thurstone Temperament Schedule*. Chicago: Science Research Associates, 1953.

Thurstone, L. L., and Jones, L. V., "The Rational Origin for Measuring Subjective Values." In L. L. Thurstone: *A Measurement of Values*. Chicago: Chicago University Press, 1959.

Tillman, R., "Semantic Differential Measurement of Consumer Images of Retail Stores." *Southern Journal of Business*, April 1967, pp. 67–73.

Tobin, J., "On the Predictive Value of Consumer Intentions and Attitudes." *Review of Economics and Statistics*, Vol. 41, 1959, pp. 1–11.

Tolman, E. C., *Purposive Behavior in Animals and Men*. New York: Appleton-Century-Crofts, 1932.

Tolman E. C., "Principles of Performance." *Psychological Review*, Vol. 62, 1955, pp. 315–26.

Torgerson, W. S., *Theory and Method of Scaling*. New York: John Wiley and Sons, Inc., 1958.

Toynbee, A., *America and the World Revolution*. London: Oxford University Press, 1962.

Treisman, A. M., "Strategies and Models of Selective Attention." *Psychological Review*, Vol. 76, 1969, pp. 282–89.

Triandis, H. C., and Fishbein, M., "Cognitive Interaction in Person Perception." *Journal of Abnormal and Social Psychology*, Vol. 67, 1963, pp. 446–53.

Triandis, H. C., Vassilou, V., and Nassiakov, M., "Three Cross-Cultural Studies of Subjective Culture." *Journal of Personality and Social Psychology*, Vol. 8, No. 4, Part 2, Monograph Supplement, 1968.

Trier, H., Smith, H. C., and Shaffer, J. D., "Differences in Food Buying Attitudes of Housewives." *Journal of Marketing*, Vol. 25, No. 3, 1960, pp. 66–70.

Triffin, F., *Monopolistic Competition and General Equilibrium Theory*. Cambridge, Mass.: Harvard University Press, 1940.

Troldahl, V. C., *The Communication of Horticultural Information and Influence in a Suburban Community*. Report No. 10 of the Communication Research Center, Boston University, Boston, 1963.

Tucker, L. R., and Messick, S., "An Individual Difference Model for Multi-Dimensional Scaling." *Psychometrika*, Vol. 26, 1963, pp. 333–67.

Tucker, W. T., "The Development of Brand Loyalty." *Journal of Marketing Research*, Vol. 1, No. 3, pp. 32–35, 1964.

Tucker, W. T., "Human Choice Behavior: The Relationship Between Effort and the Probability of Reward." In P. D. Bennett (ed.): *Marketing and Economic Development*. Chicago: American Marketing Association, 1965.

Tucker, W. T., and Painter, J. J., "Personality and Product Use." *Journal of Applied Psychology*, Vol. 45, 1961, pp. 325–29.

Tull, D. S., "The Carry-Over Effect of Advertising." *Journal of Marketing*, Vol. 29, No. 2, 1965, pp. 46–53.

Tull, D. S., Boring, R. A., and Gonsior, M. H., "A Note on the Relationship of Price and Imputed Quality." *Journal of Business*, Vol. 37, 1964, pp. 186–91.

Tversky, "Intransitivity of Preferences." *Psychological Review*, Vol. 76, 1969, pp. 31–48.

Twedt, D. W., "Consumer Psychology." In *Annual Review of Psychology*, Vol. 16. Palo Alto, Calif.: Annual Review, Inc., 1965.

Udell, J. G., "Can Attitude Measurement Predict Consumer Behavior?" *Journal of Marketing*, Vol. 29, No. 4, 1965, pp. 46–50.

Udell, J. G., "Prepurchase Behavior of Buyers of Small Electrical Appliances." *Journal of Marketing*, Vol. 30, 1966, No. 4, pp. 50–53.

Uhl, K. P., "Shareowner Brand Preferences." *Journal of Business*, Vol. 35, 1962, pp. 57–69.

Uhl, K. P., Andres, R., and Paulsen, L., "How are Laggards Different? An Empirical Inquiry." *Journal of Marketing Research*, Vol. 7, 1970, pp. 51–54.

Urban, G. L., and Karash, R., "Evolutionary Model Building." *Journal of Marketing Research*, Vol. 8, No. 1, 1971, pp. 62–66.

Venkatesan, M., "Experimental Study on Consumer Behavior: Conformity and Independence." *Journal of Marketing Research*, Vol. 3, 1966, pp. 384–87.

Venkatesan, M., "Personality and Persuadability in Consumer Decision Making." *Journal of Advertising Research*, Vol. 8, No. 1, 1968, pp. 39–46.

Venkatesan, M., and Hancock, R. S., "Credit as a Communication Process and the Consumers' Idea About Credit." In M. S. Moyer and R. Vosburg (eds.): *Marketing for Tomorrow—Today*. Chicago: American Marketing Association, 1967.

Verenis, J. S., Brandsma, J. M., and Cofer, C. N., "Discrepancy from Expectation in Relation to Affect and Motivation: Test of McClelland's Hypothesis." *Journal of Personality and Social Psychology*, Vol. 9, 1968, pp. 47–59.

Vernon, M. D., *The Psychology of Perception*. Baltimore, Md.: Penguin Books, 1962.

Vinokur, A., "Distribution of Initial Risk Levels and Group Decision Involving Risk." *Journal of Personality and Social Psychology*, Vol. 13, 1969, pp. 207–14.

Von Nemann, J., and Morgenstern, O., *Theories of Games and Economic Behavior*, Princeton University Press, 1947.

Wagner, H. M., "The Case for Revealed Preference." *The Review of Economic Studies*, Vol. 26, 1958–59, pp. 178–89.

Walker, E. L., "Psychological Complexity as a Basis for a Theory of Motivation and Choice." In D. Levine (ed.): *Nebraska Symposium on Motivation*. Lincoln, Nebraska: Nebraska University Press, 1964.

Wallace, J., "Role Reward and Dissonance Reduction." *Journal of Personality and Social Psychology*, Vol. 3, 1966, pp. 305–12.

Wallach, M. A., and Wing, C. W., Jr., "Is Risk a Value?" *Journal of Personality and Social Psychology*, Vol. 9, 1968, pp. 101–06.

Waly, P., and Cook, S. W., "Attitude as a Determinant of Learning and Memory. A Failure to Confirm." *Journal of Personality and Social Psychology*, Vol. 4, 1966, pp. 280–88.

Walster, E., "The Temporal Sequence of Post-Decision Processes." In L. Festinger: *Conflict Decision and Dissonance*. Stanford, Calif.: Stanford University Press, 1964.

Walster, E., Berscheid, E., and Barclay, A. M., "A Determinant of Preference Among Modes of Dissonance Reduction." *Journal of Personality and Social Psychology*, Vol. 7, 1967, pp. 211–16.

Walster, E., and Festinger, L., "The Effectiveness of 'Overheard' Persuasive Communications." *Journal of Abnormal and Social Psychology*, Vol. 65, 1962, pp. 395–402.

Ward, C. D., "Attitude and Involvement in the Absolute Judgement of Attitude Statements." *Journal of Personality and Social Psychology*, Vol. 4, 1966, pp. 465–76.

Warner, W. L., and Lunt, P. S., *The Social Life of a Modern Community*. New Haven: Yale University Press, Yankee City Series, Vol. 1, 1941.

Wärneryd, B., *Innovation, Inflydelse och information* (with an English summary). Stockholm, Sweden: Almquist och Wicksell, 1965.

Wärneryd, K. E., *Bilägaren och bilköpet*. Stockholm, Sweden: Institute for Economic Research, Stockholm School of Economics, 1961.

Wärneryd, K. E., and Nowak, K., *Mass Communication and Advertising*. Stockholm, Sweden: Institute for Economic Research, Stockholm School of Economics, 1967.

Waterman, C. K., and Katkin, E. S., "Energizing (Dynamogenic) Effects of Cognitive Dissonance on Task Performance." *Journal of Personality and Social Psychology*, Vol. 6, pp. 126–31.

Watson, J. B., *Behavior, An Introduction to Comparative Psychology*. New York: Holt, Rinehart and Winston, 1914.

Watts, W. A., "Commitment Under Condition of Risk." *Journal of Personality and Social Psychology*, Vol. 3, 1966, pp. 507–15.

Wax, M., "Themes in Cosmetics and Grooming." *American Journal of Sociology*, Vol. 62, 1957, pp. 588–93.

Weale, W. B., "Measuring the Customer's Image of a Department Store." *Journal of Marketing*, Vol. 37, Spring, 1961, pp. 40–48.

Webster, F. E., Jr., "The Deal-Prone Consumer." *Journal of Marketing Research*, Vol. 2, 1965, pp. 186–89.

Weick, K. E., "When Prophecy Pales: The Fate of Dissonance Theory." *Psychological Reports*, Vol. 16, 1965, pp. 1261–75.

Weick, K. E., "Dissonance and the Revision of Choice Criteria." *Journal of Personality and Social Psychology*, Vol. 3, 1966, pp. 701–5.

Weinstein, M. S., "Achievement Motivation and Risk-Preference." *Journal of Personality and Social Psychology*, Vol. 13, 1969, pp. 153–72.

Weiss, D. L., "An Analysis of the Demand Structure for Branded Consumer Products." *Applied Economics*, Vol. 1, No. 1, 1967, pp. 37–49.

Wells, W. E., "Measuring Readiness to Buy." *Harvard Business Review*, Vol. 39, No. 4, 1961, pp. 81–87.

Wells, W. D., "Computer Simulation of Consumer Behavior." *Harvard Business Review*, Vol. 41, No. 3, 1963, pp. 93–98.

Wells, W. D., "Choice Behavior." In L. G. Smith (ed.): *Reflection on Progress in Marketing*. Chicago: American Marketing Association, 1964, pp. 239–45.

Wells, W. D., "Children as Consumers." In J. W. Newman (ed.): *On Knowing the Consumer*. New York: John Wiley and Sons, Inc., 1966a.

Wells, W. D., "General Personality Tests and Consumer Behavior." In J. W. Newman (ed.): *On Knowing the Consumer*. New York: John Wiley and Sons, Inc., 1966b.

Wells, W. D., 'Patterns of Consumer Behavior." In M. S. Moyer and R. E. Vosburgh (eds.): *Marketing for Tomorrow—Today*. Chicago: American Marketing Association, 1967.

Wells, W. D., "Backward Segmentation." In J. Arndt (ed.): *Insights into Consumer Behavior*, Boston: Allyn and Bacon, 1968.

Wells, W. D., and Chinsky, J. M., "Effects of Competing Messages: A Laboratory Simalation." *Journal of Marketing Research*, Vol. 2, 1965, pp. 141–45.

Wells, W. D., and LoSciuto, L. A., "Direct Observation of Purchasing Behavior." *Journal of Marketing Research*, Vol. 3, 1966, pp. 227–33.

Welsh, G. S., and Dahlstrom, W. G., *Basic Readings on the MMPI in Psychology and Medicine*. Minneapolis: University of Minnesota Press, 1956.

West, C. J., "Results of Two Years Study of Impulse Buying." *Journal of Marketing*, Vol. 15, 1951, pp. 362–63.

Westfall, R. L., "Psychological Factors in Predicting Product Choice." *Journal of Marketing*, Vol. 26, No. 2, 1962, pp. 34–40.

Westfall, R. L., Boyd, H. W., Jr., and Campbell, D. T., "The Use of Structured Techniques in Motivation Research." *Journal of Marketing*, Vol. 22, 1957, pp. 134–39.

Wheatley, J. J., and Oshikawa, S., "The Relationships Between Anxiety and Positive and Negative Advertising Appeals." *Journal of Marketing Research*, Vol. 7, 1970, pp. 85–89.

White, I. S., "The Perception of Value in Products." In J. W. Newman (ed.): *On Knowing the Consumer*. New York: John Wiley and Sons, Inc., 1966.

Whyte, W. H., Jr., "The Web of Word of Mouth." *Fortune*, Nov. 1954, pp. 140–43 and pp. 204–12.

Wicker, A. W., "Undermanning Performances and Students' Subjective Experiences in Behavioral Settings of Large and Small High Schools." *Journal of Personality and Social Psychology*, Vol. 10, 1968, pp. 255–61.

Wicklegren, W. A., "Context-Sensitive Coding, Associative Memory, and Serial Order in (Speech) Behavior." *Psychological Review*, Vol. 76, Jan. 1969, pp. 1–15.

Wicks, J. H., and Nelson, C. C., "Preliminary Investigation of Some Psychological Determinants of Consumption Propensity." *Southern Economic Journal*, Jan. 1967, pp. 383–87.

Wickström, B., *Kosumentens Märkesval* (with an English summary). Gothenburg, Sweden: Gothenburg School of Economics and Business Administration Publications, 1965.

Wilding, T., and Bauer, R. A., "Consumer Goals and Reaction to a Communication Source." *Journal of Marketing Research*, 1968, Vol. 5, pp. 73–77.

Wilkening, E. A., "Joint Decision-Making in Farm Families; a Function of Status and Role." *American Sociological Review*, Vol. 23, 1958, pp. 187–92.

Willett, R. P., and Pennington, A. L., "Customer and Salesman: The Anatomy of Choice and Influence in a Retail Setting." In R. M. Haas (ed.): *Science, Technology and Marketing*. Chicago: American Marketing Association, 1966.

Williams, R. J., "The Relation Between Advertising Pressure and Consumer Purchases." In H. Gomez: *Innovation, Key to Marketing Progress*. Chicago: American Marketing Association, 1963.

Wilson, L. L., "Homemaker Living Patterns and Marketplace Behavior—a Psychometric Approach." In J. S. Wright and J. L. Goldstucker (eds.): *New Ideas for Successful Marketing*. Chicago: American Marketing Association, 1966.

Wind, Y., and Frank, R. E., "Interproduct Household Loyalty to Brands." *Journal of Marketing Research*, Vol. 6, 1969, pp. 430–33.

Winer, L., "Obtaining Maximum Volume From New Gasoline Outlets." *Journal of Marketing*, Vol. 31, No. 1, 1967, pp. 55–59.

Wiseman, F., "A Segmentation Analysis of Automobile Buyers During the New Model Year Transition Period." *Journal of Marketing*, Vol. 35, No. 2, 1971, pp. 42–49.

Witt, R. E., "Informal Social Essays Influence on Consumer Brand Choice." *Journal of Marketing Research*, Vol. 1, No. 6, 1969, pp. 473–76.

Wold, H., and Jursen, L., *Demand Analysis*. New York: John Wiley and Sons, Inc., 1953.

Wolfe, A., Newman, D. Z., and Winters, L., "Operant Measures of Interest as Related to Ad Lib Readership." *Journal of Advertising Research*, Vol. 9, No. 2, 1969, pp. 40–45.

Wolgast, E. C., "Do Husbands or Wives Make the Purchasing Decisions?" *Journal of Marketing*, Vol. 23, 1958, pp. 151–58.

Woodworth, R. W., and Sells, S. B., "An Atmosphere Effect in Formal Syllogistic Thinking." *Journal of Experimental Psychology*, Vol. 18, 1935, pp. 451–60.

Wooldridge, D. E., *The Machinery of the Brain*. New York: McGraw-Hill Book Co., 1963.

Wyer, R. S., Jr., and Dermer, J., "Effect of Context and Instructional Set Upon Evaluations of Personality-Trait Adjectives." *Journal of Personality and Social Psychology*, Vol. 9, 1968, pp. 7–14.

Yensen, R., "Some Factors Affecting Taste Sensitivity in Man." *Quarterly Journal of Experimental Psychology*, Vol. 2, 1959, pp. 221–48.

Young, F. W., and Torgerson, W. S., "Torsca, A Fortran IV Program for Shepart-Kruska Multi-Dimensional Scaling Analysis." *Behavioral Science*, Vol. 12, 1967, pp. 498–99.

Zabel, W. D., "What's in the Package?" *Harpers*, Aug. 1963, p. 12.

Zajonc, R. B., *Structure of the Cognitive Field*. Ann Arbor, Michigan: University of Michigan, 1954, unpublished doctoral dissertation.

Zajonc, R. B., "The Concepts of Balance, Congruity and Dissonance." *Public Opinion Quarterly*, Vol. 24, 1960, pp. 280–96.

Zajonc, R. B., "Attitudinal Effects of Mere Exposure." *Journal of Personality and Social Psychology*, Vol. 9, No 2, Part 2, June, 1968 (Monograph Supplement).

Zajonc, R. B., and Burnstein, E., "The Resolution of Cognitive Conflict Under Uncertainty." *Human Relations*, Vol. 14, 1961, pp. 113–19

Zajonc, R. B., and Burnstein, E., "The Learning of Balanced and Unbalanced Social Structures." *Public Opinion Quarterly*, 1966, Vol. 33, pp. 153–63.

Zaltman, G., *Marketing Contributions from the Behavioral Sciences*. New York: Harcourt, Brace and World, 1965.

Zander, A., and Newcomb, T., Jr., "Group Levels of Aspiration in United Fund Campaigns." *Journal of Personality and Social Psychology*, Vol. 6, 1967, pp. 157–62.

Zeilske, H. A., "The Remembering and Forgetting of Advertising." *Journal of Marketing*, Vol. 23, 1959, pp. 239–43.

Zimbardo, P. G., Cohen, A. R., Weisenberg, M., Dworkin, L., and Firestone, J., "Contro of Pain Motivation by Cognitive Dissonance." *Science*, Vol. 515, 1966, pp. 217–19.

Index